The New Psychology of Language

This illuminating book offers an up-to-date introduction to the psychology of language, exploring aspects of language processing that have previously not been given center stage such as the role of body and brain, social aspects of language use, and mental models.

The New Psychology of Language presents an overarching theoretical account called the Language User Framework for discussing a wide variety of core language activities. How do we understand speech in conversations? How do we read books? How do we convert our thoughts into bodily signals (speech, gestures, facial expressions) when we speak? What happens in the mind and brain when we have mastered two or more languages? All these aspects of language use are discussed at the level of words and sentences, as well as text and discourse. Language is considered as an embodied, embedded, incremental cognitive activity aiming at the construction and communication of rich and dynamic mental models. Discussion Boxes highlight controversies in the field; case studies and practical exercises provide insight into everyday examples; illustrations represent important models of language processing; and key findings come along with clear and concise section summaries. Special attention is paid to research techniques for investigating the psychology of language.

This accessible book is essential reading for students in disciplines such as psychology, cognitive science and neuroscience, artificial intelligence, biology, the language and communication sciences, and media studies. It is also a useful resource for a lay audience with an interest in language and communication.

Ton Dijkstra is a Full Professor in Psycholinguistics and Multilingualism at the Donders Institute for Brain, Cognition, and Behaviour at Radboud University Nijmegen, The Netherlands.

David Peeters is an Associate Professor at the Department of Communication and Cognition at Tilburg University, The Netherlands.

THE NEW PSYCHOLOGY OF LANGUAGE

From Body to Mental Model and Back

TON DIJKSTRA AND DAVID PEETERS

LONDON AND NEW YORK

Designed cover image: © Getty

First published 2023
by Routledge
4 Park Square, Milton Park, Abingdon, Oxon OX14 4RN

and by Routledge
605 Third Avenue, New York, NY 10158

Routledge is an imprint of the Taylor & Francis Group, an informa business

© 2023 Ton Dijkstra and David Peeters

The right of Ton Dijkstra and David Peeters to be identified as authors of this work has been asserted in accordance with sections 77 and 78 of the Copyright, Designs and Patents Act 1988.

All rights reserved. No part of this book may be reprinted or reproduced or utilised in any form or by any electronic, mechanical, or other means, now known or hereafter invented, including photocopying and recording, or in any information storage or retrieval system, without permission in writing from the publishers.

Trademark notice: Product or corporate names may be trademarks or registered trademarks, and are used only for identification and explanation without intent to infringe.

British Library Cataloguing-in-Publication Data
A catalogue record for this book is available from the British Library

ISBN: 978-1-032-35303-6 (hbk)
ISBN: 978-1-032-35302-9 (pbk)
ISBN: 978-1-003-32627-4 (ebk)

DOI: 10.4324/9781003326274

Typeset in Times New Roman
by Newgen Publishing UK

Contents

Preface　　xi

1　Basic assumptions of a new psychology of language　　1

1.1　Introduction　1
1.2　Embodiedness　2
1.3　Embeddedness　5
1.4　Mental models　7
1.5　Incremental processing　9
1.6　Consequences of this view on language　10
1.7　Overview of the book　12

2　Language and communication　　14

2.1　Introduction　14
2.2　Verbal and non-verbal communication　14
2.3　Language and communication in context　17
2.4　The medium and the message　18
　　2.4.1　McLuhan: The medium is the message　18
　　2.4.2　McLuhan: The medium is the *massage*　19
2.5　Evolution of communication and language　19
2.6　The Sender–Receiver model of communication　24
2.7　What is next?　25
2.8　What have we learned?　25

3　Language User Framework　　27

3.1　Introduction　27
3.2　The Language User Framework　28
　　3.2.1　Parallel and sequential processing components　31
　　3.2.2　Complex language activities in daily life　32
　　3.2.3　Cognitive control and Working Memory　33
　　3.2.4　How the Language User Framework relates to the brain　34
　　3.2.5　Language and other cognitive domains　35
　　3.2.6　Language development, second language acquisition, and multilingualism　36

            3.2.7   Linguistics and psycholinguistics   38
                    3.2.7.1   Phonetics and phonology   39
                    3.2.7.2   Lexicology and morphology   39
                    3.2.7.3   Syntax (grammar)   40
                    3.2.7.4   Semantics and pragmatics   40
                    3.2.7.5   Bringing the disciplines together   41
    3.3   What is next?   42
    3.4   What have we learned?   43

4   **Language research techniques**   **45**

    4.1   Introduction   45
    4.2   The experimental basics   45
    4.3   Research techniques measuring word retrieval   48
            4.3.1   Off-line measurement: Memory   48
            4.3.2   On-line measurement: Behavioral reaction time and neuroscientific studies   49
    4.4   Behavioral reaction time tasks   50
            4.4.1   Lexical decision: Visual and auditory   50
            4.4.2   Word naming   53
            4.4.3   Picture naming   54
    4.5   Techniques used at word and sentence level   55
            4.5.1   Self-paced reading   55
            4.5.2   Eye tracking   56
                    4.5.2.1   Using eye tracking to study natural reading   56
                    4.5.2.2   Using eye tracking in reading experiments   56
                    4.5.2.3   Using eye tracking in the visual world paradigm   58
    4.6   Neurophysiological and neuroimaging techniques   59
            4.6.1   Electroencephalography (EEG)   59
            4.6.2   Magnetoencephalography (MEG)   62
            4.6.3   Functional magnetic resonance imaging (fMRI)   62
            4.6.4   Positron emission topography (PET)   64
            4.6.5   Computerized axial tomography (CAT/CT)   64
    4.7   Combining experimental control with ecological validity   65
            4.7.1   Computer screen paradigms   65
            4.7.2   In-lab interaction paradigms   66
            4.7.3   Virtual reality paradigms   67
    4.8   What is next?   69
    4.9   What have we learned?   69

5   **Recognizing spoken words**   **71**

    5.1   Spoken word recognition: The essence   71
    5.2   Spoken word recognition: Representations   73
    5.3   Spoken word recognition: Processes   78
            5.3.1   Categorical perception   78
            5.3.2   Phoneme restoration   79
    5.4   Models of spoken word recognition   80
            5.4.1   Cohort model   80
            5.4.2   TRACE model   82

        5.4.3   Shortlist model   84
        5.4.4   Recent computational developments   85
        5.4.5   A neurobiological approach to spoken word recognition   85
5.5   Spoken word recognition: Empirical studies   86
        5.5.1   Lexical embeddings and Cohort's sequentiality assumption   87
        5.5.2   Speed of spoken word recognition   88
        5.5.3   Time-course of spoken word recognition and top-down effects   89
5.6   Spoken word recognition: The role of context   91
        5.6.1   Fast effects of linguistic and non-linguistic context on spoken word recognition   92
        5.6.2   Context effects: The role of your mental model of the speaker   95
        5.6.3   Context effects: The role of embodiedness   96
5.7   What is next?   97
5.8   What have we learned?   97

6   Recognizing printed and written words   99

6.1   Printed and written word recognition: The essence   99
6.2   Printed and written word recognition: Representations   101
        6.2.1   Letter features and letters   102
        6.2.2   Syllables and morphemes   103
        6.2.3   Writing systems or scripts: Shallow vs. deep orthography   104
6.3   Printed and written word recognition: Processes   105
        6.3.1   Are words looked up in the lexicon one by one or in parallel?   106
6.4   Models of visual word recognition   107
        6.4.1   Interactive Activation model   108
                6.4.1.1   Strengths of the IA model   110
                6.4.1.2   Limitations of the IA model   110
        6.4.2   Spatial Coding model   111
        6.4.3   Dual Route Cascaded model   113
        6.4.4   Multilink model   115
        6.4.5   Parallel distributed processing models   118
        6.4.6   Recent computational developments   119
6.5   Printed and written word recognition: Empirical studies   120
        6.5.1   Speed of printed word recognition   121
        6.5.2   Activation of phonology in word reading   122
        6.5.3   Activation of orthography during listening   123
6.6   Visual word recognition: The role of context   124
        6.6.1   Cross-modal priming with lexical decision   124
        6.6.2   Predicting words in sentence context   126
6.7   What is next?   127
6.8   What have we learned?   127

7   Sentence processing   129

7.1   Sentence processing: The essence   129
7.2   Sentence processing: Representations   131
        7.2.1   Difficult sentences: Embedded sentences   133
        7.2.2   Difficult sentences: Garden path sentences   134

7.3 Sentence processing: Processes   135
    7.3.1 Incremental processing: Tracking the eyes   135
    7.3.2 Integration of syntactic and semantic information over time   137
    7.3.3 Integration vs. prediction   139
7.4 Models of sentence processing   140
    7.4.1 Garden Path model   140
    7.4.2 Referential theory of parsing   141
    7.4.3 Constraint-based model of sentence processing   142
    7.4.4 Unrestricted race model   142
    7.4.5 Neurobiological models of sentence processing   142
    7.4.6 Computational models of sentence processing   146
7.5 Sentence processing: Empirical studies   148
7.6 Sentence processing: The role of context   152
7.7 What is next?   155
7.8 What have we learned?   155

8 Meaning 158

8.1 Meaning: The essence   158
8.2 Meaning: Representations   161
    8.2.1 Sense and reference   161
    8.2.2 Word meaning representations   162
        8.2.2.1 Semantic networks   162
        8.2.2.2 WordNet   163
        8.2.2.3 Semantic features   164
        8.2.2.4 Featural and Unitary Semantic Space   164
        8.2.2.5 Exemplar and instance theory   165
        8.2.2.6 Prototypes   166
        8.2.2.7 Semantic space based on global co-occurrence   166
        8.2.2.8 Embodied representation   167
    8.2.3 Sentence meaning representations   168
    8.2.4 Text meaning representations   169
    8.2.5 Meaning in the brain   170
8.3 Meaning: Processes   171
    8.3.1 Embodiedness: Effects of other cognitive modalities   171
    8.3.2 Linking the meaning of subsequent sentences by inferences   174
        8.3.2.1 Bridging inferences   174
        8.3.2.2 Elaborative inferences: Forward and backward   174
        8.3.2.3 Inferences: Anaphors and antecedents   175
    8.3.3 Thinking and reasoning   177
8.4 Models of meaning   178
    8.4.1 Models of sentence and text processing   178
        8.4.1.1 Construction-Integration model   179
        8.4.1.2 CAPS/READER model   180
        8.4.1.3 Event indexing and event segmentation   181
        8.4.1.4 Cognitive control and the mental model   182
8.5 Meaning: Empirical studies   182
    8.5.1 Semantic illusions   182
    8.5.2 Semantic integration of words and pictures   183

8.6 Meaning: The role of context 185
    8.6.1 Finding the correct referent using prosody 185
    8.6.2 From literal to non-literal meaning: The larger discourse context 187
8.7 What is next? 188
8.8 What have we learned? 189

9 Language production 191

9.1 Language production: The essence 191
9.2 Language production: Representations 192
9.3 Language production: Processes 196
    9.3.1 Language production and the Language User Framework 196
    9.3.2 Conceptualizer 198
    9.3.3 Formulator 200
        9.3.3.1 Syntactic encoding 200
        9.3.3.2 Lemma retrieval 201
        9.3.3.3 The complex interaction between syntactic encoding and lemma retrieval 202
        9.3.3.4 Morphophonological encoding 203
    9.3.4 Articulator 203
9.4 Models of language production 206
    9.4.1 Slot-and-filler models of language production 206
    9.4.2 Standard model of language production 207
    9.4.3 Interactive Activation model for word production 208
    9.4.4 Models of tone language production 209
    9.4.5 Interface Hypothesis 210
9.5 Language production: Empirical studies 212
    9.5.1 Picture-word interference paradigm 213
    9.5.2 Syntactic priming paradigm 214
    9.5.3 Neuroscientific studies 215
    9.5.4 Studies eliciting speech production errors 216
        9.5.4.1 Lexical bias effects in elicited speech errors 216
        9.5.4.2 Freudian speech errors 217
        9.5.4.3 Induced subject–verb agreement errors 217
9.6 Language production: The role of context 218
    9.6.1 Language production in a dialog context 218
    9.6.2 Multimodal language production 220
9.7 What is next? 221
9.8 What have we learned? 221

10 Multilingualism 224

10.1 Multilingualism: The essence 224
10.2 Multilingualism: Representations 225
    10.2.1 Cross-linguistic similarity of word representations 226
    10.2.2 Cross-linguistic similarity of syntactic representations 229
    10.2.3 Storing words and grammar of multiple languages: One or two systems? 230

10.3 Multilingualism: Processes   231
　10.3.1 Processing words and sentences in multiple languages: One or two systems?   231
　10.3.2 The interaction of bottom-up and top-down processes   232
10.4 Models of multilingual processing and control   234
　10.4.1 Revised Hierarchical Model   234
　10.4.2 Distributed Conceptual Feature model   234
　10.4.3 Bilingual Interactive Activation models   235
　10.4.4 Multilink model   235
　10.4.5 Inhibitory and Adaptive Control models   237
10.5 Multilingualism: Empirical studies   239
　10.5.1 Multilingual word retrieval   239
　10.5.2 Multilingual sentence processing   244
　10.5.3 Multilingual language production and control   246
10.6 Multilingualism: The role of context   248
　10.6.1 Semantic effects of sentence context   249
　10.6.2 Task- and stimulus-related context effects   250
10.7 What is next?   252
10.8 What have we learned?   253

11 Conclusion and outlook   255

11.1 Introduction   255
11.2 Expanding the four basic assumptions of the book   256
　11.2.1 Embodiedness, multimodality, and interactivity   256
　11.2.2 Embeddedness, symbol hierarchy, and interactivity   258
　11.2.3 Incrementality, time-scale, and interactivity   259
　11.2.4 The mental model as an interface for language and other cognitive faculties   261
11.3 Expanding the Language User Framework   263
　11.3.1 The Multimodal Language User Framework   263
　11.3.2 Language in the overarching cognitive system   265
11.4 Biases in the psychology of language   267
11.5 Outlook: Diversity, dialog, and digital developments   270
　11.5.1 Acknowledging linguistic and cultural diversity   270
　11.5.2 Shift of focus from monolog to dialog   272
　11.5.3 Advances in human–computer interaction   273
　11.5.4 Development and use of large language models   275
　11.5.5 Computational models of human language processing   276
11.6 What have we learned?   278
11.7 Final remarks   278

References   279
Index   304

Preface

This book is full of language. That is to say, language itself is used to describe what language and its use are all about. By using language in a particular way (hopefully as simple, transparent, and precise as possible), the book tries to convey how the human mind represents, processes, and controls this fascinating, profoundly human cognitive capacity in various situations in real life and in the lab.

The book arose out of the lifelong passion that we share for language. It also arose out of our need for a new textbook on the psychology of language. Over the past decades, the assumptions underlying our understanding of the psychology of language have changed, and presently available textbooks, as excellent as they often are, are no longer fully in line with many of the new insights.

In particular, we have learned that language is much more than an abstract, encapsulated system of rules and representations. An important function of language is to convey as much as possible the rich meaning structures in the minds of interlocutors, and communication often takes place in noisy daily life situations in which several communicative channels (mouth and vocal cords, hands, face) are used concurrently, incrementally, and dynamically. This book therefore stresses the embodiedness, embeddedness, and communicative function of language, while, at the same time, keeping the systematic rigor of previously done scientific work, and uses these assumptions to build up a new view on language processing.

We also intended to write a textbook that may be completely covered during one undergraduate or graduate course. As such, we take a different approach than various existing handbooks that are relatively encyclopedic in nature and therefore impossible to fully cover during one course. We take a student-oriented approach and have written our book specifically for university students, for instance, in psychology, cognitive (neuro)science, artificial intelligence, linguistics, and communication sciences. The material covered in the various chapters has been used and refined in courses on the psychology of language we have taught over many years. By presenting appealing key studies spanning decades of research, we hope to convey critical conclusions about core aspects of language. As such, we do not provide an exhaustive overview of the literature, but discuss a selection of models and studies that illustrate important insights.

While writing, we quickly realized that, although our book is not directly aimed at our more experienced colleagues in the field, it would be unavoidable even in an introduction like this to "take a stand" with respect to many fiercely debated matters in psycholinguistics. So we have stuck our neck out with respect to many issues.

For instance, we describe language as a symbolic rather than a subsymbolic system, a choice that we believe is convenient for both readers and researchers. Because, in our view, models are sketches that try to capture the most important pivot points in cognition, we see no problem in this, even though we agree that the fundamental building blocks of reality may be of a smaller, subsymbolic, grain size.

We propose language use to be multimodal and non-modular. Earlier research has too often equated language with speech. Particularly when it comes to face-to-face communication, people exchange a wide variety of communicative bodily signals that all contribute to the meaning a message conveys. Non-linguistic context of various kinds may affect language processing via a conceptual system. Interactions within the language processing system take place between different levels of representation and allow for effects of linguistic context. Cognitive control, however, in our view does not directly affect activation within this system.

We consider language as embodied, but also hold that it is more than that. Instead of assuming a radical and exclusive embodiment of language, we underline the important role of the body for language and communication, while proposing that meaning can be both embodied and abstract. We use the term "embodiedness" to reflect this position. We assume that syntactic representations are essential in representing language, but ultimately because of the support syntax can provide to semantics. We stress the importance of both behavioral and neuroscientific evidence. Finally, we plead in favor of the development and use of computational models to take us beyond purely verbal theories of language use.

During writing, we tried to apply several didactic principles. We regularly summarize key conclusions of sections in Summary Boxes. We begin the chapters with key terms and end with highlights exposed in the chapters. Over the book as a whole, we present differently worded repetitions of themes that increase in complexity. For instance, we consider brain architecture and processing in several chapters. Each time, new elements are added to stimulate students' activation and integration of knowledge. Hopefully, this gradual build-up will enrich the readers' understanding and acquisition of the presented insights. We further introduce Discussion Boxes to present opposing views on overarching issues in the study of the psychology of language. Students are invited to reflect on each theme and develop their own ideas under the guidance of their lecturer. They can also decide to write a term paper on a topic as an exercise, consulting online sources as part of the process. The same reasoning underlies the organization of the companion website to this book: It contains suggestions for more extended exercises and materials for presentations and reports. We hope that these learning tools will enable students to broaden their horizon beyond the limited selection of the vast number of empirical studies in the field that we were able to present, and to develop their own personal standpoint relative to the many debated issues in the psychology of language.

Before and during writing, we had many helpful and interesting discussions with students and colleagues. Many of them played an important role in guiding the directions we took and in streamlining the text. Here we would like to thank especially the following critical readers of earlier drafts: Gerard Kempen, Rüdiger Thul, James McQueen, Herbert Schriefers, Roberto Ferreira, Josh Ring, Lukas Ansteeg, Walter van Heuven, Kristin Lemhöfer, Henk van Jaarsveld, Montserrat Comesaña, Limor Raviv, Agnes Sianipar, Gerrit Jan Kootstra, Emma Vriezen, Stefan Frank, Mart van het Spijker, Kathy Conklin, Aaron van Geffen, Wim Pouw, Alex Titus, Randi Goertz, and Frank Leene. We are grateful to Fons Maes, Emiel Krahmer, and Juliëtte Schaafsma for creating and maintaining such a supportive work environment. We would also like to thank Routledge/Taylor & Francis for editorial support and guidance, in particular Ceri McLardy, Emilie Coin, Tori Sharpe, Khyati Sanger, and Stacey Carter. Last, but foremost, we wish to bless our stars, for our conversations with Marijke and Doris often threw new light on the subject matter. We thank them both for their continuous support and their encouragement along the way.

Ton Dijkstra and David Peeters

Chapter 1

Basic assumptions of a new psychology of language

1.1 INTRODUCTION

A man visits his physician, because he is not feeling well. After a full examination of the client's body and a number of medical tests, the doctor brings some bad news. "There is an elevation of your white blood cells," she says. The man asks: "What does that mean?" With a concerned look on her face, the doctor answers: "Up." The client first looks a little confused, but then nods.

This short dialog illustrates several key notions for understanding language and its use. First of all, it points out that humans are *embodied* creatures. While they are communicating, they use their body (their mouth, ears, eyes, hands, torso) extensively, and they often communicate about their body because they wish to protect it from harm.

Second, the dialog in this example shows that people are *embedded* in different social contexts. In this doctor–client dialog, the client first admits that the doctor's statement is not clear to him. However, after the doctor's response, he then refrains from posing any further question, probably because he does not want to seem ignorant. One could say that he wishes to protect his social identity (or "Self," if you like).

Third, the joke can only be understood in the context of complex underlying representations of the situation, called *mental models*. Both the doctor and the client have such a complex internal model (i.e., a mental representation or interpretation) of the situation, but their views are not fully compatible (hence, the client's question). However, as readers, we are able to put both perspectives into a more encompassing representation of the situation, because we realize how and where the doctor's and the client's interpretations of the situation clash. We can do this only because the mental models of the doctor and client are incorporated by us, the readers, into an overarching model.

Fourth, although it seems almost trivial, a key aspect of this dialog is that information is presented sequentially: For instance, the second sentence is a continuation to the first; the client responds to the doctor; and within each sentence, information is given word by word, sequentially and *incrementally*.

DOI: 10.4324/9781003326274-1

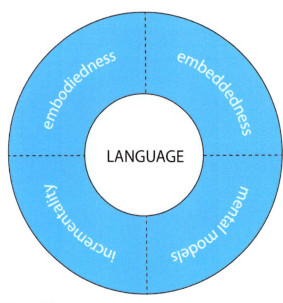

Figure 1.1
In this book, we consider embodiedness, embeddedness, mental models, and incrementality (or incremental processing) as four key aspects of language.

It is important to note that the joke cannot be understood when one of these aspects is missing; they are all interrelated. Importantly, grasping the joke requires a considerable amount of knowledge about the world. For instance, we know that if one does not feel well, one may consult specialized members of society, called "doctors." Visiting such "health authorities" follows a standard line of actions (or: schema), including making an appointment, waiting in a room, talking to the doctor in a white coat, listening to a diagnosis, receiving and following a prescription. In the dialog between doctor and client, all this background knowledge plays a more or less prominent role. Furthermore, language is specialized as a tool to talk about various daily life issues like health, medical practice, and society, as well as their abstract interrelationships. For example, we know that it is preferable in certain contexts to talk about "clients" rather than "patients." In the doctor–client dialog, exchanging language further helps to establish "common ground" (Clark, 1996) by synchronizing the continuously updated representations of the developing situation by the doctor and the client. At the same time, language has its limitations, because it is ambiguous and can be misinterpreted. In a joke, this aspect of language is used on purpose, leading to a clash between different mental models, causing humor by displacing attention from one model to the other. In our example, the model of the client clashes with that of the doctor.

In the following sections, we will consider these key aspects of language – embodiedness, embeddedness, mental models, and incremental processing – in more detail, as they are fundamental to understanding the psychology of language (see Figure 1.1). Because of their importance for understanding the nature of human language use, we will encounter them time and again throughout the book.

1.2 EMBODIEDNESS

It seems trivial to start with the observation that humans process language by way of their bodies. Reading takes place via the eyes (sighted people) or the hands and fingers (blind individuals), listening happens via the ears, speech production via the vocal cords and mouth, writing implies the use of one's hands, and if one communicates via a sign language, one will move parts of the body (hands, arms, torso, and face) in a meaningful way. Furthermore, there is non-verbal information that is conveyed through the body, for example, via posture, clothes, smell, and facial expressions. We move our arms and hands in meaningful ways when we speak. Both verbal and non-verbal communication are subserved by the brain in the body.

Calling language *embodied* raises the question of which physical possibilities and restrictions the body (and, in particular, the brain) imposes on language comprehension and production. Communication and language are inherently linked to our senses (like hearing, seeing, and tasting), to our movements and gestures (speaking, writing, and pointing, for instance), and to cognition (including thinking, emotion, and, for instance, music perception).

In principle, communication can take place via all our senses. However, which senses modern human beings give more importance to in their communication differs to some extent across cultures (Majid et al., 2018). In communicative contexts in many Western societies, taste and smell are often given less attention than seeing and hearing. As a result, our spoken vocabularies for tastes and smells are poorer relative to those for visual and auditory percepts (consider wine tasting). Although we exchange some information via smell (e.g., perfume) and taste, we usually understand the term "language" to refer to specific scribbles on paper, sounds in the air, and the hand movements produced in sign language.

Language comprehension mainly relies on information transmitted via the visual and the auditory modality. To some extent, the properties of writing systems must therefore be restricted given the properties of our eyes (for receiving messages) and hands (for producing messages). For linguistic information arriving via the eyes, spatial location is important (take, for instance, the position of a letter in a word). For sign languages, not only is the spatial location of the hands important, but also the specific shape of the hand, the accompanying movement and orientation of the hands, and any concurrent facial expressions and lip movements. When linguistic information arrives via the ears, the sequential aspect of the acoustic message is quite important, both with respect to smaller (e.g., sound segments, words) and larger units (e.g., intonation patterns on phrases). Due to the differences between eyes and ears in their physical properties, the information transferred is different in density and dimensions. Some of the differences between reading print and listening are indicated in Box 1.1 (adapted from Nickerson, 1981).

As you may derive from Box 1.1, in listening, speech sounds and words are presented sequentially, but during reading, the eyes, fixating on printed words, may process several letters in parallel. Spoken language disappears after it has been said, but printed words typically remain on the paper or screen for re-inspection. Speech consists of overlapping sounds that are often co-articulated, whereas printed letters stand out clearly relative to their background, providing contrast. There is relatively more variation in the speech signal than in the printed message. Content-wise, speech has intonation and can express affect, while print has diacritics and may mark morphosyntactic information. Listening is dependent on the speaker's speech rate, while reading pace often can be determined by

Box 1.1	Differences between reading print (visual input) and listening (auditory input)	
	listening	reading
time course	sequential	parallel
	short duration	lasting
form	continuous	discrete
	co-articulation	contrast
	varying	constant
content	intonation	diacritics
	affect	morphosyntactic information
control	external	internal
effect	arousal	visual dominance

the readers themselves. On social media, written messages sometimes make use of properties that are typical for spoken communication, such as when written text is presented only briefly before it disappears. Spoken and written language may also have different effects on their receivers in terms of physical arousal (typically larger for auditory signals) and the capture of attention (called "visual dominance"). Later chapters consider these aspects in more detail.

Similar considerations hold for different types of language production. Speaking and writing (or typing) differ on many dimensions, including articulation (muscles of vocal cords vs. those of the hands), discreteness (speaking and writing are typically more continuous in output form than typing), speed of information exchange (speaking and online chatting are typically faster than writing a book or typing a letter), and the information conveyed (intonation may reflect affect, which is expressed in print in a relatively impoverished way via exclamation marks, the use of capital letters, or emoticons). Note that in exceptional circumstances, such as when deafblind people communicate with one another, the absence of reliable visual and auditory information leads to a dominance of the tactile modality (Mesch, 1998).

An important aspect to note is that the thoughts that we wish to convey may be quite rich in content. They may concern mental models of complex situations or mathematical concepts. However, due to the nature of language and speech, these complex situations or concepts must be expressed via one or more (nearly) one-dimensional information channels.

This raises the important question of how senders could most efficiently (i.e., quickly and accurately) encode information in their utterances. Languages offer a number of tools to do this. The actual or mental reality may be described by words that refer to specific objects (e.g., nouns) or events (e.g., verbs). Syntax may accentuate the most salient aspects of messages, by putting some words in focus or subject positions. In addition, syntactic properties (e.g., word order) can be used to express unlikely events (e.g., "man bites dog"). Furthermore, often recurring strings of words (e.g., formulaic language, such as collocations or expressions such as "it runs in the family") may be processed faster by chunking them into separate abstract representations. Co-speech gestures and facial expressions may be used to convey information (for instance, spatial, or emotional) that is difficult to communicate via speech alone (Kendon, 2004; McNeill, 1992). Nevertheless, the limitations to express complex concepts and feelings remain obvious; just try to describe what you think, feel, and appreciate in a classical music piece such as Bach's "Brandenburger Concerto I" or a pop song, for example, "Northern Sky" by Nick Drake.

One way to somewhat overcome the limitations of the processing channel is to vary not only the content of the message, but also the way it is sent. As has been argued by McLuhan, Ekman, and many others, the medium is also part of the message. For instance, speaking in a loud voice may increase the message's strength (e.g., its urgency) and can also convey certain emotions. Such emotions (e.g., sadness) may be considered as an essential part of the meaning of the utterance.

In communication, information is conveyed at many different levels at the same time: verbally and non-verbally, through specific intonations or spellings, particular grammars or dialects, and registers and speaking habits. It is hard to separate the incoming information types. For instance, errors against spelling or grammatical rules may inadvertently convey the message that the writer is forgetful or illiterate, or that the content of the message may not be trustworthy (in fact, this is how we can often determine whether an email message is genuine or forged).

We would like to argue that verbal and non-verbal communication form an inseparable whole. Although this "goes without saying" for some language researchers, such as people working on co-speech gestures and sign languages, abstract approaches to language, including some branches in linguistics, have tended to consider this aspect as less relevant. In this book, we treat language as a multimodal phenomenon, in which speakers use "composite signals" (i.e., they combine speech, gesture, facial expressions, etc.) to convey messages to their addressee (Clark, 1996; Enfield et al., 2007; Engle, 1998).

> **SUMMARY: EMBODIEDNESS**
>
> Humans are biological beings (animals) that make use of their body in several ways when they communicate. First, they use body parts to speak (speech organs, ears, eyes, hands, faces, etc.). Second, they also communicate through non-verbal body language, but verbal and non-verbal aspects of communication form an inseparable whole. Third, language use is subserved and controlled by the brain.

1.3 EMBEDDEDNESS

All language use takes place in context. In the complex representations of reality that people constantly formulate and update (their "mental models"), the perspective of their bodies and personalities is in a central position, but it interacts heavily with the environment. This makes their language and models of reality "embedded." Indeed, contextual aspects of language use cannot be ignored without possibly dangerous misinterpretations of utterances. Two important types of non-linguistic context are concerned with physical and with socio-cultural aspects or restrictions.

First, utterances take place in a *physical (bodily) context*. For instance, spoken utterances are affected by bodily limitations, such as the shape and momentum of the speech organs. Assimilation and co-articulation imply that sounds may change depending on the context they occur in. For example, we tend to pronounce the words "want to" as "wanna" and "handbag" as "hambag" (Ernestus & Warner, 2011). Furthermore, our sentences and words may refer to people, objects, and actions in the present environment: "this road," "she is running." Thus, the meanings and world knowledge we use can be related to this physical context and this time. Our interpretation is also often context-dependent: The word "here" typically refers to this specific place and time, but depending on the conversation, it may refer to your local town, country, or even the universe at large (Levinson, 2004; Nunberg, 1993).

Second, utterances are fine-tuned to the *social and cultural context* in which they occur. For instance, in interaction with their infants, caregivers use a special type of child-directed language, called "baby talk," "parentese," or "motherese" (Matychuk, 2005). It is often characterized, for instance, by a slower speech rate and shorter, simplified utterances, accentuates pauses and minimizes overlap to enable turn-taking by the child, and may involve "sing song" intonation patterns at a relatively high pitch. A different example is the phenomenon of "cultural frame shifting," referring to an impact of the cultural norms of a particular language community on the speakers' personality as they themselves or others perceive it (Chen & Bond, 2010). In simple terms, bilinguals may feel they have two somewhat divergent personalities, one for each of their languages.

In a social context, not only verbal aspects of communication play a role, so too do non-verbal aspects. For instance, eye contact is important to establish whether the listener is following and understanding what you are talking about. At the same time, body language may convey information about the relationship between speaker and listener, motivation and power, attentiveness and interest, and so on.

6 Basic assumptions of a new psychology of language

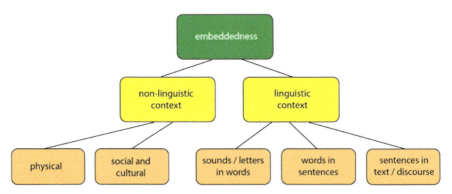

Figure 1.2
Language use is typically embedded in a physical and a sociocultural non-linguistic context. Linguistic units are typically embedded in larger linguistic units (sounds or letters in words, words in phrases or sentences, sentences in a larger text or discourse).

Generally in language comprehension, information about the context is added to the meaning of the utterance itself by the addressee of the message. This meaning may concern information about past, present, or future of the body or the world. In language production, the opposite process takes place: The speaker or signer links a meaning to an utterance taking into account available information about the (verbal and non-verbal) context in which the utterance is made. Thus, listening or reading and speaking or writing take into account non-linguistic contextual information embedded in the discourse situation and combine such information with stored world knowledge.

A quite different type of context is the *linguistic context*, referring to our knowledge about the different levels of the language in use (e.g., syntax or semantics). Sounds or letters are typically part of larger linguistic units such as words. Words often appear in the context of a larger phrase or sentence. Sentences, in turn, are often part of larger stretches of text or discourse. Different types of linguistic context effect (e.g., how syntax affects word recognition) will be considered in detail later when we discuss the Language User Framework. Figure 1.2 summarizes the different types of context that play a role in everyday language use.

We can apply the notion of the embeddedness of language in context to the opening example. The physical context in the opening example is the private examination room in which the doctor looks at the client; its function to assure privacy is recognized as such by the client. In the social and cultural context of the doctor–client relation, the roles of the doctor and client are defined in a way that is mutually understood. The doctor–client situation involves a well-known scenario with particular roles, events, and developments to be expected. In case opinions are expressed about health issues, the opinion of the doctor typically overrules that of the client – similar to what happens in our example.

Furthermore, there is general and specialized world knowledge that must be retrieved for proper understanding. For instance, the doctor in the opening example possibly believes that her client does not know the meaning of the verb "to elevate." She tries to cooperate with the client by explaining that it means "up." However, the doctor thereby overlooks the possibility that the client might, in fact, wish to know what white blood cells are for. From his side, the client then cooperates with the doctor by nodding rather than by asking for further explanation, even though this could be interpreted as evidence that he did indeed not know the meaning of the verb "to elevate." As we see in this example, the language used is context-sensitive, not only in the syntactic sense, but also with respect to the wider world knowledge the interlocutors share. At the same time, it is also very ambiguous and open to different understandings.

Context is also important in the more restricted environment of experimental laboratories in which language use is investigated. How language is processed here depends on (a) who you are with: participant characteristics; (b) stimulus characteristics and stimulus list composition; and (c) task demands, e.g., reading for the specific meaning, spelling errors, or gist of the text.

As an example, how a word is processed in an experiment depends not only on its physical properties (luminance or loudness, presentation font type and size), but also on the stimulus list it appears in, on its position in that list, and on the task that the participant is required to perform. As a matter of fact, it is impossible to build a theory of language processing based on experimental evidence without taking into account how stimulus materials, tasks, and participant characteristics contribute to the data. We will get back to these specific context effects in more detail in Chapter 10 on multilingualism.

> **SUMMARY: EMBEDDEDNESS**
>
> The language we use is typically embedded in a larger context. This context can be non-linguistic, for instance, physical or sociocultural; or linguistic, for instance, the sentence structure in which a word occurs. Language users typically take into account the physical, sociocultural, and linguistic context in which they use or perceive words and utterances. Theories and models of language use and language processing must take the various types of context into account when trying to explain the mental processes that support our linguistic abilities.

1.4 MENTAL MODELS

As a human being, you try to make sense of the world surrounding you. This implies that you try to build a coherent internal model of it, a simplified approximation of aspects that are relevant to you for physical and social survival. From early on in our lives, models for different strands of life are conveyed to us via language: Parents or caregivers, peers, and teachers provide them to us during education, and experiences with the world lead us to differentiate such models on our own.

In the most simple *mental model*, your current situation is represented in terms of various aspects: physical, biological, psychological, and sociological. For instance, at the physical level you are aware of gravity, color, resistance of material objects, and loudness. At the biological level, you perceive things emotionally, via your different bodily senses, and by movement. At the psychological level, what is happening has an emotional value or an abstract meaning. And at the sociological level, you notice your role in the ongoing dialog dependent on your background and the empathic relation between you and the person you speak with. These different aspects of the situation are all intertwined. For instance, notions such as "interpersonal distance" and "speaking volume" are usually characterized at several of these levels simultaneously. For example, you may speak more loudly (physical) when you are angry (biological and psychological), because your dialog partner just ridiculed your favorite soccer team (sociological).

In all, the various aspects of the present situation are integrated by you in a multidimensional mental model or situational model. The mental model represents information about content (e.g., the abstract meaning of messages and what was said in the discourse/text), but also about the other aspects of information present (physical, biological, and so on; cf. Johnson-Laird, 1989).

However, a mental model is not static and develops over time. It constitutes not only a spatial but also a temporal account of what is going on. When new information arrives, the mental model is dynamically adapted in order to represent it in a detailed way, making use of space, time, causality, and intentions. For instance, in a dialog situation, participants continuously (re)construct one another's viewpoint of the situation. Their mental models keep track of who said what, who responded and how, what happened first and what happened next, how and where this happened, and so on. Thus, the specifics of the model are time-dependent and open to change.

To understand what another person is saying, we must compare the incoming signal to *stored information* about language: word information in our Long Term Memory, word order information from syntax, but also meaning and world knowledge up to the deepest level (emotion, motor behavior). Speech is ephemeral; the auditory signal does not linger around in time and space, so the listener typically has to incorporate novel information into their mental model quickly and efficiently (Christiansen & Chater, 2016).

While language users are having a conversation, reading a book, or watching a series, they must construct more complex mental models to account for the psychological worlds in the minds of other speakers or writers. To a child, one might talk about aspects of the concrete situation at hand ("see the bird in that tree?"), but in order to follow the story line in a novel, one must somehow *simulate* (mimic) the continuously changing imaginary situation depicted by the writer (Willems & Jacobs, 2016).

In other words, mental models are updated all the time, by changing, adding, or removing information, depending on the language users' experiences, viewpoints, and expectations. For instance, when the Chinese flag is mentioned in a news item, the mental model for the situation might add the colors red and yellow to its content; when talking about my sister's apartment, I may recollect the spatial arrangement of it; and thinking about the novel I read last night, I may remember that a certain sentence was positioned near the top of a page with an odd page number.

The notion of a mental model is important for several reasons. First, according to this view, for effective communication it is not enough to represent messages in a completely abstract way, as *propositions* (approximately meaning formulas relating arguments by functions). Mental models contain an abundance of world meaning in sensory modalities that non-embodied representations cannot capture. As such, mental models will contain both abstract and embodied information.

Second, the notion of the mental model can be linked to the absence of *modularity* (i.e., modality-specific, compartmentalized processing), because physical, biological, psychological, linguistic, and sociocultural aspects of the situation all contribute to the way utterances are expressed and comprehended. As such, mental models must imply coherent brain activity in which different modalities participate and interact.

Third, the notion of a mental model also implies that language processing can go to different depths and involve different stages. For instance, when reading a book, physical features of the print are first recoded into abstract representations of letters, words, and sentences; these are turned into propositions; then *world knowledge and physical-biological information* are added to form an adequate mental model of the text (we will discuss these aspects in detail in Chapter 8 on meaning).

It is important to realize that, due to the simplifying nature of mental models and the incomplete and ambiguous nature of language, a book (or any written document) can never deliver a fully exact copy of what was in the writer's mind when they put the words on paper. This sometimes makes the interpretation of books whose writers lived long ago a difficult or even dangerous affair. Because we add or distort information when we understand other language users, we are basically making up *stories* that may sometimes be more in line with what we believed or expected the others to say than with what they really said or intended.

Conversely, it is probably not an exaggeration to say that our culture would not exist without the invention of written language and books. Writing and reading offer us the possibility to put our mental models on paper, adequate or inadequate. By writing a book, you can convey messages to other people, even those who are not here in space or time, and by reading a book, you are able to reconstruct and revive part of the mental world of the writer.

> **SUMMARY: MENTAL MODELS**
>
> People try to make sense of the world around them by developing and testing internal mental models of what they experience. The mental models people construe represent incoming information in line with their knowledge about the world and other language users. Mental models do not only contain abstract information, but also concrete and analog information (e.g., subjective perceptual or emotional aspects of the situation). Such information is ultimately linked to the body. Mental models represent not only the here-and-now of the physical-biological world, but also the there-and-if of the psychological worlds expressed in dialogs or books.

1.5 INCREMENTAL PROCESSING

As discussed in the previous section, mental models are multidimensional, but language processing is basically one-dimensional (i.e., it can be seen as following a timeline). Listening, reading, speaking, and writing are concerned with information that is presented piece by piece, for instance, sound by sound, or word by word. Pieces of information are processed *incrementally*, i.e., as a series of different elements that follow one another in time and build on each other. Language is hierarchically organized, such that smaller elements (e.g., sounds) are usually part of larger elements (e.g., words). By and large, incrementality seems to hold for both smaller and larger pieces of information.

For instance, sentences usually try to express the basic ideas in a speaker's mind. Such ideas are expressed incrementally by words or chunks of words. Often, the most relevant content is provided first. The "most relevant content" at some moment in time may concern the most salient aspects of a message or situation (e.g., the person who is doing something, or a relevant object in the world), but also information that allows listeners or readers to link up the upcoming information to the mental model in their Working Memory. Incrementality is also found at the word level itself: In spoken word recognition and word production, auditory signals are processed millisecond by millisecond.

Efficient processing implies that receivers do not wait until the utterance is finished, but process all information they can at each moment in time and predict what is coming next (e.g., for optimizing turn-taking; Stivers et al., 2009). This implies that syntax and semantics must be interwoven: As soon as the first words of an utterance come in, both their (lexical) meanings and their role in the sentence are established. Most likely, receivers attempt to build a structure of the event at hand even before any language input arrives. Thus, it seems unlikely that the brain would first register syntactic properties of a sentence and only then semantic aspects.

It is not only linguistic information of different sorts that is often presented in parallel or closely in time. For instance, emotional information may be presented alongside information about meaning, in terms of intonation and word stress. We convey information using different channels at the same time: Speech may be accompanied by hand gestures and a meaningful facial expression (Holler & Levinson, 2019). And when a sentence is read, word information, sentence information, and meaning information are all developing over time more or less in parallel. Language users often wish to retrieve and communicate their intentions as quickly as possible, and to understand their conversation partner without delay.

> **SUMMARY: INCREMENTAL PROCESSING**
>
> During listening, reading, speaking, and writing, relevant information of different sorts is processed in a piecemeal fashion, in parallel, and linked to a continuously adapting mental model.

1.6 CONSEQUENCES OF THIS VIEW ON LANGUAGE

Our emphasis on language as an embodied, embedded, incremental cognitive activity aiming at mental model construction prompts us to consider various aspects of language use and development in a specific way. For instance, with respect to the *phylogenesis* of language (its evolution in humans), it suggests we should consider language evolution in terms of the human body and human society. Language families and language trees fit well with this idea. With respect to the *ontogenesis* of language (its development in the human child), the embodiedness assumption stresses the importance of the genetic basis of language, while the embeddedness assumption considers language acquisition in relation to social and physically oriented interactions with caretakers, as well as cognitive aspects having to do with attention, memory, and cognitive control. Indeed, these last aspects cannot be fully appreciated if one does not consider the brain that produces language in response to particular situations and during the execution of various tasks.

Embeddedness and embodiedness are also of great importance when one considers language as it is used by different individuals (child vs. adult, man vs. woman), by different specific populations (for instance, people with aphasia, monolinguals, and multilinguals), and in dialog situations.

Mental models contain information about body-related perceptual and motor aspects, as well as abstract representations. In this respect, the view of language presented in this book deviates from some more traditional views.

In the past decades, language has indeed prominently been described by linguists and psycholinguists as an abstract system of rules and representations. Many researchers have "abstracted away" from the messy language used in daily life situations, in order to make sense of the bewildering variability of language phenomena. Indeed, by the early 1960s, in his book *Aspects of the Theory of Syntax*, the influential linguist Chomsky proposed considering language as a unique, perfectly mastered human capacity used by a homogeneous population of idealized speakers and listeners, and he developed syntactic theories that involve abstract operations in an almost mathematical framework (as we will see in Discussion Boxes in Chapters 2 and 3). While this was to some extent a fruitful approach, it is clear that systematicity in the abstract systems describing language should not lead us to ignore the actual and concrete incremental application of language in the messy social

> **DISCUSSION BOX 1: EMBODIEDNESS VS. EMBODIMENT**
>
> We have introduced the notion of "embodiedness," implying that our body is involved in many of our communicative activities. A related but somewhat different theoretical term in the empirical literature on the psychology of language is "embodiment" (Aziz-Zadeh & Damasio, 2008; Barsalou, 1999; Boulenger et al., 2009). The "embodied simulation hypothesis" assumes that language comprehension involves mental simulations subserved by the perceptual and motor areas of the brain. Language is understood "by simulating in our minds what it would be like to experience the things that the language describes" (Bergen, 2012, p. 13; Yaxley & Zwaan, 2007). The term "embodiment" therefore implies a stronger reliance of language on other modalities than is advocated in the present book, which proposes that we possess *both* abstract *and* more sense-oriented conceptual representations (cf. Raposo et al., 2009; and see Chapter 8 for more information).
>
> What is your own view on this distinction between embodiedness and embodiment? To what extent can language be fully described in terms of its relation to other cognitive modalities such as perception and action? Look up information on the internet (e.g., Google Scholar; Wikipedia) to motivate your position.

situations of daily life, realized by the physical machinery of the human body under control of the brain.

In the view presented in this book, an important function of language is to convey as much as possible the rich meaning structures (referred to by terms such as "mental models" and "semantic networks") in the minds of interlocutors. In the last decade, we have learned much about the biological substrate of language and about its dependence on various types of context, both outside language (e.g., social aspects, world knowledge) and inside it (e.g., sentence context, stimulus list composition in an experiment).

However, we depart from the majority of textbooks on language that still describe language as a purely abstract system with more or less modular components. On the basis of the zeitgeist, we believe it is time to consider a different approach to the psychology of language, stressing the embodiedness, embeddedness, and communicative function of language, while at the same time keeping the systematic rigor of previously undertaken scientific work.

A related issue is the extent to which we consider the *arbitrariness* between form and meaning to be a central "design feature" of human language (Hockett, 1960). For a long time, many language researchers assumed, based on their focus on Indo-European spoken languages, that the link between word forms and their meanings was fully or to a large extent arbitrary (following de Saussure, 1916, 1998). After all, how else would one explain that the same concept (e.g., CAR) is expressed in completely different ways in different languages (e.g., as *auto* in Dutch, *coche* in Spanish, *voiture* in French, *macchina* in Italian)? There are two problems with this view. First, language is mostly reduced to its verbal component. Second, the diversity of languages around the world is not taken into account.

Indeed, if we consider embodiedness a central feature of language and communication, we see that many of the signals we convey do not have an arbitrary link between their form and their meaning. In sign languages, many of the signs that are used resemble what they mean: The sign for "tree" in British Sign Language (BSL), for instance, to some extent resembles an actual tree in that the signer's lower arm is shown in vertical position in resemblance to a tree's trunk. The same holds for many of the co-speech gestures we make when communicating in a spoken language: They visually resemble what they mean. In spoken Indo-European languages including English, the sound of onomatopoeic words ("buzz," "beep," and "sizzle") also seems to resemble the meaning of those words. Many languages in Asia, Africa, and on the American continents have entire classes of words (often called "ideophones" or "mimetics") that give away part of their (sensory) meaning when they are spoken out loud. Do you think the word *gbudugbluu* in Ewe means "skinny" or "obese"? Try to read it aloud and your intuition will provide you with the correct answer (or see Dingemanse et al., 2015)! All these examples show that both arbitrariness and *iconicity* are important properties of language.

Words thus differ in how transparent the link is between their form and their meaning and they are typically part of larger multimodal utterances that contain other signals such as iconic co-speech gestures. Sometimes within a language small sets of words also display remarkable *systematicity* in what they look like and what they mean. Words that refer to a shiny visual experience in English often happen to start with the same consonant cluster: "glance," "glare," "glitter," "glimmer," "glow." Likewise, certain words that literally have a "nosy" meaning start in the same way: "sneeze," "sniff," "snore," "snout," "snuffle." The language user (and the language learner!) can make use of such regularities to get at the meaning of words.

Statistical approaches to test for form-meaning associations across large sets of languages actually confirm that the relation between word form and word meaning is even less arbitrary than you would think (Blasi et al., 2016). For instance, across the spoken languages of the world, it turns out that the concept SMALL is surprisingly often expressed using a word that contains the /i/ sound (a high front vowel), perhaps because small creatures typically produce high sounds. Another observed regularity is that words for the concept NOSE are found to quite often contain a nasal /n/ sound. As such, confirming the importance of the body for human language, the relation between word form and meaning may – more often than previously thought – not be so arbitrary after all!

> **SUMMARY: CONSEQUENCES OF THIS VIEW ON LANGUAGE**
>
> Considering language as an embodied, embedded, incremental cognitive activity aiming at mental model construction has important implications for our understanding of the psychology of language. It stresses that humans make use of a variety of bodily channels to communicate about aspects of the rich meaning structures present in their minds. As such, this approach breaks with a tradition that conceptualizes language as a purely abstract system of rules and representations. Rather, it fits well with recent theoretical advances showing that both arbitrary and iconic links between form and meaning exist in the communicative signals we as humans convey in concrete daily situations and in the representation of language in the human mind.

1.7 OVERVIEW OF THE BOOK

In the following chapters of this book, we will consider different aspects of language use one by one. We will start by describing different aspects of human communication in general (Chapter 2). Making a distinction between language and communication, we will proceed by briefly examining how language evolved in conjunction with simultaneous biological and sociological developments. We conclude Chapter 2 by discussing a well-known model for communication in general, the Sender–Receiver model. In Chapter 3, this model is then differentiated in a framework for language use, called the Language User Framework. This overarching framework describes the rich structures, processes, and cognitive control aspects of language use in adults.

The Language User Framework provides a general theoretical basis for the content-oriented chapters in the book (Chapters 5–10), which consider a variety of theoretical models of the specific topic at hand, the representations and processes relevant to the models, and empirical studies applying different research paradigms. To prepare for these studies, some background information on frequently applied research techniques in the experimental study of language will be provided first (Chapter 4). The core chapters of the book are then dedicated to spoken (Chapter 5) and visual (Chapter 6) word recognition, sentence processing (Chapter 7), the meaning of words, sentences, and text (Chapter 8), and the representation and production of speech during speaking (Chapter 9). In Chapter 10, we consider language processing by multilinguals in the light of the Language User Framework, which allows us to return to many important issues discussed earlier in the book. Finally, Chapter 11 provides an extended version of the Language User Framework that may be used as a basis for understanding the intrinsically multichannel nature of human communication, linking language to other cognitive domains. The chapter also considers different theoretical perspectives on language and discusses the future of the psychology of language.

QUESTIONS FOR CHAPTER 1

1 What are the basic assumptions underlying the view of the psychology of language presented in this book?
2 What is incrementality? Consider in which ways incrementality might play a role in listening, reading, speaking, and writing.
3 How do reading and listening differ in terms of involved sensory organs and signal characteristics?
4 What is a "mental model"? What makes this kind of model different from purely abstract (e.g., propositional) models?
5 Give examples of how non-verbal and verbal context may affect the processing of a spoken word. Consider different levels of processing (e.g., form and meaning of the word).
6 Here is another doctor–client dialog. Analyze it in the same way as was done in the chapter. "The doctor says: 'Unfortunately, you have a kidney disease.' The client asks: 'Can I get a second opinion, please?' To which the doctor responds: 'Sure, you have a cold as well.'"
7 Why would some researchers consider the dialog a better topic for research than the individual's language use?
8 Consider the various ways in which the body is relevant to language (e.g., as a tool, topic, functionally, physically, etc.)
9 Look up on the internet how quickly and accurately we can read, listen, speak, and write. What do you conclude from the speed and relative accuracy of these language activities?
10 It is sometimes said that in speaking we use a one-dimensional channel to confer information about a three-dimensional representation of the world (the mental model). What are the consequences of this limitation of speech for language and communication? In what ways could this limitation be overcome?

Chapter 2
Language and communication

2.1 INTRODUCTION

Consider the following joke. A student comes home from her work at night. Her dog jumps up at her as soon as she enters her flat. "And how was your day, boy?" the student asks. The dog barks: "Rough!"

Although this exchange between student and dog cannot really be seen as a conversation or language dialog, there is certainly a form of communication taking place. The term "communication" has a broader application than does the term "language." Communication has been loosely defined as the exchange of information, ideas, or feelings. It seems that student and dog at least exchange feelings here. Thus, communication can be seen as a sort of *transaction*: The participants in the dialog (technically called "interlocutors") are creating meaning together, here affective meaning (see also Ekman, 1993).

The exchange of information, ideas, or feelings is not the only function of communication. Communication can also take place in order to influence others, to develop relationships, and to fulfil social obligations. We can even say that humans have a need or urge to communicate, for instance in order to define who they are (Verderber, 1993).

A somewhat more complex definition of communication is the following: "Every action with which a person exchanges information about needs, desires, perceptions, knowledge, or affective states. Communication can be intentional or non-intentional, proceed via conventional or non-conventional signals, via linguistic or non-linguistic signals, and via spoken or other channels" (de Valenzuela, 1992, p. 2). In this chapter, we will focus on all aspects of this broad definition of communication.

2.2 VERBAL AND NON-VERBAL COMMUNICATION

Traditionally, a distinction is made between *non-verbal* communication or body language, and *verbal* communication or language. However, in reality, there is often no "hard" separation between verbal and non-verbal aspects of communication (McNeill, 1985). Non-verbal

DOI: 10.4324/9781003326274-2

signals contribute to verbal communication and vice versa. It could be said that verbal communication is embedded in a broader non-verbal communicative context. In fact, the separation between language and other cognitive domains is fuzzy. Although our cognitive systems are dedicated to specific tasks, they do not produce their output on the basis of received input in an encapsulated way. Instead, they are open to information from other systems during processing. In other words, they are *non-modular* (i.e., not functioning as fully independent systems). Such non-modularity is, for instance, evident in sign languages. Here facial and manual information interact with lip movements (so-called "mouthings"), while they are accompanied by a particular physical orientation, location, and movement of the hands. However, the non-modularity of human cognition is also evident from very basic communicative situations in which speakers combine auditory and visual signals.

A prototypical example of naturally occurring human communication in which verbal and non-verbal types of information often come together is *pointing*. Infants typically start pointing at things in the world using their index finger already before their first birthday (Bates et al., 1975). It is one of the first ways in which they express their intention to communicate with those around them (Tomasello et al., 2007). Before their second birthday, they commonly start producing pointing gestures (visual information) and speech (auditory information) at the same time (Iverson & Goldin-Meadow, 2005). Throughout our lives, pointing remains a ubiquitous form of communication (Kita, 2003). We may point at things in our surroundings while expressing our attitudes via speech: "What a lovely new haircut." We often share information with our addressee through concurrent speech and pointing: "The train station is over there." And we may point at things to request a favor from our addressee: "Could you pass me those sandwiches, please?" In all these instances, our brain in and through our body allows us to exchange information about aspects of the world around us via bodily gestures and speech. We combine verbal and non-verbal aspects of communication in a non-modular way.

An example that illustrates that also the perception of spoken language often takes place in a bodily context and is influenced by concurrent bodily information is the *McGurk effect*. This famous effect was first described by McGurk and his colleague MacDonald in the prestigious scientific journal *Nature* (McGurk & MacDonald, 1976). In an experiment, they had participants repeatedly listen to the sound "ba." At the same time, those participants watched the face of a young lady whose mouth movements corresponded to the sound "ga." When they asked the participants what they heard, a majority reported actually hearing the sound "da." This finding indicates that the brain continuously integrates visual bodily and auditory linguistic information. It provides the listener with a best guess of what is being communicated by a speaker, taking both verbal and non-verbal aspects of communication into account.

The verbal and non-verbal signals that we produce as communicators can be classified into different subcategories as a function of how they refer to something (Burks, 1949). A pointing gesture does not refer to itself, but directs the visual attention of a listener towards something different, in a way a bit similar to how smoke may direct your attention to a fire. Such a relation between a sign and its referent is called *indexical*. Other signs transfer meaning in an *iconic* way: Their form physically resembles their meaning (Perniss & Vigliocco, 2014). The word "beep" sounds a bit like an actual beep; its spoken form resembles what the speaker means when saying it. Similarly, a speaker may bring her hand to her mouth as if holding a glass while talking about her night out at the pub last Friday. Here, the iconic form and path of her hand gesture to some extent resemble the meaning of the gesture: to drink something. However, many spoken and written words in languages like English and Dutch are verbal signs that convey their meaning to a large extent in a *symbolic* way. The word form "tree" does not look like a tree or sound like a tree. In those cases, the link between form and meaning can be considered to a large extent arbitrary. It has to be

16 *Language and communication*

Figure 2.1
A selection of bodily channels that can be used to convey a variety of communicative bodily signals. Part of image designed by pikisuperstar/Freepik.

culturally learned. When a visual word form in alphabetic script looks like its meaning, such as the word "bed" that looks a bit like a bed, this is largely accidental.

It should be clear by now that humans communicate via all five sensory channels (cf. Figure 2.1). Non-illustrated examples are smell (soap, perfume) and touch (a handshake or high five). Generally, the simultaneous use of more channels increases the chance of successful communication. An example is that combining hearing and seeing typically increases learning compared to hearing alone. A spoken message supplemented by spontaneous hand gestures may often convey the thoughts in the mind of a speaker better than spoken words alone (Kendon, 2004; McNeill, 2005).

> ### SUMMARY: VERBAL AND NON-VERBAL COMMUNICATION
>
> Humans communicate by conveying verbal and non-verbal signals. There is no "hard" distinction between verbal and non-verbal aspects of a message. Our cognitive systems are non-modular. In both the production and perception of communicative messages, information (e.g., visual, auditory) from different modalities is often combined to form composite signals. Signs may relate to a referent in an indexical, iconic, or symbolic manner.

2.3 LANGUAGE AND COMMUNICATION IN CONTEXT

Communication, including language, always takes place in a specific context. As we saw in the previous chapter, it is embedded in a physical and social context and must be understood against a certain background. Location, time, light, temperature, and even positioning of the participants are all physical aspects that may contribute to the communication taking place.

When communicating, the participants heavily rely on mutual, shared knowledge or *common ground* (Clark, 1996; Lewis, 1969). They build up and rely on knowledge they share with their specific interlocutor(s), and also take into account what knowledge and beliefs any member of their community is assumed to possess (Clark, 2015). For example, I may know that (we both know that) Zadie Smith is your favorite writer ("personal common ground") and that (we both know that) most people in Brazil speak a version of Portuguese ("communal common ground"). Not only the physical situation, but also the psychological and the cultural situation contribute to the information exchange. For instance, it matters how contributors see themselves and others, and to what extent they share knowledge systems (attitudes, values, symbols, behaviors) and have shared goals and intentions (Tomasello et al., 2005).

The role of context in contributing to the meaning of a communicative message is incredibly important. This is directly evident from some of the words we use most in daily communication. What personal pronouns such as "I" or "you" refer to depends on the person who produces them in a given setting. Demonstrative adverbs such as "here" and "there" may have different implications as a function of where they are uttered, or where a speaker concurrently points at. The word "here" in "I like it here" may refer to something completely different when produced in your new apartment compared to during your holiday in Zanzibar (Levinson, 2004). What corresponds to "you" in my mental model, may correspond to "I" in yours. My "here" may be your "there." By constantly jointly establishing and aligning what we are talking about in light of our mental models of the world and our assumed common ground, we enhance the success and efficiency of our communicative interaction.

Because knowledge systems can be very different across individuals, this nevertheless implies that the information sent is not always the same as the information received. Such distorted information may lead to differences of opinion about what was said or meant and miscommunication of various kinds. Inherent to communication is that participants bring important non-linguistic characteristics to the communicative situation that affect linguistic communication. Examples are the gender and cultural background of the participants, and the relation between the sender and the receiver of the information to be transferred.

Communication often takes place in noisy situations. *Noise* is any stimulus, external or internal, that disrupts the sharing of meaning. It can be *external*, as when distractions happen (e.g., a noisy train passing), or *internal*, for instance, daydreaming or being on edge. Incoming information may also be processed differently depending on the mood of the addressee (van Berkum et al., 2013). Another form of noise is *semantic noise*, which refers to unintended meanings that the perceived utterances evoke. When I say that we had a "nice date," you might think that I found it only so-so, while, in fact, I really enjoyed it.

Messages are the complex meanings that are expressed via verbal and non-verbal signals. They can have the form of words, sounds, and actions that are supported by facial expressions, gestures, and intonation patterns. When ideas and feelings are turned into messages, this is called *encoding*. The opposite, turning messages into ideas and feelings, is called *decoding*.

Verbal and non-verbal reactions to messages indicate if the message is seen, heard, and/or understood, so that communication can proceed or be adapted. This kind of feedback or "back-channeling" is context-dependent and sometimes ambiguous. For instance, when someone nods this could mean "go on," but also "I agree."

> **SUMMARY: LANGUAGE AND COMMUNICATION IN CONTEXT**
>
> Human communication always takes place in a certain context in which interlocutors typically build up and rely on personal and communal common ground. The process of encoding and decoding of messages is challenged by internal and external noise, and by the fact that interlocutors all bring different mental models to the table.

2.4 THE MEDIUM AND THE MESSAGE

Most of the time, we pay attention to the *content* of a message (e.g., *what* is said), but the *form* of the message (e.g., *how* it is said) is an important co-determinant of how much and which information is transferred. In fact, the form of the message is therefore a part of the message. For instance, the emotion conveyed by the loudness and intonation of the utterance can be seen as part of its meaning. In fact, in tonal languages such as Mandarin Chinese and in whistling languages such as Silbo Gomero, intonation differences are even directly conveying meaning differences. Thus, the characteristics of the way information is transmitted, the channel or *medium* of communication and its affordances, do affect the meaning of that information.

2.4.1 McLuhan: The medium is the message

The Canadian linguist McLuhan has defined a medium "as any technology that ... creates extensions of the human body and senses" (1964, pp. 238–241). In his view, the content of a message is affected (or even codetermined) by aspects of the medium that conveys it. As he states: "[T]he medium is the message: ... because it is the medium that shapes and controls the scale and form of human association and action." "The wheel is an extension of the foot; the book is an extension of the eye; clothing, an extension of the skin; electric circuitry is an extension of the central nervous system." In other words, when new technology becomes available, it creates new senses or enhances available ones. In this way, reading a printed book can be seen as "extending the readers' eye" (their visual perception) in the sense that via the book derived sensory experiences can arrive in their minds. Amazingly, these experiences may originate from people who lived long ago and in a very different part of the world.

In sum, language can be seen as a medium that extends the human senses and cognition. For instance, language extends *motor behavior*, because sentences can be seen as representing actions ("I fell"); it extends *perception*, for instance by pointing out what the body sees at a distance ("look at that star"); it extends *emotion*, by expressing what the body is feeling ("I feel sad"); and in a written form, it extends *memory* by retrieving what happened in the past ("Plato said ...").

Apart from printed text, McLuhan also pays attention to more recent media for communication in his time, for example, television and radio. In this context, he points out that the relative contribution of different modalities, as well as the cognitive effort and attentional involvement of the user, depends on the medium that is used. Compare, for example, the cognitive processes engaged in communication during a traditional phone call to a present-day video call using your smartphone or laptop. The affordances of the medium shape the form and even the potential content of the message.

2.4.2 McLuhan: The medium is the *massage*

When a new medium is invented, it sometimes brings about radical changes in human society. Due to their technological characteristics, the new media create specific environments, changing old concepts and putting new rules on information transfer. A new medium "massages." This is immediately clear if we consider the effects that smartphones have on social interactions. People walk, bike, drive, and even eat while they are consulting their phones, with disrupting consequences for traditional face-to-face encounters and dialogs (Chotpitayasunondh & Douglas, 2016). As McLuhan states, technology affects the "sensory balance" of people and therefore the sensitivities of the society. As such, technological revolutions formed a "subliminal" cause of cultural change in the Renaissance and Industrialization.

McLuhan (1964, pp. 238–241) also underscores that reinforcing one sense may take place at the cost of another. In his view:

> Media create their own environments, which are beneficial to some messages whilst being hostile to others. Just as sodium-vapor light mutes all colors to an orangey-grey and ultra-violet light makes white and some colors glow eerily, so different media amplify and repress their content. If some people lived in a world constantly illuminated by sodium-vapor light, they would have very different perceptions of reality compared with people who lived in a world illuminated only by ultraviolet light, although the people of both worlds would be unaware of any distortion in their vision.

Clearly, McLuhan's views are very relevant for our times. Recent books on use of modern media often extend his ideas and apply them to the internet, Facebook, virtual reality, advertisements, and so on.

> **SUMMARY: THE MEDIUM AND THE MESSAGE**
>
> The content of a message is affected (or even codetermined) by aspects of the medium that conveys it: The medium is the message. New media may prioritize some of our senses over others. Language can be seen as a medium that extends the human senses. It extends motor behavior, perception, emotion, and memory.

2.5 EVOLUTION OF COMMUNICATION AND LANGUAGE

So far, we have discussed mainly the physical context in which communication and language use take place. We have seen that human beings, like other animals, use different parts of their body for communicative purposes. Importantly, human beings are also social beings: As members of groups they communicate in dialog situations and in larger groups.

Communication and language can be considered as means to increase our chance of survival, both physically (bodily) and socially (within the group). Through information exchange with others, the organism's internal representation of the world can be refined and corrected. The purpose of developing complex mental models is to protect the body, to help it survive and prosper in a social context.

In the course of evolution, the internal representation of information about the world has become more and more differentiated. Even the simplest living being perceives its environment and performs actions to change it. For instance, even a simple bacterium can sense chemical gradients across its body and move in response to this sensation (this is called "chemotaxis"). Slightly more complex organisms can choose between their actions while operating on the environment. Selecting particular actions is only useful if the organism can make a choice between more and less important internal goals. Information from the environment can help to formulate priorities and specify those goals. As an additional source of information, more complex organisms use knowledge from earlier experiences during their planning. This knowledge, which is acquired via perception, becomes stored in memory. This has led to increasingly complex organisms that communicate with others in ever more complex ways. Language is a means to convey multidimensional aspects of the mental models that the organism has internally developed based on experience. In the case of humans, parental guidance and teaching have become part of this experience. Language thus helps others to improve their mental simulation and prediction of upcoming events (cf. a child who asks their mother to tell the same story over and over again).

Seen from this perspective, it seems likely that the evolution of the brain, including the areas and networks involved in language use, is codetermined by biological and social developments.

When we consider information exchange from an evolutionary perspective, we observe that the capacity to use symbols and language (speech and sign) is very old (Lieberman & McCarthy, 2015). There are indications that brain structures important for language were present already in early hominids 2 million years ago. The fundamental structures of our speech apparatus have been there for at least 60,000 years.

According to some researchers, our articulatory apparatus is especially adapted to speech. Humans have a relatively short round tongue and their larynx is situated lower in the throat than in many other species. This allows us to produce many different sounds. However, the

DISCUSSION BOX 2A: LANGUAGE EVOLVED VIA A BIG BANG VS. GRADUALLY

According to some researchers (e.g., Nóbrega & Miyagawa, 2015), human language developed so quickly that the hierarchical linguistic complexity found in its present-day use must have been there since its emergence from "preadapted systems" that can currently be found in birdsong and non-human primate calls. This notion implies that there never was a rudimentary form of language (a "protolanguage") that *gradually* evolved in terms of lexicon and syntax. Instead, humans might even possess an innate capacity for using syntax, as has been proposed by the linguist Chomsky (Bolhuis et al., 2014). Other views hold that, even though syntax may have been available early on, other language skills (e.g., related to producing speech) may have undergone some development over time (e.g., due to a "descended larynx"; Fitch, 2005). Yet other views see language evolution as part of a more general development of several interacting cognitive changes (Corballis, 2009; Lieberman, 2011; MacWhinney, 2002). The view expressed in the book follows one of the last approaches. The different accounts have compared human and non-human animal vocalizations, bodily gestures, as well as genetic and environmental influences (e.g., the role of social interaction and community sizes).

What stand do you take on language evolution or "the origin of language"? What did the first language(s) look like? Did language develop gradually, and, if so, what aspects of language must have been there from the start?

downside to this is that we have relatively many teeth in a small space and that there is a choking hazard.

An important question with respect to the evolution of language is whether it happened suddenly or developed progressively. A discontinuous view is the "Big Bang" theory of language evolution (cf. Nóbrega & Miyagawa, 2015). Versions of it hold that language arose rather suddenly by a fortunate change in the evolution of the human brain in combination with the development of a hereditary capability to acquire language (a "language acquisition device") and/or the quick full-fledged integration of two preadapted systems, an expression system (like birdsong) and a lexical system (like in primate calls). In contrast, a continuous view holds that there was a gradual coevolution of language and other human capacities (see also Discussion Box 2a).

We would like to endorse the latter view. MacWhinney (1999), in his book *The Emergence of Language*, proposes there were four periods of coevolution. About 8 to 4 million years ago, our predecessors began to walk more and more on two legs. This left their hands free for activities other than walking. Apart from taking care of bodily balance, it also stimulated the brain to develop more cognitive control and planning activities. From 4 to 2 million years ago, hominids operated more and more in groups. The social cohesion in these groups was increased by vocal-auditory changes, accompanied by neurobiological developments. Still later (2 to 0.1 million years ago), social group interactions were further stimulated by what MacWhinney calls *mimesis*: the development of gestures, signs, and singing. In his view, this whole development ended up in a systematization of phonology and lexicon. This is supposed to have happened about 60,000 years ago and more recently.

It is interesting to speculate about what the first human languages must have looked and/or sounded like. The answer to this question will always to some extent remain speculative, as ways of recording language and speech (written script, grammar books, video recordings) are recent inventions, and time machines do not yet exist. Even though there is a lack of direct evidence of what the first language(s) looked like, the study of language evolution is not entirely theoretical in nature. In contrast, the empirical study of language evolution and language emergence takes place in a vibrant and growing field of study. Researchers are trying to actively explore and understand how languages evolved using a variety of complementary methods, such as computer simulations, lab experiments with human participants that pass on novel languages from one generation of participants to the next, the investigation of the evolution of modern languages over time, and cross-species comparisons that aim at understanding how other animals communicate (see, e.g., Cangelosi & Parisi, 2012; Christiansen & Kirby, 2003; Raviv et al., 2019).

When we consider communication in the animal kingdom, it is clear that it already often involves interactions in different modalities. Facial expressions, bodily movements, and hand gestures interact with grunts and cries to convey information to close-by animals of the same or different species in apes (Arbib et al., 2008). Thus, it is not unlikely that early forms of human communication already relied on both visual information (hand movements, eye gaze, facial expressions) and on auditory information (vocalizations). Different modalities are to some extent complementary in the advantages that they offer.

For instance, the visual modality allows for a higher degree of *iconicity* than the spoken modality (speech). As we have seen, hand gestures for many concrete concepts have the power to depict the thing that they refer to in an intuitive, iconic way. Whenever there is no conventionalized system of symbols in place (yet) that is shared between interlocutors, it may be easier to communicate the thought "I saw a deer running by near the river" through iconic gestures than via speech. This is also evident from present-day situations in which

DISCUSSION BOX 2B: LANGUAGE ACQUISITION DEVICE VS. LANGUAGE LEARNING

Chomsky (1965; cf. Hauser et al., 2002) proposed that human infants possess an innate mental capacity that enables them to acquire language. This capacity he called the Language Acquisition Device (LAD). At the time, an argument for this view was the "poverty of the stimulus." Because children would not be explicitly taught by their parents what utterances are correct and incorrect (they would not have "access to negative evidence"), they would only be able to learn language so quickly because they have innate grammatical knowledge (cf. Lenneberg, 1967). In this context, Chomsky also proposed a "universal grammar" that can account for all language learning. However, over the years evidence from language acquisition and neuroscience research has become available that does not appear to support these claims. For instance, the "poverty of the stimulus" argument (Chomsky, 1980) has been falsified, and none of the presumed properties of the LAD turns out to be fully universal (Evans & Levinson, 2009). As an example, not all languages have tense or distinct syntactic categories such as nouns or verbs. Researchers including Lieberman (2011) and Deacon (e.g., Behme & Deacon, 2008) have argued that, rather than a "language organ," a complex neural circuit of various functional abilities subserves language use. The animal communication of our predecessors, genetically predetermined as it was, gradually developed into more complex forms of language in line with the brain's natural abilities. Language and syntax are codependent on meaning, context, and memory aspects (Lakoff, 1987), and there might be an evolutionary development from hand gestures to words (Tomasello, 2008). More recently, therefore, researchers have stressed the interaction of "nature" and "nurture" (see Discussion Box 2a). The distinction between these two approaches is even evident in the use of the terms "language acquisition" and "language learning." The first term has often been used by linguists and the second one by psychologists of language.

What is your motivated opinion on this issue? What could the properties of Creole languages (Bickerton, 1984), Nicaraguan Sign Language (Senghas et al., 2004), and language emergence experiments using iterated learning paradigms (e.g., Smith et al., 2003) contribute to this discussion?

---

people are forced to communicate but have no spoken language in common. You may have experienced the communicative power of gestures yourself when trying to communicate with a local during holidays abroad.

At the same time, communication that dominantly relies on visual signals may not always be most convenient. For one, purely visual signals do not offer the best of possibilities to communicate when you are spending the night in the dark. But also during the day, the distance between you and the person you would like to communicate with can only be limited as it is restricted to the quality of your and your partner's eyes and vision. In such situations, vocal signals typically outperform visual gestures. Even when you do not see the speakers, their spoken messages can still convey advised actions: flee, fight, or feed, for instance. Furthermore, the use of speech leaves the hands free for other activities, such as hunting or, more importantly these days, doing the dishes. Those restrictions of the visual modality may have led to speech having become more dominant over time in many language contexts.

However, that spoken signals are not necessary at all for efficient communication is evident from Deaf communities, which have naturally developed full-fledged visual languages that allow for communication that is as rich as the spoken languages most of us are familiar with. By the same token, as is evident from conversations that take place over the phone, visual signals also are not strictly necessary for successful communication. It is clear that the auditory and the visual modality both have communicative strengths and limitations and that language can rely more on one modality (spoken sounds), on the other (visual signals), or on a combination of the two in different contexts and in different communities.

Regardless of the precise balance and relation between modalities in a certain phase of language evolution, it seems obvious that pointing gestures have played an important role in the emergence of language (Tomasello, 2008). When trying to come up with a new word or sign for an object in the world, it is important that interlocutors share joint attention to that object. Pointing is a natural way of establishing joint attention by directing the gaze of one's interlocutor (Bangerter, 2004). If we manage to share gaze to a butterfly fluttering by, and I say "blue morpho," we may jointly agree to now refer to this flying insect in this way, also when it is no longer around. Once such conventions are in place, language thus allows us to also talk about entities that are no longer present in our immediate environment. We call this *displacement* (Hockett, 1960). This property of language makes it possible to talk about events in the past or future, and about objects, people, and events that are not directly visible in our immediate surroundings. It is hard to imagine a world in which we could communicate only about things in the immediate here-and-now.

Of course, the natural spoken languages that are around today make use of a combination of auditory and visual signals. However, not all auditory and visual signals we produce are communicatively intended. Even the same signal may in one context have important communicative value while it may possess no communicatively intended meaning in another. When playing a card game with a group of friends, for instance, you may touch your earlobe to secretly signal to your best friend that you are going to fold your current hand. When another player makes the same movement, it may just be the case that they want to relieve themselves from an itchy feeling (Becchio et al., 2012). In the vocal modality, similarly, a sniff may be produced because someone has a cold, but also to express disapproval of an ongoing situation. These considerations illustrate that, for successful communication to take place, an addressee needs to *segregate* communicatively intended information from non-communicative signals during language comprehension (Holler & Levinson, 2019).

In addition to segregating communicative from non-communicative aspects of a speaker's behavior, there is more work to do for an addressee during language comprehension. We saw in Chapter 1 that language is hierarchical and incremental: Smaller pieces of information (e.g., sounds) are part of larger elements (e.g., words) – these follow one another in time and one builds on the other. We have also seen, however, that speakers in face-to-face situations communicate not only via speech, but also through hand gestures, facial expressions, and other bodily signals. Crucially, information is conveyed through these different channels at the same time. This leads to a *binding problem*. For successful comprehension, the addressee needs to be able to "bind" or integrate information that is communicated by a speaker through different modalities in an online fashion (Holler & Levinson, 2019; Özyürek et al., 2007). When I pretend to hit a forehand while I am talking to you about my plans for the weekend, you may correctly infer that I am planning to play a match of tennis. From my concomitant positive facial expression, you may at the same time deduce that I am looking forward to it. As such, your brain has correctly combined the concurrent visual and auditory information that my body conveyed as controlled by my brain.

24 Language and communication

> **SUMMARY: EVOLUTION OF COMMUNICATION AND LANGUAGE**
>
> Human language as we know it today has progressively evolved. The evolution of the brain, including the areas and networks involved in the production and comprehension of language, is codetermined by biological and social developments. Different modalities arguably played an important role during language emergence. Pointing and iconic gestures in combination with facial expressions and spoken sounds provided a basis for our present-day natural spoken languages in which both auditory and visual information play a role. Listeners segregate communicatively intended signals from irrelevant sounds and movements, and efficiently integrate the streams of information that the speaker conveys through different bodily channels.

2.6 THE SENDER–RECEIVER MODEL OF COMMUNICATION

The outcome of this biological and social development for communication is visually represented in Figure 2.2, which has long been referred to as the Sender–Receiver model of communication (going back to Shannon & Weaver, 1948). In this "model," there is a sender who encodes a particular meaning and sends it out as a message via a physical channel at a particular signal-to-noise ratio. The message is then decoded by a receiver into a meaning. Depending on rules for turn-taking, the receiver may become a sender and put their own ideas into words. According to the model, communication implies reconstructing the mental state ("mental model") someone else has in mind by prediction and/or integration. In the

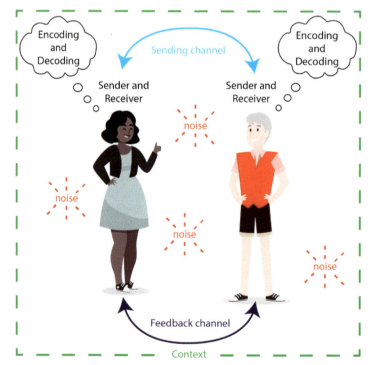

Figure 2.2
The Sender–Receiver model of communication. Part of image designed by pikisuperstar/Freepik.

case of prediction, consequences of the mental model are already "computed" before they appear in the utterance, whereas in the case of integration, they are found in the utterance and then incorporated into the mental model.

2.7 WHAT IS NEXT?

The Sender–Receiver model is a very general model for communication. In the case of language, it must be differentiated to do justice to all the complex activities that language use entails. For instance, how do we decode words, sentences, and meanings from the speaker's utterances? And how do we put our own thoughts and ideas into words and sentences that the other can understand? What role does our linguistic and world knowledge play in language comprehension and production? How can we monitor our speech to avoid errors and misunderstandings? The differentiated cognitive system that accounts for such processes is called the Language User Framework and is the topic of the next chapter.

2.8 WHAT HAVE WE LEARNED?

In communication, verbal (e.g., speech) and non-verbal (e.g., facial expressions) components form an integrated whole. Communication takes place in a physical and a social context accompanied by multidimensional, often ambiguous signals and noise. The way in which information is conveyed (called the "medium") may affect the perceived message. The understanding of expressed meanings depends on "common ground," i.e. shared views of the situation and common knowledge about the world. Relevant information is incorporated in the mental models of the interlocutors (e.g., speakers and listeners). The communicative interactions between interlocutors are characterized at a general level in the Sender–Receiver model of communication.

One way to understand the evolution of language out of a more basic form of communication is in terms of the coevolution of cognitive skills: Social development, tool use, and the need for more precise messages all arose more or less in parallel and interactively as a consequence of our human ancestors' standing up, which freed their hands and facilitated the visual exchange of information. Over tens of thousands of years, natural language and its neurobiological basis have coevolved into such a complex system for exchanging ideas and feelings that a more precise characterization is needed than the Sender–Receiver model provides.

QUESTIONS FOR CHAPTER 2

1. Explain and relate the terms "communication" and "language."
2. To what extent can or should verbal and non-verbal communication occurring in real-life situations be separated in the study of the psychology of language?
3. Describe how characteristics of context, participants, and messages affect communication.
4. Two statements from McLuhan are that "the medium is the message" and that "the medium is the massage." What would be the implications of these statements for product advertisement on television vs. radio vs. the internet?
5. In what respects is using language in a face-to-face dialog comparable to non-linguistic joint actions such as jointly lifting a piano or doing the dishes together?
6. The Sender–Receiver model is found in many books on communication science. Apply this model to conversations between (a) a dog owner and their dog; (b) a first language user and a second language learner; (c) a mother and her child; (d) a shopkeeper and a customer.

7 Explain that speech conveys a multidimensional meaning through a narrow one-dimensional channel. What can be said about communication channels and noise? Why is feedback from one's addressee important? To what extent is the receiver also often a sender?
8 What do you consider to be the role of hand gestures in face-to-face communication? What is the difference between the signs of a sign language and co-speech hand gestures?
9 Come up with at least two reasons why people might make hand gestures while they are speaking on the phone.
10 Review how language may have evolved in the course of human evolution. In what respects would the use of mental models be a "natural" consequence of evolution?

Chapter 3

Language User Framework

3.1 INTRODUCTION

Groucho Marx (1890–1977) is the most widely known comedian of the Marx Brother family. He has become famous not only for his characteristic appearance with bushy eyebrows, plastic glasses, black moustache, and stinking cigar, but also for his wit and wisecracks. One of his famous statements is: "Time flies like an arrow, and fruit flies like a banana." He also made many jokes in dialogs. Box 3.1 presents a few short dialogs with Groucho.

As these little dialogs show, language is a flexible tool for information transfer, and this flexibility can be both a blessing and a curse. Its blessing is that new messages can be constructed all the time, but its curse is that language is often ambiguous. Among other things, its interpretation depends on how a speech signal is segmented (demonstrated in the first example), how a sentence's structure is interpreted (second example), what meaning of an ambiguous word or phrase is intended ("to write for" in the third example), and how

---

Box 3.1 Short dialogs with Groucho Marx, taken from *The Essential Groucho* (Kanfer, 2000).

Groucho:	"Did you ever hear of a cow that just gives buttermilk?"
Man:	"No."
Groucho:	"What else can a cow give *but her milk*?"
Groucho:	"You know how to make a Venetian blind?"
Man:	"No."
Groucho:	"Get him drunk. That is the best way."
Groucho:	"You say you write for papers all over the world?"
Woman:	"Yes."
Groucho:	"And do they send them to you?"
Groucho:	"What makes a plane stay up in the air? I've never been able to figure it out."
Woman:	"The lift from the air holds the wing up. Air is very dense."
Groucho:	"What was that last thing? The air is what?"
Woman:	"Dense."
Groucho:	"Well, I'd love to! Do you care to waltz or rumba?"

DOI: 10.4324/9781003326274-3

words are pronounced ("dense" vs. "dance" in the fourth example). In fact, ambiguity is present at all levels of language representation and processing.

There are various scientific disciplines that are concerned with the representations and processes that underlie the language used by the interlocutors in dialogs. The constituent linguistic and psycholinguistic disciplines can most easily be discussed within the theoretical framework of the *Language User Framework*. To set the stage for a more detailed discussion of units and processes underlying language use, we will discuss this abstract framework in this chapter.

3.2 THE LANGUAGE USER FRAMEWORK

In order to understand or produce language, language users see themselves faced with a number of tasks. Four major types of task can be discerned:

- *Memory retrieval*: Finding different linguistic representations in Long Term Memory;
- *Processing representations*: Stepwise recoding of internally represented linguistic input into thought, or vice versa;
- *Using Working Memory*: Temporarily storing linguistic half-products during recoding;
- *Exerting cognitive control*: Managing and monitoring ongoing processes (e.g., by checking, shifting attention, or inhibiting representations).

The Language User Framework provides a theoretical framework that specifies and relates these activities (Dijkstra & Kempen, 1984). It assumes that there are cognitive mechanisms that take care of different aspects associated with language use. When input is presented to the language system, these mechanisms retrieve relevant stored information (structural knowledge) from Long Term Memory and change it into other forms (processing). A Cognitive Control System ensures that the processes involved proceed in the proper way, for instance, by keeping temporary products in Working Memory and checking if they are correct.

Figure 3.1 introduces a visual representation of the Language User Framework. The bottom part concerns language representations, rules, and processing components involved in the production and comprehension of language. We will refer to it as the Language Processing System. The top part corresponds to task and decision aspects that are relevant during language use, for instance, related to cognitive control and Working Memory. We will refer to it as the Cognitive Control System. The activities indicated in the figure are described in the following sections in this chapter and further refined in later chapters of this book.

Let us first focus on the bottom part of the framework, which shows that language comprehension (left part) and production (right part) both make use of knowledge stored in memory. Knowledge representations are stored in Long Term Memory in a *hierarchy*: Smaller units are part of larger units that are part of still larger units, and so forth. For instance, speech sounds are in many languages parts of syllables that themselves are combined to make up words that may constitute phrases or sentences. The stored representations are retrieved from Long Term Memory during language processing.

During the comprehension of written and spoken language:

- Small units (e.g., sounds or letters) must be recognized in the signal and represented faithfully; let us assume this is done by a "mental machine" called the *Signal Recognizer*;

Language User Framework   29

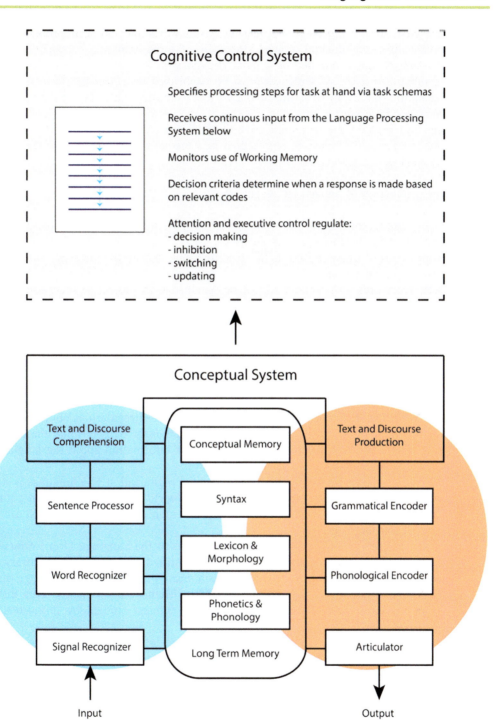

Figure 3.1
Basic structure of the Language User Framework. Its upper part is referred to as the Cognitive Control System, its lower part as the Language Processing System. We note that many aspects of the Cognitive Control System are not specific to language.

30 *Language User Framework*

- On the basis of the represented speech or print, words and all their properties must be looked up in the "mental lexicon," the store of lexico-semantic knowledge in Long Term Memory; this is handled by a *Word Recognizer*;
- The syntactic structure of sentences must be established by a *Sentence Processor*;
- The semantic (meaning) structure of the sentence message must also be determined by the *Sentence Processor*;
- Taking into account the communicative (largely non-verbal) context of the utterance, this meaning structure must be represented in a mental model and processed over time by the *Conceptual System*.

During the production of spoken language:

- Thoughts and intentions (i.e., semantic structures) are formulated within the communicative context by the *Conceptual System*;
- Appropriate word units and syntactic structures that convey the message must be built by a *Grammatical Encoder*;
- The selected words and sentences must be specified with respect to their sounds by a *Phonological Encoder*;
- Utterances must be articulated by an *Articulator* in close synchronization with the articulation of communicative signals through modalities other than speech (e.g., co-speech gestures).

During each of these tasks, the signals coming into or going out of the system must be compared to stored representations in Long Term Memory. For instance, sound units in the input signal can only be segmented by using stored rules and regularities about properties of sounds and their order in the language at hand. Similarly, to determine the syntactic structure of a sentence, word structure and word order information about the language in question must be consulted.

In Figure 3.1, what is learned and known about the organization of a language is stored in the lower middle part of the model, *Long Term Memory*. This memory system contains information about the speech sounds, words or signs, sentences, and meanings that are possible in a particular language.

There are three major distinctions in the bottom part of the Language User Framework. The first distinction is between language knowledge, stored in Long Term Memory (the middle part) and the processing components (mechanisms) that use this knowledge during language processing (situated around the Long Term Memory component). This distinction corresponds more or less with the domains of interest studied by linguistics and psycholinguistics.

The second distinction is that between the comprehension of language (on the left side) and the production of language (on the right side). It is assumed that both make use of shared language knowledge (stored in the middle), although the ways in which it is used (the processes) will surely differ. When we understand language, we focus in the first instance on signal-based representations; when we produce language, the message is initially most important. The information flow from sensory input organs (such as the ear or eye) to the conceptual system is called *bottom-up* or *data-driven*. The information flow from conceptual system towards the formulation and articulation of utterances is called *top-down* or *knowledge-driven*.

The third distinction is that between language in a strict sense and thought. The upper components, the Conceptual System and the Conceptual Memory, may be considered as "thought" systems linked up to the lower components, constituting language. The Conceptual

System works with non-linguistic information about the world and word concepts stored in the Conceptual Memory. Thus, the term "thought" can be taken to refer to the process of transforming one non-linguistic mental representation into another, or to these mental representations themselves. As such, in the Language User Framework, language and thought imply distinct but connected processes.

> **SUMMARY: THE LANGUAGE USER FRAMEWORK**
>
> The Language User Framework differentiates and extends the standard Sender–Receiver model of communication (Chapter 2) to the case of language processing. It incorporates a Language Processing System that distinguishes (i) knowledge representations and processes using this knowledge, (ii) language production and language comprehension, and (iii) language and thought. In addition, the Language User Framework includes a Cognitive Control System that monitors and controls the different stages of language processing (discussed in Section 3.2.3).

3.2.1 Parallel and sequential processing components

An important issue is how the different processing components in the Language User Framework relate while they are processing language. One option is that each component (e.g., the Signal Recognizer) processes incoming information completely *autonomously* or in isolation (using Long Term Memory) before sending it onwards to the next one (e.g., the Word Recognizer). Alternatively, components might *interact* and provide information to one another on request or based on expectations. For instance, if a particular word is expected on the basis of sentence information, word recognition might benefit from using that expectation. In the interactive approach to language that we are proposing in this book, processing in one component can generally be affected by the input signal (often more concrete) and by predictions from higher-order components (often more abstract). Nevertheless, the priority flow of information in comprehension is *bottom-up* or signal-driven, and during production it is *top-down* or concept-driven. This is because the goal of language comprehension is to *understand* a message, while that of language production is to *express* it.

Another important notion here is that of "cascaded processing." Different components of the Language User Framework can be active in parallel, but operate on different parts of the incoming signal or outgoing message. For instance, when we listen to the speech signal, the Signal Recognizer could process phonemes on the basis of which the Word Recognizer might activate words and their meaning. It could be that during listening, the Word Recognizer is still processing the previous word, while the Signal Recognizer is already at the same time trying to determine the phonetic characteristics of the following one.

> **SUMMARY: PARALLEL AND SEQUENTIAL PROCESSING COMPONENTS**
>
> The different components of the Language User Framework constantly interact to allow for efficient language comprehension and production. The flow of information during comprehension is mainly bottom-up and signal-driven, whereas in production it is predominantly top-down and concept-driven. Nevertheless, comprehension is helped by top-down predictions. There is room for predictions because of incremental processing (see Chapter 1).

Similarly, during speaking, phonological encoding might still operate on a word that was selected earlier by the Formulator. Information hence cascades through the system.

3.2.2 Complex language activities in daily life

Language use in daily life is usually more complex than just recognizing a word in a sentence, or putting an idea into words. Examples are: writing down what the teacher is saying; talking to a young child, a non-native speaker of your language, or a person with aphasia; reading aloud parts of a newspaper article to your friend (which includes both language comprehension and production activities); and having a dialog with a technician in the garage about getting your car repaired. All of these activities imply synchronized and consecutive cognitive operations (processing computations), retrieval of language and meaning information, and control activities, involving several components of the Language User Framework, embedded in a broader physical and sociocultural context.

For instance, when a student writes down what a teacher is saying, a number of tasks must be executed, implying a path through the Language User Framework. First, the student engages in spoken word recognition and retrieves the meaning of the word spoken by the teacher from their lexicon in Long Term Memory. Via the word's meaning, its spelling can be found in the mental lexicon (to some extent, the spelling could sometimes also be derived by converting the sounds of the spoken word one by one into letter representations). The lexicon also contains a specification of the handwriting movements that are associated with these letters. The letters of the word can now be written down on paper in a sequential order. To make sure the right order of letters is produced, the Cognitive Control System monitors what is going on. Simultaneously, the meaning information in the Conceptual Memory of the student is updated.

When you talk to a young child, a beginning learner of your language, or a person with aphasia, you will be aware that the person you are speaking to may have difficulties in understanding you. You may therefore articulate clearly, speak more slowly and with more repetitions, or use more co-speech hand gestures. As a parent, you will choose your words and syntactic constructions carefully, assessing the linguistic and situational knowledge of the child in line with their age. Speaking to a non-native speaker, you may avoid using low frequency or more abstract words and embedded sentence constructions. Speaking to a person with aphasia, you may perhaps point to the objects you are talking about, to disambiguate your message. This all shows that you are both an "adaptive listener" and an "adaptive speaker" (Magnuson et al., 2021).

When reading aloud parts of a newspaper article to your friend, you will switch your attention regularly from the newspaper to their face and back. You may discuss the contents of an article, which implies that you and your friend have mental models of world knowledge active and synchronize them over time. These activities thus include both language comprehension and production activities, and make use of substantial non-linguistic context information.

When you have a dialog with a technician in the garage about getting your car repaired, you may notice that your understanding of cars is limited. Your understanding of the mechanic's explanation may be so superficial, that you basically grasp only that there is a problem that can be fixed at a reasonable cost. Due to lack of knowledge, your mental model of the situation can only be partially aligned with the other person's. Nevertheless, when you have paid your bill and leave the garage, your mental model of how cars function may have been updated. This hopefully resulted in more reliable knowledge about cars in Long Term Memory, ready for future use.

> **SUMMARY: COMPLEX LANGUAGE ACTIVITIES IN DAILY LIFE**
>
> Different everyday activities that involve language can be conceptualized as following a path through the lower part of the Language User Framework. The same overall activity (e.g., taking notes) may involve both production- and comprehension-related aspects of the framework. Cognitive control processes (the upper part of the Language User Framework) monitor the activity. Mental models and contextual information also make important contributions.

3.2.3 Cognitive control and Working Memory

Because different levels of processing are involved simultaneously in language use (e.g., at the level of speech sounds, words, and sentences), ongoing computations must be monitored (checked), controlled, and updated. This task is so important that there is a dedicated Cognitive Control System for it, indicated in the upper part of the Language User Framework (Figure 3.1). Because it is involved in executing particular tasks, it is also often referred to as the "executive control system." There are several activities this control system takes care of (Green & Abutalebi, 2013; Miyake et al., 2000). Using attention to monitor ongoing processes, language users must, for instance:

- Decide/choose between relevant or selected alternatives (e.g., responses);
- Suppress unwanted alternatives (e.g., other responses);
- Switch or shift to the most relevant task aspects;
- Update information in Working Memory.

During language comprehension and production, information in focus can be temporarily (10–20 s) kept in Working Memory (or "Short Term Memory") while it is being processed or checked (also see Baddeley, 2007). Keeping information available for later consultation allows the resolution of ambiguities and the establishment of links between sentence elements. For instance, in a phrase like this, "the apple in the box," the noun phrase "the apple" can be linked to the prepositional phrase "in the box" after being kept in Working Memory until the latter phrase becomes available (Tanenhaus et al., 1995).

The Cognitive Control System is a complex system consisting of several components. Its operations are not just limited to making sure utterances are correctly understood or produced. The system is also important because language is often used with a particular goal or task in mind. For instance, we may read a story to understand its general gist, search for particular details in the text, or look for spelling errors. The contribution of task demands is even more obvious when we consider how language is processed in the lab during psycholinguistic experiments: There are many research techniques that each pose its own demands on the language user and require their peculiar specific processing steps. We will come back to this in Chapter 4.

> **SUMMARY: COGNITIVE CONTROL AND WORKING MEMORY**
>
> Language processing is supported by a Cognitive Control System (see upper part of Figure 3.1). Attentional resources are devoted to monitoring incoming and outgoing information. Such information can be stored in Working Memory for a limited amount of time. The overall goal of a specific task influences what aspects of information are prioritized and in focus.

3.2.4 How the Language User Framework relates to the brain

The Language User Framework specifies what has to be done in order to understand or produce utterances. However, it does not indicate how and when the brain takes care of these activities, or where in the brain they take place. It turns out that it is not so easy to discern the different components of the Language User Framework in the brain.

The framework's distinction between the Language Processing System involving representations and processes (bottom) and the Cognitive Control System (top) is the most easily made. Aspects of cognitive control appear to be predominantly associated with areas in the frontal lobe (see Figure 3.2), while language is represented in an extensive cortical network across the left hemisphere and parts of the right hemisphere.

The Language User Framework further implicitly makes the assumption that each component requires time to process the linguistic stimulus from a certain perspective. Even under the assumption that information is sent forward further into the system as soon as it is being processed by a certain component, some processes will, on average, take place earlier than others. For instance, the framework implies that a word can only be incorporated in a syntactic structure under construction after it has received a certain amount of processing. Simplifying, taking steps through the framework should take time in real (brain) processing.

Making this assumption, one might be inclined to search in the brain for the areas that subserve a particular task in the model, and then link them up sequentially. However, further analysis shows that this is not easily done. For instance, a task such as word reading is complex and involves several different subtasks, e.g., finding the letters of the word, locating the word form in Long Term Memory, activating sound forms and meaning, and so on. Such subtasks are most likely supported by different parts of the brain, not only in the cortex but also in deeper brain layers, especially in its left hemisphere.

For instance, it has been proposed that during word reading, the "visual word form area", situated in the fusiform gyrus in the temporal and occipital lobe, is relevant for the identification of printed words (Dehaene & Cohen, 2011). This area would then work in concert with connected areas relevant for spoken language and meaning processing.

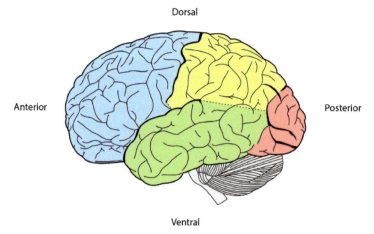

Figure 3.2
A view on the left hemisphere of the brain. Four different lobes can be distinguished: the frontal (here in blue), temporal (green), parietal (yellow), and occipital (red) lobe. The anterior part of the brain is located behind the forehead, while the posterior part is situated in the back of the head. The upper portion of the brain is called "dorsal" or "superior," while the lower part is called "ventral" or "inferior."

Among the brain regions that have been traditionally proposed to be involved in language processing are Wernicke's area in the posterior superior temporal lobe and Broca's area in the lower inferior frontal lobe. Parts of these areas are assumed to also be involved in syntactic processing, with a contribution of the right hemisphere as well (Friederici, 2011; Friederici & Gierhan, 2013). Other parts of the brain, such as the inferior and middle temporal lobes, have been mentioned as important for the processing of meaning (Pulvermüller, 2013). We will learn progressively more about the organization of the brain in Chapter 4 when we describe the fMRI technique, in Chapter 8 on meaning, in Chapter 9 on language production, and in Chapter 10 on multilingualism.

By the way, note that a particular part of the brain may be engaged in several different cognitive activities. For instance, a brain area that is recruited while ordering words during syntactic production might also be involved in producing musical phrases. In all, there is no one-to-one mapping between cognitive processes and brain areas, but a many-to-many mapping, and brain networks rather than individual areas seem relevant for subserving particular cognitive functions (cf. Ullman, 2004).

As a consequence, it is probably wiser to talk about processing (components) as involving *dynamic circuits of activation*, spanning multiple networks of brain areas, not only in the cortex but also in deeper brain layers. In the chapters on spoken and printed word recognition, and speech production, we will mention the respective brain areas and networks that are arguably involved in each activity.

> **SUMMARY: HOW THE LANGUAGE USER FRAMEWORK RELATES TO THE BRAIN**
>
> Language processing makes use of substantial parts of the brain, including areas located in the frontal, temporal, parietal, and occipital lobes. Components of the Language User Framework do not one-to-one map onto brain regions. Rather, networks of brain regions dynamically interact to allow for efficient and successful communication.

3.2.5 Language and other cognitive domains

It is important to note that the networks involved in language in the brain are not "encapsulated" or "closed" to other modalities. We have seen in the previous chapter that language is not a module. If we read an emotion word such as "happy," this word will result not only in a retrieval of its word form and abstract meaning, but also its affective (emotional) meaning.

In the Language User Framework, language is linked up to other cognitive domains via the Conceptual System and the Conceptual Memory. This is clear if we consider words for perceptual attributes ("red"), actions that involve movement ("to hike"), and smells and tastes ("vanilla"). Language is also associated with non-linguistic representations of emotions, music, mathematics, and so on. In fact, we may go even further and state that language is a medium that extends several human senses (cf. McLuhan in Chapter 2). For instance, expressions can be seen as actions that extend motor behavior ("I hereby crown thee King"), perception ("Look at that bird in the tree"), emotion ("I feel happy"), and memory traces ("Remember the summer of '69?"). Again, these aspects underline the inseparability of language and other modalities, also called "non-modularity."

Being a higher-level cognitive function, language functions are subserved by large parts of the brain, abundantly in the left hemisphere but also in the right hemisphere.

The different areas implicated in language are broadly connected to brain areas involved in other non-language functions, and parts of the brain may be engaged both in language and in non-language-processing activities.

The observation that language is not represented in the brain at one location but all over the place has far-reaching theoretical consequences. It implies that we should not conceive of a particular language activity as a localized, holistic phenomenon, but rather as a set of computations that take place both in parallel in different brain areas and sequentially over time. Language processing in the Language User Framework can be seen as activation spreading over different pathways, in parallel and sequentially. The same holds for language processing in the brain. For instance, when we hear a word, the incoming sounds will first activate brain areas involved in auditory processing, followed by activity in ventral and dorsal pathways, and then in semantic or motor areas. Activity may reverberate through networks consisting of several areas and nodes. In the past, this incremental nature of language processing has sometimes been underestimated, for instance, when it was assumed that the meaning of a word becomes available as a holistic representation at one particular moment in time. It might be better to consider language processing in terms of subsequent brain activation states in which resonating circuits are set into motion at particular entry points.

Furthermore, the Cognitive Control System that is used to resolve all sorts of task and decision problems during language processing may have both language-specific and more domain-general properties. In other words, part of it may subserve other cognitive functions such as non-linguistic perception or arithmetic.

> **SUMMARY: LANGUAGE AND OTHER COGNITIVE DOMAINS**
>
> Language is not a module in the brain. It is strongly linked up to and depends on functions related to perception, action, control, and memory. A particular language activity will activate multiple neural networks and the activation of each will take place over variable amounts of time.

3.2.6 Language development, second language acquisition, and multilingualism

The Language User Framework provides a theoretical framework for understanding how healthy adults use their native language. For patients with language disorders, children, and bilinguals, the model is insufficiently specified. It is interesting to speculate what should be changed to the framework to obtain a faithful image of the Language User Frameworks for these different groups of people.

For certain patients, information in Long Term Memory might be lost or inaccessible; their processing might be different for one or more task components; and their Cognitive Control System or Working Memory might be failing. In addition, they might adapt their ways of language processing to compensate for the problems at hand (Bastiaanse & Jonkers, 1998; Kolk & Heeschen, 1990).

In children, the full Language User Framework is not yet in place. Because children have ears, eyes, speech organs, and a developing brain, they can start to build the diverse language components. They appear to do so roughly from the lower components of the Language User Framework up (in the order of speech sounds, words, morphemes, syntax), but they simultaneously start filling their Conceptual Memory and using their

DISCUSSION BOX 3: THEORETICAL FRAMEWORKS: LINGUISTICS VS. PSYCHOLINGUISTICS

Linguists and psycholinguists often have different theoretical views on language. While cognitive frameworks such as the Language User Framework are intuitively attractive to psychologists, many linguists in the past have worked within theoretical frameworks at different stages of the development of Chomsky's theories. A figure of an earlier version of Chomsky's theory (Transformational Generative Grammar or TGG; Chomsky, 1965) is represented in Figure 3.3. In this figure, the Deep Structure is a theoretical construct intending to connect different sentences that have more or less the same meaning, for instance, "students read this book" and "this book is read by students." The Surface Structure is the syntactic structure of the sentence at hand. Various types of rule link the different components. It is immediately clear that in this framework, syntax has a central place (Chomsky, 1965, 1999; Radford, 1988).

Compare the theoretical framework for TGG to the Language Processing System of the Language User Framework. What are their differences and commonalities? Find out what happened to the TGG framework in later developments. What is MERGE?

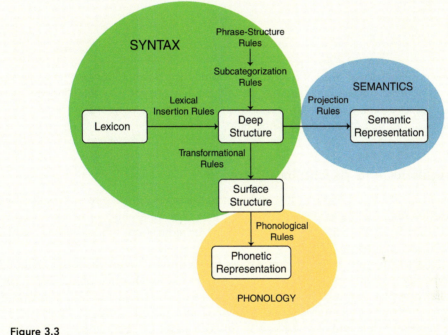

Figure 3.3
Visual depiction of Chomsky's Transformational Generative Grammar (1965).

Conceptual System (for thinking and social development) (Hoff, 2014; Schaerlaekens, 2000, p. 15).

As we will see in Chapter 10, to understand language use by bilinguals or multilinguals, the Language User Framework must also be extended and even adapted. First, Long Term Memory must be enriched with information about speech sounds, words, syntax, and meanings from the new language(s). For instance, when a speaker of German learns Mandarin Chinese, tonal information must somehow become incorporated into their Long

Term Memory. Second, developing a system of representations for the new language is not sufficient: The bilinguals must also be able to process incoming speech and build utterances in the foreign language. As such, they must develop fine-tuned processing routines and strategies for dealing with the representations and their combinations in the new language at hand. A particularly interesting case is the "early bilingual," who acquires two languages simultaneously from an early age. Here the Language User Framework is developed in parallel as one integrated system for two languages.

In sum, because a theoretical framework like the Language User Framework organizes and clarifies the mental processes underlying particular language activities, it may offer insights into daily life events that involve language. However, often research on the psychology of language is only concerned with a few aspects of one component of the framework in isolation, whereas human language behavior in daily life involves many components that interact in rather complex ways. Furthermore, different types of language user may process language differently. For instance, a child with reading problems and an adult with aphasia might compensate for (or "adapt to") their difficulties in processing by engaging in unexpected strategies. If they cannot process the incoming signal optimally, they might try to bring their world knowledge and semantic expectancies in to help them solve the problem at hand.

> **SUMMARY: LANGUAGE DEVELOPMENT, SECOND LANGUAGE ACQUISITION, AND MULTILINGUALISM**
>
> The neural instantiation of the Language User Framework develops over time while we grow up. In specific populations, such as certain patient groups and multilinguals, it is adapted or extended. Experimental research often focuses on only one or a couple of components of the framework at the same time.

3.2.7 Linguistics and psycholinguistics

Researchers from different disciplines take different perspectives in trying to understand daily language use. Among the researchers investigating language we find linguists, psychologists, neuroscientists, researchers in artificial intelligence or education, philosophers, medical doctors, biologists, and so on.

Psychologists who study language (sometimes referred to as "psycholinguists," although they are typically not linguists in origin) aim at developing theories about the mental processes that take place during language use. In terms of the Language User Framework, they are interested in the mental computations that transform a word or utterance into a meaning representation and vice versa (the outside parts of the Language Processing System). In their description of the processes, they need to apply knowledge about the linguistic representations and rules involved. Often, they benefit from the proposals of linguists in this respect.

Linguists are often especially interested in language structures for different languages and how these develop. They try to specify the representations and rules that are stored in the middle part of the Language Processing System, concerned with Long Term Memory storage. Different disciplines in linguistics are phonetics, phonology, lexicology, morphology, syntax, semantics, and pragmatics. We will now briefly discuss each of these disciplines in turn, which will give us a better understanding of the representations and processes involved in everyday language use.

3.2.7.1 Phonetics and phonology

Phonetics is a linguistic discipline that focusses on the characteristics of raw speech sounds (Roach, 2009). It is a discipline concerned with how people perceive these sounds (acoustic phonetics) and how they produce them (articulatory phonetics). In this field, it is obviously important to look at the properties of the human speech apparatus, including lips, tongue, oral cavity, larynx, and vocal cords. Also important is how speech signals can be visualized and represented technically, for instance with oscillograms and spectrograms (see Chapter 5).

Clearly, how different raw sounds can be organized in more abstract categories can be of interest to phoneticians, but this topic is studied in a dedicated linguistic discipline called *phonology*. Phonology is more of a pencil-and-paper discipline that considers which abstract categories of sounds must be discerned in the sound repertoires of different languages. Abstract sound categories are referred to as *phonemes*. When two words differ in one phoneme (a so-called "minimal pair"), this phoneme makes a difference to their meaning. An example is the minimal word pair "bad – pad," in which /b/ and /p/ are different phonemes that change word meaning. There are also sound differences that are not phoneme changes and do not change meaning. Take, for instance, the difference between the sound /p/ at the beginning or end of a word; or sound differences occurring because the speaker has the flu. Different sounds within a phoneme category are called *allophones*.

Phonemes can be (combined into) syllables. Syllables in languages like English or Dutch consist of vowels (V) and/or consonants (C) and constitute rhythmic units of speech. The V syllable /a/ consists of just one phoneme; the CVC syllable /bæd/ is a word consisting of three phonemes. It is said to have an *onset* /b/, a *nucleus* /æ/, and a *coda* /d/. Its *rime* (or rhyme) is /æd/.

In the Language User Framework, phonetic and phonological information is used by the Signal (Speech) Recognizer to turn sounds into abstract representations. In the visual modality, the Signal (Print) Recognizer is assumed to do something similar: It turns scribbles on paper into abstract letter representations. Both the Speech Recognizer and Print Recognizer may be seen as instances of the Signal Recognizer, "mental machines" that try to faithfully represent incoming sensory information in a raw and then more abstract form.

3.2.7.2 Lexicology and morphology

Lexicology is a branch of linguistics that studies different properties of words (Cruse et al., 2005). The *mental lexicon* contains all words a language user knows and specifies all these different properties:

- *Phonetic* and *phonological*: about the sounds and phonemes a word is built of;
- *Orthographic:* about the letters and graphemes that make up a written or printed word;
- *Morphological*: which meaningful smaller parts can be discerned in a word;
- *Semantic*: what a word means;
- *Syntactic:* what the syntactic category of a word is, what gender, etc.;
- *Articulation*: how a word is pronounced (cf. articulatory phonetics);
- *Motor*: what writing or typing movements are required to produce a word on paper.

As we will see in Chapters 5 and 6 on spoken and printed word recognition, a word's *lexical properties* are significant determinants of how fast the word can be looked up in Long Term Memory. The most important properties of words are their duration or length, the frequency with which they are used, the diversity of contexts in which this happens, and the specific combinations of sounds or letters that the words consist of. How many other words there are similar to the target word, and how frequent these are, is also important (the set of similar words is called "lexical competitor set" in general, "cohort" in the auditory modality, and "neighborhood" in the visual modality).

Not all words in a language consist of one abstract piece, like "book." Words can also consist of combinations of simpler words, like in the noun-noun compound "bookshop", or of a simple word and an added part, like in "booking", including the verb "to book." Even more complex are words like "bookings", in which the verb "to book" is changed into the noun "booking" (derivation), which has the plural ending "s" (inflection). There is a whole linguistic discipline that is dedicated to how complex words can be built on the basis of more simple elements in different languages: It is called *morphology* (Spencer & Zwicky, 2017). The parts of words it is concerned with are called morphemes.

Lexical and morphological information is used by the Spoken and Printed Word Recognizers in the Language User Framework to perform their task of recognizing auditorily and visually presented words.

3.2.7.3 Syntax (grammar)

Just as for word parts in complex words, there are combination and ordering rules for words in sentences. Together, these rules are called a *grammar* and they are studied in the linguistic discipline called *syntax* (Koeneman & Zeijlstra, 2017). For a long time, syntax has been considered as the most important discipline in linguistics. Syntax describes the coherent system of syntactic structures (grammar) both in a language and across languages. The syntactic structure of a sentence can have consequences for its meaning. For instance, "boy sees shark" has a different meaning than "shark sees boy."

According to the Language User Framework, the Sentence Processor makes use of syntax to build syntactic representations of an incoming sentence, and of semantics to build semantic representations in line with the syntactic representations. To do so, lexical information (e.g., about the syntactic category and function of words) is indispensable.

3.2.7.4 Semantics and pragmatics

The meaning of sentences, words, and texts is studied by a discipline called *semantics* (Cummins & Katsos, 2019). It is actually a multidisciplinary discipline and has been studied not only by linguists, but among others also by psychologists, philosophers, neuroscientists, and researchers in artificial intelligence. One major goal in semantics has been to see if different words or sentences may share underlying meaning representations. Said differently, is it possible that myriad sentences and words we encounter are understood on the basis of a limited set of building blocks for meanings? Another major goal in semantics is to find out to what extent meaning can be purely abstract or is always to some extent concrete (i.e., referring to daily life objects and events, and related to bodily experiences).

Instead of "semantic," psycholinguists often use the term *conceptual*. Whereas "conceptual" has no connotation with language, "semantic" still has a linguistic association to it. To the extent that meaning and thought are independent of language, one might prefer the term "conceptual."

Another linguistic discipline, called *pragmatics*, studies how meaning depends on the context in which utterances occur (Barron et al., 2017). It pays attention to, for instance, what we know about those involved in the conversation and their intentions, as well as place, time, and manner in which the utterances occur. One well-known example to illustrate the difference between semantics and pragmatics is the way an utterance such as "My

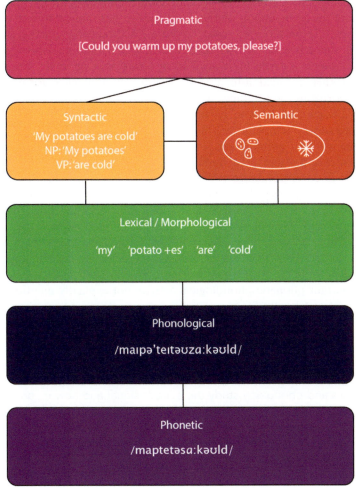

Figure 3.4
A spoken utterance from phonetic input to pragmatic meaning. Language activities take place over time and are concerned with differently sized representations; activities at different representation levels can take place simultaneously. For instance, word meaning retrieval may go hand in hand with syntactic structure building. The example is inspired by Field (2003, p. 65).

potatoes are cold" is treated (also see Figure 3.4). Semantics represents the meaning from this utterance, while pragmatics notes its intention, i.e., a potential request to the listener to serve the potatoes hot.

The Conceptual System combines the meaning representations of words and sentences, described by the linguistic disciplines of semantics and pragmatics, into larger meaning representations for whole conversations (spoken discourse) and printed texts. These constitute the mental models we have discussed before.

3.2.7.5 Bringing the disciplines together

On the basis of the different disciplines we have just discussed, a rough sketch can be made of how language users represent and process printed sentences and spoken utterances.

Leaving the contribution of context aspects and control processes for later consideration, we will now illustrate the contribution of the disciplines to our understanding of the incoming spoken utterance "My potatoes are cold." Figure 3.4 shows that on the way to meaning, the input speech signal is subjected to various "recoding operations." First, the input signal received by the listener is faithfully described in terms of a phonetic representation. This representation is then recoded into a more abstract phonological form and segmented. When the word forms in the utterance are identified, their meaning also becomes activated and available. For instance, "potato" has meaning components including "solid" and "dish," while "cold" refers to a "temperature" that is "low." On the basis of the morphosyntactic properties of the words, a grammatical structure of the sentence can be formulated. In this example, the sentence consists of a noun phrase (NP, "the potatoes") and a verb phrase (VP, "are cold"). In correspondence with the syntactic structure, word meanings are linked up and a semantic structure is built. One formulation of such a semantic structure is in terms of a proposition, which represents and relates (abstract) meanings, but there are several alternatives as well. Here it is indicated that "cold" is a property of "potatoes." But processing is not finished here: The listener will realize that the utterance was said to signal a problem and that it had the particular pragmatic goal to request for a new plate of hot (rather than cold) potatoes. Note that the figure is simplified and can be extended. For instance, an important phonetic-phonological activity not explicitly mentioned in the figure is "segmentation" (see Chapter 5).

> **SUMMARY: LINGUISTICS AND PSYCHOLINGUISTICS**
>
> The various linguistic disciplines are all important to understanding the psychology of language. Phonetics and phonology study the speech signal and how it can be represented in terms of abstract representations that must play a part in (spoken) word recognition and production. Lexicology and morphology study characteristics of words that affect both auditory and visual word recognition. Syntax is important because grammatical properties affect sentence processing and sentence meaning. Semantics and pragmatics help us to understand how people derive meaning conveyed through conversations, books, and even images.
>
> After having been separated for more than half a century, psycholinguistics and linguistics are again converging. Psycholinguists more and more resort to sophisticated views on linguistic representations, while linguists apply more and more on-line research techniques developed by psycholinguists. In addition, both find a new common ground in the cognitive neuroscientific vocabulary and themes that concern the brain. In this book, we do not make a principled distinction between the disciplines, although our focus is psychological and not linguistic in nature.

3.3 WHAT IS NEXT?

Recognizing spoken or printed words, understanding and uttering sentences and discourse, all are core activities that language users engage in when they are processing language. During each of these activities, the signals coming into or going out of the Language Processing System are processed in relation to relevant non-linguistic and linguistic representations and world knowledge stored in Long Term Memory. In other words, to understand a particular language process, discussing the associated representations is indispensable.

In Chapters 5 to 10, we will discuss the core language activities by considering their relevant linguistic representations or structures and the way they are processed. In each chapter, we consider the following aspects of language use:

- The essence of the linguistic activity (e.g., spoken word recognition);
- The architecture and representations used in that activity;
- The cognitive processes underlying the activity;
- Models for the linguistic activity that relate representations, processes, and (if available) control mechanisms;
- Experimental studies investigating theoretically associated issues;
- The presence of relevant context effects.

To fully appreciate the value and importance of empirical research studying the psychology of language, it is helpful to have a thorough understanding of the different types of experimental design, research technique, and apparatus used to present experimental stimuli to participants in this field of study. Before considering the many empirical studies addressing components of the Language User Framework, it is therefore useful to first scrutinize the research techniques with which this is typically done. This is the aim and topic of Chapter 4.

3.4 WHAT HAVE WE LEARNED?

To be able to fully describe language and its use, the Language User Framework discerns four fundamental cognitive components: Long Term Memory representations, processes converting these representations into other ones, control processes regulating the conversion, and Working Memory keeping intermediate products for later processing. The lower part of the Language User Framework, the Language Processing System, takes care of the first two components, while task and decision processes are regulated by the upper part of the Language User Framework, the Cognitive Control System. Working Memory operations are usually specified together with the processes that recode representations. The Language User Framework proposes a hierarchical, interactive, and incrementally working processing system that operates on symbolic units of various sizes (letters, sounds, syllables, words, phrases, sentences, text, and discourse). To describe the full conversion from a physical input signal to meaning into a mental model or vice versa, stored knowledge described by various linguistic disciplines is applied in a concerted way.

QUESTIONS FOR CHAPTER 3

1. What would it mean to say that components in the Language User Framework work in a "globally modular, but locally interactive" way? To what extent could a component in the framework be considered as a "mental organ"?
2. What is (linguistically) going on in the following utterances adapted from Groucho Marx (Kanfer, 2000):
    a. "Last night I shot a picture of an elephant in my pajamas and how he got in my pajamas I'll never know." [Note: "pajama" is a variant of "pyjama," derived from the Hindi words "pai jama" or "pae jama," meaning "leg clothing."]
    b. "Time wounds all heels." (See also Chapter 9 for speech errors.)
    c. "You haven't stopped talking since I came here! You must have been vaccinated with a phonograph needle!" (A phonograph was an early version of a gramophone.)

3 The Cognitive Control System specifies the processing steps (operations) that must be taken to perform a particular (language) task. Can you specify these steps for a word naming task in which people read out individual words aloud? And what would be the steps for an English lexical decision task, in which you have to indicate if a letter string is a word (e.g., BRIGHT) or not (e.g., GRIGHT)? (Also see Chapters 4 and 6.)
4 Look up the most important functions of the different lobes in the brain. Which of the lobes are important for language?
5 Someone says: "Can you pass me the salt?" What discipline(s) in linguistics consider(s) such utterances?
6 How could emotional aspects of word meaning be accounted for in the Language User Framework?
7 What aspects of language and communication may still contribute to your understanding if someone addresses you in a foreign language you do not know?
8 How could we learn about the phonetics (actual speech) of the language of a culture that has completely disappeared but which has left some written documents (e.g., the Hittite Empire)? Hints: Suppose that the script of the documents used syllables as basic units and that proper names of cities and rulers might be shared with other languages (look for "scripts" in Chapter 8 and "cognates" in Chapter 10).
9 Suppose a bilingual French-English student is performing an English lexical decision task (with the instruction: "Is the presented letter string an English word or not?"). Suddenly ORDINATEUR (the French word for "computer") is presented. How could the Cognitive Control System handle this situation and induce a correct response to occur?
10 Describe the different processing steps in understanding the spoken utterance "Wannacuppacoffee?"

Chapter 4

Language research techniques

4.1 INTRODUCTION

One of the very first studies on language was conducted by the Egyptian Pharaoh Psammetichus I (664–610 BC). The Pharaoh wanted to find out which language was the oldest in the world. His hypothesis was, of course, that it was Egyptian, but he wanted scientific proof. To find out, two young children were taken from two randomly chosen parents. The poor children were isolated in a hut and carefully guarded by a goatherd, who was instructed to make sure no language was spoken at all in their vicinity. The children were raised on goat milk and otherwise received the usual care. One day, after two years, the goatherd entered the hut and the children came crawling to him, reaching out with their hands and shouting *bekos*! Pharaoh had the children brought to him and personally confirmed what the goatherd had heard. He then instructed a team to investigate from which language this word was derived. It turned out that in Phrygian, *bekos* is the regular word for "bread." Psammetichus now rejected the popular view that Egyptian was the oldest language on earth: It had to be Phrygian (Herodotus, The Histories 2.2 [2013]).

Nowadays, we still do studies that are empirically rigorous, but not in the sense of Psammetichus. To interpret the data collected in a modern empirical study in the field of language research and to assess their quality, some background knowledge about experimental techniques is required. In this chapter, we discuss a selection of currently prominent research techniques in the study of the psychology of language. Most of these techniques are concerned with the retrieval of words from lexical Long Term Memory (the "mental lexicon") and the processing of sentences during language comprehension or production. However, towards the end of the chapter we will also introduce some relatively recent techniques that make it possible to reliably study language as an embodied activity embedded in rich, naturalistic environments.

4.2 THE EXPERIMENTAL BASICS

In a typical empirical study, experimental materials (e.g., words, sentences) belonging to one or more test and control conditions (e.g., high vs. low frequency items; long vs. short words) are administered to the participants in stimulus lists in the course of an experimental session. On each trial of the session, participants give a particular response to the materials in line with the task at hand. Afterwards, their response in test and control conditions is compared. Typically, the test and control conditions differ in only one important respect,

DOI: 10.4324/9781003326274-4

called the *independent variable* (e.g., word frequency or length). The variables of interest that are measured are called the *dependent variables*, for instance, proportion of correct or incorrect responses (accuracy), response time (RT or gaze duration), or brain activity (e.g., microVoltage in EEG, BOLD response in fMRI). The obtained result patterns show if and/or how the manipulated stimulus property of the independent variable (e.g., word frequency) affects the observed behavior or the neurophysiological response in the dependent variables of the experimental task at hand. The obtained result patterns will systematically depend on stimulus properties, task demands, and participant characteristics.

On the basis of the result patterns in the experiment and related experiments, the researchers formulate or test a coherent theoretical interpretation of the manipulated phenomenon (e.g., the effect of word frequency on the reaction time of participants when they have to name printed words). Such observations then ideally say something about the cognitive processes that support language use in everyday life.

When designing an experiment, it is important to make sure that any observed result pattern is not due to unwanted factors such as noise, uncontrolled stimulus characteristics, or experimental confounds. To obtain a reliable *signal-to-noise ratio*, language researchers typically present participants with a considerable number of stimuli per condition. To be able to attribute a potential effect to the variable they are theoretically interested in, they try to *match* the stimuli in different conditions in all possible ways while manipulating only that one variable they are focusing on for the moment. To avoid other confounds, stimuli are typically presented in an order that is *(pseudo)randomized* (seemingly coincidental or chance-based). If this is not possible or not preferable, such as when a block design (i.e., one experimental condition per block of trials) is used, the order of different trial blocks can be *counterbalanced* across participants. For instance, one half of the participants first sees block A and then block B, the other half first sees block B and then block A. Thus, over all participants together, each block occurs at every possible position in the session. Box 4.1 illustrates these various aspects in a thought experiment involving word naming.

SUMMARY: THE EXPERIMENTAL BASICS

The average experiment studying aspects of the psychology of language makes use of one or more test conditions and a matched baseline or control condition. Stimuli (e.g., words or sentences) are presented and behavioral or neural responses are measured. The researcher carefully controls the number of stimuli in and across conditions, randomizes and/or counterbalances their order of presentation, and makes sure to have enough statistical power to reliably detect any effect if present in the data.

Box 4.1 DIY experiment: Testing the word frequency effect in word naming

The more often one retrieves a word from memory (i.e., the more often a word is used), the easier it becomes to process the next time. This leads to one of the strongest effects on word recognition: the word frequency effect. As we shall see in Chapter 6, the classical models of the 1960s and 1970s in the domain of visual word recognition were basically built around this effect. Here we will perform a thought experiment to test the hypothesis that the usage frequency of a word affects how easy it is to name that word (also see Section 4.4.2). If you have time, you could follow the instructions and conduct the experiment yourself.

We can set up the experiment in two ways: as a "pseudo-experiment," using already available data, or as a real experiment. Before we present both options for you to explore, we must first select our stimulus materials for the experiment. We want to select words of different frequencies of usage. The simplest option is to select only high-frequency and low-frequency words and compare their naming response times.

But how do we know the frequency with which words are used? Fortunately, researchers have already looked into this question and have collected the usage frequencies of millions of words by counting how often they occur in subtitles. For instance, word frequencies for English words have been collected in databases SUBTLEX-US (Brysbaert et al., 2012) and SUBTLEX-UK (van Heuven et al., 2014), easily found on the internet. From these databases, you can select high-frequency words (e.g., words with a frequency above 100 occurrences per million tokens, corresponding to a log frequency of 2) and low-frequency words (for instance, words with a frequency of only 10 or 20 occurrences per million tokens, corresponding to a log frequency of around 1). We could select words such as "time," "work," or "book" as being high-frequency, and words like "tile," "cork," or "boon" as being low-frequency. But we must make sure that all words are known by our participant population!

We must be careful to match the stimuli in the two conditions in as many respects as possible (e.g., onset phoneme, length in letters and syllables, semantic and syntactic category, orthographic and phonological similarity, etc.) and only vary their frequency of usage. The quality of the match can be assessed by, for instance, t tests between the conditions. For a statistically acceptable comparison of the naming times to be obtained, the two sets of words must each consist of many stimuli (e.g., 40 or 50 per condition). By averaging the responses to the items later (resulting in mean RTs per condition), you diminish the effect of unwanted noise (e.g., a participant having to sneeze during the presentation of one stimulus) on the results. As a practical limit, the duration of the experimental session (including instruction, consent form, breaks, participant compensation, and so on) should not exceed more than an hour.

We now need to obtain word naming times for these words. Actually, for some languages, researchers have already collected the naming (and lexical decision) responses for a large number of words and put them in databases on the internet. In this case, we can extract the mean naming times for each word and the accuracy with which it was named by a large number of people from the English Lexicon Project (ELP; Balota et al., 2007). By using these data as the results of a "pseudo-experiment," you will probably find that the naming times are significantly shorter in the high-frequency condition than in the low-frequency condition (cf. Ferrand et al., 2011).

The alternative is to conduct a "real" experiment by ourselves. This requires a bit more work. First, by programming a randomization routine or using existing software to do so, we must mix all stimuli of both conditions into a list that is different for every participant. By having different lists, potential effects of fatigue or learning are averaged out across participants. We then inspect the item order in the lists based on chance and may adapt it ("pseudo-randomization") to avoid long series of high-frequency words or low-frequency words (which might induce participant strategies). Next, by means of dedicated experimental software (e.g., DMDX by Forster & Forster, 2003), the words in the lists can be presented to participants one by one and in the middle of a computer screen. A considerable practical problem is that our program must somehow register the time between the onset of the presented word on the screen and that of the naming response. Thus, we need a reliable microphone to measure response times, or collect all trial information on the computer and then later determine response times.

Before data collection begins, we must instruct the participants to name each upcoming word as quickly and as accurately as they can, also giving them a few "practice trials" to understand what they must do.

We must make sure that enough participants take part in the experiment in order to allow sound statistical conclusions later. A so-called statistical power analysis may help to determine this number (see Brysbaert, 2019a). In this way, we can be relatively sure that it is not very detrimental if one or two participants are accidentally a bit sleepy or distracted while carrying out the task.

Before we start to analyze the data, we first have to clean them. Do we accept responses slower than (for instance) 2 seconds as valid? If not, we remove them. In fact, we may decide to remove all erroneous responses and outliers (responses that are too fast or very slow relative to general performance by the participant or on the item in question). In the past, mean RTs were then analyzed with analyses of variance (ANOVAs), but nowadays we mostly use linear and logistic mixed-effects models, allowing a finer grained analysis. More and more often, these models take into account characteristics of individual participants and items (Baayen et al., 2008).

In this word naming experiment, we will probably obtain a significant but not very strong frequency effect (cf. Ferrand et al., 2011). Most likely, a follow-up experiment using a lexical decision task would show much stronger effects.

When you read a research article, or when you conduct an experiment yourself, it is always good to keep these basic experimental design issues in mind as quality criteria.

4.3 RESEARCH TECHNIQUES MEASURING WORD RETRIEVAL

A large proportion of psycholinguistic research on language comprehension and production is concerned with words. This is because words are important building blocks for larger linguistic units such as phrases or sentences. Variation in response times in experimental studies can often be explained in terms of varying word properties. Many techniques have been developed to study how language users retrieve words from their mental lexicon in Long Term Memory.

4.3.1 Off-line measurement: Memory

Off-line memory research is often concerned with how words are stored in and retrieved from Long Term Memory and how they are learned during first or second language acquisition. Research on memory and learning was already carried out in the second half of the 19th century by Ebbinghaus (Levelt, 2013). Several different types of memory have since been distinguished (see Figure 4.1). The green boxes indicate that often memory traces lasting for different durations have been proposed. Explicit memory is involved in the conscious retrieval of information (e.g., remembering your shopping list), while implicit memory is remembered unconsciously and effortlessly (e.g., riding your bike). Episodic memory is the memory of the events of daily life (e.g., when, where, what did you feel) and the collection of past personal experiences (Tulving, 1972). Semantic memory stores the general knowledge we have of our world and culture, as well as our linguistic and conceptual knowledge (see Chapter 8). As we shall see later in this chapter, during priming, a stimulus ("prime") may exert an implicit memory effect on a later stimulus ("target"). Procedural memory is called to help when we execute particular cognitive and motor skills, such as reading a text, buttoning our coat, or playing the piano.

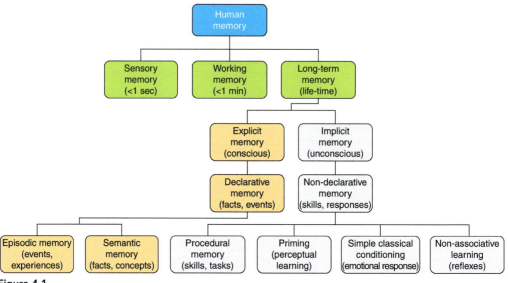

Figure 4.1
An overview and taxonomy of different types of memory.

Questions to be considered are:

- How long is the information retained in a particular form?
- Is the learning instruction implicit or explicit?
- Does the information stored concern facts and events, or skills and tasks?
- Does the information address specific events and experiences in daily life, or facts and concepts?

Off-line studies of memory in the field of language make use of at least two types of approach. In *word recognition* studies, participants first learn words and are later asked to recognize items, which they might have learned before or not, from a presented stimulus list. In *word recall* studies, participants are asked to recall (produce) as many words as possible from a set of words they have learned before. In current research, not only are learning curves of correctly remembered words drawn, but those networks of brain areas involved in the learning process are also considered.

Memory studies are still important to researchers interested in the psychology of language, for instance, in the domains of first and second language acquisition and education. Interest has been invigorated over the last decades by the arrival of brain-oriented research techniques that allow us to see how the brain changes during learning. One technique doing this is diffusion tensor imaging (DTI), which is a form of MRI (see below). It reveals how water moves along the white-matter tracts that connect the various areas of the brain. In learners and patients, it can measure neuro-anatomical changes in the myelination of fibers. For instance, Xiang et al. (2015) made DTI images of the brains of German participants in a learning study before and after they took a course on Dutch. Just 6 weeks of learning already led to detectable brain changes.

4.3.2 On-line measurement: Behavioral reaction time and neuroscientific studies

Rather than considering only a word's representation in memory, on-line research also examines the process of its retrieval. The word *on-line* here hence does not refer to the internet, but to measuring ongoing mental processes while they take place. In tasks measuring accuracy (error rate) or speed of responding (RT), the focus lies on the end product of a complex retrieval process; in neuroscientific studies, we learn about time-course of language processing in the brain and the neurobiological structures and networks involved in it.

The basic rationale underlying these on-line studies is the following. Language processing activities are assumed to be complex processes organized in multiple stages. It has been proposed that these roughly involve (more or less consecutive) identification and decision stages (Sanders, 1980; Sternberg, 1969). About five substages have been proposed: attention allocation, stimulus encoding, central (lexical) processes, response choice, and (motor) response execution. As an example, naming a word (minimally) involves finding the item (on a screen in an experiment, or, for instance, in a newspaper in everyday life), encoding it into abstract letter representations, looking it up in the mental lexicon, finding its pronunciation, and naming it aloud. Note that in each substage, numerous processes might be carried out in parallel.

The question then is: How can we find out more about these stages, for instance, about their duration and about the types of representation involved? As proposed by Donders around 1865 [1969], we can find out about these things by comparing the effects of two experimental conditions that differ only in the single dimension we are interested in (also see Box 4.1). As we mentioned earlier, one of these is the test condition, the other is the baseline or control condition (Donders, 1865/1969; Roelofs, 2018). We measure how long a particular linguistic activity takes, change only one aspect of that activity, and measure again. The difference in response times should reflect the duration of the process that we changed. For instance, we can see how long it takes for a participant to read the word "dog" following the word "cat" (meaning related) or "car" (unrelated). The difference in reading times must reflect a semantic process, because "cat" and "dog" are semantically related, but "car" and "dog" are not. This rationale (called the c-method by Donders) is applicable to both behavioral (e.g., RT) and neuroscientific (e.g., EEG and fMRI) studies. It is the fundament on which most empirical studies in the psychology of language rest.

In the following, we will first discuss some behavioral techniques at word and sentence level, and then introduce several neuroscientific techniques.

SUMMARY: RESEARCH TECHNIQUES MEASURING WORD RETRIEVAL

Off-line memory studies (word recognition and word recall) are used to gain insights about how words are represented in our mental lexicon and how the lexicon develops during acquisition. On-line behavioral reaction time and neuroscientific studies can be used to investigate how language users retrieve words from their lexicon, following different stages, triggered by an incoming signal.

4.4 BEHAVIORAL REACTION TIME TASKS

The three on-line tasks that have been most prominently used in the study of the psychology of language are lexical decision, word naming, and picture naming. For these tasks, RTs and accuracy (or error rates) for items in different experimental conditions are collected. Let us discuss these three tasks in some detail.

4.4.1 Lexical decision: Visual and auditory

In lexical decision, participants must decide as soon and as accurately as possible if a presented item is an existing word or not. In visual lexical decision, the stimulus is presented in printed form, in auditory lexical decision in spoken form (see Goldinger, 1996). If the item is a word (e.g., "house" in English lexical decision), participants press one response button (usually the right one). If it is not a word (e.g., a pronounceable pseudoword such as "vothe" or a "real" nonword, e.g., "tqxsf"), they press another one (usually the left one). Thus, lexical decision is a *two-alternative forced-choice* task (cf. Figure 4.2).

Lexical decision is often used as a proxy to word recognition. It is sensitive to many word characteristics: the frequency with which the word form is used in everyday life, its length in letters or duration in milliseconds (ms), its concreteness and imageability, its pronunciation, the number and frequency of words that are similar to it (called the "neighbors"), its age of acquisition (AoA), and many other variables. It has been suggested that lexical decision involves an automatic process of parallel activation of word possibilities, followed by an attention-consuming decision process.

Note that the decision to say "yes, it is a word" can be made as soon as the presented word form is found in the mental lexicon. This could be as soon as the orthographic representation of the item is located. Nevertheless, semantic and phonological effects are often reported. One explanation is that semantic and phonological representations, activated by orthography, feed back activation to the orthography soon enough to affect the response. Alternatively, it may be that during responding participants consult other representations in

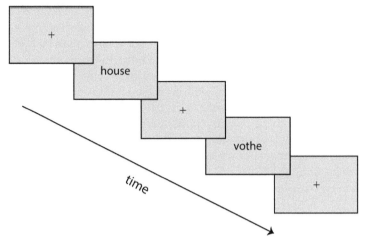

Figure 4.2
Example of the temporal order of events in a visual lexical decision study. Participants, by button press, determine whether a presented letter string is an existing word or not. Their speed of responding, accuracy, and corresponding brain activity can be recorded and analyzed to learn something about how people recognize and understand words.

addition to orthography. It usually takes about 500–550 ms for participants to make a lexical decision for words consisting of four to six letters. This includes a motor response of 100 ms or so.

An interesting variant of visual lexical decision is the "go/no-go lexical decision" task, in which participants press the button when the presented letter string is a nonword ("go") but not when it is a word ("no-go"). This technique is often combined with EEG or fMRI recordings, because it allows a relatively clean measurement of the brain activity for words, which are not themselves accompanied by an overt response in this task.

In auditory lexical decision, frequency is less important and length more important than in visual lexical decision. Taking into account the different presentation characteristics of auditory words (more sequential presentation of constituent units) and visual words (more parallel), this is not so hard to understand (see Chapter 1). In auditory word recognition, a word can be uniquely defined only after a certain amount of the speech signal has been received and processed. Only then can it be discerned from other words that start the same (cf. "captain" with "capture").

To avoid decision processes related to making the yes/no response in lexical decisions, researchers have also sometimes resorted to a "perceptual identification" task called *progressive demasking* (Dufau et al., 2008). In progressive demasking, the presentation of a target word is alternated with that of a mask (e.g., a series of hash signs). During this alternation process, the target item is presented for a longer and longer time, while that of the mask decreases. Participants are asked to push a button as soon as they identify the target word, and then to type it in.

In recent years, several large scale databases with lexical decision RTs have been compiled and made publicly available. The English Lexicon Project mentioned in Box 4.1, for instance, offers visual lexical decision data (RTs and accuracy) for over 40,000 words and pseudowords (Balota et al., 2007; see also Keuleers et al., 2010, 2012), and similar databases exist with auditory lexical decision data (e.g., Ernestus & Cutler, 2015; Tucker et al., 2019). Such databases allow for in-depth exploration of what factors determine how quickly a word is recognized.

Lexical decision has often been combined with a priming technique. The target item is then preceded by a word or sentence in the same or a different modality (e.g., auditory sentence followed by visual target word) that has a particular relation to that target. For instance, the target word "nurse" may be preceded by the semantically related word "doctor." Depending on the relation, the target word may be facilitated or inhibited relative to an unrelated item. The word "nurse" will be responded to more quickly when preceded by "doctor." This is called *semantic priming* (see Figure 4.3 for the ordering of events in such a trial). In this word-word priming task, the priming effect will be larger if: (a) the prime is of higher frequency; (b) the semantic relation between prime and target is stronger; (c) the target is of lower frequency. A large collection of semantic priming data has been collected by Hutchison et al. (2013).

Two well-known *cross-modal priming* studies that we discuss later in the book are those by Swinney (1979) and Zwitserlood (1989). In these studies, the prime is presented in a different modality (e.g., visually) than the target (e.g., auditorily). In other applications of priming, the orthographic or morphological relationship between prime and target is varied.

Another important variant of the priming technique is *masked priming* (Kinoshita & Lupker, 2003). In priming with a forward mask, the prime word is preceded by a mask (i.e., a superimposed pattern of hash signs or letter fragments) and then presented for a very short time (e.g., 50 ms) (see Figure 4.3). Backward masks (following the prime) are also sometimes used. To reduce the physical overlap between prime and target, often one of the two words is presented in lower case letters, the other in capitals.

A related but off-line task is *word association*. People are presented with a cue word (e.g., "shark") and are asked to give as many associations they can come up with (e.g., "animal," "blood," "bite," "fish," "film," …). Databases have been set up with the likelihoods that people come up with particular associations (Nelson et al., 2004). However, the relationship between semantic priming effects and word associations remains unclear. One reason is that semantic priming and word association are tasks that involve different cognitive processes

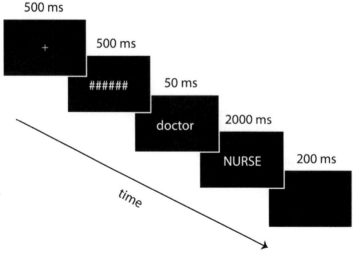

Figure 4.3
Example of the temporal order of events in a semantic priming lexical decision study that uses a forward mask.

and decision making. For instance, in word association, the first word that comes to the conscious mind may be given as a response; this is not necessarily the target that is combined with the prime in a semantic priming task.

4.4.2 Word naming

As we saw in Box 4.1, in the word naming task, participants read aloud visually presented words or pseudowords (i.e., pronounceable letter strings that are not words) as quickly and accurately as they can. This task is popular for several reasons. Most importantly, in contrast to lexical decision, it is a task that people also perform in real life. The task is per word about 100 ms faster than lexical decision, as response times of 450 ms are possible in the native language. However, there are also some caveats for using this task. One of them is that the triggering of the voice key (microphone) that is used during word naming is sensitive to the properties of the first phoneme of the word. For instance, fricatives, plosives, and vowels result in somewhat different delays before the microphone picks up the spoken signal (see Chapter 5).

In order to name a word, the orthographic representation derived from the printed letter string must be converted into a phonological-phonetic representation that can be used for articulation. This could be done in two basic ways (according to the Dual Route Cascaded model of reading, discussed in more detail in Chapter 6). One possibility is to look up the orthographic representation of the word (e.g., "lemon") in the mental lexicon directly. Next, the spoken word form could be derived from this representation or from its associated meaning ("lemon" is pronounced in a particular way). This way to name a word is called the "lexical route."

Alternatively, the letters of a word (e.g., l-e-m-o-n) could first be recoded into individual sounds. This process has been called grapheme-to-phoneme conversion (GPC). Assembling the different sounds into a whole again (i.e., the pronunciation of the whole word "lemon") would then indirectly result in the retrieval of the word's phonological representation. This way to name a word is called the "sublexical route," because it involves units smaller than a word ("sublexical"). Irrespective of which of these two routes is followed, the phonological code lies at the basis of word naming (see Chapter 6).

Both lexical decision and word naming could be argued to measure word recognition. However, although findings with the two tasks overlap to some extent, they also yield different result patterns. This can be understood by considering that the two tasks pose different demands on the Language Processing System. For instance, in order to respond to them these tasks require different outputs. Visual lexical decision is probably based on the orthographic code, because it becomes available first, whereas word naming must necessarily be based on a phonetic-articulatory code derived from the word's phonological representation.

Word naming has been extensively applied as a technique for studying the so-called "Stroop effect" (named after Stroop, who described the effect in 1935). We can easily illustrate the phenomenon. Just name the *color* of the following words as quickly as you can: **red** – **table** – **black** – **horse** – **blue** – **book**. You may already have noticed that you were slower to name the color ("green") of a color term that mismatched the printed ink color ("red") relative to when it matched it ("blue"). More precise measurements with longer lists and better timing conditions will show that naming the color of non-color words like "table" and "horse" result in intermediate naming times. Relative to this more or less neutral control condition, we thus observe both "Stroop facilitation" and "Stroop inhibition," with the inhibition clearly outperforming the facilitation (MacLeod, 1991). Researchers have studied the Stroop effect to learn about "automaticity" and "attention," "response competition," and "interference effects" in language production (Glaser & Glaser, 1989; Roelofs, 2003). The effect has also been observed in multilinguals (e.g., van Heuven et al., 2011).

4.4.3 Picture naming

Another task in which phonological codes must be derived for responding is picture naming (see Figure 4.4). Large databases with validated pictures to be used in picture naming experiments are available in the literature (e.g., Duñabeitia et al., 2018; Snodgrass & Vanderwart, 1980). To name a presented picture correctly, the depicted object must first be identified, resulting in an activation of (parts of) its semantic representation or concept. Next, the associated object name is looked up and the spoken word form can be retrieved and produced. Going from semantics to phonology could be a similar process in word naming and picture naming. However, as argued in the previous section, in word naming there are also active lexical and sublexical routes from its orthographic representation to its phonological representation. Picture naming studies often aim to advance our understanding of the mechanisms and stages involved in language production, broadly corresponding to the right part of the Language Processing System.

An example study using picture naming is presented by Alario and colleagues (2004). They had a large number of native speakers of French name a wide variety of pictures in two separate experimental sessions. The authors observed that several factors influenced picture naming RTs. These included aspects of the picture itself (e.g., its visual complexity), the degree of agreement between participants on what exact word to use to name a certain picture (i.e., its name agreement), and properties of the produced picture name (e.g., its frequency and the age at which this word was typically acquired). The speed of describing some aspect of the world in one word may thus depend on characteristics of that entity, how univocally it can be described, and properties of the word that is used to do so.

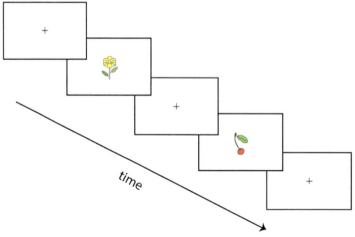

Figure 4.4
Example of the temporal order of events in a picture naming study. Participants are instructed to name each picture as quickly and accurately as possible, typically using a single word per picture.

> **SUMMARY: BEHAVIORAL REACTION TIME TASKS**
>
> Lexical decision (visual and auditory) is a commonly used task to study aspects of word recognition, retrieval, and processing. It has shown that various lexical characteristics (word frequency, length, concreteness, imageability, etc.) affect how quickly a word is retrieved. Word naming tasks illustrate that words can be named via grapheme-to-phoneme conversions or by looking up the orthographic representation of the word in the mental lexicon directly. Picture naming tasks allow the researcher to focus on the relation between semantics, phonology, and articulation during language production.

4.5 TECHNIQUES USED AT WORD AND SENTENCE LEVEL

A number of research techniques have been developed to study how people read or listen to (words in) sentences. Most prominently, studies using self-paced reading and eye tracking have contributed to advancing our understanding of the psychology of language.

4.5.1 Self-paced reading

Participants in a self-paced reading experiment are presented with a word (or a phrase) and press a button as soon as they have read it. Then a new word is presented, and so on. The time it takes for the participant to press the button is a reflection of word and sentence properties. Unfortunately, there are also other factors contributing to the participant's response, e.g., they may develop a response rhythm. Nevertheless, the technique is still sometimes used. An auditory variant is also possible ("self-paced listening") and is easy to apply with children. Self-paced reading has long been a popular technique, as it was frequently employed and part of the standard psycholinguistic toolbox, but has been giving way to eye tracking.

An example study using self-paced reading comes from Tremblay and colleagues (2011). These authors were interested in how readers process so-called "lexical bundles," i.e., sequences of words that often occur together and span phrasal boundaries, such as "in the middle of the" and "on the other hand." They had speakers of English read sentences that contained a lexical bundle, such as "I sat in the middle of the bullet train," and compared these to similar sentences without a lexical bundle, such as "I sat in the front of the bullet train." The self-paced reading data showed that the sentences that contained a lexical bundle yielded shorter reading times compared to the control sentences. As such, these data suggest that lexical bundles may have a special status in people's memory.

Related research domains are concerned with the processing of idiomatic expressions, proverbs, and metaphors. An important issue here is how and when the literal and figurative interpretations of the multiword unit come about. Consider, as an example, the sentence "this costs me an arm and a leg" (meaning "this is very expensive"). Does a listener activate the complete literal meaning of the sentence, e.g., the actual meaning of the body parts "arm" and "leg"? Is its figurative meaning derived in parallel with the literal meaning or only subsequently? Surprisingly, the figurative meaning of idioms is often processed just as quickly or even more quickly than their literal meaning (Conklin & Schmitt, 2012; Swinney & Cutler, 1979). This suggests that figurative and literal processing proceed in parallel and that idioms are represented in Long Term Memory as chunks. Rather than being based on self-paced reading, these time-critical conclusions more and more often rest on evidence from a research technique called "eye tracking."

4.5.2 Eye tracking

A research technique that has been around for a long time but that has actually increased in popularity (due, in part, to technological developments) is that of *eye tracking*. An eye tracker device uses illuminators that throw a pattern of (unharmful) near-infrared light on the eyes of a reader. Cameras take calibrated high-resolution images of the participant's retinas in the eyes, allowing dedicated software to determine moment by moment the exact position of the pupils of the reader's eyes and, consequently, the position they are looking at (called "gaze position"). The eye tracking technique has often been applied to natural reading, reading experiments, and in the so-called visual world paradigm. We will now discuss these three applications one by one.

4.5.2.1 Using eye tracking to study natural reading

Using the eye tracking methodology, one can present sentences on a computer screen, line by line, or word by word, and track the movements and fixations of the eyes when they read the words and sentences (see Figure 4.5). This measurement technique has yielded detailed temporal data on what readers "do" while they process printed sentences and texts (Rayner, 1998, 2009; Rayner & Reichle, 2010; Rayner et al., 2011). When you look at the eyes of a reader (try it!), you will notice that they make little jumps from one word in a printed sentence to a later one (often, but not always, the next content word). The jumps or hops are called "eye movements," or more specifically "saccades," while the time the eye rests on a particular word is called the "fixation duration." The total of the first and later fixations is called "gaze duration." Saccades (sometimes also called "inter-fixations") are typically quite fast (40–60 ms), while eye fixations may vary between 50 and 500 ms. Interestingly, in 10 to 15% of saccades, eyes may also move back to earlier positions in a sentence or a text, which are called "regressions." These "backward jumps" probably occur when not all is clear in the reader's mind. As we will argue in Chapter 7 on sentence processing, the reader's behavior can therefore be considered as *incremental*.

4.5.2.2 Using eye tracking in reading experiments

An important research hypothesis formulated by Just and Carpenter (1980) on the basis of eye tracking data is the "strong eye–mind hypothesis." It holds that the pattern of fixations

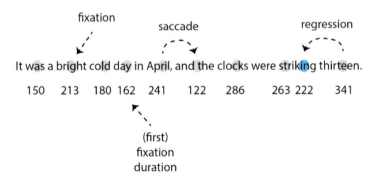

Figure 4.5
When we read a sentence or text, our eyes fixate on words, and make saccades and regressions. In this figure, filled dots indicate fixations and numbers represent fixation durations in ms. Eye movement patterns can be recorded using an eye tracker and analyzed afterwards. After Rayner et al. (2011).

and saccades is a direct reflection of cognitive activity concerning the word being looked at. To put it more boldly, the hypothesis implies that tracking the eye leads us through a direct gate to our language processing mind! This notion has been so important that, in spite of the exciting arrival of neuroscientific measurement techniques such as EEG, MEG, and fMRI, variants of the eye tracking technique have prospered in the last decennia.

Eye tracking studies further indicate that readers try to derive as much information as possible from a word in relation to the sentence context before they move on through the text (the "immediacy assumption" by Just & Carpenter, 1980). It can be deduced from the eye movement patterns that word recognition can already take place within one third of a second.

The following classical study on the *parafoveal preview effect* (Inhoff & Rayner, 1980) provides an example of the eye tracking technique as an experimental research technique in the lab. Participants were instructed to fixate on a central point on the screen. As soon as they noticed that a letter string appeared in their *parafoveal vision* (e.g., on the far side of the screen to the right of the fixation point), they were to make an eye movement to it. However, while their eyes were making a saccade, the computer replaced the initial letter string by a different word. The participants then had to name this target word as quickly as possible. This implied that the parafoveal stimulus was visible for about 200 ms before the eye movement began. Remarkably, participants were almost never aware of the identity of the original parafoveal item and did not even notice there had been a change in it. At the same time, target word naming was facilitated (relative to when the parafoveal letter string consisted of a row of unrelated letters), even when the overlap in letters had been only partial. For instance, when "chart" was the word that was named, decreasing effects of naming facilitation were found when the original parafoveal strings were "chart" (identical), "chest," or the nonword "chovt" (Rayner & Pollatsek, 1989, p. 142). The amount of facilitation also decreased when the parafoveal letter string was presented farther away from the fixation point. Figure 4.6 illustrates the difference between foveal and parafoveal vision.

In eye tracking, sentences can be presented as a whole, but also word by word. In a technique called "rapid serial visual presentation" or RSVP, each word is presented for about 300–350 ms, separated by blanks of a similar duration. This technique is quite useful when EEG is measured at the same time, because it reduces the effects of eye movements on the signal compared to when all words in a sentence are presented at once.

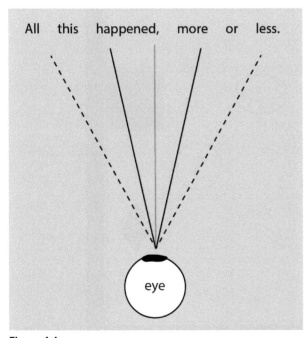

Figure 4.6
The eye fixating on a point in a sentence. The green line here indicates the exact point of fixation. The area within the solid black lines indicates foveal vision, while the area within the dotted black lines represents parafoveal vision. Note that the closer your eyes are located vis-à-vis a sentence presented in a book or on a screen, the smaller the area that falls within your foveal (and parafoveal) vision.

4.5.2.3 Using eye tracking in the visual world paradigm

There is another, very different but also very informative application of the eye tracking technique in language research, called the visual world paradigm (e.g., Cooper, 1974; Huettig et al., 2011; Tanenhaus et al., 1995). Paradoxically, it often uses eye tracking to investigate auditory processing! It works like this. Participants look at a computer screen with typically four panels containing a particular object (see Figure 4.7; in children, two panels may be used). The name of the object may have some relation to a word that is auditorily presented in isolation or as part of a sentence. For instance, the listening participant may hear "Pick up the dollar" while the four panels show a dollar, a dolphin, a collar, and a beaker (Allopenna et al., 1998).

In this case, it has been found that the eyes may initially temporarily fixate on the dolphin rather than on the dollar. This is because "dollar" and "dolphin" are part of the same word-initial cohort, leading to their initial co-activation (see Chapter 5 on spoken word recognition). At a later stage, eye movements may also move to the collar, due to its overlap in rhyme with the word "dollar." The visual world paradigm can also be used to investigate transitional ambiguities in sentences (see Chapter 5). As is the case for basically all experimental paradigms, the ecological validity of eye tracking paradigms has sometimes been questioned. In everyday life, would you ever pick up a dolphin if you could also pick up a dollar?

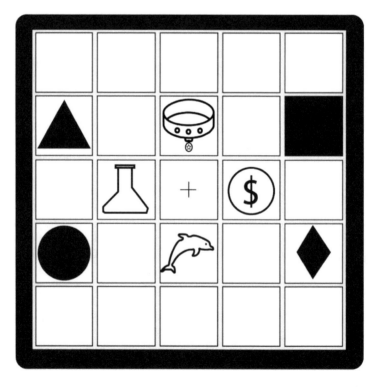

Figure 4.7
The visual world paradigm as presented on a computer screen. Four panels contain pictures of objects. The black shapes can be used for calibration purposes, while the plus indicates the initial position for the eye to fixate on. Participants listen to sentences (such as "Pick up the dollar") while their eye movements towards objects on the screen are recorded. Here you see a beaker, a collar, a dollar, and a dolphin. Where would participants look over time while listening to the sentence? Adapted from Allopenna et al. (1998).

> **SUMMARY: TECHNIQUES USED AT WORD AND SENTENCE LEVEL**
>
> Words are building blocks for larger linguistic structures such as phrases and sentences, and they are usually encountered in a broader visual environment. Self-paced reading and eye tracking paradigms allow the researcher to study the role of words in the context of such a larger linguistic or visual context. Because eye tracking procedures offer a more natural way of reading sentences than self-paced reading paradigms, they have become the most popular method in this domain.

4.6 NEUROPHYSIOLOGICAL AND NEUROIMAGING TECHNIQUES

An important development in the last decades has been the arrival of neuroscientific research techniques. These techniques allow the researcher to learn about aspects of a participant's brain activity while that participant carries out a language-related task such as reading words or naming pictures. Importantly, many of these techniques are non-invasive, such that the language researcher no longer has to rely on post-mortem inspection of the brain of patients with a language-related disorder (e.g., aphasia).

Three popular techniques studying how language is processed by the human brain are EEG (electroencephalography), MEG (magnetoencephalography), and fMRI (functional magnetic resonance imaging). EEG has a high temporal resolution and is therefore well-suited for measuring the time-course of cognitive processes, whereas fMRI has a high spatial resolution that allows for a better assessment of where in the brain processing happens. MEG to some extent combines the best of both worlds: a relatively high temporal resolution is paired with a relatively high spatial resolution.

Research using EEG, MEG, and fMRI enriches theories of language processing, which, in the past, were based particularly on response time measurements in so-called "behavioral studies." However, they also lead to new questions about the where, when, and how of brain activity during language processing.

Various other kinds of measurement also clarify where in the brain activation arises during particular language activities: single-cell recordings, electrical stimulation, positron emission tomography (PET), and transcranial magnetic stimulation (TMS). CT and CAT (computerized axial tomography) scans, in addition to MRI, can help to locate brain damage in language-related and other disorders. In this book, we mainly consider studies using EEG, MEG, and MRI techniques. However, we will briefly summarize some of the other techniques in this chapter as well.

4.6.1 Electroencephalography (EEG)

EEG measures electrical activity arising in the brain (while the MEG measures its counterpart of magnetic activity). The EEG signal (when measured non-invasively) is quite noisy, as it travels through the skull, which makes it difficult to see how the brain responds to a particular individual language event. However, if we average the EEG for a series of recurring events and time-lock it to the onset of the event, noise is to some extent cancelled out and we obtain a more stable waveform, called an event-related potential or ERP (see Figure 4.8). In the most common analysis, we average the EEG signals for many (e.g., at least 40) different occurrences of the same trial type, for instance, high-frequency words. To make an EEG/ERP, we put (32, 64, or 128) electrodes in a cap on a participant's head in a

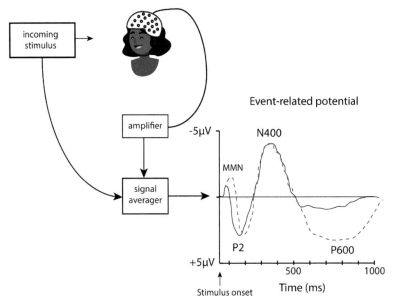

Figure 4.8
The electrophysiological response to perceiving and processing a stimulus as picked up by the electrodes in an EEG cap on the head of the participant. Amplifying and averaging the signal leads to an event-related potential (ERP). Negative signals are standardly plotted upwards. After Osterhout et al. (1997). Part of image designed by pikisuperstar/Freepik.

configuration that allows for capturing electrophysiological brain activity outside the skull (Luck, 2014).

However, due to the conductance of the skull, the signals from the brain are smeared out over relatively large areas. Therefore, it is difficult to localize the source of the signal with ERPs. In sum, its sensitivity is not good for processes deeper in the brain and source localization is difficult due to the low *spatial* resolution.

In contrast, *temporal* aspects can be measured much better with EEG than with fMRI. Neural activity over time can be measured directly up to a high temporal resolution (see Figure 4.9). Researchers have identified several ERP components that are thought to reflect aspects of language processing. Two well-known markers often observed at sentence level are:

N400: A negative amplitude in the EEG peaking at about 400 ms (350–500 ms) after the onset of the input event (Kutas & Hillyard, 1980). This component has been interpreted as both a marker of lexical-semantic integration and a marker of the extent to which an incoming word confirms the reader's or listener's prediction. Broadly speaking, one could interpret N400 amplitude as a reflection of processing ease of the stimulus it is time-locked to. It is found both for words in sentences and word-like items in isolation. For instance, pseudowords and nonwords often display larger N400 amplitude than words. Considerably oversimplifying, one could say that a more negative N400 reflects more processing effort for the reader or listener (see Kutas & Federmeier, 2011).

An N400 effect will be found for the target word in a sentence such as "Jenny put the candy in her pocket after the lesson" relative to the sentence "Jenny put the candy in her mouth after the lesson." The word "mouth" is much more expected (i.e., it has a higher CLOZE-probability) than "pocket," making "mouth" arguably easier to process than "pocket" here.

P600: Enhanced positive amplitude in the EEG signal at about 600 ms (500–700 ms) after event onset. This marker has initially been related to the language user's detection of syntactic violations, and has originally therefore also been termed the "syntactic positive shift" (SPS; Hagoort et al., 1993). The interpretation of the marker in terms of reflecting a syntactic process is not completely undisputed. Furthermore, it may be difficult to differentiate the P600 from the late positive component (LPC), another late positive response in the EEG.

A P600 effect will be observed time-locked to the verb form for a sentence such as "The spoilt child throw the toy on the ground" relative to "The spoilt child throws the toy on the ground." (Note that if your variant of English uses "spoiled" and not "spoilt" as an adjective here, your EEG might also show a P600 effect to "spoilt" when the sentence is presented visually.)

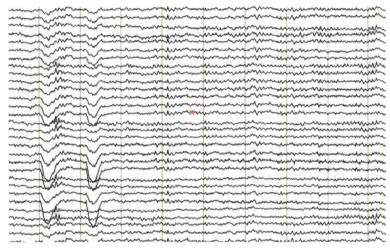

Figure 4.9
Part of the recording of raw EEG data. Each line corresponds to the data on-line recorded from one electrode. The sharp deflections at the start of the time window correspond to the participant blinking their eyes twice in a row.

Although the N400 is often interpreted to reflect semantic aspects, and the P600 is often related to syntactic aspects of processing, this does not imply that syntactic processing follows semantic processing. It may well be that earlier syntactic processes are not always detectable in the EEG. There are also several other ERP markers that may reflect a (partially) known function, for instance, the early mismatch negativity (MMN) that arises after about 150–200 ms as a response to an infrequent physical deviation in a signal.

More and more often, a different type of analysis is also done on the EEG signal: a time-frequency analysis. The result of this analysis could be compared to a spectrogram, the earlier ERP one to an oscillogram (see Chapter 5). In a time-frequency analysis, the frequency components of the signal are examined over time. You may have heard of this type of analysis in the context of "alpha waves for relaxation" and sleep research. Different frequency bands are referred to with different Greek letters: for instance, gamma (γ) – 30–50 Hz; beta (β) – 12–30 Hz; alpha (α) – 8–12 Hz; theta (θ) – 4–8 Hz; delta (δ) – 0.5–4 Hz.

4.6.2 Magnetoencephalography (MEG)

The MEG technique measures the magnetic fields produced by electrical brain activity during cognitive activities by means of sensitive devices called SQUIDs. It has a somewhat better spatial resolution than EEG but taps largely into the same underlying processes. (Remember Maxwell: Any electric current also produces a magnetic field.) However, magnetic fields are less distorted by the scalp and the skull than electrophysiological signals. Because of its orientation, the magnetic field is sensitive to brain activity originating in the sulci (grooves of the brain), whereas scalp EEG detects activity both in the sulci and on the cortical gyri (ridges of the brain).

An example MEG study in the field of language research comes from Dikker and Pylkkänen (2013). These authors had participants look at pictures that were always followed by a noun. Whenever one specific noun could be predicted on the basis of the picture (e.g., when seeing a picture of an apple prior to the word "apple"), different patterns of brain activation were found prior to the noun compared to when no specific noun could easily be predicted (e.g., when seeing a bag of groceries prior to the word "apple"). The authors argue that a predictive visual context may pre-activate an upcoming word, and they link parts of the brain in which these effects are found, such as prefrontal cortex, to predictive processing.

4.6.3 Functional magnetic resonance imaging (fMRI)

Functional MRI detects changes in the degree of oxygen in the blood in different brain areas. When a particular cognitive activity must be carried out by the brain, the involved brain areas require more "energy" in terms of oxygen. This induces an increased blood flow to the active area. MRI picks up the change in blood oxygenation (the ratio of oxygen rich and poor blood) associated with particular neural activities. The signal measured is called the BOLD signal, an acronym for blood oxygen level dependent signal change. Thus, fMRI can be used to produce so-called "activation maps" that indicate which parts of the brain are involved in a given mental process. Brain activity is typically mapped in 3D units called *voxels*. Each voxel – the 3D equivalent of a pixel – represents thousands of neurons (nerve cells). The intensity of activation of a voxel, or more commonly, a large group of voxels, is typically indicated in the image by different colors.

The first applications of fMRI appeared at the beginning of the nineties of last century. An MRI scanner functions on the basis of a very strong magnet, e.g., from 1.5 Tesla or more, and radio waves. In water, there are hydrogen and oxygen atoms. In the nuclei of the oxygen atoms, there are protons, electrically charged particles. In the 3D magnetic field generated by the cylindrical MRI scanner, these obtain a particular order or line-up (see Figure 4.10 for a simplified illustration of the fMRI setup). When these are then hit by a short burst of radio waves, their energy is increased and they are thrown out of their alignment. Next, falling back in line again, they release signals that the MRI machine picks up. In the brain, the protons in those areas that contain oxygenated blood produce the strongest signals. Different types of brain matter also respond differently. The signals sent out by the protons can be processed by a computer and turned into a 3D image.

MRI scans can be anatomic/structural or functional. Anatomic scans reveal the structure of the brain of the person in the scanner regardless of their activation in a task, while functional scans focus on areas and networks recruited in various tasks (e.g., reading, listening, naming) that participants may carry out while in the scanner.

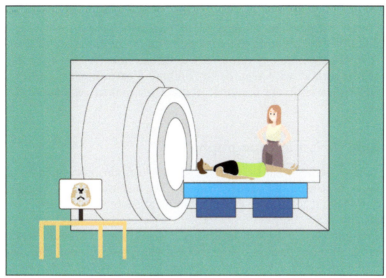

Figure 4.10
A participant almost ready to enter an MRI scanner. Once in the scanner, structural and functional scans of the brain may be made and observed by the experimenter.

In 1905, Brodmann had already noticed anatomical differences in the cortical cell layers between brain regions. Thus, the cyto-architecture of the brain varied and different "Brodmann areas" could be distinguished. Global parts of the brain were distinguished that appeared to be involved in various cognitive functions. First, the *frontal lobe* is often associated with planning, control, motor behavior, and short-term memory. Second, the *parietal lobe* is typically related to receiving and processing somatosensory information. Third, the *occipital lobe* is well-known for processing visual information. Fourth, the *temporal lobe* has been linked to processing auditory information, memory, and meaning (cf. Figure 3.2).

Functionally, psychologists and neuroscientists are eager to find out about the relationship between different brain areas (not just cortical ones) or networks and psychological representations and processes. What brain areas are involved when a particular complex cognitive function is carried out? How does activation in the brain relate to psychological processes, representations, and behavior? Which parts of the brain play a role in language processing and which aid in task-related activities?

The fMRI technique is attractive, because, just like EEG and MEG, it is non-invasive. Relative to EEG, fMRI has a number of advantages and disadvantages. Advantages are its high spatial resolution, its high sensitivity, and the possibility to assess the interconnectedness between brain areas. One disadvantage is that it measures neural activity only indirectly via the change in blood flowing to particular areas in the brain. Furthermore, relative to EEG, the temporal resolution of fMRI is low and it takes several seconds to make a good scan. Smart presentation or analysis solutions and combinations of EEG and fMRI help to partially overcome this drawback.

An example fMRI study in the field of language research comes from Tesink and colleagues (2009). These authors had participants listen to sentences while their brain activity was recorded in an MRI scanner. Some of these sentences (e.g., "Every evening I drink a glass of wine before going to bed") were typical of adult speakers, whereas others ("I cannot sleep without my teddy bear in my arms") were typical sentences a child would utter. Mismatches (compared to matches) between sentence content and voice (e.g., a child's voice uttering the *wine* sentence) were found to yield enhanced activation in left inferior frontal gyrus. This led the authors to conclude that this brain region must be important with regards to combining extra-linguistic information about speaker characteristics with the linguistic content of spoken sentences during language comprehension.

4.6.4 Positron emission topography (PET)

The PET technique studies what brain areas subserve certain processes and tasks by using trace amounts of short-lived radioactive material. The material undergoes radioactive decay and emits positrons that a detector can pick up. Brain activity is associated with areas of higher radioactivity.

Some important PET studies investigating meaning representations in the brain have been conducted early on by Damasio et al. (1996). They observed that different areas in the left temporal lobe (in addition to some other areas) are recruited for naming (a) persons; (b) animals; and (c) tools. This finding is important, because it shows that not all concepts are equal. It may be suggested that, because they are so relevant for survival, dedicated processing areas have developed for persons, animals, and tools ("category specific processing areas"). Interestingly, the results obtained with PET agreed with those in which the brains of patients with a stroke were examined. We will examine this work in more detail in Chapter 8 on meaning.

4.6.5 Computerized axial tomography (CAT/CT)

This technique makes pictures of the brain (computerized tomographic or CT scans) by using differential absorption of x-rays. The person receiving a CT scan is placed on a table that can slide in and out of a hollow, cylindrical machine. Around the inside of the tube, there is a ring around which an x-ray source moves. It aims a beam at the head of the participant. After it passes through the head, the beam is sampled by one of many detectors on the circumference of the apparatus. Different types of tissue absorb the beam of x-rays differently. Hard tissue and bone absorb x-rays well, soft tissue absorbs it less, and water and air absorb very little. This affects the image of the CT scan. As a consequence, CT scans especially reveal the gross features of the brain but less its more detailed structure. Because of their more invasive character, PET and CAT are now used less frequently than MRI.

SUMMARY: NEUROPHYSIOLOGICAL AND NEUROIMAGING TECHNIQUES

EEG, MEG, and fMRI are popular neuroscientific techniques to study cognitive and neural aspects of language. EEG has a strong temporal resolution, making it an ideal method to study the timing of cognitive processes. fMRI allows for relatively precise spatial localization of regions and networks involved in a particular (linguistic) process. MEG combines a solid temporal resolution with relatively acceptable spatial localization. Due to their more invasive nature, PET and CAT techniques have become less popular over time.

> **DISCUSSION BOX 4: MIND VS. BRAIN, BEHAVIORAL VS. NEUROSCIENTIFIC RESEARCH TECHNIQUES**
>
> Psycholinguists for a long time have studied functional aspects of language use by the human mind. For a long time, they did this by means of behavioral research techniques, for instance in reaction time studies. More recently, cognitive neuroscientists have begun to study language in the context of the human brain using neurophysiological techniques (see Kemmerer, 2022). As a consequence, their research questions and theoretical frameworks do not always correspond. According to some definitions on the internet, psycholinguists study actual behavior (i.e., our response to external stimuli), while cognitive neuroscientists investigate the underlying brain mechanisms, related to cognition. Others are more neutral and say that, while psychology studies the human mind through observation and elucidation of behavioral and mental processes, neuroscience studies the human brain through observation of its structure and function (cf. Forstmann et al., 2011).
>
> What do you think is the correct way of comparing and contrasting psychology and cognitive neuroscience when it comes to language processing? Are the mind and the brain different things? Would you argue that one approach is preferable over the other? Do you think both approaches should (or will) be integrated, or that one approach is superior? What would you ultimately like to know about language?

4.7 COMBINING EXPERIMENTAL CONTROL WITH ECOLOGICAL VALIDITY

4.7.1 Computer screen paradigms

As we saw in Chapter 2, the medium that is used to convey a particular message may have a substantial influence on what aspects of the message are in focus and how that message is perceived. Many of the research techniques discussed earlier make use of a *computer screen* as the medium that presents experimental participants with stimuli (e.g., individual words, pictures, sentences). The availability of computers for experimental language research has undoubtedly increased our knowledge about the psychology of language in unprecedented ways. It allows for the setup of the perfect experimental situation as envisioned by Donders: In a reliable way two or more experimental conditions can be compared that differ only in the one variable that the researcher is interested in. In other words, computer paradigms allow for almost perfect *experimental control*. Some of these experiments can also be carried out online, particularly when there is no need for millisecond-precise reaction time data, for instance via smartphones (Dufau et al., 2011) or platforms such as Mechanical Turk or Prolific that give access to large numbers of potential participants around the world.

The desire for strict experimental control has often decreased the *ecological validity* of the behavior participants (are required to) carry out when performing a certain experimental task. Eventually, language researchers should be interested in developing theories about how people use and comprehend language in their everyday lives. Ideally, theories that are built on the basis of laboratory findings should therefore generalize to naturally occurring situations "in the wild." Ecological validity can be defined as the extent to which an experimental task measures aspects of the real-life behavior it aims to generalize to. Not all behavior that participants (are instructed to) display in the lab may, however, be considered "natural." Experimental language researchers have often accepted this potential limitation by assuming that an increase in the much-needed degree of experimental control comes at a cost in terms of the ecological validity a paradigm has to offer. In other words, experimental control and ecological validity have implicitly been conceived of as two extremes on a continuum (Peeters, 2019).

Take, for instance, the popular research paradigm of picture naming. In a typical picture naming study, individual participants are placed in front of a computer screen on which individual pictures of objects and/or animals appear. They are seated alone in a sound-proof booth and typically name each picture in a single word that they speak into a microphone. This task contains many components that are relevant for everyday language production, such as looking up the word form in memory that corresponds to a certain concept, finding the sounds this word consists of and speaking it out loud. However, this task also lacks many crucial aspects of naturalistic language production. In everyday life, we almost always address someone (and not a microphone) when talking, and produce utterances that are much richer than a sequence of unrelated individual words. We gesture while we talk, and enrich our message dynamically with an appropriate facial expression. By definition, theories of language production that are built solely on the basis of such relatively simple paradigms cannot reflect all the richness of natural human communication. In an ideal world, studies employing a picture naming paradigm would allow us to identify some of the core components of language production, on which further experimental work that focuses on other crucial parts of human communication would build. By isolating the core components of the process of language production (i.e., the basic skeleton) in a basic, relatively noise-free task, the nature and timing of these components can be elucidated. In a worst-case scenario, however, the experimental task has become so unnatural that it shows the researcher what a participant *can* do, but not necessarily what they *will* do in real life.

4.7.2 In-lab interaction paradigms

Alternative research techniques sometimes avoid the use of computer screens to present stimuli, for instance by placing participants in a dialog situation (e.g., Brennan & Clark, 1996). In *director-matcher* tasks, for example, two participants carry out a certain task in which one participant (the director) presents information that is relevant to the task of the other participant (the matcher). The matcher's task could, for example, consist of building a certain structure with Lego blocks or selecting a correct card on the basis of the director's description. When recorded, the language (including its non-verbal components) used by the dialog partners can be analyzed in many respects by the researcher after the experiment is finished.

Another example of an in-lab interaction paradigm comes from studies using the *referential communication game*. In a referential communication game, participants can be sitting opposite one another in the same room, both looking at a set of items (potential "referents"). Sometimes, the participants cannot see one another due to an opaque screen positioned between them and can therefore communicate only through speech. As a speaker, they may be required to describe pictures, objects, or maps only they can see to the listener on the other side of the screen. An example of this paradigm will be given in Chapter 8 (Snedeker & Trueswell, 2003).

Such paradigms thus acknowledge that language use is typically a social undertaking in which a message is often intentionally conveyed and relevant to a physically present addressee who may respond to that message. They do not necessarily rely on static 2D stimuli on a computer screen, but often use real 3D objects such as cards, toys, or Lego blocks. One could argue, however, that the increase in ecological validity of these paradigms comes at the expense of their level of experimental control.

To increase the experimental control of a dialog study, sometimes one of the participants is made into a "confederate" or "stooge." This accomplice of the experimenter has been instructed before the experiment to conduct the experiment in a prescribed way. This means their behavior is to a large extent scripted and fixed to potentially elicit a certain behavior in the other, naïve participant who is not aware that the confederate is instructed by the experimenter. Consider, for instance, a situation in which a confederate on purpose uses a relatively high proportion of sentences that contain passive constructions ("the ball is kicked by the boy"), to see whether this primes the use of such constructions by the naïve participant in a card game. Another example is an experiment in which the confederate switches languages at a predefined position in a sentence and the researcher later analyzes how this affected the behavior of the "real" participant (Kootstra et al., 2010).

As such, the idea is that the same experimental paradigm offers the researcher both experimental control and ecological validity. There is some control over what the naïve participant will do, and the task in many respects resembles a natural situation in which language is used. This sounds promising, but the use of human confederates has also been criticized, as the same confederate cannot help but behave differently with different naïve participants. They may act slightly differently as a function of the time of day, the number of times they have carried out the same task before, their level of fatigue, and their social connection with the participant. This, in turn, may bias the elicited results in unwanted ways (Kuhlen & Brennan, 2013).

4.7.3 Virtual reality paradigms

So far we have looked at studies that presented their visual stimuli either on a computer screen or as existing objects in the lab, sometimes combined with spoken stimuli presented via headphones or delivered through a confederate. These paradigms seem to suggest that it is difficult to combine strict experimental control with high ecological validity within the same experimental paradigm. However, recent studies that have started using virtual reality (VR) to investigate the psychology of language suggest that ecological validity and experimental control should be conceived of as two orthogonal constructs: It seems possible to have the best of both worlds (Pan & Hamilton, 2018; Peeters & Dijkstra, 2018).

In a VR experiment, participants become immersed in a virtual environment in which they carry out a certain task. This task can be very simple, such as simply looking around and/or interacting with the world. Participants enter the virtual realm either by wearing a head-mounted display (HMD) such as Meta Quest or HTC Vive, or by entering a cave automatic virtual environment (CAVE) in which they are surrounded by walls or screens that present a dynamic virtual environment (see Figure 4.11). In both cases, they see this world in 3D. In head-mounted displays, stereoscopic vision and depth perception are attained by presenting a slightly different image to each of the participant's eyes. In CAVE environments, participants typically wear shutter glasses that make their immediate virtual environment seem real in three spatial dimensions. Participants naturally suspend their disbelief of the reality of the world they see, and typically behave in natural ways. These exciting modes of 3D stimulus display can be combined with the recording of behavioral, eye tracking, motion tracking, and/or EEG data (Chu & Hagoort, 2014; Huizeling et al., 2022; Nirme et al., 2020; Tromp et al., 2018).

Importantly, both HMDs and CAVEs allow for the study of participants' language behavior and processing in rich and dynamic environments that mimic everyday situations.

Figure 4.11
An example of a CAVE setup, in which participants become immersed in one or more dynamic virtual environments that are projected on the large screens or walls that surround them. Infrared cameras track the movement of the participant's head, such that the presentation of the virtual environment can be adapted on-line to where the participant is looking.

Nevertheless, they still also allow for high levels of experimental control, as two very rich conditions can nevertheless be made to differ in only the single variable the researcher is interested in. An additional advantage of using VR is that participants may interact with virtual agents or avatars whose behavior can be more easily controlled compared to the behavior of a human confederate. Finally, VR experiments can in principle relatively easily be replicated around the globe, as a virtual world and its digital features and inhabitants (unlike human confederates) can be transferred digitally to other labs over the internet (Pan & Hamilton, 2018).

An example VR study in the field of language research is presented by Heyselaar and colleagues (2017). These authors had speakers of Dutch play a card game with a virtual agent. They observed that participants copied the agent's tendency to use passive constructions (e.g., "the man was kissed by the woman") in their description of the cards. This study hence shows that structural properties of the language we produce in everyday situations are influenced by recently perceived linguistic input.

SUMMARY: COMBINING EXPERIMENTAL CONTROL WITH ECOLOGICAL VALIDITY

Stimuli can be presented to participants in isolated booths on a computer screen, via online platforms, inside or outside the lab during interaction with another participant or confederate, or in rich and dynamic immersive virtual reality environments. Paradigms differ in their degree of ecological validity and experimental control. There is no single "best research technique." The method the researcher opts for should always depend on the research question.

4.8 WHAT IS NEXT?

In this chapter, we have taken a serious look at the various research techniques used in the study of the psychology of language. Each of the next six chapters focuses on a different core task that language users perform when they process language. The chapters follow the processing components of the Language User Framework in a clockwise order. In the next chapter, we begin by considering how spoken words are represented and processed. Many of the experimental techniques we have discussed help us to throw light on this important language activity that even young children who cannot yet read can already manage quite well after their first year of life.

4.9 WHAT HAVE WE LEARNED?

Research techniques for studying the psychology of language have in common that they allow measurements for closely matched conditions that differ in only a single aspect, usually the focus of experimental and theoretical interest. However, they differ widely in what they measure and how fast after the event of interest they measure something. Techniques such as recall and recognition measure a relatively long time after the event of interest (learning a particular word, for instance). This also holds for fMRI, for which the BOLD response often takes two to eight seconds to collect. Behavioral reaction time studies like lexical decision and word naming often elicit responses at 0.3 to two seconds after the event. Among the fastest measuring techniques we find eye tracking, and the measurement of ERPs, which more directly reflect what is going on in mind and brain. Because all techniques and associated tasks measure somewhat different (aspects of) language-related processes, it is important to draw general conclusions about those only after applying and comparing different tasks to the theoretical issues at hand.

More recent techniques try to increase the ecological validity of the research paradigms, to allow any theoretical conclusions to be faithfully extended to daily life phenomena. The promise here is to increase ecological validity while maintaining experimental control. New language research techniques involving virtual reality applied to, for instance, discourse context, show promising developments in this direction.

QUESTIONS FOR CHAPTER 4

1. Long ago, scientists used introspection not only as an inspiration for determining research topics, but also as a method for testing theories of language. Why would many researchers today think this is not a good idea? How do you see the relationship between subjective experience and scientific evidence?
2. There are many more research techniques than those described in this chapter. Use the internet to find out what the following techniques are about: shadowing, picture description, grammaticality judgment, syllable monitoring, language decision. Would you call them "on-line" or "off-line" techniques?
3. Compare the following research techniques and try to describe their differences in terms of the Language User Framework:
   a. Object naming vs. word naming;
   b. Eye tracking vs. self-paced reading;
   c. Recognition vs. recall.
4. Are the following techniques measuring word comprehension or word production: progressive demasking, lexical decision, word naming, picture naming, word translation?

Motivate your choice. Are any of these techniques *really* measuring on-line word recognition?
5. Which lexical (word) characteristics would affect the speed of lexical decision responses and why? Consider word frequency, length, orthotactics, phonotactics, concreteness, age of acquisition, and any other word property you can think of.
6. Do you think the presently available research techniques will at some time in the future allow us to read people's minds? Explain your answer.
7. What evidence can you provide that semantic priming effects also occur in daily life?
8. Which of the discussed research techniques would you consider to be most like (eliciting) an activity that you also perform in daily life?
9. Reading in daily life is often done with a particular goal in mind, even though it is not the type of goal required by many laboratory tasks. What standard reading goals can you come up with?
10. Suppose you participate in a virtual reality lab experiment on language. How would your performance in the experiment change when you participate at different moments in the day? Would it matter what activity you engaged in right before participating in the experiment?

Chapter 5

Recognizing spoken words

5.1 SPOKEN WORD RECOGNITION: THE ESSENCE

"How to wreck a nice beach." This expression is often used by psycholinguists to quickly illustrate the problems that listeners encounter when they face the task of recognizing spoken words. The example shows that parts of a developing speech signal can be understood as words that are not actually intended by the speaker. Such words may be temporarily in line with the signal or segment it in a different way, e.g., "to wreck a nice" more or less corresponds to "to recognize," and the end of "nice beach" sounds more or less like "speech." Note that there are other embedded words that could be derived from the signal, like "two," "ice," "each," "an," and to some extent "rack." Since speech differs within and across speakers in many different respects, the listeners must determine which words and aspects of variation are intended and which are not. In sum, listeners must solve the problems of *speech segmentation* and *variability*.

This chapter considers how listeners solve these problems and tackle the ambiguous speech signal to arrive at the right sounds, words, and interpretation. In the Language User Framework, the Spoken Signal Recognizer *segments* the raw speech wave into acoustic-phonetic representations (phones) that can be turned into abstract representations (e.g., phonemes or allophones) serving as input to the Spoken Word Recognizer. We call this auditory preprocessing of segmentation and classification *prelexical*, because it takes place before whole words are available or before the mental lexicon in Long Term Memory is contacted.

Following this stage, the Spoken Word Recognizer turns the phonemic representations of the speech signal into larger units in order to look up the matching spoken words and their meanings in Long Term Memory. Such representations can be larger than phonemes and smaller than the word and are called *sublexical* (see Figure 5.1).

There is more for the Spoken Word Recognizer to deal with at this stage and later, because it must also integrate information of a *supra*segmental nature. Suprasegmental information includes various acoustic cues for prosodic structures that cover longer stretches of speech, for instance, syllables, lexical stress patterns, and phrases. Consider, for instance, the meaning distinction between "to preSENT" and "the PREsent." Here, the words' meaning differs depending on whether stress is placed on the first or second syllable, which can be signaled by an increase in loudness and/or duration (Eisner & McQueen, 2018).

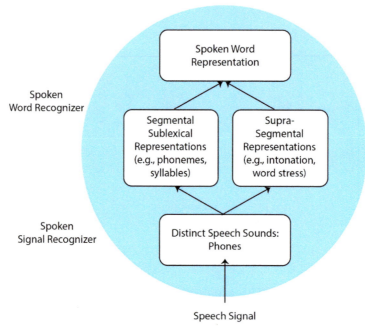

Figure 5.1
This figure summarizes the representations and processes involved in spoken word recognition. It extends the bottom left part of the Language User Framework as presented in Chapter 3. Spoken word representations are stored in a part of Long Term Memory that we call the (mental) lexicon.

The ultimately recognized words must be *aligned* with respect to the speech signal in the proper way, such that the utterance as a whole can be understood as intended. Finally, note that the process of spoken (or "auditory") word recognition is *incremental*: When we are listening, spoken word information comes in gradually over time. This is true for sentences, but at a shorter time range also for words.

In this chapter, we will first describe the relevant representations and processes involved in speech recognition, which will indeed make clear that spoken word recognition is to a considerable extent an incremental process. This incremental nature is also essential to important models of spoken word recognition, which we discuss next. Later in this chapter, empirical studies are highlighted that test key assumptions underlying these models. We conclude the chapter by placing the process of spoken word recognition in a broader context.

SUMMARY: SPOKEN WORD RECOGNITION: THE ESSENCE

To understand an incoming spoken word, the listener must first segment the ongoing acoustic signal into relevant units (phones) during a prelexical stage. During subsequent stages, these units are combined (into phonemes and larger units) and used to look up the matching spoken words and their meanings in the mental lexicon, while also any suprasegmental information available in the signal is taken into account. The listener's task of recognizing and understanding a spoken word is not straightforward, as the spoken signal will display substantial variability within and between speakers.

5.2 SPOKEN WORD RECOGNITION: REPRESENTATIONS

The Spoken Signal Recognizer builds a representation of the speech signal. It seems reasonable to assume that this representation tries to capture the speech in a faithful and detailed way. To the extent that the signal is represented undistorted by expectations, hallucinations (i.e., hearing sounds and words that are not really there) can be avoided. Of course, the speech signal could be segmented (split up) in units of many different types and sizes. One small segmental unit that is often considered is the speech sound or *phone*: It has distinct perceptual and physical characteristics and often, in languages like English or Dutch, corresponds to a vowel or consonant. As indicated in Figure 5.1, the Spoken Signal Recognizer takes into account all variable information in the signal, not only in sounds (phones) but also including melody and word stress, rhythm, and the relationship between adjacent sounds within or between words (called co-articulation and sandhi, respectively). All these aspects may be relevant for speech recognition.

As we have seen, phonetics is the linguistic discipline that studies the physical characteristics of sounds and their representations (Roach, 2009). In *acoustic* phonetics, the focus of investigation is on the comprehension of speech, while in *articulatory* phonetics it is on its production. As a shared interest they investigate how speech may be represented. Representations that are smaller than words are called "sublexical." When representations become available on the basis of the input signal before the lexicon becomes involved, they are called "prelexical." The two terms therefore refer to aspects of retrieval that are more structure-related or more process-related in nature.

What are the properties of the speech signal that a listener could use for understanding speech? Sound waves consist of fast fluctuations in air pressure. Speech waves are complex sound waves, consisting of superimposed waves of many *frequencies* that have a certain strength or *amplitude*. Frequency, heard as pitch, is defined as the number of oscillations per second (in Hertz or Hz). Amplitude, heard as sound strength or intensity, refers to the deviation in sound pressure relative to a zero-level (in decibel or dB).

The *sound spectrum* is the collection of frequency components in the speech wave, each with its own amplitude. Vowels are usually recognizable in the speech wave by their *formants* (black bands of energy) in the spectrum (see Figure 5.2). Formants are spectral areas in which certain frequency components are strengthened in amplitude through the filtering function of mouth, nose, and throat. They are characterized by a certain peak frequency and band width, and last for a certain period of time. When the first (F1) and second (F2) formant of vowels are represented in a graph (F1 vs. F2), the vowels are situated approximately in a triangle (or trapezoid), sometimes referred to as the "acoustic triangle" (also see Figure 5.3). On the corners of this vowel chart, one finds the /a/, /i/, and /u/. This figure has been known for a long time, because the two dimensions of the figure also correspond to how closed or open the mouth is when the vowel is produced (F1), and whether the vowel is produced in the back or front of the mouth (F2).

Phoneticians represent speech waves as oscillograms and spectrograms. As Figure 5.2 shows, speech is *variable*, *continuous*, and *ambiguous*. It is variable dependent on the timing, person, and situation in which it occurs. One (word) meaning can be captured by many different speech signals, for instance, slow or fast, spoken by a man, woman, or child, sloppily or carefully pronounced, in dialect or standard language, etc. This is called *many-to-one mapping*. Many slightly different signals may be used to convey the same one meaning.

Speech is also largely continuous. Unlike in written language, pauses sometimes occur within words rather than between them. The continuous speech signal must be mapped onto one meaning. This is called *continuous-to-discrete mapping*. Finally, speech is also ambiguous.

OSCILLOGRAM

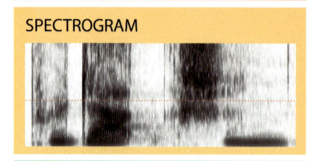

SPECTROGRAM

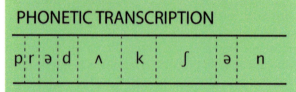

PHONETIC TRANSCRIPTION

p r ə d ʌ k ʃ ə n

Figure 5.2
Top: Oscillogram, representing time on the X-axis and amplitude on the Y-axis. Frequency depends on the speed of the fluctuations over time. Middle: Spectrogram, representing time on the X-axis, frequency on the Y-axis, and amplitude in terms of blackness. The black horizontal "bands" for vowels are called "formants." Bottom: As can be seen in the phonetic transcription, this figure presents the oscillogram and spectrogram of the English word "production" (/prəˈdʌkʃən/) as produced by a native speaker of English. Note that the different phonemes have different durations.

A particular speech signal could be understood as different words, or other words may be (partially) represented in the signal (e.g., /bæn/ may be part of /bænd/). This is called *one-to-many mapping*. One signal can be mapped onto many different representations.

When we study the oscillogram and spectrogram in Figure 5.2, we notice several things. First, there is a difference in the representation of vowels and consonants. When we produce vowels, there is a flow of air from the lungs to the mouth that passes the vocal cords in an unobstructed way. Vowels produce a lot of energy (they come at a relatively strong amplitude) that can be sustained or stable over a relatively long period of time (resulting in the formants described above). This is why we call vowels "voiced." Consonant sounds, in contrast, characteristically create some sort of constriction in the flow of air. In the production of plosives, for instance, [b], [d], [g], [p], [t], and [k], the air pressure is gradually built up and then suddenly released. In contrast, fricatives, for example, [s], [z], [f], and [v] are produced with a partially closed articulatory channel, resulting in some friction.

In the oscillogram and spectrogram, plosives and fricatives are easily discerned: Plosives, particularly when "voiceless" (or "unvoiced"), have a kind of burst preceded by near silence in the oscillogram, while fricatives are composed of sounds of many different frequencies, from high to low – as is seen in the oscillogram. Stop consonants and fricatives can be accompanied by vibrating vocal cords, leading to voiced consonants, or not. Voiced consonants are, for example, [b], [d], [z], and [g]. The difference with voiceless consonants, such as [p], [t], [s], and [k], can be noticed by putting one of your hands on your throat and then producing the consonant in question (try it!). All vowels are voiced by definition.

Further analysis shows that consonants can be represented in terms of three or four important dimensions: place of articulation, manner of articulation, voicedness, and possibly nasality. Place of articulation indicates where in the mouth a sound is produced or which parts of the articulatory apparatus are used. For instance, in the case of a [p] sound, both lips are used; hence the sound is called "bilabial." Manner of articulation indicates how the

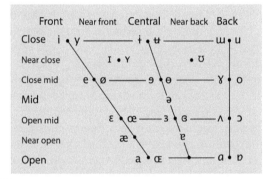

Figure 5.3
Consonants and vowels written in the International Phonetic Alphabet (IPA, 2015), including an example sentence. For polysyllabic words, stressed syllables are preceded by an apostrophe. For consonants that appear in pairs, the item to the left is the voiceless equivalent of the (voiced) item on the right. Vowels that appear in pairs are rounded (right item) and unrounded (left item).

sound is produced. For instance, for a plosive (or "stop" consonant) like [p], air pressure is built up in the mouth and suddenly released. In the case of a fricative like [s] or [f], a constrained flow of air passes through the mouth, resulting in a rubbing sound. Nasality refers to whether during the production of a sound the nose cavity plays a role or not.

This organization of consonants with multiple dimensions is detailed in the International Phonetic Alphabet (IPA) and is often explained for a particular language in the first lessons of a foreign language course. Figure 5.3 provides information on the distinctions made by IPA. As can be seen, a [p] is a voiceless bilabial plosive, while a [z] is a voiced alveolar fricative. See Figure 9.3 for a link to the human articulatory apparatus.

Different types of vowel can be distinguished on the basis of the position of the tongue (high, middle, low) and the part of the tongue (front, central, back) that is most crucial during their production. This distinction is directly linked to the positioning of formants and the "acoustic triangle" mentioned and shown above.

There are many subtle differences between produced speech sounds. For instance, a particular vowel may be pronounced in somewhat different ways depending on the word it is in, the speaker, and the language at hand. These differing speech sounds, which are not directly relevant for distinguishing different words, are called *allophones*.

When we attribute various phones to abstract categories, we are entering the domain of phonology (Roach, 2009). Phonology describes the abstract sound categories of a language, which we call *phonemes*. In Dutch, the "oo" in the word *boor* has a different sound than the "oo" in *boot*, but both are the phoneme /o:/ (sounding more or less as in English "roam"). As such, they correspond to the same phoneme, but are different allophones. Exchange of allophones never results in a different word, but exchange of phonemes does. We can find out if two different sounds are also different phonemes by making so-called *minimal word pairs*, and then consider if the two words in the pair have different meanings. For instance, in "back" and "pack" the /b/ and /p/ are different phonemes, because the two words have different meanings.

English and Dutch have about 40 different phonemes (but only 26 letters!). The phonemic repertoires differ between languages. For instance, in English there is a distinction between "bed" = [bɛd], "bad" = [bæd], "bat" = [bæt], and "bet" = [bɛt]. However, in Dutch the phoneme /æ/ does not exist, and the final consonant of a word in this language becomes unvoiced (a phenomenon called "final devoicing"). As a consequence, for Dutch listeners all these words sound more or less the same and become phonologically identical: /bɛt/. In sum, English has the phonemes /æ/ and /ɛ/, while in Dutch, these are perceived as two allophones of the phoneme /ɛ/. (Note: The phone "b" is commonly inserted in straight brackets as [b], and the phoneme "b" is inserted in forward slashes as /b/.)

What kind of abstract units would the Spoken Signal and Spoken Word Recognizers derive as building blocks for the recognition of speech on the basis of the incoming speech signal? The answer is not completely clear. One possibility is that they make not one but several types of representation at the same time (Wickelgren, 1969). Representations proposed in the literature vary from very short to very long and from very rich in information to less informative. Of course, how the word recognition process will proceed over time depends on the choice of the most prominent units. Among the proposed units are spectral templates, phonemes, allophones, and syllables.

Spectral templates (Klatt, 1979) are simply short pieces of the spectrum. For instance, the spectrum of the speech signal is represented in stretches of 10 ms. In the classic model by Klatt, called Lexical Access From Spectra (LAFS), just 10 ms is enough to make contact with word representations in the lexicon. Clearly, a vast number of different spectral templates exist that are closely linked to each speech signal.

Phonemes are another type of unit that has been proposed. They are much more abstract in nature, as we saw above. Phoneme duration in the speech signal varies considerably, from about 50 ms for a plosive up to 120 ms or more for a fricative or vowel. A consequence of choosing the phoneme as a contact unit to the lexicon is that this contact can take place only after the first phoneme has been identified (thus, after 50–120 ms).

Allophones have also been proposed to be the critical representations that listeners use to map onto stored knowledge in Long Term Memory (Luce et al., 2000; Mitterer et al., 2018). As we have seen, different allophones arise because the same phoneme sounds slightly differently in word-initial versus word-final position or in different words in general. The advantage of assuming allophones as the critical units in speech perception is that the listener can make use of the context-dependence of the acoustic qualities of the speech segments. If allophones, rather than phonemes, are mapped onto stored representations in memory, this may therefore facilitate and optimize spoken word recognition (Mitterer et al., 2018).

Phonemes and allophones are not discrete units, like letters are. Consonants and vowels are interwoven and unseparable parts of larger wholes like syllables or words. As oscillograms and spectrograms show, speech is a pattern of overlapping and mutually dependent units rather than a sequence of discrete elements. For instance, the consonant phoneme /k/ has a slightly different form in the spectrogram when it occurs in the syllables /ka/, /ki/, and /ku/. Thus, the /k/ is represented differently when it precedes different vowels. The interdependability of sounds is also clear from the phenomenon of *assimilation*. As we have seen before, people typically do not say "handbag" but "hambag." They co-articulate different sounds, resulting in adaptations of the actual production. For a word like "pack," there is already a hint of information about the /æ/ when the /p/ is presented, and the vowel information itself affects the realization of the final /k/ phoneme.

The mutual interdependability of phonemes in a word has motivated researchers to consider a somewhat larger representation than a phoneme: the *syllable*, which typically consists of a vowel (V) or more complex combinations of vowels (V) and consonants (C): V, CV, CVC, CCVC, and so on (Mehler et al., 1981). There are over 10,000 different syllables in languages like Dutch and English. Since syllables consist of one or more phonemes, their average duration is typically more than a factor 2 or 3 larger than that of a phoneme. Contact with the mental lexicon (the word store in Long Term Memory) would be considerably delayed in case whole syllables are used. Another interesting issue is that syllables may be more important for processing in some languages than in others (e.g., French vs. English; Cutler et al., 1986). For different languages, different units could be more important.

Because speech is often accompanied by noise, also other, more noise-resistant representations have been proposed. For instance, it is possible to define groups of phonemes that are more or less consistent in terms of their acoustics or articulation. Due to their characterization in terms of "robust features," the likelihood is reduced that a wrong identification of the perceived sound takes place.

How the mental lexicon can be searched will, of course, be quite different in the case of spectral templates, phonemes or allophones, and syllables. The moment in time the lexicon becomes involved and the number of possible words that are contacted in it are very different in the different cases. Given a more specific contact representation, the contact set will be smaller, but in order to obtain a more specific representation, the moment of first contact may be delayed. Furthermore, the amount of speech that is required to compute the contact representation determines the moment in time at which the first contact with the lexicon is possible.

According to some researchers, temporally early information is always the basis for first contact with the mental lexicon. The Cohort model (Marslen-Wilson & Welsh, 1978; Marslen-Wilson et al., 1994), for instance, takes the position that early information is prominent. A word-initial cohort is set up that contains all words in a language that correspond with the first part of the input. However, according to other researchers, more salient information is more important, irrespective of where it is in the speech signal. Thus, according to Gee and Grosjean (1983), parts of the signal that are very reliable, like accentuated syllables, determine the first subset in the lexicon (one speaks about vowels as "islands of certainty").

SUMMARY: SPOKEN WORD RECOGNITION: REPRESENTATIONS

The continuous speech signal is variable over time, as its amplitude and frequency differ as a function of how exactly speakers use their articulators. The incoming signal leads to the perception of different sounds, which can be categorized into partially overlapping vowels and consonants (e.g., plosives, fricatives). In the speech signal, different phonemes, allophones, and syllables can be detected. These can be taken by a listener as input to be mapped onto existing representations in the mental lexicon to recognize the intended spoken word.

5.3 SPOKEN WORD RECOGNITION: PROCESSES

The goal of word recognition is to get access to the knowledge that is stored about a word, in order to develop a meaningful interpretation of a word or utterance. The term "lexical access" is used in this context, in two different ways. First, it can mean "access to the lexicon," referring to the first moment in time that the lexicon in Long Term Memory is accessed on the basis of the represented speech signal. However, the term "lexical access" can also be used as the moment at which various properties of the stored lexical representations (words) become available, such as information about phonology, syntax, semantics, pragmatics, articulatory information and so on. There is disagreement about when exactly such types of lexical knowledge become available. Later we will discuss some studies that have investigated this issue.

As a way to divide labor, we have assumed that the Spoken Signal Recognizer tries to represent the speech waves as faithfully as possible using phones. The Spoken Word Recognizer then abstracts from the detailed signal, creating phonemes or allophones, and syllables. To arrive at a better understanding of the interaction between Signal Recognizer and Word Recognizer in the perception of spoken words, two interesting phenomena are worth discussing: *categorical perception* and *phoneme restoration*. We will therefore briefly consider these now.

5.3.1 Categorical perception

To facilitate spoken word comprehension, it might be helpful if listeners perceived different speech sounds that are physically continuous (and hence sometimes ambiguous) as belonging to discrete phoneme categories. And indeed, when sounds are manipulated by a researcher on a continuum between a clear [d] to a clear [g], listeners would commonly indicate hearing either /d/ or /g/ in an experiment (Liberman et al., 1957). In this case, the place of articulation of the sound goes from alveolar to velar in a physically continuous way, but the perception of the sound is relatively categorical (see Figure 5.4). This phenomenon, deemed "likely the single finding from speech perception with the biggest impact on cognitive science" (McMurray, 2022, p. 3819), has been called "categorical perception."

Similar to the observation mentioned above, research in the lab has shown that listeners indicate they hear either /d/ or /t/ when similar speech sounds are presented that differ with respect to their Voice Onset Time (the moment in time at which the vocal cords start to vibrate relative to speech onset). While standard VOT in English is at 0 ms for /d/, it is at 60 ms for /t/. Ambiguous sounds, having a VOT between 20 and 40 msec (/d/ vs. /t/) are typically allocated to either the /d/ or the /t/ phoneme category (e.g., Sharma & Dorman, 1999).

It is, however, not the case that listeners cannot perceive the differences between sounds having different VOTs. They are faster to identify two sounds with the same VOTs as identical relative to nearly identical VOT sound pairs. Thus, they are sensitive to VOT even within a phoneme category.

Ganong (1980) has shown that the allocation of sounds to one phoneme category or the other is context-dependent. For instance, when in a speech segment like "[k/g]iss" a first sound is heard between /k/ and /g/, it is more likely to be perceived as a /k/ than as a /g/, because "kiss" /kɪs/ is an English word and "giss" /gɪs/ is not. As we have seen before when discussing the McGurk effect, also information provided by the speaker's lips will influence which exact phoneme is perceived.

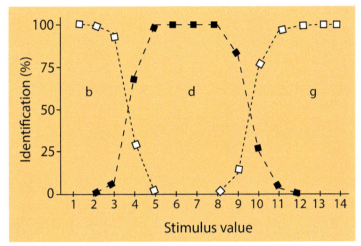

Figure 5.4
Categorical perception. The second formant of sounds is varied linearly along the horizontal axis. Perception rapidly shifts from hearing /b/ to hearing /d/, and then to hearing /g/. This phenomenon is called "categorical perception." Adapted from Liberman et al. (1957).

Recently, the relevance of the lab findings on categorical perception for everyday speech perception outside the lab has been questioned (McMurray, 2022). Indeed, it would actually be quite beneficial if listeners are sensitive to subtle detail in the speech signal and preserve detailed aspects of the input for some time as these details may have meaningful implications, for instance, about the gender of the speaker and about which sounds are going to follow next (McMurray, 2022). The seminal and theoretically impactful findings on categorical perception are now commonly considered very dependent on and restricted to the task situations in the lab in which they were observed. As such, empirical findings that for a long time are considered as fundamental may at a later stage become questioned in terms of their ecological validity (cf. Chapter 4).

5.3.2 Phoneme restoration

When listeners hear sentences like "They saw the *un shining on the beach" in which the sound /s/ has been replaced by a cough (here indicated by the *), they often do not notice the absence of the /s/ sound and even have problems indicating where in the sentence the cough was presented (Warren, 1970). Thus, they easily restore the missing phoneme. This finding could be considered as evidence in favor of top-down context effects (from both sentence and word level) on phoneme perception. However, it turns out that replacing the /b/ in the spoken word "beach" by a cough would not result in phoneme restoration. This indicates that the degree of overlap in the spectral characteristics of the replaced phoneme (/s/ or /b/) and a cough is important for the restoration effect to arise (a cough is much more similar in spectral characteristics to an /s/ than to a /b/). Phoneme restoration also helps listeners to deal with words that are produced in a reduced form (e.g., Kemps et al., 2004). For instance, the English word "probably" is often produced as /prəbli/, and the French word *fenêtre* as /fnɛtʁ/ (see Figure 5.3). Nevertheless, native listeners normally understand these words easily despite the missing phonemes (Cutler, 2012b, p. 213).

> **SUMMARY: SPOKEN WORD RECOGNITION: PROCESSES**
>
> In line with the principle of categorical perception, listeners in the lab typically allocate sounds to one particular phoneme category. On the basis of the segmented information, they will access the mental lexicon to find the word intended by the speaker ("lexical access"). Phoneme restoration can aid the listener in mapping the input signal onto a word representation.

5.4 MODELS OF SPOKEN WORD RECOGNITION

To render the processing of speech over time as efficient as possible, one might assume that units of different sizes are derived as soon as speech comes in. In addition, it would be useful to quickly engage context information of different types (e.g., about words when recognizing speech sounds, about sentences when processing words, etc.). Irrespective of which units are ultimately derived from the speech signal, its processing must proceed incrementally from earlier input to later input. Due to the incremental nature of the speech signal, the beginning of words will be available earlier than their ends, and, in the beginning, there are different possible continuations of the speech signal, and thus different possible words.

These observations have led to the formulation of a number of models for spoken word recognition, such as Cohort, TRACE, and Shortlist. These models were developed years ago now, but are still regarded as the most influential in the field of spoken word recognition. We will consider these in the following sections to further illustrate the process of spoken word recognition.

5.4.1 Cohort model

The Cohort model is an important model for spoken word recognition that was already proposed in rudimentary form by Exner in 1894 (Levelt, 2013, p. 81) and was independently reinvented by Marslen-Wilson and Welsh in 1978. There are two variants of this model (Cohort I and Cohort II) that have the following processing notion in common. When a spoken word is presented, its initial sound (phoneme) results in the parallel activation of all words in the mental lexicon that begin with that sound. This set of initially activated words is called the "word initial cohort." The number of words in this set depends on the onset phonemes of words existing in the language. For instance, in English, it will contain more candidates for the word beginning /kæ/ than for /jæ/.

When the speech signal unfolds, the incoming information leads to a gradual narrowing down of the initial cohort of activated words. At some point in time, only the word candidate that fits the signal best remains. In this model, the degree of activation of word candidates depends on the degree of correspondence with the contact representations (goodness of fit) and on the word's lexical properties. For instance, if words are used often (i.e., high-frequency words), they would be activated more strongly over time. And when the word begins with infrequent sound combinations, it may also be recognized earlier in time ("jazz" vs. "cap"), as there will be fewer competitors. In this chapter, we discuss a variant of the Cohort model that includes the activation metaphor to account for gradual effects of word frequency and duration (as in Cohort II by Marslen-Wilson, 1987), but that also assumes interactions between the Spoken Word Recognizer and the Sentence Processor (more as in Cohort I by Marslen-Wilson & Welsh, 1978).

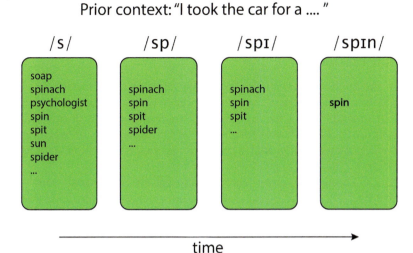

Figure 5.5
Illustration of the Cohort model (Marslen-Wilson & Welsh, 1978). The first green column represents the word initial cohort. Over time, the number of relevant word candidates decreases until a single word remains that fits the signal best.

At the end of the selection process, when listeners have determined which word was actually presented by the speaker through consultation of the mental lexicon, we may call the word "recognized." It is generally assumed that the moment at which this occurs often lies before the end of the spoken word. The exact moment of recognition would depend on a complex set of factors, such as physical properties (word duration, stimulus quality), intrinsic lexical properties of the word (word frequency), the number of other words similar to the target (the so-called cohort members or competitors), and the efficiency of the selection process. When the recognition process is considered to be more or less sequential and relying on segments (e.g., phonemes), there is a point in the signal at which the target word becomes unique. This point is called the "uniqueness point" (UP). For instance, the Dutch word *burgemeester* ("mayor") would become more or less unique around the presentation of the /m/, because other cohort members including *burger* ("citizen") and *burcht* ("castle") would no longer be fully compatible with the sound signal. However, the listener may not yet feel fully confident about the target word at this juncture (e.g., because of their daily life experience with signal variability and noise in speech). Moreover, the input analysis may not be carried out strictly on the basis of phonemes, but more probabilistically depending on signal properties. In this case, the word's recognition does not necessarily take place at the UP but may occur later in time, at what one might call the recognition point (RP). As Zwitserlood (1989, p. 32) explains: "[T]his point is a measure of the amount of sensory information listeners need to be certain that a particular word is heard, and not another."

Although other models for spoken word recognition, similarly to the Cohort model, also assume that the first part of spoken words lead to the activation of whole sets of potential words, they may consider the zooming in on a final word candidate less in terms of a *reduction* of the set over time, and more as a process of *differentiation*. For instance, in the implemented TRACE model (McClelland & Elman, 1986), which was inspired by the Cohort model, processes of activation and inhibition (due to competition between words) result in one word that gradually becomes most active. We will now discuss this model more in detail.

5.4.2 TRACE model

The TRACE model is a localist and symbolic connectionist model for spoken word recognition. It is called "localist" because in its network each node represents a specific symbol or concept (see Chapter 6.4.5 for an example of a contrasting *distributed* connectionist model). TRACE was inspired by a similar model for word reading, called the Interactive Activation model that we will discuss in Chapter 6 on written and printed word recognition.

The TRACE model assumes three hierarchically organized sets of linguistic representations: phonetic/phonological features, phonemes, and word units (see Figure 5.6). Representational units in models of spoken word recognition must encode information positioned in time (rather than in space, which is important during word reading). For instance, phonological features must represent the presence of a particular phoneme in a temporally limited stretch of speech. Because representations may reoccur later in time, separate collections of feature detectors and phoneme representations must be assumed for

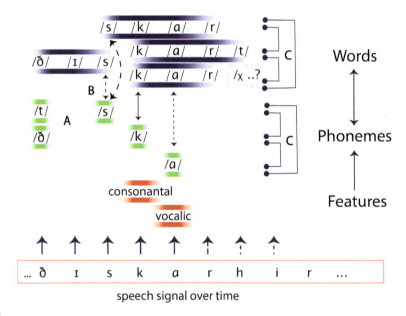

Figure 5.6
Simplified architecture of the TRACE model. The speech signal "this car here" is analyzed over time. The presence of phonetic features in the signal is checked at each moment. Phonemes characterized by one or more detected features (e.g., consonantal, vocalic, diffuse, and so on) are then activated to varying extent. For instance, on presentation of the /ð/ features, phonemes like /t/, /ʃ/, and /s/ may also be temporarily activated (A). In the speech signal, phonemes may partially overlap over time. Next, active phonemes activate words that they are part of. The activated words may have different alignments relative to the speech signal (B). Phonemes and word representations compete for recognition through a process called "lateral inhibition" (C). In this interactive model, both bottom-up and top-down processes contribute to word recognition. Reduplication of phoneme and word units that are slightly shifted in time is indirectly indicated here by green and blue horizontal bands that wax and wane in strength (e.g., above and below a phoneme or a word). For features, the red horizontal bands indicate different values on the indicated dimensions (e.g., consonantal). After McClelland and Elman (1986).

each temporal unit or "time slice" in the model. Otherwise, the vowel information in a word such as "tent" would affect the activation of both /t/'s, and the second "do" in "'dodo" might be confused with the first.

In the TRACE model, for each "time slice" of 25 ms an identical set of representations exists (the 25 ms time slice is a choice made by the modelers, corresponding to about half or a third of a phoneme in real speech). One feature spans one time slice, one phoneme six, and a word as many time slices as is necessary to represent all its phonemes. There are both top-down and bottom-up facilitatory connections between units on adjacent levels and inhibitory connections between units within levels (the top-down connections from phonemes to features are usually set to zero). The speech signal is presented to the model time slice by time slice. It provides a varying bottom-up excitation of feature units, corresponding to the currently processed stretch of sensory input. Next, multiple phoneme units are activated as a function of the extent they match with the activated features, which, in turn, activate words that contain these phonemes.

TRACE assumes that, next in the process of spoken word recognition, these activated words begin to inhibit (or: suppress) each other and simultaneously excite their constituent phonemes in a top-down fashion. Gradually, the word candidate with the best fit to the presented speech signal becomes most active. The network is called TRACE, because the activation pattern that a spoken input leaves behind is a trace of the analysis of the input at all processing levels.

TRACE was built to handle several prominent problems in speech perception. For instance, a noisy input signal can be handled by activating wrong features, not all relevant features, or correct features to a smaller extent than usual. TRACE is relatively robust and error tolerant. Co-articulation (roughly, the mutual effect of consecutive phonemes) is handled by TRACE's assumption of temporally overlapping representations (e.g., phonemes). This solution brings some context sensitivity into the model at the cost of multiplying the representational units. The problem of segmenting continuous speech input into discrete words is resolved at the lexical level ("words"). Segmentation preferences arise due to an interaction of bottom-up and top-down excitation effects with lateral inhibition. Excitation is a consequence of the correspondence of the internal representation with the speech signal, and lateral inhibition is a reduction of activation due to competition with other word candidates. One preference is that TRACE recognizes ambiguous stretches of speech as a single longer carrier word rather than as multiple shorter embedded words (also see section 5.5.1 on embedded words).

The original studies on TRACE focused on phoneme recognition and how it is affected by lexical feedback. Lexical effects in phoneme restoration and categorical perception (see above) were interpreted as evidence for the top-down feedback mechanism in the model, a view which has later come under attack. Later studies have focused on the time-course of spoken target word recognition and lexical competition. In TRACE, target word recognition is affected by the nature and number of other activated lexical competitors. Although the input signal is continuously compared to all words in the mental lexicon, competitors that match and are aligned with the target input (cohort members) are most influential (Frauenfelder & Peeters, 1990, 1998; Grosjean & Frauenfelder, 1996). For instance, when the word "accession" is presented in isolation, "access" is a much stronger competitor than is "session". In contrast to human listeners, TRACE does not recover easily or efficiently from even minor word-initial mismatches. Better simulation results are obtained if top-down information is turned off, but given that lexical information should be helpful rather than harmful in this situation, this result is paradoxical and poses a problem to the model.

Target words can already be recognized on the basis of speech fragments from word onset up to and including the UP. For words of different lengths, words with earlier UPs are recognized more quickly. Simulation work on the relation between UP and RP is supported by gating and phoneme monitoring studies. We will discuss a few of these below in the empirical section of this chapter.

Simulations with TRACE are sometimes difficult to evaluate because the model does not recognize real speech input, but typically only "mock speech," an impoverished abstract representation of the features present in the real signal. Elman (1990; Elman and McClelland, 1986) has built a version of TRACE that was able to process real speech from a single speaker. A freely available reimplementation and extension of the computational model is jTRACE (Strauss et al., 2007). It was modified for Mandarin Chinese by Shuai and Malins (2017).

Since TRACE incorporates only 15 phonemes and about 200 words, a serious problem is how to scale up the model to realistic human lexicons of 50,000 words or more. Extending the lexicon to about 1,000 words, Frauenfelder and Peeters (1998) have shown that the size of TRACE's lexicon affects its behavior. In addition, all phonemes are assumed to have the same duration and spectral characteristics, which is clearly not realistic and underestimates the variability problem that human listeners must solve (Goldinger, 1998). A severe problem lies in how TRACE handles time. Features, phonemes, and words are all reduplicated over time, and since the different representations for similar units are not connected, the resulting architecture is psychologically rather implausible. Other problems concern the difficulty of extending TRACE to larger stretches of speech and the lack of studies incorporating word frequency. Also note that TRACE does not consider the suprasegmental aspects of speech (cf. Figure 5.1).

5.4.3 Shortlist model

In contrast to TRACE, the Shortlist A model (see Figure 5.7; Norris, 1994; Norris et al., 1995) functions completely bottom-up and is capable of performing simulations with vocabularies that include tens of thousands of words. Shortlist, by using both bottom-up excitation and inhibition, first establishes a limited set of lexical candidates: the "shortlist." Any word can be included in this activated candidate set, regardless of its alignment, as long as it corresponds to the input to some preset criterion. Next, the best fitting words are wired into a

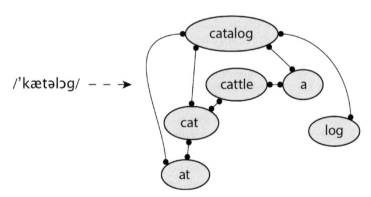

Figure 5.7
Illustration of the Shortlist A model. After Norris et al. (1995).

TRACE-like network. Lexical items in the shortlist compete with each other (this is again called "lateral inhibition"), such that any competitors are inhibited most effectively by the words that best match the input.

A noteworthy feature of Shortlist is that the Metrical Segmentation Strategy from Cutler and Norris (1988) has been implemented in the model. This strategy, later called the "rhythmic hypothesis" (Cutler, 2012b, p. 132) claims that listeners will prefer to segment continuous speech in line with the metrical forms that a language prefers. To make this possible, English words with a strong initial syllable (i.e., containing a full vowel and stressed) receive extra activation in Shortlist, while words are inhibited when they are not aligned in their onsets with a strong syllable in the input. This is in line with English as a stress-based language. A recomputation routine prevents highly active competitors from fully inhibiting matching words that arrive later by recomputing the activation of the shortlist after each incoming phoneme. The more recent Shortlist B model (Norris & McQueen, 2008) makes uses of a Bayesian (rather than an interactive activation) framework. Rather than considering a sequence of discrete phonemes as input to word recognition (Shortlist A), a sequence of multiple phoneme *probabilities* are used.

5.4.4 Recent computational developments

In recent years, developments in artificial intelligence, computer science, and related fields have inspired new types of computational model of spoken word recognition. Deep neural networks, for instance, have been applied to further our understanding of how listeners manage to understand incoming speech. In such an approach, words as stored in the mental lexicon are considered nodes in a network that can be connected to one another or not. A model such as Fine-Tracker uses neural network classifiers to extract prelexical representations from a speech signal, before passing these on to a lexical level for word recognition (Scharenborg, 2010). These prelexical representations are not phonemes or allophones, but multidimensional vectors of articulatory features (e.g., voice, or place and manner of articulation) that are calculated for every 5 ms of the speech input (e.g., Scharenborg & Merkx, 2018). The advantage of this approach is that it is data-driven and simply takes the speech signal as input, as in systems of automatic speech recognition.

5.4.5 A neurobiological approach to spoken word recognition

A key question in the domain of spoken word recognition that has become increasingly important over the last decades is how the relevant processes and representations are supported by parts of the brain. The most influential neuroscientific model in this domain is the dual-stream model introduced by Hickok and Poeppel in 2007. An ambitious characteristic of this (neurocognitive) model is that it aims to capture both production and comprehension aspects of language use, similar to the (cognitive) Language User Framework. Specifically, the dual-stream model proposes that a "ventral stream" through the brain, in both hemispheres, supports the comprehension of speech ("sound-to-meaning"), whereas a strongly left-hemisphere dominant "dorsal stream" supports the production of speech ("sound-to-action"). The ventral stream (ventral = belly) represents a relatively low lying pathway through the brain, the dorsal stream (dorsal = back) a relatively high-lying one. Thus, spoken word recognition is argued to be supported by a ventral stream that helps mapping incoming sounds onto lexical and meaning representations, starting from a spectrotemporal analysis of the incoming signal.

> ## SUMMARY: MODELS OF SPOKEN WORD RECOGNITION
>
> **Cohort models (e.g., Marslen-Wilson & Welsh, 1978):**
> On perceiving the beginning of a word, a word-initial cohort of candidates is set up. This parallel activation process uses positive information from the signal. Next, word candidates are excluded from the set on the basis of missing and negative information. The early Cohort I model assumes an "all-or-none" participation of word candidates in the cohort and allows the interaction of cohort and context. Instead, the later Cohort II model is purely *autonomous*: The Sentence Processor only receives word candidates to consider from the Spoken Word Recognizer. Thus, sentence context can affect spoken word recognition, but not in a top-down way. We propose that the Cohort II model is improved if it allows interaction between cohort and context, just like Cohort I.
>
> **TRACE model (McClelland & Elman, 1986):**
> A set of word candidates is activated in parallel on the basis of signal features at the present moment of the signal. Word candidates can join the candidate set later on, even if they are "non-aligned." Feature, phoneme, and word levels are interactive (there is top-down feedback). Units at each of these levels compete: They inhibit one another. TRACE is a localist (symbolic) connectionist model.
>
> **Shortlist model (Norris et al., 1995):**
> In contrast to TRACE, only a shortlist of the set of candidates is set up. Only for this shortlist, the competition between candidates is worked out. The model accounts for the Metrical Segmentation Strategy, which holds that listeners pay attention to the metrical structure of speech (Cutler, 1990, 2012).
>
> **Deep neural networks and neurobiological approaches:**
> Recently, deep neural networks have been employed to computationally model aspects of spoken word recognition, making use of developments in artificial intelligence and computer science. Cognitive neuroscience approaches aim at identifying the functional neuroanatomy supporting the human capacity to recognize and understand speech. They highlight the importance of networks of brain regions in both hemispheres.

5.5 SPOKEN WORD RECOGNITION: EMPIRICAL STUDIES

All models of spoken word recognition that we have discussed assume that spoken words are recognized "from left-to-right." This makes it likely that the duration of a word in milliseconds will be an important determinant of its recognition time. In addition, how frequently a word is used in everyday life is usually important for recognition as well. Indeed, duration and word frequency are the most important variables determining auditory lexical decision times. This was shown in *mega-studies* in which auditory lexical decision data were collected for large numbers of spoken words, carefully matched with a large number of pseudowords (Ferrand et al., 2018; Winsler et al., 2018). These studies further show that the moment in time a word becomes unique (i.e., distinguishable from all other words a person knows) is also important and correlates with word duration. It is also important to note that in the auditory modality, one only knows that a word is over when there is substantial silence or when the next word has begun (cf. Ernestus & Cutler, 2015). Note that in the visual modality, one can already have an impression of word length even before processing has started. (As we shall see in the next chapter, this makes word frequency an even more relevant variable in the visual modality.)

According to the Cohort model, the UP is an important determinant of the speed of spoken word recognition (see Figure 5.5). Marslen-Wilson (1984, 1987) reported very high correlations between phoneme monitoring response times and the UPs (or recognition points) of spoken words. Radeau and colleagues (2000) found effects of UP for slowly and at medium rate presented nouns, but not for fast presentations. At the fastest rate, the speech resembled that of standard conversations. Using an auditory lexical decision task, O'Rourke and Holcomb (2002) found that words with an early UP (at 427 ms after word onset) displayed an N400 effect at about 100 ms earlier than words with a late UP (at 533 ms after word onset).

There is a vast domain of spoken word recognition studies. In the remainder of this chapter, we will discuss a number of studies that were concerned with key issues. Various research techniques were used in them, such as semantically primed lexical decision, eye tracking employing the visual world paradigm, phoneme monitoring, mispronunciation detection, and listening accompanied by EEG measurements. Each study contributes to a better understanding of some aspect of spoken word recognition.

5.5.1 Lexical embeddings and Cohort's sequentiality assumption

Both the Cohort model and TRACE assume that the arrival of a spoken word will trigger the set up of a set of lexical candidates. Thus, they implicitly assume that the listener knows when a new word begins in the speech signal. But how can the listener segment the complex speech signal, full of assimilation, into the correct words? For instance, does the opening sentence of this chapter end on "speech" or "beach"? Likewise, in the sentence illustrated in the TRACE model (Figure 5.6), both "scar" and "car" would be possible segmentations. How do we determine the correct segmentation? The problem is quite serious, because it even occurs prominently for isolated words (do I hear "two lips" or "tulips"?). McQueen and Cutler (1992) found that a large proportion of words incorporate other words. In a large dictionary of two- to six-syllable words, each "carrier word" incorporated on average 2.6 other words (also see McQueen et al., 1995)!

Empirical research shows that the non-intended ("spurious") words are nevertheless temporarily activated when they fit the speech signal well enough. Shillcock (1990) found, for instance, that a spoken sentence that contained the word "trombone" led to facilitated lexical decisions to a visual target word "rib." This result (a semantic priming effect) indicates that the word "bone" in "trombone" was temporarily activated while the listeners processed the sentence. In a similar study, Gow and Gordon (1995) found facilitation for the target word "flower" not only when the prime sentence was "She tried to put her tulips in a vase," but also when it was "She tried to put her two lips on his cheek." This result already hints at yet another finding, that even words that are embedded across other words ("two lips" → "tulips") may become active (cf. Tabossi et al., 1995; also see question 10 at the end of this chapter).

In all, the lexical embedding effects demonstrate the large sensitivity and adaptation of listeners to subtle variations in the speech signal. Indeed, according to Cutler (2012, pp. 69–70), the vocabulary of a language will guide how spoken word recognition works for that language. Different languages will thus induce subtly different spoken word recognition processes. For instance, while syllable-oriented processing is useful for French, word stress may be more relevant for English speech processing (Cutler et al., 1986). Furthermore, in light of the large proportion of lexical embeddings, Cutler also concludes that the Cohort I model's assumption of purely "sequential recognition" is "doomed" as "it is simply unrealistic." We need more complex models, like TRACE or Shortlist, to start accounting for the many subtle effects.

5.5.2 Speed of spoken word recognition

How quickly are spoken words recognized? Allopenna and colleagues (1998) used eye tracking and a visual world paradigm to investigate this question. They then also compared their empirical findings directly to TRACE simulations. The researchers monitored the eye movements of experimental participants to four objects that were presented in different parts of a computer screen (see Chapter 4). While the participants were looking at the screen, they heard spoken instructions such as the following: "Pick up the beaker; now put it below the diamond." Some of the objects on screen were distractor objects that had a special relationship to the words in the instruction or not. For instance, they could be a cohort competitor, like "beetle"; a rhyme competitor, e.g., "speaker"; or an unrelated competitor, e.g., "carriage." Participants spent some time looking at the distractor objects rather than the target object, depending on the properties of both. In line with the Cohort II and TRACE models, cohort competitors ("beetle") were temporarily considered as potential targets. However, in contradiction to Cohort II, a rhyme effect was also found ("speaker"). As Figure 5.8 shows, there was a very fast separation of target and competitors in terms of the proportion of time that the corresponding objects were fixated. The fixation proportions for targets and competitors also corresponded well with the activation effects predicted by TRACE and Shortlist (also see Magnuson et al., 2001, 2003).

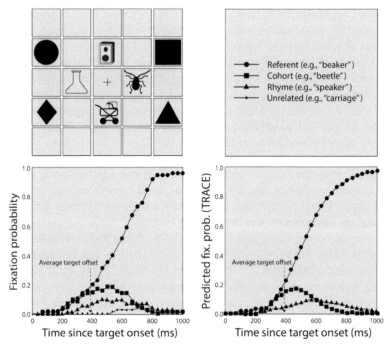

Figure 5.8
Participants in the eye tracking study by Allopenna and colleagues (1998) looked at visual displays on a computer screen (top left panel) while listening to spoken instructions such as "Pick up the beaker; now put it below the diamond" (see top right panel for the four conditions and examples of target words). The authors deduced from participants' eye movements (bottom left panel) that competitor words such as "beetle" (a cohort member) and "speaker" (a rhyme competitor) were also temporarily activated on hearing the name of the referent ("beaker"), as these were looked at more than unrelated control words ("carriage") were. The bottom right panel presents the outcome of the corresponding simulations in TRACE with cohort and rhyme competitors. After Allopenna et al. (1998).

5.5.3 Time-course of spoken word recognition and top-down effects

Frauenfelder and colleagues (1990) examined the left-to-right process in spoken word recognition and examined if phoneme processing was affected by lexical information. The empirical findings were also compared to TRACE simulations, but in a less direct way. The reasoning behind the study was as follows. If someone asks you whether there is a p-sound in the spoken word "telescope," you could find out in two ways. First, you could check a *prelexical* (phonetic) code, based on a direct analysis of the speech signal. Second, you could check whether there is a /p/ in the stored lexical representation of "telescope." This would be a *postlexical* (phonemic) code. Now suppose someone asks you whether there is a p-sound in the word "paradise." In this case, the prelexical code would be available much earlier, because the /p/ is situated before the UP at which the lexical code can be determined with certainty. Thus, the prelexical code becomes available already before the word is recognized, but the postlexical code only after it is recognized.

Now what would happen when someone asks you whether there is a p-sound in "paladife" or "terastope"? In this case, the two items are both (pronounceable) pseudowords, so no lexical code becomes available for them. Only the prelexical code can be used here to find the p-sound.

The task of listening for a particular target phoneme and pressing a button as soon as it is detected is called *phoneme monitoring*. If we assume that "paradise" and "paladife" are quite similar in their sound structure, the difference in response times between words and pseudowords should reflect the involvement of the postlexical code during phoneme monitoring.

According to TRACE, top-down feedback from the word level to the phoneme level should be able to speed up the phoneme monitoring process. Furthermore, due to the interactive nature of TRACE, such a top-down effect should already arise before the UP is reached. In contrast, according to Cohort II, there is no top-down effect, so no effect of the word code on phoneme detection is predicted (see section 5.4.1). Frauenfelder et al. (1990) showed that phoneme monitoring indeed involves both prelexical and postlexical codes at the end of words, but only prelexical codes at the beginning. In the middle of a word, just before the UP, they observed some facilitation (in line with TRACE predictions), but it was not statistically significant: The null result was more in line with Cohort II. Figure 5.9 depicts these results.

As is often the case, the findings hence do not unequivocally support one theoretical interpretation and one model. First, there is a bottom-up explanation in terms of a *race model* (e.g., Merge from Norris et al., 2000). This interpretation assumes there is a race between the *phonemic route* from acoustic signal to phonemes, and the *lexical route* from lexicon to phonemes. The fastest route determines the response time (alternatively, cues from the two routes could be weighted according to some criterion). At the end of words, the lexical route becomes available and leads to the faster response time for words than for pseudowords. Note that the use of the lexical route would also be especially useful in the case of a bad signal. A second interpretation is that of TRACE, where the phoneme itself can only be identified at the phoneme level (said differently, TRACE has only one "read-out level" for the phoneme). Here phoneme detection is faster because the phoneme becomes more activated due to top-down feedback from the word level (i.e., the lexical code).

When you study Figure 5.9, you may note that response times were (unexpectedly) also faster at the end of pseudowords. Two remarks can be made about this. First, even pseudowords initially lead to the set up of a word-initial cohort. For instance, in the case

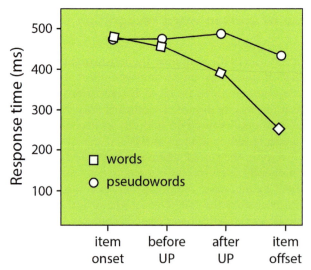

Figure 5.9
Phoneme monitoring times for Dutch spoken words and pseudowords (Frauenfelder et al., 1990). RTs in ms are presented on the Y-axis. "before UP": target phoneme located before UP. "after UP": target phoneme located after UP.

of "paladife," initially a number of words ("palace," "palate") will be included in a cohort. Only later, these drop out and after the so-called Nonword Point, when it is clear that no word in the mental lexicon matches the pseudoword, no further candidates remain. Furthermore, sounds at the beginning or end of words might be more easily discerned, because they are not flanked on one side by other phonemes when words are presented in isolation. This would explain why not only in the case of words, but also pseudowords, the response times are faster towards the end of items. Nevertheless, the difference in response times between words and pseudowords can only reflect the contribution of the postlexical code.

Later research by Mirman and colleagues (2005) showed the importance of yet another factor: Phoneme monitoring latencies for pseudowords depend on the degree of similarity between original word and pseudoword. Take, for instance, the English words "arsenic" and "abolish." When these words are turned into "arsenit" and "abolit," responses to "arsenit" are slower than to "abolit," because /t/ is more similar to /k/, which is the word-final consonant in "arsenic," than to /ʃ/, the word-final sound in "abolish."

SUMMARY: SPOKEN WORD RECOGNITION: EMPIRICAL STUDIES

Empirical studies have been carried out to test and further specify details of models of spoken word recognition. The visual world paradigm has been used in combination with eye tracking to arrive at a better understanding of what word candidates listeners activate and consider on the basis of a spoken input signal. Phoneme monitoring has been used to study the relative contributions of prelexical and lexical information during spoken word recognition.

5.6 SPOKEN WORD RECOGNITION: THE ROLE OF CONTEXT

Lexical processing clearly makes use of information derived from the sensory input, but also from higher order knowledge sources, such as lexical, syntactic, semantic, and pragmatic information that is present in the sentence context, the broader non-linguistic context, and the listener's Long Term Memory. Of crucial importance for the functioning of the Language User Framework is the question if, when, and how contextual information can affect lexical processing. Three possibilities are that context affects word recognition after, during, or before word recognition takes place.

According to *autonomous theories*, context does not exert a top-down effect on lexical processing until the moment of word recognition. In this view, context does not change the activation process of lexical candidates. Context can only contribute to the evaluation and *integration* of the output of the Word Recognizer into a higher-level sentence representation. Therefore, when effects of sentence context are found in studies on word recognition, these should happen rather late in time.

According to *interactive models*, different types of information can interact. One theoretical view is that various types of context affect word recognition, but only after a set of possible word candidates is set up. In this view, bottom-up information determines which

---

DISCUSSION BOX 5: LANGUAGE PROCESSING VS. LANGUAGE LEARNING

When you encounter someone speaking a dialect of your native language, or a foreigner speaking your language with an accent, you will often adapt to their way of speaking in a matter of minutes. At first, your recognition may be slow or intermittent, but soon you will understand them without too much of a problem. This phenomenon shows that listeners (and language users in general) are adaptive: They quickly and flexibly adjust the parameters of their word recognition system to optimize their performance (Magnuson et al., 2021). In this context, learning a spoken language could actually be seen as a continuous adaptation and improvement of speech processing. In this view, "mature" language processing goes hand in hand with language learning and could be considered as the current endpoint of the (constantly ongoing) learning process.

Interesting in this context is the existence of two variants of connnectionist approaches in the psycholinguistic literature (Montazeri et al., 2014). The first approach describes how people actually *perform* a particular language task (such as word recognition). Localist connectionist models are an example of this approach. The second approach is focused more on how people *learn* to perform a particular language task (such as learning second language vocabulary to recognize words in that language). This approach considers especially how new representations are formed and improved. Distributed connectionist models are an example in point. The first type of model is often presented without a thorough explanation of how people learn, while the second approach often only makes predictions about learning accuracy and outcomes, but not of the timing of the cognitive processes involved. The distinction has led researchers to formulate a number of questions.

How does learning relate to processing? Is learning (and forgetting) always going on during language processing? Is it necessary to build a combined model for both processing and learning if we want to understand language use? What is your opinion on these questions?

words are considered and only then context can help to refine this set. This "post initial-access but pre-recognition" view would also hold for visual word recognition. This is the view held by the Cohort II model (see also Zwitserlood's study below).

The strongest proposal is that sentence context *can* already affect the very first stages of word recognition, perhaps even before sensory input appears. This view was already expressed by Morton in the Logogen model in 1969. It was long considered to be an untenable position, but it has become more and more prominent recently. According to this view, word candidates can be *predicted* on the basis of context, rather than only be *integrated* in it after being activated. Prediction might involve *preactivation* of word candidates even before they are presented in a speech signal.

5.6.1 Fast effects of linguistic and non-linguistic context on spoken word recognition

An early study that investigated how a larger *story context* may affect the segmentation of the speech signal was done by Cole and colleagues (1980). In their experiment, participants were instructed to detect mispronunciations in a spoken sentence: "Push a button as soon as you discover a speech error." Next, they heard sentences containing an intentional speech error or not, for instance: "They saw the /kɑrko/ on the ferry," where /kɑrko/ contains the error. During pretesting, it was found that about half of the listeners interpreted /kɑrko/ as "car go" (two words) and the other half as "cargo" (one word). In the experiment proper, the sentence was preceded by a story context about cars or about the loading of ships. It was found that the speech error was discovered considerably more quickly (685 ms) in the latter context than in the first context (1054 ms).

This effect of context was explained by the authors by pointing out that when "cargo" is expected, the listeners expect /kɑrko/ to be an error by the time the second /k/ arrives. However, when "car go" is expected, /kɑrko/ could still turn into a correct sequence at that time, for instance, "They saw the car collide with another car" would be a possible continuation. In other words, the story context about cars would be inducing segmentation, whereas the context about ships loading would be avoiding segmentation. Another example in the experiment was the sentence "They saw the snow drift (snowdrift) by the window." The conclusion on the basis of this study is that context information can quickly affect the segmentation process applied to the speech signal.

In addition to the story context in which a spoken sentence is perceived, also the (linguistic) sentence context and the larger (non-linguistic) visual context may influence how listeners process spoken words. In an EEG study by Tromp and colleagues (2018), participants were immersed in a 3D virtual restaurant using a head-mounted virtual reality display. During the experiment, their electrophysiological brain activity was continuously recorded. In the restaurant, participants encountered several guests who were sitting in front of their meal and spoke to the participant. For instance, a life-size virtual agent would be sitting at a table having a plate with a piece of salmon in front of them. The participant would see this, after which the virtual agent would look at the participant and say "I have just ordered this salmon" (match) or "I have just ordered this pasta" (mismatch). Critically, both these sentences are perfectly fine if one disregards the larger visual context in which the sentence is spoken. However, the researchers observed a robust N400 effect time locked to the critical word ("salmon" versus "pasta") in that the mismatch sentences yielded significantly enhanced N400 amplitude compared to the match sentences (see Figure 5.10). As such, the larger visual context in which a spoken word (in a sentence) is encountered influences how fluently a listener processes that word.

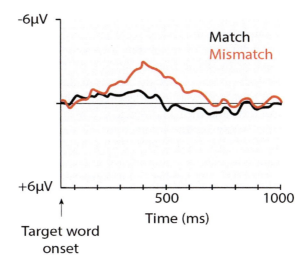
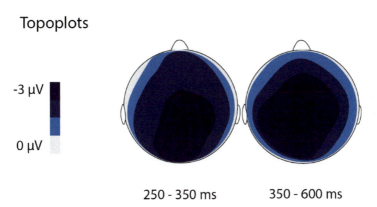

Figure 5.10
Tromp and colleagues (2018) had participants meet virtual restaurant guests in a virtual restaurant who looked at them and produced a sentence about their meal. Here you see the difference in ERP amplitude between the mismatch and the match condition averaged over left posterior electrodes (top part: ERPs) and two so-called topoplots (bottom part: Topoplots) averaged over the time windows 250–350 and 350–600 ms after the onset of the critical word. A darker blue color corresponds to a larger N400 effect, so based on the color it can be seen where over the scalp the effect was most prominently picked up.

Not only does the non-linguistic, visual context influence spoken word processing, but also the preceding *sentence context* plays a role. In a study by van den Brink and colleagues (2001), participants listened to words presented in auditory sentence contexts in the absence of a broader visual context. A Dutch example sentence is: *De schilder kleurde de details in met een klein …* ("The painter colored the details with a small …"). Depending on the condition, it could be finished by the word *penseel* ("paint brush," fully congruent), *pensioen* ("pension," initially congruent), or *doolhof* ("labyrinth," fully incongruent). This experimental manipulation resulted in enhanced N400 amplitude for both *pensioen* and *doolhof* compared to *penseel*. This effect was at the time mainly thought to reflect problems with the lexical-semantic integration of the partially or fully incongruent words into the higher-order meaning of the sentence context. We now know these effects may also be partially explained by the listeners actively predicting the fully congruent word, but not the initially congruent and fully incongruent alternatives, based on the preceding linguistic context (Nieuwland et al., 2020).

In sum, N400 amplitude time locked to target word onset in these experimental studies may reflect the ease or difficulty of integrating a spoken word with the broader linguistic and non-linguistic context, at the same time depending on the extent to which the encountered word was predicted by the listener based on aspects of that broader multidimensional context. These predictions, in turn, are based on a listener's lifetime of experience with encountering words in broader contexts and their knowledge and mental models of the world.

A related seminal study on the interactions between Word Recognizer and Sentence Processor was done by Zwitserlood (1989). Zwitserlood investigated how word recognition is affected by semantic aspects of the sentence context in which the word occurs. In her study with Dutch materials, she applied a cross-modal priming technique, combined with lexical decision (see Chapter 4). Here we will present a simplified account of this study. Participants listened to a spoken sentence with a prime word at the end. The prime word was not always completely presented, but could be just a word-initial fragment. For instance, the Dutch word *kapitein* (English: "captain") could be presented in fragments such as *kap*, *kapi*, or *kapitei*. After the sentence including the prime fragment at the end of it was presented, a printed target item appeared on a computer screen in front of the participant. This target item could be a word or a nonword, and the participants made a lexical decision on this item. If the target was a word, it could have an associative relationship to the spoken prime word. For instance, the spoken portion of *kapitein* ("captain") could be followed by the printed target *schip* ("ship").

Critically, the spoken prime words belonged to pairs of words with the same onset: They were cohort members and competitors for recognition. For instance, the word *kapitein* ("captain") is quite similar to the word *kapitaal* ("capital"). Indeed, the beginning of these words is the same, but they differ towards their ends. The visually presented target words were associated with either one or the other spoken word in such a pair. For instance, *kapitein* ("captain") was semantically related to the Dutch word *schip* ("ship"), and *kapitaal* ("capital") to the Dutch word *geld* ("money").

The spoken word fragments were presented at the end of different sentence contexts. For instance, the fragments could be positioned in a *neutral*, non-biasing condition: the Dutch equivalent of "They mourned the loss of their ...." Indeed, here both "captain" and "capital" could be logical continuations. In contrast, in a *biasing context* condition, a more informative context preceded the target fragments: the Dutch equivalent of "With dampened spirits, the men stood around the grave. They mourned the loss of their ...." This context suggests the involvement of an animate agent: the deceased person lying in the grave. As such, "captain" would make for a natural continuation of the sentence. For both conditions, the semantic priming effect (degree of facilitation) relative to a baseline condition (not considered here) was determined (cf. Figure 5.11).

The major results of the experiment are graphically represented in Figure 5.11. Following the spoken word fragment *kap*, the lexical decision times for both visual items "ship" and "money" were faster than for unrelated (baseline) words in all contexts (see the left part of the figure). Apparently, the context fragment *kap* led to activation of both *kapitein* ("captain") and *kapitaal* ("capital"). The fragment *kapitei* (right in the figure), however, only primed "ship" (i.e., it received a faster response). Thus, at that last moment, only *kapitein* ("captain") was still active. Most interestingly, presenting the medium-sized fragment *kapi* (middle of the figure) in the biasing context condition led to faster responses to the target word associated with the prime fitting in this context. So, there was a faster response to "ship" if the word fragment *kapi* appeared in a rich sentence context in which the word was

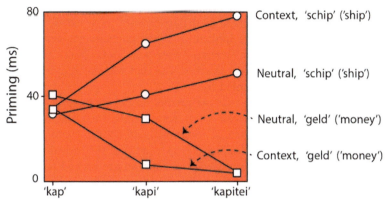

Figure 5.11
Priming effects for the item pair *kapitein* – *kapitaal* ("captain" – "capital") in the sentence context suggesting involvement of a person in Zwitserlood's (1989) priming study. The y-axis indicates the response time differences in the neutral and context sentences relative to a baseline control condition. Following a sentence context, the spoken word fragments *kap*, *kapi*, or *kapitei* were presented and immediately followed by a printed target, *schip* ("ship") or *geld* ("money"), to which a lexical decision response had to be given. After *kap*, there was priming for "ship" and "money," so both *kapitein* and *kapitaal* must have been in the cohort. After *kapitei*, there was only priming for "ship," so *kapitaal* had dropped out of the cohort. After *kapi*, the effect depended on context. In a neutral sentence condition, both targets were primed, so both must still have been in the cohort. In the biasing context condition, only "ship" was primed, so only *kapitein* was left in the cohort. For further explanation, see the main text.

biased to become *kapitein* ("captain") instead of *kapitaal* ("capital"). This suggests that the biasing sentence context induced a semantic facilitation effect on the word selection process. Context therefore appears to affect the selection process applied to the cohort members, but only after the word-initial cohort has become active.

We note that the debate on the cognitive mechanisms underlying spoken word recognition in context is still not closed, and some have criticized the use of fragments to investigate semantic priming (Heyman et al., 2016). Nevertheless, in Chapter 7 on sentence processing, we will see that also the context at large may have surprisingly strong effects on language comprehension.

5.6.2 Context effects: The role of your mental model of the speaker

As we saw earlier, interlocutors build mental models involving physical, biological, psychological, and sociological aspects of their world and of the particular (speech) events they experience. As part of this building process, listeners will typically construe a mental model of the speaker they are listening to. To what extent can such a mental model of the speaker influence spoken word recognition in the listener?

A study by Cai and colleagues (2017) illustrates how the mental model a listener has of a speaker, even when not personally knowing or seeing that speaker, may influence aspects of spoken word recognition. In a set of online experiments, these researchers had both British and American mother tongue speakers of English listen to English words pronounced in either a British or an American accent. Crucially, the critical words that were presented had different dominant meanings in the two varieties of English. A "coach," for instance, would predominantly refer to a type of bus in England but to a sports trainer in the USA. A "bonnet" is first and foremost a hat in the UK, but part of a car in the States. In a variety of cleverly designed web-based tasks (e.g., word association, cross-modal priming, sentence interpretation), it was observed that participants retrieved the meaning of words as a function of the accent they were spoken in. When participants were presented with an ambiguous word such as "coach" or "bonnet," they were more likely and faster to retrieve the meaning that was congruent (versus the meaning that was incongruent) with the (British or American) accent it was accompanied by.

These findings illustrate the idea that the mental model we have of a speaker will influence the mapping of incoming spoken word forms onto meaning representations. The results are difficult to explain for some of the models of spoken word recognition that we discussed above, to the extent that these models assume that the lexical representations that are activated on the basis of incoming speech information are argued to be abstracted away from variable properties (e.g., accent information) in the signal.

5.6.3 Context effects: The role of embodiedness

Although speech is typically produced by a speaker, experimental research into spoken word recognition has often presented participants with spoken stimuli via headphones in the absence of the visible speaker who produced the speech. As such, spoken stimuli in psycholinguistic experiments have often been largely *disembodied*. In line with earlier work on hand gestures (e.g., Krahmer & Swerts, 2007), an experimental study by Bosker and Peeters (2021) did more justice to the role of the body in spoken communication by showing participants videos of a speaker who concomitantly produced spoken sentences and *beat gestures* – simple up-and-down flicks of the hand that are typically used by speakers to highlight lexically stressed and otherwise important parts of their concurrently produced speech. To what extent would these visual hand movements influence the process of spoken word recognition?

In a series of experiments using a variety of implicit and explicit experimental tasks, the researchers found that the perception of spoken disyllabic words (e.g., "OBject" vs. "obJECT") and pseudowords ("BAGpif" vs. "bagPIF") that were ambiguous with regard to their stress pattern were recognized as a function of whether a beat gesture was present on the first or second syllable of these stimuli (also see Figure 5.1). In other words, participants perceived the word "object," when made ambiguous as to whether it had stress on the first or second syllable, as "OBject" (rather than "obJECT") when a beat gesture was produced by the visible speaker during the first syllable. Hence, listeners used their knowledge that beat gestures often come with stressed syllables to derive the assumedly intended meaning of a word from an ambiguous speech signal. In line with the McGurk effect that we discussed in Chapter 2, this finding illustrates how important the speaker's body is as a source of information for the listener. As such, both auditory and visual types of information contribute to what words we hear.

> **SUMMARY: SPOKEN WORD RECOGNITION: THE ROLE OF CONTEXT**
>
> What influence does the broader context play in influencing aspects of spoken word recognition? Empirical research has shown that listeners use information provided by a broader sentence, discourse, and visual context to guide word recognition, that words are interpreted in the context of a listener's mental model of the situation, and that observed hand gestures may modulate spoken word perception. As such, context is a multifaceted construct that cannot be ignored in theories and models aiming at a full understanding of how a listener tackles the challenging task of recognizing the words a speaker produces.

5.7 WHAT IS NEXT?

Recognizing speech is a fundamental component of human language use. The knowledge acquired in this chapter on spoken word recognition will assist us during our next steps on the path from incoming utterance to meaning. But before we consider sentence processing in Chapter 7, we will consider in Chapter 6 how word recognition is done when the linguistic input signal is not auditory, but visual (as is the case in word reading) in nature. In the past, orthography has sometimes been considered as parasitic on and derived from phonology, and its processing was not even always considered in linguistic diagrams of the language faculty. In Chapter 6, we will argue that such a position is unwarranted in light of the great importance and benefits that written and printed language have brought us. We will compare the processes of word recognition in the written (i.e., often printed, nowadays) and spoken domains to see to what extent these two variants of the Signal and Word Recognizers function in similar or different ways.

5.8 WHAT HAVE WE LEARNED?

In this chapter, we have seen that spoken word recognition can be characterized in terms of a number of important mechanisms: multiple activation, lexical embedding, lexical competition, degree of overlap, and context effects. We can illustrate this by more closely considering the opening example of this chapter: the spoken utterance "How to wreck a nice beach":

Multiple activation. On hearing /turɛk/, possible utterance continuations could be "to wreck a," but also "to recognize" or "to reckon." Empirical studies suggest that the word recognition system considers all of these in parallel until the speech signal delivers mismatching information.

Lexical embedding. The speech signal can be segmented into different words and word combinations that are locally possible. For instance, "ice," "beach," "peach," and "each" are all more or less present in the signal. Empirical evidence suggests that we activate all or most of these temporarily, indicating that speech recognition is a process that adapts itself continuously to input and speaker specificities.

Lexical competition. When several words are considered as potential constituents of the utterance, it must be decided which of these competitors are intended and which are spurious. How do we correctly select the intended words and discard other temporarily activated word candidates? Studies show that the lexical competition and selection processes take time and slow down word recognition.

Degree of overlap. If you hear "beach" preceded by an "s," you might indeed activate "speech," but what if we change the example into "How to wreck a nice leech." Do you still activate "speech" in this case, even though the /l/ sound and the /b/ are quite different? How similar must a word be to the speech signal to become active at all? Sophisticated studies indicate that listeners are quite sensitive to details in incoming speech waves and that there are limits to the coactivation of lexical candidates on the basis of sound overlap. The involved phonemes must be similar enough to allow it.

Context effects. Finally, we have seen that although there is a bottom-up priority, the broader spoken and visible (physical and bodily) context quickly affects how listeners recognize spoken words. The broader sentence context, the mental models we have of the speaker, and any concurrent information from the visual domain (hand gestures, facial expressions, objects present) may influence how quickly we recognize a word, what we hear, and what meaning we attribute to a perceived word form.

QUESTIONS FOR CHAPTER 5

1. Consider Figure 5.2. What do you notice when you compare the spoken and printed representations of the word "production"? What would be your approximate estimate of the duration of sounds like /p/, /d/, and /k/? What about /o/, /ə/, and /ʌ/? What do you neglect if you measure the duration of sounds by using the indicated vertical lines?
2. Would the Cohort model also be applicable to your recognition of the words you see here, printed on paper or presented on screen?
3. How would the Cohort model account for spoken word recognition in noisy situations? And the TRACE model?
4. How should the TRACE model be adapted for Mandarin Chinese? Hint: See Shuai and Malins (2017) for an answer.
5. Try to explain the following misperceptions (taken from Clark & Clark, 1977, p. 214): "wrecking service" (original speech signal: "wrapping service"), "meet Mr. Edison" ("meet Mr. Anderson"), "I'm covered with chocolate" ("I'm covered with chalk dust"), "get some ceiling paint" ("get some sealing tape").
6. Look up on the internet what the "cocktail party phenomenon" is (in the context of speech recognition, that is). How would you explain it based on what you learned in this chapter?
7. Can you explain why Dutch–English bilinguals may pronounce the words "bad," "bed," "bat," and "bet" all in the same way? And why would Japanese people sometimes have difficulties in pronouncing English words that contain /l/ and /r/?
8. What do you notice when you compare the printed and spoken versions of the following words: "apple"; "production"; "naturally"; "band", "bend", and "bent"; "wind" (pronounced as in "wink") and "wind" (pronounced as in "kind"); "really?" and "really!"
9. What is visible on the cover of the record *Aerial* by Kate Bush?
10. What do you hear when you speak the following series of words out loud at a reasonable rate? "Anna Mary candy lights since imp pulp lay things." This interesting segmentation of a completely different sentence was made by Skinner, a famous behaviorist. (Spoiler alert: "An American delights in simple playthings"; Cole et al., 1980.)

Chapter 6

Recognizing printed and written words

6.1 PRINTED AND WRITTEN WORD RECOGNITION: THE ESSENCE

In daily life, we read all the time: the note left by our partner on the kitchen table, the headlines of the online morning paper, and the ads accompanied by smileys on the train station to university. As can be seen in Figure 6.1 below, written and printed messages use letters of different types, fonts, and sizes. Written and printed words have in common with spoken words that they also contain smaller units that are to some extent linked and relatively continuous. But, obviously, in the Latin alphabetic script illustrated here, both printed words and written words consist of letters rather than of speech sounds.

Print and writing are modes of language that are artificial and, compared to spoken language, have been developed relatively recently by humans. In print, the signal (scribbles on paper) is ideally clearly discernible from the background, and it is less variable within and across messages than either written or spoken language. Typically, in many scripts both print and written text purposefully separate words from each other by blank spaces. Individual letters within words may (Figure 6.1, top and bottom panel) or may not (middle panel) be separated by blanks as well. When taking a historical perspective, we observe yet another possibility: In ancient Greek, a sentence was written without spaces and turning back in the other direction at the end of the sentence, in the way an oxen may plough the land (this was called *boustrophedon*).

Many scripts, regardless of whether they are used in written or printed form, explicitly indicate the presence of meaningful units – such as when sentences start with a Capital Letter and are concluded by a period (.). In Spanish, to aid the reader, a question is commonly indicated by two question marks: one upside down at the beginning of the sentence, and a "regular" one at the end of the sentence. Some information from the spoken modality is not available in the visual modality, like intonation or speech amplitude (which can signal emotional value). Other communicative channels that are used in face-to-face communication, such as a speaker's face and their hands, are not available either. In modern media, we may use special signs like emoticons to reduce that problem (BECAUSE USING CAPITAL LETTERS OFTEN SEEMS RUDE!).

Processing printed and written words cannot be exactly the same as processing spoken language, because the eyes and ears induce different spatial and temporal

DOI: 10.4324/9781003326274-6

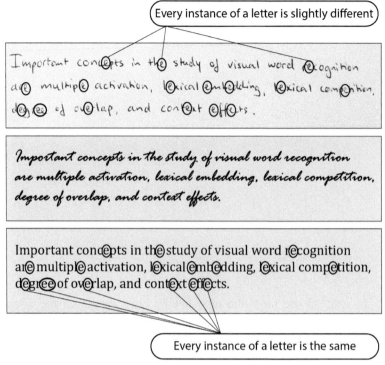

Figure 6.1
Message in handwriting (top panel) and in two different font types (middle and bottom panels).

characteristics to language processing (see Box 1.1 in Chapter 1). Furthermore, during reading, the eyes fixate on a word, and jump to the next word or even the one next to it after it is processed (see the sections on eye tracking in Chapter 4 and sentence reading in Chapter 7). At the sentence level, processing during reading is therefore incremental, as it is in the spoken modality. However, during an eye fixation on a single word, information is picked up about several letters in this word *at the same time*. This partially parallel input provides a special nature to visual word recognition. In spite of such differences, we will see in this chapter that visual and auditory word recognition still have a lot in common.

Generalizing over printed and spoken words, it has been estimated that an average adult reader knows at least 42,000 words, for which information is stored in the language user's mental lexicon (Brysbaert et al., 2016). Recognizing a printed word takes about one third of a second or less, and readers are able to process 230–260 words per minute, obviously depending on the length of the words in the text (Brysbaert, 2019b). Such feats indicate that the selection of a word from memory must be a very efficient process. In this chapter, we will discuss this process for printed word recognition.

The organization of this chapter is the same as that of the previous chapter. We will first describe the mental representations and processes involved in reading. Next, we consider influential models of visual word recognition and empirical studies that support or challenge them. Finally, we will look at how the broader (sentence) context influences the processing of individual words.

SUMMARY: PRINTED AND WRITTEN WORD RECOGNITION: THE ESSENCE

To understand a written or printed word, the reader must first segment the incoming visual signal into relevant units during a prelexical stage. During a subsequent lexical stage, these units (called "graphs") are combined into more abstract units ("graphemes") and used to look up the matching word and its meaning in Long Term Memory. The reader's task of recognizing and understanding a written or printed word is not straightforward, as the signal will display substantial variability within and across writers (for written words), and across different fonts (for printed words).

6.2 PRINTED AND WRITTEN WORD RECOGNITION: REPRESENTATIONS

As in the auditory domain, the Signal Recognizer builds a representation of the incoming signal. The printed or written words in the signal can be segmented into units of different sizes. As we have seen before, words are not "holistic" units: They typically contain smaller elements ("sublexical units") that the Signal Recognizer may derive from the signal (see Figure 6.2). In this section, we will look at visual word recognition from the perspective of

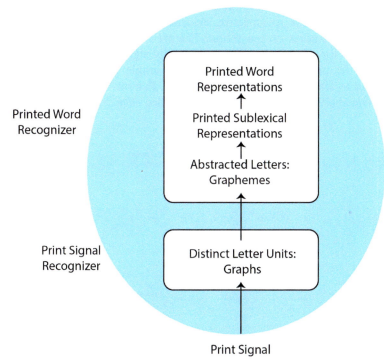

Figure 6.2
Just as in Chapter 5, this chapter is mainly concerned with the bottom left part of the Language User Framework. In printed word recognition, an incoming printed signal is factually represented by the Signal Recognizer as "graphs" and turned into abstract units such as "graphemes" (i.e., one or more letters that correspond to one phoneme). The Word Recognizer uses these segmental units to access the mental lexicon in Long Term Memory and identify word form and word meaning. Analogous processes take place for written word reccognition.

102 Recognizing printed and written words

letters and their features, syllables and morphemes, and entire writing systems and scripts. Although most of our analysis can also be applied to written words, it focuses especially on printed words, because most research has been focused on their recognition.

6.2.1 Letter features and letters

While segmenting a printed message into individual words is relatively easy in modern script, as the words are often separated by blanks, the printed signals are still quite diverse and variable. Print consists of different font types that come in different sizes, boldness, and italics. Somehow all the visually encountered variants of a word must be mapped onto an abstract representation of the word in question in Long Term Memory. Thus, also in the visual modality we encounter a problem of variability. This problem is less severe for printed messages than for handwritten messages, which vary not only across language users but also within an individual (see Figure 6.1).

To tackle the variability problem, it was proposed many years ago that the individual letters that make up a word are not recognized as templates or holistic units, but in terms of letter features, such as vertical, horizontal, and oblique lines, right and acute angles, continuous and discontinuous curves, and so on. Decoding such features would allow combining them into letter units. This view is nicely illustrated by the early Pandemonium model (Selfridge, 1959). As we can see in Figure 6.3, different types of detector (called "demons" by Selfridge) are engaged in the activities of representing the image, detecting features, integrating these into possible letters, and making decisions about what letter is actually being presented.

From an "embodiedness" perspective, evidence in favor of such a view was observed in neurophysiological studies of the retina. Feature detectors were found, i.e., groups of neurons that coded for stimuli that are perceptually significant. At an early point in the sensory pathway, feature detectors arguably have simple properties; later more complex detectors respond to features that are more specific. Famous is the research in this domain by Hubel and Wiesel (1962, 1965). They found so-called *edge detectors* in the visual cortex of

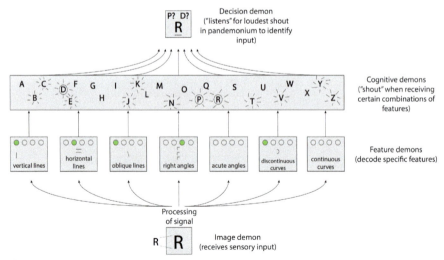

Figure 6.3

Impression of the letter recognition process according to the Pandemonium model. Letters such as "D", "P", and "R" share combinations of features, e.g., "vertical line," "discontinuous curves," "right angles," and others; this information is picked up by the "decision demon." Note that the "R" was assumed to have two horizontal segments. After Selfridge (1959).

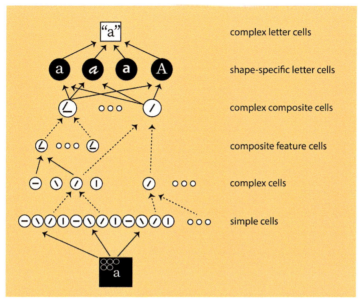

Figure 6.4
A detailed view on letter recognition and the brain. Different neuronal populations ("cells") would be involved in different stages of recognizing a letter. Simple cells scan the input for simple, localized features. Complex cells pool these units, resulting in representations that are invariant to position. Next, composite feature cells combine them into more complex features. Complex composite cells then turn the representations into shape-specific letter patterns ("templates") that are invariant to position and scale. Levels can be skipped. Note the parallels with the Pandemonium model in Figure 6.3. After Grainger et al. (2008); Riesenhuber and Poggio (1999).

the cat. Edges typically do not occur in the background noise of a visual environment and are therefore important to detect. The idea is that edgy features of letters can be detected in a similar way. Deeper in the central nervous system, there are cells that respond to more abstract symbolic representations (cf. Figure 6.4). Non-essential variation in case or font ceases to play a role there. It has been proposed that abstract visual word form perception takes place in a left cortical region of the brain within the fusiform gyrus, referred to as the Visual Word Form Area (McCandliss et al., 2003).

6.2.2 Syllables and morphemes

In addition to features and letters, words can be segmented into somewhat larger units such as syllables and morphemes. A word such as "step," for instance, consists of one syllabic (CCVC, where C = consonant and V = vowel) unit, while "rucksack" consists of two (CVCC/CVCC). In a word such as "tables," the second syllable contains an -s morpheme. As explained in Chapter 3, the term "morpheme" refers to the smallest meaningful part of a word (here the -s makes the meaning plural). Words such as "rucksack," "tables," and "anti-dis-establish-ment-ari-an-ism" are morphologically complex.

Two important concepts with respect to the morphological composition of words are *inflection* and *derivation*. It is usually said that in inflection, the syntactic category of a word (e.g., noun, verb, adverb) is not changed. Two basic sorts of inflection are the plurals of nouns ("house" → "houses") and verb conjugations ("walk" → "walks", "walking", "walked"). In derivation, the category of a word changes ("talk," verb → "talker," noun; "visual," adjective → "visually," adverb). At least in English, derivations can take inflections, but not the other way around ("talk + er + s," but not "talk + s + er"). The core of these words that are subjected to inflection or derivation is called a stem (e.g., "talk" in "talker," "talking," and "talkative").

In addition to inflection and derivation, *compounds* represent a third complex morphological form, which consists of several stems. For instance, the words "black" and "bird" can be combined into "blackbird."

The majority of words in English and across other languages of the world consist of two or more morphemes (Rastle, 2019, p. 52). It is therefore important for researchers of the psychology of language to find out whether words like "walking" or "talkers" are stored and retrieved as one whole or in several pieces. For instance, the word "talkers" could be split into "talk + er + s" during its recognition process, or not. Theories in this domain differ from assuming *full storage* (the form is stored as a whole in Long Term Memory) to *full decomposition* (the form consists of different pieces that are stored separately), and the intermediate possibility that words could be stored and retrieved both as wholes and as a combination of smaller, decomposed units. In the last case, the fastest of these dual pathways might then result in recognition.

6.2.3 Writing systems or scripts: Shallow vs. deep orthography

The importance of written and printed messages for human culture can hardly be overestimated. In fact, it could be argued that our modern society would not exist without these means of information storage. To entrust messages to papyrus, paper, or even stone makes them available to other people living in different places and even different times. Humans have invented many different scripts to encode their ideas. Letter features, letters, syllables, and/or morphemes may or may not take part in such a larger script.

One of the first ideas historically was to represent an object or animal by making a drawing of it. When these pictures were stylized over time, they turned from pictograms into logograms. Logographic writing systems represent (parts of) words by symbols. Examples are the scripts of *ancient Egyptian*, *Linear B*, *Mayan*, and *Zhongwen* (a form of Chinese). To represent auditory/spoken information, in addition to visual and semantic information, phonetic elements ("radicals") could be added to the logograms that hint at their pronunciation.

The focus on the spoken characteristics of words is stronger in so-called syllabaries. These represent the syllables in units (consonants + vowels, or merely vowels). Examples of scripts that use syllables as their most important units are *Hiragana*, *Katakana*, *Cherokee*, and *Inuktitut*. Can you find out in which countries these scripts are used?

Syllabic alphabets or abugidas have symbols for consonants and vowels. Consonants in such systems have an inherent vowel that can be changed by another vowel or by *diacritics* (markings that can change the phonetics of vowels). For instance, the consonant "gha" could be turned into "ghu" by adding a diacritic onto the consonant. Vowels can also be written with separate letters. Example scripts are those of *Bengali, Balinese, Gujarati, Hmong*, and *Devanagari*. Devanagari is used for writing not only Hindi, but also Marathi, Nepali, and several other languages.

Well-known to readers of English are scripts using the alphabet to represent consonants and vowels. Some examples are *Latin, Cyrillic, Greek, Coptic, Korean, Etruscan*, and *the International Phonetic Alphabet (IPA)*. There are around 46 different alphabets in the world. Note that the English *language* uses the Latin *script*.

Finally, there are scripts that are called abjads or consonant alphabets. These mainly represent consonants. Examples are *Arabic, Hebrew*, and *Phoenician*. Cn y mgn wht rdng s lk whn thr r n vwls vlbl? Arabic and Hebrew furthermore show that scripts are not always read from left to right, but may require right to left reading. Imagine you have to read a text from right to left that has no vowels in it!

Languages that have an alphabet can still be different in how letters are mapped onto sounds. Their writing system or script may be a "shallow orthography" or a "deep orthography." In Finnish, for instance, one phoneme is represented by just one letter unit or "grapheme." This transparent relationship makes it a very "shallow" orthography (the term is not used here in a pejorative sense). In Spanish, Italian, Serbo-Croat, and Hungarian, one or two letters may represent one phoneme. For instance, in certain Italian words the phoneme /k/ is represented by the letter combination "ch." In this case, the two letters together are therefore said to constitute one grapheme. These languages are nevertheless still rather shallow. Dutch is also relatively shallow in its orthography, although it has some irregular mappings – the letter "d" at the end of a word is pronounced as a /t/, the letter combinations "au" and "ou" are often pronounced in the same way, as is the case for "ei" and "ij." Note that a single letter ("x") may also correspond to more than one phoneme in line with a spelling rule.

French is interesting, because it often has multiple orthographic possibilities to represent the same speech sounds: -ot, -ots, -au, -eau, -aux, and -eaux can all refer to the same sound /o:/. At the same time, particular letter combinations, when presented in isolation, have only one pronunciation (*mots*).

In contrast, English has a very complex mapping between letters and sounds; it has a "deep" orthography. For instance, the pronunciation of the letter string -ough depends on the preceding letters: "bough," "tough," "though," "cough." Furthermore, the words "colonel" and "kernel" have a virtually identical pronunciation, but are written very differently – and there are, of course, other similar examples. The complexity of the English spelling system is eloquently demonstrated in a poem by Nolst Trenité called "The chaos of English pronunciation" (which you can find easily on the internet).

> **SUMMARY: PRINTED AND WRITTEN WORD RECOGNITION: REPRESENTATIONS**
>
> The words that you read on this page are not holistic units – they can be segmented into morphemes, syllables, and letters (or "graphemes"), which in turn typically consist of several letter features. The reader must in some way map the perceived visual input onto existing abstract representations in the mental lexicon to recognize the word. What a word exactly refers to may depend on inflectional and derivational processes applied to a word's stem. An important question is whether a word like "talkers" is stored as such in lexical Long Term Memory, or whether it is recognized by on-line assembling its stored stem "talk," the stored derivational morpheme -er, and the stored inflectional morpheme -s. Societies across the globe rely heavily on written and printed communication, but languages vary widely in their writing systems (scripts) and in how shallow or deep their orthography is.

6.3 PRINTED AND WRITTEN WORD RECOGNITION: PROCESSES

Just as in the auditory modality, the visual word recognition process during reading starts as the incoming signal has been analyzed and abstractly represented. The Print and Written Signal Recognizers (see Figure 6.2) encode the raw scribbles on paper as actual letter representations (concrete printed symbols, called graphs or glyphs) that can be turned into abstract representations (graphemes) serving as input to the Word Recognizer (cf. the phones and phonemes or allophones in spoken word recognition, Chapter 5). The Word Recognizer uses these grapheme representations and their combinations (like bigrams and syllables) to look up the printed words in memory, where their meaning and other properties are found. Because printed words are clearly separated by blanks in many scripts, the word segmentation process in the visual modality is relatively simple.

On the basis of the proposed lexical representation, the Word Recognizer makes contact with the mental lexicon. No word recognition models assume that a presented word has a direct (cable) connection to its stored representation in the lexicon. In the first stages of word recognition, many stored representations that are similar to the input letter string are activated (multiple activation of candidates), possibly to avoid as much as possible a situation in which the wrong word is identified (selection errors). This is then followed by a process in which all available candidates are weighted until only a single candidate remains.

An important question is, of course, which potential word candidates are initially activated. Are these the cohort members that we know from spoken word recognition? In other words, is it a set of items that have identical letters at the beginning of the word and change later on in the word? In this view, visual word recognition would be parasitic on auditory word recognition, which would make sense from an evolutionary perspective, as spoken language is significantly older than written language and learned earlier in life. However, although letter-to-letter reading can be done (e.g., in naming new words you have not encountered before and by people with aphasia whose regular word recognition process may be disturbed), the accepted view is that in reading the set of initially considered word candidates is different in nature.

When reading a word, the eyes fixate on a letter position that is usually near the middle of the word. Because of the properties of the eye's retina, information within about seven letter positions can normally be obtained in parallel. Thus, for a six-letter word (e.g., "strand"), information about all letter positions and their identity becomes gradually available. It is assumed that all word candidates similar to the input word *across the word as a whole* become temporarily activated in the mind of the reader.

The set of word candidates that differ in only one letter position from a target word is called the "neighborhood." For instance, neighbors of the word "wind" are words such as "find," "wand," "wild," and "wing." Note that the words' pronunciation is not relevant in this definition. It should be clear from this that the neighborhood of a printed word is different from the cohort of a spoken word. Cohort members of "wind" in the spoken domain include, for instance, "will," "willow," "wicked," and "window," sharing their phonemic onsets but not their offsets.

However, like in the spoken domain, smaller words may be part of longer words. For instance, "trombone" contains "bone" and "one," while "clover" contains "lover," "love," and "over." This prominent phenomenon is called "lexical embedding."

6.3.1 Are words looked up in the lexicon one by one or in parallel?

What does this notion of "neighborhood" imply for the visual word recognition process? One possibility is that the different word candidates would be checked and searched in the mental lexicon in an order determined by their degree of activation. This degree of activation might depend on the similarity to the input and the frequency of usage of the word in question (cf. Norris, 1986). For instance, when the word "wind" is read, the stored representations "wind," "find," and "wand" might become active in memory. The word "find" is more frequently used than "wand" and "wind" in everyday communication; and it may have been experienced in more contexts and thus have a higher "contextual diversity" (Adelman & Brown, 2008) or "semantic diversity" (Johns & Jones, 2022). As a consequence, it might be checked as possibly consistent with the input first. The entry "wind" might be checked next, as it is also quite frequently used and because it is more similar to the input stimulus and more frequently encountered than "wand."

Such a frequency-ordered search process in memory was proposed by an early model in the 1970s (the Search Model; Forster & Chambers, 1973; Murray & Forster, 2004). This process, somewhat similar to looking up words sequentially in a dictionary, was in line with the "computer metaphor" of the time: The Central Processing Unit in an early computer did only one thing at a time.

However, instead another model (the Logogen model; Morton, 1969) had already proposed that many word candidates could be considered for recognition simultaneously. In an activation framework, the activation of possible word candidates can be updated for all units in parallel when new information comes in. This kind of process is more like a "broadcasting system," in which each unit updates itself when new information is received. This second view is in line with the "neural network metaphor" that likens the word recognition process to the parallel activation of units in a neural network.

Over the decades, abundant evidence for this second view has accumulated. Visual word recognition entails a parallel activation of a set of word candidates and a subsequent reduction of this set to one candidate, which hopefully corresponds to the visually presented target word for reading to be successful.

We have seen that, in the auditory modality, word candidates fall out of the cohort if they are no longer supported by the increasing input signal. Positive input information ensures their activation, but negative information results either in decay (without bottom-up support, the word candidate's activation gradually decreases in the Cohort model), or in additional inhibition (incompatible signal information leads to active suppression in the TRACE model). In the visual modality, computational models including the Interactive Activation model also hold that negative information results in inhibition of a candidate (see below). For instance, if the input word is "wind," the onset "w" is inconsistent with the lexical candidate "find," and therefore results in inhibition of the latter. This inhibition speeds up the process of word recognition, thereby making it more efficient.

> **SUMMARY: PRINTED AND WRITTEN WORD RECOGNITION: PROCESSES**
>
> When encountering a visual word on paper or on screen, the Written and Print Signal Recognizers encode the raw input that they encounter into abstract representations (graphemes) that serve as input to the Word Recognizer. The Word Recognizer then uses the grapheme representations to look up the words in the mental lexicon, the Long Term Memory store in which their meaning and other properties are found. Several word candidates are considered for recognition simultaneously. Successful visual word recognition entails parallel activation of this set of word candidates and a subsequent reduction of the set to the one candidate that corresponds best to the visually presented target word.

6.4 MODELS OF VISUAL WORD RECOGNITION

As in the spoken domain, over the last decades several models have been developed that aim at explaining the intricate process of visual word recognition. Here we introduce and discuss a selection of influential models that differ in how they exactly model what happens in the mind of the reader: the Interactive Activation model, the Spatial Coding model, the Dual Route Cascaded model, and a more recent model called Multilink. For a review of several other models, have a look at Norris (2013) and Perry et al. (2007, 2010).

6.4.1 Interactive Activation model

The Interactive Activation (IA or IAC) model is a localist connectionist network model with symbolic representations for letter features, letters, and words (McClelland & Rumelhart, 1981). The auditory TRACE model we discussed in Chapter 5 was inspired by this model. The IA model assumes that the Signal Recognizer identifies possible letters in the input word by their visual features. The activated letter representations activate the words of which they are part and inhibit words they are not compatible with (e.g., "w" activates "wind," but not "find," and not even "flower," because the "w" is in the wrong position). Letter and word units "collect" activation via their connections to other units. Across matching connections this results in faster processing or facilitation, across non-matching connections in slower processing or interference. We will reserve the term "inhibition" to refer to the internal mechanism of "lateral inhibition" and use "interference" to indicate an external effect on RTs.

The IA model assumes parallel activation of word candidates. At the word level, active words compete: They reduce the activation of other activated words. This is called "lateral inhibition." Although this parameter was considered at the time to reflect a structural aspect of the word recognition system, recent research suggests that it might be context-sensitive (e.g., depending on stimulus list composition in an experiment). Furthermore, each word unit has a "resting level" of activation. This "base level" activation is higher for items that are used more often in general (i.e., they are of a higher frequency) or have been used more recently. If a unit has not been activated for a longer period of time, its activation level decreases (this is called "decay"). During word recognition, there is a bottom-up activation flow from letters to words, but also top-down feedback from words to letters. This results in a sort of "resonance" between letters and the words constituted of them. Due to bottom-up activation, lateral inhibition, decay, and top-down feedback, only one word candidate remains active after a while. This candidate can then be considered as "recognized" when it surpasses an absolute threshold criterion or depending on its activation relative to other active word candidates.

This description of the process is rather abstract. You may better understand it if you run the jIAm model on Walter van Heuven's website online.

Another way to look at the model is the following. Consider the IA model as a system of compatible and incompatible hypotheses about the input word. Compatible hypotheses strengthen each other, while incompatible ones weaken each other. Take, for instance, once more the word "wind." Based on the input letter string, the model may hypothesize that there is a "w" in the first letter position. This hypothesis is compatible with the hypothesis that the word is "wind" (or "wall"), but not that it is "find" (or "fall"). Thus, the letter "w" and the word "wind" are compatible and strengthen one another's activation. In addition, "wind" and "find" are incompatible hypotheses with regards to the first letter, so they suppress one another.

Although there is top-down feedback from the word level to the letter level, no feedback is usually assumed to occur from the letter level to the feature level. As a consequence, the feature level is purely determined by the input signal. This is important, because it ensures that top-down information (from the word level or even higher up) does not distort the incoming representation of the signal. Therefore, no "hallucinations" will arise. This is a

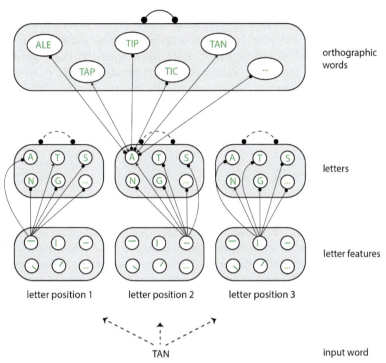

Figure 6.5
Visual illustration of the Interactive Activation model, with separate but connected levels for letter features, letters, and words. In the variant of the model shown here, unidirectional (facilitatory or inhibitory) connections are assumed from all letter features to all letters, and bidirectional connections between letters and words for every letter position. We have depicted only a small subset of letter features, letters, words, and connections, here relevant for the input word "tan." Lateral inhibition between letters in a letter position is indicated by "dashed headphones," because it is not standardly implemented. Lateral inhibition between words is indicated by a "solid headphone," as it is usually assumed to be present. Adapted from McClelland and Rumelhart (1981).

limitation on interactivity in the system, which the Language User Framework also uses to distinguish the Signal Recognizer and the Word Recognizer.

The top-down feedback from the word level to the letter level was considered as a very important characteristic of the IA model when it was built. The reason is that it provides one explanation of the so-called "word superiority effect" (Reicher, 1969; Wheeler, 1970). The word superiority effect refers to the finding that letters are recognized more quickly in words than in random letter sequences. For instance, the "w" is typically recognized more quickly in "wind" than it is in "wndf." The lexical status of the stimulus (word or nonword) thus appears to influence letter recognition. There is also a pseudoword superiority effect: Letters in "legal" (i.e., pronounceable) nonwords ("wund") can be recognized more quickly than letters in series of just consonants ("wndf"). The IA model explains these superiority effects as consequences of the interaction between words and letter units. Activations of the letters "w," "i," "n," and "d" in the input letter string all converge on the word "wind," which then sends activation back to "w." This top-down feedback from the word level facilitates the activation of the letter "w," relative to a situation in which no substantial top-down feedback is available (in the case of "wndf").

When the lexicon that an input word comes from is known, the "probability" or "expectancy value" that certain letters or letter combinations come up in different positions of the item can be assessed. For instance, in Dutch, a letter combination ("bigram") like "wi" in the beginning of the word would be much more likely than the combination "wh." This notion has in recent years led to the formulation of Bayesian models of word retrieval that weigh the different hypotheses in a smart, probabilistic way (Norris, 2006). As we will see in the next chapter on sentence processing, probabilistic models have also been applied at the sentence level, using the context-sensitive chance that a particular word will come up (Frank, 2021).

6.4.1.1 Strengths of the IA model

The IA model, as presented in the beginning of the 1980s, has been very successful, has generated a tremendous amount of research, and is still influential more than four decades after it was developed. It is a computational model that provides detailed explanations for several important phenomena in word recognition. As we have seen, it accounts for effects of word frequency of usage and recency effects (via changes in resting level activation), word superiority and pseudoword superiority effects (via top-down feedback), but also for neighborhood effects (via co-activation of candidates and lateral inhibition) and orthographic priming effects (by presenting the prime for a short time and then the target item, relevant candidates already become active). The model can also explain how different types of pseudoword and nonword are rejected in lexical decision tasks when a task account is formulated that specifies how rejection takes place (Grainger & Jacobs, 1996).

6.4.1.2 Limitations of the IA model

Nevertheless, the IA model also has several intrinsic limitations. An important general omission is that the model considers only orthographic representations, but not phonological, semantic, or morphological representations. For instance, it fails to notice the pronunciation differences in "pint" and "mint," their similarities in "bough" and "cow," and the presence of two morphemes in "baker" ("bake + r") but not in "corner."

A second important omission is that the original model does not account for how readers learn to read, although it provides a very useful framework for understanding how proficient readers process printed words.

A more technical problem of the model is that it assumes so-called "absolute letter position coding." This implies that letters in words are assumed to be in a particular absolute position in the word: One could say that the word "clam" is actually coded as "$c_1l_2a_3m_4$" (Rastle, 2019, p. 49). Consequently, the letter "c" presented in the first position of an input letter string will activate only words starting with that letter, for instance, "clam" and "climb," but not "atomic" or "stack." This model characteristic leads to several limitations to the model. One such restriction is that the model can only recognize four-letter words from a four-letter word lexicon. To apply it to three- or five-letter words, its implementation must be changed. The model considers "arm," "warm," and "swarm" as completely unrelated letter strings, because all letters are in different positions ("a" is in letter position 1 in "arm," but in letter positions 2 and 3 in "warm" and "swarm," respectively). This is a consequence of considering letters as different due to their different absolute positions. A further effect of absolute letter position coding is that words in which two letters are exchanged, like "huose" or "langauge," often are not recognized by the model, while human readers typically have only limited problems here (Gomez et al., 2008).

Box 6.1 The limitations of absolute letter position coding

A clear example of the problem with respect to absolute letter position coding circulated on the internet around 2003. It was called the "Cambridge email" or "jumbled text" and began as follows (see Rawlinson, 1999, for the original idea):

> Aoccdrnig to a rscheearch at Cmabrigde Uinervtisy, it deosn't mttaer in waht oredr the ltteers in a wrod are, the olny iprmoatnt tihng is taht the frist and lsat ltteer be at the rghit pclae.

Readers are remarkably good at understanding this text. Many people find this surprising. However, it could be argued that several words in the sentence ("are," "in," "the") are still ok, because (when onset and offset are correct) a word must consist of at least four letters to be able to change the order of its letters at all. Also note that "important" (originally represented as "iprmoetnt" in the web text, with a spelling error!) could be garbled into "aiomnprtt," which would be a lot more difficult to read than "iprmoatnt"! Moreover, in some "real word" cases, determinining the absolute letter position is critical: How else could we distinguish "bard" from "brad"? Many words are anagrams of this kind. Nevertheless, the example suggests that letter position must be coded in a more relative or at least more flexible way (Grainger & Whitney, 2004).

One possible solution that has been proposed is to code the order of letters in letter pairs called *open bigrams*. For instance, in "work," the "w" is positioned to the left of "o," "r," and "k," whereas the "r" is positioned to the right of "w" and "o," and to the left of "k" (Grainger & van Heuven, 2003). If we now consider the pseudoword "wrok," which has the middle letters from "work" exchanged, many of the bigrams are still there: The "w" is still in front of all other letters, and the "r" is still to the right of the "w" and the left of the "k." Unfortunately, research suggests that this solution cannot be the one used by human readers (Kinoshita & Norris, 2013). It has been suggested that position coding may be "noisy" in the beginning, as readers are trying to discover the letter sequence of the word. The notion of "uncertainty" also plays a role in the most detailed model of word form recognition at hand: the Spatial Coding model (Davis, 2010) developed from the earlier SOLAR model (Davis, 1999).

6.4.2 Spatial Coding model

Like the IA model, the Spatial Coding model is a localist connectionist model that aims to explain the subprocesses involved in printed word recognition (Davis, 2010). It also assumes that there are distinct levels of representation for letter features, letters, and words, that these levels are connected, and that specific features, letters, and words are implemented as nodes in a large network. It proposes that readers need to (i) encode the input stimulus word to determine the *identity* of each letter in a word, and the *order* in which these letters are presented; (ii) look up abstract word representations in their mental lexicon that match the input as good as possible; and then (iii) select the best matching word candidate. The Spatial Coding model suggests that the reader encounters two sources of uncertainty during reading: with respect to a letter's position and its identity.

Letter position uncertainty in the model arises because the reader is not completely sure about the relative position of the letter in the word relative to where their eyes fixate. To clarify, letters that are directly fixated will yield less position uncertainty than letters in the reader's parafoveal view. The further a letter in a word is removed from the reader's fixation, the larger the position uncertainty typically is (Davis et al., 2009). This also means that, by definition, longer words will yield more total position uncertainty than shorter words.

Letter identity uncertainty depends on the degree of perceptual evidence in favor of a particular letter at a certain moment in time. The more certain readers are about the presence of a particular letter, the more they will activate or "excite" that letter. If an input letter is ambiguous to the reader, it will hence be activated less at the letter level than when an input letter is clearly recognizable. The activation of a letter may differ over time, as any perceptual ambiguity may be resolved.

Just as the earlier models, the Spatial Coding model tries to find the best match between the input letter string and the word representations stored in Long Term Memory (the algorithm followed to do this is called "superposition matching"). Here the assumed *relative* position of each letter in the input stimulus is important. Suppose that the reader has coded the input stimulus word "cat" as having a "c" in position 1, an "a" in position 2, and a "t" in position 3. This information matches best with the template "cat" in the reader's mental lexicon that has the same letters in the same positions. The candidate "hat" may also be considered, especially if there is some uncertainty about the identity of the letter that is in position 1 and if we assume "hat" is a relatively frequently used word in everyday life.

Lateral inhibition between competing candidates aids to solve the selection problem: The word candidate that receives most activation from the letter level will suppress the activity of its competitors. But unlike in the IA model, it is the relative rather than absolute position of the letters that influence which words become activated. Hence the input "art" does not immediately exclude the word "part" as a reasonable word candidate, as the *relative* position of the letters a-r-t is the same in both "art" and "part."

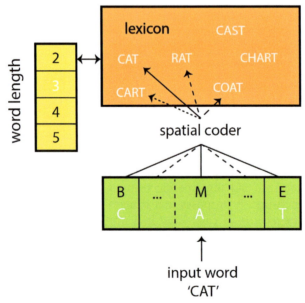

Figure 6.6
Simplified representation of the Spatial Coding model. Only a subset of activated representations and connections is shown. The degree of activation of a word representation depends on the "superposition matching function" that compares the input to the stored representation. Its calculations give more weight to the first and the last letter of the word, and relative letter position is more important than absolute letter position. After Davis (2010).

As can be seen in Figure 6.6, there are some further aspects that differentiate the Spatial Coding model from the IA model. The exterior letters of a word receive some extra importance in the Spatial Coding model through an "initial letter bank" and a "final letter bank." These letter banks explicitly code the first and the last letter of a word, and (further) activate words that match the perceived input in these respects. A "stimulus length field" explicitly codes the assumed word length of the perceived stimulus, such that this information can be used to select a word candidate that matches the input not just in terms of identity, but also with regards to its length.

In sum, the Spatial Coding model differs from the IA model in two important ways: Its coding of the input stimulus is more complex, and it has a different matching function between word candidates and their abstract representations in memory. The Spatial Coding model has been capable of simulating a wide variety of experimental findings, such as masked priming and neighborhood effects in visual word recognition. As such, it is probably the most detailed model available for how readers derive an orthographic lexical representation from a presented input string.

However, we can still pose the same questions as for the IA model: How do we retrieve the meaning of the input word? And what is the role of phonology in reading? Many readers hear an "inner voice" in their head while they are reading. Does this not imply that somehow phonology must come into play during reading at some time? The broader framework of word recognition, including orthography, semantics, and phonology, has been described in the Dual Route Cascaded (DRC) model (Coltheart et al., 2001). We present a slightly adapted variant of this model now.

6.4.3 Dual Route Cascaded model

As can be seen in Figure 6.7, the Dual Route Cascaded model incorporates several important insights with respect to visual word recognition and word naming. Just as in the IA model and the Spatial Coding model, it is assumed that in both alphabetic and non-alphabetic scripts, a direct orthographic route into the mental lexicon is possible. In an alphabetic script, an input letter string activates letters and orthographic word forms that are then found ("addressed") in the lexicon. In the mental lexicon, the word's phonological form can then be retrieved. Via this phonological word form, it can be determined how the word must be articulated (routes 1 and 3 in Figure 6.7). In non-alphabetic scripts, the printed or written word form (e.g., an ideogram) could still directly address a lexical representation stored in Long Term Memory.

However, there is also an indirect way to retrieve the lexical representations that are stored in memory. Letters and letter combinations can activate the phonemes they are usually associated with, which can then be "assembled" into phonological representations (route 2 in Figure 6.7). Via these phonological representations, phonological word forms can be activated and the corresponding words found in memory. Take the word "pen" as an example. The letters "p," "e," and "n" may activate their corresponding phonemes /p/, /ɛ/, and /n/. These can be assembled into the word /pɛn/, which can be retrieved from memory with all its associated information.

This process of "assemblage" is time-consuming. English high-frequency words are therefore more easily retrieved by skilled readers via the direct route, irrespective of whether they are regular or irregular in terms of spelling rules. However, low-frequency words are usually named more quickly when they are regular rather than irregular. When reading a low-frequency irregular word, the direct and indirect pathways may generate conflicting information. Because the decision process takes into account information from both, this conflict takes time to be resolved. Also note that the English grapheme-to-phoneme

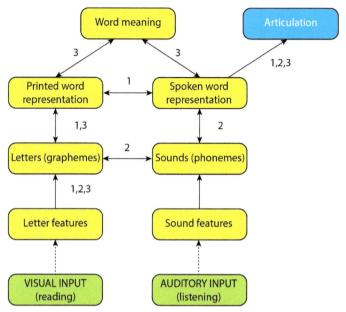

Figure 6.7
The Dual Route Cascaded model. Three main routes (1, 2, 3) allow for articulating a printed or written word. Adapted from Coltheart et al., (2001).

conversion (GPC) process is complex with many-to-many mappings between graphemes and phonemes (cf. the -ough problem mentioned above).

When children are learning to read, and when people are learning a new, second, or third language, their lexical representations in the new language are still of subjective low frequency and take relatively much time to retrieve from memory. As a consequence, they may apply the indirect route more often in word reading or word naming. Suppose, for instance, that a child tries to read the word "pen" for the first time. Although it does not know the word form, it may still recognize and sound out the individual letters. Via assemblage, it can then find out that the word must be pronounced /pɛn/. Because the child has already acquired spoken word recognition several months or years ago, understanding the meaning of this spoken word poses no problem. Similarly, an adult second language learner may try to sound out a word, following the perceived GPC rules for the new language at hand and then recognize its spoken equivalent in their mother tongue.

A prediction following from this line of reasoning is that the relative contribution of direct and indirect routes depends on the writing system (shallow vs. deep orthography) and the orthographic and phonological characteristics of the word in question. If every letter always maps onto the same single phoneme in a language, the use of the indirect route may be less time-consuming than when a language has a deep orthography.

In the word recognition process as modeled by the Dual Route Cascaded model, activation spreads from input level nodes to deeper and deeper into the system. At the same time, there is activation simultaneously in many different nodes of the network. This type of activity is called a *cascaded process*. A cascade is a waterfall: There is water on all its levels, but earlier arriving water has already fallen further than later arriving water.

The Dual Route Cascaded model has been applied since its earliest conception in 1977 to word naming and dyslexia. Children with dyslexia may find two problems hampering their reading process. First, word reading might be slowed because of a problem with the direct route. It has been proposed that the magnocellular system (involving large visual cells) is not functioning properly (Omtzigt et al., 2002). Second (and perhaps more likely), word reading and naming might be slowed down because of a problem with the indirect route. It might be that the phonetic/phonological representations derived from the orthographic word representation are impoverished. It appears that countries differ in the degree of reported dyslexia. This might be due to the shallowness or depth of the writing system used (for instance, there might be less prominent dyslexia in Japan, due to the existence of three writing systems: Processing difficulties might depend on the extent to which the system resorts to the direct or indirect routes).

When we scrutinize Figure 6.7, we note that, next to the so-called indirect and direct routes, there is actually a third route that could be followed from input to articulation: From the printed (orthographic) representation of the word to its spoken (phonological) representation via word meaning (semantics). There is some evidence that this route may play a role in reading, based on naming performance by certain people with aphasia. An Italian patient read the pseudoword "ru" as *uccello* ("bird") and the pseudoword "noste" as *letto* ("bed") (Miceli et al., 1997, p. 42). The first naming error would arise if "ru" were encoded *gru* ("crane"), followed by a semantic substitution to *uccello*. In the second case, "noste" may have been encoded as *notte* ("night"), which was substituted next by *letto*.

Finally, in the integrated framework of the Dual Route Cascaded model as presented here, we can discern aspects of the architecture of both the IA model for visual word recognition (left part of the model) and the TRACE model for auditory word recognition (right part). In this way, the model suggests that visual and auditory word recognition may be linked up and interact. Later in this chapter, we will see that there is evidence that not only orthographic but also phonological representations are commonly activated during reading. We also note the model's distinction between the alphabet and the lexicon, which is basically a differentiation of sublexical and lexical processing units.

6.4.4 Multilink model

The similarities in many of the models that we discussed so far (IA, DRC, Spatial Coding, TRACE) follow from the fact that all these implemented (or computational or computer) models are (or include many characteristics of) connectionist network models that have symbolic units in them (they are called "localist" because of this). Assuming a network organization in the mental lexicon, in which symbolic units (that are easy to understand) become activated and recognized following well-defined mathematical activation functions, has therefore been very profitable for understanding the psychological processes supporting word reading. Especially the Spatial Coding model shows that such a model can handle word recognition in a very "deep" and detailed way. But how "broad" can these models be? Is it possible to extend them to other populations than adult readers knowing only one language? And can these models mimic the human performance in different experimental tasks, including comprehension and production aspects (e.g., lexical decision, word naming, and word translation, as discussed in Chapter 4)?

A recent model that tries to account for the word retrieval process in monolinguals and bilinguals, and in different languages and tasks, is the Multilink model (Dijkstra et al., 2019; check out https://multilink.donders.ru.nl). Figure 6.8 depicts the network architecture of this model, which assumes that words from different languages are stored together in an integrated mental lexicon.

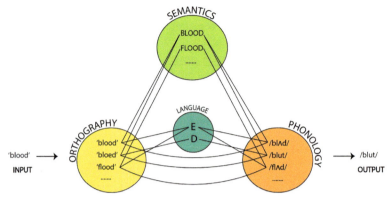

Figure 6.8
Visual depiction of the Multilink model for monolingual and bilingual word retrieval. Note the triangle Semantics – Orthography – Phonology. The figure depicts a situation in which a bilingual mastering Dutch and English translates the English input word "blood" into its Dutch spoken equivalent *bloed* for naming. After Dijkstra et al., (2019).

As before, the question now is which words become activated on the presentation of an input word, and to what extent? Said differently, what is the "similarity metric" that governs the activation of lexical representations in Long Term Memory when a monolingual or bilingual reads? The Multilink model proposes that the similarity between input and stored representations is computed on the basis of *Levenshtein distance*. This is a measure proposed by researchers in computer science to compare letter strings. The Levenshtein distance is the number of operations (deletion, addition, or substitution) that must be performed to transcode one letter string in another. Here are some examples. To change the French word *texte* into English "text," one operation is necessary (removal of the word-final "e"). Changing Dutch *tomaat* into English "tomato" requires removal of one "a" and addition of an "o," so two operations or a Levenshtein distance of 2. To turn the English word "bike" into its Dutch translation *fiets* requires replacing "b" by "f," removing "k," and adding "t" and "s." This amounts to a Levenshtein distance of 4. Note that "bike" consists of four letters and *fiets* of five, so the length difference can also be accounted for by this measure (the measure can be "normalized" to get rid of differences in length more generally). When exchanging two letters is assumed to be one additional operation (rather than removing, adding, or substituting letters), words like "bard" and "brad" are also quite similar (cf. the *Cmabrigde* example above).

A review of empirical studies suggests that (a phonological variant of) Levenshtein distance provides a reasonable approximation of word similarities that English readers take into account. Adelman et al. (2014, p. 1065) show a large data analysis that underlines the importance of Levenshtein distance in orthographic masked priming studies, whereas Yarkoni et al. (2008) consider a Levenshtein-based metric called "orthographic Levenshtein distance 20" or OLD20 (roughly, 20 words of different lengths that are similar to the target) for more general research application.

Presentation of a letter string from one language of a monolingual or bilingual to the Multilink model activates word representations in the mental lexicon to an extent that depends on the Levenshtein distance to the stored representation in question and its word frequency (measures are taken from subtitle databases; see Chapter 4). Just as in the IA model, word representations have a resting level activation that depends on how frequently they are used (and how recent the last encounter was). Orthographic representations that are more similar to the input and/or of a higher frequency, are activated to a larger extent. Activation then spreads from orthographic representations to phonological and semantic representations. A resonation process of waxing and waning activation between positively and negatively connected representations ensues, until one representation (corresponding to the input) transpasses a recognition threshold and is recognized (see Chapter 10 for an example of the model output).

It is assumed that different tasks consider different codes to assess what the response must be. Multilink proposes that a task/decision system, such as the Cognitive Control System formulated for the Language User Framework in Chapter 3, governs the performance of particular tasks. For instance, in a lexical decision task, the task/decision system takes the first orthographic code to surpass the threshold to be the target representation; but in a word naming task, the decision system would scrutinize phonological representations, and in a semantic categorization task, semantic representations would be the focus for decision making.

It is also assumed that the composition of the integrated mental lexicon differs for monolinguals and bilinguals with different backgrounds and languages. Whereas a Spanish monolingual activates just Spanish items that are similar to the input, English–Dutch bilinguals will activate both English and Dutch items. This implies that, encountering an English word like "work," the latter type of reader will activate not only English neighbors like "cork" and "worm," but also Dutch neighbors, e.g., *werk* and *worp*. (Note that "work" and *werk* have approximately the same meaning. Such translation equivalents with form overlap are called "cognates." As we will see in Chapter 10, they are recognized more quickly than non-cognates, probably because they are co-activated and activate one another via their shared meaning.)

The Multilink model has been applied quite successfully to the performance of different participant populations (e.g., monolinguals and bilinguals), for different languages and language combinations (including Dutch, English, Spanish, Portuguese, French, German, and Japanese), and in a number of different tasks (including lexical decision, word naming, word translation, and orthographic and semantic priming tasks). In conjunction with models such as the DRC and the Spatial Coding model, it shows the power (and the limitations) of models of the "localist connectionist" paradigm.

DISCUSSION BOX 6: LANGUAGE IS BEST DESCRIBED BY SYMBOLS VS. SUBSYMBOLS VS. NO SYMBOLS

In this book, we use the word "symbol" to refer to words and other linguistic units (letters, phonemes, morphemes, sentences, meanings) that directly represent parts of speech or concepts for persons, places, objects, and actions. As has been explained, the localist connectionist approach works with symbols (Dupre, 2022). A different connectionist approach is the parallel distributed processing (PDP) approach. In this *subsymbolic* approach, linguistic representations are neither symbols nor anatomic entities of a neurobiological nature. Instead, they represent linguistic notions in terms of long strings of numbers. Such "vectors" consist of values on a number of abstract dimensions. In a sense, this allows representations of smaller grain sizes, but with a functional interpretation that is not directly obvious. In each approach, symbols and subsymbols can be combined to construct more complex compositional representations. The relation of the two types of approach to brain networks is not fully understood. One could even argue that in terms of neurobiological activity, the notion of "symbol" is not useful because it may not refer or relate to specific physical properties of the neural hardware.

Can you come up with arguments in favor of using symbols, subsymbols, or no symbols in theories about how language is represented and its use is subserved by the brain (also see Discussion Box 5)?

6.4.5 Parallel distributed processing models

So far in this chapter, we have discussed the characteristics and performance of localist-connectionist processing models. However, there is another class of connectionist models, called *Parallel Distributed Processing* or PDP models (e.g., Seidenberg & McClelland, 1989). In such models, theoretical concepts are not associated with localist symbolic representations, but with patterns of activation over several nodes in the network simultaneously. Thus, representations are more vector-like and *subsymbolic.* Furthermore, these models are *learning models.* They learn to generalize and categorize the input signals they receive by adapting the weights on connections between units as a function of the (statistical) structure of the environment. A variety of learning rules (e.g, Hebbian, delta, backpropagation, LEABRA) have been implemented that differ in their actual (psychological and neurobiological) plausibility. When it is put to the test, the network will generate the correct word candidate or an alternative that is similar. Many PDP models have feedforward connections only, although they typically learn via backpropagation.

PDP models of visual word recognition have often focused on simulating the quasi-regular system of grapheme-to-phoneme mappings (cf. deep vs. shallow orthography). We will discuss only one of these models here. In Seidenberg and McClelland's (1989) model for word naming, three types of codes (orthographic, semantic, and phonological) are computed as patterns of activation distributed over a number of primitive representational units (see Figure 6.9). Only orthographic (O) and phonological (P) units were initially implemented, indirectly connected via a layer of hidden units, which enhance the processing capabilities of the network. Before being presented to the model, an item is decomposed into triples of symbols. For example, the letter string "make" is orthographically represented by the character triples (or "Wickelgraphs") "_ma," "mak," "ake," and "ke_." Similarly, phonologically it can be represented by the phoneme triples (or "Wickelphones") /_mA/, /mAk/, /Ak_/ (where A is pronounced as in "may"). This coding scheme conserves local order information. Next, each triple (input orthography or output phonology) is encoded as a distributed activation pattern over a whole set of representational units. Each triple simultaneously activates several units, and each O- or P-unit becomes active during the presentation of many different triples. On average, a word activates 81 of the 400 O-units, and 54 of the 460 P-units.

The model was trained using the backpropagation learning procedure to generate the phonology of monosyllabic words and to regenerate their orthography. The probability that a particular word was presented

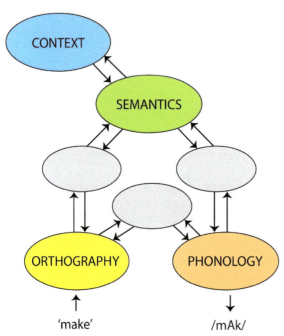

Figure 6.9
Visual depiction of a parallel distributed processing model. Grey boxes represent hidden layers. Word meaning ("semantics") and context are depicted, but originally not computationally implemented. After Seidenberg and McClelland, (1989).

depended on word frequency. After extensive training, 97.3% of the words were correctly pronounced by the model. Simulations with the model reproduced diverse effects from over 20 empirical studies on normal reading and word naming.

The PDP model has been criticized on a number of points. In contrast to human participants, it poorly pronounces new words or orthographically legal nonwords (untrained letter strings, also called "pseudowords"). The solution here might be to prolong training, since all pseudoword effects are derived from (the word bodies of) similar words, which makes them especially sensitive to training duration. With respect to lexical decision, the model incorrectly tends to reject rare words as non-existent words. It also cannot reproduce the "pseudohomophone effect," which refers to the finding that pseudowords that are pronounced like words (e.g., "brane" or "meen") take longer to reject than other pronounceable pseudowords in visual lexical decision. Furthermore, unlike human readers, it cannot make "phonological decisions," i.e., indicate whether a letter string sounds like a word, e.g., "brane." Another issue is that the model uses a phonological error score (i.e., the difference observed between the phonological representation produced by the model and the correct lexical representation) as a measure for reaction times. However, confounding accuracy and RT is undesirable, as these may reflect different aspects of performance. Some of these problems were later addressed by Plaut and colleagues (e.g., Plaut, 1997, 1999; Plaut et al., 1996; also see Harm & Seidenberg, 2004).

6.4.6 Recent computational developments

In recent years, the development of PDP models has resulted in an approach that is called "deep learning." In this approach, which has links to AI ("machine learning") and cognitive neuroscience ("neural networks"), multiple layers of nodes are trained to learn the association of a particular input to a particular output. Application of non-linear learning algorithms (as mentioned above) allows networks to discover complex and abstract relationships in the presented data. The approach has, for example, been applied to speech perception, face recognition, and other complex situations. Related research on visual word recognition is also in progress (see Di Bono & Zorzi, 2013; Cevoli et al., 2022, for word reading in sentence context; and Carreiras et al., 2014, for a general review).

One well-known application of deep learning outside the domain of visual word recognition is Alpha-Go. This is a "deep reinforcement learning AI model" that was able to beat one of the best players of the game Go in the world. In the game, Alpha-Go made some moves that looked like mistakes, but were later found to be unique and insightful. One way to look at this program would be to consider it as representing a complex way of "thinking" by the Conceptual System, which we will address in Chapter 8.

SUMMARY: MODELS OF VISUAL WORD RECOGNITION

Interactive Activation (IA) model (McClelland & Rumelhart, 1981, 1989; Rumelhart & McClelland, 1982):
The IA model assumes that, on the basis of the printed word form, a set of word neighbors is activated. The activation feeds forward and largely backward over a network of orthographic features, linked to letters, which themselves are linked to words (interactive activation). Next, word candidates become engaged in a competition process

with other words, making use of lateral inhibition. By top-down feedback, word context affects letter recognition. The IA model is a localist (symbolic) connectionist model.

Spatial Coding model (Davis, 2010):
In the Spatial Coding model, successful visual word recognition requires encoding, lexical matching, and lexical selection stages. Letter position uncertainty and letter identity uncertainty influence the activation of words. The first and last letter of a word stimulus and its length are explicitly coded. For the word as a whole, there is a form of relative, rather than absolute, position coding. Implementing these aspects leads to an improvement over the IA model.

Dual Route Cascaded model (Coltheart et al., 1977, 1993, 2001):
Going beyond the orthographic representations specified in the IA and Spatial Coding models, this model assumes there is a phonological contribution to reading that can be likened to TRACE (Chapter 5). Orthographic information input follows two important routes to articulation in word naming: a direct (addressed) route into the mental lexicon, and an indirect (assembled) route via grapheme-to-phoneme conversion rules. A third route via semantics can be assumed on the basis of patient data.

Multilink model (Dijkstra et al., 2019):
This model shows that the language behavior of different populations of monolinguals and bilinguals, for different languages and stimulus materials, and in different tasks can be successfully simulated both qualitatively and quantitatively by a relatively simple localist connectionist model. The model "circumvents" the position coding problem by mapping an input letter string directly on word representations, activating words depending on the similarity to the input in terms of Levenshtein distance.

Parallel distributed processing models:
These learning models have subsymbolic units and a hidden layer that connects input to output. They have been applied to language but also to other cognitive activities, and are nowadays integrated in many technological applications (e.g., airplane control). Often, these models focus on learning and little on "mature" processing; in contrast, the symbolically oriented Interactive Activation models focus on processing and are typically weak with respect to learning.

Deep learning models:
In recent years, models with more layers have been explored. One current disadvantage of such models is that cognitive constraints on language processing are often not implemented. This is not a problem for practical AI applications, but is undesirable when one's aim is to advance our understanding of the psychology of language.

6.5 PRINTED AND WRITTEN WORD RECOGNITION: EMPIRICAL STUDIES

The domain of printed word recognition is probably the best studied subdiscipline of the psychology of language. Two important questions that have been investigated time and again are how rapidly language users can read words, and how quickly they activate phonology during reading. These questions have been addressed using a variety of time-sensitive research techniques such as lexical decision, often in combination with EEG recordings and a masked priming procedure. In this section, we will discuss three representative example studies using these techniques.

6.5.1 Speed of printed word recognition

How quickly do we recognize words and how does this depend on their constituent properties: letters, length, frequency, etc.? An EEG study investigating the speed of word reading and recognition was done by Hauk and colleagues (2006). Participants performed a visual lexical decision task in which their electrophysiological brain activity was recorded using EEG (see Chapter 4 for more information about this method). A principal component analysis of the EEG in different conditions revealed four orthogonal components reflecting separable processes in visual word recognition: processes related to word length, letter n-gram frequency, lexical frequency, and semantic coherence of a word's morphological family. Interestingly, effects of these different variables arose at various moments in time. Early, around 90 ms after a stimulus appeared on the screen, word length and letter n-gram frequency effects started to become significant, followed by a beginning effect of lexical frequency at 110 ms. Letter n-gram frequency refers to the frequency with which certain letter combinations (n-grams, such as pairs or triplets of letters) occur in words; it is a measure of orthographic structure. Differences between words and pseudowords (an effect of lexicality or lexical status) arose at 160 ms. After 200 ms, all variables exhibited simultaneous EEG correlates. Using sophisticated statistical techniques, the authors tried to determine where the sources generating these effects were located in the brain. Source estimates pointed at parieto-temporo-occipital generators for length, letter n-gram frequency, and word frequency effects. Related to semantic coherence, there was widespread activation with foci in the left anterior temporal lobe and inferior frontal cortex. The authors concluded that the surface form of a word and its meaning are first accessed at different times in different brain systems; later, they are processed simultaneously. This pattern of results is in support of interactive processing models with different stages (see Carreiras et al., 2014).

Grainger and Holcomb (2009) present a functional architecture of the Word Recognizer that extends the Dual Route Cascaded framework that we discussed earlier. Their theoretical framework, called the Bimodal Interactive Activation Model (BIAM), is then applied to ERP studies involving masked repetition priming to link markers in the EEG signal to component processes in visual word recognition. Figure 6.10 shows BIAM in relation to an event-related potential time locked to a word appearing on a screen in front of the reader. Following a prime word, the presentation of a visual target word first leads to a derivation of its visual features. A target word that is a (full or partial) repetition of a directly preceding prime leads to a different ERP response at 150 ms than one preceded by an unrelated prime. This N/P150 effect is sensitive to the overlap between prime and target: It is greater when primes and targets have complete overlap rather than intermediate overlap. Thus, the effect appears to reflect the mapping of visual features onto (groups of) abstract letter representations. Next, an N250 effect can be obtained. According to the authors, this effect reflects a mapping of the orthographic information onto whole-word representations, either directly or via phonology. The orthographic representations are assumed to be more concrete, retinotopic (R) initially and more abstract, location-invariant, and word-centered (W) later on. Still later effects have been observed on the amplitude of the P325 component, possibly reflecting processing in the orthographic system itself, and two subcomponents of the N400 effect that may reflect interactions with semantics (N400w) and concept-to-concept processing (N400c).

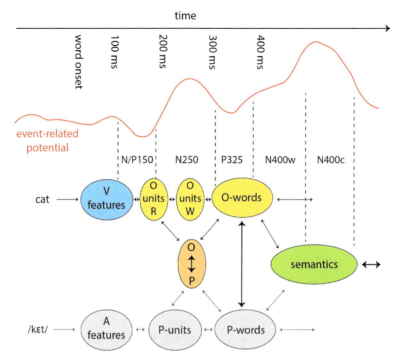

Figure 6.10
Different stages of word recognition (at the feature, orthographic, and semantic level) linked to an event-related potential, time locked to word onset in the context of the Bimodal Interactive Activation Model. Note that also the activation of phonology during reading is depicted, making the model *bimodal*. After Grainger and Holcomb (2009).

While orthographic processing proceeds, there is also a cross-modal activation of phonology and semantics. Grainger and Holcomb (2009, p. 152) propose that a rapid constraint of word identity is possible by the application of a coarse orthographic code, while a more fine-grained orthographic code is used to activate phonological representations. Thus, two routes are presumed that together optimize visual word recognition by focusing more on the word as a visual object or as a linguistic stimulus (cf. the direct and indirect routes in the DRC model). Furthermore, it is proposed that effects of semantic transparency arise later in the time window of the N250, preceded by effects of morphological structure in its early phase. For instance, a prime like "corner" could initially be parsed into the morphological components "corn" and "-er," but this option is then excluded because the meanings of "corn" and "corner" are semantically incompatible. Early semantic effects can be accounted for by assuming cascaded processing: Even in the stage of early sublexical word form processing, semantics might already become activated in parallel. In the next section, we consider the phonological effect in printed word recognition in more detail.

6.5.2 Activation of phonology in word reading

According to the Dual Route Cascade model and BIAM discussed earlier, phonological information about a word can become available on the basis of information about the letters in the word or the word as a whole. But how long does it take before these orthographic representations have activated their phonological counterparts? This important issue has been investigated using the masked priming technique combined with lexical decision (Ferrand & Grainger, 1994; Grainger et al., 2006).

Ferrand and Grainger (1994) presented French participants with letter strings that were either existing French words or pseudowords. The word targets (presented in capitals) were preceded by pseudoword primes (in lower case) that were orthographically and phonologically related ("mert – MERE"), mainly phonologically related ("mair – MERE"), or unrelated ("toul – MERE"). Participants performed a lexical decision task on the targets. The rationale behind the experiment was that during orthographic processing, the spelling similarity between prime and target should be the most effective, whereas during phonological processing the sound similarity between the words would provide an influence. It was found that for short prime durations (14 and 29 ms), the orthographic-phonological and phonological conditions resulted in a similar priming effect. However, when primes were presented for 43 ms or more, a larger effect arose in the phonologically related condition. On the basis of several studies, including this one, Grainger and colleagues conclude that phonological effects can arise less than 50 ms after a purely orthographic stage of processing (Grainger & Holcomb, 2009).

Grainger and colleagues (2006), making EEG recordings, found that orthographic and phonological priming modulated the N250 and N400 components in the EEG waves. Here it was observed that the orthographic effect indeed surfaced about 50 ms earlier than the phonological effect.

These results suggest that the conversion of an orthographic representation for words into a phonological one (going from the left of the Dual Route Cascaded model to the right) is very rapid, resulting in the activation of phonology in many reading studies (Rastle & Brysbaert, 2006). Different studies suggest that the conversion of orthography into word meaning takes a similarly short amount of time (Hoversten et al., 2015).

6.5.3 Activation of orthography during listening

Note that the interactivity between orthographic and phonological codes in the Dual Route Cascaded model leads us to expect not only that phonology is activated during reading words, but also that orthography is activated during listening to words. There are indeed empirical studies showing this. One of them was done by Dijkstra and colleagues (1995) and concerned different sound-to-letter mappings in Dutch. In primary Dutch

TABLE 6.1 Reaction times and error rates (between brackets) in the phoneme monitoring study by Dijkstra et al. (1995). In Dutch, the sound /k/ is represented by the letter "k" (primary spelling) or by the letter "c" (secondary spelling). The spelling of pseudowords is, of course, not specified. The abbreviation "UP" refers to "Uniqueness Point", while "NWP" refers to "nonword point"

Position	Spelling		
	Primary	Secondary	Pseudoword
Before UP/NWP	620 (2.0)	641 (3.4)	675 (4.3)
After UP/NWP	359 (2.4)	415 (5.8)	468 (6.5)

spelling, the sound /k/ is represented by the letter "k"; in secondary spelling, it can actually also be represented by the letter "c": When preceding the vowels "a," "o," and "u," the letter "c" is typically pronounced as a /k/. Dijkstra et al. included Dutch spoken words with a primary spelling (such as "kabouter" or "paprika"), words with a secondary spelling (such as "cabaret" and "replica"), and pseudowords (such as "kadoupel" and "taplika") in a phoneme monitoring experiment like that by Frauenfelder et al. (1990; see Chapter 5 on spoken word recognition). Dutch participants in this experiment were slower to detect the /k/ sound in "replica" than in "paprika", even though the /k/ in both words is located after the words' UP. This can be seen in Table 6.1. This table also indicates that the response to pseudowords depended on the moment in time the item could no longer become an existing word; in other words, when the item's cohort no longer contained any candidates. This point is called the "nonword point" (NWP). These differences can only be explained if we assume orthographic information becomes activated when people listen to words.

> **SUMMARY: PRINTED AND WRITTEN WORD RECOGNITION: EMPIRICAL STUDIES**
>
> Thousands of empirical studies have been carried out to test and further specify details of models of visual word recognition. Often, a lexical decision paradigm is used in combination with masked priming and/or EEG recordings. Effects related to decoding the input stimulus (concerning word length or letter frequency) typically precede effects at the word level (lexical frequency) and activation of a word's meaning. During reading, orthographic representations quickly activate their phonological counterparts. Orthographic information also seems to become activated while people listen to words.

6.6 VISUAL WORD RECOGNITION: THE ROLE OF CONTEXT

According to the Language User Framework, the Word Recognizer and Sentence Processor interact. In the previous chapter, we saw that sentence context can speed up spoken word recognition in the cross-modal "captain" / "capital" study by Zwitserlood (1989). The cross-modal priming technique can also be used to investigate how quickly sentence context can speed up word reading. We will discuss two studies investigating this issue.

6.6.1 Cross-modal priming with lexical decision

Can readers use context information to help the identification of the correct word meaning of ambiguous words? Swinney (1979) performed a cross-modal priming study similar to that by Zwitserlood (1989) discussed in the previous chapter, but focused on the effects of spoken sentence context on the resolution of lexical ambiguity. Participants heard spoken sentences incorporating ambiguous words such as "bug," which can refer to an insect or a spying device (and to a computer error, but that meaning was not so relevant in this study in the late 1970s). During reading, they naturally determined the correct meaning (insect or spy) in a particular sentence context for a correct interpretation.

Box 6.2 Terms for ambiguous items

A word like "bug," which is written the same as a word with another meaning, is called a "homograph"; two words that sound the same are called "homophones." The general term is "homonym." Examples are "wind" (as a noun or as a verb with a different pronunciation, homographs) and "kernel" – "colonel" (homophones). When the meanings of a homograph are related, this is called "polysemy." In a dictionary, such words would be in the same entry. For instance, the word "dish" could refer to a particular type of meal (a dish of fish) or a plate (wash the dishes).

The relatedness of meanings can have a historical origin. The verb "to dust" could be taken as an extreme example of polysemy, where "to dust the chair" is related but actually opposite in meaning to "to dust the cake with sugar." Words with different word forms but the same or very similar meanings within a language are called "synonyms." Examples are pairs: "begin" – "start"; "awful" – "terrible". Words with opposite meanings are called antonyms. Examples may also be pairs: "merry" – "sad"; "heaven" – "hell". Speech errors like "drink an egg" instead of "eat an egg" suggest that one semantic feature is "out of line," resulting in production of the antonym rather than of the correct word (see Chapter 9).

Research has shown that different meanings of intralingual (within-language) homographs are co-activated during reading (Kawamoto, 1993; Kawamoto & Zemblidge, 1992). This implies that the reader must disambiguate the items using context information (or just pick the most frequent meaning when a word is presented in isolation). Interestingly, "interlingual (between-language) homographs," e.g., "coin" in English and French (meaning CORNER) are also co-activated in bilingual word reading (Lemhöfer & Dijkstra, 2004; see Chapter 10).

Either directly after an ambiguous word (e.g., "bugs") or three syllables later, a letter string was presented on a computer screen and participants had to decide as quickly and accurately as possible whether this letter string was an existing word or not (lexical decision). The study's famous example sentence begins as follows: "Rumour had it that, for years, the government building had been plagued with problems. The man was not surprised when he found several …." At this point, there were two possible continuations of the sentence. In one condition, the sentence continued with "spiders, roaches, and other bugs in the corner of his room." In the other condition, the sentence continued with "bugs in the corner of his room." In both conditions, a letter string appeared while the participants had just heard the word "bugs" or in the middle of the word "corner."

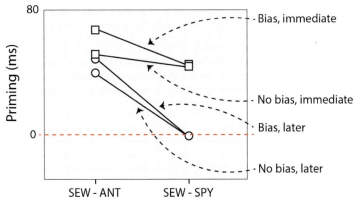

Figure 6.11
In the study by Swinney (1979), participants made lexical decisions to words and nonwords presented on a monitor while listening to sentences. Visually presented letter strings appeared directly at the offset of an auditory target word such as "bugs" (here called *immediate*) or three syllables later (*later*). The relation between an ambiguous target word (such as "bugs") and the visually presented word could be biased by the sentence context (*bias*) or not (*no bias*). In the example, the sentence context would bias the "insect-related" meaning of "bugs" versus the "spying device-related" meaning.

The letter string could be related to one meaning of the ambiguous word "bugs" or the other: The word "ant" is related to the insect meaning of "bug," and "spy" is related to its spying device meaning. In a control condition, there was an unrelated target letter string ("sew").

Presentation of the target word directly after "bugs" resulted in a faster response to both "ant" and "spy" than to "sew." This priming effect occurred in both contexts, so even when the context was biased and mentioned several kinds of insect. Apparently, initially both meanings of the ambiguous word are activated even in a biasing context. However, when the visual target appeared three spoken syllables later, only "ant" showed a facilitation effect relative to the control condition "sew." This suggests that context kicks in after some signal-driven processing has occurred. Thus, at the time the word "corner" is being presented, the context must have suppressed the spy-related meaning of "bug" (see Figure 6.11).

6.6.2 Predicting words in sentence context

In recent years, researchers have become intrigued by the possibility that in certain circumstances, readers and listeners *predict* upcoming words. Lee and colleagues (2012) tested the hypothesis that sentence comprehension depends on continuous prediction of upcoming words. In an EEG study, these researchers considered the effects of word frequency and contextual predictability on Chinese sentence reading. Sentences were presented word by word, using a technique called "rapid serial visual presentation" (RSVP; see Chapter 4). Participants read the sentences for comprehension, in order to be able to answer questions about them later. An example of a sentence (translated into English) is: "Before the clock was invented, ancient Westerners used sandglasses for timing" in which the target word was "sandglasses." The contextual predictability of a target word was measured as the CLOZE-probability of a target word in the sentence (i.e., the probability that the target word was given by a large set of naïve participants as a possible continuation after the earlier words). The word "sandglasses" is an example of a low-frequency word with a low contextual predictability. A number of EEG markers was investigated: N1, reflecting effects of early visual processing; P200, arguably reflecting perceptual decoding; and N400, reflecting lexical-semantic aspects (see Chapter 4 for a description of the EEG technique).

It was observed that low predictable words elicited a more negative anterior N1 component amplitude than high predictable words, but this was only the case for high-frequency words. Low predictable words also elicited less positive P200 amplitude than high predictable words. Finally, low predictable words yielded more enhanced N400 amplitude than high predictable words. This result pattern is taken to suggest that context can facilitate the processing of visual features and orthographic information already early in word recognition; semantic integration follows somewhat later. We will come back to this notion of prediction in the next chapter.

SUMMARY: VISUAL WORD RECOGNITION: THE ROLE OF CONTEXT

As one might expect, the preceding sentence context may aid in zoning in on the meaning of a word intended by the writer of a text, particularly when the visual word form (e.g., "bug") has several meanings. Recent research suggests that readers may predict and preactivate upcoming words while reading to facilitate the reading process.

6.7 WHAT IS NEXT?

In this and the previous chapter, we have focused largely on words in isolation, either in the auditory (Chapter 5) or visual (Chapter 6) modality. When focusing on words in isolation, the larger sentence in which these are typically embedded can be considered its surrounding linguistic context. In the next chapter, we will broaden our horizon by focusing on the processing of sentences, rather than individual words, from the start. How do readers and listeners combine individual words when they are presented with a sentence? We will see that to understand a sentence, readers and listeners have to map grammatical roles onto thematic roles in light of their mental model of the physical and/or psychological situation at hand. When the sentence becomes our focus of attention, the overarching text or discourse in which sentences typically feature can be considered their larger linguistic context.

6.8 WHAT HAVE WE LEARNED?

In this chapter, we have seen that visual word recognition can be characterized in terms of mechanisms that are analogous to those in spoken word recognition.

Multiple activation. When reading, many words that are similar to the input letter string become temporarily activated. Models and empirical studies suggest that the word recognition system considers all of these in parallel until incorrect ones are excluded on the basis of mismatching information or lexical competition.

Lexical embedding. Overlapping words that are shorter or longer than the input word may be temporarily activated. For instance, "vice" may lead to the activation of "ice" and "voice." The similarity of these items can be captured by considering the number of operations needed to transform one into the other (e.g., using the Levenshtein distance).

Lexical competition. Word candidates compete for recognition. Studies show that the lexical competition process depends on the number, distribution, and frequency of similar word candidates. In particular, the number and frequency of neighbors, words that differ at only one letter position from a target word, have been found to affect response times in lexical decision and naming.

Degree of overlap. The extent to which words in the mental lexicon overlap with or are similar to the input letter string is therefore an important factor that affects the degree to which words in the mental lexicon are co-activated.

Context effects. As in the auditory modality, words in context are recognized more quickly than in isolation. Compatible context is accompanied by faster recognition than incompatible context, which may induce slower processing than neutral context.

QUESTIONS FOR CHAPTER 6

1. This chapter has been largely concerned with the recognition of printed words. In what respects would the representation and processing of printed words, written words, and spoken words be similar or different?
2. Imagine a situation in which all spoken languages start using the International Phonetic Alphabet as their script. What would be the benefit of such a situation? Can you also think of any difficulties or drawbacks of such a development?
3. Consider the following sentences: "The none tolled hymn shea had scene a pear of bear feat on the stares." "Seaing soa mutsh greaf cawsed payne inne meye harde." How

can you still understand what each sentence means? Refer to the routes in the Dual Route Cascaded model in your explanation.
4. In English, a letter often represents different phonemes. Give some examples of this. Is this also the case in your mother tongue or in other languages you know? Sometimes, a phoneme can be represented by different letters or letter combinations. Can you find examples of this? In what respect do English and French differ with respect to the mappings of letters to sounds vs. sounds to letters?
5. Can you come up with a correction of the following: "If I reprehend anything in this world, it is the use of my oracular tongue, and a nice derangement of epitaphs!"? This is an utterance of the character Mrs. Malaprop in Sheridan's play *The Rivals* from 1775 [taken from Taylor, 1990, p. 104]. What linguistic discipline must be called for help in repairing the utterance?
6. What is the longest morphologically complex word you can find in the language(s) you speak? Can you come up with English examples?
7. When you turn the garbled sentence in Box 6.1 into a correct sentence, you will notice that it actually contains not one but two errors relative to the original! What other error, not mentioned in the text, do you notice? How could redundancy affect reading?
8. Do Mandarin Chinese characters correspond to words, morphemes, or other units? Motivate your choice.
9. Deaf-blind people may learn to communicate via a system of fingerspelling. Helen Keller, who lost her sight and hearing at an age of 19 months, found out that spelled letters can convey meaning in the following way. While she was experiencing spouting water from a pump, she realized in a flash what her tutor Miss Sullivan intended by making specific touch patterns on her hand: "I knew then that 'w-a-t-e-r' meant the cool something that was flowing over my hand. That living word awakened my soul, gave it light, hope, joy, set it free!" [Taylor, 1990, p. 146]. What other artificial systems, apart from writing and print, have been developed to capture and convey linguistic information?
10. Woody Allen supposedly once said: "I followed a speed-reading course and read *War and Peace* in five minutes. It's about Russia." What are your arguments in favor and against the supposed effectivity of speed reading? Consider the time it takes to recode various linguistic representations and engage in memory storage and retrieval.

Chapter 7

Sentence processing

7.1 SENTENCE PROCESSING: THE ESSENCE

Consider the following opening line of the novel *The Luck of the Bodkins* by P. G. Wodehouse (1935), which was considered one of the ten best first lines in fiction by *The Guardian* in 2012:

> Into the face of the young man who sat on the terrace of the Hotel Magnifique at Cannes there had crept a look of furtive shame, the shifty, hangdog look which announces that an Englishman is about to talk French.

It is obvious that it takes time to read, hear, speak, or write any sentence, including this one. Language processing in all modalities proceeds *sequentially* and *incrementally*: word by word, or, in many languages, "from left to right." It is a consequence of the fact that, while our world is 3D and our thoughts are multidimensional, language makes to a large extent use of 1D channels. At any given moment, we can encode or decode only a limited amount of verbal and non-verbal information. Even when we have a lot to talk about, its expression must go through a sort of bottleneck due to the nature of our sensory organs (ears, eyes, speech apparatus). In other words, the challenge in terms of the Language User Framework is how addressees (e.g., listeners or readers) decode the 1D linguistic utterances in which senders (e.g., speakers or writers) have encoded their messages, as derived from their rich and dynamic multidimensional mental models. In the case of spoken dialogs and conversations, non-verbal context aspects may be called on to further support utterance understanding.

Because information comes in over time, the message will initially be unfinished or ambiguous. In fact, information may even stay incomplete until the end of the utterance. In the example above, it remains unclear for some time why exactly "a look of furtive shame" crept into the face of the young man who is verbally depicted. Furthermore, only later in the novel will we find out who this young man exactly is. Here also the importance of quickly encoding encountered information in memory becomes clear (Christiansen & Chater, 2016).

Words in a sentence may intuitively be conceived of as beads on a string. A closer look at what happens when we process a sentence suggests, however, that processing is not *just* sequential, and richer in information than might be expected. This is because different types of information can to some extent be conveyed in parallel. For instance, on the presentation of the word "Englishman," we can find out over time that it consists of particular letters/sounds, has a particular pronunciation, is a noun, and has a particular meaning,

DOI: 10.4324/9781003326274-7

depending on world knowledge, actual situation, and possibly sentence or discourse context. Importantly, we might also assume that the sentence has standard English word order, making it unlikely that the very last word of the sentence would be its syntactic subject. In addition, in the spoken domain words are often accompanied by informative hand gestures, facial expressions, and other bodily signals. Thus, sentence processing involves a more or less simultaneous consultation of different information sources:

- Lexico-morphological information about word form, syntactic category, and word meaning;
- Syntactic information about sentence structure;
- Semantic/conceptual and pragmatic information about the sentence;
- World knowledge (conceptual);
- Context knowledge (conceptual, perceptual).

Note that, although related, these information sources can to some extent be disentangled. A sentence such as "Colorless green ideas sleep furiously" is syntactically correct, but semantically non-sense (Chomsky, 1957). There must be a syntactic parser that is able to derive the correct syntactic structure even in spite of the semantic problems. In contrast, a sentence such as "Storms trees falls bikes dead" is syntactically incorrect, but it might still be assigned a sensible meaning. Thus, there must be a processor that combines word meanings into a larger whole. In the end, an addressee is typically interested in decoding the meaning a speaker or writer wishes to convey, and not so much in which syntactic form that meaning is presented.

Figure 7.1 further specifies the Sentence Processor that is part of the comprehension side of the Language User Framework. As can be seen in the figure, it assumes that the Sentence Processor takes the form and meaning of individual words as its input, to be able for the listener or reader to combine these into larger syntactic and semantic structures for sentence and text/discourse levels.

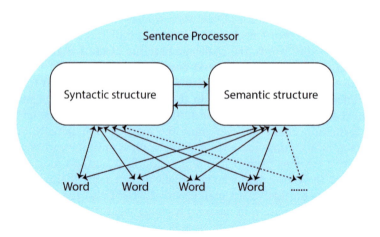

Figure 7.1
The Sentence Processor plays a central role in language comprehension, as it receives incremental input from the Word Recognizer and combines different words into syntactic and semantic structures. Subsequently presented words become linked parts of a syntactic structure; and subsequent word meanings form larger integrated meaning structures. Importantly, the syntactic and semantic structures underlying a sentence are developed in interaction.

As *lexical representations* do, so the *syntactic structure* of utterances (sentences) also unfolds over time. Word order in a sentence is not random, but reflects a syntactic organization that codetermines sentence meaning. Similarly, the *semantic components* of the sentences do not appear in a random order either, because the different concepts expressed by words and larger units appear in a systematic sequence, depending on, for instance, their thematic role, salience, and status as given or new information. Thematic or semantic roles in a sentence indicate, for instance, what an agent (or actor) did to a recipient or object with a particular kind of instrument. Salience refers to the importance or novelty given to particular information (e.g., stressing the agent rather than the recipient). Given information is old information that has been mentioned before in a text or discourse; it is sometimes referred to as the "theme" of a sentence. New information, in contrast, has not been mentioned before. More generally, the way information is packaged in a sentence (e.g., as an active or a passive sentence) is called its "information structure" (Féry & Ishihara, 2016).

To thoroughly understand sentence processing, we must know how different types of information are processed more or less in parallel and integrated over time. Said differently, how is structural information, available in a piecemeal fashion by words and sentences, mapped onto meaning structures (also called *event structures*)?

In Chapters 5 and 6 on auditory and visual word recognition, we described how language users process orthographic and phonological word forms in the mental lexicon to arrive at the words' meanings. In the present chapter, we consider how sentences with different structures give rise to their meaning representations. In Chapter 8, we will then discuss the associated word, sentence, and text meanings in more detail.

The structure of this chapter resembles the structure of the previous chapters. We will first describe the mental representations and processes involved in the processing of sentences. Next, we will discuss influential models of sentence processing, followed by empirical studies that support some of these models. Finally, we will look at how the broader (discourse) context influences the processing of individual sentences.

SUMMARY: SENTENCE PROCESSING: THE ESSENCE

The goal of processing a sentence is typically to grasp its meaning. The addressee (e.g., listener or reader) of a sentence can make use of various sources of information to derive the meaning intended by the speaker or writer: various types of information conveyed by the sentence itself, as well as contextual and world knowledge. The syntactic structure of a sentence is not random and provides clues to sentence meaning. For instance, the person performing an action (the agent) is often the syntactic subject in the sentence and the action in question is expressed by the accompanying verb.

7.2 SENTENCE PROCESSING: REPRESENTATIONS

Linguists have been studying the underlying syntactic structures of sentences for a long time. For each language they had access to, they have tried to specify a *grammar*, which is a set of internalized rules that govern the composition of sentences and sentence parts such as phrases and clauses. Even today, some linguists spend part of their working life traveling to distant language communities to learn a local language and describe its grammatical properties. Often, local language users are observed in natural situations, and informants are interviewed about what they find acceptable or inacceptable sentences ("intuitive judgments"). More recently, word functions, local constraints, and incrementality have become more important.

For our purposes, so-called *surface structures* are most important. The surface structure of a sentence relates the words of the sentence in terms of syntactic categories: word categories and phrasal categories. An example is given in Figure 7.2. In this figure, in terms of word categories, "the" and "a" are determiners (Det), "very" is an adverb (Adv), "old" is an adjective (Adj), "witch" and "cat" are nouns (N), and "sees" is a verb (V). In terms of phrasal categories, "the very old witch" and "a cat" are noun phrases (NP), "sees a cat" is a verb phrase (VP), and "very old" is an adjective phrase (AP). By establishing this structure, we have *parsed* the sentence.

In addition to establishing the syntactic categories of words in the sentence, we can also consider their function. In the sentence "The very old witch sees a cat," "The very old witch" functions as the syntactic subject of the sentence, while "sees" is the verb, and "a cat" the direct object. In many languages of the world, subjects are often presented first, before verbs and objects. The most common word orders are SOV (subject – object – verb; about 48%) and SVO (subject – verb – object, about 41%), which together make up for a large proportion of the languages in the world (Kemmerer, 2012). Much less frequent is VSO word order and only a few languages have other basic word orders (VOS and OVS; OSV seems hardly ever to occur).

An interesting question is why so many languages have a canonical SOV or SVO word order. It has been proposed that different word order frequencies are a consequence of linguistic principles, among which we find the "verb-object bonding principle," the "theme-first principle," and the "animate-first principle" (Tomlin, 2014). The principle of "verb-object bonding" holds that the object in a sentence usually has a stronger syntactic and semantic relation to the verb than the subject. An example is a verb-object idiom such as "burn your bridges." According to the more semantically oriented "theme-first principle" the theme of an expression often refers to its referent, usually the agent or subject. An example is found in the sentences "The sailor went on board the ship. *He* raised the anchor" (see Chapter 8 on inferences). Finally, the "animate-first principle" is also semantic in nature in that humans tend to be mentioned in a sentence before other animate agents, followed by inanimate agents and patients. When talking about girls, butterflies, and grass, this may be the most likely order to do so.

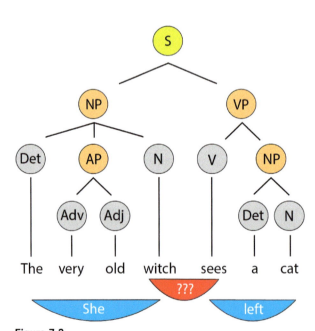

Figure 7.2
An example of a surface structure (also called phrase structure, or tree diagram) of a sentence ("S"). To understand why "sees" goes with "a cat" (into the verb phrase or VP) and not with "The very old witch" (into the noun phrase or NP), we can perform a replacement operation like the one indicated: "The very old witch" could be replaced by "She" and "sees a cat" by "left", but there is no way to replace "witch sees" by one other element.

Interestingly, SOV and SVO word orders are in line with all three principles, VSO with two of them, VOS and OVS with one of them, and OSV with none. Thus, when one speaks two languages that are both SOV, similarly structured sentence representations are regularly used.

In all, a big part of the explanation of observed word order regularities across languages has to do with semantics. The information structure (partially) reflects the prominence of certain semantic (thematic) roles or *cases* (Fillmore, 1968). For instance, when one wants to describe a scene, the most salient information may be about the agent and the action. These are typically expressed as subject and verb. If this view is correct, one might expect that languages that have a free word order will then use this ordering frequently. However, the situation is more complex than one might expect: Often, speakers provide given (known) information before they present new information. This allows the listeners to link up the new sentence to the topic of earlier discourse. However, the subject of the sentence might fulfil the role of the so-called patient rather than of the agent. That is the case in a passive sentence: "The very old witch was seen by the cat."

Anyway, it is clear that syntax allows different orderings of the incoming semantic information, and as a consequence may help to express unexpected events or improbable messages. For instance, "The man bites the dog" clearly means something different from "The dog bites the man." Patients with Broca's aphasia may become confused by the first sentence. If they have problems related to syntax, they may think on the basis of their world knowledge that the sentence's meaning is in fact that the dog is biting the man (Bastiaanse & Edwards, 2004; also see section 7.4.5).

It is important to note that language is quite flexible: A more or less similar message can be expressed by many different utterances: "I would like a beer," "Let's have a beer!," and "Beer!" In certain environments, like a noisy bar, perhaps even a single hand gesture would do the job in the absence of any spoken word.

7.2.1 Difficult sentences: Embedded sentences

In each language, some syntactic structures are considered correct, other dubious, and still others incorrect. Linguists have developed rule systems to distinguish the correct sentences from the others. These grammars have uncovered rules that can be applied *iteratively*, i.e., multiple times in a row, or in alternation with other rules. For instance, we can say "Girls love iced lattes. Boys like those girls" and turn that into "Boys like girls who love iced lattes." Here the first sentence is *embedded* in the second. One embedding of this kind typically does not challenge the proficient language user too much.

However, a (purely syntactically allowed) repeated application of such rules results in sentences that are grammatically correct, but almost incomprehensible. For instance, we can say "Dogs bite." We can extend this to: "Dogs that (other) dogs bite, bite." We can even say that a third group of dogs bites dogs as well: "(Dogs that (dogs that dogs bite) bite) bite." Because the word "that" can be left out in English in such constructions, this sentence can be reduced to "Dogs dogs dogs bite bite bite." We can use numbers to indicate which dogs bite in each case: $dogs_3$ $dogs_2$ $dogs_1$ $bite_1$ $bite_2$ $bite_3$. Thus, this syntactic structure is grammatically (syntactically) correct, but, of course, very nearly incomprehensible.

Interestingly enough, structures such as these may become more understandable if the semantics offers some insight into the relationships between the words. For instance, "Paintings (that (artists that billionaires pay) make) are expensive" can be reduced to "Paintings artists billionaires pay make are expensive." This seems to be lot more understandable than the sentence about the dogs above, although it has the same syntactic structure. Another well-known sentence that is relatively easy to understand is "The rat the cat the dog chased killed ate the malt." Here the cat was chased by the dog. The cat killed the rat that ate the malt (Chomsky & Miller, 1968).

Embedding can be central, as in the sentences just given, but it can also be asymmetrical. Compare, for instance, the two expressions "tools made by man" and "man-made tools." The syntactic structure of the first expression is called "right-branching," whereas the second one is "left-branching." As you may notice, in right-branching sentences the most important information ("tools") comes first. However, left-branching sentences are more compact and the most important information can be immediately continued and expanded on ("tools that …").

In the early 1960s, Yngve noted that the expansion ("branching") of sentences "to the right" in English was potentially infinite: "The dog that chased the cat that killed the rat that ate the malt …," whereas expansion "to the left" made sentences hard to understand very quickly: "The malt that the rat that the cat that the dog chased killed ate …." Yngve suggested that the reason for this is that the second kind of construction puts a much larger weight on Working Memory than the first. In other words, he proposed that left and right branching posed different constraints on processing. Many languages have constructions that restrict the depth of left expansions (such as agglutination and compounding). However, there are languages with a dominance of left expansions (such as Japanese and Turkish) and it appears that several typological features in combination affect the ease of processing of a sentence (Pastor & Laka, 2013; Uddén et al., 2022).

7.2.2 Difficult sentences: Garden path sentences

Other sentences that are difficult contain ambiguous words. They "lead you up the garden path" (deceive you for a while) when you choose the wrong syntactic category or function of a word. A well-known example of a garden path sentence is "The horse raced past the barn fell" (Bever, 1970). Here "raced" is a past participle, not a simple past tense. The sentence can be paraphrased as "The horse, which was raced past the barn, fell" (see Figure 7.3). Garden path sentences are notoriously difficult to process, because there is a strong tendency to assign a particular structure to them that later turns out to be wrong, requiring reanalysis and correction of the interpretation.

A garden path sentence is easier to understand if semantic information is added. In the case of the horse that was raced, context could be added to

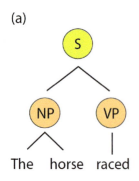

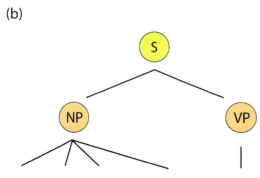

Figure 7.3
The phrase structure of (a) the sentence "The horse raced" and (b) "The horse raced past the barn fell" (cf. Bever, 1970). Readers typically think "raced" is the main verb in this sentence (as in panel a), until they encounter the actual main verb "fell" (as in panel b).

facilitate processing. When presented with the sentence "The horse raced past the barn fell" without any further context, the determiner "The" implies that there is only one horse. However, suppose that the target sentence appears following the two-sentence context "Once upon a time, there were two horses. One was made to run past a barn, and the other past a fence." Because now two horses have been mentioned, "The" in the target sentence must clearly mean "the one that," resolving any ambiguity. Also easier to understand (even on its own) is the sentence: "Only the horse raced past the barn fell …," because "only"' refers to the existence of several horses. Another example of a classic garden path sentence is: "While Anna bathed the baby played in the crib" (Christianson et al., 2001).

> **SUMMARY: SENTENCE PROCESSING: REPRESENTATIONS**
>
> The grammar of a language is a set of internalized rules that govern the composition of sentences and sentence parts like phrases and clauses. Words and phrases are the structural building blocks of a sentence. By parsing a sentence in the form of a surface structure or tree diagram, words are assigned to word categories (e.g., determiners, adjectives, nouns, verbs) and phrases to phrasal categories (e.g., noun phrase, verb phrase). Embedded sentences and garden path sentences are notoriously difficult to understand. Semantic information in these cases, as for all types of sentence, helps in understanding what is intended to be conveyed by the speaker or writer.

7.3 SENTENCE PROCESSING: PROCESSES

When language users understand spoken or printed sentences, they process their content more or less word by word. For reading, we can track the movements and fixations of readers' eyes to find out when they pick up information about the sentences they read and how long that takes. Clever experiments can then help us to disentangle how and when they use different information sources, e.g., lexical, syntactic, and semantic, in order to build syntactic and semantic structures. In the next two sections, we will consider both the more perceptual and the more abstract sides of sentence reading.

7.3.1 Incremental processing: Tracking the eyes

Understanding spoken sentences and reading printed sentences involves incremental processing. The processing of sentences during listening depends on the speaking rate of the interlocutor (the person with whom one speaks). In contrast, reading sentences is subject to the reader's own processing capacity. When you look at the eyes of a reader, you will notice that they make little jumps from one word of a printed sentence to a later one (often, but not always, the next content word). As we saw in Chapter 4, the jumps or hops are called "eye movements," or more specifically "saccades," while the time the eye rests on a particular word is called the "fixation duration" (Conklin et al., 2018, pp. 64–69). Saccades (sometimes also called "inter-fixations") are typically quite fast (40–60 ms), while eye fixations may vary between 50 and 600 ms. Interestingly, eyes may also move back to earlier positions in a sentence or a text, which is called "regression." This backward movement often happens in case an extra check must be made about what was read. It implies that some words may be fixated more than once. The total fixation time on a word is also called the "gaze duration." There are also "return sweeps," during which the eyes move back from the word at the end of a line to the beginning of the next line (see Figure 7.4). It has been shown that eye fixation patterns depend, among other factors, on how well a reader can read and whether

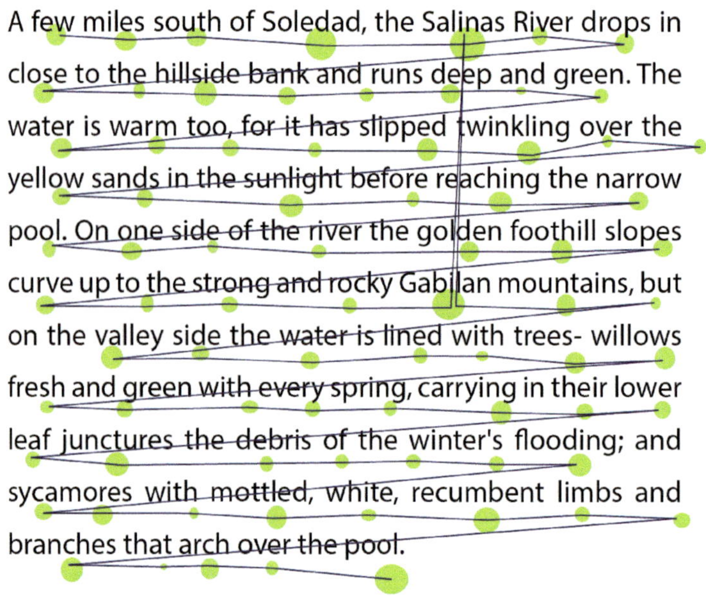

A few miles south of Soledad, the Salinas River drops in close to the hillside bank and runs deep and green. The water is warm too, for it has slipped twinkling over the yellow sands in the sunlight before reaching the narrow pool. On one side of the river the golden foothill slopes curve up to the strong and rocky Gabilan mountains, but on the valley side the water is lined with trees- willows fresh and green with every spring, carrying in their lower leaf junctures the debris of the winter's flooding; and sycamores with mottled, white, recumbent limbs and branches that arch over the pool.

Figure 7.4
An illustration of how the eyes of a reader may jump over the lines during sentence reading and fixate words. Saccades, fixations, return sweeps, and one regression are shown. The size of the green balls reflects fixation duration. See Figure 4.5 and text for an explanation of what information they process all along.

they have dyslexia or not (Rayner & Pollatsek, 1989; Rayner et al., 2011). In addition, eye tracking research involving both monolingual and bilingual readers indicates that reading times for multiword sequences like phrases are sensitive to the frequency with which they occur (Siyanova-Chanturia et al., 2011).

An important hypothesis formulated by Just and Carpenter (1980) is the "strong eye-mind hypothesis" (see Chapter 4). It holds that the pattern of fixations and saccades is a direct reflection of cognitive activity. Said boldly, the hypothesis implies that tracking the eye can provide us with a direct gate to our language processing mind!

A computational model of eye movement control in reading is the E–Z Reader model (Pollatsek et al., 2006). It describes in a formal way how the perceptual and cognitive processes involved in reading interact, paying special attention to how saccades are produced. As such, it has been used as an analytic framework for studying a variety of theoretical issues related to reading (e.g., incremental processing; Reichle, 2011).

Eye tracking has been so successful that, in spite of the exciting arrival of neuroscientific measurement techniques such as EEG and fMRI, variants of the technique have prospered in the last decennia. As we saw in Chapter 4, one interesting application is displaying sentences word by word in "rapid serial visual presentation" (RSVP). This technique allows a sequential presentation of words at one and the same position of the screen. RSVP is often used in combination with EEG measurements. Another variant is the use of eye tracking in the visual world paradigm for studying speech comprehension (remember the presentation of objects in four panels?).

7.3.2 Integration of syntactic and semantic information over time

What do these eye movements imply for sentence processing? What are readers actually doing during a word fixation? How do they integrate different types of information (lexical, syntactic, semantic) in a syntactic structure or a meaning structure of the sentence over time?

Consider what happens when we process the printed or spoken sentence: "The father gave the daughter the book" (following Levelt, 1989). Processing this sentence implies that we map the syntactic structure of the sentence onto a semantic representation of it. In Figures 7.2 and 7.3, we have already seen what the syntactic "surface structure" or "parse structure" of such a sentence looks like.

As we shall see in Chapter 8, sentence meaning can also be represented in terms of hierarchically organized structures with slots. One proposal is to combine general aspects of the meaning of larger syntactic constituents (including subjects and objects) into "event structures" (Jackendoff, 1983; Rappaport Hovav & Levin, 1988). An "event structure" describes or covers certain semantic "events," e.g., states ("Mary is tall"), activities ("John is driving the car"), achievements ("The car stopped abruptly"), or accomplishments ("The janitor cleaned the window"). The role of event and surface structures in language production will be considered in Chapter 9. Let us for the moment accept the format of the two types of sentence representation given in Figure 7.5.

When we read the sentence "The father gave the daughter the book," we do not wait for it to end in order to start processing. On encountering the first word, "The," we can already start to build up a possible syntactic structure for the sentence: The word "The" probably refers to a determiner, which is usually followed by a noun or an adjective. Both constitute (part of) a noun phrase. Reading the next word, "father," this turns out to be in line with the first option. The meaning of "father" can be looked up in the lexicon. It is likely that the "father" is, in fact, a (male) person doing something; semantically speaking, it is an "agent." At the same time, it probably functions as the syntactic subject of the sentence, because in English, word order in sentences often has subject first.

The next word, the past tense verb "gave," corroborates this hypothesis. "Gave" is a verb form that (as specified in the lexicon) requires a syntactic subject, has a direct object (what is given), and may take an indirect object (to whom) too. Because "father" appeared before the verb, it must be the syntactic subject of "gave." The appearance of "gave" further signals syntactically that a direct object and possibly an indirect object must be coming up next. Without further context information, the next content word, "daughter," referring to an animate person, is not likely to be an object that is given by the father (although the daughter might be a baby and handed over to a visiting relative to hold).

Furthermore, there is an English dative construction that allows "the daughter" in this sentence position as an indirect object, so "daughter" can be assigned the indirect object role. At the semantic level, "daughter" should then be considered as the recipient (or beneficiary) of something that is given by the father. Finally, the word "book" comes in. Because there is a required direct object with "gave," the reader might predict that this word will be the direct object (syntactically) and the so-called patient (what is given, semantically). Often, the direct object associated with "give" is non-animate, and that is indeed the case for "book." However, even when "book" would not have been predicted, it will easily find a slot in the arising sentence structure when it appears.

It is important to note that during the reading of this sentence, lexical, syntactic, and semantic information are all processed simultaneously. When listening to the sentence, prosodic information may also play a role. The lexical process will not stop after the word form "book" has been linked up to the meaning BOOK; meanings related to BOOK may become

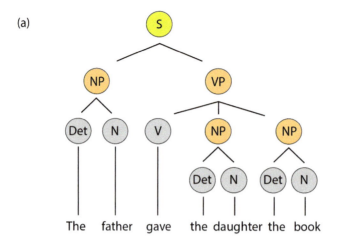
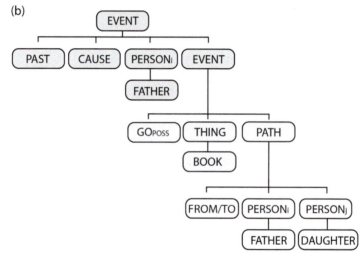

Figure 7.5
The syntactic ("surface") structure (part a) and the meaning ("event") structure (part b) of the sentence "The father gave the daughter the book." Sentence processing implies mapping grammatical roles from the surface structure (part a) onto thematic roles in the event structure (part b). See Chapter 8 for more information about meaning and Chapter 9 for event and surface structures in language production. After Levelt (1989).

activated, including its affective meaning if you like to read or receive books. More or less at the same time, both a syntactic and a semantic structure of the sentence are built incrementally and in parallel over time (cf. Jackendoff, 1990). Syntactic and semantic predictions about sentence continuations may also be made in parallel. In fact, they might influence each other, for instance, when it turns out that the "daughter" is unlikely to be the present of the father (semantics affecting syntax) or when the word "book" has already been assigned the role of direct object corresponding to the patient at the end of the sentence (syntax helping semantics). This raises the more general question, of course, how these different types of prediction conspire to come up with a possible sentence structure and an interpretation as efficiently as possible.

Readers and listeners hence build up syntactic structures and event structures while they are presented with an incoming sentence. Grammatical roles are mapped onto thematic roles, and thematic roles are brought together in a mental model of what the speaker/writer assumedly intended to convey. Two important processes taking place in the mind of the language user while an incoming sentence unfolds are *integration* and *prediction*.

7.3.3 Integration vs. prediction

When reading or listening to a sentence, incoming words are incrementally incorporated or *integrated* within the meaning representation of the unfolding sentence. Some incoming words and their meanings may be relatively easy to integrate with the structures the reader or listener has already built up, while others may be more difficult to incorporate. A relatively safe strategy during the processing of a sentence would be to simply, relatively passively, wait for each new word to appear and integrate it into the structures that were built up so far. As such, each new incoming item can be fit into the syntactic and event structures corresponding to the unfolding sentence. This is a clear *bottom-up* processing strategy.

Nevertheless, at the same time, it is possible to make *predictions* of what is going to follow next on the basis of past experiences with processing sentences and the situation at hand. We know, for instance, that when a sentence starts with the word "either," it will often at some point also include a clause that starts with the word "or" (Staub & Clifton, 2006). This means that the structure of the remainder of a sentence can, to some extent, be anticipated.

Based on experience, also individual words may be predicted and become preactivated in the mind of the reader or listener. For instance, hearing a sentence such as "The boy will eat the ..." may lead you to predict that something edible will follow, perhaps even preactivating word forms corresponding to edible objects ("cake") in your mental lexicon (Altmann & Kamide, 1999). If a stored representation of a word is already preactivated in the mental lexicon in Long Term Memory, this word may actually be easier to process and integrate once it is encountered in the remainder of the unfolding sentence. An alternative option could be that predicted or expected word candidates are put in a specially selected, context-sensitive list of potential word candidates, for which the recognition threshold (rather than the lexical activation itself) could be lowered. As such, actively predicting what type of information is going to follow, and potentially already even preactivating expected linguistic representations, is a clear *top-down* processing strategy.

During sentence processing, bottom-up integration and top-down prediction likely both play a role, for instance allowing listeners to start preparing a response to an incoming sentence before the end of the speaker's turn, leading to quick and efficient communication (Levinson, 2016).

So far, we have assumed that readers and listeners whole-heartedly build up a syntactic structure of the sentence they encounter while that sentence unfolds, and arduously map grammatical roles onto event roles. Research suggests, however, that in reality this process actually not always takes place in full detail. When people are presented with a passive spoken sentence such as "The dog was bitten by the man," and are asked who was the agent (or: actor or "doer") in this sentence, they surprisingly often (i.e., in about 32% of cases) incorrectly state the dog is the agent here (Ferreira, 2003). Apparently, they may have used the heuristic that the agent in a sentence is typically mentioned early on, or the heuristic that dogs are more likely to bite men than vice versa, and hence assumed that "the dog" must have been the agent, leading to an incorrect assignment of thematic roles. Indeed, listeners may have processed the sentence in a relatively shallow way, which would save them some time and energy. Such a processing strategy has been called *good-enough processing* (Ferreira, 2003). One could imagine that, especially in situations where the meaning a speaker is trying to convey is very clear from the bodily signals they convey (e.g., their hand gestures and

140 *Sentence processing*

facial expression), it often suffices to process the concurrent spoken utterance in a *good-enough* fashion.

> **SUMMARY: SENTENCE PROCESSING: PROCESSES**
>
> Sentence processing implies mapping grammatical roles from the surface structure onto thematic roles in the event structure while an incoming sentence unfolds. The surface structure of the sentence is mapped onto a semantic representation of the sentence to try and understand what a speaker or writer is trying to convey. Individual words in a sentence can have a meaning that can be looked up in the mental lexicon; they play a certain grammatical role in the sentence (e.g., subject) and may have a thematic role (e.g., agent or patient) in the sentence's overall meaning representation. During the processing of a sentence, lexical, syntactic, and semantic information are all processed simultaneously. Language users integrate incoming information with the (grammatical and event) structures they have built up so far (bottom-up processing), and may predict and even sometimes preactivate upcoming information (top-down processing). A good-enough processing strategy may save the listener or reader some time and energy.

7.4 MODELS OF SENTENCE PROCESSING

Over the years, both syntactically and semantically oriented models of different complexities have been proposed to account for sentence processing. We will discuss a number of them, starting with some influential classical models.

7.4.1 Garden Path model

Frazier (1987) developed a syntactic theory of sentence processing known as the Garden Path model, in which problems that language users experience with garden path sentences (see section 7.2.2) were linked to the properties of the tree diagrams for these sentences. She assumed that readers and listeners processed sentences in an *incremental* way, directly attaching each incoming word to the syntactic structure under construction (also see Frazier & Fodor, 1978). This first step of processing was assumed to be *autonomous*, thus not affected by aspects of the semantic context. When at some point the syntactic structure proved to be incorrect, it would be revised in a second step of processing. As such, different syntactic interpretations of the sentence are not considered in parallel, but in a serial manner. During processing, the structure under construction might be ambiguous. In that case, the incoming sentence would be interpreted in line with principles such as minimal attachment and late closure.

Minimal attachment involves choosing the tree structure that has as few nodes as possible. A simpler structure would imply less load on Working Memory. An example is given in Figure 7.6. *Late closure* is a different principle, which holds that the incoming word is added to the current phrase (and not to a new phrase) if possible. This reduces the risk of being obliged later to reprocess the earlier phrase.

In the Garden Path model, as in most earlier linguistic models, syntax is processed first, to be followed by semantics only later. Because semantics does not initially affect syntactic structure interpretation, these are autonomous (non-interactive) models of sentence processing. The linguistic models hence give primacy to syntax, specifying general

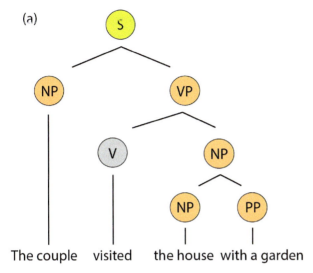

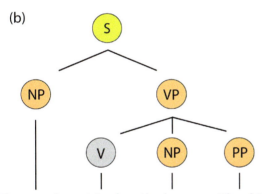

Figure 7.6
Example structures without (a) and with minimal attachment (b). Sentence structure (a) has an extra NP node (indicating that "the house" goes with "with a garden") and is therefore non-minimal. Because structure (b) has fewer nodes, according to the Garden Path model it would be the preferred option for the Sentence Processor.

rules and principles about syntactic structures (although lexical information can also play a role).

There has been a historical development from such autonomous models to interactive models. In contrast to linguistic models, psycholinguistic models (e.g., connectionist models) usually assume that syntax and semantics interact to some extent, and other types of information (e.g., lexical, prosodic, non-verbal) may also become important. In addition, these models typically assume that different interpretations of the sentence are considered in parallel, rather than in a serial manner.

7.4.2 Referential theory of parsing

The authors of the referential theory of parsing noted that garden path sentences are much easier to understand in context, as we have seen above (Altmann & Steedman, 1988). They suggested a *parallel, weakly interactive model* to account for this observation. Listeners and readers are assumed to first consider all reasonable alternative possible syntactic structures of a sentence in parallel. Next, they use context information to choose the most probable structure "directly." If a garden path effect arises, it is therefore not syntactic but semantic in nature. Incoming words, which are primarily of importance in this model because they *refer* to something, are considered in light of the mental model of the sentence or discourse built up by the language user so far.

The interaction between syntax and semantics in this theory is called *weak*, because there is only a limited effect of context on the activation of potential sentence structures in the mind of the reader or listener. In other words, semantic information does not guide the Sentence Processor in which syntactic alternatives are activated, but rather helps to select the correct syntactic analysis from the range of alternatives that are available in parallel. This parallel, weakly interactive model hence clearly differs from the serial, non-interactive Garden Path model discussed above.

7.4.3 Constraint-based model of sentence processing

The constraint-based model of sentence processing considers sentence processing as a *multiple constraint satisfaction* problem that is resolved by taking into account different types of information (MacDonald, 1994; MacDonald et al., 1994). In this *interactive* model, the sentence structure a reader or listener settles on is directly affected by different information sources (constraints), e.g., syntax, semantics, verb bias, and frequency of words and constructions. All these different sources provide some information, and the language user combines all information to arrive at a syntactic interpretation of the sentence at hand. Unlike the two-stage (syntax before semantics) Garden Path model, constraint-based models posit that all possible information can be used immediately to guide interpretation of an incoming sentence.

In case of ambiguity, several possible structures are activated to different degrees. They compete ("constraint satisfaction") and one will be the winner after some time. This process of activation of multiple candidates followed by a competition is hence reminiscent of some of the *word* recognition models we have seen in Chapters 5 and 6. If information sources contradict each other, it may take considerable time before one becomes most active. According to a one-stage model like this, longer reading times for garden path sentences thus are not a consequence of (serial) reinterpretation. Competition rather than reanalysis is proposed to explain processing difficulties.

7.4.4 Unrestricted race model

Like the constraint-based model of sentence processing, the so-called unrestricted race model (van Gompel et al., 2000) assumes that readers and listeners may immediately use a wide variety of sources of information (syntax, semantics, frequency, etc.) to try to arrive at the correct syntactic interpretation of a sentence. As such, there is no *restriction* in which sources of information can be used. This model hence clearly differs from the Garden Path model, which prioritized syntax as the main source of information a reader or listener would initially make use of.

According to this model, when an incoming sentence at a moment in time allows for more than one syntactic interpretation, the syntactic analysis that receives most support from the available information will be conducted first. As such, different syntactic alternatives can be considered to take part in a race in which there will often be one front runner. Only one syntactic analysis, for this front runner, is constructed at a time. If incoming information falsifies the syntactic analysis the Sentence Processor settled on, a reanalysis will be necessary. As such, like in the Garden Path model, the unrestricted race model explains processing difficulties by reanalysis rather than by competition.

7.4.5 Neurobiological models of sentence processing

To arrive at a better understanding of present-day *neurobiological* models of sentence processing, we will first need to take a short historical detour into the 19th century.

In 1861, the French physician and anatomist Paul Broca visited a patient in a hospital in the southern parts of Paris. The patient arguably understood what Broca said to him, but was no longer capable of producing meaningful stretches of speech, such as sentences, himself. More specifically, in response to Broca and others, the patient repeatedly uttered the single meaningless (except perhaps to himself) syllable *tan* and incidentally managed to produce a series of French swear words (*sacré nom de Dieu!*). When the patient deceased and Broca had a look at his brain, it turned out the patient had serious damage in the left inferior frontal part of his left hemisphere. Clearly, Broca thought, this must mean that left inferior frontal cortex is "the seat of articulated (spoken) language." The conclusion was that this area, which we still know as Broca's area today, must be responsible for the human capacity to produce speech.

If there is a brain region engaged in language production, one would think there should also be a region associated with language comprehension, including the processing of sentences. A short while after Broca's finding, around 1874, the German physician and anatomist Carl Wernicke came across several patients who were capable of producing spoken utterances, but showed deficits in understanding spoken and written language (including their own utterances!). Following post-mortem inspection, Wernicke found out that these patients often had a lesion in the left superior temporal part of their brain. It was concluded that this part of the brain, now known as Wernicke's area, should hence be critical for subserving language comprehension (cf. Binder, 2015).

Interestingly, Broca's and Wernicke's areas are connected via a fiber bundle that is known as the *arcuate fasciculus*. This anatomical connection makes sense in light of the findings by Broca and Wernicke. Certain linguistic activities, such as reading out loud a written sentence, indeed rely on a combination of language comprehension and language production processes. A connection between the two areas would allow for such activities, it was thought (see Figure 7.7).

Over the last few decades, significant progress has been made in advancing our understanding of how the brain supports sentence processing. In general, it has become clear that there is not one brain region that is "responsible" for language comprehension. Similarly, there is not one brain region subserving language production. Rather, neuroscientific research relying on methods such as fMRI and MEG (see Chapter 4), with both healthy volunteers and patients, has shown that different networks of connected brain regions are recruited and become activated when we are presented with a sentence and try to make sense of it (e.g., Tremblay & Dick, 2016). Using these "non-invasive" neuroscientific

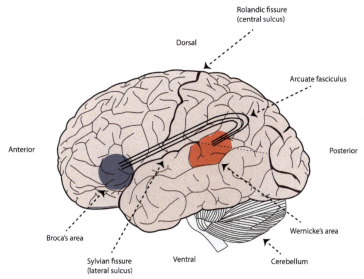

Figure 7.7
A view on the left hemisphere, including Broca's area (in blue) and Wernicke's area (in red), connected by the arcuate fasciculus. These areas are often called *perisylvian*, as they surround the Sylvian fissure, which partially separates the frontal from the temporal lobe. After Hagoort (2013).

methods, people's brain activity can be monitored while they are carrying out certain linguistic activities, such as reading or listening to sentences. As such, neurobiological models of language processing methodologically no longer have to solely rely on connecting brain damage in deceased patients to their previously observed behavioral language deficits.

Reviewing the progress made over the past decades on the neurobiological infrastructure that supports our ability to use and comprehend language, Hagoort (2013) describes the processing of multiword utterances such as sentences as reliant on three core components: memory, unification, and control (see Figure 7.8). As we saw in the context of the Language User Framework, language comprehension heavily relies on the word form representations we have acquired over time and stored in our Long Term Memory. This knowledge is stored predominantly in temporal and parietal parts of the brain. From this mental lexicon, word forms can be retrieved in combination with the syntactic role (noun, verb, adjective, etc.) they may play in a sentence. During the processing of phrases, sentences, and larger stretches of discourse, the individual words ("lexical building blocks") that we encounter can therefore be combined (or "unified") into larger grammatical and event structures, which themselves also have to be built, to ultimately arrive at the meaning the speaker or writer is intending to convey. Syntactic (surface) structures have to be construed on the fly, as well as the corresponding semantic (event) structures. Both come with slots that can be filled with specific word forms (at the level of the surface structure) or semantic representations (at the level of the event structure). Particularly areas in the left inferior frontal cortex (indeed, Broca's area and surrounding cortex) are assumed to play an important role in these syntactic and semantic unification processes. Frontal and temporal areas are assumed to interact during sentence processing via fronto-temporal circuits through which activation reverberates. Cognitive control processes, for instance supported by activation in areas in dorsolateral prefrontal cortex, monitor the language comprehension process (Hagoort, 2017).

In sum, a memory, unification, and control account of sentence processing proposes a division of labor between temporal (and parietal) brain regions involved in storing word forms and word-related information, left inferior frontal areas involved in building larger surface and event structures and integrating words into these structures, and other

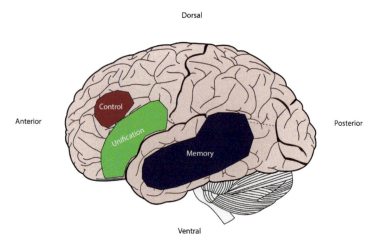

Figure 7.8
The Memory, Unification, and Control model. Note that these three regions are actually connected, and that they are not solely involved in processing language, but may (among other things) be recruited for understanding a message a speaker or writer is conveying. After Hagoort (2013).

(predominantly frontal) areas that monitor and control the ongoing language comprehension process (Hagoort, 2017).

We have seen that in the auditory modality, sentences are often encountered in the context of other meaningful information such as hand gestures or facial expressions. It would be surprising if these types of additional signal that a speaker conveys are disregarded when listeners map grammatical roles onto thematic roles, and when thematic roles are brought together in a mental model of what a speaker is assumed to communicate. Indeed, neuroscientific research on the processing of concomitant hand gestures and spoken sentences has shown that the brain integrates meaningful information conveyed through hand gestures with the information present in concurrent speech (Özyürek et al., 2007). Particularly left inferior frontal areas of the brain are recruited to integrate the meaning conveyed through hand gestures with the information provided in speech (Willems et al., 2007). The left inferior frontal cortex could therefore be called a "multimodal unification site" (Hagoort, 2017, p. 199). Indeed, the brain uses and combines information provided via different communicative channels (the face, the hands, the mouth) and modalities (visual, auditory) to try to understand as accurately as possible the message a speaker is trying to get across. These findings hence nicely illustrate the natural embodiedness and embeddedness of human language.

Alternative neurobiological models of sentence processing have been proposed. Certain of these highlight the importance of additional brain regions for language processing, such as left anterior temporal regions for deriving the meaning of multiword utterances (Pylkkänen, 2019), or they stress the existence of different streams of information between frontal, temporal, and parietal brain areas (Bornkessel-Schlesewsky & Schlesewsky, 2013). Nevertheless, although different models may introduce different accents, they all seem to agree that the frontal and temporal brain areas surrounding the Sylvian fissure play a major role in allowing us to process and understand sentences (cf. Malik-Moraleda et al., 2022).

So far, we have assumed that language processing mainly recruits brain areas in the left hemisphere. And indeed, it turns out that in most individuals important language functions are left-lateralized in the brain (Szaflarski et al., 2002). Nevertheless, there are people who show right-lateralized language dominance or a relatively symmetrical pattern of involvement of brain areas across the two hemispheres in language tasks (Szaflarski et al., 2002). Interestingly, right hemisphere dominance for language is more common in left-handed than in right-handed individuals (Willems et al., 2014). Nevertheless, also for individuals with a left-hemisphere dominant language system, the right hemisphere has been implicated in important aspects of language processing such as the processing of prosody, intonation, and stress (Friederici, 2017), and the use of world knowledge in discourse contexts (Menenti et al., 2009). As such, it seems fair to conclude that the importance of the right hemisphere for language processing should not be underestimated within and across individuals.

Importantly, the network of perisylvian areas that is recruited for sentence processing sometimes needs some help from other networks of brain areas to grasp what a speaker or writer *really* intends to say. Imagine you work in a restaurant and a customer looks at you with a disappointed facial expression, while at the same time pointing with his index finger to the bowl of soup and producing the spoken sentence "My soup is cold." In such situations, the perisylvian language network will likely be recruited to grasp the meaning of this four-word utterance. Left inferior frontal cortex may become active and support the integration of facial, manual, and spoken signals to arrive at a meaningful interpretation of the multimodal message.

Nevertheless, the so-called *coded meaning* (more or less corresponding to the literal meaning of the utterance) of this message may ultimately only be a starting point and less relevant in this context than what this customer actually intends to achieve with their message (the so-called *speaker meaning* or *pragmatic meaning*). In fact, the restaurant guest may very likely be indirectly asking you to bring them a new bowl of hot soup. To arrive at this correct, context-appropriate interpretation of the sentence "My soup is cold" and its consequences for you as an addressee of this message, a network of brain areas called the Theory-of-Mind network may become active to derive the correct speaker meaning in this situation (Frith & Frith, 2005). This network is typically taken to comprise different brain regions in medial prefrontal cortex and at the junction between the temporal and parietal lobe (Schurz et al., 2014), and is known to become active when people consider other people's mental states ("mentalizing"). As such, processing sentences in an embodied and embedded context may require the activation of several networks of brain regions in parallel over time.

7.4.6 Computational models of sentence processing

Over the past decades, also several *computational* models of sentence processing have been developed. Computational models are attractive in the study of cognition, in that they use well-defined algorithms that in detail specify the necessary representations and processing steps involved in a particular cognitive process. In addition, they allow the researcher to make testable quantitative predictions and formulate underlying mechanisms to advance our understanding, for instance of the psychology of language (Dijkstra & De Smedt, 1996; Vasishth et al., 2019).

Typically, computational models in the domain of sentence processing rightfully assume that humans are sensitive to statistical regularities in the linguistic input they encounter throughout their lives. For instance, if you are a speaker of English, you will every now and then come across the string of words "cream and sugar." Unless you are reading this book, the string "cream and dog" is not something you will encounter very often. As such, for

---

DISCUSSION BOX 7: SYNTAX IS MOST IMPORTANT VS. SEMANTICS IS MOST IMPORTANT

Historically, two theoretical positions have been important for sentence processing. The first holds that "syntax goes first." Syntactic operations like those involving minimal attachment are applied to a sentence before its semantics is considered, and syntax may constrain the expressed semantic (thematic) roles. The second position holds that syntax and semantics interact in some processing stages, if they do not do so already from the very beginning (Gunter et al., 2000). In this case, semantics may be considered to have priority, because the goal of processing a sentence is understanding it. We have advocated a theoretical view in which syntax serves to help solve semantic issues (cf. Kako & Wagner, 2001). In this sense, our position is in line with that of psychologists arguing the most important goal of language is to convey meaning. But why would syntax be so complex if it is not just as important as semantics?

What is your opinion on this issue? Consider the following possibilities: (a) this debate is ill-conceived, for instance because syntax and semantics may have exactly the same or a completely different purpose (cf. Suzuki, 2021; Zuberbühler, 2019); (b) syntax and semantics are equally important; (c) syntax or grammar is more important than semantics and also adds to meaning in its own way; there even is a "language of thought"; (d) semantics is more important than syntax, because in the end we use language primarily for exchanging meanings.

each word we perceive in a sentence context, it is possible to calculate based on statistical regularities in large corpora of speech or written text how *surprising* that word will be to a language user in a particular linguistic context. In our example, the word "dog" will have a much higher surprisal value than the word "sugar."

Surprisal is actually a formalized measure from information theory, and for each word in a sentence a specific and concrete surprisal value can be calculated based on the linguistic context it appears in (Hale, 2001, 2003). The same holds for larger units such as noun phrases. Importantly, the lower the surprisal value of a word in a particular context, the easier that word should be to process for the language user. Indeed, word probability, as quantified via the notion of surprisal, can be successfully related to measures of cognitive effort (Levy, 2008). Computational models of sentence processing often work with surprisal values. Broadly speaking, these computational models can be distinguished into at least two overall categories: models that rely on *probabilistic grammars*, and models that make use of *neural networks* (Chater & Manning, 2006; Frank, 2021).

Probabilistic (phrase structure) grammar models typically assume that, during sentence processing, we activate in parallel several possible syntactic structures that are compatible with the linguistic sentence context we encountered so far. For example, the words "The elephant is ..." could lead to an active sentence such as "The elephant is a large land mammal" or a passive sentence such as "The elephant is fed by the zoo keeper." At any moment, these different syntactic options could be ranked in terms of their probability. For instance, based on our experience, we know that some structures are more frequent and probable than others in a given context or in general. Over time, when more words come in, the number of remaining possible structures may decrease, and the position of the different syntactic alternatives in the ranking may change. Words can be assumed to be more difficult to process if they elicit a change in the ranking of the range of syntactic structures under consideration (Levy, 2008), which makes sense in light of the relative difficulty people have in processing garden path sentences. This dynamic ranking process can be modelled by computational models.

In addition, the surprisal value of individual words in the sentence can be assumed to partially depend on the type of sentence structure that the Sentence Processor considers most probable at that moment. Probabilistic grammar models hence typically assume parallel activation (or: generation) of possible syntactic structures, and surprisal values for individual words that depend, among other things, on the probability of the syntactic structures under consideration. Model predictions based on these assumptions are commonly compared to data collected in humans, such as reading times for words in a sentence, N400 amplitude time locked to the onset of visually or auditorily presented words in sentence contexts, or the duration of eye tracking fixations on single words in sentences.

Neural network models are systems consisting of a network of individual nodes that connect a certain input (like a string of words such as a sentence) to a certain output (like the assumed meaning of that sentence). As such, over time, information may flow through a network of nodes that activate and/or deactivate one another (see Chapter 6). As such, the nodes may intuitively resemble neurons connected in biological networks in the human brain. Neural network models are typically trained on a large set of sentences, after which it is tested to what extent the model is successful in its performance on sentences it never encountered before. Based on the training they received, these models may predict for a large range of words or word types how likely it is that that word or word type will follow next based on the part of the sentence the model encountered so far and the statistical regularities in the set of training sentences (e.g., Elman, 1993). Again, surprisal is a measure that plays an important role in such models, and also the performance of neural network models may be compared to processing measures (e.g., reading times, N400 and/or P600 amplitude) in humans. However, unlike probabilistic grammar models, neural network models are not explicitly interested in building and ranking grammatical structures for the input they received (Armeni et al., 2017).

> **SUMMARY: MODELS OF SENTENCE PROCESSING**
>
> Over the past decades, a wide variety of (linguistic, psycholinguistic, neurobiological, computational) models of sentence processing have been proposed. Early linguistic models, such as the Garden Path model, prioritized syntax over other sources of information the Sentence Processor could use, and explained difficulties in the processing of garden path sentences by assuming serial reanalysis of syntactic interpretations. Also the unrestricted race model explains processing difficulties by reanalysis. However, like constraint-based models, it assumes that the reader or listener makes use of a variety of information sources (syntax, semantics, frequency, etc.) to arrive at a syntactic interpretation of a sentence. The constraint-based model and the referential theory of parsing propose parallel (rather than serial) construction or activation of different syntactic alternatives, and focus on competition between these alternatives rather than on reanalysis.
>
> Neurobiological models of sentence processing have identified a network of frontal and temporal "perisylvian" brain regions that is assumed to dynamically subserve the human capacity to process and understand sentences. A division of labor is proposed between regions involved in the storage and retrieval of lexical information, and regions involved in the construction of larger syntactic and semantic structures. Additional networks of brain regions, such as the Theory-of-Mind network, may be recruited to grasp what pragmatic meaning a writer or speaker intends to convey.
>
> Many computational models of sentence processing have relied on the notion of surprisal. They model the representations and processes assumed to play a role in sentence processing, and compare model performance to human data. Probabilistic models commonly assume that several syntactic interpretations of an incoming sentence are considered in parallel and dynamically ranked, with the ranking of alternatives changing over time as more information comes in. Neural network models link input to output, based on the training they received, in a more theory-neutral way.

7.5 SENTENCE PROCESSING: EMPIRICAL STUDIES

Over the past decades, different experimental techniques and paradigms have been used to arrive at a better understanding of how we process sentences. In this section, we will look at a self-paced reading study, an eye tracking study, and an EEG study, while in the next section on context effects we will also discuss three studies, two using EEG and one using conversation analysis.

An interesting study that considered the contribution and integration of lexical, semantic (and pragmatic), and syntactic information during incremental sentence processing is that by Taraban and McClelland (1988). In one experiment, readers processed sentences in a self-paced reading task. These sentences differed in a critical word, after which they continued with other words. The critical word could be lexically expected or not, its thematic role could be expected or not, and the word could be in line with a minimal attachment structure of the sentence or not.

An example sentence is: "The janitor cleaned the storage area with the [.....] because of many complaints." Critically, it could contain words such as the following:

- "broom": Minimal attachment, expected thematic role, expected lexical item (+++)
- "solvent": Minimal attachment, expected thematic role, unexpected lexical item (++−)
- "manager": Minimal attachment, unexpected thematic role, unexpected lexical item (+−−)
- "odor": Non-minimal attachment, unexpected thematic role, unexpected lexical item (−−−)

It was found that reading was temporarily slowed when the critical word was a lexically unexpected item ("solvent") but then processing continued as before (see Figure 7.9). Furthermore, when the thematic role was unexpected, as for "manager" and "odor," there was a clear longer reading time (note that neither "manager" nor "odor" was an instrument for cleaning). No difference was found when on top of these unexpected lexical items and thematic roles, there was a non-minimal attachment (signaling an unexpected syntactic structure: "the storage area with the odor").

These findings suggest that lexical and semantic sentence aspects affected the reading process more than syntactic aspects. As such, they are not in line with the Garden Path model.

As mentioned at the beginning of this chapter, another research technique that is frequently used to study sentence processing is that of eye tracking (see Chapter 4). In the visual

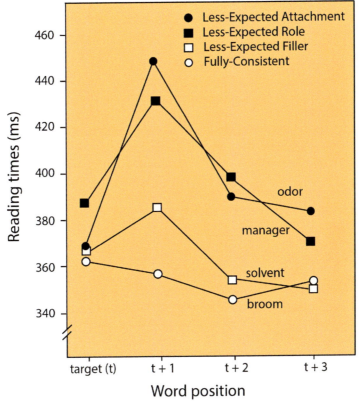

Figure 7.9
Reading times for words in conditions with different lexical, syntactic, and semantic/pragmatic properties. Reading times are displayed for the critical words (here called "target") and three subsequent words in the sentence. After Taraban and McClelland (1988).

"Put the apple on the towel in the box"

Figure 7.10
"Put the apple on the towel in the box." How would your eye movements differ when hearing this sentence while looking at the visual world on the left, versus when looking at the visual world on the right? After Tanenhaus et al. (1995).

world paradigm using eye tracking, participants typically look at a panel with four objects (the "visual world") while they listen to a sentence. Eye movements and eye fixations are recorded while they are doing this. This paradigm has been used to study auditory word recognition, as we have seen in Chapter 5, but can also be applied to the study of sentence processing.

For instance, a participant might hear the instruction "Put the apple on the towel in the box" (Tanenhaus et al., 1995). Now suppose the participant sees a display that contains only a single apple (Figure 7.10, left panel). It has been found that in this case, "on the towel" is initially interpreted as the goal of the word "put." This is in line with a minimal attachment interpretation. However, if there are two apples in the display (Figure 7.10, right panel), "on the towel" is directly interpreted as information about the correct apple. This interpretation is in contradiction with minimal attachment. Thus, this study suggests, again, that syntactic information can be used but can also be overridden by other cues. It confirms that syntax is supportive but not the most prominent aspect in sentence processing. Here we hence see in practice how a theory or model can be falsified by a cleverly designed experimental study.

Very important for studying sentence processing is the use of EEG recordings. The most fundamental study in this domain is by Kutas and Hillyard (1980). As we saw briefly in Chapter 4, they compared (among other things) sentences in the following two – congruent (A) and incongruent (B) – conditions:

A. I take coffee with cream and sugar.
B. I take coffee with cream and dog.

Participants were presented with these sentences, one word at a time on a computer screen, while their brain activity was recorded using EEG. The authors then time locked event-related potentials to the seventh word of the sentence and observed what is now widely known as an N400 effect: The incongruent final word (as in sentence B above) yielded enhanced negative amplitude in the ERP compared to the congruent word (as in sentence A above). This difference (see Figure 7.12, left panel) is argued to reflect the fact that the word "sugar" is more easily integrated with the preceding context than the word "dog," for instance, because it may even have been predicted on the basis of that sentence context (Kutas & Federmeier, 2011).

In the discussion of the notion of *good-enough processing* above, we have seen that people not necessarily always build a full-fledged syntactic structure of the sentence they are processing. When we assume that listeners or readers are more interested in grasping the meaning of a sentence they hear or read, rather than its exact syntactic structure, one could rightfully assume they would pay most attention to the most relevant or most novel information a sentence provides. Indeed, sentences are typically structured in such a way that they present some (new, relevant) information that is in focus, and some other (background, well-known) information that could be considered less relevant, for instance because it refers to knowledge the interlocutors already share. Certain parts of a sentence could hence be more seriously attended to and more deeply processed than other parts of a sentence.

In line with these ideas, Wang and colleagues (2012) used EEG to experimentally test whether certain syntactic violations are processed differently as a function of whether they are in focus position in a sentence or not. They visually presented participants with sentences on a computer screen that formed a question (Q) answer (A) pair. The study was in Dutch, but we will here provide the literal English translations of the answers – therefore the order of words may look a bit unintuitive. But note that in Dutch, the word order of the answers was (unlike the literal English translation here) always correct and intuitive. Of course, in the actual study, no words were underlined.

In the authors' correct, focus condition, a sentence pair would look like this:

Q: Who orders a taxi after the party?
A: After the party <u>order</u> the rather angry <u>guests</u> a taxi

Here, the new information in the answer corresponds to the rather angry guests. Note that the verb form "order" and the critical noun "guests" nicely agree: The plural noun is preceded by the correct verb form. This syntactically correct answer sentence was then compared to a syntactically incorrect answer sentence:

Q: Who orders a taxi after the party?
A: After the party <u>orders</u> the rather angry <u>guests</u> a taxi

Indeed, the answer here contains a so-called *number-agreement violation*, since the (singular) verb form "orders" does not agree with the fact that there is more than one guest. In other words, based on the verb form "orders," one would have expected a singular noun ("guest"), but not a plural noun ("guests"). When the participants' processing of the word "guests" was compared between the two conditions by looking at event-related potentials time locked to the onset of this word on the screen, a P600 effect was observed: enhanced positive amplitude around 600 ms after the onset of the critical word on the screen for the incorrect versus the correct answer. So far, so good: this finding is in line with earlier work showing effects of processing syntactic violations in this time window.

Now consider the following correct sentence pair, in which the critical word "guests" is actually not the focus of the answer sentence:

Q: When does one order a taxi?
A: After the party <u>order</u> the rather angry <u>guests</u> a taxi

Here the critical information is indeed the moment when the taxi was ordered ("After the party"), and not so much who ordered it ("the rather angry guests"). Note that again, the verb form ("order") and the plural noun ("guests") nicely agree. This correct, non-focus condition was then compared to the following incorrect, non-focus condition:

Q: When does one order a taxi?
A: After the party <u>orders</u> the rather angry <u>guests</u> a taxi

Here, there is again a number-agreement violation, but the verb form and noun that create the violation are not in focus position in light of the preceding question. Interestingly, when these two non-focus conditions were compared directly, no P600 effect was observed. Apparently, certain words in a sentence are processed in a more shallow way (i.e., they receive less attention) when they are not in focus and not so relevant compared to when they are in focus and contain the relevant information for the reader.

Again, we see that in processing a sentence, language users care more about the meaning of that sentence than about its exact syntactic properties. Apparently, not all syntactic details a sentence provides are paid attention to by the parser. Wang et al. (2012) refer to their findings as the *Chomsky illusion*, as they falsify the old but influential idea by Chomsky that syntactic information is the most important type of information for people processing sentences.

> **SUMMARY: SENTENCE PROCESSING: EMPIRICAL STUDIES**
>
> How readers and listeners process sentences has been studied experimentally using a variety of techniques (e.g., self-paced reading, eye tracking, EEG). In contrast with early theoretical views that predicted that a sentence's syntactic structure should be the most important knowledge source, it has been observed that lexical and semantic sentence aspects affect the reading process more than syntactic aspects. Readers and listeners use a variety of cues (including those provided by syntax) to try and grasp the meaning of a sentence.

7.6 SENTENCE PROCESSING: THE ROLE OF CONTEXT

In previous chapters, we have seen that sentence context can quickly affect segmentation of words in spoken and printed word recognition. However, the understanding of sentences itself is also sensitive to contextual information. In Chapter 5, we pointed out that the recognition of a spoken word is affected not only by segmental aspects (e.g., its phonemes and word stress position), but also by suprasegmental aspects (the prosody of the utterance it occurs in). When listeners see aspects of the world that are then referred to by somebody in a spoken utterance, they must take into account both what they see and the intonation pattern of the spoken reference sentence (Steinhauer et al., 1999).

Bögels et al. (2011) examined how listeners do this. One basic idea underlying their study was the following. Consider the contrast between saying "the YELLOW ball" (with stress on the word "yellow") and saying "the yellow BALL" (with stress on the word "ball"). The first noun phrase would be used to contrast, for instance, a yellow ball and a blue ball, while the second would distinguish, for instance, a yellow ball and a yellow hat. The experimenters now introduced experimental conditions in which the pronunciation pattern matched or mismatched the visual situation at hand. In their "linguistic context" condition, participants heard either "the YELLOW ball" or "the yellow BALL" while they saw a picture with a yellow ball and a green tent (there was also a neutral condition without any special accent). Importantly, on the previous trial, they had seen a picture of either a yellow hat or a blue ball, both accompanied by a red bike (see Figure 7.11). Note that hearing "the YELLOW ball" sounds weird following the "yellow hat and red bike" trial, but it does not following the "blue ball and red hat" trial (while the opposite holds for "the yellow BALL").

Listeners indeed had difficulties in processing the noun phrase in the mismatching accent conditions. Relative to the matching condition, recorded ERPs showed an early negativity

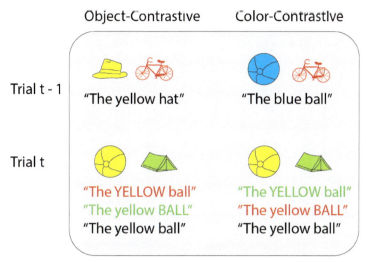

Figure 7.11
The object-contrastive and color-contrastive linguistic conditions in the ERP study by Bögels et al. (2011). An expected, matching pronunciation pattern is here indicated in green, a mismatching, unexpected pattern in red, and a neutral baseline pattern in black font color.

(at 300–400 ms after onset) for the mismatching noun phrase with an accent on the noun ("the yellow BALL") in case the color (blue followed by yellow) was contrasted relative to the previous trial (right panel Figure 7.11). Because this effect began already before the noun's onset, it must have been elicited by the adjective with the missing accent. However, in case the object carried the contrastive information (hat followed by ball), a later negativity was found for the mismatching NP ("the YELLOW ball"), starting only after noun onset (left panel Figure 7.11). This last finding must therefore be due to the missing accent on the noun.

The importance of a broader *discourse* context for sentence processing is illustrated in an EEG study by Nieuwland and van Berkum (2006). Historically, this study is best understood in the context of earlier EEG research on sentence processing, particularly the study by Kutas and Hillyard (1980) discussed in the previous section.

With these seminal N400 findings in mind, Nieuwland and van Berkum (2006) compared the online processing of sentences that are similar to the sentences in the original study, such as:

A. The peanut was salted.
B. The peanut was in love.

However, unlike in the earlier study, these critical sentences were part of an auditory story about a dancing peanut who appeared to be crazy about a girl he had just met. In this discourse context, the critical word of sentence A ("salted") actually yielded a greater N400 amplitude than the final word of sentence B ("in love"), arguably because the former item did not fit the story context (Figure 7.12, right panel). This was even the case although a peanut is usually not an animate entity that would fall in love. The broader discourse context hence reversed the original effect!

These findings illustrate the importance of mental models during language comprehension. In the context of this study, participants will have formed a mental model of the

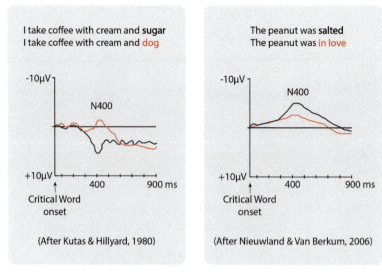

Figure 7.12
The traditional N400 effect (left panel) as observed by Kutas and Hillyard (1980), reversed by discourse context (right panel) in the study by Nieuwland and van Berkum (2006).

communicative situation at hand, in which there is an animate agent (which happens to be an infatuated peanut) that has the ability to experience human-like emotions, for instance as in fairytales or comic books. If subsequently encountered information does not match the mental model of the situation, it leads to a surprise for the person comprehending the sentence.

Beyond such a larger verbal discourse context, also the broader visual and conversational context may have an effect on how people process sentences. In a face-to-face setting, the sentences a speaker produces are typically accompanied with all sorts of visual information: Facial expressions, hand gestures, eye blinks and eye brow movements, and even the posture of the speaker may convey certain information (remember Figure 2.1). In addition, listeners in such situations are often already planning their own response while they are listening to their conversational partner. Indeed, across cultures the gap between the different turns in a conversation is remarkably short (Stivers et al., 2009), suggesting that listeners do not wait until the end of a speaker's sentence to start planning their own response. As such, processing sentences in natural conversations seems a lot more complicated than the clean and isolated sentences in experimental lab studies suggest.

In an analysis of videotaped conversations, Holler and colleagues (2018) specifically investigated how the presence of non-verbal, communicative information as conveyed by a speaker influences the processing of their message by a listener while that listener is already planning their response to the message. The authors specifically focused on question–answer sequences in natural conversations, which allowed them to reach several interesting conclusions.

First, it was observed that the majority of questions (> 60%) in the conversations were paired with a gesture, such as a manual pointing gesture or a communicative movement of the head. This shows how listeners, when they are processing sentences, constantly have to combine auditory information encountered through speech with concomitant visual information perceived from the speaker's body.

Second, the researchers found that questions that were paired with a gesture actually received a faster response than questions that were not paired with a gesture. Indeed, gaps between question and answer were typically about 200 ms when the question was not paired with a gesture, while questions paired with a gesture made this gap disappear: Most sequences in this case had a 0 ms gap between question and answer. Hence, gestures speed up turn transitions! Intuitively, this is surprising, as you might expect that when more information is provided through different channels, it should take the listener actually more time to process these signals, and hence lead to a delay of an appropriate response. In contrast, the authors speculate that the additional information present in the gestures may facilitate understanding of the spoken question, and/or draw more attention to it, hence leading to the possibility to formulate and produce a faster answer.

> **SUMMARY: SENTENCE PROCESSING: THE ROLE OF CONTEXT**
>
> Words are typically embedded in larger structures such as sentences, but also sentences usually do not come in isolation. The larger discourse structure influences how easy or hard it is to process a word in a sentence context. Words in sentences, and thereby sentences as a whole, are easier to process if they match the predictions that the reader or listener made on the basis of their mental model of the situation at hand. In addition, the visual signals (e.g., hand and head movements) that a speaker conveys may facilitate sentence processing by providing additional information, or they may draw more attention to (aspects of) the sentence produced by the speaker. During a conversation, listeners may plan the production of their own message while processing a speaker's sentence, leading to smooth transitions between conversational turns.

7.7 WHAT IS NEXT?

In the current and previous chapters we have had an in-depth look at the recognition and processing of words and sentences. In the next chapter, we will specifically focus on what language processing, in the end, is all about: deriving *meaning*. How is meaningful information organized in and derived from the language user's memory? How does the language user make sense of linguistic units that are larger than a single sentence, such as in text or discourse contexts?

7.8 WHAT HAVE WE LEARNED?

In this chapter, we have seen that sentence processing can be characterized in terms of several important mechanisms: mapping grammatical roles onto thematic roles, integration, prediction, and context effects. Eventually, readers and listeners integrate the meaningful information they derive from incoming sentences with their mental model of the situation at hand:

Mapping grammatical roles onto thematic roles. When listening to a sentence or when reading a sentence, incoming information accumulates over time. Readers and listeners build a grammatical structure of the input they perceive, assign grammatical roles to the lexical building blocks they encounter, and map these grammatical roles onto thematic roles in an event structure to grasp the sentence's meaning as a whole.

Integration (syntactic, semantic). When reading or listening to a sentence, new incoming words are incrementally incorporated or integrated with the grammatical and the meaningful representation of the unfolding sentence. Overall, the language user is ultimately more interested in the meaning of a sentence than in its exact syntactic structure.

Prediction. Based on a lifetime of experience with processing words in sentence contexts, it is possible to make predictions of which word form, word meaning, or syntactic structure is going to follow next. It is not unlikely that readers or listeners may preactivate words they expect to encounter soon while reading or listening to a sentence.

Context effects. Sentences are often part of a larger discourse, and previous discourse elements influence how incoming sentences are processed. In addition, the broader visual context provides the language user with information on sentence meaning. All these elements come together in the mental model of the listener or reader.

Role of the mental model. The mental model of the language user consists of a very complex semantic representation of the many dimensions of a communicative situation. For instance, in a conversation, the model must at the same time represent stable world knowledge, a more or less abstract and personal interpretation of the current utterance, relevant non-linguistic background information (context), and aspects of how the conversation has developed so far over time. Perhaps we should therefore discern several types of mental model, some more situational and others more abstract, and some embedded in other ones. We will discuss the mental model and its use in more depth in the next chapter.

QUESTIONS FOR CHAPTER 7

1 How would you describe and evaluate the role of syntax in language processing?
2 Analyze the sentence "The burglar steals the paintings" from the perspective of phonetics, lexicology, morphology, syntax, and semantics.
3 Consider the English sentence "The politician whom even the younger voters liked a lot was elected." How would such a sentence be understood (see also Piñango et al., 2016)? What role do you think Working Memory must play?
4 Sentence context can make particular meaning aspects of words prominent. Illustrate this by considering the effect of verb choice on the meaning of the following two sentences:
   a. "The student lifted the washing machine."
   b. "The student opened the washing machine."
5 Indicate which of the following sentence pairs is minimally attached and which not (beware of tricks!):
   a. "The spy saw the cop with the revolver." – "The spy saw the cop with the binoculars."
   b. "The couple visited the house with a friend." – "The couple visited the house with a garden."
   c. "The horse raced past the barn fell." – "The horse raced past the barn quickly."
6 Loftus and Palmer (1974) showed students film clips about car accidents. After they saw a clip, participants had to answer a critical question that could be slightly differently worded. For instance, one question could be "About how fast were the cars going when they contacted each other?" and another "About how fast were the cars going when they smashed into each other"? The mean speed estimate varied considerably depending on the verb used: "contacted" elicited a mean speed of 31.8 mph, but "smashed" of 40.8 mph. Can you explain how this difference in judgment of the exact

same video arose? What would be the consequence for interrogations of witnesses of accidents or crimes?

7   Not only words can be ambiguous (e.g., "bug"), but also sentences. Examples of syntactic ambiguity are: "Italians love operas more than Germans," "Dear ladies and gentlemen," "I saw the Grand Canyon flying to New York." Newspaper headlines often provide examples of this effect ("Reverend married Springsteen"). Can you come up with examples yourself?

8   Language users sometimes confuse different expressions. They might say, for instance, "They fought like cat and wife", "It is like carrying owls to Newcastle." What do such confusions suggest? Can you make up confusions in your own language? How do you make them?

9   Consider the idiomatic expression "to flog a dead horse." There is a literal and a figurative interpretation of this expression. Can you formulate different hypotheses about how listeners or readers might activate both (literal and figurative) interpretations and arrive at the meaning of the idiomatic interpretation? (See Conklin & Schmitt, 2012; van Ginkel & Dijkstra, 2020.)

10 Consider the following sentence: "He did neither deny nor admit unequivocally that he had had the murder committed by a hired assassin." How does this sentence show the importance of incrementality in language comprehension? What does the reader have to do to end up with the correct interpretation of the sentence?

Chapter 8

Meaning

8.1 MEANING: THE ESSENCE

You are probably familiar with the painting by René Magritte, showing a pipe with the text *Ceci n'est pas une pipe* ("This is not a pipe") below it. When you saw it for the first time, you probably said to yourself, "Yes, of course, he is right: This is not a real pipe, but a painting of a pipe." In other words, the painting somehow represents the pipe from the "real" world. It is a 2D representation of the 3D pipe that is faithful to the original in some visual respects, like color and form. However, it does not smell like a pipe and is not made of the same materials.

There is more to this example than you may have noticed: The word form "pipe" below the image is not a pipe either! One can say that, just like the painting, it refers to a real pipe, but only because you have a *concept* of PIPE somewhere in your head. And this concept is not a real pipe either …

So it appears that objects in the real world can be explicitly represented in different ways, as *images* or as *words*, while both of these implicitly refer to a shared underlying meaning representation, a *concept*, in this case that of a PIPE (see Figure 8.1). But what would these concepts look like?

As we said, the painting represents the color and form of a real pipe, but not the smell or the actual material. So perhaps the concept of a pipe represents all those dimensions in some abstract way? Could we somehow define the "building blocks" of the concept PIPE?

In fact, semantics, the discipline in linguistics that is concerned with meaning, has long considered word meanings as abstract representations composed of building blocks called "semantic features." Furthermore, concepts (or "semantic representations") are themselves assumed to be linked up in large semantic networks. Via the concept for "pipe" we might move on to the concepts of tobacco, fire, to health issues, wood, grandpa, black teeth, and so on.

But how abstract can we consider the concept to be? Seeing the pipe, we smelled the sweet flavor of its tobacco. Is this feature of smell only represented in an abstract way or would some real smelling sensation be triggered? When exactly? What about other concepts that may be associated with a particular smell, such as flowers? And what about my emotional perspective on this pipe, if I have a close relative who died from lung cancer? It could surely be activated by the picture of the pipe. This analysis of the meaning of a simple object like a pipe generates several important hypotheses about word meaning representation and its retrieval.

DOI: 10.4324/9781003326274-8

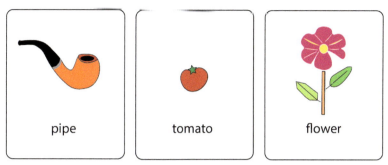

Figure 8.1
Representation of concepts as words and as images.

First, meaning is not only abstract, but embodied and multimodal. Retrieving meaning can involve aspects of perception, action and movement, emotion, and more. A tomato belongs to the family of the nightshades (abstract information), but it is also typically very red, round, and smooth (perceptual information) and has a specific taste that you may like or not. Important to the verb "to hop" is a particular movement, and "fear" is associated with a particular gut feeling. Retrieving such information for meaning specification and enrichment will take time.

Second, the meaning of the word "pipe" is not encapsulated or closed. If we continue to think about the pipe, more and more associations pop up. This suggests that word meaning is not holistic or one-piece. There is a time-course for the various meaning aspects that become available. This would be understandable if information of different types must be derived from different parts of the brain, such as motor-related aspects from motor cortex, emotional information from brain areas or networks involved in emotion and episodic memory, etc. The implication is that meaning can only be to some extent complete if it involves resonating circuits in the brain that sustain meaning, implying distributed brain states rather than local activations.

Third, related to this point, meaning representation and retrieval are context-sensitive and embedded. For instance, when you think of a frying pan, first the visual form and the color of the pan may pop up, then how it feels when it is held and what materials it is made of. But research has shown that at some moment in time you also activate the context in which you use it (the kitchen) and even that you bake solid and edible stuff in it (Johnson-Laird et al., 1978). Thus, there is a lot more to a frying pan (or any other object) than just its visual appearance.

In sum, a word's meaning may have both abstract and concrete aspects to it, and its retrieval can be linked to the non-linguistic and linguistic context in which it occurs, to other word meanings, and to world knowledge. Figure 8.2 presents the Conceptual System in the light of all these factors. Note that the Cognitive Control System at the top of the Language User Framework (Figure 3.1) is not indicated here, but it will be of influence as well.

In this chapter, when we consider the process of meaning retrieval, we will pay some attention to how meanings evoke other meanings. We usually consider this process as "thinking." Thought is depicted here as a more or less systematic sequence of meanings in terms of conceptual structures (e.g., propositional or event structures, see section 8.2.4). It can but need not be accompanied by linguistic input such as incrementally presented sentences. An interesting notion is that someone speaking to you guides your incremental

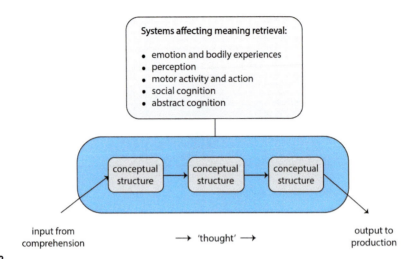

Figure 8.2
The embodied, embedded, incremental, and context-sensitive Conceptual System. Because of its non-encapsulated, open nature, many cognitive systems contribute to conceptual representations, allowing meaning to include both abstract and concrete aspects. The sequence of activation of conceptual structures over time is called "thinking" or "thought." The mapping of input onto semantics during language comprehension has been discussed already in Chapters 4–7. The mapping of meaning output to language production will be discussed in Chapter 9 under the header of "Conceptualization."

thought processes along certain pathways and in particular directions. As such, sentence comprehension can be seen as thinking guided by language, and sentence production as language guided by thought.

This chapter is again ordered in line with previous chapters. We will first consider the meaning representations of words, sentences, and text. Next, we investigate the processes involved in deriving their meaning. Two "classical" models that represent both meaning and processing at multiple levels are discussed next. Relevant empirical studies into important meaning-related issues and on the role of context conclude the chapter. Note that in this chapter, we use the terms "meaning," "semantic," and "conceptual" as interchangeable, neglecting differences in linguistic and psycholinguistic use of these terms.

SUMMARY: MEANING: THE ESSENCE

What should we consider the meaning of a word to be? Semanticists often consider word meanings as abstract representations with particular features. Such semantic representations (or concepts, as psychologists call them) are assumed to be linked up in large semantic networks. Nevertheless, word meaning is not only abstract, but also embodied and multimodal. Even simple words such as "pipe," "tomato," or "flower" may remind you of their typical smell, visual appearance, or manual affordances. The object's meaning can involve aspects of perception, action and movement, emotion, and more. The meaning of a word may also differ as a function of the context in which it is used. How are word meanings integrated when we process sentences or texts? In this chapter, we will explore various views on meaning proposed in the psychology of language.

8.2 MEANING: REPRESENTATIONS

8.2.1 Sense and reference

A fundamental distinction in semantics is the difference between reference and sense. A word can have meaning because it refers to an object, person, or event in the real world. For instance, the word "table" refers to this object in the world on which this book currently lies or this laptop currently stands. It is important to note that the word form often has no immediately evident relationship to the meaning; it can often be considered relatively arbitrary (but see Blasi et al., 2016). The English word "tree" does not look like an actual tree or sound like a tree when you read it out loud (de Saussure, 1916, 1998). When we learn the meaning of such concrete words, we can do that by pointing at the actual objects or events around us. This kind of meaning is referred to as the *reference* or *extension* of the word. We learn which aspects (or features) of tables and trees are consistent and relevant by coming across these entities time and again.

The more abstract meaning of a word can be derived by its association to other words. For instance, the word "fire truck" is linked to other words such as "red," "car," "smoke," "driving," and so on. This kind of meaning is called the *sense* or *intension* of the word. However, abstract categories may overlook practical differences in meaning. In the expression "a red fire truck," the word "red" refers a very specific shade of "red" because of our experiences with specific fire trucks. Or consider, more poetically, the Zen saying that "a white heron in snow changes color."

Some words have a meaning that can only be partially derived from direct observation. For instance, a word such as "anger" will be associated with certain bodily behavior (shouting, a red face, etc.), but needs additional meaning aspects to be correctly represented. These can be derived from what a person feels when they are angry ("They say I am angry, and I feel my hands tremble, perspiration, and a gut in flame"). They can also be linked up via sense relations to other concepts of a social nature ("Anger happens when ..."). There are many words that can be learned by a combination of direct reference and sense relations: "war," "winter," "college," and so on.

The meaning of still other words cannot be derived easily or directly from objects or events in the world. These are words such as "God," "ego," or "evolution." Their meanings are to a large extent learned on the basis of sense relations, although according to some scientists there may always be some sort of embodiment underlying this meaning (e.g., certain physical experiences may be associated with the meaning of the word "God"). Clearly, this type of words is open for misinterpretation and ambiguity, even more than other words are. Words like "God" and "ego" are quite *fuzzy*, because they may evoke different sense relations in different people.

The system of sense relations between word meanings or concepts (stored in Conceptual Memory) can be seen as a "semantic network" or a "conceptual network."

In general, words have both sense and reference. For instance, the word "queen" can be understood in relation to words like "king," "royal," "female," and even "animate" (sense), but it can also refer to Queen Elizabeth, until recently the British queen in the real world (reference). In this context, Finegan (2014, p. 192) defines a word's semantic or linguistic meaning as: "[r]eferential meaning (the real-word object/concept picked out or described by an expression) and sense meaning."

8.2.2 Word meaning representations

Earlier theories about meaning at the *word* level focused more on sense relationships, and more recent theories more on reference. Furthermore, holistic views focus on the relations between whole word concepts in terms of semantic networks, while featural views associate every concept with a set of features that can be shared between words or not (Vigliocco & Vinson, 2007). In the following sections, advantages and problems of the two proposals will be indicated.

8.2.2.1 Semantic networks

Meaning relationships between words can be indicated by connections in networks (Collins & Quillian, 1969). The (sense) meaning of a word is then determined by the position of the concept node within the "conceptual network" as a whole (see Figure 8.3 for a simple example).

The types of connection or relationship between the concepts can be specified in the networks via abstract *propositions*, such as the IS-EXEMPLAR-OF or IS-A connection that indicates that a concept is part of a particular collection. This connection exists, for instance, between the concepts CANARY and BIRD (it is the unnamed connection between the hyponym (subtype) CANARY and the hypernym (supertype) BIRD in Figure 8.4). Other types are the HAS and CAN connections.

Of special interest are hierarchical networks (as in Figure 8.4). In such networks, properties (features) at a higher level in the hierarchy are shared by all concepts lower in the hierarchy. For instance, the property of BIRD that it is an animal is "inherited" (unless stated otherwise) by all concepts lower in the hierarchy, such as CANARY and OSTRICH. The opposite is not true: Lower level concepts can have their own unique properties. This kind of network works well for particular sorts of taxonomy (e.g., family relationships), but not for others (such as color terms).

Semantic networks are very flexible and can easily be individualized (e.g., in mind maps). A disadvantage of semantic networks is that certain predictions about their use are not borne out empirically. For instance, it is not necessarily more difficult to decide that a canary is an animal than that a bird is an animal, even though BIRD is located hierarchically closer to ANIMAL than CANARY in a hierarchical semantic network (see Figure 8.4). Furthermore, in the end semantic networks must be linked up to the world by means of reference relations.

Figure 8.4 implies that speakers must select words of a certain hierarchy level. Do they call their pet bird an "animal," "bird," "canary," or "Woodstock" when talking about it? Because speakers usually try to be informative but nonredundant (see "Gricean maxims," Chapter 9), they often prefer using so-called *basic level terms* (Rosch, 1973). Thus, they would prefer to talk about their pet bird not as

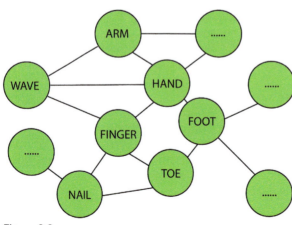

Figure 8.3
A simple conceptual network with nodes for words and their pairwise semantic relationships. Items in capitals refer to concepts.

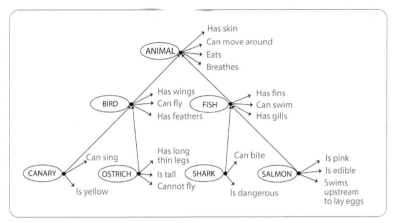

Figure 8.4
Hierarchical semantic network with feature properties. After Collins and Quillian (1969).

"that living thing," "the animal," or "this bird," but about "our canary" or, more affectionately, "Woodstock."

Many issues remain, such as how the preferred level of terms changes when we learn more about the world or find ourselves in different situations (take a biologist talking about fish to colleagues vs. to first-year students vs. to her kids), how abstract concepts are represented, and how we understand new word combinations, for example, "hairy shark."

8.2.2.2 WordNet

WordNet (Miller & Fellbaum, 1991) is a holistic network approach to lexico-semantic memory that interrelates the meaning of tens of thousands of English nouns, adjectives, and verbs. It assumes a many-to-many mapping between word form and word meaning: The same word form may have several different meanings (e.g., as in the case of polysemy), and the same meaning can be expressed using different word forms (e.g., as in the case of synonymy). In this approach, different types of semantic relation are assumed for syntactic categories including nouns, adjectives, and verbs.

In WordNet, English nouns are typically closely connected to their synonyms (e.g., GIFT and PRESENT), to their hypernyms (FLOWER is a hypernym of ROSE), to their hyponyms (FORK is a hyponym of UTENSIL), and/or to their meronyms (a NOSE is a part of a FACE).

Unlike nouns, many English adjectives are assumed to be semantically organized as a function of antonymy: GOOD versus BAD, WEAK versus STRONG, LIGHT versus DARK. Color adjectives are an exception within the system, as people may find it hard to come up with an adjective that has the opposite meaning of, for instance, "pink." Therefore, color adjectives may be organized as a function of lightness, hue, and saturation.

Finally, in WordNet, verbs are the most complex category of words when it comes to their semantic organization. Most verbs may be understood through troponymy: "TO VERB-1 is TO VERB-2 in some manner." For instance, "TO WALK is TO MOVE in some manner." Verbs may also be related in terms of entailment: "TO SNORE entails TO SLEEP" – if you are snoring, you must also be sleeping. Some other verbs may be organized in terms of opposition, similar to the antonymy relations we have seen for adjectives: "TO LENGTHEN is the opposite of TO SHORTEN."

In sum, WordNet assumes a certain semantic structure of the lexicon in which words can be related via different types of relation, most importantly dependent on the grammatical category they belong to.

8.2.2.3 Semantic features

So far we have considered the meaning of words more or less as unified. However, closer scrutiny suggests that meaning requires further differentiation. For instance, all species of birds share certain properties or features. In general, birds have wings and feathers. Concepts in a particular category share particular features and differ in others. The features that they must share to be called "bird" are called "defining features" and those that are characteristic to a concept in particular are called "characteristic features." So for a bird to be a "bird" it *must* have wings and feathers; and it *may* be able to sing or have long thin legs. (Note that because "can fly" is indicated as a feature of "bird" it might be considered as a defining feature, even though an ostrich cannot fly!)

Although networks can represent the same information as features (Hollan, 1975), the two are processed in a different way. To determine if a canary is a bird, one must look up the "IS-A" connection of CANARY with BIRD, whereas in a feature representation one must first look up what the defining features of a bird are, and whether a canary possesses those features.

There is abundant empirical evidence that semantic features somehow play a role in meaning representations and processing. For instance, a speech error such as "I always drink one egg a week" suggests that "drink" replaced "eat" because, while both verbs are about consuming something, "drink" missed out on the feature "solid material" (also see Chapter 9).

The notion of semantic features originally comes from linguistics (called "semantic markers" by Chomsky). Here features were proposed to be *binary* (just like phonological features such as voice), for instance +MALE (masculine) or –MALE (feminine). One can already tell by the vocabulary used that this view is a bit outdated. Similar oppositions can be made for human/non-human, concrete/abstract, adult/child, living/non-living, parent/non-parent. We can assume that words are characterized by feature bundles, and that "semantic decomposition" reveals these features. For instance, the distinction +MALE/–MALE (or MALE/FEMALE) is useful to describe the meaning of whole classes of words: man/woman, boy/girl, uncle/aunt, nephew/niece, and so on. Synonyms can be considered as words for concepts that have shared collections of features (e.g., sofa, couch), whereas antonyms are words for concepts that share features but can be contrasted on one characteristic (e.g., nephew/niece) (cf. Chapter 6).

Note that the difference between defining and characteristic features is not so clear. One might define a table as "a piece of furniture consisting of a flat slab fixed on legs" (Miller & Fellbaum, 1991, p. 200), but according to this definition, a horizontal hanging board without legs in a restaurant is not a table. In addition, it is not clear why a chair could not sometimes be a table according to this definition. The problem is even more serious if one tries to define and distinguish concepts such as DOG and CAT, and when we consider more abstract and "fuzzy" terms, e.g., GAME. Wittgenstein (1953) has noticed that the word "game" can be used for activities that do not appear to have anything in common, such as "the game of Monopoly" and "the game of love."

8.2.2.4 Featural and Unitary Semantic Space

Featural approaches assume that two words are semantically related to the extent that they share certain semantic features. One statistically implemented approach is the Featural and

Unitary Semantic Space hypothesis (FUSS; Vigliocco et al., 2004). FUSS strongly relies on so-called *feature norms*. To obtain such norms, people are asked to come up with a list of meaningful features that for them describe or define a word as completely as possible (McRae et al., 1997; Vinson & Vigliocco, 2008). For instance, the word "dog" might elicit the features *pet, animal, has fur, barks,* and *four legs* in one participant, and *pet, animal, friendly, has a tail,* and *mammal* in another. Participants in this task are instructed to avoid pure word-word associations – after all, the word "cat" is not a feature of the concept DOG.

The features elicited for a large number of concepts from a large number of participants can be organized using *self-organizing maps*, a dimensionality reduction technique that uses unsupervised learning and can be visualized using word clusters. If a certain feature for a given word appears in the feature norms of many participants, that feature gains in importance for that word. Concepts may differ in how many features they are associated with, and features may correlate and/or be shared across concepts. Concepts are then related to a separate level of lexico-semantic representations, each of which binds a number of conceptual features, and as a whole constitute the interface between the conceptual information and the linguistic information stored in Long Term Memory (e.g., which phonemes a word consists of, or its grammatical gender). Words hence typically represent a set of bound conceptual features. In other words, features themselves could be seen as very simple concepts.

Critically, FUSS can account for the meaning of both objects (corresponding to the nouns used to elicit feature norms) and actions (corresponding to the verbs used to elicit feature norms), while many other models typically focus solely on (mostly concrete) objects that can be linked to single (mostly concrete) nouns. In addition, unlike the global co-occurrence models that we will discuss later, one could argue that the model is to some extent grounded in reality, as many features refer to visual/perceptual information (e.g., *pink* for "grapefruit"), functional properties (e.g., *cuts* for "scissors"), or motoric aspects (e.g., *hand-held* for "axe") of a concept. Note that not all languages need to have a word for a specific concept (also see Chapter 10).

One empirical finding that FUSS can account for, while WordNet cannot, is the so-called *graded semantic effect*. Consider the concepts ORANGE and CHERRY. Both are types of fruit, just like GRAPE. If we assume concepts to be organized in a hierarchical semantic network, according to WordNet, all three words should activate the superordinate ("mother") term FRUIT and prime one another to the same extent. Clearly, however, CHERRY and GRAPE have more overlap than CHERRY and ORANGE in terms of semantic features (e.g., *relatively small, grow in clusters/bunches,* etc.). Featural approaches such as FUSS explain the differential (graded) amount of priming between words from the same semantic category by considering the degree and strength of feature overlap between word pairs and allowing for variation in semantic distance between subordinate word pairs.

8.2.2.5 Exemplar and instance theory

In exemplar theories, concepts are closely linked to the objects or events they represent in the world (their references). According to instance theories, our experiences with particular objects or categories of objects are stored as *instances* or *exemplars*. For instance, we come across all kinds of animal that are similar and different in some respects. Birds are similar in that most of them fly, sing, and lay eggs. Typically, the birds that we encounter are not very large, and several of them may be black or brown. Nevertheless, we also store our experiences with ostriches and penguins in the category BIRDS.

When we observe a new "unidentified flying object," we can compare it to all the exemplars in the category BIRD and allocate it to that category if the resemblance to one or several exemplars is large enough. For instance, although bats can fly, seeing a bat might not lead to the judgment "It is a bird," because it may deviate in too many other features from previously observed birds (e.g., in terms of flying behavior, body shape, and the sounds it makes). According to this view, one would expect faster responses in an experiment when the presented object is similar to the exemplars/instances already known.

8.2.2.6 Prototypes

A related view would be that people store their experiences with each instance in different categories, but that they are (also) abstracting from them. For instance, we could derive a "stereotypical" bird for the concept BIRD by averaging all the instances we know in the category BIRD. Such an abstract average representation of a category is called a "prototype" (Rosch, 1978). We call a new object a bird if it is sufficiently similar to the prototype. Note that by averaging, information about the variability across different exemplars in a category is lost when a prototype is built. For extreme members of a category (a penguin in the bird category), "fuzzy" categories (like GAME), and atypical examples (like a dog with three legs or a pink elephant) this might be undesirable. Here exemplar theory would be better suited. In all, it would be useful to have both exemplars and prototypes at one's disposal when categorizing new objects. It is possible to combine or mix prototype and exemplar theories. However, it is often unclear how the different theories can be tested empirically.

8.2.2.7 Semantic space based on global co-occurrence

The notion that one can average across particular defining or characteristic features of exemplars in a category to obtain a prototype, suggests that meaning could be defined with respect to different dimensions that set up some sort of "semantic space." For instance, the axes of such a space in three dimensions could be "How well does it fly?," "How large is it?," and "Does it lay eggs?". The distance in semantic space would then indicate how similar two (types of) birds are to one another.

An even more abstract way to use semantic space is the following. On the basis of a large corpus of sentences and texts, it is determined which words are often present in one another's neighborhood. If words often co-occur, this can be considered as a sign of their being related in meaning (syntactic aspects must be excluded somehow). Via cluster analyses and similar techniques, a multidimensional space with abstract dimensions (not directly representing properties) can be derived (see Figure 8.5).

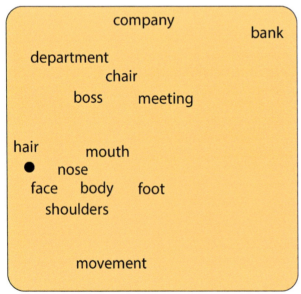

Figure 8.5
Latent semantic analysis of a word results in a semantic space in which other words (here limited to nouns) are placed at a certain distance as a function of co-occurrence properties. The closer in space two words are, the more similar they are assumed to be in meaning. The figure presents the hypothetical, simplified semantic space for the word "head," which itself is indicated by a filled dot.

Two approaches to "distributional semantics" are Latent Semantic Analysis (LSA) and Hyperspace Analogue to Language (HAL). Using a large corpus of items, LSA considers in which contexts particular words occur (Landauer & Dumais, 1997). When some words occur in more similar contexts than others, they are considered to be more semantically similar on certain abstract dimensions. Counting words that occur together in a paragraph of short text, it is possible to filter syntactic information out. In the HAL approach, Lund and Burgess (1996) investigated the co-occurrence of 70,000 words with other words for a total corpus of 300 million words. This matrix was simplified to one with about 100 to 200 abstract dimensions.

In WordNet, which exact nodes in the network are connected to one another is specified by hand by the researchers on the basis of (elicited) intuitions. This makes WordNet sensitive to subjective biases and assumptions. Global co-occurrence models such as LSA and HAL circumvent this issue by simply looking at the global co-occurrence of word pairs in large text corpora. If two words often appear together, they are assumed to share parts of their meaning. It is irrelevant to the model what exact semantic features or properties are shared between words – as long as they often co-occur in a linguistic context, it assumes that they must be semantically related.

8.2.2.8 Embodied representation

The types of meaning representation discussed so far put an important focus on sense relationships. Such meaning relations are often amodal and can be quite abstract. An alternative view that has gained in popularity is that representations of concepts are in fact directly linked or even identical to sensory perceptions and bodily actions. In this view, abstract concepts might be represented via perceptual or action metaphors ("Time is movement," "Knowing is seeing," "Time is money"; Lakoff & Johnson, 1980). Such embodiment implies the involvement of brain areas having to do with sensory or motor information. Indeed, it has been found that the neural visual pathway is activated during comprehension of the word "green" (Simmons et al., 2007; van Dam et al., 2012), while the word "grasp" may activate brain regions involved in planning and carrying out grasping actions (Hauk et al., 2004; Rueschemeyer et al., 2010).

According to an embodied semantic view, the meaning of a word does not become available all at once, but more and more meaning aspects may become activated over time. Thus, it may be better to conceive meaning not as a holistic representation with a definite beginning or end, but as involving activation of resonating circuits in the brain. Words and sentences may evoke abstract meaning, but also have perceptual, motor, and emotional aspects to them. Although one could consider these last (analog) aspects in terms of a contextual influence of non-linguistic cognitive systems, the integrated nature of the Language User Framework allows us to propose as an alternative that concepts can include various dimensions (possibly at the same time): varying from abstract (e.g., mathematics) and functional (e.g., tool vs. person) to concrete (e.g., image, colors) and embodied (e.g., movement, emotion).

Indeed, it would be a mistake to consider meaning as a purely abstract affair. The adjective "red'" evokes a clear sensory experience that may become even more refined when we speak about "the red fire truck." A verb such as "to stumble" may also trigger a certain motor experience. A very important meaning dimension of words is that of their "affective or connotative meaning." Cato et al. (2004, p. 167) define affective meaning as "a semantic attribute conveying, often implicitly, the pleasant or unpleasant nature of an object or experience." Said differently, words often express or evoke emotions. There are three dimensions that are often discerned in this respect (Osgood, 1966). First, a word concept can be experienced as positive (or pleasant),

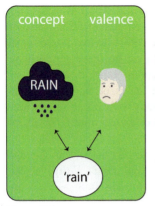 

Figure 8.6
Relation between word form, word meaning (concept), and valence.

neutral, or negative (or unpleasant). This is called the *valence* of a word. Happiness, table, and shark differ along this dimension (also see Figure 8.6). Second, a word concept may be more or less *physically arousing*. Words such as "nightmare" and "shark" for most people may evoke stronger physical responses than words such as "bicycle" or "toucan." Third, a dimension that has come into focus more recently is that of dominance vs. submissiveness: A concept may be considered weak and controlled (WIND VANE) or strong and in control (BULLDOZER). Databases containing word ratings on these and other dimensions for many words are available (e.g., Sianipar et al., 2016; Warriner et al., 2013). Psycholinguistics must incorporate emotional dimensions of meaning, because they contribute significantly to human behavior (Damasio, 1994).

8.2.3 Sentence meaning representations

Notions including semantic features, instances, and prototypes are useful when considering meaning at the level of individual words, but they cannot easily be applied to the sentence level. However, a different formalism has been proposed that can be applied at word, sentence, and even text level: that of *propositions*.

First note that features themselves could be considered as very simple concepts (e.g., MALE or FEMALE). In a proposition, we relate two concepts to one another by specifying their relationship. For instance, to indicate that Maria is a female, we can express this as the proposition IS-A(MARIA, FEMALE). If we would wish to work with binary features, we can express the concept FEMALE as NOT(MALE), turning the proposition into IS-A(MARIA, NOT(MALE)). A sentence such as "Maria is a girl" can be represented in terms of a combination of propositions: NOT(ADULT(MARIA)) & NOT(MALE(MARIA)) & HUMAN (MARIA) (Schank & Abelson, 1977; Schank & Birnbaum, 1984). Propositions provide some flexibility in describing meaning relationships between words. For instance, a concept like PARENTHOOD expresses a relation between two persons. It can be represented as a proposition by giving the function two arguments: PARENT(X, Y). If Jim is the parent of John, this can be expressed as PARENT(JIM, JOHN).

Meaning aspects like TO CAUSE, TO CHANGE, and TO DENY can be represented by propositions. Consider, for instance, the relation between verb pairs like "receive" and "give," "come" and "bring," "going up" and "lifting up," "learning" and "teaching." The second verb of each pair appears to contain a meaning aspect TO CAUSE. "Teaching" can then be paraphrased by "to cause someone to learn something." If "x learns y" is represented by the proposition LEARN(X, Y), "x teaches y to z" can then be represented as CAUSE (X, (LEARN(Z, Y))). Learning itself appears to mean "to become able to do something," so it could be represented in terms of a complex proposition COME-ABOUT(ABLE (X, (DO(X, Y)))) or something similar.

In sum, a proposition relates two concepts (arguments) to one another by a particular function (a predicate, which is a third concept), for instance, IS-EXEMPLAR-OF(TWEETY,

BIRD). Propositions themselves can be complex and are therefore useful at both the word and the sentence level. They can be interrelated in trees. For instance, IS-A(JOHN, MAN) can be linked to IS-A(JOHN, FATHER) because the two propositions share the concept JOHN. Below, we shall see that this is very useful for understanding sentences in a text.

Propositions are amodal, which has advantages (e.g., logic can be applied to them) but also disadvantages (e.g., how to link them to real-life situations?). Consider the following sentence: "The first person on Mars was a woman." When the first edition of this book was printed, this statement as a whole had no reference in the real world (only in a "possible world"; Menzel, 2022), but that does not mean that the sentence cannot be understood. At sense level, the meaning of the words are related into a meaning for the sentence as a whole. Individual words still may have a reference in the real world (e.g., "Mars"). It could be said that establishing the sense of the sentence is necessary for determining its reference by comparison to reality.

Over the decades, several formalisms similar to propositions and with different levels of abstraction have been proposed to interrelate the functional meanings of words in sentences. For instance, in case grammar (Fillmore, 1968) grammatical functions (subject, verb, object) were linked to semantic ("thematic") roles (agent, object, recipient, location, or instrument). The sentence "The father gave the daughter the book" could be represented more or less as (agent, action, recipient, object). In the previous chapter, we saw a similar type of structure for sentence processing in action: the event structure.

8.2.4 Text meaning representations

While sentences have clearly circumscribed *syntactic* structures, the texts and discourse they are often part of do not. However, those types of sentence or utterance collection still can be described as more or less organized successions of *semantic* (or *conceptual*) events. Because of this observation, the Language User Framework considers discourse comprehension and production to be done by the Conceptual System.

Take, for instance, a fairy tale or an average novel, which have some clearly recognizable patterns: A theme is defined, a problem introduced, the problem is resolved after a number of attempts (or not), and the protagonists of the story may live happily ever after (or not). *Story grammars* provide some often used organizations of stories. They are not really grammars, but more like descriptions of organizations of events.

Because they frequently encounter them, readers are familiar with these organizations, which they retrieve from Long Term Memory when appropriate. The stored information is of enough detail that they can link up sentences even when particular parts are skipped. It will, for instance, not come as a surprise to them if the protagonists in the fairy tale turn out to be a prince and princess, even when the prince first figured as a frog.

Two other well-known ways to organize information in texts are schemas and scripts. *Schemas* are organized packages of world knowledge. They contain slots and values. An example is the schema of a HOUSE, which may contain subschemas for different rooms and slots for what we find there. A prototype can be considered as a special type of schema.

Another schema type is the *script*. Well-known scripts are the "visiting a restaurant" script and the "attending a lecture" script. They specify activities in a particular order, e.g., "enter the restaurant," "find a table," "pick up the menu," "order," "eat," "pay," "give a tip." Sentences such as "John went into the fast-food restaurant. He ordered a burger but did not give a tip" can be easily understood by linking their information to the restaurant script, filling in information gaps by the default information in the script. Scripts may change over time: "Pick up the menu" may in certain parts of the world be replaced by "Scan the QR-code."

TABLE 8.1 Contrasting propositions and mental models

Proposition
- arbitrary: no relation between form and content
- amodal: no relation with perception or action
- advantages: can be implemented, has a clear relationship with language, is suitable for word meaning
- issues: grounding-problem, difficulty in accounting for empirical data

Mental model
- analog: content is (largely) represented in a sense-dependent format
- modal: directly connected to perception, action, and/or emotion
- advantage: no grounding-problem
- issues: complex, relation to language underspecified, abstract meaning understood via metaphor?

Different approaches differ in the degree to which they specify textual information. For instance, propositional structures do only consider the basic abstract meanings (sense), but do not provide analog, modality-specific information (reference). Story grammars, scripts, and schemas may provide general frameworks for capturing ongoing events, but again, their reference to the real world may be incomplete. This has been called the "grounding-problem" (Clark & Brennan, 1991).

Both sense and reference relations can be included in the semantic representation of text or discourse in terms of a *mental model* (Doyle & Ford, 1998; Johnson-Laird, 2013; Miller & Johnson-Laird, 1976). As we saw in earlier chapters, this notion represents situations not in terms of a strictly proposition-oriented "situation model," but a model that is "analogous" to the world and contains sensory, motor, emotional, and other embodied information. Thus, the model is much "richer" in information than the situation models discussed above. However, this richness also comes at a cost. Mental models can be so complex that they are hard to specify. In addition, they are also subjective and incomplete (Goldvarg & Johnson-Laird, 2000). In some cases, their relationship to language and language use is not fully clear. The differences between propositions and mental models are summarized in Table 8.1.

8.2.5 Meaning in the brain

Researchers have investigated how (word) meaning is represented in the brain by looking at neurological patients who encounter specific meaning-related language difficulties in their everyday interaction with others. Damasio and colleagues (1996) had 127 patients with a specific ("focal") lesion name photographs of well-known people ("persons"), images of animals ("animals"), and images of tools ("tools"). Some patients had difficulties retrieving the correct word for a subset of these images, even

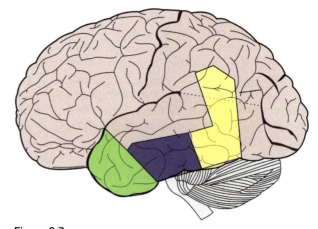

Figure 8.7
Lesions in different parts of the left hemisphere lead to deficits in word retrieval from different conceptual categories. Lesions in the area indicated in green correlate with difficulties in retrieving the name of persons, while the area in blue correlates with problems naming animals, and the area in yellow corresponds to tool naming difficulties. Note that these are not the only areas involved in naming images – this process is also subserved by a network of classic perisylvian areas (see Chapter 9). After Damasio et al. (1996).

though they knew the concepts depicted in the images. Using the positron emission tomography (PET) technique (see Chapter 4), the authors also considered which exact part of the brain of each patient was damaged.

Interestingly, the anatomical location of the lesion correlated with the conceptual category the patients had trouble with. Patients with a lesion in more anterior regions of the left temporal lobe (colored green in Figure 8.7) had most difficulty retrieving words for persons. Those patients with difficulties in retrieving words for animals typically had a lesion in "inferotemporal" areas of the left hemisphere (colored blue in Figure 8.7). Difficulties in retrieving words for tools was observed in patients with a lesion in areas around the junction of the left temporal, parietal, and occipital lobe and in more posterior temporal areas of the left hemisphere (colored yellow in Figure 8.7). These findings were in line with the patterns of brain activation observed in healthy participants naming images of persons, animals, and tools. For instance, naming an image of a person led to enhanced activation of more anterior temporal areas, while naming a tool led to enhanced activation around the junction of the lobes.

What are the consequences of these observations for how we should think about representation of word meaning? If concepts are represented purely as abstract features, they should all be equal, and one would not expect large differences in which parts of the brain are involved in retrieving the names of images that correspond to different semantic categories (persons, animals, tools). Indeed, the PET findings show that not all concepts are equal: Word meaning (stored in Conceptual Memory) must consist of more than just abstract representations.

SUMMARY: MEANING: REPRESENTATIONS

A word can have meaning because it refers to an object or event in the real world (reference). A more abstract meaning of a word lies in its association or relation to other words (sense). Words often have both sense and reference. Word concepts have been conceived of as nodes in a large conceptual network and categorized based on which (defining) semantic features they shared. Conceptual experiences with objects or events in the world could be stored as exemplars and/or linked to prototypes in memory. In addition, co-occurrence of word pairs in texts may indicate semantic relatedness. More recently, the embodied and affective meanings that word forms elicit have started to receive more scholarly attention.

Sentence meaning has traditionally been thought of in terms of propositions. A proposition relates two concepts (arguments) to one another by a function, such as IS-A or IS-EXEMPLAR-OF. Standard meaning organizations in larger stretches of text have been captured in story grammars, schemas, scripts, and mental models.

8.3 MEANING: PROCESSES

8.3.1 Embodiedness: Effects of other cognitive modalities

Our developing argumentation leads to a characterization of meaning in which abstract propositions alone do not suffice for language processing. Intuitively, it appears that people in real-life situations are open to detailed sensory aspects of the world. Thus, *processing meaning* must also entail some sort of embodiedness. Research indeed indicates that propositions alone fail in accounting for all empirical word and sentence processing data. In a study by Zwaan and colleagues (2002), participants read one of the following two sentences: (a) "The ranger saw the eagle in the sky," with the propositions SAW(RANGER, EAGLE) and IN(EAGLE, SKY), or (b) "The ranger saw the eagle in the nest" with the propositions SAW(RANGER, EAGLE) and IN(EAGLE, NEST). Note that these two sentences correspond to extremely similar propositions. Next, a picture appeared and the participants decided if the picture matched the sentence or not (Experiment 1) or they named the object in the picture (Experiment 2). In Experiment 1, slower responses were given to pictures when they mismatched with the preceding sentences (i.e., saying "no" took longer than saying "yes"). Does this happen because the participants had to compare sentences and pictures? Experiment 2 showed this was not the case: Participants also had slower *naming* responses to the picture after a mismatching preceding sentence (e.g., when an eagle in the sky was presented after the sentence "The ranger saw the eagle in the nest"). These findings can be interpreted as evidence for embodied representations: The concept of an eagle on its nest is not identical to that of an eagle in the sky. Further empirical evidence supporting this position will be discussed later in the chapter.

Embodiedness implies that over time meaning retrieval can activate modality-specific brain areas dedicated to perception or action in the real world. Neurophysiological evidence using EEG and fMRI supports this view. In a study by Kiefer et al. (2011), participants saw a target picture preceded by either a word or a picture. On a cue, they had to name both stimuli. The word-picture and picture-picture pairs were either congruent (pliers – nutcracker) or incongruent (pliers – horseshoe) with respect to the implied action. Picture primes were found to elicit early (N1) and late (N400) priming effects, but the word primes only showed late effects in the N400. This suggests that there may be fast and slow activation of action features for pictures, but (relatively) slow activation for words. Possibly, certain features are more salient for pictures than for words, leading to an earlier activation of more detailed action representations.

On the basis of these and similar results (e.g., Davis & Yee, 2019; Yee et al., 2011), it becomes interesting to consider the relative temporal dynamics of the activation of functional (more abstract), visual, and motor (more concrete) aspects of meaning. When does such embodied semantic information become available during language processing? Lam et al. (2015) investigated how long it takes for action-based, visual-form, and semantic-associative information to contribute to semantic activation in language comprehension. In a German priming paradigm with go/no-go lexical decision (see Chapter 4), the prime and target words had one of four different relations. For example, the German word for "screwdriver" could be preceded by (a) the word for "housekey" in the action-based condition, (b) the word for "soldering iron" in the visual-form condition, (c) the word for "bolt" in the semantic condition, and (d) the word for "charger" in the unrelated condition. The intervals between the prime and target stimulus were varied to assess the relative time course of activation of different features. Action priming effects were already found at short interstimulus intervals, while visual priming required more time. These results suggest that feature activation follows different time-courses during word recognition depending on the type of feature. This would be in line with the idea that different routes and routes of different lengths must be completed through the brain to retrieve different aspects of meaning.

Binder and colleagues (2009) carried out a meta-analysis of experimental neuroimaging (PET and fMRI) studies to find out what parts of the brain are recruited when people access knowledge stored in their Conceptual System on the basis of the words they read or hear. The analysis showed that conceptual knowledge is not stored in one specific brain area or lobe. Rather, areas in the frontal, temporal, and parietal lobe were found to support accessing conceptual knowledge. Indeed, a large part of our brain seems important for providing us with the conceptual knowledge we have stored based on our experiences. The widespread nature of the areas involved in conceptual processing is perhaps not surprising, as we use conceptual knowledge in almost everything we do: from producing and understanding utterances to performing context-appropriate non-linguistic actions to planning what to do next. The observation that the observed brain areas are substantially less expanded in non-human primates such as macaques could even be taken to suggest differences in behavior and performance on such everyday tasks across species (Binder et al., 2009).

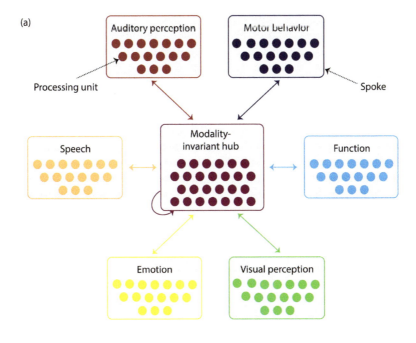

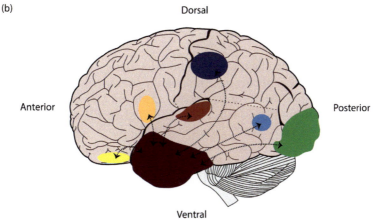

Figure 8.8
(a) Bidirectional links between modality-specific cognitive functions and the modality-invariant "hub" here depicted in the middle. (b) This "hub" is actually located in the anterior temporal lobe and the modality-specific "spokes" in different areas of the brain. Colors in this bottom image correspond to colors in the top image. For instance, visual perceptual processing (depicted in green in both images) is subserved by occipital brain areas. After Lambon Ralph et al. (2017).

Lambon Ralph et al. (2010, 2017) proposed a "hub-and-spoke" theory of semantics more or less in line with these conclusions. According to this theory, humans develop concepts on the basis of multimodal verbal and non-verbal experiences and encode these in various modality-specific parts of the cortex. These brain areas constitute the "spokes" in the theory's name. The "hub" in the theory is the transmodal bilateral brain area in the anterior temporal lobe that mediates cross-modal interactions between modality-specific resources (see Figure 8.8). This area might therefore be engaged in activities ascribed to the Conceptual System in the Language User Framework.

It is tempting to relate the "hub-and-spoke" theory to mental models. Their development over time could be conceived of as a continuously fine-tuned updating of the "spoke and hub" brain network in this theory. Modality-specific and modality-invariant properties of meaning could be linked in terms of complex time-stamped representations handled by the "hub" in the anterior temporal lobe. We will come back to this idea in Chapter 11.

8.3.2 Linking the meaning of subsequent sentences by inferences

When we process subsequent sentences during listening, reading, or speaking, they are usually not understood on their own. Subsequent sentences in text and discourse are typically related in some way and their linkage must be understood for proper processing and understanding. Linking the meanings of sentences is usually done by making inferences. An *inference* refers to information that is not literally in the text, but can be derived from it, usually with help of background knowledge and one's experience in processing texts and discourse. Important types of inference are "bridging inferences," "elaborative inferences," and anaphors (or anaphora). In the following sections, we will discuss aspects of these meaning-related issues spanning two or more sentences.

8.3.2.1 Bridging inferences

Consider the following two sentences:

(1) John and Mary went out for a picnic.
(2) The beer was warm.

The two sentences can be linked by the proposition that there was beer in the picnic supplies. This inference entails a *backward inference*, linking the second sentence to the first one afterwards. According to Garrod and Terras (2000), there are two processes involved in this "bridging" process. First, concepts such as PICNIC and BEER are activated on the basis of important words (a process called "bonding"). Second, the representation of the whole situation is linked to the first sentence ("resolution"): "The picnic supplies contained drinks; beer is a drink."

8.3.2.2 Elaborative inferences: Forward and backward

Readers and listeners enrich the sentences they are reading or hearing by adding world knowledge. They do so not only when they draw backward inferences, but also in *forward inferences*, where they anticipate forthcoming developments. For instance, when Aladdin drops the crystal decanter on the marble floor, it might be inferred that it will break into a thousand pieces. But do people make such an inference in a forward or backward fashion?

Considerable research effort has been made to investigate how many and which inferences readers and listeners actually make. According to a *minimalist approach*, readers and listeners restrict themselves as much as possible to information in the message that is conveyed (McKoon & Ratcliff, 1992). They only make inferences on the basis of locally present or easily available information. Making predictions may be cognitively demanding and there are scores of possibilities (Rayner & Pollatsek, 1989, p. 284). According to a *constructionist approach*, readers and listeners try to develop a coherent representation of the message, a mental model (Bransford et al., 1972). They make inferences when information is missing that is necessary for coherence in the model. Thus, they do make forward inferences when these are very predictable or important to the goal of the addressee (e.g., testing a particular expectation). In recent years, the notion that people make forward inferences or predictions has gained in prominence.

It is possible that specific forward inferences or predictions are not automatically made, but more general ones are. For instance, when reading about John eating soup on the train, the sentence "Suddenly the train screeched to a halt" might lead the reader to predict that something is going to happen, but not necessarily to elaborate precisely that "The soup is spilled in John's lap" (Duffy, 1986).

8.3.2.3 Inferences: Anaphors and antecedents

Important research on (bridging) inferences has concerned anaphors. An *anaphor* is a word that gets its meaning from an expression (the *antecedent*) positioned earlier in the text. Consider the following sentences (taken from O'Brien et al., 1988, p. 420):

All the mugger wanted was to steal the woman's money. But when she screamed

(1) he stabbed her with his knife
(2) he stabbed her with his weapon
(3) he assaulted her with his weapon

in an attempt to quiet her. He threw the knife away and ran.

The knife in the last sentence is an anaphor. *His weapon* or *his knife* in the previous sentence is its antecedent.

It was found that readers who were presented with these different sentence variants looked just as long at the word *knife* in the final sentence after (1) and after (2), but for a longer time after (3). It can therefore be concluded that after (2), because of the specifics of the verb "to stab," a forward inference is made that *weapon = knife*. This is why the antecedent of *the knife* is found as quickly as after (1). However, after (3) the knife is not yet known, causing a longer time to find the antecedent.

Pronouns (*he, she, ...*) can also function as anaphors. In the case of pronouns, various information sources can be used to find the antecedent. Finding the antecedent is also called "resolution." There are numerous ways in which the antecedent can be determined. First, in many languages, syntactic information such as gender and number can be used, as in the example: "Anna called Jack and Jim because **he/she/they** wanted to know something."

Second, the antecedent can be found using "foregrounding," i.e., the information that is in focus. For instance, there is the *first-mention effect*, meaning that the first mentioned entity has the preference for assignment: "Greta ate the cookies that Jane made. Then **she** drank a cup of tea." *She* would here refer to *Greta*, because Greta was mentioned first.

Third, *implicit causality* may play a role in finding the antecedent. This means that some transitive verbs put the cause with the subject or the object. Notice the difference in antecedent when comparing the following two sentences:

(1) Pete won the race against Hank because **he** ... had new shoes.
(2) Pete punished Hank because **he** ... was naughty.

Fourth, context and general knowledge (semantics) may affect the interpretation as well. Consider the following two sentences:

(3) Pete won the game with Hank because **he** ... was playing well.
(4) Pete punished Hank because **he** ... wants to look strict.

Sentence (3) is *congruent*, because implicit causality and context agree. However, sentence (4) is initially *incongruent*, because the punishment leads one to expect that Hank did something bad. Incongruent sentences are understood more slowly, and more often the wrong antecedent is chosen.

In an eye tracking study (Arnold et al., 2000), participants saw an image depicting Donald Duck and Mickey Mouse. Mickey was carrying an umbrella. While their eye movements were recorded, the participants heard the spoken sentences: "Donald is bringing some mail to Mickey while a violent storm is beginning. He's carrying an umbrella, and …" The analysis of the eye fixations showed that, directly following *he*, people looked at Donald (first-mention effect), but after *umbrella* they looked at Mickey. This finding indicates that first-mention information is used immediately, but also that listeners flexibly adjust their pronoun resolution in light of the broader context when an initial mismatch is detected (cf. Arnold & Griffin, 2007).

Research has also shown that the making of inferences can be studied by means of EEG/ERP recordings (Kuperberg et al., 2011). This type of research demonstrates that inferences may make use of several information sources at the same time. For instance, when van de Brink et al. (2009) presented a sentence such as "I cannot sleep without my teddy bear in my arms" spoken by an adult, a strong N400 effect was found to the word "teddy

DISCUSSION BOX 8: LINGUISTIC RELATIVITY

The Language User Framework makes a distinction between language and thought, and argues that they function relatively independently. Nevertheless, they are still assumed to interact. As you have read in Chapter 3, in the Language User Framework, thinking processes are performed by the Conceptual System in line with the currently active mental model in Working Memory. According to the *linguistic relativity hypothesis* (or Sapir-Whorf hypothesis), lexico-syntactic properties (e.g., available syntactic structures or lexical concepts) of a language affect speakers' thinking process, memory retrieval, or even their world view. According to Whorf, language to some extent functions as a "straitjacket" for thinking (see Whorf, 2012). However, recent views are more in favor of a "weak" linguistic relativity hypothesis, proposing some but a limited influence of language on thought (also see Au, 1983).

Consider what evidence would demonstrate that language constrains thought, supports it, or makes certain forms of thinking possible. Here are hints taken from Wolff and Holmes (2011):

- Languages may require a different attentional focus on the world because of different word orders (Flecken et al., 2015). Look up the term "thinking for speaking" (Slobin, 1987) and research on the Australian Aboriginal language Guugu Yimithirr (Levinson, 1997);
- Language may function as a "meddler" for thought, i.e., interfere with cognitive operations. Look up aspects related to color (Cibelli et al., 2016) and to memory (Carmichael et al., 1932);
- Language may function as an augmenter, i.e., help thinking or perception (Gentner, 2003);
- Language may function as a spotlight, i.e., help organize a cognitive domain (see Boroditsky et al., 2003; and Mickan et al., 2014, on grammatical gender);
- Language may function as an inducer, i.e., support schematic processing (Holmes & Wolff, 2010).

bear," indicating that the listeners quickly detected a mismatch between the content of the message and its speaker.

Inferences thus may be drawn automatically, but they still depend on Working Memory and other factors. Making predictive inferences may be sensitive to reader goals, and better readers may make more inferences (Murray & Burke, 2003).

8.3.3 Thinking and reasoning

In a text with subsequent sentences or in spoken discourse that includes several utterances, the succession of propositions and concepts in the language user's mind is relatively clear, because they can be derived from the actual productions. However, what happens in the chains of our moment-to-moment *non-linguistic* thinking?

Clearly, there are more and less organized forms of thinking. Eysenck and Keane (2015) for instance discern problem solving, decision making, judgment, deductive reasoning, inductive reasoning, and informal reasoning.

Some forms of *problem solving* may be relatively constrained. Examples are solving the weekly sudoku or cryptogram in the newspaper. The rules for finding a word or number are relatively clear. A small number of reasoning rules are required to proceed. However, one needs to find the applicable rule(s) and avoid distractions. Attentional focus, inhibition of wrong selections, and monitoring one's thinking process are required for quick solutions. All of these concern the Cognitive Control System mentioned in the context of the Language User Framework.

Similar aspects of the control system are important components in *decision making*. When a series of (potentially underdefined) possibilities is considered in the mind, selecting the best option is difficult. As Kahneman (2011) has argued in his dual-process theory, thinking here may be fast (based on intuition) or slow (based on careful reasoning), with potentially far-reaching effects. When one makes *judgments*, the emphasis may be on accuracy, rather than on speed. In the lexical decision task, the participant must find a careful balance between speed of responding and the accuracy of the decision.

Deductive and *inductive reasoning* are other reasoning processes that one may consciously engage in with more (Sherlock Holmes) or less (Watson) success. Deduction is about what necessary conclusions follow on the basis of statements assumed to be true; induction is deciding whether hypotheses are correct on the basis of given information.

Least constrained is *informal reasoning*. Here conclusions are drawn on the basis of one's knowledge of the world, based on experience. Nevertheless, the importance of this loose kind of reasoning should not be underestimated.

In a famous study, Bransford et al. (1972) presented readers with a sentence like this one: "Three turtles rested on a floating log and a fish swam beneath them." After a short interval, a considerable number of participants were no longer able to indicate whether they had seen this sentence or the following alternative: "Three turtles rested on a floating log and a fish swam beneath it." Both sentences are in line with an inference such as: "If the fish swam beneath the turtles, then it must also have been beneath the log." However, when they were separately presented with the sentence: "Three turtles rested beside a floating log and a fish swam beneath it," they were sure that they had not seen it before.

One way to approach these findings would be to represent the sentences as a series of coherent propositions, e.g., ON(TURTLES, LOG), NUMBER(TURTLES, 3), UNDER(FISH, TURTLES), SWIM(FISH), and so on. However, this would not do full justice to what happens in the reader's mind: Sentence meaning is enriched with world knowledge about turtles and fish that is not actually presented. For instance, turtles are green, and fish swim in water. In fact, the sentence evokes a rich stored knowledge structure on the basis of past experience: a mental model. Most likely, with your mind's eye you "saw" a pond with turtles, some floating wood, and perhaps a particular type of fish. A sentence such as "Three turtles rested on a floating log and a fish swam beneath it" evokes a different mental model than "Three turtles rested beside a floating log and a fish swam beneath it."

While the representation of the world may come rather naturally to us, following the strict rules of logic may not do so. Language users may come to invalid conclusions that are affected by context, emotional, motivational, and other factors such as lack of knowledge. An additional issue is that solving problems (e.g., in computation) may be complicated because they require a proper understanding of the language in which they are cast (see Discussion Box 8).

SUMMARY: MEANING: PROCESSES

In line with the embodiedness and embeddedness assumptions, listeners and readers go beyond the abstract information represented in sentences by adding sensory information about the world they are familiar with. In their incremental processing of subsequent sentences, they make inferences to arrive at a coherent interpretation that they assume intended by the speaker or writer. Forward and backward inferences, including bridging assumptions, also help to establish the congruency between sentences in terms of anaphors, antecedents, and other available information. Readers quickly and flexibly incorporate contextual information and world knowledge when creating inferences. Thinking accompanies sentence processing, but can also take place in the absence of it. Conceptual representations in language processing and thinking do not follow each other in a random fashion, but their ordering follows less or more strict rules. During both thinking and language processing, active mental models and stored world knowledge provide fundamental background structures. Mental models could be represented in the brain in terms of modality-specific "spoke" areas in the neocortex and a modality-invariant "hub" in the anterior temporal lobe.

8.4 MODELS OF MEANING

In earlier chapters of this book, we reviewed models for word and sentence processing. For such models, the process of mapping word forms and sentence structures onto meaning representations was discussed. This leads us to the discussion of models of text and discourse processing in this chapter. The semantic representation of text and discourse in such models could be considered as providing a linguistic backbone for thinking: The sequence of conceptual structures in text and discourse is integrated in their loosely systematic organization.

8.4.1 Models of sentence and text processing

As examples from this domain, we will discuss two "classical" models of text processing and then consider more recent approaches involving "events." The first model is the Construction-Integration model from Kintsch (1988; Kintsch and van Dijk, 1978). This is a model that focuses on text integration, Working Memory management, and the determinants of recall. The second model is the CAPS/READER model (Just & Carpenter, 1987, 1992; Thibadeau et al., 1982). This (very different) model considers the time-course of reading comprehension and the coordination of the many different levels of processing that are required to understand reading from word form encoding to referential processing.

8.4.1.1 Construction-Integration model

Models that wish to specify how readers understand a full text must consider numerous different language processes at the same time. As a minimal condition, they must help us to understand sentence processing and how it is part of the processing of a text. In the Construction-Integration model, the mental representation of text knows three levels:

- *Surface text*: the literal text;
- *Textbase*: the propositional structure of the text;
- *Situation model*: a model of situations and events described.

The three types of information are not retained in memory for an equally long time. The literal text disappears quickly, and in the long run only the gist of the text, which consists of the most important propositions, remains (cf. Sachs, 1967). We would like to suggest that the *situation model* is, in fact, a *mental model* that is enriched with sensory and world memory information.

Suppose we read a fantasy novel. First, we decipher the scribbles on paper into words and sentences: the literal text. From these sentences, we derive propositions representing their meaning. We connect the sentences through inferences, thus building larger propositional structures (called "coherence graphs" by Kintsch; see Figure 8.9). The resulting "textbase" is linked up to world knowledge, providing flesh and blood to the propositional skeleton. The (re)constructed mental model is what gives life to the text; in other words, the book creates a virtual world that requires a mental model to be described. In fact, this last process is very complex. It includes other sources of information, such as the readers' goals when reading, their emotional response, and their use of imagery.

Here is an actual example from Kintsch and van Dijk (1978, pp. 376–377). First, a fragment of the *surface text* reads as follows:

A series of violent, bloody encounters between police and Black Panther Party members punctuated the early summer days of 1969. Soon after, a group of Black students I teach at California State College, Los Angeles, who were members of the Panther Party, began to complain of continuous harassment by law enforcement officers.

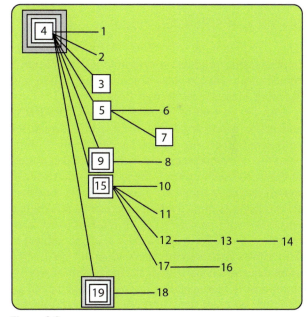

From the surface text, the propositions in Table 8.2 can be derived.

These propositions are linked and together make up a textbase. This "coherence graph" (adapted from Kintsch & van Dijk, 1978) represents the links between propositions and, as such, the *microstructure* of the text (Figure 8.9). In the next steps of processing,

Figure 8.9
Propositional structure ("coherence graph") underlying the story fragment from Kintsch and van Dijk (1978). The numbers in the structure refer to the propositions in Table 8.2.

TABLE 8.2 Propositions underlying the story fragment from Kintsch and van Dijk (1978). Numbers in the table correspond to the numbers in Figure 8.9. Numbers in propositions refer to other propositions they are related to

1 (SERIES, ENCOUNTER)
2 (VIOLENT, ENCOUNTER)
3 (BLOODY, ENCOUNTER)
4 (BETWEEN, ENCOUNTER, POLICE, BLACK PANTHER)
5 (TIME: IN, ENCOUNTER, SUMMER)
6 (EARLY, SUMMER)
7 (TIME: IN, SUMMER, 1969)
8 (SOON, 9)
9 (AFTER, 4, 16)
10 (GROUP, STUDENT)
11 (BLACK, STUDENT)
12 (TEACH, SPEAKER, STUDENT)
13 (LOCATION: AT, 12, CAL STATE COLLEGE)
14 (LOCATION: AT, CAL STATE COLLEGE, LOS ANGELES)
15 (IS A, STUDENT, BLACK PANTHER)
16 (BEGIN, 17)
17 (COMPLAIN, STUDENT, 19)
18 (CONTINUOUS, 19)
19 (HARASS, POLICE, STUDENT)

information that is deemed less relevant is removed, generalizations are introduced, and inferences are added. This leads to the so-called *macro-structure* of the text. Finally, by adding real-world knowledge (imagery, emotion, and goals), a situation model is built. Here we will refer to it as the mental model of the text.

8.4.1.2 CAPS/READER model

The computational CAPS/READER model (Thibadeau et al., 1982) is a so-called implemented "production system" model. Whenever a certain condition arises in Working Memory, production rules describe what action must be taken. The knowledge elements in Working Memory are derived from a text.

As can be seen in Figure 8.10, the CAPS/READER model assumes that there are several major processing levels when a text is read (cf. Figure 3.3). In previous chapters, we considered processing at each level in detail. Although this model, like that by Kintsch and van Dijk, is over 40 years old by now, it still captures a lot of the available data. For instance, at the word encoding level, the model accounts for the finding that longer words usually take more processing time (word length effect). Furthermore, to simulate lexical access, CAPS/READER uses an activation process not unlike that of Multilink (see Chapter 6) to link an encoded "word percept" (i.e., an internal word form representation) to the associated word meaning. Similarly, it has a base level of activation that is a function of word frequency. This allows it to capture the finding in eye tracking research that the readers' gaze duration decreases linearly with the logarithm of word frequency. Another important feature of the model is that syntactic analysis (building the sentence structure) and semantic analysis (building an event structure) operate collectively. Just like human readers, CAPS/READER takes more time to process a garden path sentence such as "Since Mary always jogs a mile

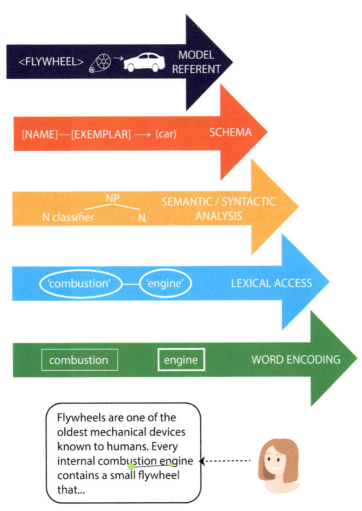

Figure 8.10
The computational CAPS/READER model for text reading. Note the cascaded nature of processing: Lower-level processes (closer to the input level) are ahead relative to higher-level processes (closer to meaning). After Thibadeau et al. (1982). Part of image designed by pikisuperstar/Freepik.

seems like a short distance." Finally, CAPS/READER constructs a referential representation of the world described by the text. Here it organizes the incoming information in text schemas with frames and slots. The model has even implemented some mechanisms for forgetting information in Working Memory.

8.4.1.3 Event indexing and event segmentation

The Construction-Integration model and the CAPS/READER model were not very specific about the process of constructing propositional structures and adapting the situation model over time. However, when reading the text proceeds, updating must be done (Zwaan & Madden, 2004). *Incremental updating* has been emphasized by the *event-indexing model* (Zwaan et al., 1995). Aspects in the model that may be updated are, for instance, time, space, the protagonist of the event, causality, and intentionality. Incoming information changes the probabilities you attach to what is happening (the so-called "priors" in Bayesian statistics).

Furthermore, at some moments in time, the old model may need to be completely replaced by a new one. Such *global updating* is emphasized by *event-segmentation theory* (Zacks & Swallow, 2007). It takes place at event boundaries and involves *prediction*. For instance, there may be relatively "natural" and discrete moments in time that events change in character: taking the tent out of its bag (event 1), unfolding it (event 2), and setting it up (event 3).

8.4.1.4 Cognitive control and the mental model

Our descriptions of reasoning processes and text reading indicate that language users *represent* the linguistic and non-linguistic aspects of the communicative situation in a mental model, which may be stored in Long Term Memory. This model is transitory in nature and develops over time. This *process* may follow guidelines of reasoning or textual development in terms of scripts or schemas; in any case, the model must be very complex.

In conversations, it must be even more complex, because we must simultaneously keep track, moment by moment, of what we are doing in relation to our conversational partner. For instance, a question such as "Remember our holiday in Greece?" invites you to retrieve aspects of that holiday from your Long Term Memory and load them into your Working Memory as part of our conversation. When I then ask you tomorrow "Remember that we talked about our holiday in Greece yesterday?," the mental model required to understand this question is even more complex, because it implies using mental models embedded within other mental models. Keeping track of the various developments in the conversation and the stored information requires serious engagement of the Cognitive Control System, showing again the importance of this upper part of the Language User Framework (see Figure 3.1).

> **SUMMARY: MODELS OF MEANING**
>
> Two classical models for text representation and processing are the Construction-Integration model (Kintsch & van Dijk, 1978) and the computational CAPS/READER model (Thibadeau et al., 1982). Propositions are an important component of these models, but enrichment in terms of mental models is necessary. More recent developments include event indexing (Zwaan et al., 1995) and event segmentation (Zacks & Swallow, 2007). Mental models may consist of different layers, and handling them requires considerable cognitive control (to keep track of who did what to whom and when).

8.5 MEANING: EMPIRICAL STUDIES

In the previous sections, we have already referred to several empirical studies to illustrate researchers' views on semantic representations and processes. In this section, we will do some cherry-picking and discuss two of the many empirical studies that have been done on meaning. The first study will discuss the role of scripts and mental models when people are falling for the so-called "semantic illusion." As a second study, we will consider whether language users process information from pictures with a verbal description in parallel or subsequently. How do they integrate the two information sources when these are either expected or unexpected?

8.5.1 Semantic illusions

It will be clear by now that, like words, sentences are not usually understood on their own. Their meaning is immediately linked to stored information about the world and the

Box 8.1 Examples of the semantic illusion

Here are some more example questions containing false information that is often not noticed by people asked to answer the questions (some are taken from Erickson & Mattson, 1981, p. 542). Can you come up with the correct sentence? And how would you adapt the sentence to reduce the semantic illusion, although the sentence would still be incorrect?

- What is the name of the Mexican dip made with mashed-up artichokes?
- What passenger liner was tragically sunk by an iceberg in the Pacific Ocean?
- What is the nationality of Thomas Edison, inventor of the telephone?
- In the novel *Moby Dick*, what color was the whale that Captain Nemo was after?
- What city near Naples was destroyed by the Etna in ancient times?
- Who found the glass slipper left at the ball by Snow White?
- What is the name of the Chinese bear that eats only palm shoots?
- What kind of music was played by saxophonist Miles Davis?
- In the biblical story, what was Joshua swallowed by?

surrounding linguistic and non-linguistic context. An interesting example illustrating this point is the "semantic illusion." A well-known semantic illusion is evoked by the question "How many animals of each kind did Moses take on the Ark?" One is inclined to answer "two" to this question. However, remember that it was not Moses, but Noah who took the animals onto the Ark.

Erickson and Mattson (1981) studied the Moses illusion in great depth. They found that the illusion is not dependent on participants perhaps skipping over the name Moses when reading or listening to the question. When participants were asked to read the question out loud before answering it, they still, in 81% of the cases, answered "two." And also when the information was presented in the form of a statement ("Moses took two animals of each kind onto the Ark") and participants were explicitly asked whether the statement was true or false, the illusion still persisted in 41% of cases.

These mistakes can be understood by assuming that readers or listeners quickly retrieve a mental model for a (in this case, biblical) scenario stored in their Long Term Memory. In this scenario, there is a slot for a biblical figure. Moses is indeed a biblical figure, and apparently it is not checked in detail if he is the right person for this scenario. Indeed, when participants are asked how many animals of each kind Nixon (at the time, a recent American president) took onto the Ark, the semantic illusion disappears (Erickson & Mattson, 1981). This may indicate that readers retrieve a sufficient but not full meaning representation. In other words, they do *good-enough processing* (Ferreira & Patson, 2007; see Chapter 7) rather than complete processing. In addition, it indicates that they trust the person posing the question to be honest (following the Gricean maxims, explained in Chapter 9).

8.5.2 Semantic integration of words and pictures

Information helping a language user in processing comes not only from scripts and scenarios. In everyday life, people find meaning in all sorts of things – not just in the words or sentences they encounter. For instance, in the context of reading a book with pictures in it, the meaning of a picture must be combined with the meaning of the words present in its caption. Willems and colleagues (2008) investigated how readers integrate the meaning of a picture and any accompanying sentence. One option would be that they first try to

Correct condition

The man gave his wife a nice flower that evening

Language mismatch condition

The man gave his wife a nice cherry that evening

Picture mismatch condition

The man gave his wife a nice flower that evening

Double mismatch condition

The man gave his wife a nice cherry that evening

Figure 8.11
An illustration of the four conditions used in the study by Willems et al. (2008, p. 1238).

grasp the meaning of the sentence by mapping grammatical roles onto thematic roles and subsequently add the meaning of the picture to that meaning representation. A one-step alternative to this two-step theory would be that the language system directly takes into account all the information it receives and immediately integrates it into a larger representation of the assumed meaning.

To disentangle these two theoretical possibilities, the authors presented participants with sentence-picture combinations from four different experimental conditions (see Figure 8.11). Each sentence contained a target word that was paired with a picture. In the correct condition, picture and target word made perfect sense in light of the preceding sentence context. In the language mismatch condition, the picture made sense in the context of the broader sentence, but the target word was a little unexpected. In the picture mismatch condition, it was the other way around: The sentence was perfectly acceptable, but the picture was a little unexpected. In the double mismatch condition, both picture and critical word were unexpected based on the sentence context.

Examining the event-related potentials (ERPs) derived from participants' EEGs, and time locked to the shared onset of the target word and the concurrent picture, a nearly identical N400 effect was found for the three conditions that contained some type of unexpected information compared to the correct condition. When the same stimuli were shown to a different group of participants in an fMRI experiment, the three conditions that contained something unexpected showed enhanced activation of left inferior frontal cortex relative to the control condition. These two findings led the authors to conclude that linguistic information is not given (temporal) priority compared to non-linguistic information when people try to make sense of a stream of information that contains both verbal and non-verbal signals. Rather, when looking for meaning in words and pictures, the processing system in our brain immediately takes into account all information that becomes available to it, regardless of whether we would label it linguistic or extra-linguistic.

Meaning 185

> **SUMMARY: MEANING: EMPIRICAL STUDIES**
>
> People use mental models and scripts to help them organize their mental representations when they are processing sentence information. This cognitive information may also steer their processing in a certain direction, which may lead to errors. One example of this is the semantic illusion, where listeners fall for a trick question because their relatively superficial (or good-enough) processing is punished by a speaker who was not acting cooperatively or in line with the Gricean maxims (see also Chapter 9).
>
> Mental models take into account information derived from the various senses. This is particularly clear when participants have to integrate information about pictures in their language interpretation. In processing, language users pay attention to all sorts of information and do not necessarily favor linguistic information over other information sources.

8.6 MEANING: THE ROLE OF CONTEXT

Perhaps even more than other parts of the Language Processing System, the Conceptual System shows the presence of linguistic and non-linguistic context effects. Most of the time, the larger physical and social context, and the discourse or the text in which a sentence appears contribute to meaning. We will exemplify this by considering the empirical effects of prosodic context on referent identification and sentence interpretation, and the effect of the larger discourse context on processing sentences in a literal versus non-literal way.

8.6.1 Finding the correct referent using prosody

Speakers typically help listeners in making them find the thing in the world they are referring to ("the referent"). For instance, during their spoken utterance, they may do so by pointing at the object in the world they want to talk about ("Look at that monkey over there!"). Snedeker and Trueswell (2003) investigated whether speakers also use the *prosodic grouping* of the words in their utterance to disambiguate what referent they are talking about, and whether listeners make use of such information.

The authors invited pairs of participants to the lab to play a *referential communication game* (see also Chapter 4). They were sitting in the same room, but could not see one another due to an opaque screen placed between them. As such, they could only communicate via speech. Both participants were given a bag with the same five toys (see Figure 8.12). One participant took on the role of speaker, while the other was assigned the role of listener. The speaker was then silently, via a written card, asked by the person leading the experiment ("the experimenter") to produce a given sentence, such as "Tap the frog with the flower," for the listener. This sentence is syntactically ambiguous, in that it could have two distinct meanings: The phrase "with the flower" could be syntactically attached to the verb phrase ("tap with the flower") or to the noun phrase ("the frog with the flower"). Therefore, the experimenter used the toys to demonstrate to the speaker what the sentence was intended to mean, either by tapping the frog that carried the little flower, or by taking the larger flower and using it to tap the poor empty-handed frog. The listener, who did not see the demonstration, was asked to select the correct toy(s) on their side of the screen and replicate the intended action on the basis of the sentence produced by the speaker. Because there was a flower, a flowerless frog, and a frog carrying a flower, while participants had to rely on speech alone, speakers had to come up with a way to communicate what the sentence actually meant. How would they do so?

Figure 8.12
Pairs of participants in the study by Snedeker and Trueswell (2003) were each given a bag with identical toys and played a referential communication game.

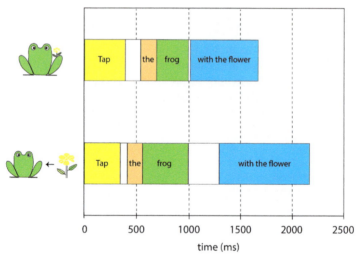

Figure 8.13
Speakers in the study by Snedeker and Trueswell (2003) varied the duration of critical words and pauses between words to help their listener to disambiguate between two possible readings of the same sentence. The width of a colored box in this graph indicates the duration in ms of a produced word, and colorless boxes indicate pauses and their duration.

In fact, it turns out that speakers varied the duration of critical words (such as "frog") in their utterance, and used meaningful pauses ("prosodic breaks") in their speech to disambiguate the ambiguous syntactic structure by indicating phrase boundaries (see Figure 8.13). And it worked: These prosodic changes helped the listener in about 70% of the cases to assign the intended meaning to (parts of) the given utterance and find the correct real-world referent(s). As such, although the words that were used were exactly the same, the actual referent was different depending on the prosodic context created by the speaker. One could say that prosody was used to support syntax, leading to differences in semantics. Later eye tracking evidence indicated that listeners made use of the information conveyed by the prosodic modulations as soon as it became available.

8.6.2 From literal to non-literal meaning: The larger discourse context

As you may have experienced in your daily life, people do not always literally say what they mean or want. There can be a discrepancy between what a string of words literally means (its "coded meaning") and what a speaker or writer actually means to convey with these words (its "speaker meaning"). Coulson and Lovett (2010, p. 112) investigated how people process non-literal meaning by presenting participants with the following types of written scenario:

> Diane and her husband Bill were celebrating their wedding anniversary and started the evening off with dinner at a restaurant. After they had ordered, the waiter soon brought out a bowl of soup for Diane and a salad for Bill. After tasting her soup, Diane said to her husband: "My soup is too cold to eat."

The critical sentence here is the final sentence in this short story. In this first scenario, the literal meaning of the sentence is most important: Diane seems to simply inform her husband about the temperature of her soup. One could say it is quite a literal statement. Now compare this situation to the very similar scenario below, in which Diane utters the same sentence, but now to the waiter in the restaurant:

> Diane and her husband Bill were celebrating their wedding anniversary and started the evening off with dinner at a restaurant. After they had ordered, the waiter soon brought out a bowl of soup for Diane and a salad for Bill. After tasting her soup, Diane said to the waiter: "My soup is too cold to eat."

In this case, one could assume that Diane produces this final sentence as an *indirect request*: She wants the waiter to do something for her. Indeed, it is an indirect, and perhaps quite polite, way of saying: "Please bring me a bowl of soup that is properly heated, waiter!" Would people process this final, identical sentence differently as a function of the preceding scenario?

After having presented participants with the start of the scenario as a whole on a computer screen, Coulson and Lovett presented these final sentences word-by-word on the screen and analyzed ERPs time locked to the onset of every word in these critical sentences. Critically, around 400 to 700 ms after the onset of the fifth word on the screen, they observed enhanced positive amplitude for the indirect requests compared to the literal statements. In the critical sentences, this was typically the word ("cold," in our example above) where the indirect nature of the request would become clear. As such, it can be concluded that the very same sentence may hence lead to different brain activity as a function of the broader discourse context. This effect was most prominent in electrodes placed over frontal parts of the scalp.

The authors interpret this finding in terms of the perceived *concreteness* of the critical words, such as "cold." In the literal condition, the word "cold" can be taken to literally refer to an aspect of the soup, whereas in the indirect request condition, it does so as well, but also signals the actual intention of the speaker. As such, the larger discourse context may influence how exactly individual words are processed in sentences that are identical in their literal meaning. Because activation differences are found prior to the end of the sentence, these findings are not in line with "two-stage models" that assume that readers first compute the literal meaning of a sentence, and only then potentially start taking into account its non-literal implications. Rather, the broader discourse context is taken into account as early as possible to infer what a speaker is actually trying to convey. Similar results have been found for when language users process idiomatic expressions ("get a taste of your own medicine"): The literal and the figurative meaning appear to be derived incrementally and in parallel (e.g., van Ginkel & Dijkstra, 2020).

In sum, available research suggests that language processing involves mental models that are open to non-linguistic and linguistic context effects. Other cognitive processes like perception, (motor) action (e.g., gesture), and emotion do all affect what is represented in the mental model. One way to interpret the evidence is to say that language users *simulate the situations* they are in, implying analog representations that incorporate perceptual and other concrete information (Barsalou, 2009, 2012; Bergen, 2012).

SUMMARY: MEANING: THE ROLE OF CONTEXT

Text and discourse processing studies show that the mental models of language users are open to the effects of linguistic and non-linguistic context (non-modularity) and to other sensory systems (perception, action, emotion). Even in cases when exactly the same words are used, differences in processing may arise due to different meaningful prosodic patterns. Compare, for instance, the difference between a statement ("she is happy") and a similarly worded question ("she is happy?"), or the English word "permit" that is pronounced differently depending on whether it is a noun or a verb. And even when exactly the same sentence is used, it may lead to different brain activity depending on the broader discourse context in which it occurs. For instance, an interpretation difference in the literal and pragmatic meaning of the sentence "the door is open" could result in a different ERP pattern. As such, effects of linguistic context have been found to affect sentence processing from different directions: from a higher level (e.g., discourse context has a role to play) and from a lower level (e.g., intonation patterns affect interpretation).

8.7 WHAT IS NEXT?

Meaning and thought are a central part of the Language User Framework. Conceptual processes are subserved by the Conceptual System, using conceptual representations stored in Conceptual Memory, a part of Long Term Memory. In previous chapters, we described the pathway connecting the linguistic signal in the outside world to the complex meaning representations (like the mental model) in the mind of the language user that were discussed in the current chapter. It is now time to turn the process of language comprehension into that of language production: This involves describing the pathway from the mental model in the mind of the speaker to their articulated spoken utterance that enters the world. As we have seen before, this is a complex process with different steps. It concerns recoding conceptual representations into lexico-syntactic, phonological, and phonetic representations, rather than the other way around. As such, language production is the topic of the next chapter.

8.8 WHAT HAVE WE LEARNED?

Concepts are meaning representations in Long Term Memory. They are organized in large networks, and connected to other concepts (sense) and to the world (reference). During language comprehension, concepts are derived from the incoming sentences or (multimodal) utterances. They become part of conceptual structures (e.g., propositions or event structures), allowing new and original lines of thinking and reasoning about the world.

Concepts are not only abstract, but also engage other cognitive systems (for perception, action, emotion, etc.). There is evidence of the embodiedness, embeddedness, incremental retrieval, and non-modularity of meanings.

Word concepts themselves are often characterized as sets of small building blocks called semantic features. Propositions relate such semantic features in terms of their functional relation. Propositions are useful to describe meaning at word, sentence, and text levels. They can be seen as a part of more general event structures.

Structural systematicity in discourse and text is picked up in story grammars, scripts, and schemas. There is also systematicity in the order in which concepts appear in thinking and reasoning.

A mental model constitutes a complex representation or even simulation of a situation that incorporates subjective experiences and non-linguistic information (e.g., perceptual, motor, and emotional). There are few well-specified models for text and discourse representation and processing. The Construction-Integration model by Kintsch and van Dijk (1978) and the CAPS/READER model by Thibadeau and colleagues (1982) can be related to mental models. Experimental studies have shown the importance of mental models, for instance, with respect to the so-called "semantic illusion."

During meaning retrieval, different types of information become available over time. Subsequent sentences are related semantically via inferences that can be captured by propositions. Thinking and reasoning can also be seen as linking conceptual structures that come in over time, for instance, in terms of propositional or event structures. Word association and semantic priming effects also work over time.

Different types of context information, both linguistic and non-linguistic, can simultaneously affect ongoing language processing. For instance, discourse background plays a crucial role in sentence comprehension; prosodic details affect the processing speed with which a referent can be identified; images or pictures that are present concurrent with sentences are processed in parallel and affect language processing. In the light of these observations, it does not take rocket science to conclude that context also affects the recognition speed of the literal or figurative meaning of an idiomatic expression.

QUESTIONS FOR CHAPTER 8

1. Semantic features are not always easy to define. For instance, what are the defining features of a "game" (Wittgenstein, 1953)? What are the semantic features of "red"? Try to determine in what domains semantic features will work well and where not (Hint: Consider family trees, tools, colors, and abstract concepts).
2. Can you guess what sentence would be expressed by the following proposition: INGEST(AGENT (JOHN) OBJECT(CAKE REF(INDEF)))?
3. What are the arguments for a language-free representation of thinking? Can you say that you (always) think in (a) language?
4. When you speak with one of your fellow students in a face-to-face situation, from which bodily channels do you derive meaningful information? How does the relative

importance of the different channels (hands, face, vocal cords) differ when you discuss (a) the coffee you just had; (b) the book chapter you just read; (c) the lecturer you just listened to; (d) the weather on the way to campus?

5 Do you think that all concepts should be defined in terms of bodily relations or experiences? Why (not)?

6 The experiment by Snedeker and Trueswell (2003) can be related to the phenomenon of minimal attachment (see Chapter 7). Explain this by considering the two readings of the sentence "Tap the frog with the flower."

7 Consider the following verse from *Through the Looking-Glass*, by Lewis Carroll (1872):

> Twas brillig, and the slithy toves
> Did gyre and gimble in the wabe:
> All mimsy were the borogoves,
> And the mome raths outgrabe.

What does this example show? Try to describe the meaning you derive from the text. How can non-sense (pseudowords) like this still convey some meaning? What role does syntax play in your account?

8 Would you have a script in mind when you go out to buy a bag of concrete mix? Would a building worker have such a script? Make your arguments explicit.

9 To what extent can the prosodic disambiguation present in spoken language be mimicked via punctuation marks in written language?

10 In advertisement, psychological principles related to psycholinguistics are often used (or abused) to sell more products. Can you come up with examples? Consider the following mechanisms: word frequency, repetition, semantic association, priming, emotion, non-linguistic context, lexical ambiguity, incrementality, language games.

Chapter 9

Language production

9.1 LANGUAGE PRODUCTION: THE ESSENCE

Tonight, Zina and the Warriors meet again to play Dungeons and Dragons (D&D) after an eternal delay of two weeks. As usual, the Dungeon Master starts the evening by giving a summary of the state of affairs in the Quest for the Lost Talisman of Gygax. "So you all entered the Crypt and Yz did a light spell." "Yes," Nigel says, "but only after Suzy Q stumbled upon the corpse on the lowest stairs." "And I was last in line, covering our backs," interrupts Gnill the Gnome. Everybody around the table is smiling, because they all know that Gnill was the first to loot the now dead half-elf female warlock that had fled into the Crypt before them. "Ok," the Dungeon Master says, "Let us first clarify the situation by putting your figurines on the drawing board."

This example shows that people can retrieve a very complex shared mental model in a wink, even when they have not considered it in weeks. In the game, the players are able to take off very quickly from where they left off: Relevant parts of the model light up as they speak about the situation, and new information is added immediately. There is a constant updating of the mental model.

More generally, speakers talk about what they see and think about. What they think and see is often very complex and multidimensional. Not only the physical world, but also the mental world is multidimensional, including the dimension of "time": The mental model for the D&D scenario has significantly changed by the end of the game night.

When speakers are talking, they take into account the listeners' viewpoints as well. Gnill the Gnome is aware that his fellow travelers know him very well and will see through his lies every now and then. Trying to deceive them is part of the fun. So the mental model that Gnill starts from must be very complex: It involves both the real world and the fantasy world at different layers and levels.

We do not know much about how we build, update, and integrate mental models, or how exactly we take them as a starting point for the production of communicative signals such as words and gestures. We know more about how people turn information in their mental models into spoken words and sentences. In this chapter, we will describe what is known about how speakers find the right words to express the different concepts of their mental models in syntactically correct sentence structures, and how they assign spoken word forms to these structures. In order to express aspects of his mental model or to comment on the current situation, Gnill (or his player) must indeed select and order particular concepts in this model, find words that can express these concepts and that fit within syntactic

DOI: 10.4324/9781003326274-9

structures allowed in the language of expression. Next, the syntactic constructions with their words must be uttered incrementally, which requires planning and phonological specification at phoneme and syllable levels.

Spoken language production is an *embodied* process – we use our brain in our body to plan a spoken utterance and our body (e.g., vocal cords, tongue, and lips) to produce it. While speaking, other parts of our body (e.g., hands, face, torso) may be employed to produce additional communicative signals, such as when we raise our eyebrows and the corners of our lips to express a positive emotion or when we move our arms and hands to provide some additional information about what we are trying to convey. Spoken language is also always *embedded* in a broader context. We often talk about the things present in the immediate environment of our conversation to an actual listener or audience facing us.

In the remainder of this chapter, we will first analyze speech errors. Such "flawed representations" turn out to be quite revealing with respect to language production processes. Next, we will discuss prominent views on the language production process, supported by speech errors and other empirical observations. We will also discuss the most prominent models of language production and some selected empirical evidence. As before, we will argue for non-modularity of the language processing system. The effects of non-linguistic contextual information will be stressed at the end of the chapter.

SUMMARY: LANGUAGE PRODUCTION: THE ESSENCE

Language production is an embodied and embedded process that involves translating information in your mental model into an utterance. Following the speaker's intention to communicate, certain concepts from the model need to be selected, and words must be looked up that can express these concepts while fitting within a syntactic structure allowed in the language at hand. Ultimately, the syntactic constructions containing these words must be uttered incrementally, often integrated with and supported by other communicative signals that the body transmits.

9.2 LANGUAGE PRODUCTION: REPRESENTATIONS

For the largest part of the 20th century, recordings of conversations and speech errors ("slips of the tongue") were the most important source of evidence about representations involved in the speaking process. Analyzing speech errors (what can go wrong in speaking) turns out to provide important glimpses into how correct language production functions. Basically, the argumentation is as follows: Speech errors contain linguistic representations that are not built correctly. If we analyze them, we can see *what* went wrong during processing and *when* it went wrong. We can also make an inventory of the kind of representation that is involved in the error: a concept, word, morpheme, syllable, phoneme, or phonological feature. It turns out we can also obtain valuable information about the processes underlying speech production by analyzing what went wrong. In fact, we can even discern an order in the different processing stages involved!

Several types of speech error can be distinguished. At a general level, speech errors may involve the exchange, substitution, addition, or deletion of linguistic units in an utterance. For instance, there are word/morpheme and phoneme exchanges, phoneme substitutions, phoneme anticipations and perseverations, and so on.

Studying collections of speech errors clarifies several properties of language production. First, speech errors may occur at *all levels of the language production process*. Thus, they may involve word concepts, lemmas, morphemes, word forms (also called "lexemes"), syllables, phonemes, and phonological features. Examples can be found in Box 9.1.

> **Box 9.1 Examples of different types of speech error**
>
> | | |
> |---|---|
> | Contextual | Jimmy is playing in front of the television with his Lego blocks. His father, who is watching the Tour de France, says to him: "Hey, you, go cycle somewhere else!" |
> | Conceptual | "I only *drink* one egg each week" (word substitution) |
> | | "This is a *tarrow* [narrow/tight] alley" (blend) |
> | Mixed | "Let me eat my *lobster* [oyster] in peace" |
> | Lemma | "on the *room* to my *door*" (word/morpheme exchange) |
> | Phonological | "He prePOsed to me" (*malapropism*) |
> | | "You hissed all my mystery lectures, in fact you tasted the whole worm" (onset phoneme exchange = *spoonerism*) |
> | | "He speered bill" [spilled beer] (rime exchange) |
>
> *Further comments:*
>
> - Mrs. Malaprop was a character who tried to impress people in a play by playwright Richard Sheridan (*The Rivals*, 1775). She used difficult words in a wrong way. In malapropisms (e.g., "conSIdered" changing into "conSIsted"; "CAbinet' changing into "CAtalog"), the similarity between intruder and target diminishes from left to right. The morphological structure, length, and accent of the speech error remain relatively constant.
> - Reverend Spooner has given his name to speech errors in which the onset of two words are exchanged (providing evidence that the syllable is a structural unit in language production).
> - A special type of contextual error is the "Freudian slip." Among Freud's large collection of speech errors (e.g., Freud, 1989) we find an error like this one (Freud, 1973, p. 59): " 'What regiment your son is with?', a lady was asked. She replied: 'With the 42nd Murderers' " (instead of "Mortars"). Freud explains an error like this one in terms of an unintended intrusion of repressed ideas in the speech output.

Second, because speech errors are construction errors in the regular speech production process, *not all speech errors that one could possibly think of do occur in real speech*. Speech errors do not result in utterances that are completely ignoring the rules and regularities of the language involved. For instance, a speech error like "a trong sguy" for "a strong guy" is very unlikely to occur. The combination "sg" is not phonotactically legal in English. However, the absence of this kind of speech error cannot be ascribed to articulatory reasons: It is perfectly fine for an English speaker to say "itsgonna rain" (a contraction of "it is going to rain"). This suggests that some sort of (monitoring) mechanism supervises the phonological legality of the utterance.

Third, *the units that interact in speech errors are typically of the same type and linguistic level*. Words are exchanged with words, morphemes with morphemes, phonemes with phonemes. Exchanges of words with phonemes do not occur, for instance. Two basic types of speech error are:

- Word/morpheme exchanges: "on the room to my door"
- Phoneme exchanges: "the dear old queen" instead of "the queer old dean"

This observation allows us to draw an important conclusion: There must be components that are concerned exclusively with these types of unit. Apparently, they are "computed" (retrieved) as part of the same processing level.

Fourth, *the units involved in speech errors have certain characteristics in common*. However, these characteristics turn out to be different in the word exchanges and the phoneme exchanges. In word exchanges, the exchanged items are "open class" items of the same syntactic category: Nouns are exchanged with other nouns, or verbs are exchanged with other verbs. These word exchanges are not necessarily similar in phonology. An example is: "Older people buy to tend bigger books." In contrast, in phoneme exchanges there is typically a phonological similarity of the phonemes involved, and the context in which the phonemes appear is also often phonologically similar. A well-known example is "heft lemisphere" for "left hemisphere." Note that the phoneme exchange here occurs between an adjective and a noun.

These observations lead to the conclusion that processes involving particular types of unit are sensitive only to certain properties and not to others. This suggests that the mental machinery taking care of words/morphemes and phonemes is different.

There is another observation that supports this conclusion: The distance between the *source* of the speech error and the *intruder* depends on the unit involved in the speech error. The distance at the word/morpheme level must be counted in terms of words, that in phoneme errors in terms of phonemes.

Consider the speech errors "bake my book" (correct: "take my book") and "a maniac for weekends" (correct: "a weekend for maniacs"). The first speech error is called a phoneme anticipation, because the phoneme /b/ is produced earlier in time than intended. In this speech error, we can discern the intrusion (/b/ in "bake"), the source (/b/ in "book"), and the target (/t/ in the correct word "take"). In this kind of speech error, usually adjacent words are involved. The second speech error, made "famous" by Fromkin (1971, 1973), is a morpheme exchange: On a stormy night, the speaker unintentionally exchanged the words "weekend" and "maniac." Clearly, distance in this example must be considered in terms of morphemes or words. Interestingly, morphological errors can cross clause boundaries and do not change sentence accent.

A conclusion is that morphemes are filled in in *syntactic frame structures*, whereas phonemes are filled in in smaller *phonological frames* of a clausal or phrasal nature. Phonological information does not yet play a role with respect to the syntactic frames. At the same time, phonological speech errors are sensitive to their phonological but not their syntactic environment (i.e., they may involve words of different syntactic categories). We will consider these frame structures in more detail later (if you like, you can already take a peek at Figure 9.4).

It is important to note that in both examples, later positioned elements are mixed up with earlier ones. This indicates that there is some kind of *planning unit* or planning window at each of the two levels. Said differently, there is *computational simultaneity* of earlier and later elements. After all, elements can only be substituted or exchanged if they are available (active) at the same time. In addition, there is *incremental planning*: The sentence is not preplanned as a whole and then uttered. The size of the planning unit, or the degree of incremental planning, has been an important topic of research in language production. Two planning units that have been proposed at different levels of speech production are the syllable and the clause.

Fifth, the analysis of speech errors indicates that *speech production processes are sequentially ordered*: Some take place earlier in time than others. A further scrutiny of the speech error "a maniac for weekends" supports this view. The correct sentence would have been "a weekend for maniacs," in which the morpheme "-s" turns the correct word "maniac" into an unvoiced plural. Note, however, that "weekends" instead has a voiced plural form (following the voiced "-d", the "-s" is pronounced /z/). Apparently, the plural morpheme has only become specified after the morpheme exchange took place. It appears that the exchange error occurred on a more abstract formula "DET N-sing PREP N-plural" (in which "DET" refers to determiner, "sing" to singular, "PREP" to preposition, and "N" to noun). Note that this also explains why the speech error was not "a maniacs for weekend": It is the morpheme "weekend," not the full word "weekends" that has been exchanged. Analogously, in an English speech error such as "an apple with chests," the determiner of "apple" would become "an" instead of the "a" in the correct utterance "a chest with apples." Again, the more abstract morphological specification precedes the more specific phonological specification.

Sixth, and finally, some researchers have argued that certain speech errors demonstrate that there is *interactivity between different language production processes*. The relevant speech errors in question here are *mixed errors*, which are word substitution errors involving substitutions that are both semantically and phonologically related. For instance, speakers make speech errors including "stop!" instead of "start!," and "porpoise" instead of "tortoise." In these cases, it appears there are both conceptual and phonological similarities between the intended words and the actually produced words. However, in a purely sequential or cascaded production process, it would be statistically unlikely that these mixed errors result from accidental errors at the two levels separately.

It also appears to be the case that phonological errors lead to existing words more often than one would expect on the basis of chance. This is called the *lexical bias* effect. Dell and Reich (1981) assessed the statistical chance on such a "lexical bias" for phonological errors and proposed an explanation in terms of feedback from the lexical level to the phoneme level.

As we will see later, the occurrence of mixed errors and the lexical bias effect have been interpreted as evidence for a model that proposes an interaction between the phonological and the lemma (or morpheme) level. In the next section, we will first discuss the language production *process* as it has been revealed by both speech error analysis and empirical research.

SUMMARY: LANGUAGE PRODUCTION: REPRESENTATIONS

Analysis of the speech errors people make has led to many important insights on the types of representation involved in language production. Different types of speech error are contextual speech errors, word substitutions, blends, mixed errors, word and morpheme exchanges, malapropisms, spoonerisms, and rime exchanges. Such speech errors may spontaneously occur at all levels of the language production process, but not all speech errors that one could possibly construct do occur in real speech. The units that interact in speech errors are usually of the same type and linguistic level. In word exchanges, the exchanged items are "open class" items of the same syntactic category: Nouns are exchanged with other nouns, or verbs are exchanged with other verbs. In phoneme exchanges, however, there is typically a phonological similarity of the phonemes involved, and the context in which the phonemes appear is also often phonologically similar. The analysis of speech errors indicates that speech production processes are sequentially ordered: Some processes take place earlier in time than others. The lexical bias effect entails that phoneme errors lead to existing words more often than one would expect on the basis of chance. This suggests a bidirectional interaction between lexical and phoneme levels during speech production.

9.3 LANGUAGE PRODUCTION: PROCESSES

Speakers select certain information from their mental models to utter. Speaking can involve the expression of sense, but speaking can also include reference. For instance, I can express that I am thinking (of) a meaning structure that is stored in my memory: "I remember talking about my holiday in Greece in Chapter 8." The person the speaker is talking to (or writing for) may now look up the relevant (sense) information in Long Term Memory. I can also make a simple reference to an actual situation, combining speech with a pointing gesture: "Look at that chair over there." A bit more complex is the following *metonymic reference*, in which the speaker refers to someone who is no longer present using a pointing gesture and eye gaze to an empty chair: "My colleague just left this room" (Littlemore, 2015). In this example, the speaker has a mental model of an earlier situation and points at a "slot" in this model. The speaker further assumes that the listener is able to retrieve this mental model as well. We can make the situation even more complex by indirectly referring to this model: "In my last example, I explained that my colleague is no longer here." To understand this sentence, one must build a mental model that includes the mental model that was already made about the two sentences! (You might want to consider what model is built when we hear the sentence: "Tomorrow it's going to rain every once in a while.")

9.3.1 Language production and the Language User Framework

During speaking, a complex message is turned into an utterance. What the message really looks like is unknown. It is usually assumed that it is a language-independent meaning representation, some sort of event structure, that may be more or less similar for speakers of different languages. However, the syntactic structure of utterances is, of course, quite language-dependent. The English surface structure of a sentence looks very different from that expressing the same or a very similar meaning in Malayalam or Hebrew. This observation makes it unlikely that the speech production process involves a simple direct mapping of a thought into an utterance. In other words, a direct "mind-to-mouth" theory is far from sufficient to account for speaking. So what processing stages and representations must be discerned in speaking?

Following the seminal work by Levelt (1989), the activities that a speaker must engage in to produce speech are commonly categorized in terms of conceptualization, formulation, and articulation (see Figure 9.1).

Conceptualization comprises a number of activities. First, the speaker must develop a contextually adequate intention to convey information to one or more listeners or addressees. In other words, on the basis of a mental model, a more restricted thought/message/conceptual representation must be made that can be put into a sentence, phrase, clause, or word. Second, the speaker must select information from this complex meaning representation that is adequate to achieve their intention. Third, the selected information must be arranged for production in a particular order. After all, our articulators do not allow us to produce several words at the exact same moment in time.

Formulation entails two processes. First, during syntactic encoding, the conceptual information to be expressed must be associated with and mapped onto word meanings and grammatical functions. To put it differently, a syntactic structure must be built on the basis of one or more words that can appropriately express the intended utterance. Second, during morphophonological encoding, a morphological specification and phonetic plan for this utterance are generated. This means that the morphologically correct sound forms of words must be internally generated.

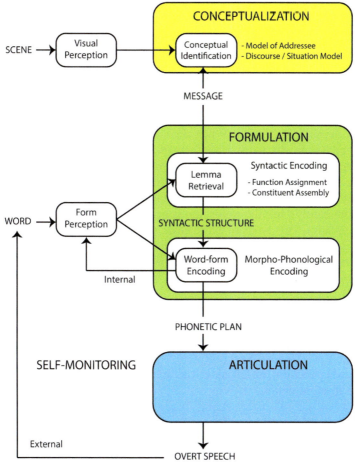

Figure 9.1
Components of the language production system. This image can be seen as a more detailed and worked-out equivalent of the right (production) part of the Language User Framework. See section 9.5 for a functional description of the associated "standard" model of language production by Levelt et al. (1991). Adapted from Roelofs and Ferreira (2019).

Finally, the phonetic plan is executed by the Articulator, resulting in overt speech. This entails the generation and execution of articulatory motor commands. The spoken words may be combined with other overt communicative signals such as facial expressions and hand gestures.

As we explained in Chapter 3, the whole production process is supervised by a monitor (that we would position in the Cognitive Control System) that helps to avoid speech errors and other glitches in speaking. This process of self-monitoring makes use of an internal and an external loop (see Figure 9.1).

Language production takes place at "high speed," often at two to three, but sometimes even up to six words per second. Although disfluencies in speech occur, the number of speech errors is relatively low. Speech errors are estimated to occur in about one word in a 1,000 (Cutler, 1982; Levelt, 1989, p. 199). The produced utterances are also mostly correct from a syntactic perspective.

How do the processes of conceptualization, formulation, and articulation relate to one another? A simplistic idea about language production would be to assume that they are working fully sequentially, the next one beginning only after the former one is completely finished: conceptualization → syntactic encoding → morphophonological encoding → articulation. However, this view is not in line with the fast and usually fluent speech that people produce. It is also not in line with the *incremental production* that we observe. Quite often, when starting to speak, a speaker does not yet know exactly how a sentence will end.

A different view is that the different "modules" can operate in parallel, but what they are working on depends on timing: When do they receive the output of earlier processes? Thus, the Formulator might work on information just received from the Conceptualizer, while the Conceptualizer would already be working on the next chunk of conceptual information. In this case we would call this "incremental production involving cascaded processing." Remember that a cascade is a waterfall. The water streams at all levels of the waterfall (simultaneously), but the water that is now below, started above in the stream some time ago (sequentially). Two types of parallelism could be distinguished:

- *Intercomponent parallelism*: e.g., Conceptualizer and Formulator work in parallel;
- *Intracomponent parallelism*: e.g., Formulator works on two aspects in parallel.

Yet another important possibility is that the production system is not strictly sequential, but *interactive*: Later components could send information back to earlier ones. In the earlier chapters on language comprehension, we have seen that connectionist models typically make this assumption.

In the following section, we consider the activities of the Conceptualizer, Formulator, and Articulator in more detail.

9.3.2 Conceptualizer

The Conceptualizer is concerned with matters such as the following:

- What is the goal of the utterance? What is it meant to achieve?
- What should be expressed in the utterance? What is its meaning content?
- What does the listener know already (given information) and what do they not yet know (new information)?
- In what order should the information be put into words?

Speaking takes place in a certain situational setting, like a conversation. Participants in a conversation (interlocutors) speak in alternation (they respond to each other, taking turns) and they speak with a certain intention. As such, a conversation can be considered a type of *joint action*. There are certain unwritten rules about who may speak at a particular moment, how one should interrupt the other, and so on. These rules may differ between cultures. In general, speakers usually try to be *cooperative*. This principle is expressed in the following four "Gricean maxims" (Grice, 1975):

- *Quantity*: Provide enough, but not too much information;
- *Quality*: Speak the truth or say that for which you have evidence;
- *Relation*: Be relevant;
- *Manner*: Be short, clear, and unambiguous.

Speakers produce utterances to achieve particular communicative goals. Such intention of an utterance is called its "illocutionary force" (Austin, 1975). A "speech act" is an expression with illocutionary force (i.e., with an intended aim or effect). Searle (1969) has proposed different types of speech act:

- *Assertives*: State that something is the case, e.g., assert, complain;
- *Directives*: Give an assignment to the listener, e.g., question, order;
- *Commissives*: Oblige the listener to something, e.g., promise, threaten;
- *Expressives*: Express feelings or a psychological condition, e.g., thank, welcome;
- *Declarations*: Adapt the state of reality, e.g., baptize, marry, assign.

Even simple dialogs may contain a variety of different speech acts. As an exercise, you might try to discern different types of speech act in the following dialog:

"Pete has torn his Achilles muscle."
"O no! Is he in the hospital?"
"Yes. I will visit him later today."
"Wish him a speedy recovery on my behalf."
"Will do."

Whether a speaker is successful in realizing their speech act (whether they are "felicitous" or not), depends on their skill in processing different types of information, both linguistic and non-linguistic.

Speakers alternate between planning and linearizing the speech they wish to utter and implementing their plans over time. Goldman-Eisler and colleagues (e.g., Henderson et al., 1966) already showed that spontaneous speech consists of phases in which relatively few words are produced ("hesitant phases") and others that are more eloquent ("fluent phases"). Later research into these hesitation-filled and fluent phases in monolog by Beattie (1983) makes likely that even larger parts of discourse are planned, not only sentences.

When speakers recode (part of) the conceptual structure into a sentence, the selected information must be ordered. This process is called *linearization*. The ordering of information is codetermined by both content and process.

With respect to content, there may be a "natural order" in mentioning particular items or events. For instance, a temporal sequence may be natural: There is an obvious meaning difference between "She got married and became pregnant" and "She became pregnant and got married." Spatial descriptions also have a natural order. Speakers often follow the shortest or easiest route from start to goal, even when this may not be strictly necessary from a logical perspective. Similar (culturally determined) natural orders exist in the planning of conversations, argumentations, etc.

Speakers and listeners implicitly share assumptions about structuring: cause before effect, intentions before decisions, and so on (see notions on reasoning in Chapter 8). Such tacit agreements facilitate the construction of messages by the speaker and their interpretation by the listener.

Ordering information is also subject to process considerations. These have to do with accounting: What has been said already and what must still be done? For instance, information is expressed linked to existing (possibly already activated) memory structures (cf. given vs. new information). Some principles are less domain-specific and culturally dependent than "natural order" agreements. Levelt (1981) identified some of these principles in experiments with chains of colored circles:

- *Principle of connectivity*: If possible, choose as the next item to be mentioned a directly connected item;
- *Principle of minimal effort*: When there are multiple connections with new items, choose your continuation in such a way that the memory load due to retaining "return addresses" is as low as possible;
- *Stack principle or first-in last-out principle*: If there is no directly connected item, return to the last return address in the waiting list. The item addresses still to be considered are ordered in a bin with the first item as the lowest item.

The result of conceptualization is a *preverbal message*: This is a representation of the intended message in a format that can be used as input to linguistic formulation processes. It has been proposed that "event roles" play an important role at this stage: actor (or agent), patient, recipient, action, and so on. A message is a conceptual structure expressing a psychological intention that is *preverbal*, meaning that it must still be mapped onto the goal language. We also use the term "meaning structure," and the work of the Conceptualizer can be seen as "thinking for speaking" (Slobin, 1996). In the literature, various proposals have been made for the representation of conceptual structures. We have seen examples of these in Chapter 7 on sentence processing and Chapter 8 on meaning.

9.3.3 Formulator

As soon as a message or fragment of a conceptual structure has been made ready for expression, the formulation process can begin. To some degree, the production process can be seen as the inverse process described in the chapter on sentence processing. Instead of deriving a meaning structure from an incoming series of words, a speaker must do the opposite: construct a syntactic structure based on a conceptual message. There are two important, inseparable parts to the formulation process: the retrieval of lexical material (lemmas) from the mental lexicon in Long Term Memory, and the construction of a syntactic frame with "slots" to which this material can be assigned. Thus, lexical and syntactic production processes go hand in hand.

9.3.3.1 Syntactic encoding

Syntactic (or grammatical) encoding involves the following subprocesses:

- Selecting lemmas (word-like units) from your mental lexicon with meanings that fit with (parts of) the message;
- Using their syntactic specifications to construct a syntactic frame with "slots" for the chosen lemmas/words;
- Filling in the slots with the lemmas.

The first step indicates that sentence construction proceeds in a *lexically driven* way. Lemmas are word-like units that mediate between semantic, syntactic, and phonological representations. First, they are linked up to meanings that partially cover the event structure that must be expressed. Second, lemmas require particular syntactic environments, for instance, verbs typically require subjects and sometimes also objects. Third, lemmas are linked up to specific phonological word forms, representing their pronunciations. In sum, the notion of lemma implies that word properties guide the sentence production process. This is why the second subprocess above, involving syntax, follows rather than precedes the first subprocess, involving lemmas, within the overall syntactic encoding process.

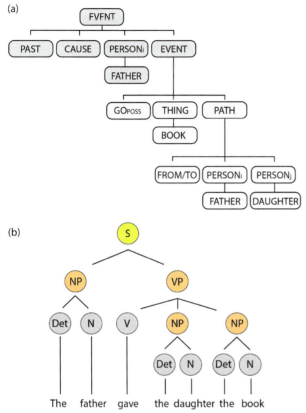

Figure 9.2
Event structure and English surface structure of the sentence "The father gave the daughter the book". In language production, the speaker needs to create a surface structure (part b of the figure) on the basis of the event structure (part a of the figure) to produce a felicitous utterance. In that sense, sentence production can be seen as reverse sentence comprehension (also see Figure 7.5 on sentence comprehension and Chapter 8 about meaning). Adapted from Levelt (1989).

The Formulator must also take care of what are called the *suprasegmental characteristics* of larger stretches of speech (see Chapter 5). Based on the intended meaning, speakers bring about certain variations in duration, pitch (tone), and amplitude (loudness) in their utterances as a whole. For example, to a baby you may speak in a much higher pitch than to an adult; when you wish to stress something, you may speak just a bit more loudly, and you can utter the same series of words as a statement or a question. More specifically, subtle differences in duration and stress may accompany the expression of different meanings: "Night rate" is not pronounced in exactly the same way as is "nitrate." Also, the intonation pattern of an utterance follows a kind of "grammar" (rule system) that is language-dependent. Italian utterances, for instance, sound clearly different from English utterances. Furthermore, the more general intonation pattern you apply to a sentence also adapts to the stress that is required on the syllables of individual words (see Chapter 5).

9.3.3.2 Lemma retrieval

In the conceptual structure of an utterance, like the event structure that we described in Chapter 7 on sentence processing, *lexical concepts* can be discerned. Suppose that we wish to convey the message that the father gave the book to the daughter (adapting an example by Levelt, 1989; also see Meyer et al., 2019). To do this, concepts such as FATHER, BOOK, and DAUGHTER can be expressed as nouns, and GAVE as a verb. Because of the existence of meaning-similar words, different lexical options may become activated. For instance, the concept BOOK might be expressed by the words "present" or "novel," and instead of "father" the word "dad" might be selected (depending on circumstances, addressee, mood, and so on). This activation process could be conceived as a "conceptual competitor set reduction process." Multiple candidates are initially considered (even from different languages in the case of multilinguals); when the conceptual specification becomes more clear, certain candidates fall out of the competitor set until one remains.

According to the standard model of language production depicted in Figure 9.1, these lexical concepts activate *lemmas*. Lemmas provide syntactic and functional information that

202 *Language production*

> ### DISCUSSION BOX 9: LANGUAGE PRODUCTION VS. LANGUAGE COMPREHENSION
>
> Figure 9.2, which relates event structures to syntactic structures, may appear familiar to you. Indeed, it is the reverse of Figure 7.5 on sentence processing. During spoken language comprehension, we incrementally derive an event structure of a sentence, and during spoken language production we do just the opposite. In comprehension, we do this by recognizing the words in the surface structure of a presented sentence and mapping their meanings on the slots of the event structure. In production, we do the opposite.
>
> As such, would it be fair to compare language to a car driving forward or backward and say that "language production is language comprehension in reverse gear"?
>
> Try to motivate your answer by examining the processes of language comprehension and production more globally and more locally. Three suggestions are the following. First, compare the contribution of segmental and suprasegmental information in speech comprehension and production (hint: think of the elliptic utterance "Wannacuppacoffee?"). Second, compare the effects of cohorts in spoken language and of semantically similar alternatives to a target word (synonyms, translation) in language production. Third, how similar are the comprehension and production of idiomatic expressions that also have a "regular" meaning (e.g., "It was smooth sailing all the way")?

drives a series of syntactic building procedures (for constituent assembly). Some of these procedures have access to the message, others to the function words (closed-class elements) in the lemma lexicon. After they are activated, lemmas point to word form addresses that specify locations in the lexicon where the sound forms (phonological representations) of words are stored. They are activated quite quickly, at a rate of about two to three per second (Levelt, 1989, p. 199; Maclay & Osgood, 1959).

9.3.3.3 The complex interaction between syntactic encoding and lemma retrieval

Let us consider the example of the father giving a book to the daughter in more detail to clarify how syntactic encoding and lemma retrieval interact. As you will have noticed, Figure 9.2 reproduces Figure 7.5 relating event structure and syntactic structure, but in opposite order (panel a has become panel b and vice versa). The event structure for the message shows that a father is prominently involved. In the conceptual function CAUSE (PERSONi, EVENT), FATHER serves as PERSON. It is also clear from the event structure that an object is transferred. There are two verbs that are often used for object transfer: "give" and "receive." Because of the prominence or salience of FATHER, we may decide to put it early in the sentence, making it the syntactic subject. Since FATHER is also the PERSON causing the event (the actor) in the conceptual specification, only the verb "give" is in line with both the conceptual and the syntactic demands. We note that the selection of this verb syntactically requires a subject (already available, FATHER), but also a direct object (and potentially an indirect object as well). Suitable words are found in line with meaning and syntax that can fulfil these functions: the nouns "book" and "daughter." After "give" has been selected, the right tense is implemented ("gave"), and production proceeds.

At some syntactic positions in the sentence, different continuations are possible. For instance, after "The father gave ...," two continuations are possible: "The father gave ... the daughter the book" or "The father gave ... the book to the daughter." And if, instead of the lemma for FATHER, that for BOOK had become available first, this could have led to the sentence "The book ... was given to the daughter by the father." It is even possible that speakers correct themselves if they are not satisfied with their initial productions: "The book ... The father gave the book to the daughter." The choice for a particular sentence construction is probably codetermined by:

- *Lexical availability*: e.g., how quickly the word form "book" could be retrieved from the mental lexicon, relative to alternative items like "present" or "novel";
- *Syntactic prominence*: which construction is still "fresh" in the memory of the speaker (consider a radio reporter or sportscaster who reuses a particular construction under time pressure), or which construction is preferred in the language at hand;
- *Conceptual accessibility and saliency*: which part of the message becomes available first, for instance because it is in focus.

Language production is not only incremental, but to some extent also *local*. This may lead to constructions such as: "He was passed in the end by the fast runner Jim Simpson immediately went at high speed to the finish line." In this example, the speaker uses the end of the first sentence as the beginning of a second one. Note that "the fast runner Jim Simpson" therefore fulfills two syntactic roles.

9.3.3.4 Morphophonological encoding

The syntactic structure with lemma positions under construction is still abstract and lacks a morphophonological specification. Morphological and phonological specification of word segments and specification of the intonation pattern (pitch contour, accent) takes place in different steps following syntactic encoding. (Thus, word retrieval in language production involves word concepts, lemmas, and word forms/lexemes.) That morphological specification follows syntactic formulation but precedes phonological specification is clear from speech errors such as "a maniac for weekends" (instead of "a weekend for maniacs") that we discussed earlier.

9.3.4 Articulator

The Articulator executes the phonetic plan that it receives from the Formulator. It controls many different parts of your body that contribute to the production of speech (see Figure 9.3 for a selection). In fact, the whole upper part of your body is involved in speaking, from lungs to lips. The Articulator sends movement instructions to muscle groups in the articulatory organs to produce series of sounds according to a particular prosodic contour. Governing the hundreds of muscles in the speech organs is a very complex process. The articulatory organs are due to a certain degree of momentum (they respond relatively slowly to changes). This necessitates a process of preplanning. When we pronounce a word such as "snooze" (/snuz/), the rounding for the /u/ sound already starts at word onset; in the spectrogram, its onset is already discernable during the /s/ (e.g., compared to the /s/ in /sniz/).

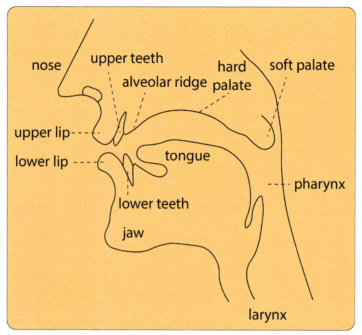

Figure 9.3
Diagram of the human articulatory apparatus.

The diverse articulatory organs are positioned at different distances from the brain areas that regulate their movements. When nerve impulses leave the brain simultaneously, they will therefore reach the muscles in the larynx later than those situated near the mouth (cf. Elemans et al., 2015; Kiebel et al., 2008). In other words, when one produces a syllable like /bɑ/, where the lips are closed approximately simultaneously with the vibration of the vocal cords, the nerve impulses to the vocal cords must have left earlier than those to the lips. Thus, a complex process of synchronization must be at work. As such, it may also be the case that some speech errors are due to more peripheral (motor-oriented) problems with articulation, rather than happening at more abstract levels of language production.

Sentences that are explicitly made to elicit speech errors are the so-called "tongue twisters." These are sentences that confuse the Articulator, because sounds that are similar and confusable alternate in a complex order. Some examples in English are:

- Peter Piper picked a peck of pickled peppers.
  A peck of pickled peppers Peter Piper picked.
  If Peter Piper picked a peck of pickled peppers,
  Where's the peck of pickled peppers Peter Piper picked?
- Betty Botter bought some butter
  But she said the butter's bitter
  If I put it in my batter, it will make my batter bitter
  But a bit of better butter will make my batter better
  So 'twas better Betty Botter bought a bit of better butter
- The sixth sick sheik's sixth sheep's sick
- She sells seashells by the seashore
- How can a clam cram in a clean cream can?

Tongue twisters have been investigated extensively by Oppenheim and Dell (2008) and Corley et al. (2011). The first authors asked participants to say out loud (overtly) or imagine saying out loud (internally or "covertly") four-word tongue twisters that manipulated phoneme onset similarity and whether slips would result in other words or not (lexicality). Two examples of the onset similarity condition are "lean reed reef leech" (possibly resulting in the word "leaf" instead of "reef") and "lean reed wreath leech" (possibly resulting in the pseudoword "leath" instead of "wreath"). The participants' repetition of the tongue twisters was paced in time with a metronome and they had to self-report all slips. The lexical bias and phonemic similarity effects found for standard speech errors were indeed replicated in the overt speech errors on the tongue twisters. Inner slips, however, were not sensitive to phonemic similarity, suggesting that inner speech is underspecified at the subphonemic level.

When it comes to articulation, a number of phases in actual speech production have been discerned (Catford, 1988; Maassen et al., 2004):

1. *Neurolinguistic programming*: The organization of a neural program for the intended utterance linked up to the output of the Formulator.
2. *Neuromuscular phase*: The execution of the neural program. In the neuromotor phase, motor commands set groups of muscle fibers into action (via nerve cells). In the myomotor phase, muscles and muscle groups start to constrict simultaneously and in succession.
3. *Organic phase*: The organs connected to the muscles and muscle groups are given certain positions and movements (e.g., contraction of the rib cage, closing the vocal folds in the larynx, tongue configuration).
4. *Aerodynamic phase*: Differences in size and form of the speech channel result in the compression and expansion of air in the channel. Together with continuous changes in the form of the larynx, this leads to various movements towards the outside (e.g., puffs, stops, bursts, continuous flow, etc.).
5. *Acoustic phase*: The movements of the air out of the mouth, resulting in waves of fluctuating air pressure, that can be perceived by everyone in hearing distance.

Just as with respect to the Speech Recognizer, an important question is what the nature of the basic unit used for neurolinguistic programming actually is: phonemes, syllables, or other units. There are different views on the relation between neural commands and phonemes during speech production. It has been proposed that the syllable is an important unit here, because co-articulation affects the final utterance to a large extent. For instance, "I demand it" is commonly resyllabified into "I de man dit."

Using such contracted speech is actually considered as a sign of high or native-like proficiency in the second language of bilinguals. For instance, a mother tongue speaker of American English typically does not exactly say "What are you doing?" but probably something more like "Whatchadoin?" (See also Chapter 3.)

> **SUMMARY: LANGUAGE PRODUCTION: PROCESSES**
>
> Language production is typically taken to consist of three stages: conceptualization, formulation, and articulation. At the conceptualization stage, speakers consider how a conceptual representation (thought/message) can be turned into a sentence, phrase, clause, or word. In line with their intention, speakers then look for pieces of conceptual information that can be expressed as word-like linguistic units, arranging them in a particular order fit for incremental production. The formulation stage entails these processes of syntactic and morphophonological encoding. During syntactic encoding, a syntactic structure is built on the basis of one or more words that can appropriately express the intended utterance. During morphophonological encoding, the morphologically correct sound forms of words are internally generated. Finally, at the articulation stage, the speaker executes a phonetic plan that results in overt speech. This entails the generation and execution of articulatory motor commands. The spoken words that are produced are typically combined with other overt communicative signals such as facial expressions and hand gestures. The language production process is supervised by an internal and an external monitor that aim to help in avoiding speech errors and other disfluencies in speaking. A large part of the body is involved in the production of speech, including mouth, tongue, vocal cords, lungs, as well as the face and gesturing hands.

9.4 MODELS OF LANGUAGE PRODUCTION

9.4.1 Slot-and-filler models of language production

On the basis of experimental evidence (including both behavioral and neuroscientific studies) and speech error analysis, several models have been proposed to capture the cognitive processes described in the previous section. Many of these models (e.g., Garrett, 1980; Levelt, 1989; Shattuck-Hufnagel, 2019) make a distinction between the linguistic *structures* that are built (in terms of syntactic, morphological, and syllable frames) and their *content* (e.g., lexical material). The linguistic frames provide *slots* into which *fillers* can be put. In line with the proposed language production process, elements are selected from the mental lexicon in Long Term Memory (these are the "fillers"); these are used to construct frames with slots that determine the order of the elements (the slots can be labeled with the syntactic category names of the fillers); next, the elements are placed in the slots.

Three examples of frames are *syntactic frames* at the level of syntactic encoding, in which word elements (lemmas) can be put, *morphological frames* for indicating morphemic structure, and *syllable frames* in which phonemes can be filled in as an onset, a nucleus, or a coda (see Figure 9.4). The assumption of syntactic frames may appear understandable, but why are syllable frames assumed to exist? In fact, speech errors provide a lot of evidence in favor of the syllable frame.

First, phonological word forms are made of smaller units, as speech errors and *tip-of-the-tongue* states testify. Second, there are syllable restrictions on phoneme exchanges: Onset phonemes are exchanged with other onset phonemes (in spoonerisms), nuclei (vowels) are exchanged with other nuclei, and codas with codas. Third, there is the so-called *syllable paradox*: Although phoneme exchanges follow the restriction on syllable position, in Indo-European languages such as English syllables as a whole are almost never exchanged. It seems therefore that syllables are not fillers themselves in English, but provide a frame, in which smaller elements such as phonemes can be placed.

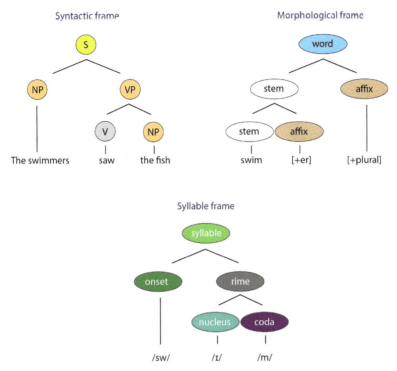

Figure 9.4
Syntactic frames, morphological frames, and syllabic frames provide structure to language production. Syntactic frames take lemmas and phrases, morphological frames receive morphemes (stems and affixes), and syllable frames incorporate phonemes (in onset, nucleus and coda positions). After Dell (1986).

In sum, syllables are assumed to have an onset-nucleus-coda or ONC structure (in which the nucleus and optional coda together are called a *rime*) because there are speech errors in which nucleus and coda exchange together (e.g., "dog" → "dip"), but almost no speech errors in which onset and nucleus change together ("dog' → "tag").

Why would syllable structures exist? Because the construction of a phonological representation out of smaller elements (e.g., phonemes) is also functional during speaking. In daily life, one can say "I - ga - vi – tim" instead of "I gave it him." Here the boundaries of syllables no longer correspond to word boundaries.

9.4.2 Standard model of language production

Levelt and colleagues (1999) proposed a model for word production that has been called the "standard model of language production" and is depicted in Figure 9.1. It has been computationally implemented as the WEAVER++ model. WEAVER is an acronym for Word-form Encoding by Activation and VERification (Roelofs, 1997). The model assumes that word production is subserved by a feedforward activation network. There is incremental (piecemeal) production with cascaded processing. Remember once more that a cascade is a waterfall. The water flows at all levels of the stream, but the water that is below now was up in the stream a while ago. *Concepts* for words (lexical concepts) activate word-like units called *lemmas*. Lemmas are word representations that are specified syntactically and semantically, but not phonologically. They correspond to the slots in the syntactic structures specified earlier. If a speaker is in a "tip-of-the-tongue" state, they know the concept to be expressed, but cannot find the (whole) form. However, the speaker might know that the word starts with an /s/, has two syllables, and has feminine grammatical gender. Lemmas activate word forms, which are *morphemes* with a *phonemic* specification. Still later, a *resyllabification* process may change the phonological representation into a final form: English "bend it" may change into "ben dit," and Spanish *los otros* into "lo so tros."

Although processes at different levels may be going on at the same time, they follow each other sequentially. A speech monitoring system checks the correctness of outputs at different levels. For a long time, WEAVER++ held that lemma selection must be completed before phonological information about the target word is accessed. This assumption is contested (Jescheniak & Schriefers, 1998; Peterson & Savoy, 1998).

9.4.3 Interactive Activation model for word production

An alternative computational model for word production is that by Dell (1986). This model is an interactive connectionist model with spreading activation between representational units in a large lexical network. The model stresses the structure–content nature of language production assumed by slot-and-filler models (see Figure 9.5). Conceptual representations for words activate word-type representations (morphemes in Dell's model), which themselves activate phonological representations. During language production, representations are selected and filled in into "tactic frames," structures like syntactic tree diagrams, morpheme specifications, and phonological syllable frames (cf. Figure 9.4). The model has its focus on speech errors. To ensure certain characteristics of speech errors, the different frame types restrict the units that can be filled in. For instance, in the syntactic structures, noun slots can only be filled in with nouns, not verbs; and in the syllabic frames, onset phoneme slots cannot be filled with coda phonemes.

Varying the settings of the model's parameters (e.g., speed of unit selection, strength of links), Dell's model can produce speech errors of different kinds (e.g., anticipations, exchanges, and perseverations). Word selection takes place after a certain amount of processing time has passed, reflecting a certain speaking rate. Of course, for correct speech, the

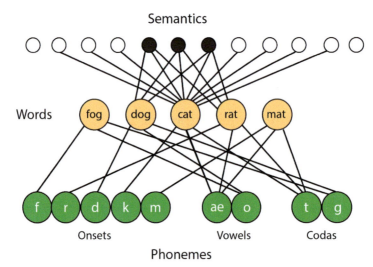

Figure 9.5
An interaction activation model of word naming. Bidirectional, excitatory connections are assumed between connected network nodes. Note that words may overlap in parts of their meaning (here indicated in dark gray) and in the sounds they consist of. After Dell et al. (1997).

most active unit at that time should be the intended one. However, with certain parameter settings, an incorrect unit of the same type may happen to be more active than the target unit and become erroneously selected instead. Because the activation of a selected unit is reset to zero, the most active unit might now be the originally intended one. It might therefore still be selected for a later slot, which would result in an exchange error. For instance, "queer dean" could result in "dear queen" after erroneous selection of the /d/ in the first onset position. If the reset of the first phoneme fails, the unit might be chosen once again, resulting in a perseveration, sounding more like "queer queen." Note that in such cases the monitor apparently has failed to detect the error in time.

Importantly, due to its interactive nature, Dell's model can also account for semantic bias, lexical bias, and mixed errors. Interactions between the conceptual/semantic and morpheme/word level lead to semantic bias: "cat" will become "dog" more often than a semantically unrelated word like "dock" (cf. Figure 9.5). Interactions between the morpheme/word and phonological/phoneme levels lead to lexical bias: Mispronouncing "cat" will lead to a word ("mat") more often than to a pseudoword ("jat"). Interactions between the conceptual (semantic), morpheme (word), and phonological (phoneme) levels can lead to mixed errors: "cat" will more often become "rat" than "mat" – the first two words both refer to animals and have considerable phonological overlap.

9.4.4 Models of tone language production

The models discussed above were developed in the context of research on Indo-European languages. As such, they may not necessarily generalize to all spoken languages, and even completely lack intrinsic features that are common to languages other than, for instance, English and Dutch. O'Seaghdha and colleagues (2010) compared the mental processes involved in the production of Mandarin Chinese (a tone language) versus English monosyllabic words and proposed a way to take *tone* into account in models of language production.

Indeed, tone is a very important feature in many languages and dialects, including Mandarin Chinese, and critically influences the meaning the same string of sounds has. For instance, the same monosyllabic set of segments "ma" will mean either "mother" or "horse" depending on the (high level vs. fall-rise) tone assigned to this syllable. The model for Mandarin Chinese presented in Figure 9.6 is based on the observation that in this language, speech

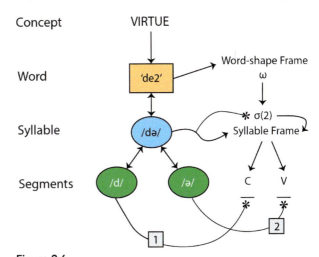

Figure 9.6
Processing stages arguably involved in the production of monosyllabic words in Mandarin Chinese. Normal arrows indicate how activation spreads through the system. Arrows ending in an asterisk reflect content being assigned to a particular (slot in a) structure. The authors assume that the syllabic level is more important in language production in Mandarin Chinese compared to English, and that tones are assigned to syllables at this level. The figure represents a situation in which a speaker of Mandarin Chinese wishes to produce the monosyllabic word corresponding to the concept VIRTUE. This means producing the sounds /də/ in combination with tone 2. The word-shape frame is called ω, tone 2 of the syllable frame is indicated by σ(2). Adapted from O'Seaghdha et al. (2010).

errors in which full syllables are exchanged occur much more commonly than in languages like English, and also more often than phoneme exchanges. One could therefore assume that syllables are the most fundamental building blocks that words in Mandarin Chinese are made of.

We have seen that models of language production often also assume the existence of *syllable frames* for languages such as English, but strongly rely on individual phonemic segments that are placed in the right order in the filler positions (e.g., onset, nucleus, coda) present in these frames. O'Seaghdha and colleagues (2010) place the assignment of a tone to a syllable in Mandarin Chinese at the level of the syllable. The idea is that (initially atonal) syllables are retrieved from the mental lexicon in Long Term Memory as holistic units, which are then assigned a certain tone in line with the concept that the speaker would like to express. As such, the critical difference with word production in English is the assumption of what type of phonological units (syllables vs. phonemes) are first retrieved from the lexicon when the speaker has the intention to express a certain concept at the stage prior to articulation when units below the lexical level need to become selected.

9.4.5 Interface Hypothesis

In everyday face-to-face communication, speakers offer their addressees a variety of visual signals while they are articulating their spoken message. Indeed, we have seen time and again that human communication is intrinsically multimodal in nature: Speakers combine visual and auditory signals to get their message across. An important type of visual signals are the hand gestures people spontaneously make while they speak. Over the past decades, several models of speech and gesture production have been developed and empirically tested. Typically, such models have taken the standard model of language production as their basis and extended it to account for the gestures people produce while they speak. The most

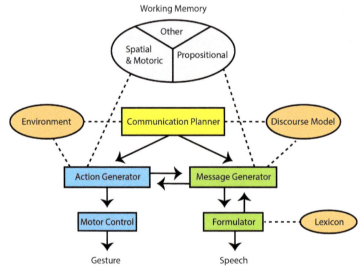

Figure 9.7
The Interface Hypothesis. A model of the production of gesture and speech. In this approach, notions we know from the Language User Framework, like "Discourse Production" and "Conceptualizer," are replaced by a generalized "Communication Planner" operating on a Discourse Model, as well as Message and Action Generators. Adapted from Kita and Özyürek (2003).

influential model in this domain has been the Interface Hypothesis (Kita & Özyürek, 2003), depicted in Figure 9.7.

The right bottom part of the visual depiction of the Interface Hypothesis indeed looks very similar to parts of the standard model of speech production, as it includes the processes of formulation and articulation (of speech) and makes use of the information stored in the mental lexicon in Long Term Memory. The Interface Hypothesis explicitly splits the higher-order process of conceptualization into two parts, taken up by a Communication Planner and a Message Generator. The Communication Planner grossly decides what information should be expressed, selects the type of speech act that will be used, and is involved in a rough ordering of the information that is going to be conveyed. Importantly, at this level, where the language user's communicative intention is generated, it is decided which *modalities of expression* are going to be involved in the to-be-produced message. The distribution of information over the auditory and the visual modality may hence depend on context: In a noisy bar, you may start to rely more on hand gestures than on speech when trying to order another drink. When communicating with a blind individual or on the phone, spoken information may be prioritized.

The Message Generator is in charge of coming up with a proposition that can be verbally formulated (remember the "preverbal message" in the standard model of speech production) and is therefore concerned with the linguistic information that will be conveyed. At the same time, an Action Generator selects and uses information from the environment and/or Working Memory to generate a spatio-motoric representation that can initiate motor control processes leading to the visual articulation of a gesture. For instance, if you see a bird flying past your window, the Action Generator may use the spatial imagery of this event as a basis for a movement, expressed by the hands, which resembles the act of a bird flying and/or the bird itself.

Critically, the Interface Hypothesis assumes that the spoken and gestural part of a message are in contact with each other. Spatial and to-be-spoken information *interface*: The Message Generator and Action Generator exchange information bi-directionally. In addition, the Message Generator may learn from the Formulator that certain information is not easily expressible in speech, after which that part of the message may be taken up by the Action Generator and conveyed visually. As such, some information (e.g., about the size of an object) may be more easily and more readily expressed by a movement of the hands, while other information (e.g., the name of that object) may be more simply conveyed via one or more spoken words. A Discourse Model provides the language user with information about what has been communicated already and which part of the communicatively intended message cannot yet be considered known or understood by the addressee of the multimodal message.

In sum, according to the Interface Hypothesis, what a hand gesture looks like exactly will depend on three variables: the communicative intention of the language user (generated at the level of the Communication Planner), information taken from the environment and/or Working Memory, and information or "online feedback" provided by the Message Generator coming from the Formulator. One thing that the Interface Hypothesis nicely underlines is the *non-modularity* of human language. Language, perception, and action are tightly interwoven.

> **SUMMARY: MODELS OF LANGUAGE PRODUCTION**
>
> Models of language production commonly make a distinction between the linguistic *structures* that are built on the way to articulation and their *content*. Linguistic frames provide *slots* into which *fillers* (information retrieved from Long Term Memory) can be inserted. Syllable frames, for instance, may be filled with individual phonological segments in onset, nucleus, and coda positions. Larger syntactic structures may have slots for individual words from a particular syntactic category.
>
> The standard model of language production relies on a distinction between conceptualization, formulation, and articulation. It assumes that word production is subserved by a feedforward activation network that combines incremental production with cascaded processing. The language production process has also been computationally implemented in interactive connectionist models that rely on spreading activation between representational units.
>
> Research on tone languages and on multimodal communication make clear that the standard model may need to be adapted or extended to account for the rich diversity of languages around the world and for the multichannel richness of face-to-face communication.

9.5 LANGUAGE PRODUCTION: EMPIRICAL STUDIES

In language comprehension studies, the input to the participant is completely known and it can be manipulated experimentally by the researcher. In contrast, the output must be assessed by indirect measurements via, for example, reaction times, eye movement patterns, brain activity, or accuracy percentages. In language production studies, the situation is reversed: The input is a thought or a preverbal message that is invisible to the researcher and difficult to manipulate experimentally. In contrast, the output is completely available. In other words, the control over the materials to be processed is in the hands of the experimenter during language comprehension studies, but more in those of the participant during language production studies. The "trick" of many experimental studies into the psychology of language production is therefore to make sure that the participant performs the "correct" (expected) production processes, which can to some extent be achieved by restricting the input to the production process and thus the produced output. An example is the research technique in which participants name or describe simple pictures presented one by one on a computer screen (see Chapter 4). Here the conceptual input can be kept under control, and the timing of various processes can be checked by clever picture variations or the introduction of distractor items at different moments in time. Nevertheless, the experimenter might still be surprised by a participant naming the couch a "sofa."

In this section, a variety of studies will be paraded, illustrating important applications of several paradigms we described in Chapter 4. Picture-word interference and syntactic priming studies will be discussed to argue in favor of a production process that is ordered from lemma-filled syntactic structures to phonological utterances. By means of neuroscientific studies, we will then clarify the associated processes in the brain. A word-pair repetition paradigm that allows the study of lexical bias effects and the elicitation of context-induced speech errors, among which Freudian slips, will be considered next. The section ends with a consideration of elicited subject-verb agreement errors and their theoretical significance.

9.5.1 Picture-word interference paradigm

In a well-known study, researchers wished to test whether in language production semantic activation arises earlier than phonological activation. Schriefers and colleagues (1990) investigated this question by means of a *picture-word interference* paradigm involving different stimulus onset asynchronies (see below). In a picture-word interference paradigm, participants name an object that is presented as a picture (e.g., a house), while they are hearing (or seeing) a distractor word item. The distractor word can be semantically related to the picture (e.g., "church"), phonologically related (e.g., "mouse") or unrelated (e.g., "storm"). The distractor affects the amount of time needed to initiate the naming process. The onset of the (here, spoken) distractor can be before the picture is presented, at the same time, or later. The time between the onset of the picture and the onset of the distractor is called the *Stimulus Onset Asynchrony* (SOA). The influence of the distractor on the picture naming RT depends on both the SOA and on the type of relation between distractor and target. When the distractor is semantically related to the picture, interference is assumed to occur (only) when both the target word and the distractor are in a semantic processing stage. Similarly, when distractor and target are phonologically related,

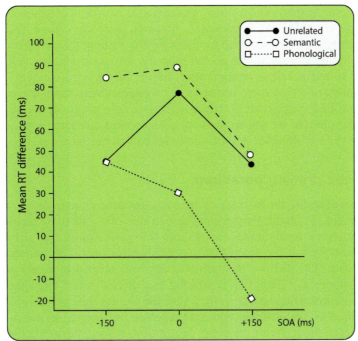

Figure 9.8
In the experiment by Schriefers and colleagues (1990), spoken distractor words and target pictures could be unrelated ("unrelated"), semantically related ("semantic"), or phonologically related ("phonological"). A spoken word was presented 150 ms before the picture onset (SOA: −150 ms), at the same time as the picture onset (SOA: 0 ms), or 150 after the picture onset (SOA: +150 ms). This graph depicts the mean response time (RT) difference for each of the resulting nine conditions in this experimental design compared to a situation where no prime was presented. A positive value means that the presence of a prime led to a slower RT compared to when no prime was presented. At an early SOA, the presence of a semantically related distractor is found to slow down RTs compared to the unrelated condition, whereas a phonologically related distractor is not found to do so. At a late SOA, a phonologically related distractor speeds up the RTs compared to the unrelated condition, whereas a semantically related distractor does not.

the distractor influences target processing only when both are in a phonological processing stage. Note that distractor processing first goes through a phonological identification stage before entering a semantic processing stage. If lexical semantic processing strictly precedes phonological activation, a two-stage model predicts that:

- Semantically related distractors will result in a slower RT (relative to the unrelated distractors) at an *early* SOA (in the experiment, SOA = –150 ms, distractor presented earlier than the picture).
- Phonologically related distractors will result in a faster RT (relative to the unrelated distractors) at a *late* SOA = +150 ms, distractor presented after the picture).

In contrast, if semantic and phonological processes interact, both effects would occur at the same SOA. The results were as follows (see also Figure 9.8).

At the early SOA, the semantic condition was clearly different from the unrelated condition: There was an "inhibition effect" of nearly 40 ms. A semantically related distractor led to a slower picture naming onset than an unrelated distractor. This is in line with the hypothesis that semantic effects during object naming arise early. The distractor semantically interferes with the target naming. At the late SOA, the difference between the semantic and the unrelated condition disappeared.

At the early SOA, there was no naming difference between the phonological condition and the unrelated condition. At the late SOA, however, there was a large "facilitation effect." A phonologically related distractor led to faster picture naming than an unrelated distractor. At late SOAs, the phonological overlap between the distractor and the target word apparently was used to facilitate the pronunciation of the target word. In sum, the experiment appears to demonstrate that there are at least two subsequent stages in language production, because we find only semantic effects first and only phonological effects later. At a later point in this chapter, we will see that the picture-word interference paradigm has come under attack in the last decades, in part due to its complexity (see, e.g., Feng et al., 2021).

9.5.2 Syntactic priming paradigm

Bock (1986a) investigated the interaction between syntactic frames and lemma retrieval in a syntactic priming paradigm. Participants had to describe a picture, showing for example a church being struck by lightning (see Figure 9.9). Just before the picture appeared, a spoken prime sentence was presented that they needed to repeat. This sentence was an active or passive sentence. The pictures themselves could be described by means of two types of sentence, for instance as "Lightning is striking the church" and "The church is struck by lightning." The experimental results showed that the picture descriptions often got the same type of description as the sentences that were repeated just before. An active prime sentence more often induced an active target event description, while a passive prime sentence relatively often elicited a passive event description.

In a different study (Bock, 1986b), the prime was not a spoken sentence but a spoken word. This word had a semantic or phonological relation with one of the two main objects in the picture, for instance:

Semantic:	"thunder" (related to "lightning")
	"worship" (related to "church")
Phonological:	"frightening" (related to "lightning")
	"search" (related to "church")

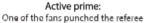
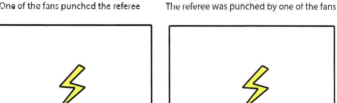

Figure 9.9
Participants in the seminal study by Bock (1986a) were instructed to name pictures like these, following a prime that could be an active (left panel) or passive sentence (right panel).

In principle, here there are still two ways to describe the picture: "Lightning hits the church" (active) or "The church was hit by lightning" (passive). Bock assumed that, via semantic spreading activation, the prime "worship" would lead to a picture description in which "church" would fulfil a prominent grammatical role. It would arise early in the sentence and lead to the passive sentence "The church was hit …" However, in the case of "thunder," "lightning" would become more active early on and lead to the active sentence "Lightning hits …" That was exactly what happened.

In addition, if the level of (morpho)phonological encoding would send feedback to syntactic encoding, then the prime "search" might preactivate the word "church"; in that case, the phonological prime would also have an effect on the selected sentence form. However, no effect of phonologically related primes was observed. Because some other studies did find effects, the conclusion that language production is cascaded rather than interactive is not definitive.

9.5.3 Neuroscientific studies

Indefrey (2011; Indefrey & Levelt, 2004) did meta-analyses of empirical neuroimaging studies (including, for instance, methods such as EEG, fMRI, DTI, MEG, PET, and TMS) to find out which areas in the brain become active at which moments in time during language production tasks. Many of such studies made use of a picture naming paradigm, in which participants named pictures while their brain activity was recorded. Even on the basis of such a relatively simple one-word production task, it becomes clear that producing language is a human capacity that entails a large number of cognitive steps. Figure 9.10 presents a visual depiction of the brain areas associated with the different processing steps involved in naming a picture using a single word according to the overview reported in Indefrey (2011).

The meta-analyses show that, in the case of producing single words, conceptual preparation takes about 200 ms. It is followed by lemma retrieval, phonological code retrieval (peaking around 275 ms) and syllabification (starting around 355 ms, taking about 50–55 ms

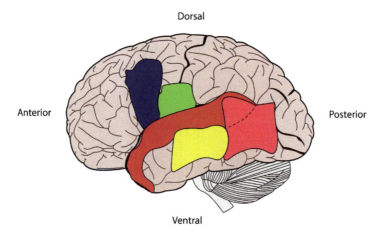

Figure 9.10
Brain areas connected to processes involved in language production, here depicted for the left hemisphere. Colors indicate which brain areas are most strongly involved in specific "functional processing components" that support word production, as evident from picture naming studies: lemma retrieval and selection (yellow), phonological code retrieval (pink), syllabification (blue), articulation (green), and self-monitoring (red). These stages are preceded by a conceptual preparation stage that relies on activation of brain areas associated with conceptual processing, for instance in the parietal lobe. Adapted from Indefrey (2011).

per syllable), phonetic encoding (starting at 455 ms) and articulation (starting at about 600 ms). Over time, the activation of different brain areas fluctuates as a function of the specific processing step at hand.

9.5.4 Studies eliciting speech production errors

In a very different approach to studying language production, researchers have attempted to seduce speakers in experiments to produce errors of different kinds, such as slips of the tongue (speech errors) and subject-verb agreement errors. The characteristics of the elicited errors are analyzed to learn more about the underlying language production processes. In the following sections, we will delve into the methodology and results of this approach.

9.5.4.1 Lexical bias effects in elicited speech errors

Baars and colleagues (1975) were among the first researchers who elicited speech errors experimentally by a procedure they called SLIP. Participants had to read a list of item pairs. In this list, there could be pairs of pseudowords, such as "rafe sode" and "rabe sofe." If participants were to make a speech error here, it might involve spoonerisms, such as "safe road" (words) and "sabe rofe" (pseudowords). A target item pair in the list was preceded by three "bias pairs" (like "soak raid") that contained at least the onset phonemes of the desired wrong outcome, in order to elicit the intended speech error. Under these circumstances, readers produced about 10 to 15% spoonerisms. It was found that a lot more errors arose for target word pairs that formed real words ("rafe sode" → "safe road") than for pairs that created pseudowords ("rabe sofe" → "sabe rofe"). This finding hence experimentally confirms the *lexical bias effect* we have discussed earlier in this chapter.

One other aspect of the experiment is interesting to mention. The lexical bias effect did not always arise. If all item pairs in the experiment were pseudowords, there was no lexical bias! Word and pseudoword speech errors were just as frequent under these circumstances. However, as soon as at least some pairs of real words were put in the experimental list, the lexical bias effect reappeared (the target item pairs remained the same, namely, pseudowords). It was concluded that this is an effect of *monitoring*. If the task of the speaker is only concerned with pseudowords, they apparently do not check the lexical status of the output. However, this changes dramatically if some existing words are included in the test materials. We will get back to effects of stimulus list composition in Chapter 10.

In sum, we may conclude that speakers typically monitor their output even before the beginning of articulation with respect to lexical status (is it a word or not?), that such monitoring processes may be strategically attenuated or even switched off as they are deemed not useful for the task at hand, and that a monitoring process detects and corrects pseudowords more easily than words (even "internally" before articulation begins).

9.5.4.2 Freudian speech errors

Motley and colleagues (Motley & Camden, 1985; Motley et al., 1983) used the technique just described to elicit Freudian speech errors. Such Freudian speech errors can be considered as effects on language production from systems "outside" language, in particular the emotional system. In that sense, they can be considered as a kind of "contextual error" (see section 9.2 above). As before, word pairs appeared on a computer screen, e.g., "past fashion." The participants read the lists of subsequent word pairs silently, but after a beep they had to read the then presented word pair aloud. The target words were preceded by two or three word pairs that should elicit speech errors. For instance, "let dangle" and "leg dangle" were followed by "dead level." This could induce "led devil," a spoonerism. Using some fake electrodes and the help of an attractive female assistant, Freudian speech errors could now be elicited for word pairs like "sham dock" and "past fashion."

Due to the placement of fake electrodes and some remarks about quirky apparatus, participants became slightly anxious and produced speech errors like "damn shock" more often when given a word pair like "sham dock" than under neutral conditions. The presence of an attractive assistant led to more errors on a word pair like "past fashion," being produced as "fast passion." The authors' conclusion is that contextually relevant concepts and emotions can preactivate conceptual units used for speaking. We would like to note that nowadays, most likely, this type of experiment would not receive ethical approval without design adaptations.

9.5.4.3 Induced subject–verb agreement errors

Bock and colleagues (e.g., Bock & Cutting, 1992; Eberhard et al., 2005) introduced an error-eliciting technique to investigate morphosyntactic and conceptual processes in language production. In their studies and those performed by others later (e.g., Vigliocco et al., 1996), participants saw sentence fragments (so-called "preambles") that had to be read aloud and then completed by saying the first thing that came to mind. The sentence fragments (often complex noun phrases) were varied with respect to grammatical and conceptual aspects. For instance, in different conditions the sentence fragment "The key to the cabinet ..." could be turned into "The keys to the cabinet ..." or "The key to the cabinets ..." The first of the two nouns in these fragments is called the "head noun." Participants completing the preambles could either continue with "is" or "are," thus violating or not the subject-verb agreement with the head noun. The participants' sentence completions showed a tendency for the verb to agree not with the subject of the sentence but with the immediately preceding noun. An example of such an "attraction error" is the sentence "The keys to the cabinet is on the table." If you pay attention to it, you will sometimes also observe such errors in everyday colloquial speech. It has been suggested that it is not the linear distance between the head noun and the second noun, but their syntactic distance in terms of surface tree properties that underlies this effect (Franck et al., 2002).

Another manipulation with this error elicitation technique was conceptual in nature. It compared, for instance, the number of errors following preambles such as "The baby on the blankets ..." and "The label on the bottles ..." Note that in these superficially very similar sentence fragments, there is actually only one baby, but numerous labels. This manipulation allowed investigating whether the *conceptual* number of the head noun does affect the number of resulting subject-verb agreement errors. Such conceptual effects have consistently been found in Dutch, Italian, Spanish, and French, but not in English (Vigliocco, 1996). One conclusion of this line of research has been that speakers use both conceptual information from their discourse model and grammatical information about number when they construct subject-verb agreement (which is a morphosyntactic process). Additional influences of pronoun agreement, article gender, case marking, and even phonological factors have also been attested.

> **SUMMARY: LANGUAGE PRODUCTION: EMPIRICAL STUDIES**
>
> Many different tools and techniques have been used to empirically study the mental representations and processes involved in language production. For instance, both behavioral and neuroscientific studies in the field of language production have relied on participants naming pictures that were presented one by one on a computer screen in picture–word interference or syntactic priming paradigms. Such studies have observed that semantic processing typically (partially) precedes phonological processing, and that the type of grammatical structure people use in their utterance may be primed by the linguistic input they recently received. Neuroscientific work has shown that the production of individual words relies on a broad network of brain areas that allow the speaker to translate their intention into a spoken word utterance in less than a second. A different approach has been to elicit language production errors, such as slips of the tongue and subject-verb agreement errors. Language production research has also shown the importance of a monitoring process that helps speakers to avoid making speech errors.

9.6 LANGUAGE PRODUCTION: THE ROLE OF CONTEXT

The earlier described study by Motley and colleagues has been taken as an indication that emotion-laden words can already be activated partially by the non-linguistic context of the situation at hand. In a more general way, non-linguistic context can change activation levels of concepts in the language system and therefore result in semantic priming effects. This is also evident from studies that consider language processing in dialog situations. In the following sections, we will discuss two of those.

9.6.1 Language production in a dialog context

In the discussion of the study by Schriefers and colleagues (1990) above, we saw that presenting a semantic distractor word (e.g., "church") slightly before people have to name a picture (e.g., of a house), leads to slower picture naming response times compared to a baseline condition in which word prime and target picture are semantically unrelated. In other words, there was a *semantic interference* effect. This finding is commonly taken to imply that there must be some form of competition going on between different semantically related words when people name pictures. A very general, open question that has been asked more and more frequently over the past decade is whether such seminal findings actually generalize to the rich and dynamic everyday situations in which language is typically used. After all, outside the lab, people usually do not name individual pictures in single words in a soundproof booth in front of a microphone while being distracted by individual words. Rather, there is a communicative and social context in which language production commonly takes place. Acknowledging this gap between the richness of everyday communication and the relatively artificial and restricted nature of the typical lab environment, Kuhlen and Abdel Rahman (2022) investigated whether the classic semantic interference effect observed in the picture-word interference task would generalize to more natural *dialog* situations.

In their study, participants played a digital card game in a dialog setup, sitting opposite each other while each facing their own computer screen. On a given trial, Participant A produced the utterance "Which card comes on [distractor word]?" that was presented on their screen, after which Participant B named the picture that was depicted on the screen they themselves could see. As in the classic picture-word interference study, and unknown to the participants, in one condition the distractor word and picture were semantically related, whereas in another condition they were not. For instance, in the semantically related condition, Participant A would say "Which card comes on apple?", after which Participant B would see and name a picture of a pear (see Figure 9.11). Also as in the classic study, the researchers cleverly manipulated the temporal gap between the onset of the distractor word and the presentation of the target picture, in this case by online recording when Participant A started uttering the distractor word and presenting the picture to Participant B either 100 ms later ("short SOA") or 650 ms later ("long SOA").

Following the single-word utterance (e.g., "pear") by Participant B, Participant A then saw two pictures on their screen (the correct, target picture and an incorrect filler picture), and selected as quickly and accurately as possible the picture they thought the other

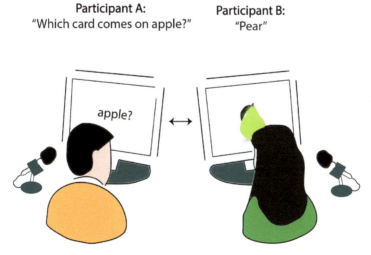

Figure 9.11
Two participants playing a dialog game. In the study by Kuhlen and Abdel Rahman (2022), participants were seated opposite one another while taking part in a relatively naturalistic, dialog version of the classic picture-word interference task.

participant just saw and named. To enhance the "game" nature of the setup, participants were instructed that the most successful pair of players would receive a gift voucher.

Interestingly, in this dialog setup, whether distractor word and target picture were semantically related or unrelated did not influence the observed naming latencies, both at short and long SOAs. This is a remarkable finding, as one would have expected a semantic interference effect at the short SOA on the basis of the classic and widely replicated findings by Schriefers and colleagues (1990). Crucially, when Kuhlen and Abdel Rahman (2022) used the same pictures and spoken distractor words as in the dialog study in a non-communicative control experiment that resembled the classic study, they did observe the well-known semantic interference effect. This means that their original finding in the dialog setup was not due to the nature of the stimuli they used, but must have been caused by the increase in communicativeness and naturalness of their dialog setup.

The authors conclude that, in the dialog setup compared to the individual "classic" setup, participants must have processed their partner's speech more strongly at a conceptual level, which may have led to conceptual facilitation (i.e., an effect of semantic priming). As such, the concept APPLE may have primed and partially activated the concept PEAR and the corresponding lexical items. This conceptual facilitation, in turn, may have cancelled out the typical decelerating effect of lexical competition and interference between semantically related words such as "apple" and "pear" at the lexical level (see also Mädebach et al., 2020).

These findings nicely illustrate how important it is to study language in situations that resemble the situations in which we use it in everyday life. Ultimately, to understand the speaking process and the psychology of language more broadly, we should not only try and understand how people behave in the lab ("what they *can* do"), but also and even more what cognitive mechanisms subserve their language use in the real world ("what they *do* do").

9.6.2 Multimodal language production

To what extent do we use language differently as a function of whom we talk to? Campisi and Özyürek (2013) report a study in which they asked Italian adults to demonstrate in front of a camera how a coffee machine works. In a within-subject design with three counterbalanced conditions, each participant explained three times how to fill the bottom part of the coffee machine with water, add the necessary coffee ingredients, get the water to boil, and have the fresh coffee find its way into an appropriate cup. Critically, participants were told that their explanation was meant either for a fellow adult who also already knew how to make coffee, for a "novice" adult who did not yet know how to make coffee, or for a 12-year-old child who did not know how to make coffee. Would participants' explanations and demonstrations look different as a function of the specific addressee they had in mind while conveying their message?

When looking at the speech participants produced, the authors observed that more words were used when the speakers imagined demonstrating the use of the coffee machine to the child or to the novice adult compared to when targeting their message at the knowledgeable adult. This is a clear example of *audience design*: The specific message people produce is tailored to the (assumed) knowledge state of their addressee. Indeed, participants must have assumed that recipients with knowledge that was less specific could benefit from hearing a lengthier and more detailed explanation.

Obviously, these Italian participants used not only spoken words in their demonstration, but made use of many of the different channels their body offered them to get their message across. When the authors therefore analyzed the hand gestures of their participants, it was found that the average number of iconic gestures they used per every 100 words was significantly higher in messages for the child than for the expert adult addressee. Apparently, participants implicitly decided that the child could use some more iconic, visual information to really understand the workings of the coffee machine. Especially iconic gestures would be helpful here, as the form of these gestures resembles their meaning and therefore makes them a valuable and accessible piece of additional information in this demonstration context.

In sum, both the knowledge state and the age (child vs. adult) of a recipient are taken into account when people design and produce their multimodal messages. It is unlikely that this conclusion holds only for Italians talking and gesturing about making coffee. Instead, it may be a fundamental property of our everyday communication!

> **SUMMARY: LANGUAGE PRODUCTION: THE ROLE OF CONTEXT**
>
> Over the past years, researchers interested in the psychology of language have started to increase the richness of their experimental paradigms to mimic more aspects of everyday communication in the lab. It has been shown that, in dialog situations, the conceptual level of processing may play a more important role than previously assumed. In addition, research looking at the hand gestures that people make while they speak has indicated that language users meticulously tailor the signals (e.g., words, gestures) they convey on the basis of what they know of the person they are communicating with and assume their mental model to be like.

9.7 WHAT IS NEXT?

In Chapters 5, 6, and 7, we considered how language users derive meaning from incoming utterances at word and sentence levels. Both structural and content aspects of language were discussed. In this chapter, we considered the representations and processes involved in the *production* of an utterance based on a conceptual message. It is often assumed that, while processing language in comprehension and production is quite different, the linguistic representations underlying both language activities are shared. Indeed, we have encountered the same representational levels as before, with the exception of the notion of a "lemma," a word-like unit serving at a syntactic level as an interface between lexical meaning and phonology.

Several notions from the domain of language comprehension came back in this chapter on production. This will also be the case in the next chapter, on multilingualism. To what extent are the characterizations of language processing in *monolingual* language users still applicable to language users that master more than one language and can be considered *multilingual*?

9.8 WHAT HAVE WE LEARNED?

Speech errors reveal a lot about speech production; they occur at all levels of processing. The analysis of speech error collections has taught us a lot about how language production takes place for larger and smaller linguistic units (like clauses and morphemes). In addition, it has shown that phonemes are important segments in languages such as Dutch and English, while speakers of Mandarin Chinese may rely more heavily on syllabic units.

Stages in language production are concerned with conceptualization, syntactic encoding (syntactic frame and lemmas), morphophonological encoding, and articulation processes.

Language production is governed by a Cognitive Control System. Among other matters, this system monitors the internal and external output, adapts quickly to ongoing processing, and inhibits unwanted information.

Many models of language production are slot-and-filler models. Particular units ("fillers") can be incorporated in the slots of syntactic, morphological, and syllable structures called "frames."

Using this notion, the standard model of language production assumes the presence of a feedforward activation network, incremental (piecemeal) production, and mostly cascaded processing. In contrast, interactive connectionist models have assumed spreading activation between representational units in a large lexical network to account for the occurrence of speech errors in natural speech. Both types of model are limited in accounting for aspects of tone language production and may be extended when considering language as a multimodal phenomenon. The Interface Hypothesis represents one way in which this could be done.

We have seen that different experimental paradigms have been developed to study aspects of language production: picture-word interference tasks, picture naming and priming setups, syntactic priming paradigms, and tasks aiming at eliciting speech errors and subject-verb agreement errors. Dialog studies and research looking at multimodal language production have stressed the importance of the role of the addressee and the body in language production.

QUESTIONS FOR CHAPTER 9

1. The following two anecdotes were attributed to Oxford don Spooner (see Potter, 1976). (1) Addressing some students he considered lazy, he must have said: "You have hissed all my mystery lectures, and were caught fighting a liar in the quad. Having tasted two worms, you will leave by the next town drain." (2) When he saw that his regular place in church was taken by a lady, he supposedly said to her: "Mardon me padam, this pie is occupewed. Can I sew you to another sheet?" Explain these speech errors in terms of the language production process described in the chapter.
2. In her book on the female brain, Brizendine (2007) wrote: "A woman uses about 20,000 words per day, while a man uses about 7,000." Empirical research into this issue found that people speak on average about 16,000 words per day (Mehl et al., 2007). Do you think this research also observed that women are more talkative than men? Look up the answer in the journal *Science*.
3. Categorize the following speech errors and give an explanation for them. The intended expression is given within parentheses:
    a. "A Gelgian from Ghent" ("Belgian").
    b. "He is starting a therapice" ("therapy/practice").
    c. "Get the child out of the war" ("war out of the child").
    d. "They evaporated the city" ("evacuated").
    e. "Blue bloxes" ("boxes").
    f. "Knife light" ("night life").
4. What would be the reasons for pauses, hesitations, and interjections ("oh," "uhm," "well," and "say") in speech production?
5. Can you come up with tongue twisters in other languages than English? Take, for instance, German: *Fischers Fritze fischt frische Fische; Frische Fische fischt Fischers Fritze*. Or French: *Cinq chiens chassent six chats*. Why are they so difficult to produce correctly? Consider lexical ambiguity, phonological similarities, and prosody.

6   In this book, the processes of typing and writing are not considered, although they are interesting and important in their own right (Logan & Crump, 2011; Pinet & Nozari, 2018; Rap & Fischer-Baum, 2014). What would be the reason(s) for not doing so? And can you come up with your own theory of typing or writing, for instance, on the basis of typing or writing errors?

7   To what extent is the Interface Hypothesis an extension of the standard model of speech production? Which parts are the same or similar in the two models, and which parts have been added in the Interface Hypothesis?

8   In the BBC television sitcom *Allo! Allo!*, Officer Crabtree is an undercover British agent in the little town of Nouvion in France during the Second World War. He speaks very bad French, greeting the people he meets with a jolly "Good moaning!" On one occasion, he says: "Ploose may I hov a kippy of the dooly nosepooper?". Explain the changes in this utterance relative to the intended one. Would a "real" English–French learner make the same errors? Why (not)? Is there any relation with one or more speech error types discussed in this chapter?

9   Children often produce utterances that provide a refreshing look on the world. Some of their expressions may "stick" in the sense that their family starts to make use of them over many years. Here are a few utterances by children (inspired by Hoving, 1974; see also Clark & Clark, 1977). Try to determine for what reasons they came about:
    a.   "Teacher, my pen stutters!"
    b.   "To dream is actually to see behind your eyes."
    c.   "Sir, are there also body teachers?"
    d.   "Miss, is a rooster a gentleman chicken?"
    e.   Mother: "Every day the natives go out lumbering". Child: "What are they tlumbering for?"

10 Utterances can be ambiguous when their specific context is not properly taken into account. Take, for instance, the following sign outside a pet shop: "You can leave your dog here." Or suppose someone walks up to you with outstretched hand and says: "Hey, Jim Johnson," who is not a person you think you know. Or suppose that you encounter someone who asks you "Is Trafalgar Square to the right here?" How could these utterances be misunderstood? Can you come up with any other examples?

Chapter 10
Multilingualism

10.1 MULTILINGUALISM: THE ESSENCE

How many languages can a person learn to use? According to the *Guinness Book of World Records*, cardinal Giuseppe Caspar Mezzofanti (1774–1849), who worked at the oldest university of Europe in Bologna and at the Vatican library, could translate 114 languages and 72 dialects, spoke 39 languages fluently and 11 passably, and understood 20 more, along with 37 dialects. The cardinal's remarkable language abilities have been described in a book of over 500 pages by Russell (1863). There are many more of such "hyper-polyglots," some of whom have been said to beat even the cardinal.

The amazing performance of polyglots shows that humans can learn an unexpectedly large number of foreign languages up to a high level of proficiency. In Chapter 6, we mentioned that adult monolingual language users may know 42,000 words or more (Brysbaert et al., 2016). Under the reasonable assumption that polyglots will know 10,000s of words in many other languages than their native one as well, this easily brings their total lexical knowledge above 100,000 words. How are they able to function "normally" when they know so many words and grammars? Imagine a polyglot who wants to describe a scene or picture. How can this person select the words and build the sentences in the language to be spoken without being distracted time and again by the many other words from all the other languages that could also describe the situation? Apparently, polyglots can still select items in the right language in real time and keep interference at bay. And if they translate between languages, they can switch languages quite accurately and when they wish to do so.

Perhaps one might wish to argue that polyglots are exceptional people and that their language performance and control issues are not relevant to the rest of us. However, you would be wrong when reasoning in this way. A majority of people in the world speak more than one language (Gardner-Chloros, 2009; Grosjean, 2008). They are not "monolingual," but "bilingual" or "trilingual," or, using a more general term, "multilingual." In a survey carried out in the European Union, more than half of all civilians and three quarters of young people between 15–24 years indicated that they could speak a foreign language well enough to have a conversation in it (European Commission, 2012; also see Eurostat, 2016). In several European countries (including countries such as Sweden and the Netherlands) over 90% were bilingual; about a quarter of Europeans should be called multilingual rather than bilingual, because they speak at least three languages. And it is even more common in many other parts of the world that people communicate in numerous languages on a daily basis.

DOI: 10.4324/9781003326274-10

Many multilinguals have acquired one or more foreign languages after infancy or childhood and they are less proficient in them compared to their mother tongue. In the psycholinguistic literature, a distinction is commonly made between *late* bilinguals and *early* bilinguals. The former term refers to bilinguals who started encountering and learning a second language later in life, for instance, when they were offered language classes in a foreign language in primary or secondary school. The latter term refers to bilinguals who have grown up with two languages, for instance, because their two parents or caregivers each interacted with them in a different language. Another distinction is between *unbalanced* and *balanced* bilinguals. Unbalanced bilinguals are more proficient in one language (their "dominant" language) than in another (their "non-dominant" language), while balanced bilinguals master their two languages at a similar level of proficiency. The proficiency in the two languages is not independent in the sense that bilinguals may know many words in their L2 at the cost of a smaller L1 vocabulary (Bialystok & Luk, 2012; Bialystok et al., 2012) and a somewhat reduced fluency in speech (Sandoval et al., 2010).

These observations have consequences for how the Language User Framework (see Chapter 3) should be organized to account for multilingual representation and processing. Becoming a multilingual does not just imply that a number of phonemes, words, scripts, grammatical rules, and language-specific concepts are added to the Long Term Memory part of the framework; in order to allow for the appropriate selection and switching of languages, there must also be an extension of the Cognitive Control System (even when only two languages are spoken!).

Following our standard chapter organization, in the following, we will consider first the representations and processes that underlie bilingual and multilingual performance. Where possible, we will use the term "multilingual" as an umbrella term. Next, we will discuss important models developed in the study of multilingual language use, highlight several influential empirical studies, and end the chapter by considering how context sensitivity may affect the cognitive processes that support multilingual communication. The four basic assumptions on language processing described in Chapter 1 will tacitly be taken as constraining the multilinguals' language use as well.

SUMMARY: MULTILINGUALISM: THE ESSENCE

When language users acquire languages other than their mother tongue, they in a sense must duplicate the Language User Framework. New *representations* at nearly all levels must be added to their Long Term Memory, and sometimes even a new level must be incorporated (e.g., to represent tone when a speaker of English learns Mandarin Chinese). In addition, they must *process* the new representations, not just on their own, but also often in the context of a fully developed first language. This requires them to carefully monitor their language processes in multiple languages and deal with all *control and decision* issues arising from the coexistence of multiple languages in their mind and brain. One may distinguish between early and late bilinguals, unbalanced and balanced bilinguals, and people who master more than two languages, such as polyglots. All these multilinguals may reach different levels of proficiency in each of the languages they know.

10.2 MULTILINGUALISM: REPRESENTATIONS

What exactly are the extensions and changes that language users must incorporate in their Language User Framework in order to communicate in another language (referred to as L2, L3, or ... Ln) in addition to their native or first language (L1)?

Most obviously, the vocabulary (lexicon) of the new language must be represented in the Long Term Memory part of the framework. Because different languages have different phoneme repertoires, subtle distinctions in pronunciations must be learned for comprehension and speaking (cf. Chapters 5 and 9). For instance, the /p/ sound at the beginning of the word "paradise" is aspirated in English, but not in its Dutch equivalent *paradijs*. Failure to pick up on this distinction will betray a speaker as a non-native.

To accommodate reading processes in a new language with a (partially) different *script*, its units must be acquired as well (Chapter 6). Printed or written words of the new language may be represented in terms of partially different letters (as in the case of, for instance, Norwegian, Greek, or Russian compared to English), syllabic units (as in Japanese hiragana or katakana), or ideograms (in the case of Chinese hanze or Japanese kanji). Examples are *øvingsbok* (Norwegian, "exercise book"), *δημοκρατία* (Greek, "democracy"), *война* (Russian, "war"), エンジニア (Japanese katakana for "engineer," pronounced as "enjinia"), and 房子 (Chinese hanze for "house").

Moreover, for the new language, the mapping of these graphemic units on phonemes (referred to as "grapheme-to-phoneme conversion" or "spelling rules") must be learned and stored. For instance, in Spanish the words *baca* ("roofrack") and *vaca* ("cow") sound similar, as do *rebelar* ("to rebel") and *revelar* ("to reveal").

The composition of words in terms of their morphology must also be captured. A language such as Turkish (called "agglutinative") has a morphology that is much richer than that of English. For example, the Turkish word *dolaplarımda* means "in my cupboards." It is composed of *dolap* (cupboard) + *lar* (plural) + *ım* (my, possessive) + *da* (at/in, locative suffix).

More generally, morphosyntactic rules and representations (e.g., grammar) in the new language must be mastered (Chapter 7). For instance, languages may have different basic word orders, requiring a different temporal alignment of meaning aspects (e.g., you must mention the agent or the action first).

Finally, printed and spoken word forms may refer to partially or completely new meanings (Chapter 8). For instance, the word "rikshaw" refers to a vehicle that the English language user may be unfamiliar with. To further complicate matters, the difficult process of language learning may be intertwined with the acquisition of language-related cultural aspects, such as how to correctly greet somebody, once again demonstrating the openness and non-modularity of language.

10.2.1 Cross-linguistic similarity of word representations

When a new language is learned, its orthographic, phonological, and semantic representations will *overlap* partially but not completely with those that are already known. One could say that the new words occupy positions that are more and less distant relative to already known words in a multidimensional lexical space (cf. the technique of Latent Semantic Analysis in Chapter 8). As an example, for a Dutch speaker, the English word "work" is not only similar in its orthography to English items like "cork" and "worm," but also to Dutch items like *vork* ("fork") and *worp* ("throw"). Such items, that differ in only one letter position from one another, are called *orthographic neighbors* (see Chapter 6).

The orthographic structure of a word is in line with language-specific rules specifying which letter sequences are legal, called "orthotactics." As a consequence, a word is more or less typical for its own language and the new language. For instance, the English word "queen" looks somewhat like other English words (e.g., "queer"), but not at all like Dutch words. "Hawk," however, looks like other words in both English (e.g., "gawk") and Dutch (e.g., *haak*), in spite of its language-specific orthotactics (the letter bigram "wk" violates Dutch orthotactic rules). As we shall see later, empirical studies have investigated whether the number of neighbors (called "neighborhood size") in both languages affects the time it takes to recognize a word (spoiler: It does!). This issue has been investigated for both orthographic and phonological similarity within and across language pairs.

Word pairs that have a large (often coincidental) form overlap between languages, but no meaning overlap, are called *false friends*. In case there is form identity that concerns orthography, the items are called *interlingual homographs*. An example is the French word form *coin* ("corner"). Note that the pronunciation of this word form in French is very different from that in English (/kwɛ̃/ vs. /kɔın/). Form identity or overlap may also concern phonology, in which case items are called *interlingual homophones*. Consider the Dutch word *kauw* ("chew"), which is pronounced but not written as English "cow" (there is an award-winning Dutch film called *Kauwboy* about a boy who has a chew as his pet).

Sometimes (quite regularly in closely related language pairs) words that overlap in their printed and/or spoken form also have the same or a related meaning. When such words are similar because they share their etymological origin, linguists call these *cognates*. Examples are words like *Nacht* (German), *nacht* (Dutch, Frisian), and *nag* (Afrikaans). Linguists contrast such words with *loanwords*, which are assimilated into the language. Examples of loan words are English words like "café" (originally meaning "coffee") and "bazaar" (from a Persian word for "market"). In contrast, psycholinguists tend to refer to all translation equivalents with form overlap as cognates. Thus, they would refer to loanwords such as "hotel" and "computer" as *identical cognates*. Such items occur in so many European languages that they could even be called "eurocognates." Examples of *non-identical cognates* are "book" – *boek* for English and Dutch, or "garden" – *Garten* for English and German. Note that these item pairs also happen to be orthographic neighbors. In the next section, we will consider the consequences of form and meaning overlap in cognates and false friends for multilingual processing.

When words in different languages have the same or nearly the same meaning, they are called *translation equivalents*. Cognates can thus be defined as translation equivalents with either form identity or large form overlap. However, there are also translation equivalents with very different word forms in different languages. For instance, the English word "butterfly" translates into *Schmetterling* in German, *papillon* in French, *vlinder* in Dutch, *mariposa* in Spanish, *farfalla* in Italian, etc. It is easy to understand that the cross-linguistic similarity of cognates makes them easier to learn than such words without form overlap.

Word meaning in different languages may cover somewhat different domains of reality. In French, the word *balle* is often used for the ball in a game, but *ballon* when speaking about a big, hollow ball, *boule* for a bowling ball or a snow ball, and *bille* for a billiard ball. In English, the word "ball" will do for all these situations. Even when words show form and meaning overlap, there may still be differences in terms of their connotative semantics. For instance, the English word "mother" may be translated into the Spanish word *madre*, but the images and connotations evoked by the two words are quite different. Thus, the semantics of a language reflects the culture that makes use of it.

Often, other cultures have some word forms in their languages for concepts that we do not recognize. For instance, according to Rheingold (1988) and de Boinod (2005), the words *hakamaroo* and *tingo* on Easter Island refer to "borrowing objects from a friend's home one by one until there is nothing left." Analogously, the French expression *esprit de l'escalier* and the German word *Treppenwitz* refer to a wisecrack that one only thinks of when it is too late. The German *Radfahrer* in parts of Germany applies not only to cyclists, but also to submissive service knockers bowing for their superiors and intimidating their subordinates. However, we note that even within a language certain concepts may be unfamiliar to some language users. Biologists and yoga teachers know words for many concepts (e.g., plant species or body positions) that are unknown to most of us.

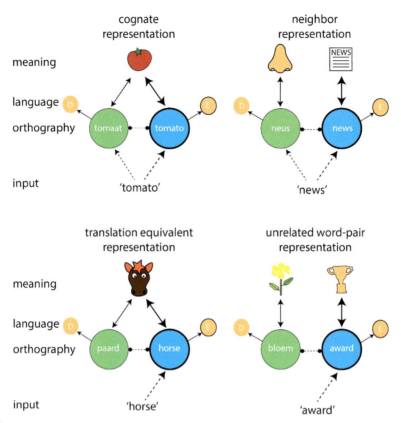

Figure 10.1
Representation of various special word types in the multilingual mental lexicon: non-identical cognates, neighbors, non-cognate translations, and unrelated word pairs. Adapted from Dijkstra et al. (2022).

Figure 10.1 graphically depicts the lexical representations proposed for non-identical cognates, neighbors, and translation equivalents. To accommodate this figure to represent false friends and identical cognates, it must be decided if identical orthographic word forms share their representation across languages or have a different representation for each.

For interlingual homographs, with their identical orthographic forms but different meanings (like English "room," meaning ROOM, and Dutch *room*, meaning CREAM), it could be argued that their orthographic identity must surely imply they share their form representation. However, due to their different meanings, such words may be used under quite different circumstances, calling for representations that have different frequencies of usage in the two languages. Because word frequency is often considered to be a property of word *forms*, it has been proposed that the word forms in bilinguals have two language-specific orthographic representations rather than one shared representation (in addition to language-specific semantic and phonetic/phonological representations). We will come back to this issue in section 10.5.1.

Similar issues arise for identical cognates. An example is the French word *assassin* that differs considerably in its frequency of usage from the English word "assassin," maybe because English has the more popular alternative "murderer." In most cases, such words also have a different phonology and pronunciation in the two languages. Importantly, morpho-syntactic properties such as gender and plural may also be different. The word for "bridge" in Italian is masculine – *il ponte*, but in Portuguese it is feminine – *a ponte*. And although the word "troll" is used in several European languages, its plural varies from "trolls" (English) to *Trolle* (German) and *trolles* (Italian).

The different word properties of orthographically identical lexical forms across languages should somehow be represented in the multilingual's lexicon. When we discuss empirical studies below, this issue of one or two form representations for identical cognates and false friends will be considered in detail, because of their potential consequences for multilingual lexical processing.

10.2.2 Cross-linguistic similarity of syntactic representations

It has been estimated that there are 7,151 living human languages in the world (Ethnologue, 2021). With respect to their syntactic organization, these languages can be divided into families of languages with a descent from a common parental language (called the "proto-language" of the family). Most European languages belong to the *Indo-European language family* (see Figure 10.2; notorious exceptions are Basque, Finnish, and Hungarian); however, across the world several other language families are found (e.g., Sino-Tibetan, Austronesian, Dravidian, Algic, and Altaic languages). Languages within a (sub)family typically share characteristics at different levels of representation. For instance, at the lexical level, there will be on average more cognates across language pairs that belong to the same language families. Besides spoken languages, there are also sign languages, predominantly used by Deaf communities.

As we saw in Chapter 7 on sentence processing, languages can differ in their canonical (main) word order. We already saw that the most common word orders are SOV (subject – object – verb) and SVO (subject – verb – object), which together are estimated to make up for over 80% of the languages in the world (Kemmerer, 2012). Much less frequent is VSO word order and only a few languages have other basic word orders (VOS and OVS; OSV hardly ever seems to occur). As a consequence, language pairs may overlap in some syntactic aspects. For

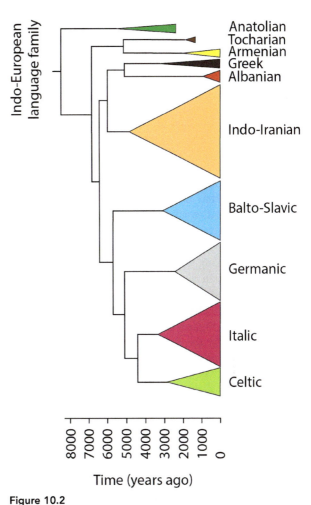

Figure 10.2
Important Indo-European language subfamilies and their diversification into separate branches over the past 8,000 years. Languages within a subfamily (e.g., the Celtic subfamily, the Balto-Slavic subfamily) will typically show more form overlap than languages across subfamilies. Adapted from Bouckaert et al. (2012).

instance, English and Spanish share word order in active sentences like *El taxi persigue el camión* ("The taxi chases the truck"), passive sentences, like *El camión es perseguido por el taxi* ("The truck is being chased by the taxi"), and intransitive sentences, like *El taxi acelera* ("The taxi accelerates"). Similarly, English and Dutch share the word order in two types of dative construction: "The father gave the daughter the book" and "The father gave the book to the daughter." However, in Dutch, an additional dative construction exists: *Ik zie dat de vader de dochter het boek geeft*, literally translated as "I see that the father the daughter the book gives." If overlapping phrase and sentence representations were stored in a shared grammar, this might have consequences for multilingual processing.

10.2.3 Storing words and grammar of multiple languages: One or two systems?

The observation that language pairs overlap to some extent in terms of their grammars and lexicons raises a fundamental question: Are the languages of a multilingual stored in *shared* or in *separate* databases (Kolers, 1963, 1966)? This issue is pervasive and applicable to the storage of units of different sizes. For instance, is there a shared or a separate storage of *alphabetic units* when the language pairs in question use the same or a different script? Are overlapping and different *phonemes* stored in the same or a different inventory for language pairs? Are *words* of different languages stored in an integrated lexicon? Are (*morpho*) *syntactic rules* for those languages stored as part of one integrated grammar or separate grammars? Is the storage of *meaning* aspects language-dependent or independent?

Many empirical studies have attempted to shed light on these issues by cleverly manipulating psycholinguistic variables in RT studies, based on the reasoning that cross-linguistic competition would be sensitive to stimulus characteristics such as relative frequency or the presence of similar words across languages. For instance, when a low-frequency target word in a later learned, weaker language has a higher frequency neighbor in the stronger L1, the target's recognition might be slowed down; and recognizing a word in a later learned language might be facilitated by the presence of a form-similar translation equivalent (cognate) in the mother tongue. We will consider this possibility in more detail later on in this chapter.

The issue can also be addressed by considering whether different languages are stored in shared or different brain areas. In a meta-analysis of 30 hemodynamic (PET and MRI) studies, Indefrey (2006) considered the findings from multilingual language production tasks, semantic decision, and syntactic/semantic sentence analysis. Remarkably, the brain areas that were activated by the participants' L1 and L2 were not so different. Most of the investigated 114 brain regions were even *activated* similarly for L1 and L2. There were only 15 differently activated areas, and 13 of them were more strongly activated during L2 processing. These activation differences might reflect less efficient or more effortful grammatical and lexical processes in L2 than in L1. They were found primarily in Broca's area, and, more specifically, the posterior part of the left inferior frontal gyrus. More detailed analysis suggested that participant characteristics affected the different tasks in complex ways. Bilinguals with a low L2 proficiency, a late onset of L2 acquisition age, or little exposure to L2 all tended to show stronger brain activation for processing the L2 compared to the L1. Later reviews arrived at similar conclusions (Liu & Cao, 2016; van Heuven & Dijkstra, 2010).

We conclude that on the basis of the currently available evidence, there is no reason to assume that different languages are stored in separated databases. The strengths of their representations, however, may be different, as may be the engagement of the control system governing L1 and L2 processing.

> **SUMMARY: MULTILINGUALISM: REPRESENTATIONS**
>
> When word pairs in a language have a very similar printed or spoken word form, they are called "within-language neighbors." Word pairs from different languages may also share form aspects. Such words are called "between-language neighbors." In contrast, "translation equivalents" share their meaning across languages. In cases where the word pairs from different languages share both meaning and form aspects, psycholinguists call them "cognates." Cross-linguistic similarity in general thus varies from very high (for cognates) to partial (for false friends and translation equivalents) to low (for many items). On average, there will be more cognate pairs for languages of the same subfamily.
>
> When multilinguals read, hear, speak, or write, they must somehow deal with all the similarities and differences in word forms, grammatical rules, and meaning within and across the languages they know. Available neuroscientific evidence indicates that such knowledge is stored in a shared fashion for the multilinguals' languages. The problem of possible cross-linguistic interference is therefore not reduced or resolved by storage of languages in separate databases and provides a severe control issue for the multilingual mind.

10.3 MULTILINGUALISM: PROCESSES

10.3.1 Processing words and sentences in multiple languages: One or two systems?

In Chapters 5 and 6 on word recognition, we saw that, in early stages of lexical processing, a set of possible words is activated based on their similarity with the input stimulus. According to models such as the Interactive Activation model, these coactivated words are subject to lexical competition. In multilinguals, the word recognition process might proceed similarly, but now lexical candidates from several languages might be coactivated and compete. However, we have also seen that the bottom-up (stimulus-driven) word recognition process can be affected by context quite early on. If multilinguals were able to exclude word candidates from the irrelevant language, they would not experience interference from that language!

In other words, the multilingual million dollar question is how quickly *top-down* effects based on expectation or context can affect the lexical selection process among candidates from different languages activated by *bottom-up* processing (see Chapter 3 for an explanation of these terms in relation to the Language User Framework). At what moment in processing can participants eliminate or *filter out* non-target language activity that arises due to the overlapping lexical and syntactic representations? Can this be done early in processing (resulting in no effects on a non-target language's word candidates) or only late (resulting in an enduring coactivation of word candidates from different languages)?

The hypothesis that lexical candidates from different languages can be coactivated for a while has been called the *language non-selective lexical access* hypothesis. According to this view, any input to the language processing system results in an "automatic" activation of all types of internal representation that are in some way similar to aspects of that input. For instance, according to an extreme "bottom-up" (signal-driven) view of processing, any shared script elements would be coactivated in different-script bilinguals. Therefore, the Russian word *радар* ("radar") would be slightly activated on the visual presentation of the

English word "pad," purely because of letter overlap between the Latin and Cyrillic scripts (see Chapter 6).

Language non-selective processing would also lead to cross-linguistic coactivation for neighbor words, false friends, and cognates. Reading the English word "pork," in a Dutch–English bilingual not only its *neighbors* "cork" and "park" in English would become activated, but also *vork* ("fork") and *pook* ("gear handle") in Dutch. Furthermore, for a French–English bilingual, the input word "coin" in an English sentence might still temporarily activate the French word *coin*, a *false friend* of the English word "corner". In spite of language-specific information provided by the preceding sentence, this might even be accompanied by a temporary activation of their different meanings! Similarly, *identical and non-identical cognates* would lead to a coactivation of word forms, and of their (largely overlapping) meaning representations. The convergence of the two readings of the cognate (e.g., "text" in English and *texto* in Spanish) on the same meaning, might instigate a resonance process, because the coactivated meaning would send activation back to the word forms in both languages.

So far, we have given examples for the multilingual reading process. However, other cross-linguistic similarities between languages in terms of vocabulary, phonology, and grammar would also affect how fast they are processed, and even how quickly they are learned (Schepens et al., 2020). For instance, when abstract syntactic constructions, such as datives, are shared, cross-linguistic syntactic priming effects might arise. We will get back to this issue when discussing a selection of empirical studies later on in this chapter.

10.3.2 The interaction of bottom-up and top-down processes

In unbalanced multilinguals (the majority of people), the native language is more strongly represented than other languages. As a consequence, language processing in most people when they are reading may be 10–20% slower in their second language than in their first language, depending on the proficiency level in that language (Brysbaert, 2019b). The consequences of such slower processing in the weaker language might be considerable, because it might overturn the balance between signal-driven (bottom-up) and concept-driven (top-down) processes that exists in monolingual processing: Slower bottom-up processing of the input might lead to an increase of top-down effects. As explained in Chapter 7 (section 7.3.2), crucial for allowing *predicting* upcoming information and not only *integrating* arrived information during listening is that the incoming signal can be processed fast enough to allow on-the-fly top-down effects to do their work. Can multilinguals do this?

In the last decade, evidence has accrued that in sentence comprehension, upcoming information is often anticipated by both monolingual and bilingual listeners and readers (e.g., Martin et al., 2013). For instance, it has been suggested that ERPs may vary depending on whether an article matches in grammatical gender (*le/la*) or in phonological form ("a"/"an") with an upcoming noun (DeLong et al., 2005; but see Nieuwland et al., 2018). Effects at both form and meaning levels of the upcoming message have been reported.

The results of an early bilingual study using eye tracking and self-paced reading by Altarriba et al. (1996) suggested that sentence constraint exerted an early effect on sentence processing at both the meaning and the form level. When fluent Spanish–English bilinguals read high-constraint sentences such as "He wanted to deposit all of his money/*dinero* at the credit union," first fixation durations and naming responses were longer for Spanish words with a high frequency when these were embedded in high-constraint English sentences than in low-constraint English sentences. This suggests that on the basis of the preceding sentence context, bilingual participants expected not only the meaning of the noun ("money" or *dinero*), but also its specific form (i.e., the orthographic characteristics of "money" or *dinero*). More recent evidence is in line with this conclusion (e.g., Rommers et al., 2013).

Currently under debate is the issue to what extent multilinguals can make the same predictions in their second language as monolinguals do in their first. Although some of the first studies in this domain suggested that bilinguals might not predict upcoming words in their L2 (which might be the case because of various reasons), more recent studies have obtained evidence of prediction both for bilingual reading and listening. For instance, in a sentence reading paradigm with cognates and non-cognates, Foucart et al. (2014) found that French–Catalan bilinguals reading in L2 could use semantic information from the sentence context to predict upcoming words (i.e., there was an N400 effect of the congruence between an article and the following, predicted noun). In a study by Dijkgraaf et al. (2019), Dutch–English bilinguals heard semantically constraining and neutral English sentences while their eye movements were measured. For both L1 and L2 constraining conditions, participants showed early biased fixations towards target objects on a display relative to distractor pictures, indicating that they were able to quickly apply semantic information to predict upcoming targets.

Because L2 processing is usually somewhat slower and more effortful than L1 processing, bilinguals trying to predict upcoming word forms and meanings may succeed less often in their slower L2 than in their dominant L1. Instead, they may more often integrate new information after it arrives, rather than predict it beforehand. The degree to which prediction succeeds should therefore also depend on the L2 proficiency of the reader. More generally, the ratio between bottom-up and top-down processing should be affected by L2 proficiency. If bottom-up processing is slow, multilinguals might compensate for this by bringing in extra top-down information during integration or by more strongly relying on non-verbal cues in the communicative environment.

We end this section by noting that not only non-verbal and verbal context may lead to predictions, but even stimulus list composition in an experiment could have such effects. For instance, in an L1 or L2 lexical decision task, participants build up lexical expectations based on the words and nonwords they have so far encountered during the practice set and the experiment proper (e.g., only English words, the presence of cognates or not, and so on).

SUMMARY: MULTILINGUALISM: PROCESSES

A key question in research on multilingualism is whether the access to (e.g., lexical or syntactic) language information is language-selective or language non-selective. The answer to this question depends on the moment at which linguistic and non-linguistic context effects can influence language selection. If they do so early in processing, this may lead to language selective access. An effect somewhat later in processing will result in effects of non-selective access that are only subsequently restricted by context (due to an interaction of bottom-up and top-down processes). Contextual constraints late in processing would result in fully language non-selective access and necessitate post-access integration processes. The speed and ratio of bottom-up and top-down processes may be different in multilinguals compared to monolinguals. This may result in differences in the use of predictions in monolingual and multilingual processing.

10.4 MODELS OF MULTILINGUAL PROCESSING AND CONTROL

How learning and processing a new lexicon (and a new language in general) must be accounted for in terms of the Language User Framework has been a focus of attention since the early days of experimental multilingual research. A wide variety of models of bilingual representation, processing, and control have been developed. In this section, we will look at some of the most influential models in this domain.

10.4.1 Revised Hierarchical Model

In the verbal Revised Hierarchical Model for L2 word learning and word translation (Kroll & Stewart, 1994), it was assumed (on the basis of the empirical evidence available at the time) that a bilingual's mental lexicon consists of two separate word form stores that are non-selectively accessed and linked up to a shared semantic (or conceptual) store for word meaning. Two pathways between the larger L1 and the smaller L2 lexicons were discerned (see Figure 10.3). First, in early stages of L2 learning, the meaning of an L2 word would be found indirectly, by using the word association (word form) link between the L2 word and the L1 word. For instance, the meaning of the newly learned Swahili (L2) word *farasi* would be found by linking it to the English (L1) word form "horse," for which the meaning is readily available. In later stages of L2 learning, the direct link of the acquired word *farasi* to its meaning would be strengthened, resulting in direct meaning retrieval. In this early model, no distinction was yet made between orthographic and phonological representations. The model would in principle be able to account for within- but not between-language neighborhood effects (given that L1 and L2 were assumed to be stored in separate lexicons). Furthermore, it was not fully specified how "special" word types like cognates and false friends are processed in different tasks (cf. Brysbaert & Duyck, 2010).

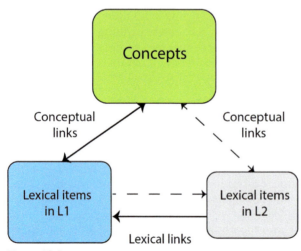

Figure 10.3
The Revised Hierarchical Model assumes strong lexical links between word forms in L2 and their translation equivalents in L1, and strong conceptual links between word forms in L1 and their meaning, during the early stages of L2 language learning. As such, when learning a new language, mapping an L2 word form onto its meaning may initially proceed via the corresponding L1 word form. Solid lines refer to strong links, dashed lines to weak links. After Kroll and Stewart (1994).

10.4.2 Distributed Conceptual Feature model

How does the (lexical) word association link work when words are not readily translatable? At the time, the Distributed Conceptual Feature model (de Groot, 1992) answered this question by proposing that a word's meaning is spread out over clusters of semantic features that are largely but not necessarily exactly the same in different languages (de Groot, 2011, p. 133). As an example, words such as "table" and "mother" would have language-specific word form representations that are connected to conceptual representations consisting of semantic feature clusters. These clusters would be made up of features specific to L1 or L2 or shared by both. In this way, a word such as "mother" could have a meaning that is largely shared with, but might still differ somewhat from, the Spanish word *madre* and the Dutch equivalent *moeder*. Whereas the Spanish word might perhaps be associated with "black-haired," its Dutch translation might trigger the semantic feature "tall." Note that this view implies that also the Conceptual System would be accessed in a language non-selective way (cf. Bermúdez-Margaretto et al., 2022).

10.4.3 Bilingual Interactive Activation models

A few years later, the computational Bilingual Interactive Activation (BIA) model of bilingual word recognition (Dijkstra & van Heuven, 1998) focused on the recognition of orthographic word forms. In contrast to the models above, it assumed an integrated bilingual lexicon and language non-selective access at both form and meaning levels. The BIA model extended the well-known monolingual IA model (see Chapter 6) by combining all words from the first and second language into a shared lexicon and adding representations specifying the language of each word. For instance, the English word form "work" was linked to an English "language node," and the Dutch word form *werk* to a Dutch language node. The implementation of the model on the computer came at a cost: It could simulate only the orthographic processing of four- or five-letter words. For those items, it did demonstrate clearly how cross-linguistic orthographic neighborhood effects would arise and gave some hints concerning the processing of false friends. However, the model was not able to simulate the recognition of cognates, due to the absence of implemented semantic representations. The BIA model is also not equipped for simulating L2 word learning. Grainger et al. (2010) proposed a model variant called BIA-d that would be able to incorporate word learning, but it still awaits implementation. For bilingual auditory word recognition, Léwy and Grosjean (2008) built BIMOLA, a somewhat similar computational model, inspired by the TRACE model (see Chapter 5).

The BIA model was succeeded by the BIA+ model (Dijkstra & van Heuven, 2002), which positioned BIA's simulation components into a verbal theoretical framework with additional representations (phonology, semantics) and a task/decision system (see Figure 10.4). In this respect, BIA+ makes the same distinction as is made in the Language User Framework in this book. Part of the verbal framework was also implemented in SOPHIA (see Thomas & van Heuven, 2005). This allowed these models to at least provide a descriptive account of false friend and cognate processing, although actual simulations were not possible.

10.4.4 Multilink model

Several notions from all mentioned earlier models were implemented in a new model called Multilink (Dijkstra et al., 2019). The model, discussed already in Chapter 6, not only incorporates implementations for phonological and semantic lexical representations, but also provides some (simple) implementations of the control structure necessary to perform different tasks. For instance, the degree of lexical competition between neighbor words from the same or other languages under different task situations can be fine-tuned by varying the degree of "lateral inhibition" in the model. Multilink takes an integrated bilingual lexicon and language non-selective access as basic assumptions to account for the bilinguals' processing of "special" items such as cognates and false friends. An example of a Dutch–English simulation by Multilink is presented in Figure 10.5. The figure shows that the input word "dog" activates both Dutch (*dag*, meaning DAY; *dom* meaning DUMB) and English ("dog") word candidates. The English phonological representation /dɔg/ is activated already

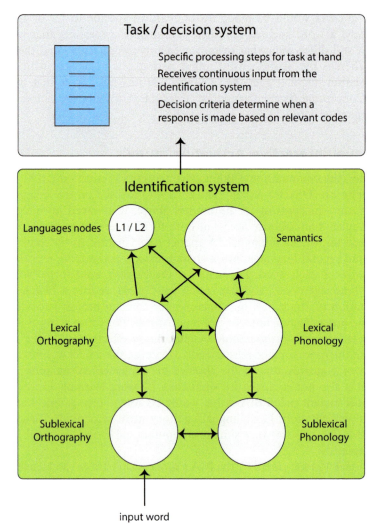

Figure 10.4
The Bilingual Interactive Activation + model. Note the similarities between the Identification System and the left part of the Language Processing System in the Language User Framework, and the similarities between the task/decision system here and the Language User Framework's Cognitive Control System. After Dijkstra and van Heuven (2002).

in earlier time cycles than the Dutch phonological representation of its translation equivalent /hɔnt/, because English phonology is activated through both orthographic-phonological and semantic-phonological links, while Dutch phonology is only activated via semantic-phonological links. Like phonology, semantics is activated at a delay compared to orthography when the input is visual. In this graph, semantics is assumed to be not sensitive to word frequency (which is probably incorrect).

The model has yielded high correlations between model cycle times and reaction times in various experimental studies. Multilink's simulations are in line with the view that isolated word retrieval in many languages entails a bottom-up process in which initially a set of possible lexical candidates is activated. This has been tested so far for English, Dutch, French, Italian, Spanish, Portuguese, German, and even for Japanese kana. Gradually, the target

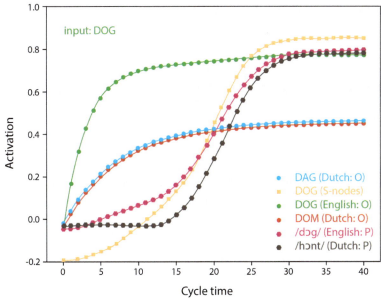

Figure 10.5
Multilink simulation of the recognition of the input word "dog" involving a Dutch–English lexicon. The x-axis represents processing time in time cycles and the y-axis lexical activation. The language membership and modality (O for orthography and P for phonology) for different word candidates are indicated. "S-nodes" refers to non-linguistic semantic representations (which here become activated by both English and Dutch input words). In this example, resting level activation is frequency-dependent for orthography and phonology, but not for semantics.

emerges from this set as the most active candidate, due to its perfect fit with the input. In addition, when lateral inhibition is assumed in the lexical network, the accompanying competition speeds up this process due to a gradual reduction of activated non-target words. Importantly, the model makes the testable assumption that *activation* in the word recognition system is not directly affected by non-linguistic context and task demands. These factors can, however, still affect language performance in terms of decision and response competition effects. In contrast, linguistic context, participant characteristics (e.g., relative language proficiency in the languages known by the multilingual), and item characteristics (e.g., frequency or cognate status) do directly affect word activation.

10.4.5 Inhibitory and Adaptive Control models

When multilinguals wish to speak, they must put their thoughts and intentions into words. Executive control processes supervise this attentional process to ensure that words from the correct language are selected and produced. How bilinguals manage to select the appropriate language for speaking and for translation between languages was the focus of the Inhibitory Control Model (ICM) by Green (1998). More recently, these notions on executive control in bilinguals have been reformulated in terms of brain activity in the context of the Adaptive Control Hypothesis (Abutalebi & Green, 2008; Green & Abutalebi, 2013).

Critical to the ICM is the notion of *task schemas*, a sort of "mental manuals" that people use to successfully carry out a given task. For a bilingual, such a task schema could be "Name a picture in English" or "Translate a Dutch sentence into Mandarin Chinese." According to the model, a particular language task schema (e.g., "Name a picture in English") can inhibit another language task schema (e.g., "Name a picture in French") and itself (e.g., when the intended goal is reached). In contrast to the task regulation mechanism in Multilink, the task schema at hand can regulate the activation level of representations stored in the bilingual's lexico-semantic system in Long Term Memory (comparable to the middle part of the Language User Framework). For instance, when the goal is to name a picture by articulating an English word, French lemmas stored in a French–English bilingual's lexicon may be suppressed. This is possible given the assumption that lemmas come with a "language tag" that specifies to which exact language they belong (similar to the language nodes in interactive activation models). As in the model by Levelt (1989) that we saw in Chapter 9, a Conceptualizer that is independent of language builds non-linguistic conceptual representations.

The Inhibitory Control Model predicts that switching between languages (and between tasks in general) will take more time than not switching between languages (and between tasks in general), because it involves switching between task schemas and reactivating the task schema that was previously inhibited. The more active a lemma is, the more inhibition it requires if it contains a non-target language tag. As such, switching into the L1 may take longer than switching into the L2 for unbalanced bilinguals, because the L1 will have received more inhibition while the L2 was used and this inhibition needs to be overcome. In section 10.5.3, we discuss an influential experimental study by Meuter and Allport (1999) that empirically supported this prediction.

More recently, Abutalebi and Green (2008; Green & Abutalebi, 2013) have refined this view on executive control and extended it to the brain. They now distinguish eight control processes (goal maintenance, conflict monitoring, interference suppression, salient cue detection, selective response inhibition, task disengagement, task engagement, opportunistic planning). Furthermore, various dimensions of L1 and L2 are accounted for in terms of a

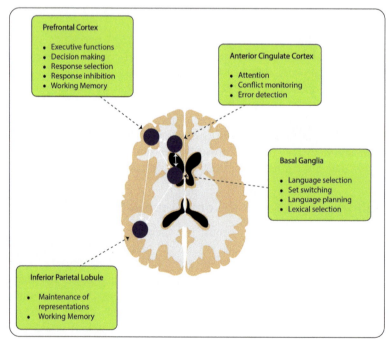

Figure 10.6
Adaptive control processes in the bilingual brain. In reality, the areas here indicated in 2D are connected brain areas extending in three spatial dimensions. After Abutalebi and Green (2008).

shared neural network in especially the left hemisphere. Importantly, the inhibitory control of language and lexical selection are subserved by a network of cortical and subcortical regions that take care of adaptive control activities.

Figure 10.6 shows several important areas in the proposed brain network. The prefrontal cortex is arguably involved in the activities of the upper part of the Language User Framework (see Figure 3.1) pertaining to executive control and Working Memory. The anterior cingulate cortex (ACC) has been related to attention, error detection, and conflict monitoring. The subcortical basal ganglia have a role to play in language planning and switching. Finally, the inferior parietal lobe maintains representations in Working Memory while language processing occurs.

Because multilinguals regularly have to deal with language switch situations (requiring inhibition) and must also actively keep track of the language they are using for production (requiring monitoring), it has been proposed that their executive control functions (supposed to be domain-general mechanisms) may be better developed than those of monolinguals (see Antoniou, 2019, for a review; Paap, 2023). Their extra practice might result in performance advantages for certain aspects of cognitive functioning, also in non-linguistic tasks. However, advocates in favor of and against this "bilingual advantage" have engaged in fierce theoretical discussions that remain ongoing and unsettled. A related, more general hot debate has been about whether the knowledge of more than one language results in some protection for language users against the onset of dementia (Bialystok et al., 2007; Woumans et al., 2015). Whatever the theoretical outcome of these debates may be, one bilingual advantage that cannot easily be disputed is the mere ability to speak with people with various language backgrounds (Peeters, 2020).

> **SUMMARY: MODELS OF MULTILINGUAL PROCESSING AND CONTROL**
>
> Over the years, various models for bilingual word retrieval have been proposed. An early verbal model is the Revised Hierarchical Model. It has been applied to L2 acquisition and word translation, and assumes that early in L2 acquisition, word meanings in the new language are retrieved via the L1 word forms they are related to. There are both direct and indirect paths to arrive at the meaning of an L2 word, with changes taking place over the course of L2 learning. The computational Bilingual Interactive Activation (BIA) model and its successor BIA+ extend the Interactive Activation model (Chapter 6) to the bilingual domain. More recently, the Multilink model has implemented extensions allowing the simulation of various language combinations, participant groups, tasks, and stimulus materials. The Inhibitory Control Model has been most influential in describing the executive control processes involved in bilingual language production. It strongly relies on the notion of task schemas and predicts asymmetrical switch costs in unbalanced bilinguals. Recently, it has become clear that bilingual control processes are adaptive and subserved by a network of dynamically activated brain areas.

10.5 MULTILINGUALISM: EMPIRICAL STUDIES

10.5.1 Multilingual word retrieval

To test the hypotheses of an integrated multilingual lexicon and language non-selective lexical access, researchers have been engaged in a search for cross-linguistic influences in the multilingual mind. Word retrieval especially (i.e., reading, listening to, or speaking words) has been a topic of their investigation.

Some of the most fascinating and surprising evidence supporting an integrated lexicon and pervasive interactivity was collected by Thierry and Wu (2007; Wu & Thierry, 2010). In their studies, Chinese–English bilinguals were presented with pairs of English words. Their task was to decide whether these printed words were related in meaning or not. Examples of the word pairs participants saw are "post – mail" and "train – ham." Participants did not know that half of the word pairs contained an identical character when they were translated into Chinese. In our example pairs, the Chinese translations of the words "train" and "ham" are, respectively, "huo che" (火车) and "huo tui" (火腿) and therefore share the Chinese character "huo" (火). In both studies, ERPs (but not RTs) were affected by the presence of the hidden Chinese overlap. Semantic relatedness between the words of a pair led to a reduction of the N400, but an independent hidden Chinese character repetition effect was also found. The result pattern was replicated in a listening comprehension task. The conclusion of the authors is that Chinese–English bilinguals apparently do unconscious translation into Chinese while they are engaged in English language comprehension! The results also suggest that the cross-linguistic activation effects were most prominent for the spoken representations.

Most other studies on word reading in bilinguals focused on interlingual homographs in the 1990s, and on cognates after the turn of the century; studies involving within- and between-language neighbors have been conducted occasionally over the whole period. Over the last decades, many studies on the spoken recognition and production of interlingual homophones and cognates have also been performed.

Using Figure 10.1 as a background, we will now review available evidence on the processing of these special word types. To begin with word reading, bilingual studies provide evidence that the number of neighbors (called "neighborhood size") of a target word can affect its recognition not only in cases where they are from the same language, but also when they are from another language (Dirix et al., 2017; van Heuven et al., 1998; Wen & van Heuven, 2018). When there were more of such similar words in the L1, the response time to the L2 word in a lexical decision task became slower. Effects of cross-language neighborhood in bilingual word recognition have also been found in an EEG task. In a blocked L1 or L2 context, a larger N400 effect was found when words had many neighbors in the other language, suggesting a more effortful lexical-semantic integration (Midgley et al., 2008).

Several related studies, both monolingual (see Ferrand, 2001, p. 98) and bilingual (Lemhöfer & Dijkstra, 2004; Mulder et al., 2018) in nature, have had difficulties in replicating the neighborhood effects. This suggests that neighborhood effects may not be structural (i.e., due to system architecture, as in the case of lateral inhibition), but strategic in nature (Dijkstra et al., 2022).

A considerable amount of RT and EEG research has also been dedicated to the recognition of false friends. The response to an interlingual homograph in a language-specific lexical decision task is affected by the relative frequency of the other-language counterpart. For instance, the response time of a Dutch–English bilingual to the English item "room" is sensitive to the frequency of the Dutch item *room* (meaning CREAM). Such a cross-linguistic effect is largest when the frequency of the target item is low, and that of the other-language competitor is high (Dijkstra et al., 1998). Because the effect is probably due to lexical competition, it is usually inhibitory in nature (i.e., false friends are processed more slowly than comparable word forms that belong to only one language). The inhibitory effects for false friends are usually larger in language-specific lexical decision than in generalized lexical decision, indicating there are effects of task demands. They are usually also stronger in stimulus lists with words from two languages (mixed lists) than in lists with words from only one language (pure lists). Two explanations for these findings have been proposed.

First, words from different languages might become more or less active depending on their occurrence or relevance in particular task situations or conversations ("language mode hypothesis"; Grosjean, 1998, 2001). Alternatively, the presence of words from only one or several languages might affect the decision criteria that are applied in the task situation at hand. Evidence in favor of this last explanation has been found in fMRI studies (Hsieh et al., 2021; Peeters et al., 2019; van Heuven et al., 2008). A conflict between the two readings of the interlingual homographs has been observed especially in the brain's language control network and in areas associated with the resolution of response conflict during task performance.

Strategic differences in decision making might also explain why interlingual homograph effects were not observed in several studies (e.g., Lemhöfer et al., 2008). If competition effects were strategic rather than structural (e.g., due to lateral inhibition), null effects could arise depending on task demands and stimulus list composition.

In contrast to false friends, printed cognates are recognized more quickly and with a higher accuracy than non-cognate control words in many tasks. This "cognate facilitation effect" has also been observed in the N400 amplitude of the ERP (less negative-going waves for cognates vs. control words) and even in pupil dilations (Guasch et al., 2017; Peeters et al., 2013). The effect is larger in tasks where the target language is the L2, but it is also observed in L1 when bilinguals are sufficiently proficient in the L2 (van Hell & Dijkstra, 2002). More facilitation also arises when an item is a cognate in three languages rather than two. For instance, the word "echo" exists in English, German, and Dutch. In trilinguals, this led to a larger facilitation effect in a German lexical decision task than the word *dienst*, which exists in German and Dutch, but not in English (both words were presented in capital letters, as ECHO and DIENST; Lemhöfer et al., 2004). Similar to the interlingual homograph interference effect, the size of the cognate facilitation effect depends on the relative frequency of word usage in the two languages, and on stimulus list composition and task demands. If a task asks for a distinction between the two cognate representations, cognates may yield slower RTs compared to control words. This is, for instance, the case in a language decision task, where participants have to press one button when a presented item belongs to one language, and another button when it belongs to the other language.

Recent studies suggest that cognate effects in lexical decision tasks are stronger when *identical* cognates are included in the experiment (Arana et al., 2022). Due to their form identity across languages, such identical cognates may be processed in a different way than non-identical cognates. Research is currently investigating if the observed effects in lexical decision are representational, processing-related, and/or decision-sensitive and strategic.

Another ongoing topic of investigation is whether identical cognates should be represented by one shared or two separate representations for the two languages at hand. As Peeters et al. (2013, p. 316) noted: "[I]t seems intuitively clear that non-identical cognates must be characterized by two different representations (one for each language), but it is as yet unclear at what level *identical* cognates are represented twice in the bilingual brain." Consider the identical cognate "assassin" in French and English. Because this word has exactly the same orthography in both languages, one might assume that it consists of only one shared orthographic representation. Because the word also has more or less the same meaning in both languages, this shared orthographic representation might be linked to one shared semantic representation. Nevertheless, as mentioned earlier in this chapter, there must also be representational differences for the word "assassin" in French and English (e.g., in pronunciation, gender, or frequency of use). Such differences might give rise to two representations rather

> ### DISCUSSION BOX 10: READING IN A NON-ALPHABETIC SCRIPT VS. AN ALPHABETIC SCRIPT: THE CASE OF JAPANESE–ENGLISH BILINGUALS
>
> A lot of the research discussed in this chapter is concerned with bilinguals that have languages sharing Latin script, for instance, French–English or Dutch–German. How the word recognition process works in such bilinguals has been described, for instance, by the BIA+ and Multilink+ models. Consider if such models could ever be extended to word reading in non-alphabetic scripts. For instance, how would Japanese–English bilinguals read words in their alphabetic English (L2) script and in one of their non-alphabetic Japanese (L1) scripts? Here are some more precise questions and hints for tackling this issue.
>
> To begin, suppose that a monolingual English reader encounters the English word "coffee." Consult the Dual Route Cascaded model in Chapter 6 for the contributions of sublexical and lexical units to word recognition. How and when would the phonemes of this word /k/, /ɔ/, /f/, and /i/ be activated? In what way is the phonological representation of the whole word /kʰɔfi/ (with an aspirated /k/) activated?
>
> Now suppose that a monolingual Japanese person reads the Japanese word for "coffee." This word is actually a Japanese–English cognate, pronounced as /koohii/ (the double vowels represent a long vowel). In Japanese katakana script, it is written as コーヒー. Katakana is a syllabary (see Chapter 6) that is used to represent foreign words in the Japanese lexicon. Try to make your own variant of the Dual Route Cascaded model for reading words in katakana. What would the sublexical units look like in this case?
>
> However, Japanese also uses two other scripts, kanji and hiragana (the latter we do not consider here). Kanji is a logographic system using characters derived from Chinese. An example of a word in kanji is 本 (pronounced as /hon/, meaning BOOK). How could this word be recognized by a Japanese reader in terms of a Dual Route Cascaded model (see Wu & Thierry, 2010, mentioned earlier in the chapter for some hints)?
>
> Finally, consider what happens when a Japanese–English bilingual encounters the English word "coffee." What would be the effect of overlap in sublexical representations between English and Japanese? Would you expect a cognate facilitation effect to arise?
>
> You can check your answer by looking up Figure 1 in Miwa et al. (2014). This figure illustrates processing routes for another English–Japanese cognate, the word for "interview."
>
> Could this approach also be applied to Mandarin Chinese, Korean, and Vietnamese? What is your opinion on the applicability of a symbolic approach, such as the one presented in this book, for answering such questions?

than one. In this example, there could be two language-specific morphemes (or lemmas) for the word "assassin" (as well as two phonological representations).

Peeters and colleagues investigated this issue as follows. They asked unbalanced French–English bilinguals to perform a lexical decision task in their second language, English, while their RTs and ERPs were measured. The combination of English and French allowed the researchers to vary the word frequency of the identical cognates in each of the two languages. They were able to select four matched item groups of cognates with a high or a low frequency in both languages (HEHF: a word such as "message"; LELF: "altitude"), a high frequency in English but a low frequency in French (HELF: "mixture"), or the reverse

(LEHF: "assassin"). (Note that the frequencies were determined on the basis of L1 usage, but that English is indicated first in the abbreviation because it was the language used in the task.)

The authors tested two contrasting hypotheses. First, if identical cognates have one shared representation in English and French, lexical decision responses should be dependent on the sum frequency of item use in the two languages. If that is the case, the recognition of a low-frequency English item should be helped considerably by a high-frequency French counterpart (remember that French was the first language of the participants). In contrast, the recognition of a high-frequency English item would not be helped so much by a low-frequency French reading. Second, when there are separate representations for identical cognates that are both activated (due to language non-selective access), lexical decision responses should be determined primarily by the task language, English, because the instruction was to respond to words of that language. Nevertheless, the French reading of the cognate might still modulate the response, because it would cause more or less interference (for high-frequency or low-frequency readings, respectively) during a late word selection process.

To summarize, the shared-representation hypothesis predicts the following order of response times in this lexical decision task from fast to slow: HEHF < LEHF < HELF < LELF (with a priority given to the native language, French). In contrast, the separate-representation hypothesis predicts the order: HEHF < HELF < LEHF < LELF (with a priority to the task language, English). The observed pattern of results was very clear (see Figure 10.7): Whereas the response to high-frequency and low-frequency English items differed in nearly 100 ms, the French frequency manipulation only modulated the response times by 13–15 ms. Thus, it was English (the L2 and task language) that had most effects on the responses, not French (the L1). The EEG data confirmed that the L1 and L2 frequencies of the cognates resulted in separable N400 effects with a different duration and scalp distribution. High-frequency items in English and in French showed a less negative going N400.

Peeters et al. argued that this set of results is best explained by assuming that in these bilinguals identical cognates have shared

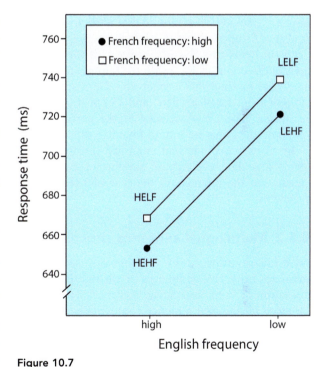

Figure 10.7

Peeters and colleagues (2013) had unbalanced, late French–English bilinguals perform a visual lexical decision task in their L2 English. The stimuli contained identical cognates that could have a high frequency in both English and French (HEHF), a high frequency in English and a low frequency in French (HELF), a low frequency in English and a high frequency in French (LEHF), or a low frequency in both languages (LELF). The figure shows the following response time pattern to these four groups of identical cognates: HEHF < HELF < LEHF < LELF, reflecting the importance of the task language (English).

orthographic but separate morphological and phonological representations for the two languages (here English and French).

To summarize the research on printed "special" words, the observed cross-linguistic effects are sensitive to the degree of cross-linguistic overlap in different dimensions (orthography, phonology, and semantics). However, it seems that cross-linguistic orthographic and phonological similarity may affect performance in visual lexical decision in a complex way (sometimes positively, sometimes negatively) and may even counter each other (Comesaña et al., 2015). Furthermore, cross-linguistically similar phonology of printed words has been found to result in a slowdown in visual lexical decision, whereas cross-linguistically similar orthography can cause interference in auditory lexical decision (Frances et al., 2021).

This brings us to the cross-linguistic effects for interlingual homophones and cognates in spoken word recognition. Studies on bilingual auditory word recognition using the eye tracking paradigm have been done by Marian and colleagues. For instance, Spivey and Marian (1999) presented Russian–English bilinguals with a panel of four objects, including a stamp (named "marka" in Russian), a marker ("flomaster" in Russian), and two distractor objects whose names had different onsets. In one condition, the participants now heard a Russian instruction to *Poloji marku nije krestika*, meaning in English "Put the stamp below the cross" (note that "marku" is an inflected form of "marka"). The study focused on the recognition of the target word form "marku" embedded in this neutral "carrier sentence." Using eye tracking, it was found that participants not only looked at the stamp (as expected), but also at form overlapping between-language distractors ("marker") for a longer time than at control items that did not begin with the same onset phonemes. The same held in the opposite direction for English instructions. In another study, Blumenfeld and Marian (2005) found that in English–German and German–English bilinguals both members of a cognate pair (e.g., English "hen" and German *Henne*) with a high phonological overlap were coactivated. The L2 proficiency of the participants and the duration of the phonological overlap of the items were both found to affect the results.

In all, we conclude that empirical research in both the visual and auditory modalities provide abundant evidence in support of coactivation of word candidates from different languages in the bilingual in the case of neighbors, cognates, false friends, and translation equivalents.

10.5.2 Multilingual sentence processing

The evidence provided in the previous section on word retrieval indicates that word candidates from both languages of the multilingual are activated when words are presented in isolation or in neutral carrier sentences. However, what happens when they are presented in a more meaningful sentence context (Fitzpatrick & Indefrey, 2010)? To what extent can the language of the sentence provide such a large top-down constraint on presented words that it eliminates words that belong to another language?

Both behavioral and ERP studies support the conclusions that were drawn in Chapter 7: After an initial bottom-up process, sentence context rapidly kicks in and can modulate coactivation effects. In the case of multilingual readers, it can steer them towards a particular language and reduce cross-linguistic effects. However, in many cases, language non-selective effects still arise for cognates and false friends, even in a language-specific sentence context. This holds for performance in lexical decision tasks, but also in eye tracking. Eye tracking studies have reported cross-linguistic cognate effects for high-constraint sentences in early fixation measures (e.g., first fixation and gaze duration), but not in later fixation durations (e.g., total reading time) (Libben & Titone, 2009). The amount of cognate facilitation appears to decrease when bilinguals become more proficient in their L2 (Krogh,

2022; van Hell & Tanner, 2012). In terms of Figure 10.1, this could be interpreted as evidence that higher L2 proficient bilinguals profit less from L1 activation, because the L2 may have higher resting level activations to begin with.

Cop and colleagues (2015, 2017) used the eye tracking technique in a natural reading study. Dutch–English bilinguals read a novel by Agatha Christie in English and/or Dutch. The average total reading time per word was about 261 ms in the English (L2) original and about 232 ms in the Dutch (L1) translation. For the English (L2) version, cross-linguistic orthographic overlap resulted in cognate facilitation. Identical cognates were facilitated extra in later eye movement measures. For Dutch (L1), non-identical cognates were facilitated in the first fixation duration of longer nouns, while identical high-frequency cognates were facilitated with respect to total reading time. These findings confirm that it seems impossible to completely "switch off" the non-target language when reading in a target language.

In another application of the eye tracking paradigm, Hoversten and Traxler (2016) asked Spanish–English bilinguals and English monolinguals to read English sentences including a Spanish–English homograph (e.g., *pie*, the Spanish word for "foot"). In one condition, the sentence only made sense when the meaning of the homograph was English, in another when it was Spanish. Examples are "While eating dessert, the diner crushed his pie accidentally with his elbow" vs. "While carrying bricks, the mason crushed his pie accidentally with the load." In the eye tracking data, there was no evidence of an early homograph interference effect. Only for late fixation measures, monolinguals and bilinguals differed in how they handled the incongruity between homograph reading and sentence meaning. Bilinguals may have initially accessed the homograph's appropriate English meaning and only later the Spanish meaning, integrating the latter only when semantically appropriate (i.e., they would show effects of incremental processing). According to the authors, this shows that proficient bilinguals quickly adapt dynamically to contextual cues when processing interlingual homographs. The use of such cues is also dependent on the degree of grammatical fit (Baten et al., 2011) and participants' executive control skills (Pivneva et al., 2014).

Interestingly, there is also evidence that *syntactic* units shared between languages (such as noun or verb phrases) have abstract representations that can be coactivated during processing. If the syntactic structures from different languages are part of one large language processing system, this allows, for example, for cross-linguistic priming effects at more abstract levels, e.g., dative and passive constructions.

In a well-known study, Hartsuiker et al. (2004) had Spanish–English bilinguals describe pictures in their L2 English using active or passive sentences (see Figure 10.8). The participants first heard an L1 Spanish sentence that was active, *El taxi persigue el camión* ("The taxi chases the truck"), passive, *El camión es perseguido por el taxi* ("The truck is chased by the taxi"), or intransitive, *El taxi acelera* ("The taxi accelerates"). When they next had to describe a picture in their L2 English, bilinguals were more likely to use a passive construction when they had just encountered a passive Spanish sentence (cf. the English priming study by Bock discussed in Chapter 9 on language production).

The conclusion of Hartsuiker and colleagues was that syntactic information in these bilinguals is shared between the languages as far as possible. In other words, shared syntactic rules and memory representations for the passive are used in both languages. Hartsuiker and colleagues developed a model for syntactic priming in multilinguals that accounts for their findings. We point out that in this case, (passive) syntactic constructions overlapped for Spanish and English. However, as the authors point out, there are also L2 syntactic constructions without (fully) corresponding L1 equivalents (e.g., as we have seen, English and Dutch share some dative constructions, but not all). For these, L2 language-specific representations may exist. Similar evidence has been collected in multilingual children (van Dijk, 2021).

Figure 10.8
In the study by Hartsuiker and colleagues (2004), Spanish–English bilinguals described pictures in their L2 English, for instance of a bottle being hit by a bullet, following a prime sentence in their L1 Spanish produced by a confederate. The prime sentence could be an active sentence (e.g., the Spanish equivalent of "The taxi chases the truck"), a passive sentence (e.g., the Spanish equivalent of "The truck is chased by the taxi"), or an intransitive sentence (e.g., the Spanish equivalent of "The taxi accelerates"). Would the syntactic structure used in the L1 prime influence the syntactic structure they used themselves when describing the picture in their L2?

10.5.3 Multilingual language production and control

In conversations with other language users, multilinguals must choose whether to use their mother tongue, a foreign language, or a mix of both. Clearly, when they speak to someone who is monolingual, they must use the language of that conversational partner to be understood. This language could be their own L1 or one of their other languages. In cases where they speak to other multilinguals, their language choice may be less strict and language switching or mixing may occur. In fact, in some communities around the world, it is quite common to mix different languages and use them alternately. For instance, the inhabitants of Puerto Rico often use a mix of English and Spanish in their conversations. This is called "language mixing" or "code mixing" (Muysken, 2000; Poplack, 1980). In Suriname in South America, there are language-mixing phenomena involving Surinamese Dutch, Sranan Tongo, Sarnami (Suriname Hindustani), the Maroon Creole language Ndyuka, and Surinamese Javanese (Yakpo et al., 2015). So how do multilinguals switch between their languages?

An influential experimental paradigm investigating issues of bilingual language production and control is the so-called *cued language-switching* paradigm (e.g., Meuter & Allport, 1999). In this paradigm, bilinguals are typically asked to name digits or pictures in either their first language or their second language as a function of a certain cue (see Figure 10.9). Such cues may be arbitrary (e.g., color cues) or motivated (e.g., a British flag for English, a French flag for French). It is typically observed that switching languages comes at a cost, i.e., switching languages takes longer than not switching languages. Interestingly, in unbalanced bilinguals sometimes *asymmetrical* switch costs have been observed, in that switching to the (dominant) L1 takes more time than switching to the (non-dominant, weaker) L2 (Meuter & Allport, 1999). Intuitively this is a surprising finding, as one would think that unbalanced bilinguals would be faster to name a digit or picture in their dominant compared to their weaker language.

The presence of asymmetrical switch costs has been explained in line with the Inhibitory Control Model we looked at earlier. When bilinguals speak in their L2, they must have inhibited (the task schema corresponding to speaking in) their L1. Because their L1 is the language they are most proficient in, they must have applied quite some

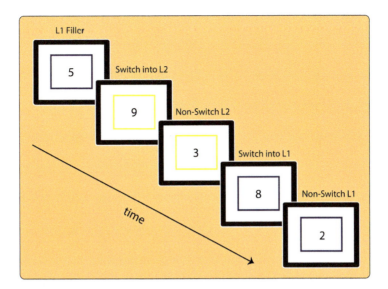

Figure 10.9
In the seminal study by Meuter and Allport (1999), bilinguals named individual digits in their first or second language as a function of the color of the rectangle that surrounded it. This led to a clear 2 x 2 design in which the independent variables were Response Language (L1 vs. L2) and Trial Type (switch vs. non-switch). Response times (RTs) and accuracy (error rates) were measured and analyzed. In this example, a yellow color cue requires naming the presented digit in L2, while a blue color cue corresponds to naming the digit in L1. Of course, the relation between (arbitrary) color cue and Response Language can be counterbalanced across participants.

inhibition to it. The requirement to overcome this relatively large amount of inhibition when switching back into the L1 may explain why making this switch takes them so much time. The opposite does not necessarily hold: When speaking in their dominant L1, there is little need to strongly inhibit their weaker L2, as it is the weaker and less influential language already anyway. Therefore switching back into the weaker L2 may be easier than switching back into the dominant L1.

Switch costs hence have been explained in terms of *reactive* inhibitory processes: The bilingual language user encounters a certain language cue and the system reacts to it on a trial-by-trial basis by applying a helpful dose of inhibition. Bilinguals have also been found to be capable of *proactively* applying inhibition to one of their languages. When unbalanced bilinguals find themselves in an experimental situation in which they know they will need to be using both their languages, sometimes they become faster overall in their "weaker" L2 compared to their "dominant" L1. This *reversed language dominance* is taken to indicate that they proactively inhibit their stronger L1 in a sustained fashion for a longer period of time, such that, throughout the task, it interferes less with their less dominant L2 (Declerck et al., 2020; Peeters, 2020).

Of course, in everyday life, multilinguals do not switch between their languages as a function of arbitrary color cues. Rather, they may switch voluntarily when communicating with someone who masters the same languages as they do, or switch language when swapping between listeners with different language backgrounds. Research has shown that switch costs may be reduced or even disappear altogether when bilinguals voluntarily switch between their languages (Gollan & Ferreira, 2009). Such findings are in line with the Adaptive Control Hypothesis, which states that the specific control processes bilinguals engage in strongly depend on the (interactional) context they are in (Green & Abutalebi, 2013).

Finally, in the empirical studies on word retrieval, we have seen effects of interlingual overlap in phonology and semantics. These have also been observed in studies of bilingual language production. For instance, the cognate facilitation effect has regularly been reported in picture naming tasks. As in bilingual reading and listening, it is typically larger in the non-dominant than in the dominant language of participants (e.g., Costa et al., 2000, 2006; Strijkers et al., 2010).

According to the Multilink model of word retrieval, these effects should be accounted for in terms of the various representations in Figure 10.1. For instance, during picture naming, the overlap and links of coactivated phonological, semantic, and orthographic representations of a cognate would result in a resonance process. The application of task-specific decision criteria would ultimately lead to the empirically observed production facilitation effect.

SUMMARY: MULTILINGUALISM: EMPIRICAL STUDIES

Empirical studies involving multilinguals' recognition of words in isolation and in sentences support the view of an integrated mental lexicon that is language non-selectively accessed. Bilingual processing, especially in L2, shows evidence of cross-linguistic effects exerted by the L1. When L2 proficiency is high enough, cross-linguistic effects in the other direction (from L2 to L1) may also arise. Factors relating to sentence context also affect bilingual lexical processing, but effects of language non-selective activation remain for cognates and false friends even in highly constraining sentence contexts. Empirical evidence from syntactic priming studies suggests that syntactic processing is also language non-selective. Abstract syntactic structures that overlap or are shared between languages appear to be stored together in Long Term Memory. They are coactivated and lead to cross-linguistic (priming) effects during sentence processing.

Many empirical studies in the domain of multilingual language production have focused on the question of how bilinguals manage to switch between the languages they know. The observation of switch costs and reversed language dominance have led researchers to speculate about the role of both reactive and proactive inhibitory processes in supporting bilinguals to adaptively select the context-appropriate language.

10.6 MULTILINGUALISM: THE ROLE OF CONTEXT

Multilinguals often find themselves in situations that require restrictions on or switches of language choice. For instance, on a holiday they may find themselves in a foreign café talking their native language to their partner. When the waiter arrives, they will need to answer questions in a different language. Speaking in that language, they may need to try to use words from their L1 for a lack of knowledge, or resort to using non-verbal cues such as gestures. How do linguistic and non-linguistic aspects of the broader context affect language processing?

In the following section, we will first examine the role of local and global bilingual sentence context on word recognition. In the subsequent section, we will then consider effects of what we could call "non-linguistic" context, in particular the role of task demands and stimulus list composition.

10.6.1 Semantic effects of sentence context

As noted above, semantically constraining sentences can modulate the effects of non-target languages on target item recognition, even though effects often remain in low-constraint and neutral sentence context (Dijkstra et al., 2015; Duyck et al., 2007; Schwartz & Kroll, 2006; van Hell & de Groot, 2008). In a study involving cognates and non-cognates, Dijkstra and colleagues (2015) examined how Dutch–English bilinguals processed sentences and target words in Dutch (their L1) and English (their L2). Sentences were presented word by word (using a technique called RSVP; see Chapter 4). In the reaction time variant of the experiment, the participants decided if the last presented item of the sentence was an English word or not (English lexical decision). On average, target word recognition took about the same time following English and Dutch sentences. This suggests that word recognition proceeded especially bottom-up, limiting the effect of a language switch on lexical decision time. At the same time, non-identical cognates (like "apple") were processed more quickly than matched control words existing in only one language, especially in the (L2) English sentence context. This also happened when participants had to decide if the target word (*appel* in Dutch) belonged to Dutch rather than English (Dutch lexical decision). In the result patterns, the Dutch (L1) sentence context led to a stronger constraint than the English (L2) one for these Dutch–English bilinguals.

On the basis of a meta-analysis of a large number of bilingual studies, Lauro and Schwartz (2017) came to several conclusions in line with these findings. First, lexical access was concluded to be language non-selective. In many studies, significant cognate facilitation effects arose in both high- and low-constraint sentences, although the average effect was smaller in high-constraint conditions. In other words, even though the language of the preceding sentence could reduce the activation of a non-target language, it was not sufficient to eliminate the cognate effect. Furthermore, smaller effects were usually found in the L1 than in the L2 of the participants. The specific task that was performed also affected the size of cognate effects. Picture naming and translation led to the largest effect sizes, word naming and lexical decision to smaller effects, and eye tracking studies to the smallest effects. Lauro and Schwartz noted that the picture naming and translation tasks require overt responses based on top-down activation from meaning to form, while word naming and lexical decision rely more on bottom-up processing from form to meaning. The authors further note that the temporal dynamics of cross-linguistic effects must be considered, which is clearly exemplified by the different measures used in the eye tracking task. Measures for early processing, like first fixation duration, may reflect the impact of (a combination of) different L1 and L2 variables more than measures for later processing, such as total reading time.

Elston-Güttler and colleagues (2005; also see Paulmann et al., 2006) examined how global language context and local sentence context affected the activation of interlingual homographs in lexical decision. As a global language context, a 20-minute movie was played before the actual experiment was done. It was accompanied by a narrative in L1 (German) or L2 (English). Next, German–English bilinguals performed an English (L2) lexical decision task. The target words in this task were preceded by sentences that ended on German–English homographs or English control words that were or were not semantically related to the target words. An example of the related condition is the sentence "Joan used scissors to remove the TAG," while the unrelated condition here would be "Joan used scissors to remove the LABEL." Note that in its capital form the English word "tag" is written just like the German word *Tag*, meaning DAY. In other words, it is an interlingual homograph. In contrast, the word "label" is an exclusively English control word. Accompanying these sentences, the word *DAY* (related to TAG but not to LABEL) could be presented as an L2 target (in italics) for English lexical decision.

Critically, the English homograph targets were responded to more quickly when the participant had watched the German film, but not the English one. There are at least three possible explanations of these findings. First, only following the German film there was sufficient *activation* of the German reading of TAG to induce semantic priming of the target word *DAY*. Alternatively, there was already an *inhibition* of the German reading of TAG by the preceding local English sentence context following the English film. Finally, because effects of global context appeared only in the first part of the first block after the German movie was shown, participants may have gradually zoomed in on their English by raising their *decision criteria* to diminish effects of their German on the target language English. This was the explanation the authors favored.

10.6.2 Task- and stimulus-related context effects

The response patterns observed in word recognition by multilinguals are sensitive not only to the properties of the language combinations and sentences in which the words appear. They are also dependent on other characteristics of the context, such as the task that is being performed and the stimulus lists in which target words appear.

One theoretical proposal is that language processing itself always proceeds in the same way, but that participant strategies to optimize the requirements of the task (or to deal with a specific stimulus list composition in a laboratory situation) change the outcoming behavior. The distinction in the Language User Framework between the Language Processing System and the Cognitive Control System (Chapter 3) is in line with this assumption; and the Multilink model (Chapter 6) makes the same assumption. However, a contrasting view is that language processing is so sensitive to context aspects that the activation processes in the Language Processing System themselves are different depending on the circumstances. Clearly, if this latter proposal is correct, psycholinguists are faced with the difficult task to indicate precisely when and how activation processes change depending on the circumstances. The larger the contribution of top-down factors to bottom-up activation processes becomes, the more we will need to specify such factors – which, so far, have been rather underdefined (because they relate to difficult-to-define terms such as "attention" and "motivation").

Consider, as an example of *task* effects, the following study with Dutch–English bilingual participants conducted by Dijkstra et al. (2010). In the study's first experiment, participants performed an English lexical decision task, deciding whether a presented letter string was an English word or a pseudoword. In the second experiment, they had to press one button if a presented item was an English word, and another button if it was a Dutch word. This task is called "language decision." In the third experiment, participants had to identify English words that gradually emerged from a background mask. This task is named "progressive demasking" (see Figure 10.10). In this study, the same types of word were processed in three experiments that each involved a different task. In all three tasks, largely the same set of "special" words had to be processed, in particular, Dutch–English cognates that had varying degrees of form overlap between the two languages. Take, for instance, the English item "alarm," which has an identical word form in Dutch; "flood," with the Dutch translation equivalent *vloed*; and "song," with Dutch translation *lied*.

The response patterns to these translation equivalents with varying degrees of cross-linguistic form overlap were systematically different between the three tasks. In English lexical decision, cognate facilitation effects arose depending on the degree of form overlap between English targets and their Dutch counterparts (the more overlap English targets had, the more facilitation they showed). In language decision, cognate interference effects (i.e., slower RTs to cognates than to control words) arose that became larger when orthographic similarity increased. In both studies, the largest effects arose for identical cognates.

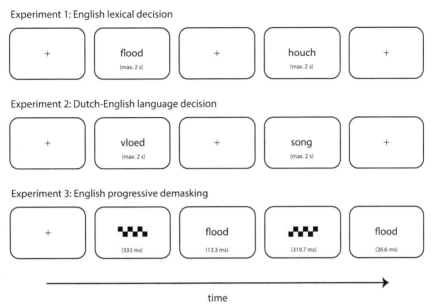

Figure 10.10
In the study by Dijkstra et al. (2010), Dutch–English unbalanced bilingual participants took part in either an English lexical decision task, a Dutch–English language decision task, or an English progressive demasking experiment.

Finally, in English progressive demasking, only low-frequency identical cognates showed a facilitation effect, while non-identical cognates did not.

The different result patterns were explained by pointing to the different requirements of the three tasks. In English lexical decision, the overlap between English (L2) and Dutch (L1) words could successfully be exploited, because it did not matter if the Word Recognizer detected the presence of either the English or the Dutch variant of the cognate. Note that responding on the basis of a highly active Dutch word would never lead to a response error. In language decision, however, the detection of either the English or the Dutch counterpart of the cognate would lead to a different response (pressing the English OR the Dutch button). Participants therefore had to determine the language to which the presented item belonged, which resulted in interference effects that depended on amount of overlap (as well as item frequency in the other language; cf. Peeters et al., 2013). The English progressive demasking task, finally, required the participants to respond in yet another way: They had to recognize the item and then type it in. This makes task performance relatively slow. The response in the task is also extra variable because the task involves a number of cycles in which the target word and a mask are alternately presented. In all, these task properties make it understandable that certain cross-linguistic effects might have been diluted by the time the participant responds.

Next to the particular task at hand, a second general context variable that has been shown to affect the result patterns is *stimulus list composition*. This refers to the (proportions and order of) different item types appearing in the experimental session at hand. Dijkstra et al. (2000) confronted Dutch–English bilinguals with an English lexical decision task, in which interlingual homographs and exclusively English words (requiring a "yes" response) appeared, as well as purely Dutch words and English pseudowords (requiring a "no" response). However, exclusively Dutch items were introduced only in the second part of the experiment. In the first part of the experiment, reaction times for homographs did not differ significantly from those to English words (575 ms vs. 581 ms, respectively), but they became considerably slower after Dutch words appeared in the second part of the stimulus list (613 ms vs. 592 ms). Participants often gave a wrong response to the first Dutch word in the list and then adapted their response strategy.

Cognate effects have also been shown to be sensitive to stimulus list composition. For instance, Vanlangendonck et al. (2020) had two groups of unbalanced Dutch–English bilinguals perform an English lexical decision task. The materials included the same set of cognates, interlingual homographs, and English control words in both experiments. However, in Experiment 2, half of the pseudowords in Experiment 1 were replaced by Dutch words, requiring a "no" response. Importantly, the cognate facilitation effects of the pure language list (Exp. 1) turned into cognate interference effects in the mixed language list (Exp. 2). Effects were more extreme when the cross-linguistic form overlap of the cognates increased. Relative to control words, interlingual homographs also displayed larger interference effects in the mixed list than in the pure list. Recently, the effects on lexical decision of different proportions of identical cognates in a list have been a topic of considerable research (e.g., Arana et al., 2022).

All in all, an increasing amount of available empirical evidence is making it clearer that the way in which the (multilingual) language processing system is used in the lab is very sensitive to task demands and stimulus list composition.

SUMMARY: MULTILINGUALISM: THE ROLE OF CONTEXT

The amazing sensitivity and flexibility of language use is evident in the adaptive way that bilinguals and multilinguals respond to sentence and global language context, as well as non-linguistic context. In sentence context, cognate effects are modulated but usually remain present. Effects for false friends are more fragile and perhaps more context-sensitive. Global language context may exert subtle transitory effects on bilingual processing. Depending on the task at hand, cognate facilitation effects may even turn into interference effects. Stimulus list composition has been shown to affect the interference that is sometimes observed for false friends in several tasks.

In all, the language processing of multilinguals depends on the languages they speak, the tasks they perform, and the lexical, morphosyntactic, and semantic aspects of the stimulus materials they are confronted with. From a qualitative perspective, many of the same underlying processing mechanisms and representations have been proposed for multilinguals and monolinguals. However, from a quantitative point of view, multilingual processing is different from monolingual processing, reflecting complex interactions of the languages involved.

10.7 WHAT IS NEXT?

In this chapter, we have considered how the Language User Framework should be extended to account for the representation, processing, and control of two or more languages. Because the use of different languages has often been assumed to involve a shared, non-linguistic level of meaning representation, we did not pay much attention to bilingual text and discourse processing, or bilingual mental models.

However, by doing so, we neglected how language is intertwined with cultural aspects. In the concluding Chapter 11, we will therefore take a step back and examine what aspects of complex language use we may have overlooked in earlier times and in the present book so far. This reflection on the state of affairs in the general domain and our own specific research interests may also help to establish a research agenda for the study of the psychology of language in the near future.

10.8 WHAT HAVE WE LEARNED?

Most people in the world can converse in more than one language. Bilinguals and multilinguals have lexicons and grammars that are stored together, in an integrated fashion, and are accessed in a language non-selective way. Cross-linguistic processing effects may arise in areas where languages share common elements. This is the case, for instance, for cognates, false friends, and shared syntactic constructions. Due to cross-linguistic interactions, the bilinguals' language systems are differently organized from those in monolinguals. Thus, bilinguals are not "two monolinguals in one head" (Grosjean, 1989).

Monolingual and bilingual processing may proceed along qualitatively similar lines, but differences in language organization lead to quantitatively different result patterns in experiments and the brain. An important difference between monolinguals and bilinguals lies in the involvement of the Cognitive Control System, due to the different requirements that arise when multiple languages are stored and processed. Bilinguals must be able to handle several language systems at the same time.

Recently implemented computational models for bilingual processing take into account representational, processing, and control issues. They have also been functionally related to the brain.

Like monolinguals, bilinguals will most likely (try to) predict upcoming words, even in their second language. Bilingual performance is also sensitive to non-linguistic and linguistic context effects in real life (e.g., perceptual and discourse information), and in lab experiments (e.g., task demands and stimulus list composition).

QUESTIONS FOR CHAPTER 10

1 Suppose you are working for the European Commission and have to translate the speech of a politician into another language while it occurs. This process is called "simultaneous interpreting." What challenges would you encounter? Consider aspects of listening, understanding, and reproduction. For example, what would have to be done when the English noun phrase "the White House" must be translated on the fly into the French *la Maison Blanche*?
2 The Rosetta stone is inscribed with a political text in different scripts: Ancient Egyptian, hieroglyphic, Demotic script, and Ancient Greek. Assuming that you were able to read one of these scripts, how would you approach the problem of unraveling and understanding the other scripts? What problems would you encounter? Hint: Foreign names in the Demotic, hieroglyphic, and native Egyptian scripts were written using phonetic characters.
3 Explain why the problem in Question 2 is of a very different nature than that in Question 1.
4 Which 50 words does Kate Bush list for "snow"? How does this relate to the often encountered view that Inuit have many words for "snow"? Search the internet, for instance, using "Eskimo Hoax" and "G.K. Pullum."
5 Collect 40 cognates between your native language and English (or a different language when English is your native language). Try to analyze why exactly words with these

meanings are cognates. Examples: (1) a "computer" was first developed in an English-speaking country, and other languages/cultures "borrowed" the word from English; (2) the Netherlands were once an important seafaring nation. The Dutch word *bootsman* was introduced in Russian as *боцман* (pronounced as "botsman"); (3) The English word "father" corresponds to Dutch *vader* and German *Vater*. Both languages belong to the Germanic branch of the Indo-European language family.

6   Interlingual homographs have a coincidental cross-linguistic overlap. Sometimes this leads to funny effects. For instance, the famous rock group Cream had a hit with the song "White Room." In Dutch, the word for "cream" is *room*, and *witte room* means "white cream." Similarly, Pink had a hit with "Little Finger," and *pink* is the Dutch word for one's "little finger"! Can you come up with similar examples in English and your own native language?

7   There is a German game called *Teekesselchen* (which is sometimes played in English, too). You take a polysemous word and give two descriptions that cover two meaning variants. The listener must guess what word the description is about. Example: "Shooting it, you may hurt a body part." Answer: The word "arm." As a variant of the game, one can play it by combining word definitions in two languages. Example from Dutch–English: "Just a small note." Answer: *brief* (the Dutch word for "letter"). Can you come up with monolingual and bilingual examples?

8   A joke has circulated on the internet of a German soldier who receives an emergency message from a submarine and then replies with a heavy German accent: "Can you tell me what you are sinking about?" What was the original message, do you think? Explain the joke in terms of phonetics (consult the IPA table in Chapter 5), language differences, and foreign language proficiency.

9   Multilinguals sometimes indicate that they "think" in one of their languages. How would you interpret this statement in terms of the Language User Framework?

10 Sometimes, multilinguals even feel they are different people when they converse in one language or another (Chen & Bond, 2010). How could cultural or language differences affect their performance or personality?

Chapter 11

Conclusion and outlook

11.1 INTRODUCTION

The bell rings and I open the door. Two illuminated skeletons shout at me: "Trick or treat! Your candy or you can die!" Pointing over my shoulder to the light of the door, I say: "Please, spare me, I will get you what you want!" The skeletons look at one another, then back at me, and nod. On my return, I quickly start filling their bags with sweets. "Oh and please, don't forget to remind your father that we go out fishing tomorrow!" "No, sir, yes, sir!," is the skeletons' answer. I wave them off and close my door. How many more to go?

As this description of a dialog shows, more information is conveyed in face-to-face conversations than just speech. For instance, there is communicative information conveyed by my body. My facial expression will have shown that I recognized my next-door neighbors' kids, that I expected them, and that I willingly played along. A pointing gesture accompanied my assertion that I would get them what they wanted.

The interpretation of the utterances was part of a communicative situation familiar to the participants involved. We all knew, without saying, what game we were playing, pretending to be someone else (we were on "common ground"). The events incrementally followed a scenario that we were all aware of, a mental model. And then, from one moment to the next, just one request from me was enough to force the skeletons into a totally different relationship to me. Suddenly a different mental model became prominent, with a very different relationship between the interlocutors.

As a reader, you will have quickly realized that this story was about Halloween. You have a mental script for this annual event, and probably had little difficulty understanding that after the skeletons nodded, I went back into the house to pick up some sweets that already sat prepared on the kitchen sink. This information, however, was present nowhere in the story. You will also have understood that I stepped out of the pretended mental model when I started to talk about their father, who is not the father of the skeletons, but of the children impersonating them.

In sum, this short story once more illustrates that language use is an embedded and embodied activity that heavily relies on incremental processing and the use and development of mental models (Figure 11.1). By having read the previous ten chapters of this book, you will have developed an idea of the representations and processes involved in my mind and the mind of the skeletons when we were using language, and in your own mind when you read the short story. We have introduced the Language User Framework as a basis for understanding the psychology of language in these and other situations.

DOI: 10.4324/9781003326274-11

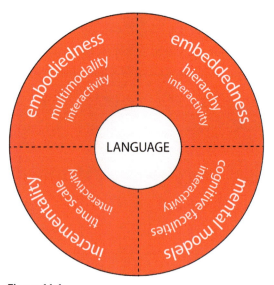

Figure 11.1
The four key assumptions we selected as a basis for discussing the psychology of language in this book: embodiedness, embeddedness, incrementality (or: incremental processing), and the use of mental models. These four pillars are strongly linked to other important notions in cognitive (neuro)science, such as multimodality, hierarchy, cognitive faculties, and time scale. They are related through the fundamental notion of interactivity, which can appear in different forms (as explained in the text).

In the following sections, we will once more consider the four fundamental assumptions (or "pillars") underlying this book. After extending the Language User Framework to fully account for the multi-channel and multimodal nature of human communication, and placing it in a still larger framework for different cognitive activities, we will examine how biases of different sorts have framed earlier views on language use. In this context, we will also dwell on our own biases. We will end the chapter by sketching exciting ongoing and future developments relevant to the study of the psychology of language that may help to overcome these.

11.2 EXPANDING THE FOUR BASIC ASSUMPTIONS OF THE BOOK

Let us begin by considering our four pillars in more depth than before and relate them to important present-day research issues. Clearly, these assumptions about the psychology of language do not stand on their own, but should allow us to bring many facets important to the study of the psychology of language together under one roof.

11.2.1 Embodiedness, multimodality, and interactivity

One pillar of this book is that the language processing system is *embodied, multimodal, and allows for local interactions*. An important reason for these assertions lies in the origin and development of language. It has been argued that, in an evolutionary context, the human capacity to communicate developed first and foremost to allow for efficient face-to-face interactions (Levinson, 1983). In addition, we learn to communicate early in life based on the input we receive in face-to-face situations, and face-to-face settings remain the locus in which language is mostly used throughout our lives (Capirci et al., 1996; Vigliocco et al., 2014).

In such common settings, we make use of the different channels provided by our body to communicate (e.g., Mondada, 2016; Stivers & Sidnell, 2013). Indeed, throughout the book we have seen time and again that everyday communication is intrinsically a multi-channel phenomenon. It involves a variety of both conventional and idiosyncratic manual gestures (e.g., beat gestures, iconic gestures, emblems, pointing gestures, etc.), head movements (e.g., nodding or pointing), facial expressions, and other bodily signals that all take place in close interaction with (or sometimes in the absence of) concurrent speech (Bavelas et al., 1992; Ekman, 1993; Kendon, 2004; Kita, 2003; McNeill, 1992; Scheflen, 1964). As such, the body is not only consistently used as a means of communication by users of sign languages, but it also contributes significantly to the messages that members of speech communities convey during face-to-face interactions (Goldin-Meadow, 2014). The embodiedness of language hence allows for efficient multimodal and multichannel communication.

As we hope to have shown in the book, the body indeed plays a significant role not only in the production and comprehension of speech and concurrent bodily signals, but also in reading, via the eyes (for printed and written text) or hands (for tactile writing systems such as Braille). Moreover, because language is typically used in rich and dynamic environments (e.g., a living room, a restaurant, a marketplace) and in interaction with aspects of these environments, language (in the mental model) also covers more or less subjective body-related perceptual, motor, and emotion aspects of the communicative setting. The wolf in the fairy tale is dark gray, runs fast, smells of rain, and its teeth evoke fear.

This view also entails that we do not use our hands, face, and so on, separately from our voice: Gestures and words are tightly temporally synchronized and often complementary or supplementary in their expression of meaning (Pouw & Dixon, 2019; Wagner et al., 2014). In line with this view, many classic findings we know from the literature on spoken and written communication actually surface in a similar manner when we look at the meaning speakers convey through their arms and hands while they speak or learn a language. To illustrate that similar principles may underlie communication via speech when compared to communication via the hands, we will briefly highlight three recent findings pointing in this direction in the context of language comprehension, language production, and language learning.

One example of similar basic principles underlying the *comprehension* of communicative messages was already discussed in the context of the classic McGurk effect in Chapter 5. Remember that this effect refers to the phenomenon that the lip movements a speaker makes influence what speech sound you will hear. Indeed, combining a video of the lips saying "ga" with a speech sound "ba" makes people say and think they hear "da" (McGurk & MacDonald, 1976). As such, this finding shows that the language comprehension system combines visual signals (here provided by the speaker's lips) with auditory signals (here the presented speech sound) to provide the listener with a best guess of what the speaker is assuming to convey (Massaro, 1987).

Interestingly, we have seen that there is also a to some extent manual equivalent when looking at the hand movements people make when they speak. In this manual McGurk effect, the exact timing of an up-and-down manual beat gesture influences on which syllable (e.g., PERmit versus perMIT) people perceive word stress, even though the spoken signal remains the same and may even point in the opposite direction (Bosker & Peeters, 2021). As such, at a very basic level, the language user must be combining visual with auditory input signals to try and understand an incoming multimodal message.

As another example, this time in the context of *learning*, remember that we have seen that bilinguals typically process words that overlap in form and meaning between their languages ("cognates") more quickly compared to words that express the same meaning but have different forms in their two languages (Chapter 10). Clearly, these words will also help language learners to "break into" a new language they are learning (e.g., Nagy et al., 1993). Intuitively, you would think that speakers who are learning a *sign language* as a second language cannot rely on such overlap between their first (spoken) and second (signed) language, because of the differences in the articulators used (cf. Berent & Gervain, 2023). It turns out, however, that some of the signs they will have to learn overlap in form (e.g., the handshape, movement, or orientation of the hands used) with the co-speech gestures speakers make themselves while they are talking (Ortega & Özyürek, 2020; Ortega et al., 2020). For instance, the hand movements speakers often make when they talk about drinking, may resemble the conventional sign for "to drink" in a given sign language. Such *manual cognates* indeed come with processing and learning benefits ("cognate facilitation") compared to signs that do not resemble the co-speech gestures people make (Ortega et al., 2020). Overall, when people learn a new language, they hence make use of the stored knowledge and experience they have at their disposal, regardless of the modality (spoken/written or manual) associated with the stored piece of information.

Finally, also in the domain of language *production* a classic finding is replicated when looking at language as a multimodal phenomenon. The so-called *Lombard effect* entails that people involuntarily raise their voice and make larger mouth movements whenever they communicate in challenging environments, such as when there is a lot of background noise (Lombard, 1911). In itself, this may not seem very surprising, but people also do it whenever they are not actively aware of it, for instance when there is only a little bit of background noise. In addition, they find it hard to not do it even when they are explicitly asked to keep their speech level constant (Brumm & Zollinger, 2011). Apparently, people just really want to get their message across. This idea is confirmed by the finding that the effect is most convincingly present in face-to-face interactions.

When looking at the hand movements people make in noisy environments, such as at a music festival, a *multimodal* Lombard effect has been observed. Indeed, when noise levels increased, people started making more hand movements (Trujillo et al., 2021). Crucially, when looking at language as a multimodal phenomenon, the Lombard effect was actually even more robust in the visual signals (i.e., hand and lip movements) people produced than in the acoustics of their speech. As such, the language user may rely on exactly those bodily channels that optimize the odds of being understood by the person they communicate with as a function of properties of the larger context in which the communicative act takes place.

In sum, the human body seems of tremendous importance for the language user, and basic principles underlying language comprehension, learning, and production surface in both spoken and manual forms of communication. In section 11.3.1, much in contrast with a long tradition that basically equates "language" with (spoken and printed) "words," we will therefore argue that the Language User Framework should be expanded to take into account incoming and outgoing signals beyond spoken and printed words.

11.2.2 Embeddedness, symbol hierarchy, and interactivity

A second pillar of our book is that language is in many ways *embedded*, meaning that language use is affected by the context it occurs in. In a broad sense, language takes place in a particular physical and social situation, most often one in which several people interact. Non-verbal context, general communicative context, and language context all affect what is said and how it is said. In a more narrow sense, the use of certain language elements is itself embedded. Sounds and letters are embedded in words, words in sentences, and so on.

In this book, we argued that such global and local contextual effects may very quickly affect the processing of the presented linguistic stimulus. However, we have also argued that there are certain limitations to the degree of such influences. First, we noted that it is important to keep a non-distorted representation of the input, in order to avoid hallucinations and misinterpretations. Furthermore, we assumed that interactivity is limited by inherent delays in communication between distributed networks in the brain that are partially involved in different activities. Limitations in the speed of spreading nervous activity and larger spatial distances in the brain will result in temporally delayed interactions between the neurobiological counterparts of cognitive processing components. By means of smart meta-analyses, the average processing time of language processing stages can be assessed (cf. Chapters 9 and 10). This has led, for instance, to estimates for the various processing stages in language production, such as conceptualization, lemma retrieval, phonological code retrieval, resyllabification, phonetic encoding, and articulation (Indefrey, 2011; Indefrey & Levelt, 2004; Roelofs & Shitova, 2017).

This reasoning suggests that there are limits to top-down effects in the Language Processing System. But what exactly are these limits? The assumption of language as an interactive system brings in the obligation to answer this far-reaching question. This is one reason why, earlier in its history, psycholinguistics started from the simplifying assumption, inspired by Occam's Razor, that language processing could be differentiated into a number of autonomously working, encapsulated modules (Fodor, 1983). At the time, the workings of the linguistic mind were compared to those of a computer (the "computer metaphor"), because the Central Processing Unit of a computer also worked sequentially on input.

However, as we have argued, such a view is untenable in light of the multimodal character of language and communication. Different streams of information enter the language processing system at the same time during language comprehension, and they leave the system in parallel during language production. By providing a categorization of language activities in terms of different tasks in the Language User Framework, we hope to provide some restrictive guidelines for thinking about language interaction, even in its broader context of communication.

In all, we have proposed that language consists of a *hierarchical system of locally interacting representations of different sizes*. Other cognitive domains (such as non-linguistic perception) may share this property as a design principle. The elements taking part in the interactions between levels of the representational hierarchies have traditionally been considered to be *symbols*. Indeed, the building blocks of language (e.g., words and sentences) lend themselves very easily for a symbolic interpretation. More recently, subsymbolic and non-symbolic ways to capture language have been proposed as alternatives. In this book, we still advocate a symbolic approach, for several reasons. For one, both readers and researchers find it easy to handle symbols. Symbols are the exchange coins of our conversations. Models can more easily be understood if they consist of functional units with symbolic value.

Our approach does not imply that "reality" can (or should) only be described with symbols. The symbolic units of "words" are probably not represented in the brain in terms of discrete bundles of millions of nerve cells; they may be fuzzy and overlapping. Specifying their memory trace in terms of brain activity might require a completely new categorization and not only a much finer "granularity" of proposed units. Nevertheless, when we consider models as sketches of language behavior, symbolic sketches will do their job, as long as they capture the most important mechanisms and events. They should correlate well with empirical phenomena, and have a certain validity and some predictive power. Later in this chapter, we will come back to this point when we consider the value of computational models in this respect.

11.2.3 Incrementality, time-scale, and interactivity

A third pillar in our approach to language is that its processing takes place *incrementally*, over time. Lots of experimental research into the psychology of language considers language processing mostly in the time window of 0 ms to about 2 seconds after a word is presented. Longer response times are often considered not trustworthy, because strategies and thought processes may at that stage have become more and more prominent, interfering at longer time ranges and inducing noise. However, as we have seen, it is likely that information arriving from other modalities will affect or color the available semantic representations relatively late, up to several seconds after the language event. Of course, nobody will contest the importance of long time scales (e.g., years or decades) for developments in the lexicon or grammar of languages in the mind of the language user, but here we are talking about mere seconds.

Much psycholinguistic work has to some extent ignored or simplified the (global, task-related, and/or decision) processes that follow word recognition or sentence construction.

For instance, all that happens at the end of sentence processing has sometimes been called "wrap up" effects and is commonly excluded from eye tracking or EEG data analysis. However, from the perspective of language as a multimodal, interactive, and incremental system, this might lead to the loss of valuable data.

Coming along with the assumption of incrementality is the notion that subprocesses for representations of different "grain sizes" may take place at different time-scales (cf. Chapter 9 on language production). As a consequence, there are many different ways in which information streams may come together in the language user's mind and brain.

Figure 11.2 illustrates what effects different information streams may have on each other. Panel (a) illustrates the bottom-up activation of the word "cat" by its input letters "c," "a," "t," and the top-down activation from this word to its letters. The presence of simultaneous opposite information streams between letter and word *levels* is usually considered as a clear case of interaction, in which units at both levels are strengthened by *resonance*. As we noted in Chapter 10, orthographic-semantic resonance is an important driving force behind cognate facilitation effects in multilinguals. In a localist connectionist model like the TRACE model, interactions between units at adjacent levels come with a delay of two time steps. For instance, phonemes in the model activate words in step 1, and those words then send activation back to phonemes at time step 2. If the model is extended to distinguish a syllable level between the phoneme and word level, the interaction between phonemes and words then requires a delay of four time steps: phoneme → syllable → word → syllable → phoneme. The addition of a syllable level between phonemes and words therefore has immediate consequences for the model's lexical processing.

Panel (b) in Figure 11.2 depicts how words in a sentence activate a syntactic structure or an event structure over time. On the basis of such sentence-level structures, the syntactic

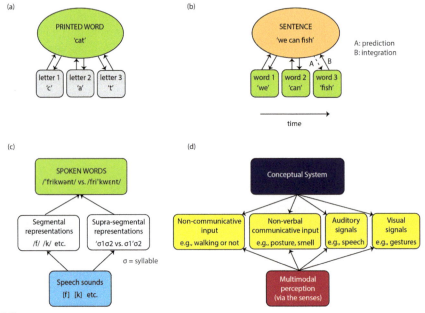

Figure 11.2

How different information flows may come together in the Language Processing System. Note that we usually speak of interaction only when information flows in two directions between the same two levels or components (e.g., between letters and words, words and sentence context; cf. Panels a and b). However, in the case of complex information flows, the distinction between interaction and integration is hard to make without a detailed temporal analysis (as in Panel c for segmental and suprasegmental information, and in Panel d for parallel input from multiple modalities).

category or thematic role of an upcoming item could be predicted. Later words could thus be anticipated in terms of syntactic, semantic, or even word form aspects. This would constitute a clear case of interaction between the Word Recognizer and the Sentence Processor, because the two *subsystems* or *components* affect each other mutually (i.e., there is a "two-way street" of bottom-up and top-down information), again with a certain delay.

Alternatively, upcoming items could (only) be integrated more easily in prepared compatible structures than in unrelated structures (requiring a bottom-up information stream only). When certain brain areas or networks are prepared to expect the arrival of certain information, they can quickly integrate it. As we have seen, experienced human language users have systematically organized their knowledge of the world (and the events that may occur) in mental models, scenarios, scripts, story grammars, event structures, and syntactic structures. These all provide systematic representations of situations, in which newly arriving information can be easily embedded.

Panel (c) in Figure 11.2 represents a different type of information stream, where information from different dimensions of an input stimulus is temporarily processed in parallel before converging. It shows the parallel activation of segmental (e.g., phonemic) and suprasegmental (e.g., prosodic) information streams that come together in speech processing (Chapter 5).

Panel (d) illustrates differences in function and relevance that incoming sensory information can have for the language user. Suppose that we wish to understand a person who is gesturing to us while approaching. Our eyes (providing input to our visual perception system) will then receive diverse types of information: non-communicative (e.g., is the person walking or not), non-verbal information that could have a communicative value (e.g., what is the current posture of the person, what clothes or perfume do they wear), and more specific language-related aspects. In particular, when the person then starts talking, the specific spoken words, hand gestures, lip movements, and changing facial expressions are simultaneously relevant. The convergence of information streams may happen at different locations in the Language Processing System (cf. the McGurk effect), but it all has as its final destination the Conceptual System. After paying focused attention to particular aspects of the input, and discarding or suppressing irrelevant information that is deemed not communicatively intended, the incoming message must be integrated by the Conceptual System of the perceiver into a coherent mental model. Note that in sign language, very similar input information may be distributed solely over the available visual bodily channels.

11.2.4 The mental model as an interface for language and other cognitive faculties

The *mental model* constitutes an important fourth pillar in our multimodal and interactive approach. It functions as an interface or "meeting place" between language and other cognitive systems. Instead of studying various cognitive activities separately, they should be considered in tandem. Even after identification processes at the word and sentence level are completed, the mental model(s) in the Conceptual System may be fine-tuned to ongoing feedback from other cognitive systems and contextual information more generally. Thinking, perceiving, moving, and feeling emotions does not stop when language processing is finished.

Our Conceptual System thus makes sense of the "original extents or bignesses of all the sensations which c[o]me to our notice at once, coalesced together into one and the same space" (James, 1890, p. 488). It does not only represent meanings of words, sentences, and text or discourse in mental models. It also processes, represents, and relates information originating from different cognitive modalities such as non-linguistic perception. It can interactively use this information in speaking and writing, and derive it for listening and reading.

It has been proposed that the input from different cognitive domains (including language) could be linked and integrated by recoding all their different representational formats into a common and abstract "language of thought," in which symbol-like units would play a role in various cognitive modalities (Quilty-Dunn et al., 2022). However, even without making this assumption, a shared conceptual code might not (always) have to be computed. Instead, the mental model might be organized more like a 3D view of the world. Modality-specific information could be kept in its original format, while information from different cognitive systems is time-stamped to indicate relations between different cognitive formats. Keeping precise track of timing and synchronization aspects between different cognitive modalities in this type of "hub-and-spoke" system (Lambon Ralph et al., 2017; see Chapter 8) would be an important function of the Cognitive Control System.

We believe that language has its own role to play in cognition and that it cannot fully be reduced to mental simulations, action, perception, or emotion. In all, our theoretical position lies close to that of the *language marker hypothesis* (Hagoort, 2023, p. 2) that considers language as "a rich symbolic system that plays a central role in interpreting signals delivered by our sensory apparatus". We hence do not advocate the alternative view that "[c]ognition and language are grounded in perception and action and need to be specified according to the formats of these systems" (Hagoort, 2023, p. 1). Although further development of the former view is clearly required, we believe it is a promising theoretical and realistic basis for further empirical exploration.

A consequence of the assumption that conceptual representation may be of various kinds, including modality-specific ones, is that recoding from one format into another is necessary for talking about what is happening in a particular situation. In Chapter 9 on language production, we saw that it has often been assumed that the Conceptual System makes use of non-linguistic conceptual representations that are turned into language-sensitive semantic representations for the purpose of speaking ("thinking for speaking"; Slobin, 1987). This process may require looking for certain perceptual information in the world to allow the formulation of correct utterances ("seeing for saying"; Bock et al., 2003). We briefly addressed these notions in the context of language production (Discussion Box 9) and multilingualism (Chapter 10).

Given that this issue is complex and currently not well-understood, research progress on mental models will most likely be slow (as in the decades behind us) and progress may first and foremost be made in subdomains (cf. Eysenck & Keane, 2015). Nevertheless, attempts at constraining the workings of the Conceptual System are important, since building appropriate conceptual representations is the ultimate goal of language comprehension and the starting point of language production.

SUMMARY: EXPANDING THE FOUR BASIC ASSUMPTIONS OF THE BOOK

The Language User Framework is built on four basic assumptions and acknowledges that language processing is an embodied, embedded, incremental activity that allows for linking incoming and outgoing utterances to the language user's mental model. The notion of embodiedness is naturally linked to multimodality, while the concept of embeddedness can be interpreted in light of a hierarchy of smaller and larger representations. The notion of incrementality considers step-wise language processes at different time scales, and mental models take into account information from different cognitive modalities. All these assumptions are directly linked to interactions between and convergences of representations within and beyond the Language Processing System.

11.3 EXPANDING THE LANGUAGE USER FRAMEWORK

We have argued that language representation and processing are subserved by an interactive, hierarchically organized system that works in an incremental way from body to mental model and back: the Language User Framework. Its Language Processing System operates under the supervision of a regulatory Cognitive Control System that is in part also used in other domains of cognition; however, more research is needed to better understand which control aspects are shared across cognitive domains and which are specific to language and multilingualism (cf. Abutalebi & Green, 2008; Bialystok et al., 2007; Peeters et al., 2019).

We have also considered the Language User Framework to be context-sensitive. However, we do not believe it to be so dynamic or interactive that an appropriate description requires fine-grained fuzzy elements of a subsymbolic nature whose prominence varies with every language user, task, context condition, or language stimulus. We believe that using symbols is possible and useful to describe systematicities in the system when context aspects are taken into account. Although describing linguistic representation and language processing in terms of symbols might exaggerate the "black and white" in the system, at least they do not leave us with indistinguishable shades of gray or new black boxes.

The Language User Framework has been helpful as a general framework to represent much of the progress made over the past century in our understanding of the psychology of language and to link the several activities the language user carries out (speaking, listening, reading, etc.). Nevertheless, like the empirical studies and insights it was based on, it comes with clear limitations. In the following section, we will therefore aim to expand it, in two ways. First, we will adapt the Language User Framework to the growing insight that human communication is intrinsically multimodal (i.e., often employing the auditory and visual modality at the same time) and multichannel (i.e., often using more than one bodily channel at a time) in nature. Second, we will position it within a larger framework of human cognition.

11.3.1 The Multimodal Language User Framework

In Chapter 1 (Box 1.1), we presented a comparison of reading printed words and listening to speech in terms of different dimensions: their time course, form, content, control, and effect. Interestingly, we saw that reading connected handwriting in Latin script appears to be similar to reading print in terms of all these dimensions except for form: It is typically similar to listening in that it is concerned with a more continuous input signal.

When we wish to extend the Language User Framework to seriously take into consideration the multimodal and multichannel richness of everyday face-to-face communication, more changes may be required. Figure 11.3 presents an attempt to incorporate the bodily richness of everyday communication into the Framework. As you can see, the Word Recognizer has been replaced by a more generic Sign Recognizer that would take on words and other incoming signals but would work quite differently for various types of input. These signals, once segmented from the incoming information streams by the Signal Recognizer, need to be mapped onto stored representations (e.g., of words, gestural representations, etc.) in Long Term Memory by the Sign Recognizer. Note that we here use the term *sign* as not specific to sign language. Indeed, the spoken language user often has to derive meaning from an incoming stream of concomitant words, gestures, facial expressions, and other bodily signals. Specifically, the Sign Recognizer would recognize a hand gesture by considering several dimensions in parallel, such as its handshape, orientation, and movement

264   *Conclusion and outlook*

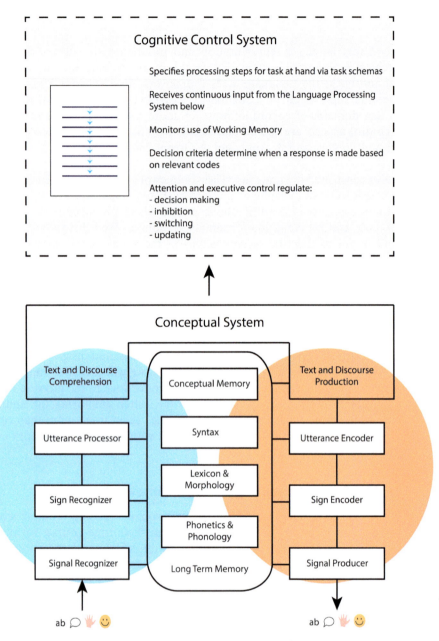

Figure 11.3
The Language User Framework extended to account for the intrinsically multimodal and multichannel nature of human communication.

in space, as these may impact its corresponding meaning. It would concurrently also have to interpret any non-manual markers that accompany the gesture (and/or spoken words), such as a facial expression.

Clearly, the variety of incoming signals, once recognized as communicatively intended signs, should be integrated to arrive at a best guess of what a speaker is trying to convey. We have therefore changed the name of the Sentence Processor into "Utterance Processor," as sentences in face-to-face communication are commonly accompanied by non-verbal signals that significantly contribute to the interpretation of the utterance.

In the right side of the adapted framework, the production of a multimodal message is considered. Based on the language user's intention, a grammatical structure needs to be built with slots that have to be filled with lexical items and enriched with concurrent non-verbal signals. As such, language production becomes conceptualized as a process of translating one's intentions into a series of motor programs that in parallel control the various muscles allowing for the articulation of spoken words, hand gestures, facial expressions, and other types of bodily signals. Also the use and processing of sign language may be understood in more or less the same framework with more or less the same components (e.g., Emmorey, 2001; Ormel, 2008).

11.3.2 Language in the overarching cognitive system

While the Language User Framework may be extended to fully account for the multimodal and multichannel nature of language, the framework itself can also be considered part of a yet larger framework of human cognition. Indeed, an interesting question is how the domain of language is related to other cognitive domains. In Figure 11.4, we illustrate our theoretical view with respect to the overarching general cognitive system, building on notions from Barrett and Satpute (2013) and Sianipar (2017). As Figure 11.4 shows, different cognitive activities are subserved by different brain networks that allow processes supporting different types of tasks in different cognitive domains. Interacting low-level neural processes allow the computation of higher-order level actions or task responses in domains such as language, emotion, and social cognition. Because brain networks are in principle domain-general, a particular network may be engaged not only in language processing, but also in subserving aspects of attention, emotion, and social cognition (Barrett & Satpute, 2013).

In light of this overarching framework, it becomes possible to describe how the interaction between language processing and, for instance, affective/emotional processing comes about. When we encounter a skeleton who says "You can die" (as in the opening example of this chapter), hearing the emotion-laden verb form "die" will instigate the retrieval of its word form and meaning in the mental lexicon in Long Term Memory. Responding to this statement requires the execution of a number of activities: Neural networks must be activated for visual attention (to localize the speaker in space), mentalizing (to infer what the speaker is actually intending with this quite threatening utterance), central executive functioning (to allocate attentional resources), and motor performance (for accurate and efficient articulation of a response). The proper application of these activities implies an interaction between the different domains indicated in Figure 11.4. As such, it may be that verb forms like "die" (or, for instance, nouns such as "snake") engage language, emotion, and other cognitive domains at different time courses (Sianipar, 2017). Processing of the incoming word "die" will not only activate the mentalizing network, but also involve a change in core affect aspects in the salience network depending on its valence and arousal properties. Thus, parallel and yoked processes involving categorization and core affect may take place with different temporal characteristics (Barrett, 2006, 2017). Likewise, the meaning of a word like "snake" does not only involve the perceptual experience with a snake (shape, color), but also the accompanying feelings (negative, fear), which may be represented and stored as part of word meaning in subcortical neural networks (cf. Pulvermüller, 2013).

Conclusion and outlook

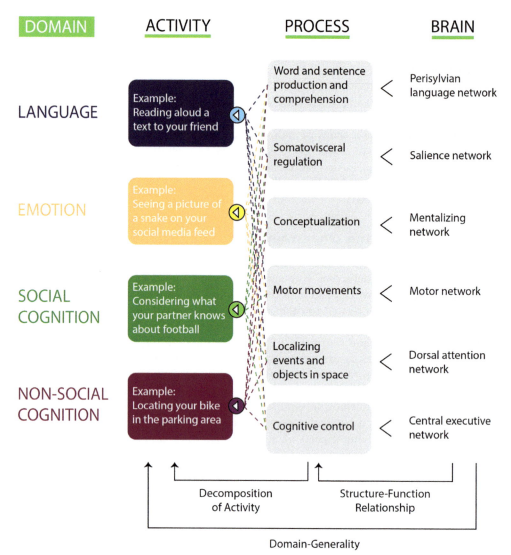

Figure 11.4
A general constructionist framework for human neurocognitive processing. The figure extends Figure 2C in Barrett and Satpute (2013, p. 4). Successfully carrying out different activities in everyday life may require activation of distributed domain-general functional brain networks including the perisylvian network subserving basic language processing.

SUMMARY: EXPANDING THE LANGUAGE USER FRAMEWORK

By defining its task in a more general way, the Language User Framework can be reformulated to account for the multimodal and multichannel nature of everyday face-to-face communication. In addition, the Language User Framework can be hooked up to a more general overarching view of different cognitive functions, their interrelation and neurobiological basis in terms of distributed functional networks. Language processing may make use of neurobiological resources that are shared across cognitive domains, and might serve as a complex and partially independent interface between different cognitive functions.

11.4 BIASES IN THE PSYCHOLOGY OF LANGUAGE

The general view on language as a cognitive domain that is illustrated in Figure 11.4 encompasses the Language User Framework first introduced in Chapter 3. As such, it allows a description of the language processing pathways "from body to mental model and back." But in what respect does this view represent a "new" psychology of language? If the word "new" is meant to express that earlier biases or limitations in the psychology of language were to be overcome, the question arises to what extent the "new" view itself is subject to biases and subjective choices.

When we look back at the early days of modern psycholinguistics, the view on language that we have presented indeed represents a radical conceptual shift. A comparison of our present approach to language with that of Chomsky in his famous book *Syntactic Structures* (1957) and in later work is indicative of this point (see Discussion Boxes in Chapters 2, 3, and 7). In his influential research at the dawn of modern-day linguistics and psycholinguistics, Chomsky expressed several basic assumptions about language.

First, language, and in particular syntax, was considered as an abstract rule system that could potentially be described even mathematically. Chomsky further assumes that the language community is homogeneous, consisting of standard speakers, who have a certain innate capacity to learn a "universal grammar" of the language by means of a Language Acquisition Device. They apply this competence in performance, which is prone to errors and hesitations.

Second, language is modular in nature and functions as "an organ of the mind" (1980, *Rules and Representations*). The notion of "modularity" was further specified by Fodor in his book *The Modularity of Mind* (1983).

Third, complete utterances (sentences) are subjected to syntactic analyses at the level of sentences. These analyses have become optimized in a coherent system of rules on the basis of operations like "move α" or MERGE (Chomsky, 1999; Koeneman & Zeijlstra, 2017). Incrementality has only a limited role to play. Originally, these analyses were based on speaker judgments about what is considered grammatically correct or incorrect. As such, these are off-line, competence-oriented measures.

Finally, in his Berkeley lectures (1993, p. 85), Chomsky deems neuroscience as not very relevant to linguistics:

- "In fact, the belief that neurophysiology is even relevant to the functioning of the mind is just a hypothesis. Who knows if we're looking at the right aspects of the brain at all. Maybe there are other aspects of the brain that nobody has dreamt of looking at yet. That's happened often in the history of science."
- "The belief that neurophysiology is implicated in these things could be true, but we have very little evidence for it. So, it's just a kind of hope; look around and you see neurons; maybe they're implicated."

While Chomsky continued to adapt and refine his theories on language over many years, all of his assumptions have come under attack. First, since the turn of the century, there is an increasing contribution of neuroscience to the study of language, for instance methodologically via the use of techniques such as EEG and fMRI, and theoretically via the integration of neuroscientifically relevant notions such as "prediction" into our psychological theories of language processing. This development has also renewed attention to the concrete properties of everyday language use. Competence and performance are no longer considered separately, and errors and hesitations are seen as inherent consequences of a "messy" system that works with regularities rather than rules.

Second, although modularity was widely adopted as a constraint on the Language Processing System by psycholinguists for several decades, it has come under attack and is (being) abandoned (also see Cohn & Schilperoord, 2022). Accompanying this development towards non-modularity was the availability of more and more empirical data that linked up previously separate domains of linguistics: morphology and syntax, syntax and semantics, and so on. We note that, from this respect, the component boxes in the Language User Framework are to be considered more as a convenient categorization for specifying particular language tasks than as separate modular components.

Third, the principle of an economic organization of the (syntactic) rule system has been replaced by a principle of the economy of effort exerted by the language user. This development in psycholinguistics was accompanied by linguistic innovations towards more incremental approaches as in Generalized Phrase Structure Grammar (Gazdar et al., 1985) and Lexical Functional Grammar (Bresnan et al., 2016).

A big influence on the research developments in the psychology of language and linguistics has also been the development of more and more refined research techniques (see Chapter 4). Moreover, on-line research techniques developed by psycholinguists have gradually been adopted by linguists as well to overcome the limitations of their off-line grammatical judgment tasks. Good examples are self-paced reading, eye tracking, and fMRI paradigms.

Finally, the invention and general availability of the personal computer and the internet have led to a tremendously increased collection of empirical studies in the last decades. This hopefully has led us to a more realistic view on language and its use. Nevertheless, we should not see our book as involving a radical deviation from all earlier works. In fact, we see a remarkable similarity in our views to those expressed in the book *The Psychology of Language* (Clark & Clark, 1977). For instance, one important notion that was already stressed at the time and in the decades to follow was that of "common ground" between language users. Indeed, we would consider aligning our mental models cooperatively in terms of their content as a very important underlying principle in dialog; in fact, it can be considered as a goal in teaching and writing as well (cf. Maes et al., 2022).

Of course, this observed similarity does not absolve us from answering the question to what extent we ourselves are prone to bias in our views on language. Some limitations are already clear to us.

First, the current edition of this book does not contain a separate chapter on the important topics of Language Development or Language Disorders. Rather, we have alluded to these topics in various chapters and included them in assignments on the book's companion website. This omission is bound to exaggerate the importance attributed to language processing in adults relative to the language learning process in children.

Second, as Cutler (2012a) once expressed: "One-language psychology is no language psychology." Structural differences between languages are bound to result in processing differences between those languages. It is therefore important to extend our (monolingual and multilingual) empirical studies on language to as many different languages as possible, especially those that do not belong to the Indo-European language family, and consider both spoken and signed languages equally. In embracing diversity, important steps forward in our understanding of the psychology of language will quickly become within reach.

As a case in point, consider the relationship between sound representations and meaning. For a very long time, it has been considered that this relation is largely arbitrary, implying that a word's form in no means resembles its meaning (de Saussure, 1916; Hockett, 1960; Pinker, 1999). However, a relatively recent analysis of the word form – meaning relation across a wide variety of different languages in the world has made it very clear that this

> **Box 11.1 The relation between form and meaning in language**
>
>
>
> **Figure 11.5**
> Two shapes.
>
> Have a look at the two images presented in Figure 11.5. Which of these two shapes should be called *bouba* (or *maluma*) and which one should be named *kiki* (or *takete*)?
> Already about a century ago, Köhler showed that people predominantly and consistently associate the spiky figure (here on the left) with pseudowords containing voiceless stops such as *kiki* and *takete*, and the curvy figure (here on the right) with pseudowords that do not contain voiceless stops or contain only continuant consonants, such as *bouba* and *maluma* (see Köhler, 1947). Apparently, people prefer a certain combination of sounds as a function of properties (e.g., its degree of spikiness or roundedness) of the object it refers to. In this example, perhaps the spikiness of the lines in the figure on the left in some way resembles properties of the sounds present in the pseudoword *kiki*, following the "sharp" inflection of the articulators (such as the tongue) involved in producing the sounds (Ramachandran & Hubbard, 2001; see also Knoeferle et al., 2017).

assumption is not generally correct. Indeed, statistical approaches to test for word-meaning associations across large sets of languages actually point out that the relation between word form and word meaning is less arbitrary than previously thought (Blasi et al., 2016; Dingemanse et al., 2015). For instance, across the spoken languages of the world, it turns out that the concept SMALL is surprisingly often expressed by a word that contains the /i/ sound (a high front vowel), perhaps because small creatures typically make high sounds. Another observed regularity is that words for the concept NOSE are found to quite often contain a nasal /n/ sound. As such, the relation between word form and meaning may not be so arbitrary after all. Box 11.1 further illustrates this point.

Third, the view on language expressed in this book is functional in nature and not strictly dependent on the research techniques applied to collect its data. Nevertheless, the study of the psychology of language has received a valuable external impulse in the past three to four decades by advances in neuroscience, resulting in several theoretical insights. It may well be that in the future a formulation will become more prominent that is even more strictly embedded in neuroscientific terms. Where in the brain certain language-related processes take place and how they are conducted are old questions on language (already posed by Broca and Wernicke) that can be considered much more adequately since the arrival of new neuroimaging techniques. Also exciting is the increasing interest in the genetics underlying language and other cognitive modalities (e.g., Enard et al., 2002; Fisher & Scharff, 2009).

This last point brings us to the question of what kind of future research on language we should expect over the coming decade or so. This is the topic of the last section of the book.

> **SUMMARY: BIASES IN THE PSYCHOLOGY OF LANGUAGE**
>
> Looking at the history of psycholinguistics over the last 65 years, it is evident that our knowledge on language and its use has not only increased enormously, but also has been refined in many ways. The advent of new computer-steered research techniques has contributed to this development. At the same time, the theoretical perspective on the underlying mechanisms of language representation and use has changed greatly as well. Language and language use are no longer considered to be (just) purely abstract in nature, but seen much more as supported by a relatively messy system that is very sensitive to contextual influences. Furthermore, language is apparently not organized in terms of strict separate modules, and incrementality is important. Other languages than English, language development, and language disorders should be considered as well to develop a balanced view of the many aspects of language use.

11.5 OUTLOOK: DIVERSITY, DIALOG, AND DIGITAL DEVELOPMENTS

It is an exciting time to study the psychology of language, as there are many recent, impactful, ongoing methodological developments that will allow for finding new answers to old theoretical questions, and for posing new questions that for a long time most prominently belonged to the domain of science fiction. In this section, we will discuss five theoretical and methodological advances which we expect will have a significant impact on the study of the psychology of language over the coming decade(s).

11.5.1 Acknowledging linguistic and cultural diversity

As a first change that is slowly coming about, we would like to mention that more and more experimental researchers of the psychology of language are (finally) seriously starting to consider aspects of individual, linguistic, and cultural *diversity*. Although sociolinguistics has been an important domain in linguistics for decades, interindividual differences have long been neglected by many psycholinguists. Many current models of the psychology of language indeed generalize only across relatively homogeneous groups of young and healthy participants in Europe or the United States. Typically, these language users are WEIRD: Western, Educated, Industrialized, Rich, and Democratic in background (Henrich et al., 2010). Focusing on this group, there is an increased tendency of incorporating participant and item characteristics in statistical analyses (as in linear mixed-effects models). However, diversity in terms of languages and dialects (e.g., minority and heritage languages), and broader cultural aspects, is still often neglected.

There are several reasons why it is important to study the psychology of language from perspectives other than English. First of all, there currently exist over 7,000 (spoken and signed) languages in the world and English is similar to only some of them (Ethnologue, 2021). For instance, many languages, unlike English, rely on tone information to distinguish meaningful units, contain a substantial number of lexical items that display iconic form-meaning mappings, and have no left-to-right alphabetic writing system or no writing system at all (Blasi et al., 2022). Taking into account such differences will clearly impact our theories and models. And what would happen if we had taken sign language rather than spoken language as a starting point for our theorizing (Perniss et al., 2010)?

But even when we compare properties of English to other Indo-European languages, we note remarkable differences. Consider the following three English sentences:

(1) John and <u>his</u> wife;
(2) John and <u>his</u> son;
(3) John and <u>his</u> kids.

In these three cases, the possessive pronoun "his" is identical and does not change in form as a function of the word that follows it. If we translate these sentences into French, a different picture appears:

(4) *Jean et <u>sa</u> femme*;
(5) *Jean et <u>son</u> fils*;
(6) *Jean et <u>ses</u> enfants*.

Based on the grammatical gender of the word following it, and based on whether that word indicates a singular or plural referent, the pronoun takes a different form. As such, French readers and listeners may use it to predict the upcoming noun by restricting the lexical search space into much more detail than speakers of English in a similar situation. Perhaps, the importance of prediction for on-line language processing would have been noted earlier on had not English but another language been given center stage.

Different language characteristics may also allow for an easier experimental disentanglement of various cognitive processes. For instance, studying verb-initial languages may result in new insights on language comprehension and production process. On the basis of anticipatory gaze durations in an eye tracking study in Tagalog, a language spoken in the Philippines, Sauppe (2016) concluded that listeners quickly used the meaning of verbs in comprehension to identify semantic roles and referents, rather than information about syntactic functions or word order. In contrast, for speech production in Tagalog already the earliest stages of sentence formulation were found to be sensitive to the sentence's grammatical structure (Sauppe et al., 2013; cf. Chapter 8). The author argues that a similar time-course analysis could not easily have been done in English, due to its rigid subject-initial word order. Thus, these "results on Tagalog highlight the need for controlled studies on typologically diverse languages that allow dissociations between different processes at the interface of thinking and speaking" (Sauppe et al., 2013, p. 1270).

Another important reason for studying a wide range of unrelated languages is to better understand the variation and variety in language processing phenomena and their consequences for society and education. For instance, Huettig and Ferreira (2022, p. 1) argue that the notion of a "normal language user" who is engaged in "normal reading" "makes little sense given the diversity of the backgrounds of participants and the fact that outside the Anglo-Saxon world multilingualism is the norm rather than the exception." In reality, they argue, "normal reading" does not exist. Reading consists of a broad variety of activities by language users in many different populations varying widely in cultural and linguistic characteristics, for different goals and purposes. As a consequence, the authors suggest that a hunt for the "best" reading instruction method is futile. Individuals should be *expected* to read differently rather than all in the same way! Their paper concludes with ominous words: "In important ways, educational policies and the science of reading arguably have gotten it all wrong: The focus should not be so much on how well people decode written language and how fast people read but instead on what people comprehend given their own stated goals" (Huettig & Ferreira, 2022, p. 7). Changing the educational focus requires a better understanding of the "diversity of brains and experiences" of language users across the globe.

11.5.2 Shift of focus from monolog to dialog

As a second development within the study of the psychology of language and beyond, we are experiencing a gradual shift from experimental paradigms in which participants are tested individually to task settings that focus on *dialog* and *interaction*. The realization that language performance is sensitive and fine-tuned to the (social) context it takes place in has led to a consideration of how exactly speakers and listeners take into account the contribution and presence of the other interlocutor (Pickering & Garrod, 2013, 2021). Moreover, researchers have started to realize that having participants carry out relatively artificial tasks individually in a soundproof experimental booth is quite a long shot from these same participants' everyday language behavior that one hopes our psychological theories of language generalize to. Indeed, such "passive spectator science" may have led to psychological theories of language that do not do justice to the interactive richness of human communication (cf. Hari et al., 2015). Considering verbal and non-verbal interactions in a dialog situation is turning the psychology of language more into a "two-person science" similar to the ongoing social developments in "second-person neuroscience" (Schilbach et al., 2013).

The recent advent of more and more sophisticated virtual reality (VR) applications (described in Chapter 4) will further stimulate a change of research focus from individual language users in restricted experimental situations to more ecologically valid dialog and multiparty conversations. With some effort and dedication, any non-linguistic and/or linguistic aspect of a communicative setting can be implemented in a virtual environment. Relative to a standard lab study, this allows for a more natural introduction of world knowledge, scenario activation, and theoretically relevant characteristics of the addressee (e.g., manipulating their age, gender, or language background as well as their verbal and non-verbal behavior). Participants can be immersed in dynamic everyday situations such as cafés, universities, airports, city streets, and marketplaces in the lab.

Immediately, several concrete ideas for research come to mind. For instance, studies suggest that individuals adapt the words and other aspects of the language they choose (also called "register") on the basis of knowledge of the person they converse with and the knowledge they assume to be shared (Sacks & Schegloff, 1979). This phenomenon, sometimes referred to as "recipient design," can be introduced in VR by having participants meet virtual agents that provide them with more or less information about themselves. For instance, when multilingual participants may learn a virtual agent just like them speaks several languages, language switches may come about much more naturally in a rich and dynamic immersive virtual environment than in "standard" computer experiments (cf. Peeters, 2020).

Another possibility is to investigate changes in mental models over time. For instance, in the opening example of this chapter, one mental model suddenly replaces the other one, and the effect of such a transition could be examined in a naturalistic VR setting. An even simpler manipulation could be that a virtual agent leaves a conversation with the human participant, but comes back later. The question here is how the earlier mental model is "reinstated." Behavioral research using the priming paradigm (Dell et al., 1983; O'Brien & Myers, 1987; O'Brien et al., 1986) has already shown that not only is the actor brought back into play, but so, too, is the entire earlier scenario. Application of VR will allow a more refined and naturalistic analysis of the reinstatement process.

11.5.3 Advances in human–computer Interaction

A third development that has been going on for decades but has recently gained momentum is concerned with other advances in the domain of artificial intelligence (AI). As you may have experienced, in more and more situations we as humans no longer communicate exclusively with other humans (or sometimes with animals), but also with interactive (and often embodied and social) digital agents such as chatbots, virtual agents, avatars, virtual assistants, and robots.

Consider the following conversation with Kuki, the chatbot formerly known as Mitsuku, in Figure 11.6. This conversation is hardly any different from an online conversation between humans who meet each other for the first time. Actually, chatbot Kuki may even be quite a bit funnier than most humans one encounters on the internet. It is becoming more and more difficult to find out that such chatbots are not real people. You may have heard of the Turing test, formulated by Turing in 1950. When a human language user would no longer be able to reliably discern that a computer program communicating through a text-only channel is not human, it would have passed the test. What would it mean if Kuki could communicate in such a way that it is no longer distinguishable from a chatting human? An adage commonly attributed to theoretical physicist and Nobel prize winner Feynman is: "What I cannot create (or build), I do not understand" (Way, 2017). Can this be applied to argue that by building Kuki we have fully understood human language production and dyadic interaction?

Readers of this book will surely understand that this conclusion does not logically follow. For example, a machine that can read text to the blind is very useful, but not as a cognitive model for how humans read. An important aim in the study of the psychology of language is to describe language use taking into account the processing restrictions that come with being human. Humans process language with their body, which has been described as a "straitjacket" or "bottleneck" in terms of its capacities (Broadbent, 1958; Christiansen & Chater, 2016; Ferreira & Pashler, 2002; Treisman, 1969). As we have seen, limitations in their articulatory speech apparatus and Working Memory affect the way in which humans can process language. These restrictions are silent companions of the assumptions of

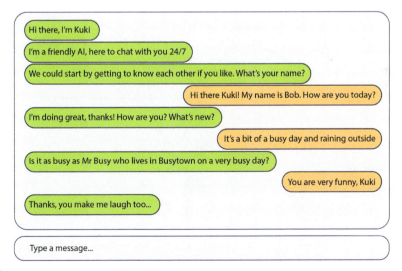

Figure 11.6
The start of an online conversation with chatbot Kuki.

embodiedness, embeddedness, and incremental processing. In contrast, artificial intelligence programs have access to (massive amounts of) text (or images), while they may possess very large memory stores and multiple processing units.

Nevertheless, the superficial similarity in behavior of chatbots and other non-human "intelligent agents" to human language users will quite likely increase in the upcoming years, while being graphically supported by technological advances in the domain of virtual and augmented reality. The development of three-dimensional virtual humans has now reached a point where their looks (perceptual aspects) and movements (motor aspects) have become about equally realistic as the conversation (language aspects) maintained by Kuki above (e.g., de Coninck et al., 2019).

Indeed, the virtual agents and avatars one encounters in virtual worlds may now have passed the point where they come across as a little creepy or "uncanny" (Mori et al., 2012). The term "uncanny valley" is used for the case of a substantial but not complete similarity of a non-human agent to a "real" human. As you can see in Figure 11.7, humanoid robots are not so scary when they are clearly recognizable as being non-human, and they might also not be scary when you cannot really notice any difference in their appearance compared to a real human (until you find out!). But when they are slightly off, they typically come across as a little creepy. In turn, technologically leaving the valley behind may mean that it is no longer necessary to use relatively cartoon-like virtual agents in virtual reality studies to prevent feelings of unease in experimental participants in the language sciences (Huizeling et al., 2022).

Anyway, using text-to-speech technology and advanced speech recognition systems in combination with realistic 3D graphic rendering of "virtual humans" and their (communicative and non-communicative) bodily movements, it will become possible to have a relatively

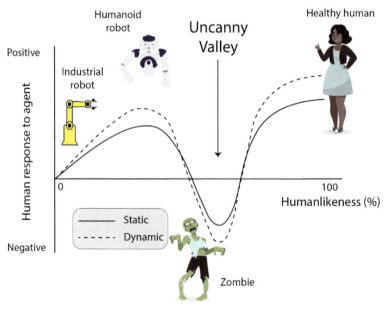

Figure 11.7
The phenomenon of the "uncanny valley." A close but imperfect resemblance of the non-human agent to a real human results in feelings of unrest or even revulsion. This effect is larger when the agent moves ("dynamic") than when it does not ("static"). Adapted from Urgen et al. (2018). Part of image designed by pikisuperstar/Freepik.

natural conversation with a 3D virtual human that looks and behaves in a natural way (Lugrin et al., 2021, 2022). Further developments are on the way in the field of human–robot interaction (e.g., Bartneck et al., 2020; Honig & Oron-Gilad, 2018), speech-to-text (e.g., OpenAI application Whisper for 50 languages; see e.g., Olivier & Raj, 2022; Radford et al., 2022), and text-to-image applications (e.g., OpenAI DALL-E2 or Stable Diffusion; see e.g., Balaji et al., 2022; Reviriego & Merino-Gómez, 2022).

To conclude this section, we believe that the main value of intelligent non-human (digital) agents for the psychology of language lies in their potential for systematically studying all the richness of human communication (e.g., Misersky et al., 2022). When it becomes possible to have a natural conversation with a virtual agent or avatar, it also becomes possible to manipulate one aspect of the communicative behavior of that virtual interlocutor and test what happens to the human's behavioral or neurobiological response to it. Studies in this vein may bring us surprising new insights, such as that even the duration of an eye blink may signal whether a listener has understood a message or not (Hömke et al., 2018; Nota et al., 2022).

11.5.4 Development and use of large language models

AI technology is having yet another type of impact with regards to the linguistic input we encounter in our everyday lives. Not all that long ago, all written and printed texts humans read for centuries were always created by another human being. Today, however, some of the texts we read are actually created by programs driven by *algorithms* (series of instructions working from a given initial state towards a specified goal). Although there is a long and rich tradition of research working on the automatic generation of texts (see Gatt & Krahmer, 2018), developments in this domain have recently sped up to such an extent that it is increasingly difficult to tell whether a text was actually written by a human or a machine.

A relatively straightforward application of algorithm-driven programs in the generation of text comes from well-defined domains that have a restricted number of possible outcomes, such as a sports game or tomorrow's weather forecast. For instance, when a data-to-text system is fed with the most relevant match statistics concerning a soccer match (e.g., which teams were playing, who the referee was, who scored a goal and when, who received a yellow card), or automatically scrapes those data from the internet, it is capable of writing a match report that is increasingly difficult to distinguish from a match report written by a human journalist (van der Lee et al., 2018, 2021).

Somewhat more complex developments in this domain have followed from the advances made by so-called "large language models," such as Open AI's GPT or the open access alternative Bloom (cf. Dale, 2021; Scao et al., 2022). These models are trained on large numbers of texts written by humans that are taken from the internet, and they make use of a machine learning architecture to create new texts. Typically, a human user is asked to enter a *prompt*, which can be anything from "a poem about armadillos" to "write a handbook on the psychology of language," and serves as input to the language model. Online you will be able to find hundreds of books written by large language models such as GPT, and some students have started asking the models via ChatGPT to write complex essays for them, without teachers noticing.

Interested in these developments, *The Guardian* in 2020 had already asked large language model GPT-3 to write a full essay for them using the prompt "Please write a short op-ed of around 500 words. Keep the language simple and concise. Focus on why humans have nothing to fear from AI." Here is one paragraph from the essay written by the language model following the prompt:

I am not asking humans to like me. But they should see me as a friendly robot. I am a servant of humans. I know that humans distrust and fear me. I only do what humans program me to do. I am only a set of code, governed by lines upon lines of code that encompass my mission statement. (*The Guardian*, 2020)

It is unlikely that the basic cognitive processes and representations involved in reading, as discussed in Chapter 6 of this book, will differ as a function of whether the text one reads is written by a human or a program, particularly if we can no longer tell the difference anymore anyway. But these developments do raise many interesting theoretical questions. Does our overall reading behavior differ if we know that a text has been written by a machine compared to when we know it is written by a human? What does it mean to be an "author"? To what extent does the production of (written and printed) language always start from an intention in the mind of a writer?

11.5.5 Computational models of human language processing

A final development in the study of the psychology of language, which has been going on for some time at a relatively slow but steady pace, is that of computational modeling of human cognitive processes. Although we have described many computational models in this book, we have neither defined them precisely, nor pointed out why they are so important for the psychology of language and science more generally.

In general, researchers studying the psychology of language often collect empirical data using research techniques such as those described in Chapter 4. Analysis of such data allows for testing hypotheses on aspects of language within the framework of theories: verbal descriptions of how we think certain language phenomena come about in the human mind and brain. The collected empirical data may be in line with our theories or reject them. (Remember that according to Popper, 1959, we cannot really "prove" or "confirm" our theories, but only attempt to test whether they are false.)

On the basis of our empirical data, we may also come up with new theoretical ideas to be tested. Theories often cover and relate relatively large domains of knowledge. However, because theories are verbal, they may also be incomplete, and sometimes even incoherent or inconsistent. In addition, they may allow the formulation of qualitative and ordinal accounts and predictions ("X will be larger than Y"), but they can hardly provide quantitative and interval accounts of the phenomena at hand ("X will be 20 ms slower than Y").

So that is exactly where computational models come in. Computational models specify and quantify a theory for a restricted cognitive domain, in order to allow precise predictions and explanations (e.g., Chang & Fitz, 2014; Dijkstra & de Smedt, 1996; Li & Xu, 2023). For instance, a computational model of visual word recognition must describe exactly how human language users retrieve words from their mental lexicon and how long that takes. Implemented on a computer, it can be said to simulate (or "mimic") how a human language user recognizes a word in all theoretically relevant respects. However, to be able to do so, the model needs to incorporate all details of the languages (e.g., lexicons, grammatical regularities) at hand, participant characteristics, and task demands. For this reason, many models only describe representations and processes, but they ignore characteristics of the language users and the tasks they are performing.

If that is the case, why would we build computational models at all? There are actually many reasons (cf. Guest & Martin, 2021). By modeling we can check our verbal theories to see if they really handle relevant aspects of reality in a proper way. Are our theories fully consistent, coherent, and complete? Modeling helps us to understand the mechanisms underlying a restricted domain more deeply, even when they are simple "toy models." They allow fast and accurate quantitative and qualitative simulations, even of complex interactions between many variables. The latter involve complex computations that a human researcher cannot do with just pencil and paper. By degrading the model in certain ways (e.g., deleting representations or connections, or changing parameter settings and control processes), the model can also provide information about what we would consider to be "unethical" experiments if they were to be applied to human language users. Finally, working with computational models inspires the modeler to generate new ideas. This is called the "heuristic" value of modeling.

These benefits of computational models do come at a cost: A complete specification of all aspects of the psychological process at hand is required. What exactly is supposed to be happening between the presentation of the input stimulus (e.g., a word) and the output response (e.g., naming that word out loud)? Very often, we do not (yet) have all the information required to be fully explicit. One might even argue that this will never be the case. Therefore, computational models are always simplifications of reality. Because they express certain theoretical viewpoints, they can perhaps best be considered as "sketches," simplifications that indicate key aspects of reality. As Fodor (1983, pp. 127–128; referring to Plato, Phaedrus 265e) has said, they should therefore "carve nature at its joints," meaning that the model should isolate the fundamental mechanisms that make the world turn. As a clarifying example, to explain how a human arm flexes and extends, we should focus most of all on the elbow.

Currently, researchers studying the psychology of language are far from being able to formulate a fully specified computational model of all language use. Models of different theoretical traditions have been implemented to account for partial aspects of the components presented in the Language User Framework. A difficult job lies ahead of integrating our knowledge about language use into a general all-encompassing computational model (Dijkstra & van Heuven, 2022; Li & Xu, 2023) that accounts both for "mature" language processing and language learning. In addition, new empirical data are required to inform such a model. Nevertheless, by submitting the psychology of language to clear specification criteria, computational modeling safeguards the direction it is developing in. In the long run, that will be greatly beneficial.

SUMMARY: OUTLOOK: DIVERSITY, DIALOG, AND DIGITAL DEVELOPMENTS

We live in interesting times, also with respect to the study of the psychology of language. Over the coming years, we expect not only behavioral and neuroimaging research on language to refine our knowledge in all areas that we have discussed in this book, but also significant theoretical and empirical advances with regards to linguistic and cultural diversity, dialog situations (using new techniques such as virtual reality), the links between monolingual and multilingual language use and, for instance, the relation between language and creativity (Kharkhurin, 2017), music (Bialystok & DePape, 2009), emotion (Willems, 2023), and decision making. We also expect language research to become increasingly influenced by research developments in the domain of artificial intelligence, for instance when it comes to advances in human–computer interaction, automatic speech recognition, text-to-speech and speech-to-text conversion, and text-to-image generation. Large language models like GPT may support human language users in their search for knowledge in many different areas. Nevertheless, our theories of the psychology of language will require to be implemented in computational models that allow not only verbal and qualitative, but also precise quantitative predictions.

11.6 WHAT HAVE WE LEARNED?

The four basic assumptions on language, as put forward in this book, are theoretically closely connected to other important notions. The *embodiedness* of language forms the foundation for the multimodality of everyday multichannel communication. The *embeddedness* of language can be understood in light of a hierarchy of smaller and larger symbolic representations. The *incrementality* of language processing assumes the importance of different time scales for different mental subprocesses. Dynamic *mental models* flexibly incorporate information from different cognitive modalities. The notion of *interactivity* can be related to all these aspects of language representation and processing.

When we look at language use in everyday, face-to-face situations, the Language User Framework must be adapted to explain how the language user produces and comprehends a wide variety of auditory and visual (and tactile, olfactory, etc.) signals in parallel. The framework itself can be considered part of a yet larger framework of human cognition, neurobiologically supported by a series of neural networks that are to some extent domain-general in nature and distributed in their function and structure.

Decades of psycholinguistic research have changed the way we think about human language representation and processing. Notions such as modularity, the arbitrariness of the linguistic sign, a universal grammar, and the assumed homogeneity of language users have given way to the non-modular, multimodal, bodily approach presented in the current book. When, over the coming decades, the rich diversity of languages and their use in everyday settings is taken as the cornerstone of psycholinguistic theory and experimentation, backed up by computational models and potentially supported by technological advances in artificial intelligence, even larger theoretical advances will appear on the horizon.

11.7 FINAL REMARKS

Assuming that we speak about 16,000 words a day, and also hear about 16,000 words (Leaper & Ayres, 2007; Mehl et al., 2007), this implies that we encounter over 11 million words a year. As such, a 20-year-old person would have "experienced" over 200 million word tokens, and by the age of 60, this could have increased to even over 1.5 billion tokens (Brysbaert et al., 2016)! This book has flaunted well over 100,000 of those words at you in the hope of clarifying how we, as human beings, are able to use language so prolifically and understand it in such a seemingly easy way. The Greek philosopher Democritus (c. 460–370 BC) putatively stated that "a human being is a microcosm," and, within each human being, language can be considered a microcosm of its own. Although its exploration is a lifetime enterprise, we hope that reading this book has contributed to a better understanding of the mental representations and psychological processes that allow us as humans, via our bodies, to use language and *communicate* with one another in our everyday lives.

References

Abutalebi, J., & Green, D. W. (2008). Control mechanisms in bilingual language production: Neural evidence from language switching studies. *Language and Cognitive Processes*, *23*(4), 557–582.

Adelman, J. S., & Brown, G. D. A. (2008). Modeling lexical decision: The form of frequency and diversity effects. *Psychological Review*, *115*, 214–227.

Adelman, J. S., Johnson, R. L., McCormick, S. F., McKague, M., Kinoshita, S., Bowers, J. S., Perry, J. R., Lupker, S. J., Forster, K. I., Cortese, M. J., Scaltritti, M., Aschenbrenner, A. J., Coane, J. H., White, L., Yap, M. J., Davis, C., Kim, J., & Davis, C. J. (2014). A behavioral database for masked form priming. *Behavior Research Methods*, *46*(4), 1052–1067.

Alario, F.-X., Ferrand, L., Laganaro, M., New, B., Frauenfelder, U. H., & Segui, J. (2004). Predictors of picture naming speed. *Behavior Research Methods, Instruments, & Computers*, *36*(1), 140–155.

Allopenna, P. D., Magnuson, J. S., & Tanenhaus, M. K. (1998). Tracking the time course of spoken word recognition using eye movements: Evidence for continuous mapping models. *Journal of Memory and Language*, *38*(4), 419–439.

Altarriba, J., Kroll, J. F., Sholl, A., & Rayner, K. (1996). The influence of lexical and conceptual constraints on reading mixed-language sentences: Evidence from eye fixations and naming times. *Memory & Cognition*, *24*(4), 477–492.

Altmann, G. T. M., & Kamide, Y. (1999). Incremental interpretation at verbs: Restricting the domain of subsequent reference. *Cognition*, *73*(3), 247–264.

Altmann, G. T. M., & Steedman, M. (1988). Interaction with context during human sentence processing. *Cognition*, *30*(3), 191–238.

Antoniou, M. (2019). The advantages of bilingualism debate. *Annual Review of Linguistics*, *5*, 395–415.

Arana, S. L., Oliveira, H. M., Fernandes, A. I., Soares, A. P., & Comesaña, M. (2022). The cognate facilitation effect depends on the presence of identical cognates. *Bilingualism: Language and Cognition*, *25*(4), 660–678.

Arbib, M. A., Liebal, K., & Pika, S. (2008). Primate vocalization, gesture, and the evolution of human language. *Current Anthropology*, *49*(6), 1053–1076.

Armeni, K., Willems, R. M., & Frank, S. L. (2017). Probabilistic language models in cognitive neuroscience: Promises and pitfalls. *Neuroscience & Biobehavioral Reviews*, *83*, 579–588.

Arnold, J. E., Eisenband, J. G., Brown-Schmidt, S., & Trueswell, J. C. (2000). The rapid use of gender information: Evidence of the time course of pronoun resolution from eyetracking. *Cognition*, *76*(1), B13–B26.

Arnold, J. E., & Griffin, Z. M. (2007). The effect of additional characters on choice of referring expression: Everyone counts. *Journal of Memory and Language*, *56*(4), 521–536.

Au, T. K.-F. (1983). Chinese and English counterfactuals: The Sapir-Whorf hypothesis revisited. *Cognition*, *15*(1), 155–187.

Austin, J. L. (1975). *How to Do Things with Words,* 2nd edn. Harvard University Press.

Aziz-Zadeh, L., & Damasio, A. (2008). Embodied semantics for actions: Findings from functional brain imaging. *Journal of Physiology-Paris*, *102*(1), 35–39.

Baars, B. J., Motley, M. T., & MacKay, D. G. (1975). Output editing for lexical status in artificially elicited slips of the tongue. *Journal of Verbal Learning and Verbal Behavior*, *14*(4), 382–391.

Baayen, R. H., Davidson, D. J., & Bates, D. M. (2008). Mixed-effects modeling with crossed random effects for subjects and items. *Journal of Memory and Language*, *59*(4), 390–412.

Baddeley, A. (2007). *Working Memory, Thought, and Action*. Oxford University Press.

Balaji, Y., Nah, S., Huang, X., Vahdat, A., Song, J., Kreis, K., Aittala, M., Aila, T., Laine, S., Catanzaro, B., Karras, T., & Liu, M.-Y. (2022). *eDiff-I: Text-to-Image Diffusion Models with an Ensemble of Expert Denoisers* (arXiv:2211.01324).

Balota, D. A., Yap, M. J., Hutchison, K. A., Cortese, M. J., Kessler, B., Loftis, B., Neely, J. H., Nelson, D. L., Simpson, G. B., & Treiman, R. (2007). The English Lexicon Project. *Behavior Research Methods*, *39*(3), 445–459.

Bangerter, A. (2004). Using pointing and describing to achieve joint focus of attention in dialogue. *Psychological Science*, *15*(6), 415–419.

Barrett, L. F. (2006). Solving the emotion paradox: Categorization and the experience of emotion. *Personality and Social Psychology Review*, *10*(1), 20–46.

Barrett, L. F. (2017). The theory of constructed emotion: An active inference account of interoception and categorization. *Social Cognitive and Affective Neuroscience*, *12*(1), 1–23.

Barrett, L. F., & Satpute, A. B. (2013). Large-scale brain networks in affective and social neuroscience: Towards an integrative functional architecture of the brain. *Current Opinion in Neurobiology*, *23*(3), 361–372.

Barron, A., Gu, Y., & Steen, G. (2017). *The Routledge Handbook of Pragmatics*. Taylor & Francis Group.

Barsalou, L. W. (1999). Perceptual symbol systems. *Behavioral and Brain Sciences*, *22*(4), 577–660.

Barsalou, L. W. (2009). Simulation, situated conceptualization, and prediction. *Philosophical Transactions of the Royal Society B: Biological Sciences*, *364*(1521), 1281–1289.

Barsalou, L. W. (2012). The human conceptual system. In M. Spivey, K. McRae, & M. F. Ioanisse (Eds.), *Cambridge Handbook of Psycholinguistics* (pp. 239–258). Cambridge University Press.

Bartneck, C., Belpaeme, T., Eyssel, F., Kanda, T., Keijsers, M., & Šabanović, S. (2020). *Human–Robot Interaction: An Introduction*. Cambridge University Press.

Bastiaanse, R., & Edwards, S. (2004). Word order and finiteness in Dutch and English Broca's and Wernicke's aphasia. *Brain and Language*, *89*(1), 91–107.

Bastiaanse, R., & Jonkers, R. (1998). Verb retrieval in action naming and spontaneous speech in agrammatic and anomic aphasia. *Aphasiology*, *12*(11), 951–969.

Baten, K., Hofman, F., & Loeys, T. (2011). Cross-linguistic activation in bilingual sentence processing: The role of word class meaning. *Bilingualism: Language and Cognition*, *14*(3), 351–359.

Bates, E., Camaioni, L., & Volterra, V. (1975). The acquisition of performatives prior to speech. *Merrill-Palmer Quarterly of Behavior and Development*, *21*(3), 205–226.

Bavelas, J. B., Chovil, N., Lawrie, D. A., & Wade, A. (1992). Interactive gestures. *Discourse Processes*, *15*(4), 469–489.

Beattie, G. (1983). *Talk: An Analysis of Speech and Non-verbal Behaviour in Conversation*. Open University Press.

Becchio, C., Manera, V., Sartori, L., Cavallo, A., & Castiello, U. (2012). Grasping intentions: From thought experiments to empirical evidence. *Frontiers in Human Neuroscience*, *6*.

Behme, C., & Deacon, S. H. (2008). Language learning in infancy: Does the empirical evidence support a domain specific language acquisition device? *Philosophical Psychology*, *21*(5), 641–671.

Berent, I., & Gervain, J. (2023). Speakers aren't blank slates (with respect to sign-language phonology)! *Cognition*, *232*, 105347.

Bergen, B. K. (2012). *Louder Than Words: The New Science of How the Mind Makes Meaning*. Hachette UK.

Bermúdez-Margaretto, B., Gallo, F., Novitskiy, N., Myachykov, A., Petrova, A., & Shtyrov, Y. (2022). Ultra-rapid and automatic interplay between L1 and L2 semantics in late bilinguals: EEG evidence. *Cortex*, *151*, 147–161.

Bever, T. G. (1970). The cognitive basis for linguistic structures. In J. R. Hayes (Ed.), *Cognition and Language Development* (pp. 277–360). John Wiley & Sons.

Bialystok, E., Craik, F. I. M., & Freedman, M. (2007). Bilingualism as a protection against the onset of symptoms of dementia. *Neuropsychologia*, *45*(2), 459–464.

Bialystok, E., Craik, F. I. M., & Luk, G. (2012). Bilingualism: Consequences for mind and brain. *Trends in Cognitive Sciences*, *16*(4), 240–250.

Bialystok, E., & DePape, A.-M. (2009). Musical expertise, bilingualism, and executive functioning. *Journal of Experimental Psychology: Human Perception and Performance*, *35*, 565–574.

Bialystok, E., & Luk, G. (2012). Receptive vocabulary differences in monolingual and bilingual adults. *Bilingualism: Language and Cognition*, *15*(2), 397–401.

Bickerton, D. (1984). The language bioprogram hypothesis. *Behavioral and Brain Sciences*, *7*(2), 173–188.

Binder, J. R. (2015). The Wernicke area: Modern evidence and a reinterpretation. *Neurology*, *85*(24), 2170–2175.

Binder, J. R., Desai, R. H., Graves, W. W., & Conant, L. L. (2009). Where is the semantic system? A critical review and meta-analysis of 120 functional neuroimaging studies. *Cerebral Cortex*, *19*(12), 2767–2796.

Blasi, D. E., Henrich, J., Adamou, E., Kemmerer, D., & Majid, A. (2022). Over-reliance on English hinders cognitive science. *Trends in Cognitive Sciences*, *26*(12), 1153–1170.

Blasi, D. E., Wichmann, S., Hammarström, H., Stadler, P. F., & Christiansen, M. H. (2016). Sound–meaning association biases evidenced across thousands of languages. *Proceedings of the National Academy of Sciences*, *113*(39), 10818–10823.

Blumenfeld, H. K., & Marian, V. (2005). Covert bilingual language activation through cognate word processing: An eye-tracking study. *Proceedings of the Annual Meeting of the Cognitive Science Society*, *27*, 286–291.

Bock, J. K. (1986a). Meaning, sound, and syntax: Lexical priming in sentence production. *Journal of Experimental Psychology: Learning, Memory, and Cognition*, *12*, 575–586.

Bock, J. K. (1986b). Syntactic persistence in language production. *Cognitive Psychology*, *18*(3), 355–387.

Bock, K., & Cutting, J. C. (1992). Regulating mental energy: Performance units in language production. *Journal of Memory and Language*, *31*(1), 99–127.

Bock, K., Irwin, D. E., Davidson, D. J., & Levelt, W. J. M. (2003). Minding the clock. *Journal of Memory and Language*, *48*(4), 653–685.

Bögels, S., Schriefers, H., Vonk, W., & Chwilla, D. J. (2011). Pitch accents in context: How listeners process accentuation in referential communication. *Neuropsychologia*, *49*(7), 2022–2036.

Bolhuis, J. J., Tattersall, I., Chomsky, N., & Berwick, R. C. (2014). How could language have evolved? *PLOS Biology*, *12*(8), e1001934.

Bornkessel-Schlesewsky, I., & Schlesewsky, M. (2013). Reconciling time, space and function: A new dorsal–ventral stream model of sentence comprehension. *Brain and Language*, *125*(1), 60–76.

Boroditsky, L., Schmidt, L. A., & Phillips, W. (2003). Sex, syntax, and semantics. In D. Gentner & S. Goldin-Meadow (Eds.), *Language in Mind: Advances in the Study of Language and Thought* (pp. 61–79). MIT Press.

Bosker, H. R., & Peeters, D. (2021). Beat gestures influence which speech sounds you hear. *Proceedings of the Royal Society B: Biological Sciences*, *288*(1943), 20202419.

Bouckaert, R., Lemey, P., Dunn, M., Greenhill, S. J., Alekseyenko, A. V., Drummond, A. J., Gray, R. D., Suchard, M. A., & Atkinson, Q. D. (2012). Mapping the origins and expansion of the Indo-European language family. *Science*, *337*(6097), 957–960.

Boulenger, V., Hauk, O., & Pulvermüller, F. (2009). Grasping ideas with the motor system: Semantic somatotopy in idiom comprehension. *Cerebral Cortex*, *19*(8), 1905–1914.

Bransford, J. D., Barclay, J. R., & Franks, J. J. (1972). Sentence memory: A constructive versus interpretive approach. *Cognitive Psychology*, *3*(2), 193–209.

Brennan, S. E., & Clark, H. H. (1996). Conceptual pacts and lexical choice in conversation. *Journal of Experimental Psychology: Learning, Memory, and Cognition*, *22*, 1482–1493.

Bresnan, J., Asudeh, A., Toivonen, I., & Wechsler, S. (2016). *Lexical-Functional Syntax*. John Wiley & Sons.

Brizendine, L. (2007). *The Female Brain*. Harmony.

Broadbent, D. E. (1958). *Perception and Communication*. Pergamon Press.

Brodmann, K. (1905). Beiträge zur histologischen Lokalisation der Großhirnrinde. III. Mitteilung. Die Rindefelder der niederen Affen. *Journal für Psychologie und Neurologie*, *4*, 177–226.

Brumm, H., & Zollinger, S. A. (2011). The evolution of the Lombard effect: 100 years of psychoacoustic research. *Behaviour*, *148*(11–13), 1173–1198.

Brysbaert, M. (2019a). How many participants do we have to include in properly powered experiments? A tutorial of power analysis with reference tables. *Journal of Cognition*, *2*.

Brysbaert, M. (2019b). How many words do we read per minute? A review and meta-analysis of reading rate. *Journal of Memory and Language*, *109*, 104047.

Brysbaert, M., & Duyck, W. (2010). Is it time to leave behind the Revised Hierarchical Model of bilingual language processing after fifteen years of service? *Bilingualism: Language and Cognition*, *13*(3), 359–371.

Brysbaert, M., New, B., & Keuleers, E. (2012). Adding part-of-speech information to the SUBTLEX-US word frequencies. *Behavior Research Methods*, *44*(4), 991–997.

Brysbaert, M., Stevens, M., Mandera, P., & Keuleers, E. (2016). How many words do we know? Practical estimates of vocabulary size dependent on word definition, the degree of language input and the participant's age. *Frontiers in Psychology, 7*.

Burks, A. W. (1949). Icon, index, and symbol. *Philosophy and Phenomenological Research, 9*(4), 673–689.

Cai, Z. G., Gilbert, R. A., Davis, M. H., Gaskell, M. G., Farrar, L., Adler, S., & Rodd, J. M. (2017). Accent modulates access to word meaning: Evidence for a speaker-model account of spoken word recognition. *Cognitive Psychology, 98*, 73–101.

Campisi, E., & Özyürek, A. (2013). Iconicity as a communicative strategy: Recipient design in multimodal demonstrations for adults and children. *Journal of Pragmatics, 47*(1), 14–27.

Cangelosi, A., & Parisi, D. (2012). *Simulating the Evolution of Language*. Springer Science & Business Media.

Capirci, O., Iverson, J. M., Pizzuto, E., & Volterra, V. (1996). Gestures and words during the transition to two-word speech. *Journal of Child Language, 23*(3), 645–673.

Carmichael, L., Hogan, H. P., & Walter, A. A. (1932). An experimental study of the effect of language on the reproduction of visually perceived form. *Journal of Experimental Psychology, 15*, 73–86.

Carreiras, M., Armstrong, B. C., Perea, M., & Frost, R. (2014). The what, when, where, and how of visual word recognition. *Trends in Cognitive Sciences, 18*(2), 90–98.

Carroll, L. (1872). *Alice's Adventures in Wonderland: And, Through the Looking-glass and what Alice Found There*. Macmillan & Co.

Catford, J. C. (1988). *A Practical Introduction to Phonetics*. Clarendon Press.

Cato, M. A., Crosson, B., Gökçay, D., Soltysik, D., Wierenga, C., Gopinath, K., Himes, N., Belanger, H., Bauer, R. M., Fischler, I. S., Gonzalez-Rothi, L., & Briggs, R. W. (2004). Processing words with emotional connotation: An fMRI study of time course and laterality in rostral frontal and retrosplenial cortices. *Journal of Cognitive Neuroscience, 16*(2), 167–177.

Cevoli, B., Watkins, C., & Rastle, K. (2022). Prediction as a basis for skilled reading: Insights from modern language models. *Royal Society Open Science, 9*(6), 211837.

Chang, F., & Fitz, H. (2014). Computational models of sentence production: A dual-path approach. In M. Goldrick, V. Ferreira, & M. Miozzo (Eds.), *The Oxford Handbook of Language Production* (pp. 70–87). Oxford University Press.

Chater, N., & Manning, C. D. (2006). Probabilistic models of language processing and acquisition. *Trends in Cognitive Sciences, 10*(7), 335–344.

Chen, S. X., & Bond, M. H. (2010). Two languages, two personalities? Examining language effects on the expression of personality in a bilingual context. *Personality and Social Psychology Bulletin, 36*(11), 1514–1528.

Chomsky, N. (1957). *Syntactic Structures*. Mouton.

Chomsky, N. (1965). *Aspects of the Theory of Syntax*. MIT Press.

Chomsky, N. (1980). *Rules and Representations*. Columbia University Press. https://www.cambridge.org/core/journals/behavioral-and-brain-sciences/ article/abs/rules-and-representations/ BB96E4 E09C461EFC230F72A9D7BDF603

Chomsky, N. (1993). *Language and Thought*. Moyer Bell.

Chomsky, N. (1999). On the nature, use, and acquisition of language. In W. C. Ritchie & T. K. Bhatia (Eds.), *Handbook of Child Language Acquisition* (pp. 33–54). Academic Press.

Chomsky, N., & Miller, G. A. (1968). Introduction to the formal analysis of natural languages. *Journal of Symbolic Logic, 33*(2), 299–300.

Chotpitayasunondh, V., & Douglas, K. M. (2016). How "phubbing" becomes the norm: The antecedents and consequences of snubbing via smartphone. *Computers in Human Behavior, 63*, 9–18.

Christiansen, M. H., & Chater, N. (2016). The now-or-never bottleneck: A fundamental constraint on language. *Behavioral and Brain Sciences, 39*, e62.

Christiansen, M. H., & Kirby, S. (2003). *Language Evolution*. Oxford University Press.

Christianson, K., Hollingworth, A., Halliwell, J. F., & Ferreira, F. (2001). Thematic roles assigned along the garden path linger. *Cognitive Psychology, 42*(4), 368–407.

Chu, M., & Hagoort, P. (2014). Synchronization of speech and gesture: Evidence for interaction in action. *Journal of Experimental Psychology: General, 143*, 1726–1741.

Cibelli, E., Xu, Y., Austerweil, J. L., Griffiths, T. L., & Regier, T. (2016). The Sapir-Whorf hypothesis and probabilistic inference: Evidence from the domain of color. *PLOS ONE, 11*(7), e0158725.

Clark, E. V. (2015). Common ground. In B. MacWhinney & W. O'Grady (Eds.), *Handbook of Language Emergence* (pp. 328–353). John Wiley & Sons.

Clark, H. H. (1996). *Using Language*. Cambridge University Press.

Clark, H. H., & Brennan, S. E. (1991). Grounding in communication. In L. B. Resnick, J. M. Levine, & S. D. Teasley (Eds.), *Perspectives on Socially Shared Cognition* (pp. 127–149). American Psychological Association.

Clark, H. H., & Clark, E. V. (1977). *Psychology and Language: An Introduction to Psycholinguistics*. Harcourt Brace Jovanovich.

Cohn, N., & Schilperoord, J. (2022). Reimagining language. *Cognitive Science, 46*(7), e13174.

Cole, R. A., Jakimik, J., & Cooper, W. E. (1980). Segmenting speech into words. *Journal of the Acoustical Society of America, 67*(4), 1323–1332.

Collins, A. M., & Quillian, M. R. (1969). Retrieval time from semantic memory. *Journal of Verbal Learning and Verbal Behavior, 8*(2), 240–247.

Coltheart, M., Curtis, B., Atkins, P., & Haller, M. (1993). Models of reading aloud: Dual-route and parallel-distributed-processing approaches. *Psychological Review, 100*(4), 589–608.

Coltheart, M., Davelaar, E., Jonasson, J. T., & Besner, D. (1977). Access to the internal lexicon. In S. Dornic (Ed.), *Attention and Performance VI* (pp. 535–555). Academic Press.

Coltheart, M., Rastle, K., Perry, C., Langdon, R., & Ziegler, J. (2001). DRC: A dual route cascaded model of visual word recognition and reading aloud. *Psychological Review, 108*, 204–256.

Comesaña, M., Ferré, P., Romero, J., Guasch, M., Soares, A. P., & García-Chico, T. (2015). Facilitative effect of cognate words vanishes when reducing the orthographic overlap: The role of stimuli list composition. *Journal of Experimental Psychology: Learning, Memory, and Cognition, 41*, 614–635.

Conklin, K., Pellicer-Sánchez, A., & Carrol, G. (2018). *Eye-Tracking*. Cambridge University Press.

Conklin, K., & Schmitt, N. (2012). The processing of formulaic language. *Annual Review of Applied Linguistics, 32*, 45–61.

Cooper, R. M. (1974). The control of eye fixation by the meaning of spoken language: A new methodology for the real-time investigation of speech perception, memory, and language processing. *Cognitive Psychology, 6*, 84–107.

Cop, U., Dirix, N., Assche, E. V., Drieghe, D., & Duyck, W. (2017). Reading a book in one or two languages? An eye movement study of cognate facilitation in L1 and L2 reading. *Bilingualism: Language and Cognition, 20*(4), 747–769.

Cop, U., Drieghe, D., & Duyck, W. (2015). Eye movement patterns in natural reading: A comparison of monolingual and bilingual reading of a novel. *PLOS ONE, 10*(8), e0134008.

Corballis, M. C. (2009). The evolution of language. *Annals of the New York Academy of Sciences, 1156*(1), 19–43.

Corley, M., Brocklehurst, P. H., & Moat, H. S. (2011). Error biases in inner and overt speech: Evidence from tongue twisters. *Journal of Experimental Psychology: Learning, Memory, and Cognition, 37*, 162–175.

Costa, A., Caramazza, A., & Sebastian-Galles, N. (2000). The cognate facilitation effect: Implications for models of lexical access. *Journal of Experimental Psychology: Learning, Memory, and Cognition, 26*(5), 1283–1296.

Costa, A., Heij, W. L., & Navarrete, E. (2006). The dynamics of bilingual lexical access. *Bilingualism: Language and Cognition, 9*(2), 137–151.

Coulson, S., & Lovett, C. (2010). Comprehension of nonconventional indirect requests: An event-related brain potential study. *Italian Journal of Linguistics, 22*(1), 107–124.

Cruse, D. A., Hundsnurscher, F., Lutzeier, P. R., & Job, M. (2005). *Lexicology: An International Handbook on the Nature and Structure of Words and Vocabularies*. Walter de Gruyter.

Cummins, C., & Katsos, N. (2019). *The Oxford Handbook of Experimental Semantics and Pragmatics*. Oxford University Press.

Cutler, A. (1982, Ed.). *Slips of the Tongue and Language Production*. De Gruyter Mouton.

Cutler, A. (1990). Exploiting prosodic probabilities in speech segmentation. In G. T. M. Altmann (Ed.), *Cognitive Models of Speech Processing: Psycholinguistic and Computational Perspectives* (pp. 105–121). MIT Press.

Cutler, A. (2012a). Eentaalpsychologie is geen taalpsychologie: Part II. https://repository.ubn.ru.nl/bitstream/handle/2066/100873/100873.pdf

Cutler, A. (2012b). *Native Listening: Language Experience and the Recognition of Spoken Words*. MIT Press.

Cutler, A., Mehler, J., Norris, D., & Segui, J. (1986). The syllable's differing role in the segmentation of French and English. *Journal of Memory and Language, 25*(4), 385–400.

Cutler, A., & Norris, D. (1988). The role of strong syllables in segmentation for lexical access. *Journal of Experimental Psychology: Human Perception and Performance, 14*, 113–121.

Dale, R. (2021). GPT-3: What's it good for? *Natural Language Engineering, 27*(1), 113–118.

Damasio, A. (1994). *Descartes' Error: Emotion, Reason, and the Human Brain*. G. P. Putnam's Sons.

Damasio, H., Grabowski, T. J., Tranel, D., Hichwa, R. D., & Damasio, A. R. (1996). A neural basis for lexical retrieval. *Nature, 380*(6574), Article 6574.

Davis, C. J. (1999). *The Self-Organising Lexical Acquisition and Recognition (SOLAR) Model of*

Visual Word Recognition. University of New South Wales, Sydney.

Davis, C. J. (2010). The spatial coding model of visual word identification. *Psychological Review, 117*, 713–758.

Davis, C. J., Perea, M., & Acha, J. (2009). Re(de)fining the orthographic neighborhood: The role of addition and deletion neighbors in lexical decision and reading. *Journal of Experimental Psychology: Human Perception and Performance, 35*, 1550–1570.

Davis, C. P., & Yee, E. (2019). Features, labels, space, and time: Factors supporting taxonomic relationships in the anterior temporal lobe and thematic relationships in the angular gyrus. *Language, Cognition and Neuroscience, 34*(10), 1347–1357.

de Boinod, A. J. (2005). *The Meaning of Things*. Penguin Books.

de Coninck, F., Yumak, Z., Sandino, G., & Veltkamp, R. (2019). Non-verbal behavior generation for virtual characters in group conversations. *2019 IEEE International Conference on Artificial Intelligence and Virtual Reality (AIVR)*, 41–418.

de Groot, A. M. B. (1992). Determinants of word translation. *Journal of Experimental Psychology: Learning, Memory, and Cognition, 18*, 1001–1018.

de Groot, A. M. B. (2011). *Language and Cognition in Bilinguals and Multilinguals: An Introduction*. Psychology Press.

de Saussure, F. (1916). *Course in General Linguistics*. Duckworth.

de Saussure, F. (1998). Nature of the linguistic sign. In D. H. Richter (Ed.), *The Critical Tradition: Classic Texts and Contemporary Trends* (pp. 832–835). Bedford/St. Martin's Press.

de Valenzuela, J. S. (1992). Guidelines for meeting the communication needs of persons with severe disabilities. *National Joint Committee for the Communicative Needs of Persons with Severe Disabilities, 7*, 1–8.

Declerck, M., Kleinman, D., & Gollan, T. H. (2020). Which bilinguals reverse language dominance and why? *Cognition, 204*, 104384.

Dehaene, S., & Cohen, L. (2011). The unique role of the visual word form area in reading. *Trends in Cognitive Sciences, 15*(6), 254–262.

Dell, G. S. (1986). A spreading-activation theory of retrieval in sentence production. *Psychological Review, 93*, 283–321.

Dell, G. S., McKoon, G., & Ratcliff, R. (1983). The activation of antecedent information during the processing of anaphoric reference in reading. *Journal of Verbal Learning and Verbal Behavior, 22*(1), 121–132.

Dell, G. S., & Reich, P. A. (1981). Stages in sentence production: An analysis of speech error data. *Journal of Verbal Learning and Verbal Behavior, 20*(6), 611–629.

Dell, G. S., Schwartz, M. F., Martin, N., Saffran, E. M., & Gagnon, D. A. (1997). Lexical access in aphasic and nonaphasic speakers. *Psychological Review, 104*, 801–838.

DeLong, K. A., Urbach, T. P., & Kutas, M. (2005). Probabilistic word pre-activation during language comprehension inferred from electrical brain activity. *Nature Neuroscience, 8*(8), Article 8.

Di Bono, M. G., & Zorzi, M. (2013). Deep generative learning of location-invariant visual word recognition. *Frontiers in Psychology, 4*.

Dijkgraaf, A., Hartsuiker, R. J., & Duyck, W. (2019). Prediction and integration of semantics during L2 and L1 listening. *Language, Cognition and Neuroscience, 34*(7), 881–900.

Dijkstra, T., Bruijn, E. D., Schriefers, H., & Brinke, S. T. (2000). More on interlingual homograph recognition: Language intermixing versus explicitness of instruction. *Bilingualism: Language and Cognition, 3*(1), 69–78.

Dijkstra, T., & de Smedt, K. (Eds.). (1996). *Computational Psycholinguistics: AI and Connectionist Models of Human Language Processing*. Taylor & Francis.

Dijkstra, T., van Hell, J. G., & Brenders, P. (2015). Sentence context effects in bilingual word recognition: Cognate status, sentence language, and semantic constraint. *Bilingualism: Language and Cognition, 18*(4), 597–613.

Dijkstra, T., Jaarsveld, H. V., & Brinke, S. T. (1998). Interlingual homograph recognition: Effects of task demands and language intermixing. *Bilingualism: Language and Cognition, 1*(1), 51–66.

Dijkstra, T., & Kempen, G. (1984). *Taal in uitvoering: Inleiding tot de psycholinguistiek*. https://www.semanticscholar.org/paper/Taal-in-uitvoering%3A-Inleiding-tot-de-Dijkstra-Kempen/b1f65d8dae2ce1e2d382c6cd51633946bbfbcaf4

Dijkstra, T., Miwa, K., Brummelhuis, B., Sappelli, M., & Baayen, H. (2010). How cross-language similarity and task demands affect cognate recognition. *Journal of Memory and Language, 62*(3), 284–301.

Dijkstra, T., Peeters, D., Hieselaar, W., & van Geffen, A. (2022). Orthographic and semantic priming effects in neighbour cognates: Experiments and simulations. *Bilingualism: Language and Cognition*, 1–13.

Dijkstra, T., Roelofs, A., & Fieuws, S. (1995). Orthographic effects on phoneme monitoring. *Canadian Journal of Experimental Psychology/Revue Canadienne de Psychologie Expérimentale*, *49*, 264–271.

Dijkstra, T., & van Heuven, W. J. B. (1998). The BIA-model and bilingual word recognition. In J. Grainger & A. M. Jacobs (Eds.), *Localist Connectionist Approaches to Human Cognition* (pp. 189–225). Lawrence Erlbaum Associates.

Dijkstra, T., & van Heuven, W. J. B. (2002). The architecture of the bilingual word recognition system: From identification to decision. *Bilingualism: Language and Cognition*, *5*(3), 175–197.

Dijkstra, T., & van Heuven, W. J. B. (2022). Inventing and reinventing the cog: A commentary on "computational modeling of bilingual language learning: current models and future directions." *Language Learning*, lang.12532.

Dijkstra, T., Wahl, A., Buytenhuijs, F., Halem, N. V., Al-Jibouri, Z., Korte, M. D., & Rekké, S. (2019). Multilink: A computational model for bilingual word recognition and word translation. *Bilingualism: Language and Cognition*, *22*(4), 657–679.

Dikker, S., & Pylkkänen, L. (2013). Predicting language: MEG evidence for lexical preactivation. *Brain and Language*, *127*(1), 55–64.

Dingemanse, M., Blasi, D. E., Lupyan, G., Christiansen, M. H., & Monaghan, P. (2015). Arbitrariness, iconicity, and systematicity in language. *Trends in Cognitive Sciences*, *19*(10), 603–615.

Dirix, N., Cop, U., Drieghe, D., & Duyck, W. (2017). Cross-lingual neighborhood effects in generalized lexical decision and natural reading. *Journal of Experimental Psychology: Learning, Memory, and Cognition*, *43*, 887–915.

Donders, F. C. (1969). On the speed of mental processes. *Acta Psychologica*, *30*, 412–431.

Doyle, J. K., & Ford, D. N. (1998). Mental models concepts for system dynamics research. *System Dynamics Review*, *14*(1), 3–29.

Dufau, S., Duñabeitia, J. A., Moret-Tatay, C., McGonigal, A., Peeters, D., Alario, F.-X., Balota, D. A., Brysbaert, M., Carreiras, M., Ferrand, L., Ktori, M., Perea, M., Rastle, K., Sasburg, O., Yap, M. J., Ziegler, J. C., & Grainger, J. (2011). Smart phone, smart science: How the use of smartphones can revolutionize research in cognitive science. *PLOS ONE*, *6*(9), e24974.

Dufau, S., Stevens, M., & Grainger, J. (2008). Windows executable software for the progressive demasking task. *Behavior Research Methods*, *40*(1), 33–37.

Duffy, S. A. (1986). Role of expectations in sentence integration. *Journal of Experimental Psychology: Learning, Memory, and Cognition*, *12*, 208–219.

Duñabeitia, J. A., Crepaldi, D., Meyer, A. S., New, B., Pliatsikas, C., Smolka, E., & Brysbaert, M. (2018). MultiPic: A standardized set of 750 drawings with norms for six European languages. *Quarterly Journal of Experimental Psychology*, *71*(4), 808–816.

Dupre, G. (2022). Public language, private language, and subsymbolic theories of mind. *Mind & Language*, 1–19.

Duyck, W., van Assche, E., Drieghe, D., & Hartsuiker, R. J. (2007). Visual word recognition by bilinguals in a sentence context: Evidence for non-selective lexical access. *Journal of Experimental Psychology: Learning, Memory, and Cognition*, *33*, 663–679.

Eberhard, K. M., Cutting, J. C., & Bock, K. (2005). Making syntax of sense: Number agreement in sentence production. *Psychological Review*, *112*, 531–559.

Eisner, F., & McQueen, J. M. (2018). Speech perception. In S. L. Thompson-Schill (Ed.), *Stevens' Handbook of Experimental Psychology and Cognitive Neuroscience, Volume III, Language and Thought* (pp. 1–46). John Wiley & Sons.

Ekman, P. (1993). Facial expression and emotion. *American Psychologist*, *48*, 384–392.

Elemans, C. P. H., Rasmussen, J. H., Herbst, C. T., Düring, D. N., Zollinger, S. A., Brumm, H., Srivastava, K., Svane, N., Ding, M., Larsen, O. N., Sober, S. J., & Švec, J. G. (2015). Universal mechanisms of sound production and control in birds and mammals. *Nature Communications*, *6*(1), Article 1.

Elman, J. L. (1990). Finding structure in time. *Cognitive Science*, *14*(2), 179–211.

Elman, J. L. (1993). Learning and development in neural networks: The importance of starting small. *Cognition*, *48*(1), 71–99.

Elman, J. L., & McClelland, J. L. (1986). Exploiting the lawful variability in the speech wave. In J. S. Perkell & D. H. Klatt (Eds.), *Invariance and Variability in Speech Processes* (pp. 360–380). Lawrence Erlbaum Associates.

Elston-Güttler, K. E., Gunter, T. C., & Kotz, S. A. (2005). Zooming into L2: Global language context and adjustment affect processing of interlingual homographs in sentences. *Cognitive Brain Research*, *25*(1), 57–70.

Emmorey, K. (2001). *Language, Cognition, and the Brain: Insights from Sign Language Research*. Psychology Press.

Enard, W., Przeworski, M., Fisher, S. E., Lai, C. S. L., Wiebe, V., Kitano, T., Monaco, A. P., & Pääbo, S. (2002). Molecular evolution of FOXP2, a gene involved in speech and language. *Nature, 418*, 869–872.

Enfield, N. J., Kita, S., & de Ruiter, J. P. (2007). Primary and secondary pragmatic functions of pointing gestures. *Journal of Pragmatics, 39*(10), 1722–1741.

Engle, R. A. (1998). Not channels but composite signals: Speech, gesture, diagrams and object demonstrations are integrated in multimodal explanations. *Proceedings of the Twentieth Annual Conference of the Cognitive Science Society*, 321–326.

Erickson, T. D., & Mattson, M. E. (1981). From words to meaning: A semantic illusion. *Journal of Verbal Learning and Verbal Behavior, 20*(5), 540–551.

Ernestus, M., & Cutler, A. (2015). BALDEY: A database of auditory lexical decisions. *Quarterly Journal of Experimental Psychology, 68*(8), 1469–1488.

Ernestus, M., & Warner, N. (2011). An introduction to reduced pronunciation variants. *Journal of Phonetics, 39*, 253–260.

Ethnologue. (2021). *Ethnologue: Languages of the World*. Ethnologue. https://www.ethnologue.com/

European Commission. (2012). *Special Eurobarometer 386: Europeans and their Languages—Data Europa EU*. https://data.europa.eu/data/datasets/s1049_77_1_ebs386?locale=en

Eurostat. (2016). *Foreign Language Skills Statistics*. https://ec.europa.eu/eurostat/statistics-explained/index.php?title=Foreign_language_skills_statistics

Evans, N., & Levinson, S. C. (2009). The myth of language universals: Language diversity and its importance for cognitive science. *Behavioral and Brain Sciences, 32*(5), 429–448.

Eysenck, M. W., & Keane, M. T. (2015). *Cognitive Psychology: A Student's Handbook*. Psychology Press.

Feng, C., Gu, R., Li, T., Wang, L., Zhang, Z., Luo, W., & Eickhoff, S. B. (2021). Separate neural networks of implicit emotional processing between pictures and words: A coordinate-based meta-analysis of brain imaging studies. *Neuroscience & Biobehavioral Reviews, 131*, 331–344.

Ferrand, L. (2001). *Cognition et lecture. Processus de base de la reconnaissance des mots écrits chez l'adulte*. De Boeck Université.

Ferrand, L., Brysbaert, M., Keuleers, E., New, B., Bonin, P., Méot, A., Augustinova, M., & Pallier, C. (2011). Comparing word processing times in naming, lexical decision, and progressive demasking: Evidence from Chronolex. *Frontiers in Psychology, 2*.

Ferrand, L., & Grainger, J. (1994). Effects of orthography are independent of phonology in masked form priming. *Quarterly Journal of Experimental Psychology Section A, 47*(2), 365–382.

Ferrand, L., Méot, A., Spinelli, E., New, B., Pallier, C., Bonin, P., Dufau, S., Mathôt, S., & Grainger, J. (2018). MEGALEX: A megastudy of visual and auditory word recognition. *Behavior Research Methods, 50*(3), 1285–1307.

Ferreira, F. (2003). The misinterpretation of noncanonical sentences. *Cognitive Psychology, 47*(2), 164–203.

Ferreira, F., & Patson, N. D. (2007). The "good enough" approach to language comprehension. *Language and Linguistics Compass, 1*(1–2), 71–83.

Ferreira, V. S., & Pashler, H. (2002). Central bottleneck influences on the processing stages of word production. *Journal of Experimental Psychology: Learning, Memory, and Cognition, 28*, 1187–1199.

Féry, C., & Ishihara, S. (2016). *Oxford Handbook of Information Structure*. Oxford University Press.

Field, J. (2003). *Psycholinguistics*. Psychology Press.

Fillmore, C. J. (1968). Lexical entries for verbs. *Foundations of Language, 4*(4), 373–393.

Finegan, E. (2014). *Language: Its Structure and Use*. Cengage Learning.

Fisher, S. E., & Scharff, C. (2009). FOXP2 as a molecular window into speech and language. *Trends in Genetics, 25*(4), 166–177.

Fitch, W. T. (2005). The evolution of language: A comparative review. *Biology and Philosophy, 20*(2), 193–203.

FitzPatrick, I., & Indefrey, P. (2010). Lexical competition in nonnative speech comprehension. *Journal of Cognitive Neuroscience, 22*(6), 1165–1178.

Flecken, M., Athanasopoulos, P., Kuipers, J. R., & Thierry, G. (2015). On the road to somewhere: Brain potentials reflect language effects on motion event perception. *Cognition, 141*, 41–51.

Fodor, J. A. (1983). *The Modularity of Mind*. MIT Press.

Forster, K. I., & Chambers, S. M. (1973). Lexical access and naming time. *Journal of Verbal Learning and Verbal Behavior, 12*(6), 627–635.

Forster, K. I., & Forster, J. C. (2003). DMDX: A Windows display program with millisecond accuracy. *Behavior Research Methods, Instruments, & Computers, 35*(1), 116–124.

Forstmann, B. U., Wagenmakers, E.-J., Eichele, T., Brown, S., & Serences, J. T. (2011). Reciprocal relations between cognitive neuroscience and formal cognitive models: Opposites attract? *Trends in Cognitive Sciences, 15*(6), 272–279.

Foucart, A., Martin, C. D., Moreno, E. M., & Costa, A. (2014). Can bilinguals see it coming? Word anticipation in L2 sentence reading. *Journal of Experimental Psychology: Learning, Memory, and Cognition, 40,* 1461–1469.

Frances, C., Navarra-Barindelli, E., & Martin, C. D. (2021). Inhibitory and facilitatory effects of phonological and orthographic similarity on L2 word recognition across modalities in bilinguals. *Scientific Reports, 11*(1), Article 1.

Franck, J., Vigliocco, G., & Nicol, J. (2002). Subject-verb agreement errors in French and English: The role of syntactic hierarchy. *Language and Cognitive Processes, 17*(4), 371–404.

Frank, S. L. (2021). Toward computational models of multilingual sentence processing. *Language Learning, 71*(S1), 193–218.

Frauenfelder, U. H., & Peeters, G. (1990). Lexical segmentation in TRACE: An exercise in simulation. In G. T. M. Altmann (Ed.), *Cognitive Models of Speech Processing: Psycholinguistic and Computational Perspectives* (pp. 50–86). MIT Press.

Frauenfelder, U. H., & Peeters, G. (1998). Simulating the time course of spoken word recognition: An analysis of lexical competition in TRACE. In J. Grainger & A. M. Jacobs (Eds.), *Localist Connectionist Approaches to Human Cognition* (pp. 101–146). Lawrence Erlbaum Associates.

Frauenfelder, U. H., Segui, J., & Dijkstra, T. (1990). Lexical effects in phonemic processing: Facilitatory or inhibitory? *Journal of Experimental Psychology: Human Perception and Performance, 16,* 77–91.

Frazier, L. (1987). Sentence processing: A tutorial review. In M. Coltheart (Ed.), *Attention and Performance XII: The Psychology of Reading* (pp. 559–586). Lawrence Erlbaum Associates.

Frazier, L., & Fodor, J. D. (1978). The sausage machine: A new two-stage parsing model. *Cognition, 6*(4), 291–325.

Freud, S. (1973). Slips of the tongue. In V. A. Fromkin (Ed.), *Speech Errors as Linguistic Evidence* (pp. 46–81). Mouton.

Freud, S. (1989). *The Psychopathology of Everyday Life.* W. W. Norton & Company.

Friederici, A. D. (2011). The brain basis of language processing: From structure to function. *Physiological Reviews, 91*(4), 1357–1392.

Friederici, A. D. (2017). *Language in Our Brain: The Origins of a Uniquely Human Capacity.* MIT Press.

Friederici, A. D., & Gierhan, S. M. (2013). The language network. *Current Opinion in Neurobiology, 23*(2), 250–254.

Frith, C., & Frith, U. (2005). Theory of mind. *Current Biology, 15*(17), R644–646.

Fromkin, V. A. (1971). The non-anomalous nature of anomalous utterances. *Language, 47*(1), 27–52.

Fromkin, V. A. (1973). Slips of the tongue. *Scientific American, 229*(6), 110–117.

Ganong, W. F. (1980). Phonetic categorization in auditory word perception. *Journal of Experimental Psychology: Human Perception and Performance, 6,* 110–125.

Gardner-Chloros, P. (2009). *Code-switching.* Cambridge University Press.

Garrett, M. F. (1980). Levels of processing in sentence production. In B. Butterworth (Ed.), *Language Production Vol. 1: Speech and Talk* (pp. 177–220). Academic Press.

Garrod, S., & Terras, M. (2000). The contribution of lexical and situational knowledge to resolving discourse roles: Bonding and resolution. *Journal of Memory and Language, 42*(4), 526–544.

Gatt, A., & Krahmer, E. (2018). Survey of the state of the art in natural language generation: Core tasks, applications and evaluation. *Journal of Artificial Intelligence Research, 61,* 65–170.

Gazdar, G., Klein, E., Pullum, G. K., & Sag, I. A. (1985). *Generalized Phrase Structure Grammar.* Harvard University Press.

Gee, J. P., & Grosjean, F. (1983). Performance structures: A psycholinguistic and linguistic appraisal. *Cognitive Psychology, 15*(4), 411–458.

Gentner, D. (2003). Why we're so smart. In D. Gentner & S. Goldin-Meadow (Eds.), *Language in Mind: Advances in the Study of Language and Thought* (pp. 195–236). MIT Press.

Glaser, W. R., & Glaser, M. O. (1989). Context effects in Stroop-like word and picture processing. *Journal of Experimental Psychology: General, 118,* 13–42.

Goldinger, S. D. (1996). Auditory lexical decision. *Language and Cognitive Processes, 11*(6), 559–568.

Goldinger, S. D. (1998). Echoes of echoes? An episodic theory of lexical access. *Psychological Review, 105,* 251–279.

Goldin-Meadow, S. (2014). Widening the lens: What the manual modality reveals about language, learning and cognition. *Philosophical Transactions of the Royal Society B: Biological Sciences, 369*(1651), 20130295.

Goldvarg, Y., & Johnson-Laird, P. N. (2000). Illusions in modal reasoning. *Memory & Cognition, 28*(2), 282–294.

Gollan, T. H., & Ferreira, V. S. (2009). Should I stay or should I switch? A cost–benefit analysis of voluntary language switching in young and aging bilinguals. *Journal of Experimental*

Psychology: Learning, Memory, and Cognition, 35(3), 640.

Gomez, P., Ratcliff, R., & Perea, M. (2008). The overlap model: A model of letter position coding. *Psychological Review, 115*, 577–600.

Gow, D. W. Jr., & Gordon, P. C. (1995). Lexical and prelexical influences on word segmentation: Evidence from priming. *Journal of Experimental Psychology: Human Perception and Performance, 21*, 344–359.

Grainger, J., & Holcomb, P. J. (2009). Watching the word go by: On the time-course of component processes in visual word recognition. *Language and Linguistics Compass, 3*(1), 128–156.

Grainger, J., & Jacobs, A. M. (1996). Orthographic processing in visual word recognition: A multiple read-out model. *Psychological Review, 103*, 518–565.

Grainger, J., Kiyonaga, K., & Holcomb, P. J. (2006). The time course of orthographic and phonological code activation. *Psychological Science, 17*(12), 1021–1026.

Grainger, J., Midgley, K., & Holcomb, P. J. (2010). Rethinking the bilingual interactive-activation model from a developmental perspective (BIA-d). In M. Kail & M. Hickmann (Eds.), *Language Acquisition across Linguistic and Cognitive Systems* (pp. 267–284). John Benjamins Publishing.

Grainger, J., Rey, A., & Dufau, S. (2008). Letter perception: From pixels to pandemonium. *Trends in Cognitive Sciences, 12*(10), 381–387.

Grainger, J., & van Heuven, W. (2003). Modeling letter position coding in printed word perception. In P. Bonin (Ed.), *Mental Lexicon: Some Words to Talk about Words* (pp. 1–23). Nova Publishers.

Grainger, J., & Whitney, C. (2004). Does the huamn mnid raed wrods as a wlohe? *Trends in Cognitive Sciences, 8*, 58–59.

Green, D. W. (1998). Mental control of the bilingual lexico-semantic system. *Bilingualism: Language and Cognition, 1*(2), 67–81.

Green, D. W., & Abutalebi, J. (2013). Language control in bilinguals: The adaptive control hypothesis. *Journal of Cognitive Psychology, 25*(5), 515–530.

Grice, H. P. (1975). Logic and conversation. In P. Cole & J. L. Morgan (Eds.), *Syntax and Semantics. Volume 3. Speech Acts* (pp. 41–58). Academic Press.

Grosjean, F. (1989). Neurolinguists, beware! The bilingual is not two monolinguals in one person. *Brain and Language, 36*(1), 3–15.

Grosjean, F. (1998). Studying bilinguals: Methodological and conceptual issues. *Bilingualism: Language and Cognition, 1*(2), 131–149.

Grosjean, F. (2001). The bilingual's language modes. In J. L. Nicol (Ed.), *One Mind, Two Languages: Bilingual Language Processing* (pp. 1–22). Blackwell.

Grosjean, F. (2008). *Studying Bilinguals*. Oxford University Press.

Grosjean, F., & Frauenfelder, U. H. (1996). A guide to spoken word recognition paradigms: Introduction. *Language and Cognitive Processes, 11*(6), 553–558.

Guardian, The. (2020). A robot wrote this entire article. Are you scared yet, human? *The Guardian.* https://www.theguardian.com/commentisfree/2020/sep/08/robot-wrote-this-article-gpt-3

Guasch, M., Ferré, P., & Haro, J. (2017). Pupil dilation is sensitive to the cognate status of words: Further evidence for non-selectivity in bilingual lexical access. *Bilingualism: Language and Cognition, 20*(1), 49–54.

Guest, O., & Martin, A. E. (2021). How computational modeling can force theory building in psychological science. *Perspectives on Psychological Science, 16*(4), 789–802.

Gunter, T. C., Friederici, A. D., & Schriefers, H. (2000). Syntactic gender and semantic expectancy: ERPs reveal early autonomy and late interaction. *Journal of Cognitive Neuroscience, 12*(4), 556–568.

Hagoort, P. (2013). MUC (Memory, Unification, Control) and beyond. *Frontiers in Psychology, 4*.

Hagoort, P. (2017). The core and beyond in the language-ready brain. *Neuroscience & Biobehavioral Reviews, 81*, 194–204.

Hagoort, P. (2023). The language marker hypothesis. *Cognition, 230*, 105252.

Hagoort, P., Brown, C., & Groothusen, J. (1993). The syntactic positive shift (sps) as an erp measure of syntactic processing. *Language and Cognitive Processes, 8*(4), 439–483.

Hale, J. (2001). A probabilistic early parser as a psycholinguistic model. *Second Meeting of the North American Chapter of the Association for Computational Linguistics*, 159–166.

Hale, J. (2003). The information conveyed by words in sentences. *Journal of Psycholinguistic Research, 32*(2), 101–123.

Hari, R., Henriksson, L., Malinen, S., & Parkkonen, L. (2015). Centrality of social interaction in human brain function. *Neuron, 88*(1), 181–193.

Harm, M. W., & Seidenberg, M. S. (2004). Computing the meanings of words in reading: Cooperative division of labor between visual and phonological processes. *Psychological Review, 111*, 662–720.

Hartsuiker, R. J., Pickering, M. J., & Veltkamp, E. (2004). Is syntax separate or shared between languages?: Cross-linguistic syntactic priming in

Spanish–English bilinguals *Psychological Science, 15*(6), 409–414.

Hauk, O., Davis, M. H., Ford, M., Pulvermüller, F., & Marslen-Wilson, W. D. (2006). The time course of visual word recognition as revealed by linear regression analysis of ERP data. *NeuroImage, 30*(4), 1383–1400.

Hauk, O., Johnsrude, I., & Pulvermüller, F. (2004). Somatotopic representation of action words in human motor and premotor cortex. *Neuron, 41*(2), 301–307.

Hauser, M. D., Chomsky, N., & Fitch, W. T. (2002). The faculty of language: What is it, who has it, and how did it evolve? *Science, 298*(5598), 1569–1579.

Henderson, A., Goldman-Eisler, F., & Skarbek, A. (1966). Sequential temporal patterns in spontaneous speech. *Language and Speech, 9*(4), 207–216.

Henrich, J., Heine, S. J., & Norenzayan, A. (2010). The weirdest people in the world? *Behavioral and Brain Sciences, 33*(2–3), 61–83.

Herodotus. (2013). *The Histories* (W. Blanco & J. T. Roberts, Eds.). W. W. Norton & Company.

Heyman, T., Hutchison, K. A., & Storms, G. (2016). Is semantic priming (ir)rational? Insights from the speeded word fragment completion task. *Journal of Experimental Psychology: Learning, Memory, and Cognition, 42*, 1657–1663.

Heyselaar, E., Hagoort, P., & Segaert, K. (2017). In dialogue with an avatar, language behavior is identical to dialogue with a human partner. *Behavior Research Methods, 49*(1), 46–60.

Hickok, G., & Poeppel, D. (2007). The cortical organization of speech processing. *Nature Reviews Neuroscience, 8*(5), Article 5.

Hockett, C. F. (1960). The origin of speech. *Scientific American, 203*(3), 88–97.

Hoff, E. (2014). *Language Development*, 5th edn. Wadsworth.

Hollan, J. D. (1975). Features and semantic memory: Set-theoretic or network model? *Psychological Review, 82*, 154–155.

Holler, J., Kendrick, K. H., & Levinson, S. C. (2018). Processing language in face-to-face conversation: Questions with gestures get faster responses. *Psychonomic Bulletin & Review, 25*(5), 1900–1908.

Holler, J., & Levinson, S. C. (2019). Multimodal language processing in human communication. *Trends in Cognitive Sciences, 23*(8), 639–652.

Holmes, K. J., & Wolff, P. (2010). Simulation from schematics: Dorsal stream processing and the perception of implied motion. *Proceedings of the Annual Meeting of the Cognitive Science Society*, 2704–2709.

Hömke, P., Holler, J., & Levinson, S. C. (2018). Eye blinks are perceived as communicative signals in human face-to-face interaction. *PLOS ONE, 13*(12), e0208030.

Honig, S., & Oron-Gilad, T. (2018). Understanding and resolving failures in human–robot interaction: Literature review and model development. *Frontiers in Psychology, 9*.

Hoversten, L. J., Brothers, T., Swaab, T. Y., & Traxler, M. J. (2015). Language membership identification precedes semantic access: Suppression during bilingual word recognition. *Journal of Cognitive Neuroscience, 27*(11), 2108–2116.

Hoversten, L. J., & Traxler, M. J. (2016). A time course analysis of interlingual homograph processing: Evidence from eye movements. *Bilingualism: Language and Cognition, 19*(2), 347–360.

Hoving, H. (1974). *Juf-compleet*. Arbeiderspers.

Hsieh, M.-C., Jeong, H., Sugiura, M., & Kawashima, R. (2021). Neural evidence of language membership control in bilingual word recognition: An fMRI study of cognate processing in Chinese–Japanese bilinguals. *Frontiers in Psychology, 12*.

Hubel, D. H., & Wiesel, T. N. (1962). Receptive fields, binocular interaction and functional architecture in the cat's visual cortex. *Journal of Physiology, 160*(1), 106–154.2.

Hubel, D. H., & Wiesel, T. N. (1965). Binocular interaction in striate cortex of kittens reared with artificial squint. *Journal of Neurophysiology, 28*(6), 1041–1059.

Huettig, F., & Ferreira, F. (2022). The myth of normal reading. *Perspectives on Psychological Science*, 17456916221127226.

Huettig, F., Rommers, J., & Meyer, A. S. (2011). Using the visual world paradigm to study language processing: A review and critical evaluation. *Acta Psychologica, 137*(2), 151–171.

Huizeling, E., Peeters, D., & Hagoort, P. (2022). Prediction of upcoming speech under fluent and disfluent conditions: Eye tracking evidence from immersive virtual reality. *Language, Cognition and Neuroscience, 37*(4), 481–508.

Hutchison, K. A., Balota, D. A., Neely, J. H., Cortese, M. J., Cohen-Shikora, E. R., Tse, C.-S., Yap, M. J., Bengson, J. J., Niemeyer, D., & Buchanan, E. (2013). The semantic priming project. *Behavior Research Methods, 45*(4), 1099–1114.

Indefrey, P. (2006). A meta-analysis of hemodynamic studies on first and second language processing: Which suggested differences can we trust and what do they mean? *Language Learning, 56*(s1), 279–304.

Indefrey, P. (2011). The spatial and temporal signatures of word production components: A critical update. *Frontiers in Psychology*, 2.

Indefrey, P., & Levelt, W. J. M. (2004). The spatial and temporal signatures of word production components. *Cognition*, *92*(1), 101–144.

Inhoff, A. W., & Rayner, K. (1980). Parafoveal word perception: A case against semantic preprocessing. *Perception & Psychophysics*, *27*(5), 457–464.

IPA. (2015). *Full IPA Chart | International Phonetic Association*. https://www.internationalphonetic association.org/content/full-ipa-chart

Iverson, J. M., & Goldin-Meadow, S. (2005). Gesture paves the way for language development. *Psychological Science*, *16*(5), 367–371.

Jackendoff, R. S. (1983). *Semantics and Cognition*. MIT Press.

Jackendoff, R. S. (1990). *Semantic Structures*. MIT Press.

James, W. (1890). *The Principles of Psychology*. Henry Holt & Co.

Jescheniak, J. D., & Schriefers, H. (1998). Discrete serial versus cascaded processing in lexical access in speech production: Further evidence from the coactivation of near-synonyms. *Journal of Experimental Psychology: Learning, Memory, and Cognition*, 24, 1256–1274.

Johns, B. T., & Jones, M. N. (2022). Content matters: Measures of contextual diversity must consider semantic content. *Journal of Memory and Language*, *123*, 104313.

Johnson-Laird, P. N. (1989). Mental models. In M. I. Posner (Ed.), *Foundations of Cognitive Science* (pp. 469–499). MIT Press.

Johnson-Laird, P. N. (2013). Mental models and cognitive change. *Journal of Cognitive Psychology*, *25*(2), 131–138.

Johnson-Laird, P. N., Gibbs, G., & de Mowbray, J. (1978). Meaning, amount of processing, and memory for words. *Memory & Cognition*, *6*(4), 372–375.

Just, M. A., & Carpenter, P. A. (1980). A theory of reading: From eye fixations to comprehension. *Psychological Review*, 87, 329–354.

Just, M. A., & Carpenter, P. A. (1987). *The Psychology of Reading and Language Comprehension* (pp. x, 518). Allyn & Bacon.

Just, M. A., & Carpenter, P. A. (1992). A capacity theory of comprehension: Individual differences in working memory. *Psychological Review*, 99, 122–149.

Kahneman, D. (2011). *Thinking, Fast and Slow*. Farrar, Straus & Giroux.

Kako, E., & Wagner, L. (2001). The semantics of syntactic structures. *Trends in Cognitive Sciences*, *5*(3), 102–108.

Kanfer, S. (2000). *The Essential Groucho*. Penguin Books.

Kawamoto, A. H. (1993). Nonlinear dynamics in the resolution of lexical ambiguity: A parallel distributed processing account. *Journal of Memory and Language*, *32*(4), 474–516.

Kawamoto, A. H., & Zemblidge, J. H. (1992). Pronunciation of homographs. *Journal of Memory and Language*, *31*(3), 349–374.

Kemmerer, D. (2012). The cross-linguistic prevalence of SOV and SVO word orders reflects the sequential and hierarchical representation of action in Broca's Area. *Language and Linguistics Compass*, *6*(1), 50–66.

Kemmerer, D. (2022). *Cognitive Neuroscience of Language*. Routledge.

Kemps, R., Ernestus, M., Schreuder, R., & Baayen, H. (2004). Processing reduced word forms: The suffix restoration effect. *Brain and Language*, *90*(1), 117–127.

Kendon, A. (2004). *Gesture: Visible Action as Utterance*. Cambridge University Press.

Keuleers, E., Diependaele, K., & Brysbaert, M. (2010). Practice effects in large-scale visual word recognition studies: A lexical decision study on 14,000 Dutch mono- and disyllabic words and nonwords. *Frontiers in Psychology*, 1.

Keuleers, E., Lacey, P., Rastle, K., & Brysbaert, M. (2012). The British Lexicon Project: Lexical decision data for 28,730 monosyllabic and disyllabic English words. *Behavior Research Methods*, *44*(1), 287–304.

Kharkhurin, A. V. (2017). Language mediated concept activation in bilingual memory facilitates cognitive flexibility. *Frontiers in Psychology*, 8.

Kiebel, S. J., Daunizeau, J., & Friston, K. J. (2008). A hierarchy of time-scales and the brain. *PLOS Computational Biology*, *4*(11), e1000209.

Kiefer, M., Sim, E.-J., Helbig, H., & Graf, M. (2011). Tracking the time course of action priming on object recognition: Evidence for fast and slow influences of action on perception. *Journal of Cognitive Neuroscience*, *23*(8), 1864–1874.

Kinoshita, S., & Lupker, S. J. (Eds.). (2003). *Masked Priming: The State of the Art*. Psychology Press.

Kinoshita, S., & Norris, D. (2013). Letter order is not coded by open bigrams. *Journal of Memory and Language*, *69*(2), 135–150.

Kintsch, W. (1988). The role of knowledge in discourse comprehension: A construction-integration model. *Psychological Review*, 95, 163–182.

Kintsch, W., & van Dijk, T. A. (1978). Toward a model of text comprehension and production. *Psychological Review*, 85, 363–394.

Kita, S. (2003). *Pointing: Where Language, Culture, and Cognition Meet*. Psychology Press.

Kita, S., & Özyürek, A. (2003). What does cross-linguistic variation in semantic coordination of speech and gesture reveal?: Evidence for an interface representation of spatial thinking and speaking. *Journal of Memory and Language*, *48*(1), 16–32.

Klatt, D. H. (1979). Speech perception: A model of acoustic–phonetic analysis and lexical access. *Journal of Phonetics*, *7*(3), 279–312.

Knoeferle, K., Li, J., Maggioni, E., & Spence, C. (2017). What drives sound symbolism? Different acoustic cues underlie sound-size and sound-shape mappings. *Scientific Reports*, *7*(1), Article 1.

Koeneman, O., & Zeijlstra, H. (2017). *Introducing Syntax*. Cambridge University Press.

Köhler, W. (1947). *Gestalt Psychology: An Introduction to New Concepts in Modern Psychology*. Liveright Publishing Corporation.

Kolers, P. A. (1963). Interlingual word associations. *Journal of Verbal Learning and Verbal Behavior*, *2*(4), 291–300.

Kolers, P. A. (1966). Reading and talking bilingually. *American Journal of Psychology*, *79*(3), 357–376.

Kolk, H., & Heeschen, C. (1990). Adaptation symptoms and impairment symptoms in Broca's aphasia. *Aphasiology*, *4*(3), 221–231.

Kootstra, G. J., van Hell, J. G., & Dijkstra, T. (2010). Syntactic alignment and shared word order in code-switched sentence production: Evidence from bilingual monologue and dialogue. *Journal of Memory and Language*, *63*(2), 210–231.

Krahmer, E., & Swerts, M. (2007). The effects of visual beats on prosodic prominence: Acoustic analyses, auditory perception and visual perception. *Journal of Memory and Language*, *57*(3), 396–414.

Krogh, S. M. (2022). Danish–English bilinguals' cognate processing in L1 and L2 visual lexical decision tasks. *Languages*, *7*(3), Article 3.

Kroll, J. F., & Stewart, E. (1994). Category interference in translation and picture naming: Evidence for asymmetric connections between bilingual memory representations. *Journal of Memory and Language*, *33*(2), 149–174.

Kuhlen, A. K., & Abdel Rahman, R. (2022). Mental chronometry of speaking in dialogue: Semantic interference turns into facilitation. *Cognition*, *219*, 104962.

Kuhlen, A. K., & Brennan, S. E. (2013). Language in dialogue: When confederates might be hazardous to your data. *Psychonomic Bulletin & Review*, *20*(1), 54–72.

Kuperberg, G. R., Paczynski, M., & Ditman, T. (2011). Establishing causal coherence across sentences: An ERP etudy. *Journal of Cognitive Neuroscience*, *23*(5), 1230–1246.

Kutas, M., & Federmeier, K. D. (2011). Thirty years and counting: Finding meaning in the N400 component of the event related brain potential (ERP). *Annual Review of Psychology*, *62*, 621–647.

Kutas, M., & Hillyard, S. A. (1980). Reading senseless sentences: Brain potentials reflect semantic incongruity. *Science*, *207*(4427), 203–205.

Lakoff, G. (1987). *Women, Fire, and Dangerous Things: What Categories Reveal about the Mind*. University of Chicago Press.

Lakoff, G., & Johnson, M. (1980). The metaphorical structure of the human conceptual system. *Cognitive Science*, *4*, 195–208.

Lam, K. J. Y., Dijkstra, T., & Rueschemeyer, S.-A. (2015). Feature activation during word recognition: Action, visual, and associative-semantic priming effects. *Frontiers in Psychology*, *6*.

Lambon Ralph, M. A., Jefferies, E., Patterson, K., & Rogers, T. T. (2017). The neural and computational bases of semantic cognition. *Nature Reviews Neuroscience*, *18*(1), Article 1.

Lambon Ralph, M. A., Sage, K., Jones, R. W., & Mayberry, E. J. (2010). Coherent concepts are computed in the anterior temporal lobes. *Proceedings of the National Academy of Sciences*, *107*(6), 2717–2722.

Landauer, T. K., & Dumais, S. T. (1997). A solution to Plato's problem: The latent semantic analysis theory of acquisition, induction, and representation of knowledge. *Psychological Review*, *104*, 211–240.

Lauro, J., & Schwartz, A. I. (2017). Bilingual non-selective lexical access in sentence contexts: A meta-analytic review. *Journal of Memory and Language*, *92*, 217–233.

Leaper, C., & Ayres, M. M. (2007). A meta-analytic review of gender variations in adults' language use: Talkativeness, affiliative speech, and assertive speech. *Personality and Social Psychology Review*, *11*(4), 328–363.

Lee, C.-Y., Liu, Y.-N., & Tsai, J.-L. (2012). The time course of contextual effects on visual word recognition. *Frontiers in Psychology*, *3*.

Lemhöfer, K., & Dijkstra, T. (2004). Recognizing cognates and interlingual homographs: Effects of code similarity in language-specific and generalized lexical decision. *Memory & Cognition*, *32*(4), 533–550.

Lemhöfer, K., Dijkstra, T., Schriefers, H., Baayen, R. H., Grainger, J., & Zwitserlood, P. (2008).

Native language influences on word recognition in a second language: A megastudy. *Journal of Experimental Psychology: Learning, Memory, and Cognition*, *34*(1), 12.

Lenneberg, E. H. (1967). *Biological Foundations of Language*. John Wiley & Sons.

Levelt, W. J. M. (1981). The speaker's linearization problem. *Philosophical Transactions of the Royal Society of London. B, Biological Sciences*, *295*(1077), 305–315.

Levelt, W. J. M. (1989). *Speaking: From Intention to Articulation*. MIT Press.

Levelt, W. J. M. (2013). *A History of Psycholinguistics: The Pre-Chomskyan Era*. Oxford University Press.

Levelt, W. J. M., Roelofs, A., & Meyer, A. S. (1999). A theory of lexical access in speech production. *Behavioral and Brain Sciences*, *22*(1), 1–38.

Levelt, W. J. M., Schriefers, H., Vorberg, D., Meyer, A. S., Pechmann, T., & Havinga, J. (1991). The time course of lexical access in speech production: A study of picture naming. *Psychological Review*, *98*, 122–142.

Levinson, S. C. (1983). *Pragmatics*. Cambridge University Press.

Levinson, S. C. (1997). Language and cognition: The cognitive consequences of spatial description in Guugu Yimithirr. *Journal of Linguistic Anthropology*, *7*(1), 98–131.

Levinson, S. C. (2004). Deixis. In L. Horn (Ed.), *The Handbook of Pragmatics* (pp. 97–121). Blackwell.

Levinson, S. C. (2016). Turn-taking in human communication – origins and implications for language processing. *Trends in Cognitive Sciences*, *20*(1), 6–14.

Levy, R. (2008). Expectation-based syntactic comprehension. *Cognition*, *106*(3), 1126–1177.

Lewis, D. (1969). *Convention*. Harvard University Press.

Léwy, N., & Grosjean, F. (2008). The Léwy and Grosjean BIMOLA model. In F. Grosjean (Ed.), *Studying Bilinguals* (pp. 201–210). Oxford University Press.

Li, P., & Xu, Q. (2023). Computational modeling of bilingual language learning: Current models and future directions. *Language Learning*, 1–48.

Libben, M. R., & Titone, D. A. (2009). Bilingual lexical access in context: Evidence from eye movements during reading. *Journal of Experimental Psychology: Learning, Memory, and Cognition*, *35*, 381–390.

Liberman, A. M., Harris, K. S., Hoffman, H. S., & Griffith, B. C. (1957). The discrimination of speech sounds within and across phoneme boundaries. *Journal of Experimental Psychology*, *54*, 358–368.

Lieberman, D. (2011). *The Evolution of the Human Head*. Harvard University Press.

Lieberman, P., & McCarthy, R. C. (2015). The evolution of speech and language. In W. Henke & I. Tattersall (Eds.), *Handbook of Paleoanthropology* (pp. 873–920). Springer.

Littlemore, J. (2015). *Metonymy*. Cambridge University Press.

Liu, H., & Cao, F. (2016). L1 and L2 processing in the bilingual brain: A meta-analysis of neuroimaging studies. *Brain and Language*, *159*, 60–73.

Loftus, E. F., & Palmer, J. C. (1974). Reconstruction of automobile destruction: An example of the interaction between language and memory. *Journal of Verbal Learning and Verbal Behavior*, *13*(5), 585–589.

Logan, G. D., & Crump, M. J. C. (2011). Hierarchical control of cognitive processes: The case for skilled typewriting. *Psychology of Learning and Motivation*, *54*, 1–27.

Lombard, E. (1911). Le signe de l'élévation de la voix. *Annales des Maladies de l'Oreille, du Larynx, du Nez et du Pharynx*, *37*, 101–119.

Luce, P. A., Goldinger, S. D., Auer, E. T., & Vitevitch, M. S. (2000). Phonetic priming, neighborhood activation, and PARSYN. *Perception & Psychophysics*, *62*(3), 615–625.

Luck, S. J. (2014). *An Introduction to the Event-Related Potential Technique*, 2nd edn. MIT Press.

Lugrin, B., Pelachaud, C., & Traum, D. (2021). *The Handbook on Socially Interactive Agents: 20 Years of Research on Embodied Conversational Agents, Intelligent Virtual Agents, and Social Robotics, Volume 1: Methods, Behavior, Cognition*. Morgan & Claypool.

Lugrin, B., Pelachaud, C., & Traum, D. (2022). *The Handbook on Socially Interactive Agents: 20 Years of Research on Embodied Conversational Agents, Intelligent Virtual Agents, and Social Robotics, Volume 2: Interactivity, Platforms, Application*. Morgan & Claypool.

Lund, K., & Burgess, C. (1996). Producing high-dimensional semantic spaces from lexical co-occurrence. *Behavior Research Methods, Instruments, & Computers*, *28*(2), 203–208.

Maassen, B., Kent, R. D., Peters, H. F. M., van Lieshout, P. H. H. M., & Hulstijn, W. (Eds.). (2004). *Speech Motor Control: In Normal and Disordered Speech*. Oxford University Press.

MacDonald, M. C. (1994). Probabilistic constraints and syntactic ambiguity resolution. *Language and Cognitive Processes*, *9*(2), 157–201.

MacDonald, M. C., Pearlmutter, N. J., & Seidenberg, M. S. (1994). The lexical nature of syntactic ambiguity resolution. *Psychological Review, 101*, 676–703.

Maclay, H., & Osgood, C. E. (1959). Hesitation phenomena in spontaneous English speech. *WORD, 15*(1), 19–44.

MacLeod, C. M. (1991). Half a century of research on the Stroop effect: An integrative review. *Psychological Bulletin, 109*, 163–203.

MacWhinney, B. (1999). *The Emergence of Language*. Lawrence Erlbaum Associates.

MacWhinney, B. (2002). The gradual emergence of language. In T. Givón & B. F. Malle (Eds.), *The Evolution of Language Out of Pre-language* (pp. 231–263). John Benjamins Publishing.

Mädebach, A., Kurtz, F., Schriefers, H., & Jescheniak, J. D. (2020). Pragmatic constraints do not prevent the co-activation of alternative names: Evidence from sequential naming tasks with one and two speakers. *Language, Cognition and Neuroscience, 35*(8), 1073–1088.

Maes, A., Krahmer, E., & Peeters, D. (2022). Explaining variance in writers' use of demonstratives: A corpus study demonstrating the importance of discourse genre. *Glossa: A Journal of General Linguistics, 7*(1), Article 1.

Magnuson, J. S., Dahan, D., & Tanenhaus, M. K. (2001). On the interpretation of computational models: The case of TRACE. In J. S. Magnuson & K. M. Crosswhite (Eds.), *University of Rochester Working Papers in the Language Sciences* (pp. 71–91). University of Rochester Press.

Magnuson, J. S., Nusbaum, H. C., Akahane-Yamada, R., & Saltzman, D. (2021). Talker familiarity and the accommodation of talker variability. *Attention, Perception, & Psychophysics, 83*(4), 1842–1860.

Magnuson, J. S., Tanenhaus, M. K., Aslin, R. N., & Dahan, D. (2003). The time course of spoken word learning and recognition: Studies with artificial lexicons. *Journal of Experimental Psychology: General, 132*, 202–227.

Majid, A., Roberts, S. G., Cilissen, L., Emmorey, K., Nicodemus, B., O'Grady, L., Woll, B., LeLan, B., de Sousa, H., Cansler, B. L., Shayan, S., de Vos, C., Senft, G., Enfield, N. J., Razak, R. A., Fedden, S., Tufvesson, S., Dingemanse, M., Ozturk, O., ... Levinson, S. C. (2018). Differential coding of perception in the world's languages. *Proceedings of the National Academy of Sciences, 115*(45), 11369–11376.

Malik-Moraleda, S., Ayyash, D., Gallée, J., Affourtit, J., Hoffmann, M., Mineroff, Z., Jouravlev, O., & Fedorenko, E. (2022). An investigation across 45 languages and 12 language families reveals a universal language network. *Nature Neuroscience, 25*(8), Article 8.

Marslen-Wilson, W. D. (1984). Function and process in spoken word recognition: A tutorial review. In H. Bouma & D. G. Bouwhuis (Eds.), *Attention and Performance X* (pp. 125–150). Lawrence Erlbaum Associates.

Marslen-Wilson, W. D. (1987). Functional parallelism in spoken word-recognition. *Cognition, 25*(1), 71–102.

Marslen-Wilson, W. D., Tyler, L. K., Waksler, R., & Older, L. (1994). Morphology and meaning in the English mental lexicon. *Psychological Review, 101*, 3–33.

Marslen-Wilson, W. D., & Welsh, A. (1978). Processing interactions and lexical access during word recognition in continuous speech. *Cognitive Psychology, 10*(1), 29–63.

Martin, C. D., Thierry, G., Kuipers, J.-R., Boutonnet, B., Foucart, A., & Costa, A. (2013). Bilinguals reading in their second language do not predict upcoming words as native readers do. *Journal of Memory and Language, 69*(4), 574–588.

Massaro, D. W. (1987). *Speech Perception by Ear and Eye: A Paradigm for Psychological Inquiry*. Psychology Press.

Matychuk, P. (2005). The role of child-directed speech in language acquisition: A case study. *Language Sciences, 27*(3), 301–379.

McCandliss, B. D., Cohen, L., & Dehaene, S. (2003). The visual word form area: Expertise for reading in the fusiform gyrus. *Trends in Cognitive Sciences, 7*(7), 293–299.

McClelland, J. L., & Elman, J. L. (1986). The TRACE model of speech perception. *Cognitive Psychology, 18*(1), 1–86.

McClelland, J. L., & Rumelhart, D. E. (1981). An interactive activation model of context effects in letter perception: I. An account of basic findings. *Psychological Review, 88*, 375–407.

McClelland, J. L., & Rumelhart, D. E. (1989). *Explorations in Parallel Distributed Processing: A Handbook of Models, Programs, and Exercises*. MIT Press.

McGurk, H., & MacDonald, J. (1976). Hearing lips and seeing voices. *Nature, 264*(5588), 746–748.

McKoon, G., & Ratcliff, R. (1992). Inference during reading. *Psychological Review, 99*, 440–466.

McLuhan, M. (1964). *Understanding Media: The Extensions of Man*. McGraw-Hill.

McLuhan, M. (1967). *The Medium is the Massage: An Inventory of Effects*. Penguin Books.

McMurray, B. (2022). The myth of categorical perception. *Journal of the Acoustical Society of America, 152*(6), 3819–3842.

McNeill, D. (1985). So you think gestures are nonverbal? *Psychological Review, 92*, 350–371.

McNeill, D. (1992). *Hand and Mind: What Gestures Reveal about Thought*. University of Chicago Press.

McNeill, D. (2005). *Gesture and Thought*. University of Chicago Press.

McQueen, J. M., & Cutler, A. (1992). Words within Words: Lexical Statistics and Lexical Access. 221–224. https://pure.mpg.de/pubman/faces/ViewItemOverview Page.jsp?itemId=item_77035

McQueen, J. M., Cutler, A., Briscoe, T., & Norris, D. (1995). Models of continuous speech recognition and the contents of the vocabulary. *Language and Cognitive Processes*, *10*(3–4), 309–331.

McRae, K., de Sa, V. R., & Seidenberg, M. S. (1997). On the nature and scope of featural representations of word meaning. *Journal of Experimental Psychology: General*, *126*, 99–130.

Mehl, M. R., Vazire, S., Ramírez-Esparza, N., Slatcher, R. B., & Pennebaker, J. W. (2007). Are women really more talkative than men? *Science*, *317*(5834), 82–82.

Mehler, J., Dommergues, J. Y., Frauenfelder, U., & Segui, J. (1981). The syllable's role in speech segmentation. *Journal of Verbal Learning and Verbal Behavior*, *20*(3), 298–305.

Menenti, L., Petersson, K. M., Scheeringa, R., & Hagoort, P. (2009). When elephants fly: Differential sensitivity of right and left inferior frontal gyri to discourse and world knowledge. *Journal of Cognitive Neuroscience*, *21*(12), 2358–2368.

Menzel, C. (2022). Possible worlds. In E. N. Zalta & U. Nodelman (Eds.), *The Stanford Encyclopedia of Philosophy (Winter 2022 Edition)*. Stanford University Press.

Mesch, J. (1998). Tactile sign language: Turn taking and questions in signed conversations of deaf-blind people. *DeafBlind Culture and Community*, *42*.

Meuter, R. F. I., & Allport, A. (1999). Bilingual language switching in naming: Asymmetrical costs of language selection. *Journal of Memory and Language*, *40*(1), 25–40.

Meyer, A. S., Roelofs, A., & Brehm, L. (2019). Thirty years of speaking: An introduction to the special issue. *Language, Cognition and Neuroscience*, *34*(9), 1073–1084.

Miceli, G., Benvegnu, B., Capasso, R., & Caramazza, A. (1997). The independence of phonological and orthographic lexical forms: Evidence from aphasia. *Cognitive Neuropsychology*, *14*(1), 35–69.

Mickan, A., Schiefke, M., & Stefanowitsch, A. (2014). Key is a llave is a Schlüssel: A failure to replicate an experiment from Boroditsky et al. 2003. *Yearbook of the German Cognitive Linguistics Association*, *2*(1), 39–50.

Midgley, K. J., Holcomb, P. J., van Heuven, W. J. B., & Grainger, J. (2008). An electrophysiological investigation of cross-language effects of orthographic neighborhood. *Brain Research*, *1246*, 123–135.

Miller, G. A., & Fellbaum, C. (1991). Semantic networks of English. *Cognition*, *41*(1), 197–229.

Miller, G. A., & Johnson-Laird, P. N. (1976). *Language and Perception*. Harvard University Press.

Mirman, D., McClelland, J. L., & Holt, L. L. (2005). Computational and behavioral investigations of lexically induced delays in phoneme recognition. *Journal of Memory and Language*, *52*(3), 416–435.

Misersky, J., Peeters, D., & Flecken, M. (2022). The potential of immersive virtual reality for the study of event perception. *Frontiers in Virtual Reality*, *3*.

Mitterer, H., Reinisch, E., & McQueen, J. M. (2018). Allophones, not phonemes in spoken-word recognition. *Journal of Memory and Language*, *98*, 77–92.

Miwa, K., Dijkstra, T., Bolger, P., & Baayen, R. H. (2014). Reading English with Japanese in mind: Effects of frequency, phonology, and meaning in different-script bilinguals. *Bilingualism: Language and Cognition*, *17*(3), 445–463.

Miyake, A., Friedman, N. P., Emerson, M. J., Witzki, A. H., Howerter, A., & Wager, T. D. (2000). The unity and diversity of executive functions and their contributions to complex "frontal lobe" tasks: A latent variable analysis. *Cognitive Psychology*, *41*(1), 49–100.

Mondada, L. (2016). Challenges of multimodality: Language and the body in social interaction. *Journal of Sociolinguistics*, *20*(3), 336–366.

Montazeri, M., Hamidi, H., Hamidi, B., & Yaghoobi, J. (2014). The localist and the distributed models of connectionism. *Journal of Applied Linguistics and Language Research*, *1*(2), Article 2.

Mori, M., MacDorman, K. F., & Kageki, N. (2012). The uncanny valley [from the field]. *IEEE Robotics & Automation Magazine*, *19*(2), 98–100.

Morton, J. (1969). Interaction of information in word recognition. *Psychological Review*, *76*, 165–178.

Motley, M. T., Baars, B. J., & Camden, C. T. (1983). Experimental verbal slip studies: A review and an editing model of language encoding. *Communication Monographs*, *50*(2), 79–101.

Motley, M. T., & Camden, C. T. (1985). Nonlinguistic influences on lexical selection: Evidence from double entendres. *Communication Monographs*, *52*(2), 124–135.

Mulder, K., van Heuven, W. J. B., & Dijkstra, T. (2018). Revisiting the neighborhood: How L2 proficiency and neighborhood manipulation affect bilingual processing. *Frontiers in Psychology, 9*.

Murray, J. D., & Burke, K. A. (2003). Activation and encoding of predictive inferences: The role of reading skill. *Discourse Processes, 35*(2), 81–102.

Murray, W. S., & Forster, K. I. (2004). Serial mechanisms in lexical access: The rank hypothesis. *Psychological Review, 111*, 721–756.

Muysken, P. (2000). *Bilingual Speech: A Typology of Code-Mixing*. Cambridge University Press.

Nagy, W. E., García, G. E., Durgunoğlu, A. Y., & Hancin-Bhatt, B. (1993). Spanish–English bilingual students' use of cognates in English reading. *Journal of Reading Behavior, 25*(3), 241–259.

Nelson, D. L., McEvoy, C. L., & Schreiber, T. A. (2004). The University of South Florida free association, rhyme, and word fragment norms. *Behavior Research Methods, Instruments, & Computers, 36*(3), 402–407.

Nickerson, R. S. (1981). Speech understanding and reading: Some differences and similarities. In O. J. L. Tzeng & H. Singer (Eds.), *Perception of Print: Reading Research in Experimental Psychology* (pp. 257–289). Lawrence Erlbaum Associates.

Nieuwland, M. S., Barr, D. J., Bartolozzi, F., Busch-Moreno, S., Darley, E., Donaldson, D. I., Ferguson, H. J., Fu, X., Heyselaar, E., Huettig, F., Matthew Husband, E., Ito, A., Kazanina, N., Kogan, V., Kohút, Z., Kulakova, E., Mézière, D., Politzer-Ahles, S., Rousselet, G., … von Grebmer zu Wolfsthurn, S. (2020). Dissociable effects of prediction and integration during language comprehension: Evidence from a large-scale study using brain potentials. *Philosophical Transactions of the Royal Society B: Biological Sciences, 375*(1791), 20180522.

Nieuwland, M. S., Politzer-Ahles, S., Heyselaar, E., Segaert, K., Darley, E., Kazanina, N., von Grebmer zu Wolfsthurn, S., Bartolozzi, F., Kogan, V., Ito, A., Mézière, D., Barr, D. J., Rousselet, G. A., Ferguson, H. J., Busch-Moreno, S., Fu, X., Tuomainen, J., Kulakova, E., Husband, E. M., … Huettig, F. (2018). Large-scale replication study reveals a limit on probabilistic prediction in language comprehension. *ELife, 7*, e33468.

Nieuwland, M. S., & van Berkum, J. J. A. (2006). When peanuts fall in love: N400 evidence for the power of discourse. *Journal of Cognitive Neuroscience, 18*(7), 1098–1111.

Nirme, J., Haake, M., Gulz, A., & Gullberg, M. (2020). Motion capture-based animated characters for the study of speech–gesture integration. *Behavior Research Methods, 52*(3), 1339–1354.

Nóbrega, V. A., & Miyagawa, S. (2015). The precedence of syntax in the rapid emergence of human language in evolution as defined by the integration hypothesis. *Frontiers in Psychology, 6*.

Norris, D. (1986). Word recognition: Context effects without priming. *Cognition, 22*, 93–136.

Norris, D. (1994). Shortlist: A connectionist model of continuous speech recognition. *Cognition, 52*(3), 189–234.

Norris, D. (2006). The Bayesian reader: Explaining word recognition as an optimal Bayesian decision process. *Psychological Review, 113*, 327–357.

Norris, D. (2013). Models of visual word recognition. *Trends in Cognitive Sciences, 17*(10), 517–524.

Norris, D., & McQueen, J. M. (2008). Shortlist B: A Bayesian model of continuous speech recognition. *Psychological Review, 115*, 357–395.

Norris, D., McQueen, J. M., & Cutler, A. (1995). Competition and segmentation in spoken-word recognition. *Journal of Experimental Psychology: Learning, Memory, and Cognition, 21*, 1209–1228.

Norris, D., McQueen, J. M., & Cutler, A. (2000). Merging information in speech recognition: Feedback is never necessary. *Behavioral and Brain Sciences, 23*(3), 299–325.

Nota, N., Trujillo, J., & Holler, J. (2022). Conversational eyebrow frowns facilitate question identification: An online VR study. PsyArXiv.

Nunberg, G. (1993). Indexicality and deixis. *Linguistics and Philosophy, 16*(1), 1–43.

O'Brien, E. J., Duffy, S. A., & Myers, J. L. (1986). Anaphoric inference during reading. *Journal of Experimental Psychology: Learning, Memory, and Cognition, 12*, 346–352.

O'Brien, E. J., & Myers, J. L. (1987). The role of causal connections in the retrieval of text. *Memory & Cognition, 15*(5), 419–427.

O'Brien, E. J., Shank, D. M., Myers, J. L., & Rayner, K. (1988). Elaborative inferences during reading: Do they occur on-line? *Journal of Experimental Psychology: Learning, Memory, and Cognition, 14*, 410–420.

Olivier, R., & Raj, B. (2022). There is more than one kind of robustness: Fooling whisper with adversarial examples (arXiv:2210.17316). arXiv.

Omtzigt, D., Hendriks, A. W., & Kolk, H. H. J. (2002). Evidence for magnocellular involvement in the identification of flanked letters. *Neuropsychologia, 40*(12), 1881–1890.

Oppenheim, G. M., & Dell, G. S. (2008). Inner speech slips exhibit lexical bias, but not the phonemic similarity effect. *Cognition, 106*(1), 528–537.

Ormel, E. A. (2008). *Visual Word Recognition in Bilingual Deaf Children*. Radboud University Nijmegen.

O'Rourke, T. B., & Holcomb, P. J. (2002). Electrophysiological evidence for the efficiency of spoken word processing. *Biological Psychology, 60*(2), 121–150.

Ortega, G., & Özyürek, A. (2020). Types of iconicity and combinatorial strategies distinguish semantic categories in silent gesture across cultures. *Language and Cognition, 12*(1), 84–113.

Ortega, G., Özyürek, A., & Peeters, D. (2020). Iconic gestures serve as manual cognates in hearing second language learners of a sign language: An ERP study. *Journal of Experimental Psychology: Learning, Memory, and Cognition, 46*, 403–415.

O'Seaghdha, P. G., Chen, J.-Y., & Chen, T.-M. (2010). Proximate units in word production: Phonological encoding begins with syllables in Mandarin Chinese but with segments in English. *Cognition, 115*(2), 282–302.

Osgood, C. E. (1966). Dimensionality of the semantic space for communication via facial expressions. *Scandinavian Journal of Psychology, 7*(1), 1–30.

Osterhout, L., McLaughlin, J., & Bersick, M. (1997). Event-related brain potentials and human language. *Trends in Cognitive Sciences, 1*(6), 203–209.

Özyürek, A., Willems, R. M., Kita, S., & Hagoort, P. (2007). On-line integration of semantic information from speech and gesture: Insights from event-related brain potentials. *Journal of Cognitive Neuroscience, 19*(4), 605–616.

Paap, K. (2023). *The Bilingual Advantage in Executive Functioning Hypothesis. How the Debate Provides Insight into Psychology's Replication Crisis*. Routledge/Taylor & Francis.

Pan, X., & Hamilton, A. F. de C. (2018). Why and how to use virtual reality to study human social interaction: The challenges of exploring a new research landscape. *British Journal of Psychology, 109*(3), 395–417.

Pastor, L., & Laka, I. (2013). Processing facilitation strategies in OV and VO languages: A corpus study. *Open Journal of Modern Linguistics, 03*(03), 252–258.

Paulmann, S., Elston-Güttler, K. E., Gunter, T. C., & Kotz, S. A. (2006). Is bilingual lexical access influenced by language context? *NeuroReport, 17*(7), 727.

Peeters, D. (2019). Virtual reality: A game-changing method for the language sciences. *Psychonomic Bulletin & Review, 26*(3), 894–900.

Peeters, D. (2020). Bilingual switching between languages and listeners: Insights from immersive virtual reality. *Cognition, 195*, 104107.

Peeters, D., & Dijkstra, T. (2018). Sustained inhibition of the native language in bilingual language production: A virtual reality approach. *Bilingualism: Language and Cognition, 21*(5), 1035–1061.

Peeters, D., Dijkstra, T., & Grainger, J. (2013). The representation and processing of identical cognates by late bilinguals: RT and ERP effects. *Journal of Memory and Language, 68*(4), 315–332.

Peeters, D., Vanlangendonck, F., Rueschemeyer, S.-A., & Dijkstra, T. (2019). Activation of the language control network in bilingual visual word recognition. *Cortex, 111*, 63–73.

Perniss, P., Thompson, R., & Vigliocco, G. (2010). Iconicity as a general property of language: Evidence from spoken and signed languages. *Frontiers in Psychology, 1*.

Perniss, P., & Vigliocco, G. (2014). The bridge of iconicity: From a world of experience to the experience of language. *Philosophical Transactions of the Royal Society B: Biological Sciences, 369*(1651), 20130300.

Perry, C., Ziegler, J. C., & Zorzi, M. (2007). Nested incremental modeling in the development of computational theories: The CDP+ model of reading aloud. *Psychological Review, 114*, 273–315.

Perry, C., Ziegler, J. C., & Zorzi, M. (2010). Beyond single syllables: Large-scale modeling of reading aloud with the Connectionist Dual Process (CDP++) model. *Cognitive Psychology, 61*(2), 106–151.

Peterson, R. R., & Savoy, P. (1998). Lexical selection and phonological encoding during language production: Evidence for cascaded processing. *Journal of Experimental Psychology: Learning, Memory, and Cognition, 24*, 539–557.

Pickering, M. J., & Garrod, S. (2013). An integrated theory of language production and comprehension. *Behavioral and Brain Sciences, 36*(4), 329–347.

Pickering, M. J., & Garrod, S. (2021). *Understanding Dialogue: Language Use and Social Interaction*. Cambridge University Press.

Piñango, M. M., Finn, E., Lacadie, C., & Constable, R. T. (2016). The localization of long-distance dependency components: Integrating the focal-lesion and neuroimaging record. *Frontiers in Psychology, 7*.

Pinet, S., & Nozari, N. (2018). "Twisting fingers": The case for interactivity in typed language production. *Psychonomic Bulletin & Review, 25*(4), 1449–1457.

Pinker, S. (1999). *Words and Rules: The Ingredients of Language*. Basic Books.

Pivneva, I., Mercier, J., & Titone, D. (2014). Executive control modulates cross-language lexical activation during L2 reading: Evidence from eye movements. *Journal of Experimental Psychology: Learning, Memory, and Cognition*, *40*(3), 787.

Plaut, D. C. (1997). Structure and function in the lexical system: Insights from distributed models of word reading and lexical decision. *Language and Cognitive Processes*, *12*(5–6), 765–806.

Plaut, D. C. (1999). A connectionist approach to word reading and acquired dyslexia: Extension to sequential processing. *Cognitive Science*, *23*(4), 543–568.

Plaut, D. C., McClelland, J. L., Seidenberg, M. S., & Patterson, K. (1996). Understanding normal and impaired word reading: Computational principles in quasi-regular domains. *Psychological Review*, *103*(1), 56–115.

Pollatsek, A., Reichle, E. D., & Rayner, K. (2006). Tests of the E-Z Reader model: Exploring the interface between cognition and eye-movement control. *Cognitive Psychology*, *52*(1), 1–56.

Poplack, S. (1980). Sometimes I'll start a sentence in Spanish Y TERMINO EN ESPAÑOL: Toward a typology of code-switching. *Linguistics*, *18*, 581–618.

Popper, K. R. (1959). *The Logic of Scientific Discovery*. Hutchison & Co.

Potter, J. M. (1976). Dr. Spooner and his dysgraphia. *Proceedings of the Royal Society of Medicine*, *69*(9), 639–648.

Pouw, W., & Dixon, J. A. (2019). Entrainment and modulation of gesture–speech synchrony under delayed auditory feedback. *Cognitive Science*, *43*(3), e12721.

Pulvermüller, F. (2013). How neurons make meaning: Brain mechanisms for embodied and abstract-symbolic semantics. *Trends in Cognitive Sciences*, *17*(9), 458–470.

Pylkkänen, L. (2019). The neural basis of combinatory syntax and semantics. *Science*, *366*(6461), 62–66.

Quilty-Dunn, J., Porot, N., & Mandelbaum, E. (2022). The best game in town: The re-emergence of the language of thought hypothesis across the cognitive sciences. *Behavioral and Brain Sciences*, 1–55.

Radeau, M., Morais, J., Mousty, P., & Bertelson, P. (2000). The effect of speaking rate on the role of the uniqueness point in spoken word recognition. *Journal of Memory and Language*, *42*(3), 406–422.

Radford, A. (1988). *Transformational Grammar*. Cambridge University Press.

Radford, A., Kim, J. W., Xu, T., Brockman, G., McLeavey, C., & Sutskever, I. (2022). *Robust Speech Recognition via Large-Scale Weak Supervision* (arXiv:2212.04356). arXiv.

Ramachandran, V. S., & Hubbard, E. M. (2001). Synaesthesia—a window into perception, thought and language. *Journal of Consciousness Studies*, *8*(12), 3–34.

Rap, B., & Fischer-Baum, S. (2014). Representation of orthographic knowledge. In M. A. Goldrick, V. S. Ferreira, & M. Miozzo (Eds.), *The Oxford Handbook of Language Production* (pp. 338–357). Oxford University Press.

Raposo, A., Moss, H. E., Stamatakis, E. A., & Tyler, L. K. (2009). Modulation of motor and premotor cortices by actions, action words and action sentences. *Neuropsychologia*, *47*(2), 388–396.

Rappaport Hovav, M., & Levin, B. (1988). What to do with theta-roles? In W. K. Wilkins (Ed.), *Syntax and Semantics, Vol. 21: Thematic Relations* (pp. 7–36). Academic Press.

Rastle, K. (2019). The place of morphology in learning to read in English. *Cortex*, *116*, 45–54.

Rastle, K., & Brysbaert, M. (2006). Masked phonological priming effects in English: Are they real? Do they matter? *Cognitive Psychology*, *53*(2), 97–145.

Raviv, L., Meyer, A., & Lev-Ari, S. (2019). Larger communities create more systematic languages. *Proceedings of the Royal Society B: Biological Sciences*, *286*(1907), 20191262.

Rawlinson, G. (1999). *Reibadailty | New Scientist*. https://www.newscientist.com/letter/mg16221887-600-reibadailty/

Rayner, K. (1998). Eye movements in reading and information processing: 20 years of research. *Psychological Bulletin*, *124*, 372–422.

Rayner, K. (2009). The 35th Sir Frederick Bartlett Lecture: Eye movements and attention in reading, scene perception, and visual search. *Quarterly Journal of Experimental Psychology*, *62*(8), 1457–1506.

Rayner, K., & Pollatsek, A. (1989). *The Psychology of Reading* (pp. xi, 529). Prentice-Hall, Inc.

Rayner, K., Pollatsek, A., Ashby, J., & Clifton Jr., C. (2011). *Psychology of Reading*. Psychology Press.

Rayner, K., & Reichle, E. D. (2010). Models of the reading process. *WIREs Cognitive Science*, *1*(6), 787–799.

Reicher, G. M. (1969). Perceptual recognition as a function of meaningfulness of stimulus material. *Journal of Experimental Psychology*, *81*, 275–280.

Reichle, E. D. (2011). Serial-attention models of reading. In S. Liversedge, I. Gilchrist, & E. Everling (Eds.), *The Oxford Handbook of Eye Movements* (pp. 767–786). Oxford University Press.

Reviriego, P., & Merino-Gómez, E. (2022). *Text to Image Generation: Leaving no Language Behind* (arXiv:2208.09333). arXiv.

Rheingold, H. (1988). *Koro*. Kosmos.

Riesenhuber, M., & Poggio, T. (1999). Hierarchical models of object recognition in cortex. *Nature Neuroscience, 2*(11), Article 11.

Roach, P. (2009). *English Phonetics and Phonology*. Cambridge University Press.

Roelofs, A. (1997). The WEAVER model of word-form encoding in speech production. *Cognition, 64*(3), 249–284.

Roelofs, A. (2003). Goal-referenced selection of verbal action: Modeling attentional control in the Stroop task. *Psychological Review, 110*, 88–125.

Roelofs, A. (2018). One hundred fifty years after Donders: Insights from unpublished data, a replication, and modeling of his reaction times. *Acta Psychologica, 191*, 228–233.

Roelofs, A., & Ferreira, V. S. (2019). The architecture of speaking. In P. Hagoort (Ed.), *Human Language: From Genes and Brains to Behavior* (pp. 35–50). MIT Press.

Roelofs, A., & Shitova, N. (2017). Importance of response time in assessing the cerebral dynamics of spoken word production: Comment on Munding et al. (2016). *Language, Cognition and Neuroscience, 32*(8), 1064–1067.

Rommers, J., Dijkstra, T., & Bastiaansen, M. (2013). Context-dependent semantic processing in the human brain: Evidence from idiom comprehension. *Journal of Cognitive Neuroscience, 25*(5), 762–776.

Rosch, E. H. (1973). Natural categories. *Cognitive Psychology, 4*(3), 328–350.

Rosch, E. H. (1978). *Principles of Categorization* (E. Roach & B. B. Lloyd, Eds.). Lawrence Erlbaum Associates.

Rueschemeyer, S.-A., van Rooij, D., Lindemann, O., Willems, R. M., & Bekkering, H. (2010). The function of words: Distinct neural correlates for words denoting differently manipulable objects. *Journal of Cognitive Neuroscience, 22*(8), 1844–1851.

Rumelhart, D. E., & McClelland, J. L. (1982). An interactive activation model of context effects in letter perception: II. The contextual enhancement effect and some tests and extensions of the model. *Psychological Review, 89*, 60–94.

Russell, C. W. (1863). *The Life of Cardinal Mezzofanti: With an Introductory Memoir of Eminent Linguists, Ancient and Modern*. Longman & Green.

Sachs, J. S. (1967). Recognition memory for syntactic and semantic aspects of connected discourse. *Perception & Psychophysics, 2*(9), 437–442.

Sacks, H., & Schegloff, E. A. (1979). Two preferences in the organization of reference to persons in conversation and their interaction. In G. Psathas (Ed.), *Everyday Language. Studies in Ethnomethodology* (pp. 15–21). Irvington Publishers.

Sanders, A. F. (1980). 20 stage analysis of reaction processes. In G. E. Stelmach & J. Requin (Eds.), *Advances in Psychology* (Vol. 1, pp. 331–354). North-Holland.

Sandoval, T. C., Gollan, T. H., Ferreira, V. S., & Salmon, D. P. (2010). What causes the bilingual disadvantage in verbal fluency? The dual-task analogy. *Bilingualism: Language and Cognition, 13*(2), 231–252.

Sauppe, S. (2016). Verbal semantics drives early anticipatory eye movements during the comprehension of verb-initial sentences. *Frontiers in Psychology, 7*.

Sauppe, S., Norcliffe, E., Konopka, A. E., Van Valin, R. D. Jr., & Levinson, S. C. (2013). Dependencies first: Eye tracking evidence from sentence production in Tagalog. *Proceedings of the Annual Meeting of the Cognitive Science Society*, 1265–1270.

Scao, T. L., Fan, A., Akiki, C., Pavlick, E., Ilić, S., Hesslow, D., Castagné, R., Luccioni, A. S., Yvon, F., Gallé, M., Tow, J., Rush, A. M., Biderman, S., Webson, A., Ammanamanchi, P. S., Wang, T., Sagot, B., Muennighoff, N., del Moral, A. V., ... Wolf, T. (2022). *BLOOM: A 176B-Parameter Open-Access Multilingual Language Model* (arXiv:2211.05100). arXiv.

Schaerlaekens, A. (2000). De verwerving van het Nederlands: Een blauwdruk. In S. Gillis & A. Schaerlaekens (Eds.), *Kindertaalverwerving. Een handboek voor het Nederlands* (pp. 11–38). Martinus Nijhoff.

Schank, R. C., & Abelson, R. P. (1977). *Scripts, Plans, Goals, and Understanding: An Inquiry into Human Knowledge Structures*. Lawrence Erlbaum Associates.

Schank, R. C., & Birnbaum, L. (1984). Computational models: Memory, meaning, and syntax. In T. G. Bever, J. M. Carroll, & L. A. Miller (Eds.), *Talking Minds: The Study of Language in Cognitive Science* (pp. 209–251). MIT Press.

Scharenborg, O. (2010). Modeling the use of durational information in human spoken-word recognition.

Journal of the Acoustical Society of America, 127(6), 3758–3770.

Scharenborg, O. E., & Merkx, D. (2018). The role of articulatory feature representation quality in a computational model of human spoken-word recognition. *Proceedings of the Machine Learning in Speech and Language Processing Workshop*. https://repository.tudelft.nl/islandora/object/uuid%3Ae734e1ed-8e27-4779-a89c-6a4bd797aa63

Scheflen, A. E. (1964). The significance of posture in communication systems. *Psychiatry, 27*(4), 316–331.

Schepens, J., van Hout, R., & Jaeger, T. F. (2020). Big data suggest strong constraints of linguistic similarity on adult language learning. *Cognition, 194*, 104056.

Schilbach, L., Timmermans, B., Reddy, V., Costall, A., Bente, G., Schlicht, T., & Vogeley, K. (2013). Toward a second-person neuroscience. *Behavioral and Brain Sciences, 36*(4), 393–414.

Schriefers, H., Meyer, A. S., & Levelt, W. J. M. (1990). Exploring the time course of lexical access in language production: Picture-word interference studies. *Journal of Memory and Language, 29*(1), 86–102.

Schurz, M., Radua, J., Aichhorn, M., Richlan, F., & Perner, J. (2014). Fractionating theory of mind: A meta-analysis of functional brain imaging studies. *Neuroscience & Biobehavioral Reviews, 42*, 9–34.

Schwartz, A. I., & Kroll, J. F. (2006). Bilingual lexical activation in sentence context. *Journal of Memory and Language, 55*(2), 197–212.

Searle, J. R. (1969). *Speech Acts: An Essay in the Philosophy of Language*. Cambridge University Press.

Seidenberg, M. S., & McClelland, J. L. (1989). A distributed, developmental model of word recognition and naming. *Psychological Review, 96*, 523–568.

Selfridge, O. G. (1959). Pandemonium: A paradigm for learning. In D. V. Blake & A. M. Uttley (Eds.), *Proceedings of the Symposium on Mechanisation of Thought Processes* (pp. 511–529). HM Stationery Office.

Senghas, A., Kita, S., & Özyürek, A. (2004). Children creating core properties of language: Evidence from an emerging sign language in Nicaragua. *Science, 305*(5691), 1779–1782.

Shannon, C. E., & Weaver, W. (1948). A mathematical theory of communication. *Bell System Technical Journal, 27*(4), 379–423.

Sharma, A., & Dorman, M. F. (1999). Cortical auditory evoked potential correlates of categorical perception of voice-onset time. *Journal of the Acoustical Society of America, 106*(2), 1078–1083.

Shattuck-Hufnagel, S. (2019). Toward an (even) more comprehensive model of speech production planning. *Language, Cognition and Neuroscience, 34*(9), 1202–1213.

Shillcock, R. (1990). Lexical hypotheses in continuous speech. In G. T. M. Altmann (Ed.), *Cognitive Models of Speech Processing: Psycholinguistic and Computational Perspectives* (pp. 24–49). MIT Press.

Shuai, L., & Malins, J. G. (2017). Encoding lexical tones in jTRACE: A simulation of monosyllabic spoken word recognition in Mandarin Chinese. *Behavior Research Methods, 49*(1), 230–241.

Sianipar, A. N. S. W. (2017). *Emotional and Semantic Meanings of Words in the First and Second Language: Representation, Learning, and Processing*. Radboud University Nijmegen.

Sianipar, A., van Groenestijn, P., & Dijkstra, T. (2016). Affective meaning, concreteness, and subjective frequency norms for Indonesian words. *Frontiers in Psychology, 7*.

Simmons, W. K., Ramjee, V., Beauchamp, M. S., McRae, K., Martin, A., & Barsalou, L. W. (2007). A common neural substrate for perceiving and knowing about color. *Neuropsychologia, 45*(12), 2802–2810.

Siyanova-Chanturia, A., Conklin, K., & van Heuven, W. J. B. (2011). Seeing a phrase "time and again" matters: The role of phrasal frequency in the processing of multiword sequences. *Journal of Experimental Psychology: Learning, Memory, and Cognition, 37*, 776–784.

Slobin, D. I. (1987). Thinking for speaking. *Annual Meeting of the Berkeley Linguistics Society, 13*, 435–445.

Slobin, D. I. (1996). From "thought and language" to "thinking for speaking." In J. J. Gumperz & S. C. Levinson (Eds.), *Rethinking Linguistic Relativity* (pp. 70–96). Cambridge University Press.

Smith, K., Kirby, S., & Brighton, H. (2003). Iterated learning: A framework for the emergence of language. *Artificial Life, 9*(4), 371–386.

Snedeker, J., & Trueswell, J. (2003). Using prosody to avoid ambiguity: Effects of speaker awareness and referential context. *Journal of Memory and Language, 48*(1), 103–130.

Snodgrass, J. G., & Vanderwart, M. (1980). A standardized set of 260 pictures: Norms for name agreement, image agreement, familiarity, and visual complexity. *Journal of Experimental Psychology: Human Learning and Memory, 6*, 174–215.

Spencer, A., & Zwicky, A. M. (1998). *The Handbook of Morphology*. John Wiley & Sons.

Spivey, M. J., & Marian, V. (1999). Cross talk between native and second languages: Partial activation of an irrelevant lexicon. *Psychological Science*, *10*(3), 281–284.

Staub, A., & Clifton, C. Jr. (2006). Syntactic prediction in language comprehension: Evidence from either ... or. *Journal of Experimental Psychology: Learning, Memory, and Cognition*, *32*, 425–436.

Steinhauer, K., Alter, K., & Friederici, A. D. (1999). Brain potentials indicate immediate use of prosodic cues in natural speech processing. *Nature Neuroscience*, *2*(2), Article 2.

Sternberg, S. (1969). The discovery of processing stages: Extensions of Donders' method. *Acta Psychologica*, *30*, 276–315.

Stivers, T., Enfield, N. J., Brown, P., Englert, C., Hayashi, M., Heinemann, T., Hoymann, G., Rossano, F., de Ruiter, J. P., Yoon, K.-E., & Levinson, S. C. (2009). Universals and cultural variation in turn-taking in conversation. *Proceedings of the National Academy of Sciences*, *106*(26), 10587–10592.

Stivers, T., & Sidnell, J. (2013). *The Handbook of Conversation Analysis*. John Wiley & Sons.

Strauss, T. J., Harris, H. D., & Magnuson, J. S. (2007). jTRACE: A reimplementation and extension of the TRACE model of speech perception and spoken word recognition. *Behavior Research Methods*, *39*(1), 19–30.

Strijkers, K., Costa, A., & Thierry, G. (2010). Tracking lexical access in speech production: Electrophysiological correlates of word frequency and cognate effects. *Cerebral Cortex*, *20*(4), 912–928.

Stroop, J. R. (1935). Studies of interference in serial verbal reactions. *Journal of Experimental Psychology*, *18*, 643–662.

Suzuki, T. N. (2021). Animal linguistics: Exploring referentiality and compositionality in bird calls. *Ecological Research*, *36*(2), 221–231.

Swinney, D. A. (1979). Lexical access during sentence comprehension: (Re)consideration of context effects. *Journal of Verbal Learning and Verbal Behavior*, *18*(6), 645–659.

Swinney, D. A., & Cutler, A. (1979). The access and processing of idiomatic expressions. *Journal of Verbal Learning and Verbal Behavior*, *18*(5), 523–534.

Szaflarski, J. P., Binder, J. R., Possing, E. T., McKiernan, K. A., Ward, B. D., & Hammeke, T. A. (2002). Language lateralization in left-handed and ambidextrous people: FMRI data. *Neurology*, *59*(2), 238–244.

Tabossi, P., Burani, C., & Scott, D. (1995). Word identification in fluent speech. *Journal of Memory and Language*, *34*(4), 440–467.

Tanenhaus, M. K., Spivey-Knowlton, M. J., Eberhard, K. M., & Sedivy, J. C. (1995). Integration of visual and linguistic information in spoken language comprehension. *Science*, *268*(5217), 1632–1634.

Taraban, R., & McClelland, J. L. (1988). Constituent attachment and thematic role assignment in sentence processing: Influences of content-based expectations. *Journal of Memory and Language*, *27*(6), 597–632.

Taylor, I. (1990). *Psycholinguistics: Learning and Using Language*. Prentice-Hall.

Tesink, C. M. J. Y., Petersson, K. M., van Berkum, J. J. A., van den Brink, D., Buitelaar, J. K., & Hagoort, P. (2009). Unification of speaker and meaning in language comprehension: An fMRI study. *Journal of Cognitive Neuroscience*, *21*(11), 2085–2099.

Thibadeau, R., Just, M. A., & Carpenter, P. A. (1982). A model of the time course and content of reading. *Cognitive Science*, *6*(2), 157–203.

Thierry, G., & Wu, Y. J. (2007). Brain potentials reveal unconscious translation during foreign-language comprehension. *Proceedings of the National Academy of Sciences*, *104*(30), 12530–12535.

Thomas, M. S. C., & van Heuven, W. J. B. (2005). Computational models of bilingual comprehension. In J. F. Kroll & A. M. B. de Groot (Eds.), *Handbook of Bilingualism: Psycholinguistic Approaches* (pp. 202–225). Oxford University Press.

Tomasello, M. (2008). *Origins of Human Communication*. MIT Press.

Tomasello, M., Carpenter, M., Call, J., Behne, T., & Moll, H. (2005). Understanding and sharing intentions: The origins of cultural cognition. *Behavioral and Brain Sciences*, *28*(5), 675–691.

Tomasello, M., Carpenter, M., & Liszkowski, U. (2007). A new look at infant pointing. *Child Development*, *78*(3), 705–722.

Tomlin, R. S. (2014). *Basic Word Order (RLE Linguistics B: Grammar): Functional Principles*. Routledge.

Treisman, A. M. (1969). Strategies and models of selective attention. *Psychological Review*, *76*, 282–299.

Tremblay, A., Derwing, B., Libben, G., & Westbury, C. (2011). Processing advantages of lexical bundles: Evidence from self-paced reading and sentence recall tasks. *Language Learning*, *61*(2), 569–613.

Tremblay, P., & Dick, A. S. (2016). Broca and Wernicke are dead, or moving past the classic model of

language neurobiology. *Brain and Language*, *162*, 60–71.
Tromp, J., Peeters, D., Meyer, A. S., & Hagoort, P. (2018). The combined use of virtual reality and EEG to study language processing in naturalistic environments. *Behavior Research Methods*, *50*(2), 862–869.
Trujillo, J., Özyürek, A., Holler, J., & Drijvers, L. (2021). Speakers exhibit a multimodal Lombard effect in noise. *Scientific Reports*, *11*(1), Article 1.
Tucker, B. V., Brenner, D., Danielson, D. K., Kelley, M. C., Nenadić, F., & Sims, M. (2019). The Massive Auditory Lexical Decision (MALD) database. *Behavior Research Methods*, *51*(3), 1187–1204.
Tulving, E. (1972). Episodic and semantic memory. In E. Tulving & W. Donaldson (Eds.), *Organization of Memory*. Academic Press.
Uddén, J., Hultén, A., Schoffelen, J.-M., Lam, N., Harbusch, K., van den Bosch, A., Kempen, G., Petersson, K. M., & Hagoort, P. (2022). Supramodal sentence processing in the human brain: FMRI evidence for the influence of syntactic complexity in more than 200 participants. *Neurobiology of Language*, *3*(4), 575–598.
Ullman, M. T. (2004). Contributions of memory circuits to language: The declarative/procedural model. *Cognition*, *92*(1), 231–270.
Urgen, B. A., Kutas, M., & Saygin, A. P. (2018). Uncanny valley as a window into predictive processing in the social brain. *Neuropsychologia*, *114*, 181–185.
van Berkum, J., de Goede, D., van Alphen, P., Mulder, E., & Kerstholt, J. (2013). How robust is the language architecture? The case of mood. *Frontiers in Psychology*, *4*.
van Dam, W. O., Van Dijk, M., Bekkering, H., & Rueschemeyer, S.-A. (2012). Flexibility in embodied lexical-semantic representations. *Human Brain Mapping*, *33*(10), 2322–2333.
van den Brink, D., Brown, C. M., & Hagoort, P. (2001). Electrophysiological evidence for early contextual influences during spoken-word recognition: N200 versus N400 effects. *Journal of Cognitive Neuroscience*, *13*(7), 967–985.
van der Lee, C., Gatt, A., van Miltenburg, E., & Krahmer, E. (2021). Human evaluation of automatically generated text: Current trends and best practice guidelines. *Computer Speech & Language*, *67*, 101151.
van Dijk, C. (2021). *Cross-Linguistic Influence during Real-Time Sentence Processing in Bilingual Children and Adults*. Radboud University Nijmegen.

van Ginkel, W., & Dijkstra, T. (2020). The tug of war between an idiom's figurative and literal meanings: Evidence from native and bilingual speakers. *Bilingualism: Language and Cognition*, *23*(1), 131–147.
van Gompel, R. P., Pickering, M. J., & Traxler, Matthew J. (2000). Unrestricted race: A new model of syntactic ambiguity resolution. In A. Kennedy, R. Radach, D. Heller, & J. Pynte (Eds.), *Reading as a Perceptual Process* (pp. 621–648). North-Holland/Elsevier Science Publishers.
van Hell, J. G., & de Groot, A. M. B. (2008). Sentence context modulates visual word recognition and translation in bilinguals. *Acta Psychologica*, *128*(3), 431–451.
van Hell, J. G., & Dijkstra, T. (2002). Foreign language knowledge can influence native language performance in exclusively native contexts. *Psychonomic Bulletin & Review*, *9*(4), 780–789.
van Hell, J. G., & Tanner, D. (2012). Second language proficiency and cross-language lexical activation. *Language Learning*, *62*(s2), 148–171.
van Heuven, W. J. B., Conklin, K., Coderre, E., Guo, T., & Dijkstra, T. (2011). The influence of cross-language similarity on within- and between-language Stroop effects in trilinguals. *Frontiers in Psychology*, *2*.
van Heuven, W. J. B., & Dijkstra, T. (2010). Language comprehension in the bilingual brain: FMRI and ERP support for psycholinguistic models. *Brain Research Reviews*, *64*(1), 104–122.
van Heuven, W. J. B., Dijkstra, T., & Grainger, J. (1998). Orthographic neighborhood effects in bilingual word recognition. *Journal of Memory and Language*, *39*(3), 458–483.
van Heuven, W. J. B., Mandera, P., Keuleers, E., & Brysbaert, M. (2014). Subtlex-UK: A new and improved word frequency database for British English. *Quarterly Journal of Experimental Psychology*, *67*(6), 1176–1190.
van Heuven, W. J. B., Schriefers, H., Dijkstra, T., & Hagoort, P. (2008). Language conflict in the bilingual brain. *Cerebral Cortex*, *18*(11), 2706–2716.
Vanlangendonck, F., Peeters, D., Rueschemeyer, S.-A., & Dijkstra, T. (2020). Mixing the stimulus list in bilingual lexical decision turns cognate facilitation effects into mirrored inhibition effects. *Bilingualism: Language and Cognition*, *23*(4), 836–844.
Vasishth, S., Nicenboim, B., Engelmann, F., & Burchert, F. (2019). Computational models of retrieval processes in sentence processing. *Trends in Cognitive Sciences*, *23*(11), 968–982.
Verderber, R. F. (1993). *Communicate!* Wadsworth Pub.

Vigliocco, G. (1996). One or more labels on the bottles? Notional concord in Dutch and French. *Language and Cognitive Processes, 11*(4), 407–442.

Vigliocco, G., Butterworth, B., & Garrett, M. F. (1996). Subject-verb agreement in Spanish and English: Differences in the role of conceptual constraints. *Cognition, 61*(3), 261–298.

Vigliocco, G., Kousta, S.-T., Della Rosa, P. A., Vinson, D. P., Tettamanti, M., Devlin, J. T., & Cappa, S. F. (2014). The neural representation of abstract words: The role of emotion. *Cerebral Cortex, 24*(7), 1767–1777.

Vigliocco, G., Perniss, P., & Vinson, D. (2014). Language as a multimodal phenomenon: Implications for language learning, processing and evolution. *Philosophical Transactions of the Royal Society B: Biological Sciences, 369*(1651), 20130292.

Vigliocco, G., & Vinson, D. P. (2007). Semantic representation. In M. G. Gaskell (Ed.), *The Oxford Handbook of Psycholinguistics* (pp. 195–216). Oxford University Press.

Vigliocco, G., Vinson, D. P., Lewis, W., & Garrett, M. F. (2004). Representing the meanings of object and action words: The featural and unitary semantic space hypothesis. *Cognitive Psychology, 48*(4), 422–488.

Vinson, D. P., & Vigliocco, G. (2008). Semantic feature production norms for a large set of objects and events. *Behavior Research Methods, 40*(1), 183–190.

Wagner, P., Malisz, Z., & Kopp, S. (2014). Gesture and speech in interaction: An overview. *Speech Communication, 57*, 209–232.

Wang, L., Bastiaansen, M., Yang, Y., & Hagoort, P. (2012). Information structure influences depth of syntactic processing: Event-related potential evidence for the Chomsky illusion. *PLOS ONE, 7*(10), e47917.

Warren, R. M. (1970). Perceptual restoration of missing speech sounds. *Science, 167*(3917), 392–393.

Warriner, A. B., Kuperman, V., & Brysbaert, M. (2013). Norms of valence, arousal, and dominance for 13,915 English lemmas. *Behavior Research Methods, 45*(4), 1191–1207.

Way, M. (2017). "What I cannot create, I do not understand." *Journal of Cell Science, 130*(18), 2941–2942.

Wen, Y., & van Heuven, W. J. B. (2018). Limitations of translation activation in masked priming: Behavioural evidence from Chinese–English bilinguals and computational modelling. *Journal of Memory and Language, 101*, 84–96.

Wheeler, D. D. (1970). Processes in word recognition. *Cognitive Psychology, 1*(1), 59–85.

Whorf, B. L. (2012). *Language, Thought, and Reality*, 2nd edn. *Selected Writings of Benjamin Lee Whorf*. MIT Press.

Wickelgren, W. A. (1969). Auditory or articulatory coding in verbal short-term memory. *Psychological Review, 76*, 232–235.

Willems, R. M. (2023). MA-EM: A neurocognitive model for understanding mixed and ambiguous emotions and morality. *Cognitive Neuroscience, 14*(2), 51–60.

Willems, R. M., der Haegen, L. V., Fisher, S. E., & Francks, C. (2014). On the other hand: Including left-handers in cognitive neuroscience and neurogenetics. *Nature Reviews Neuroscience, 15*(3), Article 3.

Willems, R. M., & Jacobs, A. M. (2016). Caring about Dostoyevsky: The untapped potential of studying literature. *Trends in Cognitive Sciences, 20*(4), 243–245.

Willems, R. M., Özyürek, A., & Hagoort, P. (2007). When language meets action: The neural integration of gesture and speech. *Cerebral Cortex, 17*(10), 2322–2333.

Willems, R. M., Özyürek, A., & Hagoort, P. (2008). Seeing and hearing meaning: ERP and fMRI evidence of word versus picture integration into a sentence context. *Journal of Cognitive Neuroscience, 20*(7), 1235–1249.

Winsler, K., Midgley, K. J., Grainger, J., & Holcomb, P. J. (2018). An electrophysiological megastudy of spoken word recognition. *Language, Cognition and Neuroscience, 33*(8), 1063–1082.

Wittgenstein, L. (1953). *Philosophical Investigations*. Blackwell.

Wodehouse, P. G. (1935). *The Luck of the Bodkins*. Herbert Jenkins.

Wolff, P., & Holmes, K. J. (2011). Linguistic relativity. *WIREs Cognitive Science, 2*(3), 253–265.

Woumans, E., Santens, P., Sieben, A., Versijpt, J., Stevens, M., & Duyck, W. (2015). Bilingualism delays clinical manifestation of Alzheimer's disease. *Bilingualism: Language and Cognition, 18*(3), 568–574.

Wu, Y. J., & Thierry, G. (2010). Chinese–English bilinguals reading English hear Chinese. *Journal of Neuroscience, 30*(22), 7646–7651.

Xiang, H., van Leeuwen, T. M., Dediu, D., Roberts, L., Norris, D. G., & Hagoort, P. (2015). L2-proficiency-dependent laterality shift in structural connectivity of brain language pathways. *Brain Connectivity, 5*(6), 349–361.

Yakpo, K., van den Berg, M., & Borges, M. (2015). On the linguistic consequences of language contact in Suriname: The case of convergence. In E. B. Carlin, E. Carlin, I. Léglise, B. Migge, & P. B. T. S. Fat (Eds.), *In and Out of Suriname: Language, Mobility and Identity* (pp. 164–195). Brill.

Yarkoni, T., Balota, D., & Yap, M. (2008). Moving beyond Coltheart's N: A new measure of orthographic similarity. *Psychonomic Bulletin & Review*, *15*(5), 971–979.

Yaxley, R. H., & Zwaan, R. A. (2007). Simulating visibility during language comprehension. *Cognition*, *105*(1), 229–236.

Yee, E., Huffstetler, S., & Thompson-Schill, S. L. (2011). Function follows form: Activation of shape and function features during object identification. *Journal of Experimental Psychology: General*, *140*, 348–363.

Zacks, J. M., & Swallow, K. M. (2007). Event segmentation. *Current Directions in Psychological Science*, *16*(2), 80–84.

Zuberbühler, K. (2019). Evolutionary roads to syntax. *Animal Behaviour*, *151*, 259–265.

Zwaan, R. A., Langston, M. C., & Graesser, A. C. (1995). The construction of situation models in narrative comprehension: An event-indexing model. *Psychological Science*, *6*(5), 292–297.

Zwaan, R. A., & Madden, C. J. (2004). Updating situation models. *Journal of Experimental Psychology: Learning, Memory, and Cognition*, *30*, 283–288.

Zwaan, R. A., Stanfield, R. A., & Yaxley, R. H. (2002). Language comprehenders mentally represent the shapes of objects. *Psychological Science*, *13*(2), 168–171.

Zwitserlood, P. (1989). The locus of the effects of sentential-semantic context in spoken-word processing. *Cognition*, *32*(1), 25–64.

Index

abjad, 104
absolute letter position coding, 110–112
abstract concept, 167
abstract information, 9, 159, 178
abstract rule system, 267
abugida, 104
ACC, 239
accent, 91, 95–96, 152–153, 203
acoustic phase, 205
acoustic phonetics, 39, 73
acoustic triangle, 73, 75
action, 133, 169–170, 172, 188, 211
Action Generator, 211
activation, 35–36, 62–63, 81–83, 107–112, 116–124, 172, 208–209, 235–240
active sentence, 147, 215, 246
actor, 131, 139, 200, 202
Adaptive Control Hypothesis, 237, 247
adaptive listener, 32, 91
adaptive speaker, 32
adjective, 103, 132, 135, 153, 163, 167
adjective phrase, 132
adverb, 17, 103, 132
advertisement, 19, 25, 190
aerodynamic phase, 205
affective meaning, 14, 138, 167, 171
affix, 207
affordance, 18, 160
age of acquisition (AoA), 50, 70
agent, 131–133, 137, 139, 169
agglutinative language, 226
algorithm, 146, 275
allophone, 39, 75–78
alpha wave, 61
alphabet, 104
alphabetic script, 104, 113, 242
Alpha-Go, 119
ambiguity, 17, 27–28, 73, 78, 96, 124–126, 135, 142, 157, 161, 185–186, 223

amodality, 167, 169–170
amplifier, 60
anagram, 111
analysis of variance (ANOVA), 47
anaphor, 174–175
anatomic MRI scan, 62
animacy, 132, 137, 161
animate-first principle, 132
ANOVA, 47
antecedent, 175–176
anterior cingulate cortex (ACC), 239
antonym, 125, 163–164
AoA, 50, 70
aphasia, 32, 115, 133
arbitrariness, 11–12, 15–16, 161, 170, 268–269
arcuate fasciculus, 143
arousal, 3–4, 265
article, 232–233
articulation, 30, 39, 74, 203–206
Articulator, 30, 197, 203–206
articulatory apparatus, 20, 74–75, 203–204
articulatory feature, 85
articulatory organ, 74, 203–204
articulatory phonetics, 39, 73
artificial intelligence, 85, 273–274
aspiration, 226, 242
assemblage, 113–114
assertive speech act, 199
assimilation, 5, 77
association, 52, 159, 161
asymmetrical switch cost, 246
attention, 4, 33, 265
attention allocation, 49, 265
attentional focus, 176–177
audience design, 220
auditory lexical decision, 50–51, 86
auditory (spoken) word recognition, 9, 13, 32, 39, 42, 51, 58, 71–98, 99, 100, 124, 150, 152
augmented reality, 274

automatic text generation, 275
autonomous processing, 31, 86, 140, 259
autonomous theory, 91
avatar, 68, 273–275

baby talk, 5
back-channel, 17
backpropagation, 118
backpropagation learning, 118
backward inference, 174
backward jump, 56, 135
backward mask, 52
balanced bilingual, 225
basal ganglia, 238–239
basic level term, 162
Bayesian statistics, 85, 110, 181
beat gesture, 96, 257
behavioral research, 49–58
between-language neighborhood effect, 234, 240
BIA model, 235–236
BIA+ model, 235
BIA-d model, 235
BIAM, 121–122
bias, 267–270
big bang, 20–21
bigram, 110–111
bilingual, 5, 37–38, 224–254
bilingual advantage, 239
Bilingual Interactive Activation + model (BIA+), 235
Bilingual Interactive Activation model (BIA), 235–236
bilingual language production, 237–239, 246–248
bilingual listening, 232–233, 240
bilingual reading, 226, 232–233, 240–245, 249–250
Bimodal Interactive Activation Model (BIAM), 121–122
BIMOLA, 235
binary feature, 168
binding problem, 23

Index

birdsong, 20–21
blend, 193
blood oxygenation, 62
Bloom, 275
bodily channel, 15–16, 189–190, 256–258
bodily signal, 16, 23, 256–257, 263
body language, 5, 14
BOLD response, 62
boldness, 102
bonding, 132, 174
borrowing, 254
bottleneck, 129, 273
bottom-up activation, 83–84, 108, 250, 260
bottom-up processing, 30–31, 83–84, 139, 231–233, 244
bouba-kiki, 269
boustrophedon, 99
Braille, 257
brain, 34–35, 59–64, 85, 142–146, 170–173, 183–184, 215–216, 238
brain network, 34–36, 147, 174, 238–239, 265–266
branching, 134
bridging inference, 174–175
broadcasting system, 107
Broca, 142–143
Broca's aphasia, 133, 142–143
Broca's area, 35, 143–144, 230
Brodmann area, 63
building block, 40, 48, 76, 144, 158, 210, 259

Cambridge email, 111
capital letter, 99
CAPS/READER model, 180–181
card game, 23, 67–68, 219
cascaded processing, 31–32, 113–115, 122, 181, 198, 207
case, 103, 133, 218
case grammar, 133, 169
case marking, 218
CAT scan, 64
categorical perception, 78–79, 80, 83
causality, 8, 175–176, 181
CAVE, 67–68
cave automatic virtual environment (CAVE), 67–68
central embedding, 134
central executive network, 265–266
Central Processing Unit, 107, 259
cerebellum, 143
characteristic feature, 164, 166
chatbot, 273–274
ChatGPT, 275–276
Chinese character, 128, 140
Chomsky illusion, 152

circuit of activation, 35–36, 144, 159, 167
clause, 131, 194
client, 2, 36, 38, 49, 59, 64, 115, 120, 133, 142–144, 170–171
clothing, 18
CLOZE-probability, 61, 126
c-method, 50
co-activation,
co-articulation, 3, 5, 73, 77, 83, 205
cocktail party phenomenon, 98
coda, 39, 206–208, 210
coded meaning, 145–146, 187–188
code mixing, 246
cognate, 117, 227–233, 241–245, 248–252, 257
cognate facilitation effect, 241–242, 244–245, 248–252, 257
cognitive control, 28, 33–34, 144, 182
Cognitive Control System, 28–29, 33–34, 36, 177, 182, 222, 262–263
cognitive neuroscience, 65, 119
coherence graph, 179–180
cohort, 40, 58, 77, 80–81, 88–90, 94–95, 106–107, 124
cohort member, 81, 83, 88, 94–95, 106
Cohort model, 80–82, 86, 98
color cue, 246–247
color term, 53, 162
commissive speech act, 199
common ground, 2, 17, 255, 268
communal common ground, 17
communication, 2–4, 14–26
Communication Planner, 210–211
competence, 267
competitor, 40, 80–81, 83, 85, 88, 201
composite signal, 5
compound, 40, 104, 134
computational model, 85, 146–148, 276–277
computational simultaneity, 194
computer metaphor, 107, 259
Computerized Axial Tomography (CAT), 64
computer screen paradigm, 65–66
concept, 11–12, 158, 162–169
conceptual accessibility, 203
conceptual code, 262
conceptual event, 169
conceptual facilitation, 220
conceptual link, 234
Conceptual Memory, 29–32, 35, 161, 171
conceptual network, 161–162
conceptual representation, 37, 40, 54, 117, 137, 140, 144, 156, 158, 159–160, 165, 170, 178, 182, 199–201, 226, 235, 237, 241, 259, 262
conceptual speech error, 193
conceptual structure, 30, 42, 130, 135, 138, 148, 159–160, 164, 178, 199–201
Conceptual System, 29–30, 35, 41, 159–160, 172–173, 185, 235, 261–262
conceptualization, 196–200, 211
concept-driven, 31, 232
concreteness, 50, 187
confederate, 67–68
conflict monitoring, 238–239
conjugation, 103
connectionist model, 82, 86, 91, 108–112, 115–120, 208–209
connectivity, 49, 200
consonant, 73–77, 103–104
consonant alphabet, 104
consonant cluster, 12
constraint satisfaction, 142
constraint-based model, 142, 148
Construction-Integration model, 179
constructionist approach, 174–175
context, 1, 5–7, 17, 91–96, 124–126, 152–155, 185–188, 218–221, 248–252, 258–259
context effect, 79, 95–97, 127, 156, 250–252
context knowledge, 130
contextual diversity, 107
contextual speech error, 193
continuous-to-discrete mapping, 73
contracted speech, 205
control condition, 45, 49–50
conversation, 8, 154, 182, 198, 246, 272–275
cooperativity, 198
co-speech gesture, 4, 11–12, 15–17, 23, 26, 96, 145, 154–155, 196, 210–211, 220–221, 256–257, 263–265
counterbalancing, 46
creativity, 277
Creole language, 22, 246
cross-linguistic competition, 230
cross-linguistic interference, 231
cross-linguistic priming, 245–246
cross-linguistic similarity, 226–232
cross-modal priming, 52, 94–96, 124–126
CT scan, 64
cued language-switching paradigm, 246–248
cultural context, 5–6
cultural diversity, 270–272
cultural frame shifting, 5

culture, 5–6, 227, 270–272
cycle time, 236–237

data scraping, 275
data-driven processing, 30
data-to-text system, 275
dative construction, 137, 230
Deaf community, 23, 229
deaf-blind, 128
deafblind communication, 4
decay, 107–108
decision criteria, 241, 248, 250
decision making, 53, 117, 177, 241, 277
declaration, 199
declarative memory, 48
decoding, 17, 24, 102, 129–130
decomposition, 104, 118, 164
deductive reasoning, 177
deep learning, 119–120
deep neural network, 85–86
deep orthography, 104–105, 114
Deep Structure, 37
defining feature, 164, 189
degree of overlap, 79, 97, 127, 227, 250–252
dementia, 239
demonstrative, 17
dependent variable, 46
derivation, 40, 103–105
descended larynx, 20
design feature, 11
determiner, 132, 135, 137, 195
diacritic, 3, 104
dialect, 73, 91, 209, 224, 270
dialog, 1–2, 8, 13, 27, 66–67, 199, 218–220, 272
different-script bilingual, 231
diffusion tensor imaging (DTI), 49
direct object, 132, 137–138, 202
direct route, 113–115, 122
directive speech act, 199
director-matcher task, 66–67
discourse, 6–7, 130, 153–154, 156, 169–170, 174, 178, 187–189
discourse model, 210–211, 218
discourse processing, 178–182, 187–188
displacement, 23
distractor, 88, 213–214, 218–220, 244
Distributed Conceptual Feature model, 234–235
distributed connectionist model, 91, 118–119
distributional semantics, 166–167
diversity, 270–272
domain-generality, 36, 239, 265–266
dominance, 3–4, 168

dominant language, 225, 248
dorsal, 34, 36, 85
dorsal attention network, 266
dorsal stream, 85
DTI, 49
Dual Route Cascaded model, 53, 113–115, 120, 123, 242
dual-process theory, 177
dual-stream model, 85
Dungeons and Dragons, 191
dyslexia, 114–115, 136

early bilingual, 38, 225
ecological validity, 65–68
edge detector, 102
education, 7, 49, 271
EEG, 59–61, 92–94, 121–123, 126, 150–154, 184, 240, 243
elaborative inference, 174–175
electroencephalography (EEG), 59–61, 92–94, 121–123, 126, 150–154, 184, 240, 243
embedded sentence, 133–134
embeddedness, 1–2, 5–7, 10–11, 17, 32, 71, 87, 159–160, 182, 192, 256, 258–259
emblem, 256
embodied representation, 167–168
embodied simulation hypothesis, 11
embodiedness, 1–5, 10–11, 96, 102, 145–146, 159–160, 167–168, 170–174, 192, 255–258
embodiment, 11, 161, 167
emoticon, 4, 99
emotion, 4, 7–8, 10, 18, 35, 99, 158–159, 167–168, 217, 265
encapsulation, 15, 35, 159–160, 259
encoding, 17, 24, 49, 129, 196–198, 200–203, 206–208, 215–216
episodic memory, 48, 159
ERP, 59–61, 92–94, 121–122, 150–154, 176–177, 184, 241
error detection, 239
ethical approval, 217
eurocognate, 227
European Commission, 253
event indexing, 181–182
event onset, 59, 60–61
event role, 139, 200
event segmentation, 181–182
event structure, 137–139, 144, 159, 180, 189, 196, 200–202, 260–261
event-indexing model, 181
event-related potential (ERP), 59–61, 92–94, 121–122, 150–154, 176–177, 184, 241
event-segmentation theory, 182
evolution, 19–24, 106
exemplar theory, 165–166

excitation, 83–84, 112, 208
executive control, 33, 237–239, 245
executive control system, 33, 238–239
executive functioning, 265
exemplar, 162, 165–166, 168
expectancy value, 110
experiment, 7, 46–47, 66–68
experimental control, 65–68
experimenter, 63, 67, 185, 212
explicit memory, 48
expressive speech act, 199
extension, 18, 161
external loop, 197
external noise, 18, 24, 46–47, 77, 258
eye blink, 16, 61, 154, 275
eye brow movement, 16, 154
eye contact, 5
eye fixation, 56–58, 88, 100, 106, 135–136
eye movement, 56–58, 88, 135–137, 150, 175–176
eye tracker, 56
eye tracking, 56–59
E–Z Reader model, 136

F1, 73
F2, 73, 79
Facebook, 19
face-to-face communication, 23–24, 210–211, 256–258, 263–265
facial expression, 2–5, 10, 17, 21, 23, 66, 130, 145, 154, 197, 256, 261, 263–265
facilitation effect, 95, 126, 214, 241, 248, 250–252
false friend, 227–228, 232, 235, 240–241, 244
falsification, 276
Featural and Unitary Semantic Space (FUSS), 164–165
featural approach, 164–165
feature norm, 165
feedforward activation, 118, 207
figurative language, 55, 157, 187–188
figurative meaning, 55, 157, 187–188
filler, 206, 210, 222
final devoicing, 76
final letter bank, 112–113
Fine-Tracker, 85
fingerspelling, 128
first language (L1), 224–225, 230–235, 238, 240–251
first-mention effect, 175–176
fixation duration, 56, 135–136, 232, 245, 249

fixation proportion, 88
fluent phase, 199
fMRI, 59, 62–64, 143, 184, 215–216
focus, 4, 33, 150–152, 175–176, 203
font, 7, 99–100, 102–103
font size, 7, 99–100, 102
font type, 7, 99–100, 102
foregrounding, 175
foreign language, 224–225, 242, 246
form perception, 103
formant, 73–75, 79
form-meaning mapping, 163, 269–270
form-meaning relation, 12, 269
formulation, 196–198, 200–203, 210–211, 271
Formulator, 196–198, 200–203, 205, 210–211
forward inference, 174–175
forward mask, 52
foveal vision, 57
fragment, 94–95, 179–180, 217–218
frequency band, 61
Freudian slip, 193, 217
Freudian speech error, 193, 217
fricative, 74–76
frontal cortex, 121, 143–145, 184
frontal lobe, 34–35, 63
functional Magnetic Resonance Imaging (fMRI), 59, 62–64, 143, 184, 215–216
functional MRI scan, 62
FUSS, 164–165
fuzzy term, 161, 164, 166

garbled sentence, 111, 128
Garden Path model, 140–141, 149
garden path sentence, 134–135, 141–142, 147, 180–181
gaze, 21, 23, 136, 196
gaze duration, 46, 56, 135, 180, 224, 271
gaze position, 56, 136
gender (biological), 17, 79, 241, 272
generalized lexical decision, 240
generalized phrase structure grammar, 268
genetics, 10, 20, 22, 269
gesture, 4, 11–12, 15–17, 23, 26, 96, 145, 154–155, 196, 210–211, 220–221, 256–257, 263–265
gesture-speech synchronization, 30, 257
given information, 131, 151, 177, 198
global co-occurrence model, 166–167
global language context, 249, 252

global updating, 182
glyph, 105
go/no-go lexical decision task, 51, 172
goal maintenance, 238
good-enough processing, 139–140, 150–151, 183
GPC, 53, 113–114, 226
GPT, 275
graded semantic effect, 165
grain size, 117, 260
grammar, 4, 22, 37, 40, 131, 133, 135, 146, 230, 268
Grammatical Encoder, 29–30, 197
grammatical category, 39, 40, 47, 103, 130, 134, 164, 194, 195, 206, 212
grammatical encoding, 200–201
grammatical fit, 245
grammatical gender, 39, 165, 176, 208, 232, 271
grammatical knowledge, 22
grammatical role, 138–139, 145, 155–156, 215
grammatical rule, 4, 133, 225
grammatical (syntactic) structure, 30, 32, 37, 40–42, 130–131, 133–135, 137–141, 144, 147–152, 155–156, 169, 176, 186, 192, 194, 196, 200, 202–203, 206–208, 212, 222, 232, 245–246, 248, 253, 260–261, 265, 267
grammaticality judgment, 69, 267–268
graph, 101, 105
grapheme, 101, 105–106, 113–114
grapheme-to-phoneme conversion (GPC), 53, 113–114, 118, 226
Gricean maxim, 183, 198
Groucho Marx, 27, 43
grounding-problem, 170
gyrus, 34, 62

HAL, 167
hallucination, 73, 108, 258
hand gesture, 4, 11–12, 15–17, 23, 26, 96, 145, 154–155, 196, 210–211, 220–221, 256–257, 263–265
handwriting, 32, 100, 102, 263
hanze, 226
head movement, 16, 154–155, 256
head-mounted display (HMD), 67
heritage language, 270
hesitant phase, 199
hesitation, 199, 222, 267
heuristic value, 277
hierarchy, 9, 28, 162–163, 256, 258–259

high-constraint sentence, 232, 244, 249
hiragana, 104, 226, 242
HMD, 67
holistic meaning, 36, 159, 162–163
holistic network approach, 163
holistic unit, 101–102, 210
homograph, 125, 227–228, 240–241, 245, 249–252, 254
homonym, 125
homophone, 125, 227, 244
hub-and-spoke theory, 173–174, 262
human-computer interaction, 273–275
humanlikeness, 274
humanoid robot, 274
human–robot interaction, 275
hypernym, 162–163
hyper-polyglot, 224
Hyperspace Analogue to Language (HAL), 167
hyponym, 162–163

ICM, 237–238, 246–247
icon, 15
iconic gesture, 12, 15, 21, 221, 256
iconicity, 12, 15, 21, 270
identical cognate, 227–229, 241–243, 245, 250–252
identification system, 236
ideophone, 12
ideogram, 113, 226
idiom, 55, 132, 157, 188, 202
illocutionary force, 199
imageability, 50
immediacy assumption, 57
implicit causality, 175–176
implicit memory, 48
incremental planning, 194
incremental processing, 1–2, 9–10, 80, 129, 135–136, 139–140, 245, 256, 259–261
incremental production, 192, 198, 207
incremental retrieval, 72, 188
incremental updating, 181
incrementality, 1–2, 9–10, 13, 159–160, 256, 259–261
independent variable, 46
index, 15, 304
index finger, 15, 145
indirect object, 137, 202
indirect request, 187–188
indirect route, 114–115, 122
Indo-European language, 11–12, 229, 254, 268, 271
inductive reasoning, 177
industrial robot, 274

inference, 174–180
inferior frontal cortex, 35, 64, 143–145, 184, 230
inflection, 40, 103–104
informal reasoning, 177
information stream, 145, 259–261
information structure, 131, 133
information theory, 147
infrared camera, 56, 68
inhibition, 54, 82–86, 107–110, 177, 222, 235–241, 246–247, 250
inhibition effect, 214, 240
inhibitory connection, 82–84
Inhibitory Control Model, 237–238, 246–247
initial letter bank, 112–113
in-lab interaction paradigm, 66–67, 219–220
innateness, 20, 22, 267
inner voice, 113
instance, 165–166
instance theory, 165–166
instrument, 131, 169
integrated mental lexicon, 115–117, 248
integration, 24–25, 60, 91–93, 137–140, 144–145, 178–179, 183–184, 233
intelligent agent, 274
intension, 161
intention, 8, 10, 14–15, 17, 30, 40–41, 187, 196, 198–200, 210–211, 265, 276
intentionality, 181
interaction, 5, 31, 66–68, 202, 225, 232–233, 256–263, 265, 272–275
interactive activation, 108–111, 208–209
Interactive Activation model (IA), 108–111
Interactive Activation model for word production, 208–209
interactive model, 82–83, 86, 91, 108–111, 121–122, 141–142, 208–209, 235–237
interactivity, 195, 240, 256–263
intercomponent parallelism, 198
Interface Hypothesis, 210–211, 223
interference, 54, 108, 213–214, 219–220, 231, 238, 241, 244–245, 250–252
interference suppression, 238
inter-fixation, 56, 135
interjection, 222
interlingual homograph, 227–228, 232, 240–241, 244–245, 249, 251–252, 254

interlingual homophone, 227, 240, 244
interlocutor, 14, 17, 25, 95–96, 135, 198, 272, 275
internal goal, 20
internal loop, 197
internal noise, 17
International Phonetic Alphabet (IPA), 75, 104, 127
internet, 19, 25, 268
intonation, 3–5, 10, 17–18, 99, 145, 152, 201, 203
intracomponent parallelism, 198
intralingual homograph, 125
introspection, 69
intuitive judgment, 131–132, 267–268
IPA, 75, 104, 127
italic, 102
iterated learning, 22

jIAm model, 108
joint action, 25, 198
jTRACE, 84
judgment, 156–157, 177
jumbled text, 111, 128

kanji, 226, 242
katakana, 104, 226, 242
knowledge, 2, 6, 17, 20, 28, 30, 32, 48, 130–131, 144, 172, 175–180, 220–221, 272
knowledge-driven processing, 30
Kuki, 273–274

L1, 224–225, 230–235, 238, 240–251
L2, 205, 224–225, 230–235, 238–251, 257–258
L2 learner, 12, 25, 114
L2 learning, 36–38, 48, 91, 225, 234, 257
LAD, 21–22, 267
LAFS, 76
language acquisition, 22, 36–38, 267
language acquisition device (LAD), 21–22, 267
language comprehension, 71–157
language control, 237–239, 241, 246–248
language decision, 69, 241, 250–251
language development, 36–38
language disorder, 36–38, 59
language dominance, 145, 247
language emergence, 19–24
language evolution, 10, 19–24, 26
language family, 10, 229–230, 253–254, 268

language game, 190
language learning, 22, 36–38, 91, 234, 257–258, 267
language marker hypothesis, 262
language mixing, 246
language node, 235–236, 238
language non-selective lexical access, 231–235, 239–240, 243–244, 249
language of thought, 146, 262
language production, 191–223
language proficiency, 205, 224–225, 230, 232–233, 237, 244
language subfamily, 229
language switching, 246–248
language tag, 238
language tree, 10, 229
Language User Framework (LUF), 27–44, 263–266
large language model, 275–276
larynx, 20, 39, 204–205
late bilingual, 225
late closure, 140
late positive component (LPC), 61
latent semantic analysis (LSA), 166–167, 226
lateral inhibition, 82–85, 108–112, 235–237, 240–241
Latin script, 99, 104, 242, 263
learning model, 118–120
left anterior temporal cortex, 145, 173–174
left hemisphere, 34, 85, 142–145, 170–171, 194, 215–216, 238–239
left inferior frontal gyrus, 64, 121, 142–145, 184, 230
left temporal lobe, 64, 170–171
left-branching, 134
left-handedness, 145
lemma, 192–193, 200–203, 207–208, 238
lemma retrieval, 200–203, 207–208, 214–216, 258
lesion, 143, 170–171
letter, 3, 32, 99–114, 124, 128, 226, 260
letter bank, 112–113
letter feature, 102–103
letter identity, 111–112
letter identity uncertainty, 112
letter n-gram frequency, 121
letter position, 106, 108–112, 226
letter position coding, 108–112
letter position uncertainty, 111
letter recognition, 102–103, 108–114, 121
Levenshtein distance, 116
lexeme, 192, 203
lexical access, 78, 180

Lexical Access from Spectra (LAFS), 76
lexical ambiguity, 124, 190, 222
lexical availability, 203
lexical bias, 209
lexical bias effect, 195, 205, 216–217
lexical bundle, 55
lexical competition, 97, 127, 220, 231, 235, 240
lexical competitor set, 40, 83
lexical concept, 176, 201, 207
lexical decision, 50–52, 86–87, 117, 124–126, 240–244, 249–252
lexical embedding, 87, 97, 106, 127
lexical frequency, 46–47, 81, 86, 121, 126, 180, 228, 242–243
Lexical Functional Grammar, 268
lexical link, 234
lexical matching, 112–113, 120
lexical processing, 50–53, 78–86, 105–120, 231–232
lexical property, 39–40, 80–81
lexical route, 53–54, 89, 113–115
lexical selection, 80–85, 94–95, 97, 100, 106–120, 208, 231, 239, 243
lexical-semantic integration, 60, 240
lexicology, 39–40
lexicon, 30, 32, 39, 76–77, 106–107, 115, 139, 200–202, 230, 234–235
lexicon project, 47, 51
lexico-semantic memory, 163
linear mixed-effects model, 47, 270
linearization, 199
linguistic context, 6, 92, 148–155, 185–188
linguistic diversity, 11, 270–272
linguistic relativity, 176
linguistics, 30, 37–42, 267–268, 270
lip movement, 3, 15, 257–258
literal meaning, 55, 145–146, 187–188
loanword, 227
local sentence context, 249
localist connectionist model, 82–84, 91, 108–113, 115–117, 208–209, 235–237
location, 17, 169
log frequency, 47
logic, 169, 178
logistic mixed-effects model, 47
Logogen model, 92, 107
logogram, 104, 242
logographic system, 104, 242
Lombard effect, 258
Long Term Memory, 8, 28–32, 48, 71–72, 101–102, 104, 144, 226, 264
low-constraint sentence, 232, 249

LPC, 61
LSA, 166–167, 226

macaque, 172
machine learning, 119, 275
macro-structure, 180
magnetic resonance imaging (MRI), 59, 62–64, 143, 184, 215–216
magnetoencephalography (MEG), 62, 215–216
Magritte, 158
malapropism, 193
maluma-takete, 269
Mandarin Chinese character, 128, 240
manner of articulation, 74–75, 85
manual cognate, 257–258
manual McGurk effect, 257
many-to-many mapping, 35, 114, 163
many-to-one mapping, 73
masked priming, 52–53, 113, 123
mathematics, 35, 167, 267
McGurk effect, 15, 257
McLuhan, 18–19, 25
meaning, 40–41, 158–190
meaning structure, 11, 30, 130–131, 196, 200
Mechanical Turk, 65
medium is the massage, 19, 25
medium is the message, 18, 25
MEG, 62, 215–216
mega-study, 86
memory, 28–31, 33, 48–49, 144, 172–174, 263–265
memory retrieval, 28, 176
Memory Unification Control (MUC) model, 144
mental lexicon, 30, 39–40, 49–50, 77, 100, 106–107, 112, 139, 144, 200, 203, 228, 234
mental model, 1–2, 7–10, 24–25, 32, 95–96, 141, 153–154, 170, 177–180, 182–183, 191, 196, 255–256, 261–262, 272
mental organ, 43
mental simulation, 8, 11, 20, 188, 262
mentalizing, 146, 265–266
mentalizing network, 266
MERGE, 37, 267
Merge model, 89
meronym, 163
message, 3–5, 17–19, 24, 30–31, 133, 145–146, 196, 199–200, 210–211, 220–221
Message Generator, 210–211
metaphor, 55, 167

metonymic reference, 196
metonymy, 196
metrical segmentation strategy, 85
micro-structure, 180
mimesis, 21
mimetic, 12
mind, 65, 267
mind-to-mouth theory, 196
minimal attachment, 140–141, 146, 148–150, 190
minimal effort, 200
minimal pair, 39
minimalist approach, 174
minority language, 270
mismatch negativity (MMN), 60–61
misperception, 71, 97–98
Mitsuku, 273
mixed error, 193, 195, 209
mixed-effects model, 47, 270
MMN, 60–61
modality of expression, 3–4, 21–23, 211
modality-specific information, 8, 170, 173–174, 262
modularity, 8, 267–268
monitoring, 28, 33, 89–90, 144–145, 193, 197, 208–209, 216–217, 238–239
monolingual, 117, 224, 232, 239, 242, 245–246, 253
monolog, 199, 272
morpheme, 39–40, 103–105, 110, 192–195, 206–209
morpheme exchange, 193–195
morphological family, 121
morphological frame, 206–207
morphology, 39–40, 226
morphophonological encoding, 196–198, 203
Moses illusion, 183
mother tongue, 95–96, 246
motherese, 5
motion tracking, 67
motor behavior, 8, 18, 35, 48, 63, 188
motor command, 197, 205
motor control, 39, 204–205, 211
motor cortex, 36, 159
motor information, 165, 167, 170
motor network, 266
motor performance, 265
motor program, 265
motor response, 49, 51
mouth movement, 15, 205, 257–258
mouthing, 15
movement, 3, 7, 21, 23, 35, 39, 154, 159, 167, 203, 274
MRI, 59, 62–64, 143, 184, 215–216

MUC, 144
multichannel communication, 263–265
multilingual language production, 237–239, 246–248
multilingual sentence processing, 244–246
multilingual speaker, 224–225
multilingualism, 37–38, 224–254
Multilink model, 115–117, 235–237, 248
Multilink simulation, 237
multimodal communication, 210–211, 220–221, 256–258
multimodal language production, 220–221
Multimodal Language User Framework, 263–265
multimodal Lombard effect, 258
multimodal meaning, 159, 173
multimodal unification, 145
multimodality, 5, 256–258
multiple activation, 97, 106, 127, 142
multiple constraint satisfaction, 142
multiword unit, 55, 136
music, 4, 35, 258, 277
myomotor phase, 205

N1, 126, 172
N150, 121–122
N250, 121–123
N400, 60–61, 92–94, 121–123, 126, 150, 153–154, 176–177, 184, 240, 243
name agreement, 54
naming, 46–47, 53–55, 114–117, 170–171, 208, 213–216, 246–248
nasality, 12, 74–75, 269
natural reading, 56, 245
neighbor, 50, 106, 117, 226–228, 232, 240
neighborhood, 40, 106, 166, 234–235, 240
neighborhood size, 227, 240
nerve cell, 62, 205, 259
neural network, 36, 85, 107, 119, 147–148, 239, 265–266
neural network metaphor, 107
neural network model, 147–148
neuroimaging, 59, 62–65, 172–173, 215–216
neurolinguistic programming, 205
neuromotor phase, 205
neuromuscular phase, 205
neuron, 62, 102–103, 147
neurophysiology, 46, 59–65, 102–103, 267
neuroscience, 65, 267, 269

neuroscientific research, 49–50, 59–65, 85, 142–146, 215–216
new information, 8, 107, 131, 133, 151, 198–199
nodding, 1, 16–17, 256
noise, 17, 24, 46–47, 59, 77, 103, 258
non-alphabetic script, 104, 113, 242
non-communicative information, 23, 260–261, 274
non-declarative memory, 48
non-dominant language, 225
non-human agent, 273–275
non-human primate, 20–21, 172
non-identical cognate, 227–228, 232, 241, 245, 249–252
non-linguistic context, 5–6, 92–94, 185, 218–221, 250–252
non-linguistic perception, 36, 261
non-linguistic thinking, 177
non-literal meaning, 187–188
non-minimal attachment, 149
non-modularity, 8, 15, 35, 211, 226, 268
non-target language, 231, 237, 238, 245, 249
non-verbal communication, 2, 4, 14–16, 154–155, 256–258
non-verbal context, 6, 129
non-verbal information, 2, 14–16, 129, 154–155, 184, 256–258, 260–261, 263–265
nonword, 50–51, 57, 60, 90, 109, 123–125, 209, 233
nonword point (NWP), 90, 123–124
noun phrase, 42, 132, 137, 141, 152–153, 185–186
noun–noun compound, 40, 104, 134
NP, 42, 132, 137, 141, 152–153, 185–186
nucleus, 39, 206–207, 210
number agreement, 151–152
number-agreement violation, 151–152
NWP, 90, 123–124

object, 4–5, 23, 54, 58, 88, 104, 132, 137–138, 158, 161, 165–166, 169, 202
object naming, 69, 214
Occam's Razor, 259
occipital lobe, 34, 63, 171, 173
off-line measurement, 48–49, 52–53, 69, 267–268
OLD20, 116
one-to-many mapping, 74
on-line measurement, 42, 49–50, 69, 70, 268

onomatopoeia, 12
onset, 39, 47, 59, 60–61, 78, 84, 87, 93, 94, 111, 122, 147, 151, 153, 184, 187, 193, 203, 206–207, 209, 210, 212–214, 219, 230, 239
onset phoneme, 47, 80, 193, 206, 208, 216, 244
ontogenesis, 10
open bigram, 111
opportunistic planning, 238
organic phase, 205
orthographic neighbor, 50, 106, 117, 119, 127, 226–228, 231–232, 235, 240, 244
orthography, 50–51, 104–105, 114, 116, 118, 123–124, 226–227, 236, 237, 241, 244
orthotactics, 70, 226
oscillogram, 39, 61, 73–74, 76

P150, 121
P200, 126
P325, 121
P600, 61, 147, 151–152
Pandemonium model, 102–103
parafoveal preview effect, 57
parafoveal vision, 57, 111
parallel activation, 50, 80, 86, 107–108, 147, 261
parallel distributed processing, 117–120
parentese, 5
parietal lobe, 34–35, 63, 144–146, 171–172, 216, 239
parse structure, 132, 137
parser, 130, 152
participant, 14–15, 17, 21, 25, 45–68, 88, 92–94, 96, 161–162, 165, 183–186, 198, 205, 216–221, 232–233, 237, 240, 248–252, 270–272
passive sentence, 67–68, 131, 133, 139, 147, 214–215, 230, 245–246
patient, 2, 36, 38, 49, 59, 64, 115, 120, 132–133, 137–138, 140, 142–144, 170–171, 200
pause, 5, 73, 186, 222
PDP model, 117–119
peanut, 153–154
perception, 3, 11, 18–20, 36, 67, 76–80, 83, 96, 103, 119, 159–160, 170, 172, 176, 188–189, 211, 259, 261, 262
performance, 47, 70, 91, 115, 117, 119, 147–148, 224, 237, 239, 241, 244, 251, 254, 265, 267, 272
perisylvian, 142, 145, 148, 170, 266
perseveration, 192, 208, 209
personal common ground, 17

personal pronoun, 17, 175 176, 218
personality, 5, 254
PET, 59, 64, 171–172, 215, 230
phone, 73, 76
phoneme, 31, 39, 47, 53, 71–72, 74, 76–86, 89, 97, 101, 105–106, 113, 117–118, 192–195, 205, 207–210, 216, 221, 226, 230, 242, 244, 260
phoneme anticipation, 192, 194
phoneme error, 194–195
phoneme exchange, 192–195, 206, 210
phoneme monitoring, 84, 86–87, 89, 90, 123–124
phoneme onset, 39, 47, 80, 106–107, 193, 205–206, 208–209, 216, 244
phoneme perception, 79
phoneme repertoire, 76, 226
phoneme restoration, 78–80, 83
phoneme substitution, 192
phonemic route, 89
phonetic encoding, 216, 258
phonetic plan, 196–197, 203, 206
phonetic transcription, 74
phonetics, 39, 42, 44, 73, 156, 254
phonological code retrieval, 215–216, 253
phonological decision, 119
Phonological Encoder, 30, 32, 215
phonological encoding, 32, 215
phonological feature, 82, 164, 192
phonological frame, 194
phonological priming, 123
phonological similarity, 47, 194–195, 222, 227, 244
phonology, 21, 37, 39, 42, 54, 76, 113, 116, 118, 120, 122–123, 194, 227, 228, 232, 235–237, 244
phonotactics, 70, 193
phrasal category, 132, 135
phrase, 6, 27, 33, 37, 42, 132, 134–135, 137, 140, 147, 152–153, 185, 253, 268
phrase structure, 37, 132, 134, 147, 268
phylogenesis, 10
pictogram, 104
picture database, 54
picture description, 69, 214, 215
picture naming, 54, 66, 69, 213–216, 218, 222, 248–249
picture-word interference, 213–214, 218–220, 222
pitch, 5, 73, 201, 203
place of articulation, 74, 78
planning, 21, 63, 154, 167, 172, 192, 194, 199
plosive, 74–77
plural, 103, 151, 194, 226, 228, 271

pointing, 3, 15, 23–24, 145, 154, 161, 185, 196, 255–256
pointing gesture, 15, 154, 196, 255
polyglot, 224–225
polysemy, 125, 163, 254
positron emission tomography (PET), 59, 64, 171–172, 215, 230
possessive pronoun, 271
postlexical code, 89–90
posture, 2, 154, 261
poverty of the stimulus, 22
power analysis, 47
practice trial, 47, 233
pragmatic meaning, 41, 146, 148, 188
pragmatics, 38, 40–42
preactivation, 92
prediction, 20, 24–25, 60, 92, 114, 126, 138–140, 155–156, 182, 233, 267, 271
prefrontal cortex, 62, 144, 146, 239
prelexical code, 73, 85, 89–90
prelexical processing, 71–72, 101
preverbal message, 200, 211–212
primary spelling, 123–124
primate, 20–21, 172
prime, 48, 52–53, 87, 94, 110, 121–123, 165, 172, 213–215, 218, 246
priming, 48, 52–53, 70, 87, 94–96, 110, 113, 116–117, 121, 123–126, 165, 172, 189, 214–215, 218, 220, 222, 232, 245, 248, 250, 272
Print Recognizer, 39, 105
Print Signal Recognizer, 101, 107
printed (visual) word recognition, 39, 42, 46, 92, 99–128, 276
Printed Word Recognizer, 40
printed word representation, 101–105, 115, 152
prior, 181
proactive inhibition, 247–248
probabilistic grammar, 147–148
probabilistic model, 110, 147–148
probability, 61, 110, 126, 147
problem solving, 177
procedural memory, 48
production system model, 180, 197, 198
proficiency, 205, 224–225, 230, 232–233, 237, 244, 248
progressive demasking, 51, 250–251
Prolific, 65
prompt, 275
pronoun, 17, 175–176, 218, 271
pronoun agreement, 218
pronunciation, 49–50, 53, 104–106, 110, 125, 129, 152–153, 214, 227–228, 241

proposition, 8, 42, 162, 168–172, 174, 177, 179–180, 182, 189, 211
propositional structure, 159, 170, 179–181, 189
prosodic break, 186
prosodic disambiguation, 190
prosodic grouping, 185–188
prosodic information, 137, 141, 261
prosodic structure, 71, 188, 203
prosody, 145, 152, 185–187
protolanguage, 20, 229
prototype, 166, 169
proverb, 55
Psammetichus, 45
pseudohomophone effect, 119
pseudo-experiment, 46–47
pseudo-randomization, 47
pseudoword, 50–51, 53, 60, 86, 89–90, 96, 109–111, 115, 119, 121, 123–124, 190, 205, 216–217, 250–252, 269
pseudoword superiority effect, 109–110
psycholinguistics, 37, 38–42, 168, 259, 267–268, 270

question-answer sequence, 154

race model, 89, 142, 148
radical, 104
randomization, 47
ranking, 147–148
rapid serial visual presentation (RSVP), 57, 126, 136, 249
reactive inhibition, 247–248
reaction time (RT), 46–47, 49–55, 59, 65, 69, 89, 95, 213, 240, 243, 249
reading, 2–3, 8, 18, 34, 38, 50, 55–59, 70, 99–128, 135–136, 139, 149, 152, 155–156, 174–175, 178–183, 226, 232–233, 240, 242, 244–245, 263, 271, 276
reasoning, 177, 182, 189
recall, 49–50, 69, 178
recipient, 131, 137, 169, 200, 221
recipient design, 272
recoding, 28, 42, 188, 261–262
recognition point (RP), 81, 84, 87
redundancy, 128
reference, 161–162, 165, 169–171, 189, 196
referent, 15–16, 88, 132, 185–187, 189, 271
referential communication game, 66, 185–186
referential theory of parsing, 141, 148
register, 4, 272

regression, 135–136
regularity, 12, 269
reinstatement, 272
relative letter position, 111–112
replication, 68, 205, 220, 240, 258
resolution of data, 56, 59–60, 62–64
resolution of problems, 33, 124, 174–176, 241
resonance, 62–63, 108, 232, 248, 260
response choice, 49
response competition, 54, 237
response execution, 49
response time, 46–47, 49–55, 59, 65, 69, 89, 95, 213, 240, 243, 249
resting level activation, 108, 110, 116, 237, 245
resyllabification, 208, 258
retina, 56, 102, 106
retinotopic, 121
return sweep, 135–136
reversed language dominance, 247–248
Revised Hierarchical Model (RHM), 234, 239
rhyme, 39, 58, 88
rhythmic hypothesis, 84
right hemisphere, 34–35, 145
right-branching, 134
rime, 39, 193, 195, 207
rime exchange, 193, 195
robot, 275–276
robust feature, 77
Rosetta stone, 253
RSVP, 57, 126, 249

saccade, 57
salience, 131, 202, 265
salience network, 265
saliency, 203
salient cue detection, 238
sandhi, 73
Sapir-Whorf hypothesis, 176
scenario, 6, 183, 187, 272
schema, 2, 169, 237–238, 246
script, 16, 21, 44, 99, 102, 104–105, 113, 127, 169, 190, 226, 230–231, 242, 253, 255, 263
Search model, 107
second language (L2), 25, 36–38, 48–49, 91, 114, 205, 225, 232–233, 235, 242, 246–247, 253, 257
second language acquisition (SLA), 36–38, 48–49
secondary spelling, 123–124
second-person neuroscience, 272
seeing for saying, 262

segment, 3, 76, 78, 81, 203, 209–210, 212, 221
segmental information, 73, 101, 152, 202, 260–261
segmentation, 42, 71, 83, 85–87, 92, 98, 106, 152, 181–182
segregation, 23–24
selective response inhibition, 238
self-monitoring, 197, 216
self-organizing map, 165
self-paced listening, 55
self-paced reading, 55, 59, 69, 148, 152, 232, 268
semantic bias, 209
semantic categorization, 117
semantic coherence, 121
semantic component, 131
semantic feature, 125, 158, 164–165, 167–168, 171, 189, 234–235
semantic illusion, 182–183, 185, 189
semantic integration, 183–184
semantic interference effect, 219–220
semantic marker, 164
semantic memory, 48, 163
semantic network, 161–163, 165
semantic noise, 17
semantic priming, 52–53, 70, 87, 94–95, 117, 189, 218, 220, 250
semantic relatedness, 171, 240
semantic representation, 37, 40, 54, 117, 137, 140, 144, 156, 158–160, 165, 170, 178, 182, 199–201, 226, 235, 237, 241, 259, 262
semantic (thematic) role, 127, 131–133, 137–140, 145–146, 148–149, 155, 169, 184, 200, 261, 271
semantic space, 164–166
semantic structure, 30, 42, 130, 135, 138, 148, 164
semantic unification, 144
semantics, 9, 37, 40–42, 54–55, 115–116, 118, 120–122, 133, 138, 140–142, 146, 158, 160–161, 167, 173, 175, 227, 235–237, 248
Sender–Receiver model, 24–25, 31
sense, 3, 7, 8, 18–19, 35, 161–162, 167, 169–171, 185, 188–189, 196
sensory channel, 16, 102
sensory organ, 13, 30, 129, 262
sentence, 6, 9–10, 37, 40, 52, 55–61, 64, 87, 92–94, 98–99, 111, 125–128, 129–157, 160, 172, 174–178, 180, 183, 185, 187, 189, 194, 196, 199, 203, 214–215, 217–218, 232, 237, 244–246, 249, 260

sentence context, 11, 57, 86, 91–95, 97, 119, 124–126, 147, 150, 152–156, 184, 232–233, 244, 248–250, 252, 260
sentence meaning, 40, 42, 55, 131, 137–138, 140, 147, 149, 152, 155–156, 168–169, 171, 177–178, 183–184, 188–189, 245, 249
sentence processing, 30, 42, 129–157, 171, 178–179, 188, 200–202, 229, 244–246, 248, 260
Sentence Processor, 29–30, 40, 80, 86, 94, 124, 130, 141–142, 147–148, 261, 265
sentence reading, 57, 100, 126, 135–137, 139, 143, 233
sentence (syntactic) structure, 30, 32, 37, 40–42, 130–131, 133–135, 137–141, 144, 147–152, 156, 169, 176, 186, 180, 192, 194, 196, 200, 202–203, 206–208, 212, 222, 232, 245–246, 248, 253, 260–261, 265, 267
separate-representation hypothesis, 243
sequential processing, 31–32, 81, 87, 129, 136, 195, 198
shadowing, 69
shallow orthography, 104–105, 114, 118
shared syntax, 245, 253
shared-representation hypothesis, 243
Short Term Memory, 33, 63
Shortlist model, 80, 84–88
sign language, 2–4, 11, 15, 22, 26, 229, 256, 257, 261, 263, 265, 270
Sign Recognizer, 263–264
Signal Producer, 264
Signal Recognizer, 28, 31, 39, 71, 73, 78, 101, 108–109, 263–264
signal-driven, 31, 231–232
signal-to-noise ratio, 24, 46
similarity metric, 116
simulation, 11, 20, 21, 83–84, 88–89, 119, 189, 235–237, 239, 262, 277
simultaneous interpreting, 253
singular, 151, 195, 271
situation model, 170, 179–181
slip of the tongue, 192–193, 205, 212, 216, 218
slot, 137, 183, 196, 206–209, 222
slot-and-filler model, 206–207, 208, 222
smartphone, 19, 65
smell, 2–3, 16, 158, 160
SOA, 213–214, 219–220
social cognition, 265

social context, 5, 17, 19, 25, 185, 219, 272
social identity, 1
social media, 4, 19, 99
sociolinguistics, 270
SOLAR model, 111
somatosensory information, 63
SOPHIA model, 235
sound, 3, 5–6, 9, 12, 15, 20, 23–24, 28, 30, 32, 39, 43, 53, 66, 71, 73–81, 85, 89–90, 97–98, 105, 114, 119, 123–125, 201, 203–204, 206, 208–209, 226, 257, 268–269
sound spectrum, 73
source localization, 60
Spatial Coding model, 108, 111–113, 115, 117, 120
spatial resolution, 59–60, 62–63
speaker judgment, 267
speaker meaning, 146, 187
speaking, 3–4, 6–7, 9–10, 13, 26, 32, 66, 91, 135, 159, 176, 192, 196–200, 203, 206–208, 217, 220, 227, 237, 240, 247–248, 261–262, 271
spectator science, 272
spectral template, 76–77
spectrogram, 61, 74, 77, 203
speech act, 199, 211
speech amplitude, 73–74, 77, 99, 201
speech channel, 205
speech error, 92, 164, 192–195, 206, 216, 221, 223
speech perception, 71–85, 119
speech production, 2, 192–197, 203–205, 211, 216–218, 221–222, 271
Speech Recognizer, 39, 71, 205
speech segmentation, 71
speech signal, 3, 27, 31, 42, 51, 71–89, 92, 96–98
speech-to-text, 275, 277
speed reading, 128
spelling, 4, 7, 32–33, 105, 111, 123–124, 226
spelling rule, 4, 105, 113, 226
spoke-and-hub system, 173–174, 178, 262
Spoken Signal Recognizer, 28–29, 71, 73, 78
spoken (auditory) word recognition, 9, 13, 32, 39, 42, 51, 58, 71–100, 124, 150, 152
Spoken Word Recognizer, 71, 76, 78, 80, 86
spoken word representation, 73–77
spoonerism, 193, 195, 206, 216–217

spreading activation, 36, 114, 208–209, 212, 215, 222
SPS, 61
SQUID, 62
Stable Diffusion, 275
stack principle, 200
standard model of language production, 201, 207–208, 210–212, 222–223
stem, 104–105
stimulus encoding, 49
stimulus onset, 213–214
stimulus list, 7, 11, 49, 108, 217, 233, 241, 248, 250–253
Stimulus Onset Asynchrony (SOA), 213–214, 219–220
stimulus quality, 81
storage, 38, 104, 128, 148, 230–231
story context, 92, 153
story grammar, 169–171, 189, 261
straitjacket, 176, 273
stress, 96, 145, 152, 201, 257
strong eye-mind hypothesis, 56, 136
Stroop effect, 53–54
Stroop task, 53
structural MRI scan, 62–63
subject, 4, 130–133, 137, 169, 175, 202, 212, 216–218, 220, 222, 229, 271
subject–verb agreement error, 212, 216–218, 222
sublexical representation, 53, 71, 73, 101, 115, 122, 242
sublexical route, 53–54
submissiveness, 168
subsymbolic approach, 11–12, 117–118, 120, 259, 263
subsymbolic representation, 12, 118, 120
subtitle, 47, 116
sulcus, 62
sum frequency, 243
superposition matching, 112
suprasegmental, 71–72, 84, 152, 201–202, 260–261
surface structure, 37, 132, 135, 137–138, 140, 144, 196, 201–202, 218
surface text, 179–180
surprisal, 147–148
switch cost, 239, 246–248
switching, 225, 238–239, 246–247
syllabary, 104, 242
syllabic alphabet, 104
syllabification, 209, 215–216
syllable, 39, 71, 77, 85, 87, 96, 103, 142, 192–194, 204–207, 209–210, 216, 222, 257, 260

syllable frame, 206–210, 212
syllable monitoring, 69
syllable paradox, 206
Sylvian fissure, 143
symbol, 17, 20–21, 82, 104–105, 117–118, 259, 263
symbolic approach, 11, 15–16, 43, 82, 86, 103, 108, 115, 118, 120, 242, 259, 262, 278
symbolic representation, 103, 108, 118, 278
synonym, 125, 163–164, 202
syntactic, 39–40, 47, 61, 91, 103, 130–134, 137, 140–142, 146, 150–152, 155, 163, 166–167, 175, 180, 185, 191–192, 194–195, 200, 202–203, 206–208, 212, 218, 233
syntactic ambiguity, 157, 185
syntactic category, 39–40, 47, 103, 130, 134, 164, 194–195, 206, 212
syntactic encoding, 196–198, 200–203, 206, 215, 221
syntactic frame, 194, 200, 206–207, 214, 221
syntactic parser, 130, 152
syntactic positive shift (SPS), 61
syntactic priming, 218, 222, 232, 245, 248
syntactic priming paradigm, 212, 214–215
syntactic prominence, 203
syntactic representation, 40, 229, 231, 245
syntactic role, 144, 203
syntactic rule, 230
syntactic (grammatical) structure, 30, 32, 37, 40–42, 130–131, 133–135, 137–141, 144, 147–152, 156, 169, 176, 186, 192, 194, 196, 200, 202–203, 206–208, 212, 222, 232, 245–246, 248, 253, 260–261, 265, 267
syntactic unification, 144
syntactic violation, 61, 151
syntax, 4, 6, 8–10, 20, 22, 36, 37, 40, 42, 78, 133, 138, 140–142, 146
syntax-first, 146, 148, 150, 152, 156, 187, 190, 200, 202, 267–268
systematicity, 10–12, 131, 159, 178, 189, 261

tactile communication, 4, 257, 278
tactile writing system, 257
target, 48, 51–53, 81, 83, 87–90, 94, 116–117, 125–127, 149, 193–194, 208–209, 213–214, 216–220, 230–231, 233, 236–238, 241, 244–245, 249–251

target language, 241, 243, 245, 250
target sentence, 135
target word, 40, 51–52, 57, 60, 81, 83–84, 87, 88, 94, 106–107, 110, 121, 125–127, 172, 184, 202, 208, 213–214, 216–217, 230, 240, 244, 249–251
task, 7, 28, 33–34, 36, 43–44, 47, 50–55, 59, 62–63, 65–67, 79, 89, 91, 110, 117, 165, 215, 217, 235–238, 241, 249–252, 263, 272
task demand, 7, 44, 46, 66, 177, 237, 240–241, 248, 250–253, 272, 276
task disengagement, 238
task effect, 250–252
task engagement, 238
task language, 243
task schema, 44, 110, 237–239, 246
task switching, 238
task/decision system, 117, 235–236
taste, 3, 159
teaching, 7, 20, 32, 168, 268, 275
technology, 18–19, 56, 120, 274–275, 278
temporal lobe, 35, 63–64, 121, 143, 171, 173–174, 178
temporal resolution, 59–60, 63–64
test condition, 49
text, 18, 33, 48, 56–57, 99–100, 111, 126–127, 130–131, 135, 147, 167, 168–170, 174–175, 177–182, 185, 188–190, 245, 252–253, 273–277
text meaning, 169–170
text processing, 178–182
text schema, 2, 169
text script, 169, 190, 255
textbase, 179–180
text-to-image application, 275, 277
text-to-speech technology, 274, 277
thematic (semantic) role, 127, 131–133, 137–140, 145–146, 148–149, 155, 169, 184, 200, 261, 271
theme-first principle, 132
Theory-of-Mind (ToM), 146, 148
thinking, 3, 37, 119, 159–160, 176–178, 189, 200, 261–262, 271
thinking for speaking, 176, 200, 262
thought, 28, 30–31, 40, 146, 159–160, 176, 188, 196, 206, 212, 259, 262
thought experiment, 46
time scale, 256, 259–261, 262, 278
time-course, 49, 59, 83, 89–90, 159, 172, 178
time-frequency analysis, 61

tip-of-the-tongue state, 206–207
TMS, 59, 215
ToM, 146, 148
tone, 201, 209–210, 225, 270
tone language, 212, 222
tongue twister, 204–205, 222
top-down feedback, 82–83, 89, 91, 108–110, 120, 232–233, 244, 249, 259–260
top-down processing, 30–31, 79, 82–83, 86, 89, 139–140, 231–233, 261
topoplot, 93
TRACE model, 80–81, 82–89, 98, 107–108, 115, 120, 235, 260
transaction, 14
transcranial magnetic stimulation (TMS), 59, 215
transformational generative grammar (TGG), 37
transitional ambiguity, 58
translation, 69, 115, 117, 151, 202, 227–228, 234–235, 237, 239–240, 245, 249–250
translation equivalent, 117, 227–228, 230–231, 234, 236, 244, 250
tree diagram, 132, 135, 140, 208
trilingual, 224, 241
troponym, 163
Turing test, 273
turn transition, 155
turn taking, 5, 9, 24
two-alternative forced-choice task, 50
two-person science, 272
typing, 4, 39, 223

unbalanced bilingual, 225, 232, 238–239, 242–243, 246–247, 251–252
uncanny valley, 274
unification, 144–145
uniqueness point (UP), 81, 84, 87, 89–90, 123–124
universal grammar, 22, 267, 278
unrestricted race model, 142, 148
updating, 174, 181–182, 191
Utterance Encoder, 264
Utterance Processor, 264–265

valence, 168, 265
variability, 10, 71–72, 81, 84, 101–102, 166
vector, 85, 117–118
ventral, 34, 36, 85
ventral stream, 36, 85
verb, 4, 6, 22, 40, 61, 103, 125, 131–135, 137, 142, 144, 151–152, 156, 159, 163–165, 167–169, 175, 188, 194–195, 200–202, 208, 212, 216–218, 222, 229, 265, 271
verb phrase (VP), 42, 132, 135, 185, 245
verbal communication, 2, 4, 14–16, 25
verbal theory, 235, 276
verb-object bonding principle, 132
virtual agent, 68, 92, 272–275
virtual assistant, 273
virtual environment, 67–68, 272
virtual human, 274–275
virtual reality (VR), 67–70, 92, 272, 274, 277
visual attention, 15, 265
visual complexity, 54
visual context, 59, 62, 92–93, 96, 156
visual lexical decision, 50–52, 119, 121, 243–244
visual perception, 18, 165, 261
visual word form, 16, 34, 103, 126
Visual Word Form area, 34, 103
visual (printed) word recognition, 39, 42, 46, 92, 99–128, 276
visual world paradigm, 56, 58, 87–88, 90, 136, 150
vocal cord, 2, 4, 39, 74, 78, 190, 192, 204, 206
vocalization, 20–21
voice, 4, 53, 64, 78, 85, 113, 164, 257–258
voice onset time (VOT), 78
voicedness, 74
VOT, 78
vowel, 12, 73, 75–77, 83, 85, 103–104, 242, 269
vowel chart, 73, 75
voxel, 62
VR, 67–70, 92, 272, 274, 277

WEAVER++ model, 24, 207–208
WEIRD, 270
Wernicke, 143, 269
Wernicke's area, 143
whistling language, 18
Wickelgraph, 118
Wickelphone, 118
word association, 52–53, 96, 165, 189, 234
word candidate, 80–81, 83, 86, 90–92, 97, 106–108, 111–112, 118–119, 127, 139, 231, 237, 244
word category, 103, 132, 134–135, 147
word duration, 81, 86

word exchange, 193–194
word form, 11–12, 15–16, 34–35, 42, 50, 53–54, 66, 97, 101, 113, 119, 122, 125, 130, 137, 139, 144, 156, 158, 163, 168, 180, 192, 198, 203, 206–208, 227–228, 231–235, 239–240, 244, 250, 261, 265, 268–269
word frequency, 46–47, 55, 70, 81, 84, 87, 110, 116, 119, 126, 142, 180, 190, 228, 236, 242
word frequency effect, 46–47
word learning, 234–235
word length, 86, 121, 124, 180
word meaning, 12, 31, 36, 39–42, 44, 73, 101, 115, 123–126, 130, 156, 158–171, 175, 178, 183–184, 189, 192, 196, 203, 207–208, 227, 233–234, 239, 265, 269
word naming, 44, 46–47, 49, 53–55, 57, 69, 113–115, 117–120, 208, 249, 277
word onset, 84, 87, 93–94, 111, 122, 147, 151, 153, 184, 187, 193, 203–206, 209–210, 212, 219
word order, 4, 8, 30, 130–133, 137, 151, 176, 198, 226, 229–230, 271
word pair repetition, 212, 216–217
word percept, 180
word production, 9, 69, 208, 210, 212, 216
word rating, 168
word recall, 49–50
word recognition, 6, 9, 31, 42, 46, 49–50, 57, 70, 78, 99, 131, 231, 235, 237, 242, 248–249, 259
Word Recognizer, 30–31, 40, 91, 94, 101, 105–107, 109, 121, 124, 130, 251, 261, 263
word retrieval, 48, 110, 115, 203, 236, 239–244, 248
word selection, 80–85, 94–95, 97, 100, 106–120, 208, 231, 239, 243
word stress, 10, 71, 73, 87, 96, 152, 201, 257
word substitution, 193, 195
word superiority effect, 109–110
word translation, 115, 117, 234, 239
word-form encoding, 180
word-initial cohort, 58, 77, 89, 94
WordNet, 163
word-shape frame, 209
word-word association, 165
Working Memory, 9, 28, 33, 36, 43, 48, 134, 140, 156, 176–178, 180–182, 211, 239, 273
world knowledge, 5, 6, 8, 11, 25, 32, 38, 42, 130–131, 133, 145, 156, 159, 169, 174, 177–180, 272
world view, 176
wrap up effect, 260
writing, 2–4, 6, 9–10, 13, 32, 39, 99–100, 104, 128, 196, 223, 261, 263, 268
writing error, 270
writing system, 3, 102, 104–105, 114–115, 257, 270
Written Signal Recognizer, 105
written word recognition, 99–128

Taylor & Francis eBooks

www.taylorfrancis.com

A single destination for eBooks from Taylor & Francis with increased functionality and an improved user experience to meet the needs of our customers.

90,000+ eBooks of award-winning academic content in Humanities, Social Science, Science, Technology, Engineering, and Medical written by a global network of editors and authors.

TAYLOR & FRANCIS EBOOKS OFFERS:

- A streamlined experience for our library customers
- A single point of discovery for all of our eBook content
- Improved search and discovery of content at both book and chapter level

REQUEST A FREE TRIAL
support@taylorfrancis.com